MEDIEVALIA ET HUMANISTICA

MEDIEVALIA ET HUMANISTICA

STUDIES IN MEDIEVAL & RENAISSANCE CULTURE

NEW SERIES: NUMBER 11

EDITED BY
PAUL MAURICE CLOGAN

1982
ROWMAN AND LITTLEFIELD
TOTOWA, NEW JERSEY

First published in the United States 1982 by Rowman and Littlefield,
81 Adams Drive, Totowa, New Jersey 07512.

Distributed in the U.K. and Commonwealth by
George Prior Associated Publishers Limited
37-41 Bedford Row
London WC1R 4JH, England

ISBN: 0-8476-7105-4
ISSN: 0076-6127
LC 81-173800

Printed in the United States of America

Contents

Contents

Editorial Note

Since 1970, this new series has sought to promote significant scholarship, criticism, and reviews in the several fields of medieval and Renaissance studies. It has published articles drawn from a wide variety of disciplines and has given attention to new directions in humanistic scholarship and to significant topics of general interest. This series has been particularly concerned with exchange between specializations, and scholars of diverse approaches have complemented each other's efforts on questions of common interest.

Medievalia et Humanistica is sponsored by the Modern Language Association of America, and publication in the series is open to contributions from all sources. The Editorial Board welcomes scholarly, critical, or interdisciplinary articles of significant interest on relevant material and urges contributors to communicate in a clear and concise style the larger implications, in addition to the material of their research, with documentation held to a minimum. Texts, maps, illustrations, diagrams, and musical examples will be published when they are essential to the argument of the article. In preparing and submitting manuscripts for consideration, potential contributors are advised to follow carefully the instructions given on page xii. Articles in English may be submitted to any of the editors. Books for review and inquiries concerning *Fasciculi* I-XVII in the original series should be addressed to the Editor, *Medievalia et Humanistica*, P.O. Box 13348, North Texas Station, Denton, Texas 76203.

Inquiries concerning subscriptions should be addressed to the publisher.

Preface

This volume, the eleventh in the series, is a special collection of original articles focusing mainly on theology and literature. The range of subjects represented by the articles should afford the scholar and serious student with new insights into current research in fields other than their own. Each article makes a contribution to its own specialized field but is presented in such a way that its significance may be appreciated by nonspecialists. In its review articles significant new publications are surveyed, and the progress of studies in medieval eschatology and apocalyptic, 1974–1981, is reported.

As usual, I am grateful to the Editorial Board and Rowman and Littlefield for their ready cooperation.

P. M. C.
July 1981

MEDIEVALIA ET HUMANISTICA

New Series

Paul Maurice Clogan, EDITOR
North Texas State University

EDITORIAL BOARD

Articles for Future Volumes Are Invited

Articles may be submitted to any of the editors, but it would be advisable to submit to the nearest or most appropriate editor for consideration. A prospective author is encouraged to contact his editor at the earliest opportunity to receive any necessary advice and a copy of the style sheet. The length of the article depends upon the material, but brief articles or notes are normally not considered. The entire manuscript should be typed, double-spaced, on standard 8½" x 11" bond paper with ample margins and documentation should be held to a minimum. Endnotes, prepared according to *A Manual of Style*, twelfth edition (University of Chicago Press), should be double-spaced and numbered consecutively and appear at the end of the article. All quotations and references should be carefully verified before submission. The completed article should be in finished form, appropriate for printing. Only the original manuscript (not photocopy or carbon) should be submitted, accompanied by a stamped, self-addressed manuscript envelope.

The addresses of the American editors can be determined by their academic affiliations. The addresses of the editors outside the United States are:

Professor Agostino Paravicini Bagliani, 13 chemin de Riettaz, CH-1030 Bussigny-Près-Lausanne, Switzerland (Church History)

Mr. Peter Dronke, Clare Hall, Cambridge CB3 9DA, England (Medieval Latin Poetry and Thought)

Professor J. R. Hale, Department of Italian, University College London, Gower Street, London WC1E 6BT, England (Renaissance History)

Professor Denys Hay, Department of History, University of Edinburgh, William Robertson Building, George Square, Edinburgh EH8 9JY, Scotland (Renaissance History)

Professor Ian D. McFarlane, Wadham College, Oxford OX1 3NA, England (Renaissance French and Neo-Latin Literature)

Professor Jean-Claude Margolin, 75 Bld Richard-Lenoir, 75011 Paris, France (Humanism, Renaissance Philosophy and Neo-Latin)

Virgil's Wisdom in the Divine Comedy

CHRISTOPHER J. RYAN

The commonly accepted view of Virgil's role in the *Divine Comedy* is that, while he may not be reduced to a pure symbol or cypher, he represents and acts as the spokesman of reason as distinct from faith, of the human order as distinct from the christian. Clearly, he does not draw on purely human powers in his guidance of Dante: he undertakes his journey only as the result of an initiative from heaven, and he is always aware that he is the executor of a special grace given to Dante.[1] None the less, most readers of the *Comedy*, in my view correctly, regard the knowledge that Virgil uses to guide Dante during his journey as being essentially that of human reason. His is the wisdom that can be attained by man on earth independently of the christian dispensation. What I should like to do in this essay is to specify more closely the nature of Virgil's human wisdom by highlighting certain aspects of his knowledge which have not been given the attention by critics that they merit.[2] Above all, I wish to highlight the fact that there is in Virgil's wisdom a limitation of which he himself is at best only dimly aware. This limitation begins to become apparent in two incidents in the *Inferno*, the entry to the city of Dis (VIII.82ff), and the encounter with the demon-guardians of the barrators (XXI). Its full measure and significance, however, emerge only at the point of transition from Virgil to Beatrice, and it is to Dante's presentation of that moment that I shall devote most attention. It can be claimed that the single most revealing speech of Virgil to Dante is the final one in which he, in effect, sums up his own role. A striking feature of this speech, considered in the light of the events recorded earlier in *Purgatorio* XXVII, is that it reveals Virgil to be, in an important sense, mistaken with respect to Dante's state and to the coming of Beatrice. It can also be claimed that the final disappearance of Virgil and the appearance of Beatrice (*Pg.* XXX–XXXI) contain *in nuce* the theology of the *Paradiso*. Certainly, an accurate understanding of that scene is crucial for a correct understanding of the *Comedy* as a whole, and it can be no matter for surprise that Dante should deploy his powers of art most sharply and subtly there. One significant feature of Dante's artistry there is his weaving into the narrative of several lines of Virgil's poetry. While

I

Medievalia et Humanistica, New Series, Number 11 (Paul Maurice Clogan, ed.). Rowman and Littlefield, Totowa, NJ, 1982.

the presence of these Virgilian echoes has always been noted, their significance has scarcely been recognized: Dante is, in fact, employing them to
make a critique of Virgil, not merely to pay him a tribute. It is my belief
that by adverting to the indications of the limitations in Virgil's guidance,
and by examining closely, in the light of the underlying theology of grace
and revelation, the nature of Dante's echoing of these Virgilian passages,
we can come to a richer and more nuanced understanding of Virgil's
wisdom in the *Comedy* than is commonly the case. Thereby we can come
to a greater appreciation of the depth of the transition from Virgil to
Beatrice, and of the quality of Dante's art in describing it.

I shall not here attempt to justify in detail the commonly accepted view
that Virgil is portrayed by Dante as essentially voicing the wisdom of the
human as distinct from the christian order.[3] Like most readers of the
Comedy, I take as emblematic Virgil's statement with respect to free choice:
" 'Quanto ragion qui vede / dirti poss' io; da indi in là t'aspetta / pur a
Beatrice, ch' è opra di fede' " (*Purg.* XVIII.46–8).[4] This view accords with
Virgil's saying about himself that he will guide Dante as far as his school
can lead (ib.XXI.32–3); with his declaration to Dante as he prepares to
leave him on the threshold of Beatrice's coming and of the journey through
heaven: " 'se' venuto in parte / dov' io per me più oltre non discerno' "
(ib.,XXVII.128–9); and with the fact that in almost all the instances in
which he speaks at length on doctrinal issues (leaving aside questions
concerning the afterlife) he draws almost entirely on what can be known
through reason unaided by revelation.[5]

Before going on to consider more specifically how Virgil essentially
represents human reason, it is worth dwelling for a moment on the fact
that he shows a considerable knowledge of what man on earth comes to
know only through revelation. I shall return later to the significance of this
knowledge, but it should be clearly recognized that upholding the view
that Virgil represents human reason should not obscure the fact that the
objective content of his knowledge includes important points of christian
doctrine. His knowledge in this respect is, understandably, fullest with
regard to life after death. He is clear from the outset that only they enter
heaven who have been chosen for this by God (*Inf.*I.129),[6] and he knows
that he and others have been excluded from "seeing the High Sun" because they lack the theological virtues (*Pg.* VII.34–6).[7] It is particularly
noteworthy that he is aware that man's nature is marked by hereditary
sinfulness which cuts him off from God: this is directly implied in a
number of places, as when he speaks of the companions of the virtuous
pagans in Limbo, the *pargoli innocenti*, as " 'dai denti morsi de la morte
avante / che fosser da l'umana colpa essenti' " (ib.31–3).[8] Certainly, we
must assume from his amazement at the sight of Caiphas
(*Inf.* XXIII.124–6), and at the pageant that unfolds in the Earthly Paradise

(*Pg.* XXIX. 57), that he is ignorant alike of the details of Christ's life and of many important facets of revelation.[9] But he is aware of the two basic tenets of christianity, namely the Trinity and the Incarnation-Redemption. He speaks explicitly of the Trinity (*Pg.* III. 36), and the latter is implied when he goes on to talk of Mary's having had to give birth for mankind to attain the beatific vision (37–44), and in his description of Christ as " 'l'uom che nacque e visse sanza pecca' " (*Inf.* XXXIV. 115).[10] Similarly, some knowledge of the redemption is entailed in his awareness that " 'a powerful one, crowned with victory' " shrove hell (ib. IV. 52–63; cf. ib. VIII. 128–30).[11]

Dante, then, certainly presents Virgil as knowing in some measure important features of what can be known on earth only through christian revelation. Yet this aspect of Virgil's knowledge is counterbalanced by another on which I shall concentrate. Dante portrays him as being limited to a surprising degree in his knowledge, as having a blindness or naivety with regard to the depth of evil. Equally strikingly, this is a limitation of which Virgil himself becomes only painfully and partially aware during the journey. Critics frequently say of Virgil that he, being of the purely human order, cannot reach up to the heights of heaven and that it is because of this that he must cede to Beatrice. With this I have no quarrel, but I wish to argue that his exclusion from the supernatural order, which is in essence a lack of direct, personal knowledge of the loving God, entails also an inability fully to reach down to the depths of evil. Virgil becomes a more intriguing figure, and the *Comedy* a more complex and interesting work, when we recognize that Virgil is not only innocent of heaven and perfect goodness, but also and thereby naive with regard to the full depths of evil. While Virgil would, so to speak, have had little difficulty in accepting the appraisal of him as unable to lead Dante up to heaven, I suspect that he would have been not a little surprised to be described as unable to lead his pupil to full knowledge of evil, including, crucially, to full knowledge of the evil in Dante himself. Yet no less than this is implied, I believe, if we take with adequate seriousness the manifestations of the limitations in Virgil's knowledge that his poetic creator depicts in the course of describing the journey through hell and up the mountain of purgation. Virgil's blindness with regard to the supernatural order begins in fact much earlier than the point where he declares "più oltre non discerno".

This blindness is seen most obviously in two incidents in the *Inferno.* While Virgil's limitation is evident in them, the precise nature and the degree of limitation in his knowledge are commonly not adverted to. The first incident is that of the pilgrims' entry to the lower part of hell, the City of Dis, recorded at *Inf.* VIII. 82–IX. 106. When challenged angrily by the devils who stand guard over the gates to the city (no light sentinel detach-

ment this: "più di mille", Dante tells us: VIII.82), Virgil appears confident
that his speaking to them will gain the poets entry. To the devils' irate
words, he replies by signalling that he wishes to speak secretly to them
(ib.86–7). Certainly, he calms Dante's fear by saying that his and Dante's
progress cannot be halted, because God wills it (" 'da tal n'è dato' ",
ib.104–5), but he evidently thinks that their advance will be effected by
his secret parley with the devils. These, however, give him short shrift,
for they accord him only a curt hearing before flying back inside and
shutting the doors (ib.113–6). Virgil's reaction is described in terms denot-
ing surprise, dismay and even personal affront:

> . . . rivolsesi a me con passi rari.
> Li occhi a la terra e le ciglia avea rase
> d'ogne baldanza, e dicea ne' sospiri:
> "Chi m'ha negate le dolenti case!"
>   (ib.117–20)

Yet significantly he is not dismayed to the extent that he feels compelled to
acknowledge fully his helplessness to bring about the desired entry. When
he turns to Dante to reassure him by speaking of the power of the one who
threw back the gates of hell itself, and of the help of one who will open the
city (*la terra*) to them (ib.124–30), he prefaces reference to this by the
curious remark that he, Virgil (with an emphatic *io*), will be victorious in
the struggle:

> "Tu, perch' io m'adiri,
> non sbigottir, ch'io vincerò la prova,
> qual ch'a la difension dentro s'aggiri."
>   (ib.121–3)

Again, while waiting on the "da ciel messo" (IX.85),[12] Virgil continues to
speak as if he will be, in part at least, responsible for the victory over the
devils: " 'Pur a noi converrà vincer la pugna' " (ib.7).[13] Characteristically,
Dante does not spend the time of waiting in useless silence. He asks Virgil
if anyone has been from Limbo to lower hell before, and Virgil's positive
reply that *he* has contains the intended reassurance to Dante not to worry
for he knows the road well (ib.30).[14] This contrasts markedly with Virgil's
actual inability to further their journey.

We have clear evidence that to see the limitation of Virgil in this incident as an important feature of Dante's portrayal of him is not idiosyncratic or special pleading. Shortly after this scene, Dante, addressing
Virgil as they witness the punishment of those who did violence to God,
begins: " 'Maestro, tu che vinci / tutte le cose, fuor che ' demon duri / ch'a
l'intrar de la porta incontra uscinci . . .' " (*Inf.*XIV.43–5). One cannot

resist the impression that this qualifying remark, while being entirely accurate, is hardly in accord with the laws of courtesy. Its presence can only be explained if Dante the pilgrim was keenly conscious of Virgil's mistaken confidence at the gates of Dis, and is only poetically justified if Dante the poet wishes to draw our attention to this.

The comic atmosphere of the scene described in *Inf.* XXI is far removed from the violent, nervous drama played out at the gates of Dis. The incident, however, is not simply an amusing interlude designed merely to rest the reader from the grim seriousness of the journey. Comic the incident and its sequel certainly are, and I have no doubt that part of Dante's intention is to ensure the continued interest of the reader by varying the tone of the narrative in this way. But Dante's mastery of comic technique enables him to harness it to an underlying moral purpose, not the least part of which is to sketch subtly but firmly the proneness of Virgil to become overinvolved in the comedy and overconfident of his own powers.[15] Here I shall confine myself to noting briefly the feature relevant to the present theme, the limitation in Virgil's knowledge with respect to evil.

In this incident the pilgrims have to deal with demons, who make one of their surprisingly rare appearances in the *Inferno*, as guardians of the fifth trench of Malebolge where the barrators are punished. Far from being put specially on his guard by the presence of devils, Virgil displays a marked confidence throughout the episode, a confidence which in the event turns out to be misplaced and almost leads to disaster. Seeing the grotesquely comical spectacle of the demons poking at the sinners like cooks around a massive pot of boiling meat, Virgil, before confronting them, turns to reassure Dante that he will not be hurt when he goes out alone to meet them. His are the words of a confident man, and his confidence is based on his own previous experience of lower hell:

> "e per nulla offension che mi sia fatta,
> non temer tu, ch'i' ho le cose conte,
> per ch'altra volta fui a tal baratta."
> (loc.cit.61-3).

When the devils rush towards him, he speaks in ringing tones, though here, it is true, he bases his assurance on God's willing the journey (ib.79-84). He shows neither caution nor wary diffidence in accepting Malacoda's offer of guidance towards a nonexistent bridge over the sixth bolgia (ib.106ff). He accepts, despite the clear signs of malignity and coarse bravura in the demons (vv.100-2, 131-9). It is significant that in doing so he puts aside as unfounded the reservations of Dante, who here displays a fearful respect for the demons which they entirely merit (vv.91–99; 127–32). The incident is drawn to a close at the end of c. XXIII. Virgil is seen ruminating, with a somewhat puzzled dignity,[16] on having been misled by Malacoda:

> Lo duca stette un poco a testa china;
> poi disse: "Mal contava la bisogna
> colui che i peccator di qua uncina."
> (vv. 139–41)

This draws from the former friar with whom he has been speaking the tart rejoinder: " 'Io udi' già dire a Bolgona / del diavol vizi assai, tra ' quali udi' / ch'elli è bugiardo e padre di menzogna' " (ib. 142–4). This is, of course, no abstruse piece of legal information; it is a verse familiar to any christian, John VIII.44. Its being a commonplace of christian knowledge sets off all the more clearly the naivety of Virgil in accepting help from demons, and failing to discriminate truth from falsehood in the ingenious pastiche which was Malacoda's offer of help.

A more important limitation than that shown in these two episodes in the *Inferno*, but perhaps less readily perceptible, is Virgil's mistakenness with regard to the coming of Beatrice and to Dante's fitness to be received by her. The evidence points to Virgil's thinking that Beatrice when she comes will welcome Dante, and that Dante will merit this welcome as one who has been fully purified through his journey under Virgil's tutelage. This attitude of Virgil is first suggested at *Pg.*VI.46–8. After giving an explanation of his words in the *Aeneid* regarding the nonacceptability of prayer offered to God by pagans, he adds that Dante ought not to dwell on any doubt he might still have until she speaks who will be " 'a light between the truth and your intellect' " (ib.45). Suspecting that the reference might escape his pupil, he adds: " 'Non so se 'ntendi: io dico di Beatrice; / tu la vedrai di sopra, in su la vetta / di questo monte ridere e felice' " (ib.46–8). Dante immediately expresses his desire to press on more quickly, saying that he no longer feels the tiredness that he did, and that he sees the shadow being thrown by the mountain (as the day declines). Virgil replies that they will continue on that day, but cautions Dante that the sun will rise again before they are "là sù" (ib.55), picking up his earlier reference to Beatrice's appearance at the top of the mountain. Significantly, that is the extent of his caution; there is no warning that Dante will have to undergo a further purgation, a further spiritual lightening of his weight of sin, beyond what he must undergo on the journey to the top. The text here gives no reason to believe that Virgil thought any such further purification would be required.

What is strongly suggested in c. VI is amply confirmed in the canto describing the end of Virgil's guidance. Virgil's words in c. XXVII betray no hint that Dante needs further purgation; on the contrary, they consistently indicate that he believes that Beatrice will come happy to meet her beloved, who will have been fully purified. This is apparent in the return, at greater length and in more dramatic form, of the encouragement motif that appeared in c. VI, and in the final words to Dante when they at last step onto the plateau at the top of the mountain.

Dante, faced with having to pass through the walls of purifying fire which girds the topmost cornice of Mount Purgatory, balks at the prospect (XXVII. 10–18). Virgil encourages him to overcome his fear by saying that the fire may hurt but cannot kill nor even physically harm him, and by reminding him that he has been guided successfully through realms much further from God (ib. 20–30). Neither the assurance of safety nor the mention of their being nearer God is enough to break Dante's troubled immobility; his mentally and physically stricken stance is described in a lapidary line: "E io pur fermo e contra coscienza" (v. 33).[17] Virgil, his elaborate encouragement having failed, switches tack and succeeds with the simple observation: " 'Or vedi figlio: / tra Beatrice e te è questo muro' " (vv. 35–6). The poetry opens out into the lovely simile comparing the effect of Virgil's mention of Beatrice's name on Dante to that of Thisbe on Pyramus (vv. 37–42), its tone matching the softening of Dante's *durezza*. It is a smiling Virgil who then asks in mild irony: " 'Come! / volenci star di qua?' " (vv. 43–4). Virgil continues to speak of the approaching meeting with Beatrice to support Dante in the agony of the fire, and in terms which, for all their brevity, indicate clearly that Virgil thinks that it will be a happy Beatrice who will come:

> Lo dolce padre mio, per confortarmi
> pur di Beatrice ragionando andava,
> dicendo: "Li occhi suoi già veder parmi."
>
> (vv. 52–4)

Virgil's words as he prepares to terminate his guidance are of a piece with the earlier encouragement of Dante to look forward to a welcoming Beatrice. There is no direct reference to Beatrice in the short address of Virgil to Dante when the latter awakens from his dream in which Lia has spoken to him, but his promise contains no suggestion that further purgation is necessary:

> "Quel dolce pome che per tanti rami
> cercando va la cura de' mortali,
> oggi porrà in pace le tue fami."
>
> (vv. 115–7)

Though the *pome* in the context is most naturally to be understood as referring either to Christ or more broadly to human happiness,[18] we can scarcely forget that Beatrice has been referred to indirectly by this figure shortly before; Virgil had smiled at Dante when his opposition had crumbled on hearing Beatrice's name "come al fanciul si fa ch'è vinto al pome" (v.45).

When they step onto the mountain top and Virgil addresses Dante for the last time, he speaks as to one who does not face further purifying pain: " 'lo tuo piacere omai prendi per duce' ", he tells his pupil, adding, in what can only be taken as indicating a belief that Dante has come to the end of his painful purgation: " 'fuor se' de l'erte vie, fuor se' de l'arte' " (vv.131–2). A similar thought seems to underlie his following words, for they convey the impression that Dante is aptly in Eden (the locus of man's innocence), and indeed in the reference to the sun's playing on Dante's face, that he is aptly there because God is pleased with him:

> "Vedi lo sol ch 'n fronte ti riluce;
> vedi l'erbette, i fiori e li arbuscelli
> che qui la terra sol da sè produce.
>
> Mentre che vegnan lieti li occhi belli
> che, lagrimando, a te venir mi fenno,
> seder ti puoi e puoi andar tra elli."
> (vv.133–8)

The description of the imminently awaited Beatrice through reference to her happy eyes comes as no surprise in this context. The contrast Virgil draws between these and her tearful eyes when she first commissioned him to help rescue Dante from his sinful state [19] only strengthens the impression that she will welcome Dante as one who has been purified fully. The famous final lines, with their proudly ringing tones betokening someone who has finished well a deeply loved task, simply sum up what has preceded. Dante is crowned and mitred over himself and declared independent of further tutelage because his power of choice is free, straight and whole:

> "Non aspettar mio dir più né mio cenno;
> libero, dritto e sano è tuo arbitrio,
> e fallo fora non fare a suo senno:
> per ch'io te sovra te corono e mitrio."

We are in no way led to expect either that Beatrice will be displeased, or that Dante must undergo further repentance and purification; quite the contrary. And with those lines, epitomizing the attitude of Virgil, the poet has at once heightened the drama of the narrative and prepared for further development of the underlying theology—for, as we know, when she comes Beatrice is far from pleased, and Dante turns out to be very much in need of further purification.

There is no need to dwell here on the nature of the further purgation that Dante must undergo. My scope is the narrower one of elucidating the nature of Virgil's wisdom and in particular the limitation in human reason which is evidenced in the blindness to evil that we have seen. But before going on to consider the pointers to the nature of that limitation in c.XXX preceding Virgil's quiet disappearance, it is worth noting clearly that Dante *is* presented as still being in a state of sin when Beatrice comes.[20] Dante's sinfulness is most evident in the words of Beatrice, whose accusation Dante finally and with great difficulty acknowledges.[21] It is implied in her harsh words of greeting, where Dante's lamenting Virgil's disappearance is contrasted with his need to cry because of another word, the word of God (XXX.55–7; cf. *Hebrews* IV.12), and again in the sharply ironical " 'Come degnasti d'accedere al monte? / non sapei tu che qui è l'uom felice?' " (ib.74–5). Her address to the angels describing Dante's sinfulness after her death in turning from her and from God begin and end with the words which indicate that the sin is still present. Her aim in speaking is that in Dante " 'sia colpa e duol d'una misura' " (ib.108), and she ends by declaring:

> "Alto fato di Dio sarebbe rotto,
> se Letè si passasse e tal vivanda
> fosse gustata sanza alcuno scotto
> di pentimento che lagrime spanda."
>   (ib.142–5)

With insistence she requires that Dante admit the truth of her accusation: " 'dì, dì se questo è vero; a tanta accusa / tua confession conviene esser congiunta' " (XXXI.5–6). When that confession is finally forthcoming, Beatrice speaks in terms which unquestionably mean that before the admission of his guilt Dante was still marked by that sin:

> "Ma quando scoppia de la propria gota
> l'accusa del peccato, in nostra corte
> rivolge sé contra 'l taglio la rota."
>   (ib.40–2)

Dramatically more striking evidence of Dante's still being in a state of sin is found in the difficulty with which he is drawn to confession of it. The extremely painful psychological process, of which the external details are such an eloquent witness, is only intelligible if Dante had indeed lodged deep in his psyche something shameful to hide. Had he been purified of his sin in respect of Beatrice and all that she implies for his relation to God, on the mountain, then the agony he has to undergo would be devoid of both plausibility and meaning. The only explanation of that agonizing movement to partial then fuller [22] expression of sinfulness (see XXX.82–99, XXXI.7–9, 13–21, 31–36) is that until his confession his soul was still marked, still warped by the unconfessed sin.

If the whole import of Dante's initial meeting with Beatrice in the *Comedy* is to cleanse him from sin through Beatrice's stern exactment of the confession of his unrepented faithlessness towards her and to God,[23] and if, as I have argued, Virgil had envisaged Beatrice as coming happy to welcome a fully purified Dante, the conclusion is inescapable that Virgil was mistaken about the centrally important matter of the state of Dante's soul and the profundity of his need of purification. Just as in hell Virgil naively overestimated his own powers and underestimated the power and depth of evil in the devils, so here he finally appears naive in overestimating his own ability to guide Dante to complete purification and in underestimating the degree of evil in him. Accepting further that Virgil's wisdom is essentially that of the human and natural as distinct from the christian, we must also accept that the difference between the natural and supernatural is of a kind and depth which escapes the insight of which that human wisdom is capable. Virgil's is a worldly wisdom where the world must stand not simply for the limitation of the temporal as distinct from the eternal, but for the further limitation of sinfulness as distinct from innocence and purity, an innocence of which Virgil, as man marked by original sin, is himself in a critically important way unaware.[24] In short, while Virgil's complete fulfilment of the natural virtues eminently qualifies him to lead Dante to full natural purification, his being marked by original sin prevents him from recognizing fully the degree of evil involved in the culpable rejection by a christian of the God who loves his creatures so much as to offer them full participation in his eternal life, an offer given to the angels and to men to whom christian salvation is offered. It is this which precludes him from leading Dante to full purification.[25]

This double limitation in Virgil, of exclusion from eternal life and in his knowledge of evil, both stemming from being marked mysteriously by a fault of which he was not the perpetrator, are themes to which, I suggest, Dante returns subtly but powerfully when, at canto XXX, Virgil finally must make way for Beatrice and Dante the poet pays his final tribute to his poetic master. It is there that the full import both of the extension of Virgil's knowledge beyond what man can know on earth without christian revelation, and of the limitation in his wisdom, are revealed, within the context of a reverential love for the greatness of Dante's human, and tragically human, guide.

At two points in c.XXX Dante unmistakably adopts verses from the *Aeneid*. *Pg.*XXX.21 is, with the addition of the exclamatory "oh" for the sake of metre, a citation of a hemistich of *Aeneid* VI.883: " 'Manibus, oh, date lilia plenis' "—all the more striking for being the only instance in the *Comedy* in which a nonbiblical work is quoted, and for coming immediately after a biblical text. *Pg.*XXX.48, " 'conosco i segni de l'antica fiamma' " is a translation [26] of Dido's words at *Aeneid* IV.23: " 'adgnosco veteris vestigia flammae.' " There is no serious doubt in my mind that E. Moore was correct in proposing that we see in verses 49–51 of this canto a reflection of *Georgics* IV.525–7, but the omission of any reference to this by many commentators writing since this proposal was made would seem to indicate that his view has not gained universal acceptance. [27] Certainly Dante is not as evidently indebted to Virgil here, and for this reason, and since these verses are not as germane to the line of thought that I wish to develop, I shall leave verses 49–51 out of consideration for the present.

Either tacitly or expressly commentators and critics almost uniformly take the two uses of the *Aeneid* at *Pg.*XXX.21 and 48 simply as a final tribute by Dante to the poetic, or more generally human, achievement of Virgil. [28] This is especially true of Dante's citing *Aen.*VI.883 at *Pg.*XXX.21, which is taken as being put by Dante on a level with the citation of the *Benedictus* at v.19, and hence is regarded simply as it stands as perfectly befitting the scene which is unfolding. The recent commentary of Bosco-Reggio may be taken as reflecting the common mode of regarding Dante's use of the *Aeneid* here: "La presenza, nel canto degli angeli, di un verso profano in mezzo a tutta una serie di citazioni scritturali, non deve stupire: anche il linguaggio classico ha una sua sacralità. D'altronde esso è segno del sincretismo dantesco . . ."; "Significativo che anche qui, proprio rivolgendosi a Virgilio e nel momento in cui sta per constatarne dolorosamente la scomparsa, il poeta ricorra testualmente a un verso virgiliano. Come quella del v.21 questa citazione [v.48] è un estremo omaggio al poeta latino." [29]

While one must hesitate to modify significantly an interpretation so widely shared, I feel bound to say that in my opinion this interpretation does less than justice to the artistry of Dante. It fails to discriminate in the attitude of Dante towards Virgil between respectful gratitude and regretful recognition of his limitations, and obscures the development in the underlying thought. I entirely agree that Dante *is* paying a tribute of thanks and admiration to Virgil in these lines. But that is only part of the story. That there is another part to the story I shall attempt to establish, and since, as far as I am aware, my view finds only slight corroboration in the tradition, there is some advantage in stating clearly the nature of the general viewpoint I adopt, and the general grounds for so doing, before examining the texts in detail.

It seems to me that the differences between the use of the two lines in their original and their use in the *Divine Comedy* are so great as to cause a considerable aesthetic incongruity were Dante's use intended simply as a tribute to Virgil. I am not, of course, suggesting that critics have been unaware of these differences. What I am suggesting is that not to see an incongruity in the use of these lines regarded purely as a tribute is possible only if one assumes that Dante is ignoring the differences between the original use and his own, or treating those differences as insignificant as regards the *Comedy*. These differences are not, however, those of mere detail; they are substantial and easily observed. Thus that Dante should ignore them or treat them as insignificant for the development of his thought is *prima facie* unlikely: he is a poet of great subtlety; his high respect for poetry in all its ramifications and allusions as a medium of thought cannot be doubted; and consistently in his own poem he makes narrative skill and poetic artistry subserve the overriding moral and religious purpose of the work. Furthermore, we are in *Purgatorio* XXX, it is commonly acknowledged, at the spiritual centre of the *Comedy*, and Dante is here doing something that is of the deepest importance to him: preparing to meet Beatrice, and at the same time paying tribute and bidding farewell to Virgil. It is unlikely, I would submit, that at this point he should wish to do less than complete justice to any reference he makes to the *Aeneid* by ignoring important differences between his use and the original stemming from the very different contexts in which the lines occur. By contrast, it is entirely in keeping both with Dante's general practice in the *Comedy*, and with the importance of the scene taking place, that he should *make use of the very differences* between the function of the lines in his poem and their function in the *Aeneid* to develop the thought of his own poem and clarify his stance vis-à-vis his poetic master, and moral and intellectual tutor. Dante's citation and translation of the *Aeneid* are not, then, evidence of an undifferentiated "cultural syncretism",[30] but an implicit statement of Dante's way of seeing both the harmony and distinction of the human and the christian.[31]

The words spoken by the angels as part of the invocation to Beatrice are in the *Aeneid* spoken by Anchises, bewailing the premature death of Marcellus. Beatrice and the Roman youth have this in common: each died relatively young,[32] their promise cut off before it could fully flower on earth. But this similarity is set within, and serves to highlight, the differences which are equally if not more evident. The overarching and outstanding difference between the two scenes is that where death and sadness dominate in the portrayal of Marcellus, it is life and joy that characterize the anticipated figure of Beatrice.[33] Marcellus appears enshrouded in sadness. Contrasting with his youthful beauty and the brilliance of his arms is his " 'frons laeta parum et deiecto lumina voltu' " (VI.862).[34] His presence is noble, but " 'nox atra caput tristi circumvolat umbra' " (v.866).[35] The cause of this dominant note of sadness is that Marcellus' early death precludes him from fulfilling what was, in the perspective of the principal theme of the *Aeneid* as a whole and of book VI in particular, his essential function, namely to enhance the fortunes of Rome through his warrior prowess. " 'Ostendent teris hunc tantum fata, nec ultra / esse sinent' ", begins Anchises' eulogy, his grief centring on the fact that:

> "nec puer Iliaca quisquam de gente Latinos
> in tantum spe tollet avos, nec Romula quondam
> ullo se tantum tellus iactabit alumno."
>
> (vv.875–7)[36]

This leads him to cry:

> "heu pietas, heu prisca fides, invictaque bello
> dextera! non illi se quisquam impune tulisset
> obvius armato, seu cum pedes iret in hostem,
> seu spumantis equi foderet calcaribus armos.
> heu! miserande puer, si qua fata aspera rumpas,
> tu Marcellus eris!"
>
> (vv.878–83)[37]

The call of Anchises for flowers that follows immediately does not reverse but rather climaxes the sadness of his eulogy, for he wishes in strewing the flowers on the youth's tomb to express his grief in what he recognizes to be *a fruitless gesture:*

> "manibus data lilia plenis,
> purpureos spargam flores animamque nepotis
> his saltem accumulem donis et fungar inani
> munere."
>
> (vv.883–6)[38]

It is on this note that the eulogy closes, and indeed these are the last words of Anchises that we are given.

As noted, the dominant tone of sadness flows from the principal theme of the *Aeneid* as a whole. The work is designed to record the origins of a people whose glorious role is distinctly and exclusively intrawordly, a role summed up in the famous words of Anchises:

> "tu regere imperio populos, Romane, memepto
> (hae tibi erunt artes) pacique imponere morem,
> parcere subiectis et debellare superbos."
>
> (VI.851–3)[39]

It is no accident that these words are found in the mouth of Anchises, in book VI, for although that book records a journey to the underworld, and contains the brief but intriguingly attractive description of the Elysian fields and of the purification of mankind in the afterlife, the basic thematic perspective of exalting the people of Rome and their function through relating their history is not departed from even there. It is within that perspective that the role of Marcellus is judged and his death lamented. However much Anchises' short disquisition on the spirit that pervades all things, including the human race, and on purification before and after death (VI.724–51, especially 743–7) may have caught the interest of readers, particularly christian readers, the fact remains that Aeneas is not shown the dead so that he might desire eternal life, but, as Anchises says pointing to the vast throng in the grove on the shores of Lethe:

> "has equidem memorare tibi atque ostendere coram,
> iampridem hanc prolem cupio enumerare meorum,
> quo magis Italia mecum laetere reperta."
>
> (vv.716–8)[40]

When the review of the future Romans closes with the description of Marcellus, Anchises and his son "through the whole region . . . freely range"; the words of the father as he prepares to bid farewell place the visit of Aeneas to the underworld again firmly within a perspective bound by life on earth:

> incenditque animum famae venientis amore,
> exin bella viro memorat quae deinde gerenda . . .
>
> (vv.889–90)[41]

The contrast between the central perspective of the *Aeneid* and that of the *Comedy*, and between the essential function of Marcellus and Beatrice which these perspectives entail, is sufficiently evident not to require my dwelling on it. I should like, however, to draw attention to the way in which Dante emphasizes Beatrice's role as the one who brings *eternal* life precisely at this point where he refers to a Virgilian passage in which death is seen above all as a cause for sadness and the end of hopes placed in Marcellus.

The hundred angels who herald Beatrice's coming by uttering the words from the Gospel and the *Aeneid*, at vv.19–21, are described at v.18 as "ministri e messaggier di vita etterna", and it is entirely apt to regard them as fulfilling their function in heralding Beatrice. Furthermore, v.18 culminates the comparison, begun at v.13, of the rising in song of the angels to the resurrection of the saints at the end of time. The association of the angels with eternity, itself suggested by their incorruptible nature, is twice taken up again by Dante in this canto. He describes them as "quei che notan sempre / dietro a le note di li etterni giri" (vv.92–3), and Beatrice begins to address them: " 'Voi vigilate ne l'etterno die . . .' " (v.103).[42]

Nor should we forget that the context in which the angels' greeting to Beatrice is uttered is suggestive of eternal life. Immediately, the scene is irradiated by the seven streams of light, which are referred to thus in the opening lines of c.XXX: "il settentrion del primo cielo, / che né occaso mai seppe né orto / né d'altra nebbia che di colpa velo". More broadly, the setting of the scene is Eden, and Dante has twice shortly before associated Eden with eternity. Matelda, telling the pilgrim of the state of Adam before his sin, says:

> "Lo sommo Ben, che solo esso a sè piace,
> fè l'uom buono e a bene, e questo loco
> diede per arr' a lui d'etterna pace."
> (*Pg.*XXVIII.91–3)

The poet describes his wandering in Eden thus: "Mentr' io m'andava tra tante primizie / de l'etterno piacer tutto sospeso . . ." (ib.XXIX.31–2).

Beatrice herself is first invoked by the angels in terms which unmistakably link her to Christ: " 'Benedictus qui venis' " (v.19).[43] Christ is, of course, for Dante above all the one who "opened heaven",[44] and thus obtained again for man the gift of eternal life lost by Adam. This was in christian tradition universally regarded as the essence of Christ's work, but it is a feature on which Dante focuses particularly sharply,[45] attributing as he does the guidance of man's life in this world to the Empire, and describing the nature of the Church as being "nothing other than the life of Christ" (*Mon.*III.xiv.3), so that her role involves renouncing all power over the goods of this world (ib.passim). It is in keeping with this view of Christ that Statius should describe the preaching of the early christians as " 'la vera credenza, seminata / per li messaggi de l'etterno regno' " (*Pg.*XXII.77–8).

The particular words in which Beatrice, representing Christ, is heralded ("Benedictus qui venis") carry strongly this connotation of eternal life. The very fact of these words being uttered when Christ's death is an event of the remote past naturally connotes, as commentators have noted, the second coming of Christ, when the eternal kingdom will finally be inaugurated. But there are several other factors which, even without this reference forward to the second coming, make these words evocative of Christ as the one who brings eternal life. It is probable that *Benedictus qui venis* would recall first to the christian audience at whom Dante directed them not the biblical story but the Eucharist, for these words were used as the people's response to the Preface to the central moment in the Mass, the Canon.[46] They would, therefore, refer in the minds of his readers primarily not to the historical Christ as he was about to enter Jerusalem, but to the Christ whose heavenly sacrifice is re-presented in the Eucharist, and who was to be received in communion as the "bread of angels".[47] There is a further liturgical setting which Dante may have had in mind, and in which the *Benedictus* evokes Christ as the one who brings eternal life through breaking the bonds of death. In the liturgy of Palm Sunday which opens the most solemn of the liturgies of the year (those of Holy Week), the ceremony begins with the reading of the account of Christ's triumphal entry to Jerusalem. It is an unusual, indeed a unique, feature of this liturgy that it has two gospel readings; on all other occasions, there is a single reading which takes place after the initial rites and the reading of a passage or passages from elsewhere in the Bible.[48] The function of the special gospel reading of Christ's entry to Jerusalem at the beginning of the liturgy is to act as a joyful anticipation of the kingship of Christ to be achieved through his breaking of the bonds of death on Easter Sunday.[49] It is on this joyful note (the joy being continued in the procession imitating the strewing of the palms which immediately follows) that the Palm Sunday liturgy begins, before proceeding to the sombre accents of the reading of the passion narrative (the second gospel passage in the same liturgy), and the muted tones of subsequent liturgies of Holy Week.

The note of joyful anticipation of Christ's victory over death is not absent from the biblical account itself. The greeting of Christ can be regarded in its immediate historical setting as no more than the expression of popular enthusiasm, which soon evaporated in the face of opposition to Jesus from the Jewish leaders. But as presented by the evangelists in the context of the resurrection, the people's joyful cry appears as a providentially willed, if ironically unconscious, tribute by the Jewish people to Christ who is about to become the king victorious over even death. Looked at in the perspective of faith in the risen Jesus from which the evangelists wrote, the *Benedictus* appears not as being negated and mocked by his death, but as having its ultimate justification in that death, through which eternal life is attained by Jesus for mankind, who may now look forward to his second coming.[50]

In a variety of ways, then, it is Beatrice as representing Christ as the one who has attained eternal life through death who is greeted by the angels' cry of "Benedictus qui venis". Dante, therefore, by quoting from the *Aeneid* where he does, after the description of the angels as ministers and messengers of eternal life, and their citation of the *Benedictus*, indicates strongly that Virgil's wisdom can lead only as far as death, where christian wisdom by contrast brings life in a deeper sense, the new life whose richness carries it beyond death into the fulness of life in eternity.

No reader of the *Divine Comedy* will wish to quarrel with the view that for its author, as for any orthodox christian of his time, what essentially distinguishes the human from the christian order is the promise of eternal happiness made by God in Christ. There is, therefore, a considerable aptness in Dante's so firmly drawing the line in terms of eternal life between Virgil, as he is about to disappear, and the coming of Beatrice. The author of the *Aeneid*, we know, was only marginally concerned with life after death and has but a shadowy knowledge of it. But even granted this, it might still legitimately be asked why Dante has chosen to portray Virgil *as he is in the afterlife* as not having led Dante to repent of his sin of having turned from God's offer of eternal life. We may recall here the observation with which this paper began, that Virgil in the *Comedy* has a not insignificant knowledge of truths of revelation, and in particular he knows about heaven, both what it essentially consists in,[51] and how it is gained.[52] We may work towards an answer to the question just posed by considering Dante's second use of the *Aeneid* in *Pg.* XXX, for, as I shall try to show, Dante there draws forward his critique of Virgil and of the human order (while, of course, paying a further tribute to him). Having indicated the gulf that separates him (*qua* christian) from Virgil in quoting *Aeneid* VI.883 at *Pg.* XXX.21, Dante now goes on to a more nuanced use of Virgil at v.48, for there is a strong element of similarity between Dido's and Dante's love, as well as a profound dissimilarity.

An outstanding difference between the love of Dido and that of Dante which should alert us to the fact that Dante the poet is not simply at *Pg.* XXX.48 making his own the thought of Virgil at *Aen.* IV.23 (nor, therefore, simply paying him a tribute), is that whereas in the *Aeneid* passage Dido's love for Sychaeus is about to die, Dante's love is stirred once more by the same person, Beatrice. Where "adgnosco veteris vestigia flammae" is ambivalent in that Dido's love (once aroused by Sychaeus, now fanned into life by Aeneas) is both old and new, "conosco i segni de l'antica fiamma" refers to one and the same old love. Dido's old love, in the strictest sense, is about to cede to a new; Dante's love is *antico* in a full and positive sense ("antica fiamma" of v.48 picks up "antico amor" of v.39).[53] However, what clearly links the two figures is that both betray their "first love" through infidelity. It is, I believe, in the suggested interplay between similarity and dissimilarity in their unfaithfulness that a critique of Virgil by Dante is implicitly carried forward. Both Dido and Dante pledged to continue their love despite the death of their beloved, and neither remains faithful to that promise. As with Dante in respect of his love of Beatrice, Dido's failure to continue to love Sychaeus is presented by Virgil as involving culpability on her part. Before she allows her love of Aeneas full play, she recognizes that she has pledged herself to be faithful to Sychaeus by eschewing any further marriage: " 'si mihi non animo fixum immotumque sederet, / ne cui me vinclo vellem sociare iugali / . . . huic uni forsan potui succumbere culpae' " (IV.15–6,19).[54] Nor is it that she hesitates to yield to the new attraction simply because she had become " 'utterly weary of the bridal bed and torch' " (v.18). Acknowledging the " 'veteris vestigia flammae' ", she turns to *pudor* as her reason for not yielding, and in very strong terms. She declares that she wishes to be hurled by the "almighty father" to the shades " 'ante, Pudor, quam te violo aut tua iura resolvo. / ille meos, primus qui me sibi iunxit, amores / abstulit; ille habeat secum servetque sepulchro' " (v.27–29).[55] It is only under the persuasion of her sister that she succumbs. Anna, holding out the attraction of children and of "venus", asks scornfully: " 'id cinerem aut Manis credis curare sepultos?' " (vv.31ff.)[56] When Aeneas has left the shores of Carthage, Dido condemns herself despairingly: " 'non servata fides cineri promissa Sychaeo' " her repeated lament ends (v.552).[57] After describing her suicide, Virgil comments "nam quia nec fato, merita nec morte peribat, / sed misera ante diem subitoque accensa furore . . ." (vv.696–7),[58] thus enclosing his narrative with the thought with which it had begun: "At regina gravi iamdudum saucia cura / vulnus alit venis et caeco carpitur igni" (vv.1–2).[59]

Yet while the implication of Virgil's account at these points in the narrative clearly is that Dido ought to have preserved her faith vowed to Sychaeus, her situation differs from Dante's in that there is no active help from beyond the grave from her husband [60] or from friendly gods to enable her to fulfil her vows. On the contrary, it is the goddess Venus who, as the opening lines of book IV quietly remind us, is the ultimate cause of her love for Aeneas. Venus, fearing that Juno will again attempt to bring harm to Aeneas during his wandering, tries to secure his safety by encompassing his permanent stay in Carthage. Her aim is to make Dido fall so deeply in love with Aeneas, through the agency of Cupid, that she will induce the Trojan to settle permanently in Carthage with Dido (I.657–719, esp. 672–5). Cupid readily obeys so that "paulatim abolere Sychaeum / incipit et vivo temptat praevertere amore / iam pridem resides animos desuetaque corda" (ib.720–22).[61]

By contrast, Dante betrays both God and Beatrice despite Beatrice's influencing him from heaven to remain faithful. This hardly needs to be spelled out. It will be sufficient to note that the testimony of the concluding chapters of the *Vita Nuova* is fully in accord with the words of Beatrice in the accusation recorded shortly after Dante's recognizing "the signs of the old love":

> "Né l' impetrare ispirazion mi valse,
> con le quali e in sogno e altrimenti
> lo rivocai: sì poco a lui ne calse!"
>
> (XXX.133-5)

Her bringing about Dante's journey through the afterlife is 'only' a culminating grace, necessary because her previous attempts proved fruitless
(ib.136ff.). These interventions by Beatrice in turn are but special manifestations of the grace of God,[62] and epitomize its meaning, for Dante has
been touched and formed by grace from his infancy, and indeed in a
particularly favoured way. Not merely was he formed by sanctifying
grace through baptism, but God had within the grace-filled dispensation
of Christianity specially blessed him. It is to this that Beatrice turns his
attention when she begins her lengthy accusation:

> "Non pur per ovra de le rote magne,
> che drizzan ciascun seme ad alcun fine
> secondo che le stelle son compagne,
>
> ma per larghezza di grazie divine,
> che sì alti vapori hanno a lor piova,
> che nostre viste là non van vicine,
>
> questi fu tal ne la sua vita nova
> virtualmente, ch'ogne abito destro
> fatto averebbe in lui mirabil prova."
>   (ib.109–17)

When we reflect on the implications of this, the distinction between Dido's fault and Dante's becomes clear, and with this the gravity of Dante's
sin, and the reason for Virgil's inability to appreciate the depth of that
sinfulness and lead him to repent of it. The absence in Dido's case of the
active presence of the eternal in time enabling her to remain faithful to a
love beyond the grave points to the absence among mankind outside of the
christian order of that personal presence of the eternally loving God which
is the heart of christian revelation. That nonchristian order is represented
by Virgil, and not even his knowledge of truths belonging to the christian
dispensation has brought him the kind of 'contact' with God that is specific
to christian revelation.[63] As I shall try to elaborate in the light of medieval
theology, Virgil remains for Dante outside christian revelation, for all his
knowledge of individual truths pertaining to christianity. Lacking the
experience of the presence of God proper to christian revelation and the
knowledge of Him that is intrinsic to that experience, he lacks the ability
to help Dante where he most needs it: to repent of the sin of having
rejected the eternally loving God manifest in Christ and in Dante's *alter
Christus*, Beatrice.

The most evident difference between Virgil's knowledge of God even in
the afterlife and that which Dante had had during life stems from the
nature of the love of God for each. Virgil knows that God's love for
mankind is such that through the redemption some have been elected to be

sharers in the fulness of God's eternal life. A line which takes on its full poignancy only when we come to share some of Dante's affection for Virgil is his exclamation in the opening canto: " 'oh felice colui cui ivi elegge' " (v. 129). It is the cry of one who senses something of what that might mean had he been among the elect, but it is still the cry of an outsider, of someone who has never been the recipient of the kind of love for the individual implied in that mysterious election.[64] Dante, however, had known and turned away from the offer of divine love made in its simplest and absolute sense: God's offer of Himself as the perfect, eternal good. Aquinas admirably sums up the fundamental meaning of christianity and grace when he begins his discussion of the essence of grace in the *Summa Theologiae*. Distinguishing the love of God for those to whom he gives grace from the love with which he loves all his creatures, Aquinas writes: "Alia autem est dilectio specialis, secundum quam [Deus] trahit creaturam rationalem supra conditionem naturae, ad participationem divini boni. Et secundum hanc dilectionem dicitur aliquem diligere simpliciter: quia secundum hanc dilectionem vult Deus simpliciter creaturae bonum aeternum, quod est ipse" (I–II,q. 110,a. 1).[65]

This central difference in the nature of God's love for each entails substantial differences in the mode by which Virgil and Dante know God. Dante's situation as a baptized and believing christian bespeaks an experiential base absent in the one who has guided him through the first two realms of the afterlife. In the theology of Dante's time, to have faith in the saving God is not simply to believe *that* God wishes to save through Christ's redemptive work; it is to accept the truth of the revelation of God's love *on the testimony of God himself*. Whatever the difficulties in understanding the precise nature of the doctrine, the essential point common to the medieval theology of faith is clear: in adhering in faith to christian revelation as true, man comes in contact with, and relies on, God himself, as the first being or truth. Aquinas writes in the opening article of his consideration of faith in the *Summa:* "non enim fides de qua loquimur assentit alicui nisi quia est a Deo revelatum; unde ipsi veritati divinae innitur tanquam medio" (II–II,q. 1,a. 1).[66] That God himself as first truth is that on which faith is based is a recurrent theme in Aquinas' discussion of faith; it is perhaps most tersely summed up in the statement that "ratio formalis obiecti fidei est veritas prima" (ib.a. 3).[67] The meaning of this terse formulation is more fully explained later: "Sed tamen considerandum est quod in obiecto fidei est aliquod formale, scilicet veritas prima super omnem naturalem cognitionem creaturae existens; et aliquid materiale, sicut id cui assentimus inhaerendo primae veritati" (ib.,q. 5,a. 1).[68] Furthermore, it will be recalled, this personal though obscure 'contact' with the living God in faith is not given to the christian merely on occasion, as a special aid from outside when he consciously adverts to revelation; God's self-revelation through the preaching of the church and its sacramental ministry effects a transformation in man, giving his intellectual faculty a new permanent form or habit: "Ad secundum dicendum quod sicut homo per naturale lumen intellectus assentit principiis, ita homo virtuosus per habitus virtutis habet rectum iudicium de his quae conveniunt virtuti illi. Et hoc modo etiam per lumen fidei divinitus infusum homini homo assentit his quae sunt fidei, non autem contrariis. Et ideo nihil periculi vel damnationis inest his qui sunt in Christo Iesu (Rom.8,1), ab ipso illuminati per fidem" (ib.,q.2,a.3,ad 2um).[69] Through the new power in his intellect man is able to begin eternal life here on earth: "fides est habitus mentis qua inchoatur vita aeterna in nobis, faciens intellectum assentire non apparentibus" (ib.,q.4,a.1).[70]

"Qual si lamenta", Dante comments as he witnesses the joy of the saints in the heaven of the sun "perché qui si moia / per viver colà sù, non vide quive / lo refrigerio de l'etterna ploia" (*Par.* XIV.25–7).[71] The dialogue between Dante and Peter on faith in part I of Dante's celestial final examination brings out what is suggested by that passage, that the rain brings refreshment through the presence of God himself; "eternal rain" is an imaging by Dante of the docrine on faith we have noted common to his time. When asked by his 'examiner' what is the basis of the fundamental virtue of faith, Dante replies eagerly:

> "La larga ploia
> de lo Spirito Santo, ch'è diffusa
> in su le vecchie e 'n su le nuove cuoia,
>
> è silogismo che la m'ha conchiusa
> acutamente sì, che 'nverso d'ella
> ogne dimostrazion mi pare ottusa."
> (*Par.* XXIV.91–6)

This explanation had already been encapsulated in a line of an earlier reply in the examination: " 'La Grazia che mi dà ciò ch'io mi confessi . . . ' " (ib.58), and the affective overtones of this terse statement are hinted at by St. Peter in the densely beautiful parenthesis which echoes that earlier statement: " 'La Grazia, che donnea / con la tua mente, la bocca t'aperse . . .' " (ib.118–9).

It is against the background of such ideas, gradually revealed to us, and coming to their most explicit expression in *Par.* XXIV,[72] that we come to understand more fully the implications of the opening words of Beatrice's accusation recorded at *Pg.* XXX.109ff, which in turn illuminate the difference between Virgil's guidance and hers. There Dante is said to have been in his new life potentially such that " 'ogne *abito* destro fatto averebbe in lui mirabil prova' ", not only because of the influence of the "great wheels", but " 'per larghezza di grazie divine / che sì alti vapori hanno a lor *piova*, / che nostre viste là non van vicine.' " In turning from Beatrice he had turned from knowledge of the living God in her; she had represented, made present, the God-man, Christ, for Dante. In a poet whose use of adjectives is notably sparing, we may be sure that they carry their full significance when, at the close of the scene that began with her accusation, he apostrophizes at the sight of her second beauty: "O isplendor di *viva* luce *etterna*" (XXXI.139). What separates the wisdom of the christian from the wisdom of Virgil is indicated by that line, which alone Dante allows himself in describing Beatrice there, disclaiming the ability to say more. He will press on to make some attempt to give expression to that beauty in the *Paradiso*. Success in that enterprise (at least the success at which Dante was principally aiming) will depend not only on his technical expertise, but on his being able to call upon a range of experience in his readers which Virgil lacked. The words addressed by Dante to Piccarda in the lowest heaven signal the source of the limitation of Virgil's wisdom and of his inability to lead Dante to full repentance, for they speak of what, in Dante's eyes, separates the least in the kingdom of heaven from even the greatest representative of the pagan order: personal experience and knowledge of the eternal life of God:

> "O ben creato spirito, che a' rai
> di vita etterna la dolcezza senti
> che, non gustata, non s'intende mai . . ."
> (*Par*.III.37–9)[73]

Furthermore, in the light of such lines, and of the medieval doctrine of grace and revelation whose sharing by Dante they bespeak, we are able to see that not even Virgil's knowledge of *facts* pertaining to revelation, to which allusion was earlier made, puts him in the position to lead Dante to knowledge of the deepest evil. The essence of revelation is personal knowledge and experience of the love of God, or better, of the loving God. Christianity is not essentially knowledge of facts about God and his plan of salvation, but knowledge of, or contact with, God himself revealing himself and his love in facts, events and persons. We do not know how Virgil came to such facts pertaining to revelation as he possesses. It would be idle to speculate on whether he was able to conclude to the knowledge he has from acquaintance with other souls in Limbo and from the events he witnessed there, or whether he gained it from some special knowledge gien by God to him or to all virtuous pagans after death. What we can certainly say, and it is of major importance for assessing his role vis-à-vis Dante, is that his mode of knowledge differs essentially from that of any christian: he has never known God revealing himself in person, however dimly and obscurely, as He who loves with that love of friendship which wishes to bring a person to eternal enjoyment of His company. Considered in terms of affectivity, Virgil's situation after death is essentially a continuation of that which he had before death: he does not love God supernaturally, with charity. What Virgil does not possess is caught in the distinction that Aquinas draws between natural and supernatural love of God: "caritas diligit Deum super omnia eminentius quam natura. Natura enim diligit Deum super omnia, prout est principium et finis naturalis boni: caritas autem secundum quod est obiectum beatitudinis, et secundum quod homo habet quandam societatem spiritualem cum Deo" (I–II, q.109,a.3, ad lum).[74] For all his knowledge of specific facts, Virgil lacks participation in the "spiritual communion" with God from which Dante had turned in turning from Beatrice, and it is therefore essential that he should cede to her and to her strictures on Dante if the latter is fully to repent and be re-established in the communion of saints.

In considering Dante's third and final borrowing from Virgil in *Pg.*XXX, from *Georgics* IV.525–7, we may leave aside the question of whether Dante was familiar with the *Georgics* as a whole. He may, as Moore suggested, have found the Eurydice episode in a florilegium.[75] As I have noted, some critics would seem to be hesitant to accept the parallel since they omit any mention of it when discussing *Pg.*XXX.49–51,[76] though none, so far as I am aware, has adduced positive arguments against it. It seems to me that the similarity of thought in the two passages, taken together with the threefold occurrence of Virgil's name in the same metrical positions as those in which "Eurydice" is found in *Georgics* IV, puts the parallel beyond reasonable doubt:

> (volveret) *Eurydicen* vox ipsa et frigida lingua,
> a miseram *Eurydicen!* anima fugiente vocabat.
> *Eurydicen* toto referebant flumine ripae.[77]

> Ma *Virgilio* n'avea lasciati scemi
> di sé, *Virgilio* dolcissimo patre,
> *Virgilio* a cui per mia salute die'mi.

Here the similarity in the dominant meaning and tone of the two passages enable us to see Dante as climaxing his tribute to Virgil by the definite subordination or difference to similarity. Both passages speak of overwhelming sadness at the loss of someone deeply loved. Orpheus' loss of his wife is readily able to evoke a response in us, and no one who has followed the journey of the two poets in the *Comedy* can doubt Dante's depth of feeling when he discovers that his "dolcissimo patre" has disappeared. Both Eurydice and Virgil are lost because they must return to the melancholy underworld of the shades.

We are not, in this final echo of a Virgilian passage, so arrested by dissimilarity as to require our seeing the narrative and development of ideas progressing only through immediate resolution of the tension, in the meeting with Beatrice and Dante's repentance. But there is one undeniable difference between the loss of Eurydice and the loss of Virgil which is given just sufficient prominence in the Dantean tercet as to leave us with a hope at the back of our minds that Dante will attempt later to ease our disquiet. The difference is, of course, that where Eurydice is forced to return to the underworld through Orpheus's breaking of the condition that he must not look back, Virgil's disappearance is not caused by Dante's turning to him. Dante turns after Virgil has left; Virgil is portrayed as the agent of his own disappearance: "Ma Virgilio n'avea lasciati scemo di sè". It is, however, an agency not without its element of unwillingness, for we must assume that there would be in Virgil a desire, *ceteris paribus*, to accompany Dante to the realm of happiness. Things, we know, are not equal. He goes in accord with God's will. But God's will cannot be equated with the " 'immitis rupta tyranni foedera' " [78] whose harsh injustice leads Eurydice to cry out against the " 'crudelia . . . fata' " (vv.492–6). We have heard on several occasions during the poets' journey Virgil's own account of why he has been condemned to eternally unfulfilled desire. The account he gives is coherent, but retains all the mystery of an intelligibility whose nodal point is the inscrutable providence of God. This will be not merely (relatively) intelligible but affectively acceptable to the degree that one appreciates that divine providence is the providence of a loving God. Such knowledge of providence we have not yet attained in the *Divine Comedy*, I would submit; we do not yet know God in a way that will enable us readily to accept that his providential will is indeed the will of one who loves more deeply than we who, with Dante, have something in us that balks at the sight of human goodness denied divine fulfillment. Dante will return to the theme (*Par*.XIX–XX,esp.XIX.67–90) after we have become familiar with the overflowing goodness of God displayed in the joy of the saints in heaven, and will attempt to lead us with himself to that knowledge (and acceptance), but it will be a knowledge stemming from and dependent on contact with God as he reveals himself supernaturally in the christian dispensation, [79] and Virgil will not be there.

The hint is given by Dante at *Pg*.XXX.49–54 and earlier that the Virgil who disappears necessarily, yet with such fine descretion, at the coming of Beatrice is a figure of great melancholy not simply because he is denied beatitude, but also because the ultimate reason for the justice of that denial, the justice of a loving God, escapes being known in the only way that would bring him anything like trustful and 'satisfactory' understanding. Just as the lack of experience of immediate contact with the loving God precludes Virgil from leading Dante to full repentance, so it leaves him, even at the end, lacking understanding of himself and his own eternal fate; he remains in a real sense a mystery even to himself.[80]

All three reminiscences of Virgil's works in *Pg.* XXX serve to draw a line between the wisdom of Virgil and christian wisdom, though in a graded way: the difference is stark at v.21, less marked at v.48, and softened into the overriding sense of mystery and melancholy loss at vv.49–51. Each in its own way accentuates a central truth of the *Comedy*, to which the limitations in Virgil's guidance discussed in the first part of this paper also called attention: it is the glory and the burden of Virgil to be essentially in death as in life *worldly*-wise, no less and no more.

NOTES

1. See, for example, *Inf.* I and II passim; VIII.104–5; XXI.79–84; *Pg.* I.52–69. Clearly, too, Virgil is given the task of guiding Dante because he is now an inhabitant of the world that waits beyond death; when explaining his presence to Statius, it is to this, in the context comparatively pedestrian, fact that Virgil first refers. Speaking of Dante, Virgil tells Statius: " 'l'anima sua ch'è tua e mia serocchia, / venendo sù, non potea venir sola, / però ch'al nostro modo non adocchia. / Ond'io fui tratto fuor de l'ampia gola . . .' ", *Pg.* XXI.28–31.

2. It may be worth stating here that throughout this essay when theological terms such as 'christian', 'supernatural', 'revelation' are used, they refer to Dante's understanding of these terms, or to their meaning as commonly accepted in the middle ages. The use of these terms has changed significantly over the centuries, but it is not part of my purpose to note such changes, nor to attribute to christians today acceptance of the medieval meaning of the terms or of the theology implied therein.

3. For recent discussions of Virgil as representing reason, see D. Consoli, *Il significato del Virgilio dantesco* (Florence, 1967), especially pp. 59ff (and cf. id., s.v. "Virgilio", *Enciclopedia Dantesca*, vol. 5 [Rome, 1976], pp. 1034–43); A. Vallone, *Dante* (Milan, 1971), pp. 394–410.

4. Though this statement is one of the major grounds for regarding Virgil as voicing what reason unaided by faith can know, it should be noted that it is not couched in universal terms; indeed the qualifying *qui* would seem to be emphasized: Virgil will *on this topic* (free choice) say what reason knows. J. Pelikan is, I suspect, reflecting a common reading of this passage when, accepting "The identification of the role of Vergil in the *Divine Comedy* as, among other things, that of reason leading to revelation", he cites in support this passage without the qualification: " 'I can speak to you', Dante had Virgil say, 'only as far as reason sees; beyond that, you must wait for Beatrice, for that is the business of faith' ", *The Christian Tradition, 3: The Growth of Medieval Theology (600–1300)* (Chicago, 1978), p. 291.

5. The following certainly qualify as major doctrinal passages: *Inf.* VII.73–96 (on fortune and providence); XI.22–111 (on the divisions of hell); XIV.94–120

(the Old Man of Crete); *Pg.*XV.46–57 and 64–81 (on prayer and on the highest good); XVII.85–139 (on the divisions of Purgatory); XVIII.16–75 (on love and free choice). In these, the only point at which Virgil is possibly voicing knowledge beyond what unaided reason can know is when he speaks of God's running to charity and increasing its eternal worth (*Pg.*XV.70–72), though even here he acknowledges that for clear knowledge of this subject Dante may have to await Beatrice, and in terms that may denote that he is speaking from reason alone: " 'E se la mia ragion non ti disfama, / vedrai Beatrice, ed ella pienamente / ti torrà questa e ciascun' altra brama.' " (ib.76–78); cp.ib.XVIII. 46–8 cited above. It is true that Virgil refers to *Genesis* at *Inf.*XI.106–7, but this is by way of embellishment and confirmation; his argument does not depend intrinsically on the bible here.

6. Virgil goes on to recognize that mankind is able to live in 'regions beyond the moon' only in virtue of a heavenly power (*Inf.*II.67–8. With N. Sapegno [*La Divina Comnedia*, vol. 1, 2nd ed. (Florence, 1968), p. 24] and others, I take *sola* in v.76 to refer to *virtù* and not to *donna*, but the same doctrine is implied if the alternative sense is understood). Cf. also Virgil's addressing the avaricious on Mt. Purgatory as "eletti di Dio" (XIX.76).

7. In this passage, Virgil describes himself as having lost the right to see God " 'non per far, ma per non far' " (vv.25–6), and this lack of activity is later identified as that of "not having put on the three holy virtues" (vv.34–5). These three, contrasted with "the other virtues", are clearly the theological as distinct from the natural. Earlier, Virgil says that only those are in heaven who, during their mortal life, had received baptism, the gate of faith (*Inf.*IV.35–6). He knows that he and others who lived before the coming of Christ are confined to Limbo because they did not adore God *debitamente* (ib.37–9). In *Inf.*I he describes himself as "ribellante a la sua [God's] legge' " (v.125). Neither from this nor from elsewhere is it clear whether Virgil's sinfulness is restricted to being marked by original sin or includes a personal element. For the purposes of this paper it is not essential to determine which is the more likely. What is important here is to clarify the consequences of his sinfulness, with regard to his wisdom and his ability to guide Dante. For a recent consideration of the nature of Virgil's sin, and that of the good pagans generally, see the careful, if inconclusive, study by K. Foster, "The Two Dantes" in *The Two Dantes and Other Studies* (London, 1977), pp. 156–253 (on which see n.64).

8. See also his justification of the words on prayer he had put into the mouth of the Sybil in the *Aeneid* (" 'desine fata deum flecti sperare precando' ", VI.376); his words were accurate, he tells Dante, " 'perché 'l priego da Dio era disgiunto' " (*Pr.*VI.28–42). Similarly, knowledge of some original and universal fault lies behind his pensive words that if mankind had had the capacity to reach up to knowledge of the Trinity " 'mestier non era parturir Maria' " (ib.III.34–9). He does not merely know the essential point that man is by nature cut off from God through hereditary sin. He knows of Adam's existence (*Inf.*III.115 and *Pg.*XI.44), and of the tower of Babel and the linguistic disharmony that resulted from the sin there (*Inf.*XXXI.91ff). He is aware that Satan is the great sinner and the origin of all evil (ib.XXXIV, esp. 108; and

ib.I.111), and of Michael's battle in heaven (ib.VII.11–12). Nor is Virgil's knowledge of matters recorded in the Old Testament confined to the fall. He is able to name a number of the figures who appear there, and, somewhat surprisingly, he refers *nominatim* to the book of *Genesis* (ib.XI.107).

9. Although J.H. Whitfield performs a service when he emphasizes that Virgil's knowledge includes awareness of revealed matters, he is much too sweeping when he writes: "Non è dunque soltanto il Vecchio Testamento che Virgilio ha studiato: anche il Nuovo Testamento, con tutta quanta la dottrina cristiana, gli è venuta a conoscenza", "Dante e Virgilio", *Le parole e le idee* 7(1965), p.10. Even with regard to the Old Testament, it is going beyond the evidence to accredit Virgil with deep knowledge of it all, as Whitfield does (ib.p.9; cf. also p.15).

10. This terse description singles out the uniqueness of Christ: it distinguishes him from all men in that he was sinless, and from Adam who is later described as "quell'uom che non nacque" (*Par.* VII.26). Although he is ignorant of Caiphas' part in encompassing the crucifixion, Virgil is aware of Judas' betrayal (*Inf.* XXXIV.61ff).

11. Virgil also shows knowledge of things belonging to the time after Christ's death. He knows historical facts pertaining to individuals in hell who lived after the time of Christ: see his comments on the avarice of the clergy (*Inf.* VII.40–48), and his naming of Michael Scot, Guido Bonatti and Asdente (ib.XX.115–8). It is hardly likely that he learned of these from other Limbo dwellers, as he had learned of Statius' affection for him from Juvenal (*Pg.* XXII.13–15). Also and notably he is able to predict the coming of the Veltro. With the prophetic aspect of his knowledge I shall not be concerned. Virgil is not portrayed during the rest of the journey as one whose guidance depends essentially on a special prophetic power; indeed the role of prophesying concerning Dante's own life is given to others, not to Virgil. The prophecy regarding the Veltro is a unique case; and neither this nor the knowledge he shows of individuals in hell who lived after the time of Christ requires altering the view that his wisdom in the *Comedy* is essentially that which mankind can gain on earth through its own powers.

12. In contrast to Virgil, the heavenly agent opens the gates of Dis effortlessly ("con una verghetta / l'aperse" IX.89–90), thus in a sense both fulfilling and belying Virgil's words: " 'la città dolente / u' non potemo entrare omai sanz'ira' " (ib.32–3). This latter aspect is hinted at by Dante when he comments that after the opening of the door "Dentro li 'ntrammo sanz'alcuna guerra" (ib.106). The devils are implicitly contrasted with the heavenly agent, who so easily affects the opening, in the use of the phrase *da ciel*. While he is the instrument of God's power as "da ciel messo", they have been banished from heaven; they are "da ciel piovuti" (VIII.83), or, in Virgil's words " 'cacciati del ciel' " (IX.91). The identity of the one sent from heaven is disputed, but this problem is not germane to the theme of this paper.

13. The hesitation implied in the immediately subsequent " 'se' non . . .' " is overcome by his remembering Beatrice and the help that is on its way: " 'Tal ne s'offerse. / Oh quanto tarda a me ch'altri qui giunga!' " (IX.8–9).

14. Dante's principal aim in having Virgil speak of this journey may have been to

portray him as confidently reassuring the pilgrim. This journey of Virgil seems to have been a creation of Dante, without warrant in classical or medieval tradition: see Sapegno, p. 100, who surmises that Dante must have taken "il primo spunto alla sua invenzione" from Lucan, *Pharsalia*, VI.508–827.

15. I have considered these themes in detail in *"Inferno* XXI: Virgil and Dante. A study in contrasts", forthcoming in *Italica*.

16. This contrasts with the undignified scramble with which he had helped Dante escape from the deluded demons: see *Inf.* XXIII.37–51. Again, significantly, it was Dante who first expressed anxiety about the possibility of being overtaken once more by the demons (ib.21–4), and who alerted Virgil to their actual approach (ib.34–36).

17. Note the repetition of "pur fermo" in the following line ("Quando mi vide pur fermo e duro"), and contrast Beatrice's being "pur ferma" with respect to the pitying angels, and thus indirectly with respect to Dante himself: *Pg.* XXX.100. On this see the comment in C.J. Ryan "Grace, merit and *buona volontade*", *Italian Studies* 34(1980), p. 10.

18. Christ in his glory is referred to in the image of the *pome* at *Pg.* XXXII.74: "Quali a veder de' fioretti del melo / che del suo pome li angeli fa ghiotti / e perpetue nozze fa nel cielo . . ." The meaning of *pomi* at *Inf.* XVI.61 is not specified, but it seems to refer to the virtues or ingredients of perfection and happiness: " 'Lascio lo fele e vo per dolci pomi / promessi a me per lo verace duca.' " The same may be implied in a possible connection between the *pomi* which hang on trees whose sustenance comes from heaven, and which are denied to the gluttonous, and the fruit of the tree of Eden: cf. *Pg.* XXII.132, XXIII.34 and 68; and cp. the inversion of these trees with that of the tree of justice (ib.XXII.133–5 and XXXII.40–2).

19. It is with reference to Beatrice's tearful eyes that Virgil, at *Inf.* II, closes his description to Dante of his encounter with her: "Poscia che m'ebbe ragionato questo, / li occhi lucenti lagrimando volse, / per che mi fece del venir più presto' " (vv.115–7).

20. It is advisable to state this point clearly since commentators and critics, when speaking of Dante at the end of his journey up the mountain, frequently speak as if he were now faultless. The relation between that sinfulness still to be purged and the forgiveness which apparently occurred at the gate of Purgatory, and between it and the purification on the mountain, raise delicate and interesting problems, but they are not my concern here.

21. The words of Beatrice lose their most serious significance with respect to Dante's purification if they are considered as voicing spite or jealousy, or even simply personal hurt. B. Stambler, speaking of Beatrice's command to Dante to "raise his beard", regards her as talking "with almost fishwife spite"; and, commenting more broadly on the meeting, he believes that "all these [allegorical] significances are secondary to our first and dominant attention to the lashings out of a woman whose self-esteem has been wounded" (*Dante's Other World. The Purgatorio as Guide to the Divine Comedy* [London, 1958], pp. 264–5). I agree entirely with Charles Williams' comment regarding Beatrice when she

meets Dante: "Beatrice is not to be supposed to be vulgarly and extremely jealous", *The Figure of Beatrice* (2nd ed., New York, 1957), p. 186.

22. 'Fuller' rather than 'full': even Dante's final confession is marked by the sinner's wish to minimize his guilt. See Ryan, art.cit., p.11.

23. J.S. Scott has argued, convincingly, that the puzzling comparison of Beatrice to an admiral (*Pg.*XXX.58–60) is designed by Dante, through the disconcerting masculinity of the term of comparison, to prevent the reader from forgetting the analogical level by shocking him "into recognition of Beatrice's role" as analogue of Christ ("Dante's admiral", *Italian Studies* 27[1972], p.40). I would add that the masculinity and sternness of the image serve also to draw attention more sharply to the shift in tone between Virgil and Beatrice in their attitude to Dante. Where Virgil in his final words has been proud and congratulatory, so that Dante at the approach of Beatrice can turn spontaneously to him "col respitto / col quale il fantolin corre a la mamma /quando ha paura o quando elli è afflitto" (*Pg.*XXX.43–5), Beatrice rebukes him and will not speak with pleasure to him until he repents. The contrast between Virgil and Beatrice's attitudes is all the more striking for Dante's successive and contrasting association of feminine and masculine roles with people of the 'other' sex.

24. This conclusion is not overturned by Matelda's words at the end of *Pg.*XXVIII. Addressing Virgil, Statius and Dante, she says: " 'Quelli ch' anticamente poetaro / l'età de l'oro e suo stato felice, / forse in Parnaso esto loco sognaro. / Qui fu innocente l'umana radice; / qui primavera sempre e ogne frutto; / nettare è questo di che ciascun dice' " (vv.139–44). Dante adds: "Io mi rivolsi 'n dietro allora tutto / a' miei poeti, e vidi che con riso / udito avean l'ultimo costrutto." The *forse* hardly implies a real doubt; it seems clear that in Matelda's gracious parenthesis Dante is certainly attributing to the ancient poets some knowledge of Eden and human innocence. The key word is *sognaro*, which implies, in consonance with the rest of the *Comedy*, that they had no more than a vague knowledge of the primeval state. As Grandgent puts it: they "had some inkling of the truth. When they sang of Parnassus and the golden age, they may have been dimly conscious of the real origin of man", *La Divina Commedia*, ed. and annotated by C.H. Grandgent, revd by C.S. Singleton (Cambridge, Mass., 1972), p.569. A similar imperfect awareness of man's first state is implied in Virgil's speaking of the Old Man of Crete (*Inf.*XIV.94–120). It is entirely compatible with such knowledge that he should be unaware of the full measure of God's gift to man in his original innocence or in the state restored by Christ, and hence of the evil involved in the sin committed by Adam or a christian. Just as his knowledge of the fact of original sin and of the primal sin of the devils does not make him fully sensitive to the evil of the devils, so neither does his partial awareness of original innocence and the christian dispensation bring him to full appreciation of the love of God for the christian, and of what sinning involves for the christian.

25. I agree with R. Guardini when he remarks that under Virgil Dante can "comprendere il male, e, nel levarsi contro di esso, il bene, ma tutto serba una certa indeterminatezza", and that the experience of Purgatory becomes for

Dante "conoscenza aperta e piena soltanto alla luce di Beatrice", "La figura di Virgilio nella *Commedia*", in *Maestro Dante* (Milan, 1962), pp.58–9.

26. The translation may have been intended by Dante to be not quite exact: see n.53.

27. See pp. 35–6.

28. Singleton, Landino and Pézard are, up to a point, exceptions: see below, notes 32 and 33. The suggestion by L. Pietrobono, *La Divina Commedia*, vol. 2 (Turin, 1952), p.404, that Dante in citing *Aen.* VI.883 may intend the line, in harmony with its original sense, to refer not to Christ nor to Beatrice but to the future Veltro has, rightly, not been taken up by critics.

29. U. Bosco-G. Reggio, *La Divina Commedia*, vol.2 (Florence, 1979), pp.514 and 516. Sapegno, commenting on v.21, writes: "La citazione poetica, in bocca agli angeli, è un altro segno del sincretismo culturale di Dante, che si fa più vistoso nei passi di intonazione volutamente più solenne" (op.cit., p.331). S.A. Chimenz, commenting on the same verse, writes: "La frase virgiliana . . . vuol essere indirittamente un supremo omaggio di Dante a Virgilio, la cui parola è messa sullo stesso piano di quella del vangelo", *La Divina Commedia*, vol. 2 (Turin, 1965), p. 261. (This author runs contrary to the common viewpoint when he adds: "ma appunto questa così scoperta contaminazione di cristiano e pagano, per sè assai significativa, sulla bocca degli angeli non si può dire proprio conveniente." Any incongruence disappears if, as I argue, Dante is not merely juxtaposing the bible and Virgil, but making a creative critique of the latter to draw forward his thought.) Less explicitly, A. Momigliano has commented: "Le parole con cui Beatrice è invocata ed accolta sono sempre latine, come richiede la solennità del momento: e qui dove non soccorrono quelle dei testi sacri, Dante ricorre ad una frase di Virgilio . . . che, interpolata da un *o*, acquista l'apparenza d'un versetto di coro sacro." (*La Divina Commedia*, vol. 2 [repr., ed. F. Mazzoni, Florence, 1973], p.685). Similarly, M. Porena: "Dante non poteva onorare Virgilio più che con questo far cantare da angeli, in un momento così solenne, parole sue insieme con parole del Vangelo!" (*La Divina Commedia*, vol. 2 [2nd ed., Bologna, 1973], p.289).

30. Similarly, I think that it is inappropriate to speak of Dante's citation of Virgil simply as "underlining" the physical abandonment of Dante to Virgil spoken of at *Pg.*XXX.43–5, as do Sapegno (p.333,n.48) and, echoing him, Bosco-Reggio (p.516,n.51). The *abbandono* within the narrative, indicated in the child-mother image, turns out to be fruitless and inappropriate because Virgil cannot succour Dante in his deepest need. Dante the poet, the creator of that narrative, turns poetically to Virgil at the points discussed in *Pg.*XXX not in an uncritical abandonment, but with an admiration touched with clear awareness of his Latin master's limitations.

31. Work on this paper was far advanced when I was struck by a passage in E.R. Curtius' *European Literature and the Latin Middle Ages*. While his claims concerning the would-be critic do not apply in the relatively narrow context of this paper, the view he expresses broadly confirms the one adopted here: "To cite Dante's hundreds of imitations of the *Aeneid*, and especially of Book VI; to point out his taking over of Virgilian persons and other world localities; to pursue the transposition of Virgil's verses into Dante's lines (Aen.,IV,23=

Purg.,XXX,48; Aen.,VI,883= Purg.,XXX,21)—these tasks cannot be attempted here. Whoever undertakes them will need the most delicate tact, together with intensive scholarship. He would have to raise the question of which elements of the *Commedia* were borrowed from the *Aeneid* or based upon it, *and how they were modified*" (ET [London, 1953], p.359; italics mine).

32. The similarity is noted by A. Pézard: "Cette réminiscence est bizarre à première vue . . . Mais Dante songeait sans doute à d'autres expressions de Virgile qu'il ne cite pas: 'egregium forma iuvenem' (VI.861), et surtout les deux vers de regret: 'ostendent terris hunc tantum fata, neque ultra esse sinent' (869–870), qui pourraient s'appliquer au passage de Béatrice en ce monde et à sa disparation soudaine" (*Dante. Oeuvres complètes* [Paris, 1965], p.1331). However, the strangeness in the contrast is not sufficiently explained by this parallel between the situations of Marcellus and Beatrice: a christological reference is needed, and the essential difference between Marcellus' death and that of Christ must be brought out.

33. The difference between the two scenes is not only passed over but obscured by commentators who speak *tout court* of the Virgilian passage as being in honour of, or in praise of, Marcellus: see Scartazzini-Vandelli ("Anchise . . . parla in onore del giovane Marcello", p.567); Gmelin ("Anchises zum Preise des Marcellus spricht", p.476); Chimenz ("parole di Anchise in lode del giovinetto Marcello", p.261). Certainly Anchises does praise the young Roman in the course of the passage (VI.867–886) (and, of course, historically the passage may have been a later addition by Virgil; see: *The Sixth Book of the Aeneid*, ann. H.E. Butler [Oxford, 1920], p.263; for a different view see: *Aeneidos Liber Sextus*, ann. R.G. Austin [Oxford, 1977], p.265), but the praise is situated within a dominant tone of sorrow and regret. The passage begins on this note: " 'o gnate, ingentem luctum ne quaere tuorum' ", and ends as it began; it is from the concluding lament that Dante's citation is taken. Pietro di Dante is certainly straying from the truth when he comments on *Pg.*XXX.21: "Simile dicit Virgilius *de beatitudine* Marcelli", *Petri Allegherii super Dantis ipsius genitoris comoediam commentarium, nunc primum in lucem editum* (Florence, 1845), p.511. (We may surmise from this and from his comment on v.48, where he says that the words of Dido were spoken "de amore Sichaei praeterito in recessu Aeneae" [ib.p.512] that the commentator was not at this point working "testo alla mano"!) Benvenuto is, similarly, wide of the mark when he comments: "Modo ad propositum Anchises fecit magnam commendationem supra Marcellum et *volens facere festum dixit . . .* ", *Benevenuti de Rambaldis de Imola Comentum super Dantis Alligherii Comoediam nunc primum integre in lucem editum*, ed. J.C. Lacaita, vol. 4 (Florence, 1887), p.208. Singleton is, as far as I am aware, unique among both ancient and modern commentators in regarding Dante as intending us to bear in mind the sadness of the Marcellus scene. But rather than see Dante as contrasting the tone of the original with that of *Pg.*XXX.21, he regards him as bringing across the sadness of the *Aeneid* to the *Purgatorio* scene, through the verse's being directed to Virgil: "This most remarkable farewell verse, taken from *Aen.*VI.883, is turned toward Virgil, though it serves in the literal meaning as an utterance of the welcoming angels, who, as will be seen, toss flowers for Beatrice. It bears the haunting sadness of

its context in the *Aeneid* and functions as a climax to the whole strain of pathos that has attached to the figure of the 'sweet father', as he will now be called when suddenly he is no longer by Dante's side" (p.734). This seems to me to require forcing a more direct reference to Virgil than the text will bear at this point, and to fail to give adequate account of the contrast in tone between the principal sense of the two passages. One way in which the scene in the *Aeneid* may be likened to that of the *Comedy*, but still within the context of a basic contrast, is that suggested by the comment of Landino: "Manibus, o, date lilia plenis, È sententia presa di Virgilio, il quale, deplorando la morte di Marcello, conforta, che tali ossequie sieno ornate di gigli, onde dice nel Sesto . . . Et in tal modo per transito ci ammonisce, che *honoriamo la passione di Cristo*", *Dante con l'espositioni di Christophoro Landino et d'Alessandro Vellutello* (Venice, 1596), p.264.

34. "his face was sad and his eyes downcast". All translations of Virgil's works are taken from *Virgil*, trans. by H.R. Fairclough, vol. 1 (Cambridge, Mass., 1967).

35. "but black night hovers about his head with its mournful shade".

36. "No youth of Ilian stock shall exalt so greatly with his promise his Latin forefathers, nor shall the land of Romulus ever take such pride in any of her sons."

37. "Alas for goodness! alas for old-world honour and the hand invincible in war! Against him in arms would none have advanced unscathed, whether on foot he met the foe, or dug his spurs into the flanks of his foaming horse. Ah! child of pity, if haply thou couldst burst the harsh bond of fate, thou shalt be Marcellus!"

38. "Give me lilies with full hand; let me scatter purple flowers; let me heap o'er my offspring's shade at least these gifts and fulfil an unavailing service."

39. These lines may have been the conclusion of Anchises' speech in an earlier draft of the *Aeneid*: see n.33. That Dante was well aware of the thematic importance of these lines we know from his citation of them at *Mon.* II.vi.9.

40. "These in truth I have long yearned to tell and show thee to thy face, yea, to count this, my children's seed, that so thou mayest rejoice with me the more at finding Italy."

41. "And when Anchises . . . fired his soul with love of fame that was to be, he tells him then of the wars he must thereafter wage . . ."

42. See also the description of the angelic boatman by Virgil at *Pg.* II.34–6: " 'Vedi come l'ha dritte verso 'l cielo, / trattando l'aere con l'etterne penne, / che non si mutan come mortal pelo.' "

43. Connected with the theme of eternal life in *Pg.* XXX is the note of joy that runs throughout the verses anticipating and describing Beatrice's coming. The biblical figures turn to the gryphon and its chariot "come a sua pace" (v.9). One of them sings "Veni, sponsa, de Libano" (v.11), evocative not of the rapturous pleasure of purely human love which the *Song of Songs* records, but of the spiritual nuptials between God and the Church, and between Christ and the individual soul which Christian tradition had read into the biblical work (as witness St. Bernard's well known series of sermons commenting on this work). The angels who strew the flowers are compared in their singing to the blessed who "alleluia" at the end of time (vv.13–18).

44. *Par.* VII.48; cf. also ib.XXXIII.7–9, and next note.

45. K. Foster has drawn attention to the strong emphasis which Dante gives to Christ's work as being that of bringing man to eternal happiness; see, for example, his entry *Cristo* in the *Enciclopedia Dantesca*, vol. 2 (Rome, 1970), pp.262–9. There he speaks of Dante's "insistenza, tutta personale, sulla 'ultramondanità' del fine ultimo cristiano, teso essenzialmente a una vita eterna e trascendente" (p.264). Later in the same article he writes: "Una sintesi della natura e della missione di Cristo è contenuta nelle parole che Beatrice rivolge a Dante nel Cielo stellato: 'Quel che ti sobranza / è virtù da cui nulla si ripara. / Quivi è la sapienza e possanza / ch'aprì le strade tra 'l cielo e la terra, / onde fu già sì lunga disianza (XXIII.35–39; cfr *Pg.* X.34–42)" (p.269).

46. This liturgical background has been noted by J.S.P. Tatlock, "The last cantos of the *Purgatorio*", *Modern Philology* 32(1934–5), p.122, Grandgent-Singleton, p. 584, and Singleton, p. 734.

47. This title applied to Christ in the Eurcharist (originally used of manna: *Ps.* 77/78, v.25; cf. *Wisdom* XVI.20) was a traditional one. It is used by Dante of Christ, though not specifically of him in his Eucharistic presence, at *Par.* II.11 (and contrast *Conv.* I.i.7).

48. The structure of the Palm Sunday liturgy in the Latin rite of the Roman Catholic church has remained unchanged in essentials from the middle ages. On the structure of the Palm Sunday liturgy in the middle ages, see *Le Pontifical romain au moyen-âge, Tome I: Le pontifical romain du XIIe siècle*, ed. M. Andrieu (Vatican City, 1938), p.211.

49. On the liturgical significance of this gospel reading, see P. Parsch, *The Church's Year of Grace*, vol. 2 (ET, Collegeville, Minn., 1953), pp.291–6.

50. J.C. Fenton, *St. Matthew* (London, 1963), p.329; C.E.B. Cranfield, *The Gospel according to St. Mark* (Cambridge, 1972), p. 354; R.E. Brown, *The Gospel according to John, I-XII* (New York, 1966), pp.462–3. A feature of Luke's account of the crowd's cry (XIX.38) calls for particular attention. There the phrase which follows the *Benedictus* is not the simple "hosanna in altissimis/excelsis" of Matthew (XXI.9) or Mark (XI.10; John omits the phrase), but the longer: "pax in caelo et gloria in excelsis" (XIX.38). Here Luke portrays the crowd as echoing in part (albeit unconsciously) the words of the angels to the shepherds at the beginning of the gospel story: " '*Gloria* in altissimis Deo, et in terra *pax* hominibus bonae voluntatis' " (II.14): see C. Stuhlmueller, "The Gospel according to Luke" in *The Jerome Biblical Commentary* (London, 1970), part II, p.153; cf. also A.R.C. Leaney, *The Gospel according to St. Luke* (London, 1958), p.246, E.J. Tinsley, *The Gospel according to Luke* (Cambridge, 1965), p.175, and G.W.H. Lampe, "Luke", *Peake's Commentary on the Bible* (revd ed., London, 1962), p. 838. The words which formed part of the joyful introduction to the whole life of Christ are now adopted as part of the introduction to the final phase of that life: the ministry in Jerusalem, the passion and resurrection (*Luke* XIX.29–XXIV.53). And it may be that Dante had the Lucan account particularly in mind, for not only does Luke appear to have been something of a favourite with him (he calls him "scriba mansuetudinis Christi", *Mon.* I.xvi.2), but also, we may reasonably assume, the echo by the crowd of the angels' song would not have escaped Dante's ear, readily attuned as it was to verbal artistry. Where the crowds echo the angelic *gloria* and *pax* in

the gospel, Dante places the *Benedictus* of the crowds on the lips of angels in the *Comedy*.

51. The attaining of "il ben de l'intelletto", *Inf*. III. 18.

52. Through love of God whose eternal *valor* is drawn to that love: see esp. *Pg*. XV. 67–75.

53. This difference may be hinted at in Dante's use of *segni* for *vestigia*, whereby he safeguards his love from the possible nuance in the Latin that one love is about to cede to another. The alternative would seem to have been open to him: he uses *vestigge* and *vestige* at *Pg*. XXXIII. 108 and *Par*. XXXI. 81, as well as *vestigio* at *Inf*. XXIV. 50, *Pg*. XXVI. 106 and *Par*. V. 11. B. Nardi comments on Dante's use of Dido's words: "sulle sue labbra acquista più verità che non su quelle di Didone", *Dal Convivio alla Commedia* (Rome, 1960), p. 131.

54. "Were the purpose not planted in my mind, fixed and immovable, to ally myself with none in bond of wedlock . . . to this one weakness, perchance, I might have yielded."

55. "Before, O Shame, I violate thee or break thy laws! He, who first linked me to himself, has taken away my heart; may he keep it with him, and guard it in the grave!"

56. "Thinkest thou that dust or buried shades give heed to that?"

57. "The faith vowed to the ashes of Sychaeus I have not kept."

58. "For since neither in the course of fate did she perish, nor by a death she had earned, but hapless before her day, and fired by sudden madness . . ."

59. "But the queen, long since smitten with a grievous love-pang, feeds the wound with her life blood, and is wasted with fire unseen."

60. Sychaeus, like Beatrice, is faithful to his beloved beyond the grave (*Aen*. VI. 473–4); the difference lies in the former's impotence to help.

61. "But he . . . little by little begins to efface Sychaeus, and essays with a living passion to surprise her long-slumbering soul and heart unused to love."

62. On the journey itself as being willed by God, see especially, in addition to the loci in *Inf*. VIII–IX and XXI discussed above, *Inf*. I. 91 and the recurring description of the journey as a *grace*: *Pg*. VIII. 66, XIV. 14 and 79–80, XVI. 40, XX. 42; *Par*. X. 54 and 83, XXIV. 4. As Dante's long journey nears its end, Beatrice addresses him: " 'Figliuol di grazia . . .' " (*Par*. XXXI. 112).

63. What I say here of the christian dispensation applies to the whole judaeo-christian order. In medieval theology, God's presence to the Jews before Christ was of a kind superior to his presence in nature or in other religions. Jewish history before Christ formed a single whole with Christ's life and the history of the christian church, as the medium in which God supernaturally revealed himself.

64. Virgil cannot be said not to be loved by God. For Dante, all of creation is the result of God's love (*Par*. XXIX. 10ff). Even hell is created by divine love: "fecemi la divina potestate / la somma sapienza e 'l primo amore" (*Inf*. III. 5–6). Though all of God's actions are guided by his perfect will, it remains a mystery to man why only some are given grace sufficient to overcome the evil of original sin (cf. *Par*. XIX. 67–90). It will be evident that I cannot agree with K. Foster when he proposes that Virgil and all pagans have been offered, and

have refused, sanctifying grace (*The Two Dantes*, cit., pp. 245–52). This is too large a theme to enter here; for a brief indication of why I disagree, I may refer to my review of Dr. Foster's book: *New Blackfriars* 59(1978), pp.190–2.

65. "there is, however, another [love], the special love by which [God] draws a rational creature above his natural condition to participation in the divine good. And it is as loving in this way that he is said to love someone simply speaking because it is as loving in this way that God simply speaking wills for the creature the eternal good, which is himself."

66. "for the faith of which we are speaking here does not assent to anything except on the ground that it is revealed by God; and so it rests on the divine truth itself as the medium of its assent." The same truth is expressed in different language when Aquinas calls God the source of faith: "Fides ergo facit hominem Deo inhaerere in quantum est nobis principium cognoscendi veritatem; credimus enim ea vera esse quae nobis a Deo dicuntur" (*Summa Theologiae*, II.II.q.17,a.6).

67. "the formal object of faith is the First Truth".

68. "it should however, be borne in mind that in the object of faith there is what can be termed a formal element, namely the First Truth, which surpasses all knowledge natural to a creature, and a material element, which is that to which we assent by adhering to the First Truth." God's being the basis or motive of human faith is signified in the second part of the pseudo-Augustinian formula: "credere Deum, credere Deo, credere in Deum" (see T. Camelot, " 'Credere Deo, credere Deum, credere in Deum.' Pour l'histoire d'une formule traditionelle", *Revue des sciences philosophiques et théologiques* 30[1941–2], pp.149–55). Aquinas comments on this formula: "Differt enim dicere credere Deum, sic enim designo obiectum; et credere Deo, quia sic designo testem; et credere in Deum, quia sic designo finem: ut sic Deus possit haberi ut obiectum fidei, ut testis et ut finis" (*Super Ev. S. Johannis Lectura*, cap.VI, lect.3, pars 7). For a detailed discussion of the Thomistic view of faith, and particularly of God as the basis of faith, see J. Alfaro, "Supernaturalitas fidei iuxta sanctum Thomam", *Gregorianum* 44(1963), pp.501–42 and 731–87. The essence of Thomas' position was shared by other medieval theologians: see, for example, Bonaventure, *In Sent.*, lib.III, dist. XXIII,dub.3: "Nam credere Deum respicit divinam Veritatem ut obiectum; credere Deo, ut motivum; credere in Deum, ut finem ultimum"; ib.,a.1,q.3: "una est ratio credendi in omnibus, videlicet ipsa summa Veritas, cui ipsa fides innititur propter se et super omnia"; Albert the Great, *In Sent.*, lib.III,dist.XXIII,a.8: "Fides enim innititur primae veritati . . . Ad primum ergo dicendum, quod virtus una est fides, et habet unum obiectum, quod est prima veritas, et unam rationem quae est eadem veritas, et innititur primae veritati propter seipsam."

69. "As regards the second point it must be said that just as man by means of the natural light of the intellect assents to principles [in deductive reasoning], so the virtuous man by means of the habit of virtue judges rightly concerning what is in keeping with that virtue. And in this way, too, by means of the light of faith divinei infused into man, man assents to what pertains to faith and not to the opposite. And so there is no danger or damnation for those who are

in Christ Jesus (*Rom.* 8:1), illumined by him by means of faith." In traditional doctrine, man is brought to faith through a conjunction of a supernatural mode of God's presence (as the direct motive of faith) and a supernatural principle in man by which his intellectual power is raised to be able to recognize God's presence. As Aquinas puts it: "de divinis duplex scientia habetur . . . Alia secundum modum ipsorum divinorum, ut ipsa divina secundum se ipsa capiantur; quae quidem perfecte nobis in statu viae est impossibilis, sed fit nobis in statu viae quaedam illius cognitionis participatio et assimilatio ad cognitionem divinam, in quantum per fidem nobis infusam inhaeremus ipsi Primae Veritati propter se ipsam" (*In Boeth. De Trinitate*, q.2,a.2).

70. "Faith is the habit of mind whereby eternal life is begun in us, bringing the intellect to assent to things that are not seen." Through faith man begins even on earth to participate in God's own knowledge of himself. Knowledge through the 'informing' of the intellect by God himself is the defining characteristic of the beatific vision; this vision is the perfect realization of the supernatural mode of knowledge, through God's perfect, unclouded actuation of the intellect by his own form or essence. But already on earth man begins, through faith, to share in God's own knowledge of himself: "homo participat cognitionem divinam per virtutem fidei" (Aquinas, I–II,q.110,a.4); faith is a "participatio et assimilatio ad cognitionem divinam" (*In Boeth. De Trinitate*, loc.cit.).

71. As this passage indicates, man *on earth* is refreshed by this "eternal rain". For Dante, as for medieval theologians, the beatific vision makes God present in higher degree, infinitely more clearly; it does not make him directly and personally present for the first time. See notes 69, 70 and 73.

72. The centrality of these ideas is seen in their recurrence as underlying the light imagery employed in the final canto to describe Dante's entry into the vision of God; see especially vv.53–4: "e più e più intrava per lo raggio / de l'alta luce che da sé è vera."

73. The knowledge or experience of eternal life of which Dante is speaking is not confined to its perfect realization in the saints in heaven; he is referring also to the partial sharing of it by christians on earth. This seems clearly implied in the passage; such an interpretation harmonizes with his programmatic statement in *Par.* I, where his experience of heaven is likened to that of christians on earth, so that the latter is necessary for appreciation of his journey: "Trasumanar significar per verba / non si poria; però l'essemplo basti / a cui experienza grazia serba" (vv.70–2). At an important moment later in the *Paradiso*, recording his meeting with Cacciaguida, Dante makes a similar call on christian experience to supply for the inability of his reason (*ingegno*, man's natural intellectual aptitude) to grasp the memory he is recalling: "Qui vince la memoria mia lo 'ngegno; / ché quella croce lampeggiava Cristo, / sì ch'io non so trovare essempro degno; / ma chi prende sua croce e segue Cristo, / ancor mi scuserà di quel ch'io lasso, / vedendo in quell' albor balenar Cristo" (XIV.103–8).

74. "Charity loves God above all things in a higher way than nature. For nature loves God above all things by way of his being the source and end of natural

good; charity, on the other hand, loves him by way of his being the object of beatitude, and according as man has a certain spiritual communion with God."

75. "There is, it is true, very little evidence that Dante was familiar with the *Georgics*, but the episode of Orpheus and Euridice [sic] was one very likely to have been included in collections of 'Extracts' or 'Florilegia' ", *Studies in Dante I* (Oxford, 1896), p.178.

76. Moore writes "But I must not omit to call attention to the beautiful and touching 'echo' of a quotation which has been pointed out in the parting scene of Dante and Virgil in *Purg.* XXX.49–51, as compared with that of Orpheus and Euridice [sic] in *Georg.* IV.525–7 . . . The pathetic repetition of the beloved name in three successive lines and in the corresponding position in each line is very striking", op.cit., pp.20–21. The words "which has been pointed out" are not explained by Moore, but seem to refer to his own earlier remark: "[Dante] shows little, if any, knowledge of the *Georgics*, except one beautiful instance of reminiscence and imitation, which will be quoted below", ib.p.9. See also ib.pp.177–8. Of the major commentators writing since Moore, only T. Casini-S.A. Barbi (*La Divina Commedia*, vol. 2 [repr., ed. F. Mazzoni, Florence, 1973], p.689), G.A. Scartazzini-G. Vandelli (*La Divina Commedia* [19th ed., Milan, 1965], p.569), H. Gmelin (*Die Göttliche Komödie. Kommentar*, vol. 2 [2nd ed., Stuttgart, 1968], p.478), and C.S. Singleton (*The Divine Comedy*, vol. 2, part 2 [Princeton, 1973], p. 741) have taken up his suggestion; others are silent on the point. None of the early commentators makes any allusion to the *Georgics* here. The only critic earlier than Moore whom I know to have made a connection between the two passages is Daniello: "Et usa qui il Poeta una bellissima repetitione, e piena di maraviglia, ripetendo tre volte questo nome Virgilio: così Virgilio nella Georgica;—'Eurydicen vox ipsa . . .' ", *Dante con l'espositione di M. Bernardino Daniello di Lucca, sopra la sua Comedia dell'Inferno, del Purgatorio et del Paradiso; nuovamente stampato, et posto in luce* (Venice, 1568), p.451.

77. "the bare voice and death-cold tongue, with fleeting breath, called Eurydice—ah, hapless Eurydice! 'Eurydice' the banks re-echoed, all adown the stream."

78. "the ruthless tyrant's pact . . . broken."

79. Note the *sovra* in "se la scrittura sovra voi non fosse" (*Par.* XIX.83). This is an elliptic attribution to the objective medium of faith, the Scriptures, of a quality of the subjective virtue of faith, namely its being a higher mode of understanding than that attainable by reason unaided by supernatural illumination: see *Mon.* II.vii.4: "Quedam etiam iudicia Dei sunt, ad que etsi humana ratio ex propriis pertingere nequit, *elevatur* tamen ad illa cum adiutorio fidei eorum que in Sacris Licteris nobis dicta sunt, sicut ad hoc: quod nemo, quantumcunque moralibus et intellectualibus virtutibus et secundum habitum et secundum operationem perfectus, absque fide salvari potest, dato quod nunquam aliquid de Cristo audiverit."

80. It is a commonplace that in presenting Virgil as a figure of deep sadness Dante is being faithful to the historical Virgil as revealed in his poetry. One aspect of Dante's faithful portrayal may be that the lack of understanding inherent in

Virgil's situation in the *Comedy* reflects the deepest source of melancholy in his own poetry: the sadness may stem, in part at least, from his inability fully to see or accept that the world is governed by any ultimate intelligibility, any eternal providence. It might, *mutatis mutandis*, be said of Virgil what G.L. Bickersteth wrote of his chief poetic character, Aeneas: "He accepts his destiny; phrases such as 'Italiam sequimur', 'tendimus in Latium', 'poscor Olympo' are ever on his lips: but, even so, he still leaves us with the impression that he does not really understand, and is consequently never wholly reconciled to, the will of God", *Dante's Virgil. A Poet's Poet* (Glasgow, 1951), pp. 21–2. Later Bickersteth commented: "though like any good Stoic . . . Virgil worships and prays to that spirit and feels impelled to love it, yet his joy in so doing is frustrated by the feeling that, since it is an impersonal presence it cannot return his love, or rather he cannot be sure that it does—'di, *si* qua est caelo pietas, quae talia curet' . . . It is the depth of this passionate but unsatisfied *Sehnsucht* for a God of Love—love being essentially a relation between persons—that imparts such poignancy to the expression of his 'spes incerta futuri' " (ib.,p. 26, author's italics). Something of the lack of understanding, as well as the unfulfilled longing, is, I suggest, retained in Dante's portrayal.

The Power of Discourse:
Martyr's Passion and Old French Epic

ALISON GODDARD ELLIOTT

In the martyrs' *passiones* and the *chansons de geste*, direct speech constitutes an act of the first importance.[1] Both passion and epic involve intense physical suffering, but the necessary prelude to physical *agon* is verbal *agon*: the ritual contest prefigures the literal. Martyr and epic hero alike must triumph over their adversaries in word as well as deed. Direct discourse, moreover, is unambiguous, and it serves as the primary means by which the polarities of the narrative are established. As a result, characters whose significant actions do not include important speech acts tend to be eliminated from the drama.

The speeches in the works under consideration do not function entirely as they do in "real life." The poems of Prudentius, for example, are literary texts obedient to their own laws——laws based on, but not wholly coincident with, those of non-literary discourse. Writing of "the specific problems raised by the interpretation of texts because they are texts and not spoken language," Paul Ricoeur utilizes the terminology of J. L. Austin and J. R. Searle [2] to distinguish three levels of subordination in speech acts: the locutionary or "propositional act," the illocutionary act or force, "that which we do *in* saying," and the perlocutionary, "that which we do *by* saying." He illustrates these distinctions as follows:

When I tell you to close the door, for example, "Close the door" is the act of speaking. But when I tell you this with the force of an order and not of a request, this is an illocutionary act. Finally, I can stir up certain effects, like fear, by the fact that I give you an order. These effects make my discourse act like a stimulus producing certain results. This is the perlocutionary act.[3]

What we have, I suggest, in the *passiones* and in some instances of discourse in the *chansons de geste* is a skewing of function, a tension or disparity between the type of speech act as far as the dramatic situation *within* the text is concerned (that is, with the speech act treated as if it were not literary but actual discourse) and as it is perceived by an audience to function *outside* the text.

In these poems direct speech often performs a function beyond the

Medievalia et Humanistica, New Series, Number 11 (Paul Maurice Clogan, ed.). Rowman and Littlefield, Totowa, NJ, 1982.

purely denotative (the locutionary act). Both in the martyr's speech of defiance and confession of faith during the confrontation scene and in the epic warrior's prayer and theological argument prior to battle, the words are directed beyond the seemingly intended receiver in the text (exceeding, therefore, their apparent dramatic function) to the audience at large. Speeches which seem from the actor's point of view important for their perlocutionary effects (those designed to persuade, convert, or intimidate) are, from the audience's perspective, statements of belief, incapable of alteration and proof against mediation. For the audience, then, they are illocutionary acts. On the other hand, discourse which appears within the context of the poem to be purely declarative may have perlocutionary effects for the listeners. The two types of act, illocutionary and perlocutionary, are present in the same speech; [4] which aspect predominates is a function of the decoder—it depends whether we are looking at the actor or the audience.

The purpose of the present study is to investigate some functions of direct discourse in both passion narrative and epic. In specific we shall explore the pattern of structural oppositions established by the speeches, examine some uses of illocutionary and perlocutionary discourse, and suggest common features and possible influences.

The dramatic climax of many accounts of the martyrs is not, as one might expect, the moment of death but the prior confrontation between saint and persecutor. In a recent article Charles Altman has called attention to the significance of this scene.[5] He notes that the *passiones* are organized in accord with principles of diametrical opposition, as is medieval epic. The confrontation scene, according to Altman, serves to identify the opposing values of the *passio* not with the individual actors in the hagiographic drama but with the religions which they represent. Good and evil are polar opposites and there is no middle ground, no meditation. To quote the *Chanson de Roland,* "Paien unt tort e chrestïens unt dreit." [6]

In the confrontation scene the tyrant attempts to persuade the saint to recant; the saint defiantly refuses, confesses his faith, and assails pagan religion. Then follow torture and death. The prominence of such scenes in hagiography probably owes as much to literary criteria as to historical fact. In the comparatively few "historic" accounts which remain, this section of the narrative is usually brief.[7] In later *Acta*, however, those dating to the fourth and fifth centuries which Hippolyte Delehaye has christened "epic," [8] we find a far different situation. The scene is long and dramatic, its function dialectical. Two facts about the "epic" *Acta* are significant here: they were composed after the Peace of Constantine ended the days of literal martyrdom, and they were largely based on oral traditions since many Church documents had been destroyed during the persecution of Diocletian.[9] Consequently, for the epic *Acta* there is the possibility of adherence to ideal, as well as to actual, standards of behavior. The text primarily is a literary work, not a historical document.[10]

The first fully developed poetic narratives of triumphant Christian heroism are the fourteen hymns in honor of the martyrs entitled collectively the *Peristephanon* (*On the Crown* [*of Martyrdom*]) composed by Aurelius Prudentius Clemens around 405 A.D.[11] The most interesting hymn for our purposes is the fifth, dedicated to St. Vincent of Saragossa, martyred during the reign of Diocletian. A very popular saint, Vincent and his cult moved from Spain to France when the Franks, fighting against the Visigoths during the reigns of Childebert and Clothair I, transferred his body from Saragossa to Paris.[12] Vincent became one of the best-known Spanish martyrs; his adversary, Dacian, provincial governor of Tarragona, acquired great repute as a savage persecutor, a fame he largely owed to his connection with Vincent.[13] The two serve as useful templates for the ideal martyr-hero and the stereotyped tyrant.

There are four closely related versions of the *passio* of St. Vincent: the prose *Acta* published in the *Acta Sanctorum* which served as Prudentius' source;[14] *Peristephanon* V; and two hymns in the Mozarabic liturgy.[15] The first Mozarabic hymn, a contemplative survey of the legend, includes the last forty lines of *Per.* V, while the second consists of the first half of Prudentius' poem, with only minor alterations. Of the Mozarabic hymns, the second alone will concern us. In all versions, Vincent's story is one of triumphant heroism. The *Acta Vincenti*, a good example of epic *Acta*, give the most detailed account and contain the largest cast of characters. The hero is bold and defiant, the tyrant an insane monster, "furore caecus, . . . fervens insania." [16] Vincent replies to Dacian's threats with polemical sermons. There are many actors in the drama. Vincent's nobly-born parents are named; Bishop Valerius of Saragossa, whose archdeacon Vincent was, figures prominently; a throng of guards witnesses the miracle of the blooming potsherds and the appearance of the band of angels in prison. Each subsequent poetic version narrows the focus of the story, reducing the number of actors involved. The result is to emphasize the saint's heroic action and to increase the importance of discourse. Speech becomes *the* significant action, the means by which the polar oppositions are established. In the speeches, moreover, we see most clearly revealed the distinction between Prudentius' poetic creation and a historical document; the poet does not simply versify his source, the *Acta*, even allowing for alternations due to exigencies of meter, but feels free to transform them to suit *his* purpose.

After a brief, hymnal proem, Prudentius plunges into his drama with Dacian's first speech interrogating the saint, omitting entirely the arrest of Vincent and Valerius and the bishop's exile. Dacian abruptly orders Vincent to sacrifice. In his refusal Vincent professes his faith with a speech

which Prudentius has taken from the *Acta* but has shortened so that the
binary opposition between Christian and pagan stands out clearly.[17]

> "Tibi ista praesint numina,
> tu saxa, tu lignum colas,
> tu mortuorum mortuus
> fias deorum pontifex;
> "nos lucis auctorem patrem
> eiusque Christum filium
> qui solus ac uerus deus,
> Datiane, confitebimur."
>
> (33–40)

["Let these by your masters; you may worship stones and wood and
become the dead priests of dead gods. We shall confess the Father, the
author of light, and Christ His Son, who is the only and true God,
Dacian."]

This speech is not intended to convince Dacian of his folly, nor does it do
so. Its purpose is to remind the audience at the outset of the drama of the
polarities. It is therefore an illocutionary speech act.

Dacian grows angrier, Vincent more defiant. In the *Acta* Dacian immediately orders Vincent to be tortured, but Prudentius prolongs the
interrogation scene, giving his hero a thirty-nine line attack on pagan
superstition. Indeed, 86% of this scene (21–208) consists of direct discourse, as the tyrant challenges the saint, and Vincent counters with
scornful polemics. Then actions replace words as the torture begins. The
transition between these two sections of the hymn makes plain the opposition:

> Ventum ad palestram gloriae;
> spes certat et crudelitas,
> luctamen anceps conserunt
> hinc martyr illinc carnifex.
>
> (213–216)

[They come together on the athletic field of glory; hope and cruelty
struggle; the martyr on one side, the torturer on the other, they join in
dubious contest.]

The athletic metaphor (a hagiographic commonplace) stresses the active
nature of the saint's role in the ensuing action. It signals the change from
verbal to physical *agon*. Of his own accord (*sponte*, 221), Vincent ascends
the pyre, unafraid. He is no passive victim, but a willing, energetic par-

ticipant in the contest. But more is at stake than the fate of one man. Hope and Cruelty, Good and Evil, are pitted against one another in mortal combat.[18]

Finally, as the ultimate torture, Dacian orders Vincent placed in a totally dark prison, there to rest his mangled body on the sharp edges of broken potsherds. The sherds, however, suddenly burst into flower, and a crowd of angels appears to the saint, one of whom welcomes him into heaven with a joyous triple anaphora:

> "Exsurge, martyr inclyte,
> exsurge securus tui,
> exsurge et almis coetibus
> noster sodalis addere!"
> (285–288)

["Arise, illustrious martyr, arise, free of care for yourself, arise and join our kindly band as our companion!"]

There have been no speeches in this second section which depicts the physical *agon*. Prudentius has recast portions of the narrative which in the *Acta* were in direct discourse (e.g. the order to thrust the saint into prison) into indirect speech. Consequently, the Angel's words ring out in brilliant contrast to the surrounding narrative. The triple anaphora, *exsurge*, underlines the solemnity of the occasion. The speech is important, for immediate entry into Heaven prior to the Last Judgement was the specific reward for martyrdom, a doctrinal point which the structure of the poem thrown into high relief.

After Vincent's death, the remainder of the hymn concerns the tyrant's vain attempts to destroy the saint's corpse, attempts foiled by a series of miracles. A crow defends the exposed body from marauders; when the soldier Eumorphio throws it into the sea, weighted by a millstone, it floats to shore. The poem closes with a prayer to the martyr to have pity on those venerating his holy day and to intercede with Christ on their behalf.

In Prudentius' drama, direct discourse is unproblematic. There is little gap between interior and exterior, actual (or intended) and apparent meaning. Characters—their speeches and actions—are diametrically opposed, their differences irreconcilable. But here history and the generic expectations of hagiographic narrative are in conflict. In the "historic" *Acta*, some Roman magistrates, with apparent sincerity, tried to persuade the martyrs to recant. Prudentius, however, is careful that we do not think Dacian anything but dedicated to the cause of evil. The narrator characterizes the tyrant's first speech as mild and flattering:

> Ac uerba primum mollia
> suadendo blande effuderat,
> (17–18)

[But first he had poured out soft words, gently persuading.]

These lines, however, are immediately followed by a simile which undercuts the apparent softness of Dacian's words:

> capator ut uitulum lupus
> rapturus adludit prius.
> (19–20)

[just as the hunting wolf first plays with the calf it is going to capture.]

The future active participle, *rapturus*, excludes any possibility of doubt
about Dacian's intentions. He has no genuine desire at all to convince. At
best the tone of Dacian's first speech might be characterized as matter-of-
fact: it is neither particularly soft (*mollia*) nor flattering (cf. *blande*). The
Roman monarch, says Dacian, has ordered the Christians to sacrifice; the
imperatives are peremptory:

> "Vos, Nazareni, adsistite,
> rudemque ritum spernite.
> Haec saxa quae princeps colit
> placate fumo et uictima."
> (25–28)

["You Nazarenes, attend, and reject your crude rite. Propitiate with
smoke and sacrificial victims those stones which the prince worships."]

His second speech is more emotional (*commotior*, 41). Dacian threatens
immediate death if the appointed sacrifices are not made (50–52), and
flattery is nowhere apparent. Overt threats and orders—illocutionary
speech acts—are Dacian's normal mode of discourse. He is incapable of
effective perlocutionary speech; *his* orders fail to frighten or persuade.

The apparent conflict between the tone of Dacian's speech and the
interpretative preface to it (17–20) is not a sign of failure or lack of artistic
control on Prudentius' part. The historical tradition indicated that the
opening speeches of Roman officials were often mild; the later hagiographic tradition admitted no stance but that of total commitment. Intention and appearance must coincide. Consequently, the simile (19–20) focuses the reader's attention on the predatory nature of Dacian's verbal
play. In lines 17–18, Prudentius bows to expectations aroused by history,
in 19–20 undercuts them.[19]

The world of hagiography is black and white. Words mean what they say; what men say corresponds to what they do.[20] The saint confesses his faith, then translates words into actions. The tyrant cannot carry out *his* threats, but it is not for the lack of trying. There is, then, no conflict between word and deed. In fact the hero might be defined in this context as the actor capable of achieving his expressed goals, his opponent as the one who is impotent. The narrator hopes to find himself ultimately aligned with the hero. The concluding lines of the hymn express the hope that the hymnal performance will aid in winning clemency and absolution of sin. Specifically, it is the act of veneration, involving both purity of heart *and* performance of the hymn, which the narrator-poet hopes will obtain him his desired end: [21]

> Si rite sollemnem diem
> ueneramur ore et pectore. . . .[22]
> paulisper huc inlabere
> Christi fauorem deferens,
> (561–562, 565–566)

[If we properly reverence the day of your festival with mouth and heart . . . , come down here for a little while, bringing the favor of Christ.]

Prudentius has written the hymn which will provide the means for venerating the saint *ore et pectore*, the hymn which provides the possible mediation between sin and salvation. By the end of the poem the poet-creator, the poet-audience (one of the faithful witnessing the hagiographic drama), and the poet-performer and -worshipper (one of the congregation venerating the saint) have been harmoniously united into a single person, the Christian poet, an active participant in the hagiographic text.[23] For a Christian, the performance of such a hymn is a significant act, a form of unambiguous discourse. If the poet succeeds in obtaining by his hymn the saint's intercession, his poem itself has become an effective perlocutionary speech act. Unlike the martyr's illocutionary discourse, such speech is capable of effecting mediation, and the role of mediator between good and evil, sin and salvation, is played by the text itself, together with its poet. The poet then will have achieved his goal, literally aligning himself with the side of the Saints and Angels.

The second hymn of the Mozarabic liturgy, a curtailed version of *Per.* V, ends at line 288 after the exultant first strophe of the Angel's speech to Vincent quoted above. Ruth Messenger has suggested that the ensuing portions of Prudentius' hymn were omitted as "perhaps too prolonged and too gruesome to be used as a hymn." [24] On the contrary, one suspects that the end of the poem is too undramatic, too descriptive and lyrical. The

Mozarabic hymn includes the frightful details of Vincent's torture, details more horrible than those depicting Dacian's attempts, unsuccessful after all, to desecrate the saint's body. The hymn-writer perceived what the modern scholar has not, that the true climax of the poem occurs at the Angel's speech of welcome. The Mozarabic hymn ends when the significant *action* of the account has concluded. The scenes which follow the saint's death, with their attendant miracles, testify to Vincent's sanctity, but they are not integral to the narration of triumphant, active heroism.

Both poetic versions of the *passio* have condensed the account contained in the prose *Acta*, eliminating minor details and characters. There is, moreover, a consistent pattern to the omissions. By eliminating the peripheral, the poet focuses the audience's attention more sharply upon the essential action, and in particular upon discourse. The Mozarabic hymn, for example, leaves out the final scenes of the drama which contain only three speeches, two of them short (4 and 10 lines); it ends with the Angel's words of welcome. Prudentius has eliminated non-speaking characters contained in the *Acta* (the saint's parents, Bishop Valerius).

The martyr is one who witnesses (Gk. MARTYREIN 'to witness'), but Christian witnessing is active, not passive. The Christian confession of faith is an act which the speaker must be willing to back up with deeds. Vincent voluntarily ascended the pyre. Prudentius has limited his cast to those who act unambiguously in word and deed. In this respect the Old French epic resembles the martyr's *passio*. Altman, we saw, noted that the martyr's *passio*, like the *chanson de geste*, is binary in structure. Good and evil are diametrically opposed. Larry S. Crist has written that the world of medieval epic "is one in which oppositions are great and exclusive: one is A or X; there are no tenable non-A or non-X categories." [25] We can diagram such a universe using the "semiotic square" elaborated by A. J. Greimas [26] (in fact a version of the "logical square" of Apuleius).[27]

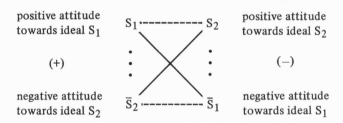

positive attitude towards ideal S_1 S_1 ----------- S_2 positive attitude towards ideal S_2

(+)   (−)

negative attitude towards ideal S_2 $\bar{S}_2$ ----------- $\bar{S}_1$ negative attitude towards ideal S_1

In such a schematization, S_1----------S_2 represents the axis of contraries, S_1 _____ $\bar{S}_1$ the axis of contradictories (the affirmation or negation of a seme), and S_1..............$\bar{S}_2$ indicates implication. Positions, moreover, have moral values attached; the left-hand side of the square represents positively valued ideals (S_1 and, less good, $\overline{S}_2$), while the right-hand values are negative (S_2 and, less bad, S_1). For hagiography (and medieval epic) such attitudes might be semanticized:

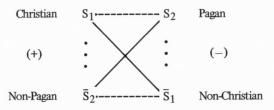

Christian S_1 ----------- S_2 Pagan

(+)   (−)

Non-Pagan $\overline{S}_2$ ----------- $\overline{S}_1$ Non-Christian

Applying this taxonomy to early *chansons de geste* such as the *Chanson de Roland* and the *Chançun de Willame* reveals the following deep structure.[28]

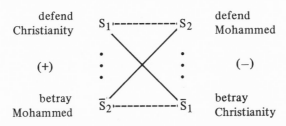

defend   defend
Christianity S_1 ----------- S_2 Mohammed

(+)   (−)

betray   betray
Mohammed $\overline{S}_2$ ----------- $\overline{S}_1$ Christianity

In the early epics, the lower two positions of the square $\overline{S}_2$ and $\overline{S}_1$, numbered 2 and 3) are not tenable on a permanent basis. Allegiances must be unambiguous, not defined by implication. Shifts between the top two positions (1 ⟷ 4) are possible (i.e. conversion or apostasy, treason),[29] and to alter positions a character moves through the bottom positions; he is not, however, permitted to remain there (at 2 or 3). He either moves up or dies. In the *Chanson de Roland* the traitor Ganelon, whose final position is 3 ("betray Christianity") is killed. For the principal actors of this epic we might represent the action as follows:

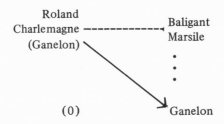

Roland
Charlemagne ------------- Baligant
(Ganelon)   Marsile

(0)   Ganelon

Bramimonde, the Saracen queen, converts to Christianity (as do most pagan women in epic), moving first to a position of lack of sympathy with the pagan cause (4 → 3), then to more active support for the Christian cause (3 → 2), and finally to conversion and baptism (2 → 1). At the end, the cast of characters is neatly divided into the two polarized camps with the majority, of course, occupying the Christian position.

Prudentian hagiography is even more sharply polarized than medieval epic. The prose *Acta* upon which Prudentius relied for his account of Vincent present more actors than does *Per. V*. The saint's parents are named; Bishop Valerius is an important figure; there are many jailors; a throng of Christians hear Vincent's dying speech. Prudentius has eliminated from his poem all characters who take no important action or who might be considered to occupy one of the two lower positions of the semiotic square (2 or 3). In the *Acta* Vincent's parents are named only; they *do* nothing. A single jailor does duty for the rest. The crowd listens passively; Prudentius leaves this scene out but includes their *act* of preserving relics of the saint.

More significant is the omission of Valerius. Bishop Valerius suffered from a speech impediment,[30] and Vincent was therefore compelled to serve as his spokesman. In suffering the punishment of exile rather than the supreme penalty (and reward) of a martyr's death, Valerius might seem to have slipped down to the "Non-Pagan" position (2). That is, he was not a "Non-Christian" (3) or a Pagan (4), but his position has not been affirmed by clear-cut, Christian action. His relationship toward the ideal, Christianity (1), is defined by implication and is, potentially at least, problematic. He opposed the ideal, Paganism (4), along the axis of contradictories, not contraries. The positions of characters in the *Acta Vincenti* could then be represented:

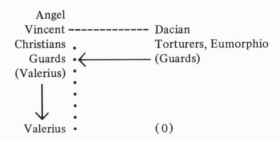

In *Per.* V the situation is simpler; note, moreover, that the poet-narrator, by challenging Dacian verbally (421–432), earns inclusion among those occupying the position S_1:

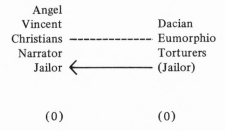

The polarized world of Prudential hagiography (like medieval epic) does not admit a permanent stance such as that assigned to Valerius in the *Acta*. Figures occupying one of the two lower positions of the square must either move up or die. Valerius, incapable of effective speech and exiled, does neither; therefore he has been eliminated from the narrative.

In *Per*. V movement from one position to another in the semiotic square occurs in the horizontal plane, along the axis of contraries (i.e. the sudden conversion of the jailor).[31] Prudentius' ethos, however, appears to be a literary, not a historically accurate, representation. The more historical accounts of the years of persecution, contained in the letters of various bishops, tell of many who occupied "Non-Christian" or "Non-Pagan" positions—those Christians who backslid or managed to escape confrontation, or, on the pagan side, those who retained their belief in the old ways but avoided open persecution.[32] Toleration and compromise may be admirable qualities in real life; they are not positively valued in medieval epic or in the *Peristephanon*.

Several other hymns of the *Peristephanon* reveal a similar emphasis upon heroically unambiguous speech and action. *Per*. II, for instance, opens with a situation potentially parallel to that of Valerius and Vincent; Pope Xystus has been arrested together with his Spanish-born archdeacon, St. Lawrence. Prudentius includes the arrest in his hymn to St. Lawrence; in the first scene of *Per*. II, Prudentius, following St. Ambrose,[33] depicts the martyred Xystus addressing Lawrence from the cross, predicting that he too will be martyred within three days. The account appears to be at variance with history at this point; Xystus was beheaded, not crucified, but since a victim of the former punishment cannot speak *during* his execution, the mode of death has been altered.

Per. III, celebrating the martyrdom of twelve-year-old St. Eulalia of Mérida, gives an especially vivid picture of saintly heroism.[34] Eulalia, who has sought out the tribunal of her own accord,[35] impetuously bursts into speech without waiting to be questioned ("uociferans: 'quis furor est?' " 66). Her parents, who would keep her safe from persecution, are mentioned in passing but only as a foil to the young martyr's triumphant zeal for persecution.

Per. XIV, dedicated to another young virgin martyr, St. Agnes, follows the now familiar pattern. Agnes, martyred like Eulalia at the age of twelve, is first urged by a seemingly mild judge to relent and sacrifice, then, in the very next line, threatened with cruel tortures.

> Temptata multis nam prius artibus
> nunc ore blandi iudicis inlice
> nunc saeuientis carnificis minis. . . .
>
> (15–17)

[First she was tempted by much guile, now by the enticing words of a flattering judge, now by the threats of a cruel executioner. . . .]

Agnes stands firm ("stabat feroci robore pertinax," 18). Significantly, the enticing words (a perlocutionary speech act) of the judge are not quoted; the first direct speech is overtly hostile and cruel (an illocutionary speech act), and the speaker is characterized as a "trux tyrannus" (21). He threatens to put Agnes in a brothel since she is not swayed by fear of pain; she will cherish her virginity, he thinks, more than her life. But he fails to persuade. To his threat Agnes, confident that Christ will not permit her dishonor, replies boldly (31–37); she has a second, longer speech at her execution in which she eagerly welcomes death (69–84).

The hymns of the *Peristephanon* under consideration here follow a consistent organizational plan. In them all, speech figures prominently. The fifth is particularly symmetrical, although its carefully balanced structure is not readily apparent.[36] The interrogation scene (Section I) is usually the longest, and in it direct discourse plays a major role, as the following table shows:

	Section I: *Percent of Poem*	*Percent Speech in* *Section I*
Per. II	61	76
Per. III	61	56
Per. V	36	86
Per. XIV	51	35

For Prudentius, then, the high point of the account is not the martyr's gruesome suffering, as has sometimes been maintained,[37] but rather the confession of faith prior to torture and the heroic opposition to pagan superstition. Deeds are important; the martyrs actively embrace their deaths. But acts alone do not suffice; the martyrs' outspoken confessions

prior to suffering are necessary parts of the narrative. The verbal *agon*—
the ritual contest—must precede the physical.[38]

The emphasis on speech is not wholly to be explained in terms of the
importance of preaching in early Christianity (although Prudentius himself testifies eloquently to the vital need for spreading Christian doctrine in
Per. XIII, dedicated to St. Cyprian of Carthage, a voluminous writer).
Not all the *Peristephanon* feature direct discourse so prominently. It is
precisely in those hymns which stress most clearly the heroic character of
the martyr that speech constitutes such an important act.

I have discussed elsewhere some of the similarities between Prudentius'
dynamic *passiones* and the Old French epics.[39] The prominence of direct
discourse is one of the shared features. Indeed, the importance afforded to
the martyr's verbal challenge to his adversary may explain a seemingly
anomalous use of discourse in certain *chansons de geste*.

Contemporary theorists have introduced two concepts which help to
clarify what has occurred—"horizon of expectation" (Jauss, Nichols),[40]
and "vraisemblance" (Todorov).[41] In the discussion of the *Couronnement de
Louis* which follows, I am not suggesting that the jongleur necessarily
"imitated" hagiographic narrative, if by "imitation" we understand the
sort of conscious poetic cross-reference which, for example, we admit
when we say that a classical poet such as Vergil "imitated" Homer. But
passion narratives were familiar to all, whether from reading or perform-
ing Latin hymns such as those of Prudentius,[42] from hearing vernacular
poems such as the *Vie de saint Léger* or the *Canczon de sancta Fides*, or from
listening to sermons, preached in the vernacular from the ninth century.
These well-known stories set up a particular horizon of expectation in poet
and audience alike with respect to proper heroic behavior and to the
proper function of discourse. The depiction of the Christian hero finds its
norms, as this paper has suggested, in literary, not historical, realities.
These norms are determined by the "supra-reality" of *vraisemblance*, of
which Todorov writes:

One can speak of the *vraisemblance* of a work in so far as it attempts to make us
believe that it conforms to reality and not to its own laws. In other words, the
vraisemblable is the mask which conceals the text's own laws and which we are
supposed to take for a relation with reality.[43]

Citing this statement of Todorov, Stephen G. Nichols adds: "*Vraisemblance* belongs, by this definition, to the same kind of internal structure
as 'poetic language.' However, it differs from the latter in pointing outward, beyond the text, to other texts and objects in the world." [44] The
"laws" of hagiographic narrative have extended "outward" to influence the
"laws" of epic composition. Both genres, in the case of heroic discourse,
reveal similar conceptions of the *vraisemblable*.

The heroes of the *chansons de geste* are angry, impetuous, argumentative. Much of the narrative in the epics takes the form of direct speech, the most dramatic way to recreate an event. But the uses of discourse in the epic are varied, their significance exceeding a desire for vivid mimesis. Of the speeches in the epics, Michel-André Bossy has stated:

Two types of verbal encounter shape the hero's career in the early *chansons de geste:* (1) the battlefield confrontation in which the hero insults his enemies and praises the violence he has or will inflict on them; (2) the council-scene confrontation in which the plain binary opposition between Christian society and its pagan antithesis unfolds into a contradiction within society itself.[45]

Bossy notes that discourse is the second instance, unlike the speeches on the battlefield or in the martyr's *passio*, is problematic. In the council-scene confrontations, appearance and reality do not coincide.

One important subspecies of battlefield confrontation may reveal a great debt to norms of *vraisemblance* and horizons of expectation acquired from hagiography, not from history. Although in the press of battle there was probably little opportunity for long prayers and debates, let alone for hearing the enemy's reply, such interchanges are stock epic incidents. In the martyr's trial, however, verbal encounters did occur, even if the historical documents suggest that the interrogations actually took a form simpler than that presented in the epic *Acta* or in hymns like the *Peristephanon*. Occasionally on the battlefield we find an epic hero appearing to assume a role more appropriate to the martyr than the warrior, as he turns preacher, expounding religious doctrine and engaging in theological debates with his pagan adversary prior to combat (e.g. the argument between Guillaume and Corsolt which prefaces the first battle of the *Couronnement de Louis*, and the theological debates in the *Pseudo-Turpin Chronicle* between Charlemagne and Agolant, Roland and the giant Ferragut).[46]

Before we turn to the encounter in the *Couronnement de Louis*, it is useful to consider a text intermediate between Latin hagiography and vernacular epic, the Provençal *Canczon de sancta Fides*, composed around 1060. In defiance of history, the tormenter of the young martyr is none other than Dacian, who has become, largely thanks to his association with Vincent of Saragossa, the torturer *par excellence*. Much of this *passio* takes the form of direct discourse; in particular, the saint has several speeches in which she boldly defies her persecutor. Dacian threatens her with the fire which burnt St. Lawrence (289–290). In reply Fides utters her *credo* in the form of a prayer: [47]

"Deus, nostre Donz, lo glorios,
De totas res es poderos.
Del Cel czai deissended per nos

E fez dess homen molt ginnos;
Guerilz malaves els lebros,
Baptismenz ded en l'agua jos.
Pres fol seus corps, lo precios;
Judeu l'aucidrum enveios.
Destruiss Enfern, lo tenebros;
Los seus en traiss, ge connog pros.
Aqel volri' aver espos.

(Laisse 30, 301–311)

[God, our Lord, the glorious one, of everything is He master. From heaven He descended here for our sake, and made Himself into a superior man; He cured the leprous and gave baptisms in the lowly water. His precious body was taken; the envious Jews killed Him. He destroyed shadowy Hell, taking out His own people, for which I know Him valiant. This one I want to have for my bridegroom.]

The martyr's confession of faith rehearses Christ's history, concluding not with the Resurrection but with the Harrowing of Hell, as Christ is depicted as a valiant warrior (*pros*, 310), destroying the forces of evil. The speech is not primarily designed to convert Dacian or even to win God's mercy (although the latter is admittedly an important goal); its function is to restate the polarities of the drama at a climactic moment, reminding the audience once again of the ideological basis of the conflict. From the listener's perspective, then, it is first and foremost an illocutionary speech, although apparently perlocutionary.

In the *Couronnement de Louis*, there are two instances of discourse which demonstrate a horizon of expectation concerning the role of heroic speech (in specific the use of illocutionary and perlocutionary discourse) which has possibly been created by familiarity with the martyrs' *passiones*. Prior to his fight with Corsolt, Guillaume dismounts and speaks a long "epic prayer" [48] (695–789), which resembles that of Saint Fides in the prominent position afforded the Harrowing of Hell, for Guillaume concludes with the Harrowing, which he places *after* the Resurrection: [49]

"Et al tierz jor fustes resuscitez.
Dreit en enfer fu voz chemins tornez.
Toz voz amis en alastes jeter,
Qui longement i aveient esté.
Si com s'est veir, bels reis de majesté,
Defent mon cors, que ne seie afolez." [50]

(779–784)

Such rearrangement of scriptural chronology is, indeed, typical of epic prayers.[51] A similar alteration occurs, for example, in Aude's prayer prior to the combat between Roland and Olivier in *Girart de Vienne* (5710ff.). In her prayer in the *Poema de Mío Cid* (330ff.), Ximena inserts references to Old Testament figures into her recital of Christ's life; like Guillaume, she concludes with the Harrowing of Hell.[52]

During the actual combat, Guillaume pronounces a second prayer in which chronology is again disordered; after mentioning Christ's resurrection, Guillaume reflects on the Last Judgment, and he concludes this prayer with references to a mélange of saints and Old Testament heroes, ending with Moses.[53] The chronology of these epic prayers has been altered to highlight particular Biblical events which have special appropriateness as models or paradigms for the careers of both martyr and epic hero.[54] We have seen the prominence of the Harrowing of Hell in the prayer of Saint Fides where Christ was depicted as a brave warrior. The Last Judgment was the most significant event in any Christian's spiritual life; the scene was dramatically displayed for worshippers to contemplate on the tympanon of many romanesque churches. The Harrowing of Hell prefigures this event as Christ assaults the Devil's stronghold and releases his friends from captivity. But all Christians, *except for the martyrs and those heroes who died in battle against the infidel*, must await the Day of Judgment for their deliverance. Some of Prudentius' hymns (e.g. II and IV) conclude with specific prayers to the martyrs to intercede on that dreadful *dies irae*. An evocation of the Harrowing of Hell reminds the faithful of Christ's mercy towards his allies (cf. *Sancta Fides*, "los seus"; *CL*, "voz amis"), and encourages them to hope. Moses, known for his violent opposition to pagan superstition, prefigures the martyr diametrically opposed to paganism.

The devil, vanquished by Christ in the Harrowing of Hell, is the enemy of every Christian. Like the martyr, the epic hero must conquer his adversary in word as well as deed. After Guillaume's first prayer, the devil-like Corsolt, "hisdos com aversier" (505, 673), asks Guillaume to whom "he has so long been talking" (794). When Guillaume tells him, Corsolt replies that Guillaume is a fool if he thinks that his God will help him, and a spirited theological debate is under way. The issue is whether God concerns himself in an active fashion with the destiny of mankind. The opposition is absolute. Corsolt cries out, "Chrestiienté est *toz* foleiemenz" (844).[55]

The debate between Roland and another giant, Ferragut, in the *Pseudo-Turpin Chronicle*, is even more expressly concerned with theology, as Ferragut questions the triune nature of the Trinity, which seems to him a logical impossibility. In his rebuttal, Roland emphasizes the significance for all Christians of the Last Judgment. In combat the question of God's intervention in human affairs is raised as Roland calls out, "Oh Jesus, son of the blessed Virgin Mary, help me!" [56] He then fatally wounds Ferragut who in turn screams, "Mafumet, Mafumet, help me for I am dying." The pagan's plea goes unanswered.

For Roland and Guillaume to turn theologian is perhaps surprising. Both heroes are, like all epic warriors, good Christians, but they appear to be men of action rather than of speech.[57] Although Guillaume, whose legend is conflated with that of St. William of Aniane, eventually makes a pious end, and Roland dies a martyr's death at Rencesvals, both heroes seem more at home with the sword than the book. Guillaume in particular makes a strange cleric (in the *Moniage Guillaume I* [130–137], we discover that the hero cannot even read!); he is a Hercules figure—an oversized, gluttonous, impetuous soldier who is nothing averse to using fists if he does not have a sword handy. Yet it is important for both epic heroes to take verbal as well as physical action against the enemy.

Battlefield discourse performs for the epic the same function, in terms of defining both the work's oppositional structure and the role of the hero, that speech does in the confrontation scenes of the *passiones*. The audience, listening to either genre, has similar horizons of expectation concerning heroic behavior. Here, for once, all discourse is unproblematic. The function of such speeches, however, exceeds their apparent dramatic purpose. The prayers and debate of the *Couronnement de Louis* are not primarily intended to inculcate Christian doctrine nor to stress Guillaume's piety; both can be taken for granted, just as they could in the *passiones* of St. Vincent and St. Fides. From the dramatic perspective *within* the text, or from a more "historical" viewpoint, the debates and prayers of the epics and passions seem designed to convince or persuade—to convert a pagan adversary, to win God's mercy. But the saints and heroes in their speeches frequently fail to engage their interlocutors in genuine, responsive exchanges; St. Fides, for example, rehearses Scriptural history as a reply to Dacian's threats, answering his challenge only indirectly. But viewing the text as an artifact composed *after* a well-known historic encounter took place (or is imagined to have taken place), we may find that the purpose of such discourse differs. The real decoder of such speeches is not the actor but the audience, an audience who knows that Dacian was not, could not be, converted, that saints Vincent and Fides did obtain, must obtain, God's blessing. From this vantage point, therefore, the speeches are illocutionary—declarative, unambiguous statements of belief. Their purpose is to identify the speakers once more with the beliefs which they espouse. They are champions, representatives of diametrically opposed ideologies: as Guillaume falters, the bishop cries out, "Sainz Pere, sire, secor ton champion" (1062). The perlocutory functions of such discourse differ from the dramatic one: exhortation to steadfastness and to imitation, not to conversion.

The speeches, then, establish the binary opposition between Good and

Evil, Christian and Pagan, Spes and Crudelitas. The martyrs' and heroes' illocutionary speeches, in this instance, are not a mediating force but its opposite, the means of asserting unalterable polarity. The mediation, or resolution, at least in the case of hagiography, occurs outside of the dramatic context, at the Last Judgment. Martyrs are known for their heroic but gruesome deaths, epic warriors for the brave deeds on the battlefield. Yet for both groups of heroes, defiant, illocutionary speech must precede action. Saint and hero alike have earned their place in Heaven by triumphant words as well as deeds. The power of discourse equals the power of the sword.

NOTES

1. I gratefully acknowledge the generous help afforded me in the preparation of this essay by my colleagues Michel-André Bossy and Charles Segal, and by Stephen G. Nichols of the editorial board of *Medievalia et Humanistica*.
2. J. L. Austin, *How to Do Things with Words* (Oxford, 1962); J. R. Searle, *Speech Acts: An Essay in the Philosophy of Language* (Cambridge, 1969), esp. chs. 2 and 3. Perlocutionary acts involve the consequences illocutionary acts may have on the hearers: i.e. by arguing one may persuade, by warning one may alarm, etc. (see Searle, op. cit. p. 25).
3. Paul Ricoeur, "The Model of the Text: Meaningful Action Considered as a Text," *New Literary History*, 5 (1973–74), 93–94 (author's italics).
4. See Michael Hancher, "Beyond a Speech-Act Theory of Literary Discourse," *MLN*, 92 (1977), 1081–1098, esp. 1084.
5. "Two Types of Opposition and the Structure of Latin Saints' Lives," *Medievalia et Humanistica*, 6 (1975), 1–12.
6. Line 1015: all citations of *Roland* are from the edition of F. Whitehead (Oxford, 1975).
7. Adolf Harnack, *Militia Christi: Der christliche Religion und der Soldatenstand in der ersten drei Jahrhunderten* (Tübingen, 1905), gives a good collection of texts.
8. *Les Passions des martyres et les genres littéraires* (Subsidia Hagiographica, 20, 1966), p. 171ff.
9. Prudentius comments on this destruction, *Per.* I, 73ff.
10. In "The Interaction of Life and Literature in the *Peregrinationes ad Loca Sancta* and the *Chansons de Geste*," *Speculum*, 44 (1969), Stephen G. Nichols suggests that instead of emphasizing "the progression from the historical event to the literary event, as though there actually were a logical sequence, proceeding from the one to the other," we should realize that in the *chanson de geste*, "we have to do rather with a number of different literary perceptions of events *thought to be historic*" (p. 51, author's italics). The distinction is, if anything, even more important for hagiography. See also Barbara Hornstein Smith, "Poetry as Fiction," *New Literary History*, 2 (1970–71), 259–281.
11. The earliest hymns in honor of the martyrs were written a generation earlier by St. Ambrose; his hymns all consist of 32 lines of iambic dimeter.

12. Ruth E. Messenger, "Mozarabic Hymns in relation to Contemporary Culture in Spain," *Traditio*, 4 (1946), 157.

13. B. de Gaiffier, *"Sub Daciano Praeside:* A Study of Some Spanish *Passios,"* *Classical Folia*, 21 (1967), 6ff.

14. *AA.SS.*, II (Jan 22), 6–10.

15. *PL* 86, 1066, "Adest miranda passio," and 1073, "Beate Martyr prospera."

16. *Acta Vincenti*, p. 7.

17. All quotations of Prudentius are from the edition, Maurice Cunningham, *Aurelii Prudentii Clementi Carmina*, Corpus Christianorum, Series Latina, 126 (Turnhout, 1966).

18. I discuss this passage at greater length in "The Martyr as Epic Hero: Predentius' *Peristephanon* and the Old French *chanson de geste," Proceedings* of the Third Annual Conference on Patristic, Medieval and Renaissance Studies, Villanova University (1978), 119–135.

19. Similarly the *Acta* of Saint Fides of Agen (whose tormentor is, in violation of history, none other than Dacian), the tyrant first attempts to talk the saint into relenting, but the narrator characterizes him in this instance as "callidissimus simulata tranquillitate" (*AA.SS.* 51 [Oct. III], 288E). This interpretation is perpetuated in the metrical life composed by Hildebert of Lavardin (1056?–1133), "mentem tranquillam simulans" (*AA.SS.* 56 [Oct. VIII], 827A).

20. Only villains attempt (unsuccessfully) to lie; cf. Dacian's dissimulation discussed above. In the *Chanson de Roland*, Ganelon tries to misrepresent the truth of Roland's horn-blast; see the discussion of Sarah Kay, "Ethics and Heroics in the 'Song of Roland,' " *Neophilologus*, 62 (1978), 480–491, esp. note 21.

21. At the conclusion of a number of the *Peristephanon* (e.g. II, III, VI), Prudentius specifically comments on the mediating role of his poetry in obtaining salvation.

22. The martyr's confession also involves coincidence of heart and speech; in *Per.* III, 75, Eulalia declares, "pectore et ore Deum fateor."

23. For the significance of hagiographic performance and its role in validating belief, see Karl D. Uitti, *Story, Myth and Celebration in Old French Narrative Poetry, 1050–1200* (Princeton, 1973), pp. 25ff. In "Levels of Identification of Hero and Audience," *New Literary History*, 5 (1973–74), 296, Hans Robert Jauss notes that in ceremonial performances such as the religious drama of the Middle Ages (and, I suggest, performance of hagiographic hymns), "the opposition between work and audience, between actors and spectators, is suspended." While I discuss below a way in which audience and actor are distinguished as decoders of certain illocutionary speeches, the comment is nonetheless valuable for hagiography. Prudentius, moreover, participates *actively* in his text; the narrator of *Per.* V addresses Dacian (421–432), and the tyrant replies directly to his questions.

24. *Mozarabic Hymns* (above, n. 12), p. 157.

25. "Deep Structures in the chansons de geste: Hypotheses for a Taxonomy," *Olifant*, 3, (1975), 6.

26. A. J. Greimas and F. Rastier, "The Interaction of semiotic constraints," *Yale French Studies*, 41 (1966), 86–105.

27. See Claude Calame, "L'univers cyclopéen de l'Odyssée entre le carré et l'hexagone logiques," *Versus*, 14 (1976), 106.

28. Pierre van Nuffel, "Problèmes de semiotique interpretative: l'Épopée," *Lettres Romanes*, 27 (1973), 150–162. Note, however, that epic admits *far more* ambiguity than does hagiography. Such diagrams are unsatisfactory for later *chansons de geste*, and even for the early poems are not intended as fully adequate representations of the epic world.

29. Paul Zumthor, *Essai de poétique médiévale* (Paris, 1972), p. 326.

30. "Episcopus impeditoris linguae fuisse dinoscitur," *Acta Vincenti*, p. 7.

31. In this respect Prudentius, in contrast to the epic, presents a more restricted set of possible actions.

32. See W. H. C. Frend, *Martyrdom and Persecution in the Early Church* (Oxford, 1965), pp. 409ff.

33. A. S. Walpole, *Early Latin Hymns* (Cambridge, 1922), pp. 94–100; the same version is followed by the Mozarabic hymn, *PL* 89, 1179.

34. The *Acta* of Eulalia have not survived, and Prudentius' hymn is our earliest record of this saint. The Mozarabic liturgy includes all of *Per.* III. For a further discussion of Eulalia's violent heroism, see "The Martyr as Epic Hero" (n. 18 above). The "Séquence de ste. Eulalie" appears to be independent of Prudentius' hymn.

35. In fact the Church in the third century often discouraged voluntary martyrdom; see Frend, *Martyrdom and Persecution*, p. 415ff.

36. The interrogation scene comprises 36% of the whole, the torture and death of the martyr 28%, the aftermath of death and conclusion 36%. Charles Witke demonstrates a like symmetry for the fourth hymn; *Numen Litterarum*, Mittellateinische Studien und Texte, V (Leiden, 1971), 129–138.

37. Critics, calling attention to the common Spanish origin of Seneca, Lucan, and Prudentius, have sometimes attributed Prudentius' "delight in descriptions with horrible details," to his Hispanicity, a view rejected by Josep Vives, "Prudentiana," in *Homenatges a Rubió i Lluch* (Barcelona, 1936), p. 3; for this view of Prudentius, see Gaston Boisier, *La Fin du paganisme* (Paris, 1891), II, 143. For the four poems under consideration (II, III, V, XIV), the scene of the martyr's torture and death is shorter than the confrontation scene; for *Per.* II it constitutes 23% of the total, for III 14%, for V 28%, for XIV 18%.

38. Cf. the athletic metaphor in *Per.* V, "ventum ad palestram gloriae."

39. "The Martyr as Epic Hero" (above, n. 18). Also my thesis, "Saints and Heroes: Latin and Old French Hagiographic Poetry," University of California, Berkeley, 1977.

40. H. R. Jauss, "Littérature médiévale et théorie des genres," *Poétique*, I (1970), 79–101, and "Literary History as a Challenge to Literary Theory," *New Literary History*, 2 (1970–71); Stephen G. Nichols, "A Poetics of Historicism?: Recent Trends in Medieval Literary Study," *Medievalia et Humanistica*, 8 (1977), 77–101.

41. Tzvetan Todorov, "Introduction," *Le Vraisemblable, Communications* 11 (1968). I attach, however, no pejorative connotations to pursuit of *vraisemblance*.

42. Bernard M. Peebles (*The Poet Prudentius*, Boston College Candlemas Lectures on Christian Literature, 2 [New York, 1951], p. 156), points out that at least

nine of the *Peristephanon* (including both III and V) attained some liturgical use in Spain. The Mozarabic liturgy was not replaced by the Roman Rite in Spain until the closing years of the eleventh century (Messenger, "Mozarabic Hymns," 149).

43. Quoted by Nichols, "A Poetics of Historicism?" p. 97.

44. Nichols, p. 97.

45. "Heroes and the Power of Words in the *chansons de geste*" (an abstract) in "The Myth of the Hero: Classical and Medieval Epic (A Report on a Conference)," *Olifant*, 7 (1980), 235–247.

46. Chs. 15 and 21; *The Pseudo-Turpin*, ed. H. M. Smyser (Cambridge, Mass., 1937).

47. Text from A. Thomas, *La Chanson de Ste. Foy*, (Paris, 1925). There is no real parallel for this prayer in the *vita*. There the only prayer is brief, uttered *before* the saint voluntarily presents herself to Dacian. She does not rehearse the creed but prays for support ("adesto nunc famulae tuae, et praebe ori meo sermonem acceptabilem, quem in conspectu tyranni hujus respondeam," *AA.SS.* 51 [Oct. III], 288D–E). This Latin prayer is more perlocutionary than the Provençal one.

48. Cf. Edmond-René Labande, "Le 'Credo' épique: À propos des prières dans les chansons de geste," *Recueil de travaux offert à M. Clovis Brunel*, II (Paris, 1955), 62–80; Jacques de Caluwe, "La 'prière épique' dans les plus anciennes chansons de geste françaises," *Olifant*, 4 (1976), 4–20. Critics have failed to note that Sancta Fides' prayer is the earliest example (ca. 1060) of the type.

49. Donald Maddox and Sara Sturm-Maddox, among others, have commented on the chronological rearrangement in Guillaume's prayer; "Le chevalier à l'oraison: Guillaume dans *Le Couronnement de Louis*," in *Charlemagne et l'épopée romane*, Actes du VIIᵉ Congrès International de la Société Rencesvals, *Congrès et Colloques de l'Université de Liège*, 76 (Liège, 1978), 609–615. The Maddoxes write: "La Descente en Enfer préfigure le courage de Guillaume qui doit vaincre un adversaire démoniâque avant de libérer les fidèles captifs des Sarrasins" (p. 614).

50. Quotations of *Le Couronnement de Louis* are from the edition of Ernest Langlois (2nd ed.; Paris, 1968). The edition of Yvan G. Lepage (Droz, 1978) of the *AB* manuscripts is unfortunately not available to me.

51. See Antoinette Saly, "Le thème de la descente aux enfers dans le 'credo' épique," *Travaux de linguistique et de littérature de Strasbourg*, 7 (1969), II, 47–63. Saly traces the rearrangement back to the popular "Gospel of Nicodemus." In Prudentius' *Cathemerenon* IX, the narration of the Harrowing of Hell precedes that of Christ's death!

52. Saly (p. 50) notes that the references to the Harrowing frequently form the conclusion of such prayers.

53. In this reference to Moses, the Maddoxes (above, n.49) see a prefiguration of Guillaume's two most important roles, protector and liberator.

54. Guy Raynaud de Lage suggests that the prototype of the "epic prayers" is ultimately a text close to the religious "climate" of the *chansons de geste*, the Biblical account of the exploits of the Macabees: "L'inspiration de la prière 'du plus grand péril,' " *Romania*, 93 (1972), 568–70.

55. Of this scene Jean Frappier writes: "Corsolt avait engagé la controverse en théologien," *Les Chansons de geste du cycle de Guillaume d'Orange*, II (Paris, 1967), 126. Frappier notes that there are other scenes of theological debate in the epics (e.g. *La Chanson de Guillaume*, (ed. Wathalet-Willem), 2111–24, and *Aliscans* (ed. Weinbeck), 1223–28. These confrontations conform less closely to the pattern of the *passio*. They are brief and do not serve as preludes to the ensuing dramas.

56. I quote from the medieval Catalan translation since both speeches are there given as direct address (*Història de Carles Maynes e de Rottlà: Traducció català del segle XV*, ed. Martí de Riquer [Barcelona, 1960], p. 82). In the Latin text published by Smyser, Roland's cry is not quoted directly.

57. Sarah Kay, "Ethics and Heroics in the 'Song of Roland,' " (above, no. 20), studies Roland's use of language and concludes that he "uses language as an extension of physical action rather than as a primarily mental or psychological tool" (p. 483). She attempts (p. 484) to establish a sharp dichotomy between words (Ganelon as a man of words) and deeds (Roland as a man of deeds), which is, I believe, something of an oversimplification.

St. Bonaventure's Debt to Joachim

E. RANDOLPH DANIEL

Recent scholarship has established that Abbot Joachim saw the history of redemption through two complementary patterns, the *prima* and *secunda diffinitiones*. Earlier scholarship had interpreted Joachim's theology of history exclusively in terms of the *prima diffinitio*, according to which history unfolded in three successive *status*, identified respectively with the Father, the Son and the Holy Spirit. This pattern, popularized and radicalized by the Pseudo-Joachite *Expositio super Hieremiam* (before 1248) and by Gerard of Borgo San Donnino in his *Liber introductorius in evangelium eternum* (1254) has been understood as the sole source of Franciscan Joachitism.[1]

Since the publication of Joseph Ratzinger's *The Theology of History in St. Bonaventure*, it has become clear that in the *Collationes in Hexaemeron* Bonaventure developed a theology of history which was significantly indebted to Abbot Joachim. Scholars have assumed that Bonaventure was borrowing from Joachim's *prima diffinito*, although the Franciscan doctor had to avoid the radical implications associated with the *status* of the Holy Spirit.[2]

The purpose of this study is to demonstrate that Bonaventure borrowed Joachim's *secunda diffinitio*, not the *prima*. By 1270 the *prima diffinitio* was associated with radical Joachitism which expected the abolition of the existing sacraments and the papal church in favor of a mendicant spiritual church. By adopting the *secunda diffinitio* Bonaventure was able to envision a final *status* of peace and revelation within history, surpassing and consummating the present state of the church but not abolishing or superceding it. St. Bonaventure in his *Collationes* of April and May, 1273 was setting a more orthodox, but legitimate interpretation of Joachim against the views of Gerard of Borgo San Donnino.

Bonaventure's apocalyptic eschatology developed in three stages. In his *Commentary on the Sentences* (1251–1253) and his *Breviloquium* (1257), Bonaventure utilized only the Augustinian six ages which represent the six days of the creation-week and the six *aetates* of man. The seventh or sabbath *aetas* was understood as contemporaneous with the sixth, referring to the rest of those souls who have died in Christ, and was, therefore, seen by Bonaventure as being outside history. Bonaventure did not mention either St. Francis himself or the Franciscan Order in connection with this Augustinian pattern.[3]

Medievalia et Humanistica, New Series, Number 11 (Paul Maurice Clogan, ed.). Rowman and Littlefield, Totowa, NJ, 1982.

The publication of Gerard's *Liber introductorius* in 1254, the controversy with the secular masters at Paris and Bonaventure's election to be minister general of the Franciscan Order in 1257 compelled Bonaventure to consider the eschatological significance of St. Francis and his Order.[4] In his *Quaestiones disputatae de perfectione evangelica* (1254–1256), the *Itinerarium mentis in deum* (1259), and the *Legenda maior* (1261), Bonaventure developed a Franciscan eschatology. He identified St. Francis, who bore the stigmata, with the angel of the sixth seal who bears the sign of the living God (Apocalypse 7:2). Francis is the exemplar of evangelical perfection, the model for those who would conform themselves to Christ by humility, poverty and obedience. Francis has made the *transitus*, the passover from the speculative level of the cherubim to the affective unity of the seraphim. As the initiator of evangelical renewal, Francis is John the Baptist or Elijah, the herald of the coming of Christ in glory. The role of the Franciscans who have embraced poverty is to mark the foreheads of the servants of God with the *tau*, the sign of the living God. In other words the friars are sent by Christ to renew the apostolic life in this last hour of the world as a preparation for the end.[5]

Both Guido Bondatti and Ratzinger have detected in these works an element of Joachitism. According to the latter these texts "(betray) the traces of the Joachimite-eschatological interpretation of the Order of St. Francis." [6] Bernard McGinn has seen Bonaventure as "appropriating the force of the Joachite vision in the services of the Franciscan Order without falling into the errors of the radical Joachites." [7] In my opinion Bonaventure was defending a genuinely Franciscan eschatology which ultimately derived from Francis himself. Bonaventure developed this eschatology in reaction against the eschatologies of William of St. Amour on the one side and of Gerard of Borgo San Donnino on the other. Specific Joachite influence is missing. There is no trace of Joachim's *concordia* of the Old with the New Testament, nor does Bonaventure suggest a series of historical *tempora* since Christ, especially a final historical sabbath, surpassing the present age. There is no hint of a future *ordo* which would characterize such a future age. St. Francis and the Franciscans have an eschatological mission but it is set in the framework of an Augustinian sixth *aetas*. The friars' mission is to renew the evangelical life in anticipation of the end of history.[8]

When in 1269 Bonaventure wrote his *Apologia pauperum*, he restated his Franciscan eschatology. Christ had conferred the stigmata on Francis because Francis had served and taught the perfection of the gospel fully. Francis is thus a model of evangelical perfection "against the dangerous darkness of these final times." By him "we are led back to Christ, to the exemplar and end of perfect virtue." [9]

Nevertheless, a new note had already emerged in the eschatology of

Bonaventure. In his *Collationes de decem praeceptis* (1267), Bonaventure had attacked theses regarding the eternity of the world and the unity of the intellect in all men. Here Bonaventure discerned a threat, emerging at Paris in the heart of Latin Christendom. This danger is the teaching of an Aristotelian philosophy, independent of and counter to evangelical perfection. In this philosophy Bonaventure saw an eschatological counterpart to the Franciscan eschatological role. The philosophers were preparing the way for Antichrist with their radical Aristotelianism, just as Francis had set the stage for Christ himself.[10]

The controversy at Paris regarding radical Aristotelianism motivated Bonaventure to give his *Collationes in Hexaemeron* in 1273. Unfortunately Bonaventure did not complete his original plan. There are no lectures on the sixth day which would logically have been the most important for bringing together Bonaventure's views on apocalyptic eschatology. Furthermore, we have no text prepared by Bonaventure himself. The *Collationes* survive in the form of two *reportationes*, that is sets of notes taken by auditors, neither of which is stenographic but instead often appear to summarize or paraphrase what Bonaventure said. In most instances there is no clear reason to prefer one version to the other. The nature of these *reportationes* makes their meaning allusive especially in certain key passages and, therefore, the best course seems to be to examine both versions.[11]

As was noted in the beginning of this article, Ratzinger has demonstrated convincingly that Bonaventure borrowed significantly from Joachim in these sermons, especially in *Collationes* fifteen and sixteen. In the fifteenth *Collatio*, commenting on the text, "the earth brought forth vegetation, every kind of seed-bearing plant" (Genesis 1:11), Bonaventure says that:

> As in the gathering of the waters, there was a symbol of the many forms of intelligent beings, and in the germination of the earth, a symbol of the multiplicity of sacramental images, so also in the seeds is shown a kind of infinity in the heavenly theories that are pointed to by these same seeds. For the principal intelligences and figures exist in certain determined numbers, while the theories are almost infinite . . .
>
> This consideration of the theories exists between the two mirrors of the cherubim (cf. Exodus 37: 7–9), that is, of the two testaments, that shed light on each other, so that man 'be transformed . . . from glory to glory' (2 Corinthians 3:18). But this germination of the seeds procures the understanding of the different theories through adaptation to the different times; and the man who overlooks the times cannot know the theories. For one who ignores the past cannot know the future. If, indeed, I do not know from which tree a seed comes, I cannot know what tree is to grow from it. Hence the knowledge of future events depends on the knowledge of those of the past.[12]

The meaning of the terms intelligences and figures (*intelligentiae, figurae, sacramenta, mysteria*) on the one hand and the term theories (*theoriae*) on the other is certainly not immediately clear. In my opinion intelligences and figures here refer to historical events recorded in the Old Testament which typologically foreshadow events in the New Testament. Theories are the spiritual understandings which are seminally contained in these typologized events. If, as I will argue subsequently, Bonaventure was here summarizing the hermeneutical basis of Joachim's *secunda diffinitio*, then the meaning of this text will become clear when Joachim's use of these cherubim has been elucidated.[13]

Using these theories, Bonaventure constructed a number of patterns of history, beginning with the Augustinian six ages and culminating in two series of seven *tempora* each. The first seven *tempora* extend from Adam to Christ, corresponding to the Old Testament. The second series extends from Christ to a *tempus pacis postremae*, a future sabbath of peace and contemplation within history. Bonaventure placed his own present within the sixth *tempus* of the New Testament series, which corresponds to the Old Testament era from Hezekiah through the Babylonian Exile to the return to Jerusalem in the reign of Cyrus. The sixth *tempus* began in the days of Charlemagne, who corresponds to Hezekiah. Under Charlemagne the church enjoyed a zealous, Christian ruler who promoted Christian learning. Tribulation followed at the hands of the hostile emperors, Henry IV, Frederick I Barbarossa, and most recently Frederick II. Bonaventure suggested that the aim of these persecutors, or at least of Frederick II was to exterminate the church but he was prevented from this by the angel of the sixth seal, that is St. Francis.[14] Bonaventure, however, expected yet another tribulation to occur within the sixth *tempus*. During this future tribulation, "knowledge and revelation or the key of David and the understanding of scripture will be given to one person or to a multitude as if it were given to the angel of the church of Philadelphia."[15] Robert Lerner has argued that this angel of Philadelphia should also be understood as Francis, but it is possible that Bonaventure had in mind the future seraphic order about which he speaks in *Collatio* Twenty-Two.[16] There Bonaventure describes the hierarchy of the militant church which corresponds to and exemplifies the heavenly hierarchy. The earthly hierarchy is, however, not static but dynamic, moving toward a yet unrealized goal. The Benedictines correspond to the thrones, because they devote themselves entirely to prayer, devotion, and praise. The Franciscans and Dominicans correspond to the cherubim, because the mendicants combine speculation with piety, the Dominicans placing greater emphasis on speculation, the Franciscans more emphasis on piety. The seraphim stand on a higher level because they "attend to God by means of elevation, that is, through ecstasy and rapture." [17] Francis already belonged to this seraphic *ordo* but Bonaventure believed that the *ordo* itself will appear only after the end of the future tribulation.[18] Whether this *ordo* will appear within the sixth *tempus* or in the final seventh is unclear.

The sixth *tempus* is unmistakably a period of apocalyptic transition. The pattern is one of initial peace, then tribulation which in turn is followed by a second period of peace before the second persecution. During this sixth *tempus* full revelation of the spiritual meaning of scripture will be given to the faithful. As Ratzinger has shown, this final revelation moves from the *sapientia multiformis*, the spiritual meaning of scripture, toward the *sapientia nulliformis*, the mystical, unitive stage where the intellect must be abandoned because the light has become blinding. Bonaventure merged this Pseudo-Dionysiac notion with the belief that this ultimate revelation will be given only to the *paruuli*, only to those who on the model of Francis himself are truly humble and poor. Thus this revelation will be "non-discursive and non-scholastic in character. It will be a simple, inner familiarity with the mystery of the Word of God." [19]

After the sixth *tempus* there will be only the seventh time, a final sabbath of peace. In this *tempus:*

> There will be a rebuilding of divine worship and a restoration of the city. Then will be fulfilled the prophecy of Ezekiel (Ezekiel 40–45: 8), when the city will come down from heaven, not indeed that city which is above, but the one below, that is, the church militant: when it will be conformed to the church triumphant, as far as it is possible on the pilgrim way. Then there will be a building of the city, and a restoration of it as it was in the beginning. And then there shall be peace. But how long this peace will last, God knows.[20]

The system of concords between the two Testaments, the two series of *tempora*, the division of the sixth *tempus* into two persecutions, the expectation of a full revelation of the spiritual meaning of scripture, the final *tempus* of peace, and the notion of a final *ordo* are all elements adapted from Joachim which Bonaventure fused with or better transformed by his Franciscan eschatology as well as his Pseudo-Dionysiac mysticism. Ratzinger demonstrated Bonaventure's debt to Joachim's *concordia*, but he assumed that Bonaventure had adapted Joachim's *prima diffinitio*. Moreover, Ratzinger understood the *prima diffinitio* on the basis of the works of Ernst Benz. For Benz only one of Joachim's patterns of history is historically important, that of the three *status*. The third status of the Holy Spirit, according to Benz, would be not only a new historical age, but it would have a new *ecclesia spiritualis*, a spiritual church, which would supercede the existing clerical church.[21] Ratzinger, therefore, was forced to conclude that:

If Joachim was above all concerned with bringing out the movement of the second age to the third, Bonaventure's purpose is to show, on the basis of the parallel between the two ages, that Christ is the true center and the turning-point of history. Christ is the center of all. This is the basic concept of Bonaventure's historical schema, and it involves a decisive rejection of Joachim.[22]

According to Ratzinger, Joachim had made Christ the turning-point from the first *status* to the second, but he had also introduced a second turning-point from Christ to the Holy Spirit. Thus Bonaventure had to borrow a radical pattern of history without adopting its radical implications.[23] Bonaventure thus was a Joachite *malgre lui.*[24]

The assumption that Bonaventure borrowed Joachim's *prima diffinitio* is incorrect. Bonaventure, on the contrary, clearly borrowed Joachim's *secunda diffinitio.*

Joachim viewed the *prima diffinitio* as a scheme in which the three *status* correspond to internal relationships between the three persons of the trinity and to the development of the three orders, those of the laity, the clergy, and the monks. The first *status* belongs to the Father and to the laity. Out of it proceeds the second *status* which is shared by the Son and the Holy Spirit—although the Son is pre-eminent—and by the clergy and the monks. Thus it corresponds to the generation of the Son by the Father and to the procession of the Holy Spirit from the Father and to the procession of the clergy and the monks from the laity. The third *status* belongs to the Holy Spirit, proceeding from the Son, and to the monks, who proceed from the clergy. Theologically, the *prima diffinitio* emphasizes the equality of the trinitarian persons. Historically it explains the evolution of the orders from the married laity to the final future society in which monks will be pre-eminent.[25]

The *secunda diffinitio* expresses the correspondence between the intratrinitarian relationships, the procession of the spiritual understanding from the Old and New Testaments, and the derivation of the *uiri spirituales* from the Jewish and Gentile peoples. The Father generates the Son. The Holy Spirit proceeds from both the Father and the Son. Likewise the Old Testament was the source of the New Testament. The spiritual understanding proceeds from both Testaments. The Christian people are the heirs of the Jewish people. Beginning with Elijah and Elisha the *uiri spirituales* have emerged out of both peoples.[26]

The differences between the two *diffinitiones* should not be exaggerated. The underlying pattern is the same but the nuances are different. Both are trinitarian and both point forward to a future sabbath of peace and spiritual comprehension. For Joachim they were complements, not alternatives.[27] Nevertheless, in the 1260's and 1270's, the *prima diffinitio* was associated with the views of Gerard of Borgo San Donnino who had transformed it into three successive ages, each alloted to a different person of the trinity and had identified the principal works of Joachim with the Eternal Gospel of Apocalypse 14:6, thus suggesting a spiritual gospel which would supercede the New Testament. Bonaventure explicitly rejected this interpretation when he wrote: "After the New Testament, there will be no other, nor can any sacrament of the new law be eliminated, for this is an Eternal Testament." [28]

No such connotations were attached to the *secunda diffinitio* which Gerard had apparently neglected. Bonaventure's reference in the fifteenth *Collatio* to the two cherubim, who were placed facing each other above the ark of the covenant demonstrates clearly that he was using the *secunda diffinitio*, because Joachim explicitly associated these two cherubim with this *diffinitio*, as symbols of the *concordia* of the two Testaments.

For we have spoken above about the three *status* of this world, as they are signified by the three great patriarchs and the three angels who appeared to one of them, that is, to Abraham (Genesis 18:1–21); but we have not spoken about the significance of Moses and Aaron and of the two cherubim of whom mention was made above. Hence it is necessary to assign the *status* of the world in another way on account of another mystery of the trinity; in order that we, who have concerned ourselves with the assignment of three *status* of the world according to the three persons of the deity, according to this other way may assign not three *tempora* but only two.[29]

Joachim referred here to the preface of the *Liber de concordia* in which the two cherubim who face each other are the two Testaments, the Old and the New.[30] He explained his meaning more fully when he said:

We have said above that the two Testaments are signified in the two cherubim who, spreading their wings, overshadow the ark of the Lord's covenant which remains hidden within them (Exodus 37:7–9). For a cherub is interpreted as the fullness of knowledge. This fullness of knowledge is, moreover, the whole of the Old Testament and the whole of the New Testament. But if knowledge and knowledge have been signified in the two cherubim, namely the letter of the Old Testament and the letter of the New Testament, which are letter from letter and knowledge from knowledge, what is signified in the ark of the Lord's covenant . . . except that we say that here is understood that orthodox and spiritual understanding, which in the type of the Holy Spirit proceeds from both Testaments?[31]

Bonaventure, as has been noted above, was indebted to Joachim in his use of the two cherubim who face each other above the ark of the covenant. For Joachim the cherubim symbolize the letter of the Old and the letter of New Testament, which are related to each other as type and fulfillment. These Testaments contain *mysteria* or *sacramenta* within themselves, that is the letters of the Testaments conceal the *spiritualis intelligentia*. Bonaventure's meaning is clear if his *intelligentiae* or *figurae* are the same as Joachim's *litterae*, and if his *theoriae* comprise Joachim's spiritual understanding. Both for Joachim and for Bonaventure the primary element in this *spiritualis intelligentia* is an awareness of the future course of redemptive history, an awareness gained from the *concordia* of the two Testaments. Both assume that the New Testament must be understood to include the history of the church from its beginnings to its consummation at the end of history.

For Joachim the two Testaments are, therefore, two *tempora*. On the basis of these two *tempora*, Joachim constructed an elaborate series of sub-patterns. In the concluding chapters of Book Two of the *Liber de concordia* the two times are subdivided into two series of persecutions culminating in final sabbaths.[32] In Book Three, Joachim alloted the seven seals to the Old Testament *tempus* and their openings to the New Testament *tempus*. Here Joachim treated the relationship of the Holy Spirit to the Son at great length. The relationship is graphically depicted in the figure of the *Pavimentum*, according to which seven pairs of men are sent within the six seals. One member of each pair represents the Son and one the Holy Spirit. In the first six pairs the Son and the Spirit alternate in pre-eminence but in the seventh pair they are equal. In the sixth pair, for example, Ezekiel represents Christ, Daniel represents the Holy Spirit. Both of these prophets wrote in symbols, but Daniel openly explained his. Thus Ezekiel stands for Christ who said according to John 16:12–14: "I have many things to say to you but you are not able to receive them now. When, however, the spirit of truth will come, he will teach you all of the truth. For he will not speak from himself, but whatever he hears he will speak, and he will proclaim those things which are to come. He will glorify me, because he will receive what is mine and proclaim it to you."[33]

Joachim's Christology is both kenotic and pleromatic. In Jesus, Christ has emptied himself of his glory by assuming human flesh in order to reveal himself to carnal men who like spiritual infants could only perceive him in tangible form.[34] The ultimate goal of redemptive history is the realization of the mystical body of Christ, the achievement of which is the work of the Holy Spirit. The pleromatic side of Joachim's Christology is most clearly expressed in connection with the *prima diffinitio*, but it is equally fundamental to his concept of the *uiri spirituales* in the *secunda diffinitio*.[35]

Bonaventure's theology of history is christocentric. Christ is the exemplar which all creation mirrors, the center of history and its goal. Ratzinger, however, says of Bonaventure: "Certainly the two final *ordines* are orders of the Holy Spirit; and the Spirit certainly achieves a particular power in the final age; but this age, as such is an age of Christ."[36] No theologian could describe Joachim's theology of history as christocentric in the same sense, but the relationship between the Son and the Holy Spirit in the *secunda diffinitio* points in a similar direction. the final sabbath belongs to the Son but it is realized by the full revelation of the Holy Spirit.

Joachim was most intensely interested in the sixth seal and in its opening. In both he discerned a pattern of two persecutions, those recorded by Judith and Esther in the Old Testament, the fall of the *noua Babylon* in the New.[37] The image of the New Babylon is explained more fully in Book Four where Joachim treated the two *tempora* according to the *generalis concordia*, that is, he set each of the forty-two generations from Jacob to Zorobabel and from Christ onward side by side in order to show the *concordia* generation by generation. In the latter part of this exposition Joachim treated the conflict between the papacy and the emperors from Pope Leo IX through the pontificate of Urban III. As persecutors of the reformed papacy, the emperors embody the new Babylon, the fall of which will take place under the forty-first generation by means of the two persecutions of the sixth opening. Then the forty-second generation will see a reform of the church under a new Zorobabel, a pope to whom will be given "full liberty to reform the Christian religion and to preach the word of God."[38] This reform will initiate the final sabbath.[39]

The identification of St. Francis with the angel of the sixth seal certainly induced Bonaventure to emphasize the pattern of the seven seals. His treatment differs from Joachim's. Joachim treated the period from Adam to Isaac as a preparatory phase and began the first seal with Jacob, whereas Bonaventure began the first seal with Adam. Bonaventure's sixth seal began with Hezekiah and with Charlemagne who initiate Joachim's fifth seal. Nevertheless, the pattern of twin persecutions and the role of the German emperors are clear indications that Bonaventure was borrowing from Joachim's *secunda diffinitio*.[40]

Bonaventure's expectation of a future seraphic *ordo* appears to be borrowed from Joachim's future order of monks associated with the third *status* in the *prima diffinitio*. Nevertheless, the *uiri spirituales* and the spiritual understanding which they will receive in the final sabbath may be the source of Bonaventure's notion.

While it cannot be proven that Bonaventure read the *Liber de concordia*, it is clear that the *Liber* was available to him in Paris. That a manuscript was in Paris before 1250 is clear from William of Auvergne's reference to the *Liber* in his *De uirtutibus*.[41] Two late thirteenth century manuscripts of the *Liber de concordia* have survived which belonged to masters at the Sorbonne.[42]

In his *Collationes in Hexaemeron* Bonaventure turned to the *secunda diffinitio* and to Joachim's treatment of the seven seals, which enabled Bonaventure to fuse into his already-developed Franciscan eschatology a hermeneutic of the Two Testaments, series of seven *tempora*, a final historical sabbath, and a future seraphic order. Because Bonaventure was conscious of the connotations associated with the third *status* of the Holy Spirit, since Gerard's publication of his *Introductio*, Bonaventure returned to Joachim to find there a pattern much closer to his own theology of history. Bonaventure did not in the last analysis reject Joachim, he restudied him.

NOTES

1. On the *prima* and *secunda diffinitiones* see Marjorie Reeves, *The Influence of Prophecy in the Later Middle Ages: A Study In Joachimism* (Oxford, 1969), pp. 16–27; idem, *Joachim of Fiore and the Prophetic Future* (New York, 1976), pp. 1–28; Marjorie Reeves and Beatrice Hirsch-Reich, *The Figurae of Joachim of Fiore* (Oxford, 1972), pp. 1–19; E. R. Daniel, "The Double Procession of the Holy Spirit in Joachim of Fiore's Understanding of History," *Speculum* Vol. 55, 1980, pp. 469–483. Henry Mottu, however, concentrated almost entirely on the *prima diffinitio* in his *La manifestation de l'Esprit selon Joachim de Fiore* (Neuchatel and Paris, 1977), pp. 105–112. On the *Expositio super Hieremiam* and Gerard of Borgo San Donnino see Reeves, *The Influence of Prophecy*, pp. 56, 59–66; Heinrich Denifle, "Das *Evangelium aeternum* and die Commission zu Anagni," *Archiv fur Literatur- und Kirchengeschichte des Mittelalters*, Vol. 1, 1885, pp. 49–142. Marjorie Reeves argued for a Cistercian or Florensian origin for the *Expositio* in "The Abbot Joachim's Disciples and the Cistercian Order," *Sophia* Vol. 19, 1951, pp. 355–371 (reprinted in Delno West, *Joachim of Fiore in Christian Thought*, 2 vols. [New York, 1975], 1:151–167). B. Topfer, "Eine Handschrift des *Evangelium aeternum* des Gerardino von Borgo San Donnino," *Zeitschrift fur Geschichtswissenschaft*, Vol. 7, 1960, pp. 156–163, suggests that Dresden, Sachs. Landesbibl., A. 121 is a copy of Gerard's work which retains the glosses but from which the *Liber introductorius* has been removed. M. M. Dufeil, *Guillaume de Saint Amour et la polemique universitaire parisienne, 1250–1259* (Paris, 1972) retains the conventional view of Gerard.
2. Joseph Ratzinger, *The Theology of History in St. Bonaventure*, trans. by Zachary Hayes, O.F.M., (Chicago, 1971).
3. Ratzinger, *Theology of History*, pp. 109–110; Bernard McGinn, "The Abbot and the Doctors: Scholastic Reactions to the Radical Eschatology of Joachim of Fiore," *Church History*, Vol. 40, 1971, p. 41 (reprinted in Delno West, *Joachim of Fiore in Christian Thought*, 2 vols. (New York, 1975, 2:461); E. R. Daniel, "St. Bonaventure: Defender of Franciscan Eschatology," *S. Bonaventure: 1274–1974*, 5 vols. (Grottaferrata, 1974), 4:796–797; Bonaventure, *IV Sent.* d. 40, dub. 3, *Opera theologica selecta*, vol. 4, p. 845; idem, *Breviloquium*, prol. section 2, *Opera theologica selecta*, vol. 5, pp. 7–9. On the chronology of Bonaventure's Sentence Commentary see John F. Quinn, C.S.B., "Chronologie de saint Bonaventure, 1217–1257," *Etudes franciscaines*, Vol. 21, Supplement Annuel, 1971, pp. 87–104.

4. See above footnote 1. See also Decima L. Douie, "St. Bonaventure's Part in the Conflict Between Seculars and Mendicants at Paris," *S. Bonaventure: 1274–1974*, 5 vols. (Grottaferrata, 1974), 2:585–612.

5. Daniel, "St. Bonaventure," pp. 797–801; Bonaventure, *Questiones disputatae de perfectione evangelica, Opera omnia*, vol. 5, p. 164; Ratzinger, *Theology of History*, pp. 113–114.

6. Guido Bondatti, *Gioachinismo e Francescanesimo nel Dugento* (Assisi, 1924), pp. 137–140; Ratzinger, *Theology of History*, pp. 113–114.

7. McGinn, "The Abbot and the Doctors," p. 42 (p. 462).

8. Daniel, "St. Bonaventure," p. 801; E. R. Daniel, *The Franciscan Concept of Mission in the High Middle Ages* (Lexington, Ky., 1975), pp. 26–36.

9. Bonaventure, *Apologia pauperum*, chp. 3, sections 2–10, *Opera omnia*, vol. 8, pp. 244–247; Daniel, "St. Bonaventure," pp. 801–802.

10. Ratzinger, *Theology of History*, pp. 134–163.

11. One of the *reportationes* has been edited by the Collegio S. Bonaventure in the *Opera omnia*, vol. 5, pp. 329–449 (hereafter cited as *Collationes in Hexaemeron, Opera omnia*); the other was edited by F. Delorme, O.F.M., in the *Bibliotheca Franciscana scholastica medii aevi*, vol. 8 (Grottaferrata, 1934), which is hereafter cited as *Collationes in Hexaemeron, Delorme*, The *Opera omnia* version has been translated by Jose de Vinck, *Collations on the Six Days*, in *The Works of Bonaventure*, vol. 5 (Paterson, N.J., 1970), which is hereafter cited as *Collations*.

12. Bonaventure, *Collations*, col. 15, sections 10–11, pp. 222–223. The translation is of the version of the *Collationes in Hexaemeron, Opera omnia*, p. 400 which reads:

> Sicut enim in congregatione aquarum significatur multiformitas intelligentiarum, et in germinatione terrae multiplicitas sacramentalium figurarum; sic in seminibus ostendit, se habere infinitatem quandam caelestium theoriarum, quae significantur per semina. Intelligentiae enim principales et figurae in quodam numero certo sunt, sed theoriae quasi infinitae . . .
>
> Haec consideratio theoriarum est inter duo specula duorum cherubim, duorum scilicet testamentorum, quae refulgent in invicem, ut "transformetur" homo a "claritate in claritatem." Haec autem germinatio seminum dat intelligere secundum diuersas temporum coaptationes diversas theorias; et qui tempora ignorat istas scire non potest. Nam scire non potest futura qui praeterita ignorat. Si enim non cognosco, cuius arboris semen est; non possum cognoscere, quae arbor debet inde esse. Unde cognitio futurorum dependet ex cognitione praeteritorum.

The *Collationes in Hexaemeron, Delorme*, visio 3, col. 3, sections 10–11 p. 172, differs in wording but not significantly in meaning, although it omits the word *cherubim*.

> Sicut aquae omnes continentur in utre maris, sic intelligentiae et sacramenta sive mysteria et theoriae ad modum seminum in herba continentur in ventre sacrae scripturae. Sacramenta autem et mysteria sunt in numero quodam determinato sicut species specialissimae cuiuslibet generis. Sed theoriae, sicut multiplicatio seminum in infinitum procedit . . .

Haec autem theoriarum inspectio est inter duo specula duorum testamentorum scripturae sacrae, quae refulgent in invicem, ut transformetur homo de "claritate in claritatem, 2 Cor. 3, 18. Haec germinatio sementiva dat secundum diversitates coaptationis temporum sive secundum diversas temporum coordinationes intelligere potissime theorias in scriptura, quae dat potissime providentiam futurorum. Qui enim ignorat praeterita, nullo nuntio potest scire futura; ut si cognosco hoc semen, cognosco quam arborem germinabit, et si nescio cuius arboris est hoc semen, consequenter nescio quam arborem generabit. Ideo cognitio praeteritorum est quoddam semen respectu futurorum.

13. See below pp. 66–68.
14. Bonaventure, *Collationes in Hexaemeron, Opera omnia,* Col. 16, section 29, p. 408:

Hoc autem tempus est geminum, unde, sicut in passione Domini fuit primo lux, deinde tenebra, postea lux; sic necesse est, ut primo sit lux doctrinae, et succedat Iosias Ezechiae, post quam facta est tribulatio Iudaeorum per captivitatem. Necesse est enim, ut surgat unus princeps zelator ecclesiae, qui vel erit, vel iam fuit—et addidit; Utinam iam non fuerit—post quem fit obscuritas tribulationum. Hoc tempore similiter Carolus exaltavit ecclesiam et eius successores oppugnaverunt eam; tempore Henrici quarti fuerunt duo papae, similiter tempore Frederici magni, duo. Et certum est, quod aliquis inter eos voluit exterminare ecclesiam; sed "angelus ascendens ab ortu solis clamavit quatuor angelis; nolite nocere terrae et mari, quousque signemus servos dei nostri in frontibus eorum." (Apocalypse 7:2–3).

The *Collationes in Hexaemeron, Delorme,* visio 3, col. 4, section 29, p. 192, adds Frederick II:

Sed hoc tempus est geminum; nam processus religionum in ecclesia primo fulget dignitatibus et ex eis praelati in ministerium ecclesiae assumuntur et multipliciter dilatantur, sed sequitur tribulatio maxima et deinde iterum pax. Sicut Iosias successit post tribulationem Manasse patris sui et religiosus fuit, ante quem Ezechias fuit religiosus et rectus, et intermedium fuit tempus tenebrae; sic post pacem quam habuit ecclesia per Carolum religiosissimum, qui libros multos scripsit, sequebatur tribulatio ecclesiae. Nam tempore Henrici quarti imperatoris fuerunt diu duo papae et tempore Frederici magni. Similiter et iste ultimus Fredericus, si posuisset, omnino exterminasset ecclesiam, sed angelus Domini clamavit ne noceret etc.

15. Bonaventure, *Collationes in Hexaemeron, Opera omnia,* col. 16, section 29, p. 408:

Unde adhuc restat ecclesiae tribulatio. Et dictum est angelo Philadelphiae, qui sextus est: "Haec dicit sanctus et verus, qui habet clavem David; qui aperit, et nemo claudit; claudit, et nemo aperit. Scio opera tua, quia ecce, dedi coram te ostium apertum" (Apocalypse 3:7–8).—Et dixit, quod adhuc intelligentia scripturae daretur vel revelatio vel clavis David personae vel multitudini; et magis credo, quod multitudini.

The final sentence is a good example of the difficulty in dealing with a *reportatio* where we have the reporter's summary of what he understood Bonaventure to say, rather than Bonaventure's words.

The *Collationes in Hexaemeron, Delorme,* visio 3, col. 4, section 29, p. 192, suggests that Bonaventure left the identification of the angel of Philadelphia open.

Post cuius mortem [the death of Frederick II] est aliqua pax ecclesiae, et tamen tribulatio adhuc expectatur per quam status ecclesiae rectificabitur, in quo tempore dabitur uni personae vel multitudini quasi angelo ecclesiae Philadelphiae scientia et revelatio sive clavis David et intelligentia scripturae, cui dicitur; "Quia servasti verbum patientiae meae, et ego te servabo ab ira, Apoc." (Apocalypse 3:10). Alternationes istae in ecclesia quantum ad pacem et tribulationem elegantissime significantur per hoc quod, Christo in cruce pendente, primo fuit lux sive dies, deinde tenebrae in universa terra et iterum adhuc eo pendente lux rediit.

On the two series of *tempora* see Ratzinger, *Theology of History,* pp. 19–31.

16. Robert Lerner, "An 'Angel in Philadelphia' in the Reign of Philip the Fair: The Case of Guiard of Cressonessart," in *Order and Innovation in the Middle Ages: Essays in Honor of Joseph R. Strayer,* edited by William C. Jordan, Bruce McNab and Teofilio F. Ruiz (Princeton, New Jersey, 1976), pp. 352–353. Brian Tierney, *Origins of Papal Infallibility 1150–1350* (Leiden, 1972), p. 78, also identifies Francis with both angels. Bonaventure also refers to the angels of the sixth seal and of the church of Philadelphia in *Collationes in Hexaemeron, Opera omnia,* col. 20, section 29, p. 430. The angel of Philadelphia is paralleled with Joseph in *Collationes in Hexaemeron, Opera omnia,* col. 23, section 29, p. 449. It is also possible that Bonaventure understood both Francis and the seraphic order as the angel of Philadelphia, because Francis belonged to and was a prototype of that order.

17. Bonaventure, *Collationes in Hexaemeron, Opera omnia,* col. 22, sections 20–22, pp. 440–441; *Collationes in Hexaemeron, Delorme,* visio 4, col. 3, sections 20–23, p. 256; *Collations,* col. 22, sections 20–22, pp. 350–352.

18. Bonaventure, *Collationes in Hexaemeron, Opera omnia,* col. 22, section 23, p. 441.

19. Ratzinger, *Theology of History,* pp. 59–71. The quotation is from p. 71.

20. Bonaventure, *Collationes in Hexaemeron, Opera omnia,* col. 16, section 30, p. 408; *Collationes in Hexaemeron, Delorme,* visio 3, col. 4, section 30, pp. 192–193; *Collations,* col. 16, section 30, pp. 249–250.

21. Enrst Benz, *Ecclesia spiritualis* (Stuttgart, 1934; reprinted Stuttgart, 1964), pp. 4–48; Henry Mottu, *La manifestation de L'Esprit,* pp. 224–264.

22. Ratzinger, *Theology of History,* p. 118.

23. Stephan Otto, "Bonaventuras christologischer Einwand gegen die Geschichtslehre des Joachim von Fiore," *Miscellanea Mediaevalia,* vol. 11, 1977, pp. 113–130, takes a similar view.

24. Reeves, *The Influence of Prophecy,* pp. 179–181; Nachman Falbel, "Sao Boaventra e a theologia de historia de Joaquim de Fiore: Un resumo critico," *S. Bonaventure: 1274–1974,* 5 vols. (Grottaferrata, 1974), 2:584.

25. See above, footnote 1. My treatment of these two *diffinitiones* is based on E. R. Daniel, "The Double Procession," pp. 471–477, where I have argued that these two *diffinitiones* were complements of each other. From the beginning readers of Joachim tended to adopt one or the other but not both. On the early

diffusion of the *secunda diffinitio*, see Marjorie Reeves and Morton Bloomfield, "The Penetration of Joachism into Northern Europe," *Speculum* Vol. 43, 1954, pp. 772–793 (reprinted in Delno West, *Joachim of Fiore in Christian Thought*, 2 vols. [New York, 1975], 1:107–128).

26. Daniel, "The Double Procession," pp. 477–480.
27. Ibid., pp. 471, 480–482.
28. Bonaventure, *Collationes in Hexaemeron*, col. 16, section 2, p. 403; *Collations*, col. 16, section 2, p. 232; Ratzinger, *Theology of History*, pp. 117–118.
29. Joachim of Fiore, *Liber de concordia novi ac veteris testamenti* (Venice, 1519; reprinted Frankfurt a. Main, 1964), Book 2, Part 1, chp. 6, fol. 9ra. The following text is from my edition which will be published by the American Philosophical Society.

> Locuti namque sumus de tribus statibus huius mundi secundum id quod significant tres magni patriarche et tres angeli qui apparuerunt uni eorum, hoc est Abrahe; non secundum id quod significant Aaron et Moyses et duo cherubin quorum supra fecimus mentionem. Unde necesse est alio modo assignare status mundi propter aliud mysterium trinitatis ut, qui tres status mundi propter tres personas deitatis assignare curavimus, alio modo non tria tempora set duo tantum modo assignemus, quia sic oportet fieri et ita se habet causa et manifestatio veritatis.

The translation is my own.

30. Ibid., *Praefatio* (fol. 2vb). The folios of the preface are not numbered in the printed edition.

> . . . opere pretium estimavimus ex veteribus et novis hystoriis opus istud componere in quo, Ezechielis rotis diligenter inspectis (Ezekiel 1:15–17, 10:1–19), quanta sit in utrisque concordia luculenter ostendimus, et que duo illa cherubin mutuis se uultibus contemplantia designabant (Exodus 37:7–9), in duorum testamentorum consonantia assignare curavimus . . .

See also Book 1, chp. 1, fol. 1vb: ". . . utpote qui secundum plenitudinem illam scientie quam duo significant cherubin de duorum testamentorum concordia tractaturi sumus . . ."

31. Ibid., Book 2, Part 1, chp. 29, fol. 18ra-rb:

> Diximus superius significari duo testamenta in duobus cherubin que, expansis alis suis, archam federis domini, manentem intrinsecus, obumbrabant. Interpretatur enim cherubin plenitudo scientie. Est autem plenitudo scientie integritas testamenti novi. Sed si scientia et scientia significata est in duobus cherubin—littera scilicet testamenti veteris et littera testamenti novi, que est littera de littera et scientia de scientia—quid in archa federis domini, in qua locutus est dominus Moysi continens infra seipsam decem precepta legis, intelligendum dicimus nisi illam orthodoxam et spiritualem intelligentiam, que in typo Spiritus Sancti ab utraque procedit?

32. Ibid., Book 2, Part 2, chps. 9–10, foll. 23rb–25rb.
33. Ibid., Book 3, Part 1, chp. 2, fol. 26va and chp. 20, fol. 37va-vb. On Joachim's use of John 16:12–14 see Daniel, "The Double Procession," pp. 479–480 and footnote 21. Henri Mottu, *La manifestation de l'Esprit*, p. 204, argued that Joachim used only verses 12–13 but not verse 14. Actually Joachim quotes

both although he never quotes the entire text at one time.

34. Joachim uses the classic text for Kenotic Christology Philippians 2:5–11. See for example, *Liber de concordia*, Book 3, Part 1, chp. 5, fol. 27vb; chp. 6, fol. 28rb; chp. 8, fol. 28vb; chp. 9, fol. 29rb.

35. Joachim uses both of the classic texts, Ephesians 4:13 and 1 Corinthians 12:14–20. See Joachim of Fiore, *Liber figurarum*, edited by L. Tondelli, M. Reeves and B. Hirsch-Reich, 2nd revised edition (Turin, 1953), tav. 12. Joachim cites Ephesians 4:13 in the *Liber de concordia*, *Praefatio*, (fol. 3^{ra-rb}); Book 2, Part 1, chp. 8, fol. 9va. See also Daniel, "The Double Procession," pp. 475–476.

36. Ratzinger, *Theology of History*, p. 117. On the Christology of Bonaventure see also Zachary Hayes, O.F.M., "Incarnation and Creation in the Theology of St. Bonaventure," in *Studies Honoring Ignatius Charles Brady Friar Minor*, edited by R. S. Almagno, O.F.M. and C. L. Harkins, O.F.M. (St. Bonaventure, N.Y., 1976), pp. 309–329.

37. Joachim, *Liber de concordia*, Book 3, Part 2, chp. 6, fol. 40^{va-vb}.

38. Ibid., Book 4, Part 1, chps. 18–31, fol. 53ra–56va. The quotation is from chp. 31, fol. 56rb, where Joachim identifies this future *pontifex* also with the angel of the sixth seal of Apocalypse 7:2. See also Joachim of Fiore, *Expositio in Apocalypsim* (Venice, 1527; reprinted Frankfurt a. Main, 1964), Part 2, fol. 120vb–121ra, where in treating Apoc. 7:2 Joachim makes the same identification.

39. Joachim, *Liber de concordia*, Book 4, Part 1, chps. 31–32, fol. 56va.

40. Joachim, *Liber de concordia*, Book 3, Part 1, chp. 19, fol. 36va–37va. It should also be remembered that Bonaventure saw himself as living within the sixth *tempus*, but Joachim expected it to begin in the imminent future, shortly after 1200.

41. Reeves, *The Influence of Prophecy*, pp. 41–42, quotes the relevant passage. W. Schacten, "Die Trinitatslehre Bonaventuras als Explication der Offenbarung vom personalen Gott," *Franziskanische Studien*, Vol. 56, 1974, p. 213, suggests that Bonaventure used Joachim's commentary on the Hexaemeron, which forms Part 1 of Joachim's *Liber de concordia*, Book 5, chps. 1–30, fol. 60va–73va, but gives no proof of this dependence.

42. Paris, Bibliotheque nationale, Lat. 16280 belonged to Peter of Limoges who was at Paris as an M.A. from 1262 and died in 1306. Paris, Bibliotheque nationale, Lat. 15254, belonged to Gerald of Utrecht.

Imagination as the First Way to Contemplation in Richard of St. Victor's Benjamin Minor

RAYMOND D. DiLORENZO

In each of his two major treatises on comtemplation, *Benjamin minor* and *Benjamin major*, Richard of St. Victor (d. 1173) presents a remarkable theory of imaginative activity.[1] Though rather different in character, the theories are not only quite elaborate, but also, in their general assessment of imaginative activity, surprisingly positive. The imagination depends upon the senses, and they in turn depend upon the world of concrete singular things. But the discipline of the contemplative man turns him away from the world of visible things. It turns him toward the invisible, transcendent reality of God, who is spirit. In fact, the overall contemplative discipline taught by Richard does not depart from this fundamental orientation of Christian spirituality. Nonetheless, there do remain in his teaching important and positive functions of imagination.

The entire teaching of Richard on imagination has not received the concentrated study it deserves.[2] Not only must the different treatments of it in the *Benjamin* treatises be understood and compared, but they need to be assessed in relation to Richard's theological thinking as a whole and to the tradition of mystical theologians, especially Augustine, Gregory the Great, Dionysius, and Hugh of St. Victor, whose thoughts on imagination may have influenced Richard's own. Toward this rather ambitious goal, my intention here is to take a very modest step: to explain the activities of imagination personified in the *Benjamin minor* by the biblical figures Bala, handmaiden of Rachel, and by Dan and Nephtalim, the sons that Bala bears to Jacob for Rachel's adoption. This small part of Richard's general teaching is sufficiently complex to warrant a study restricted to it.

Richard's primary concern in the *Benjamin minor* is the way leading toward contemplation and not contemplation itself. His basic thesis regarding imagination is that imaginative activity, when properly con-

Medievalia et Humanistica, New Series, Number 11 (Paul Maurice Clogan, ed.). Rowman and Littlefield, Totowa, NJ, 1982.

trolled, is the first way or *prima via* for anyone proceeding toward contemplation. But we ought to be aware that in the *Benjamin major*, the later of the two treatises, Richard treats contemplation itself, not the way leading toward it; and he claims here that imaginative activity is an integral part of the first three of six kinds (*genera*) of contemplation. In the latter three, the higher kinds, imagination has no part whatsoever. There is contemplation in imagination and according to imagination (first genre), in imagination according to reason (second genre), in reason and according to imagination (third genre), in reason and according to reason (fourth genre), above reason but not excluding reason (fifth genre), and above reason and even excluding it (sixth genre).[3] I shall not undertake an analysis of the *Benjamin major* here. Its doctrine of kinds or genres of contemplation, in so far as they involve imagination, clearly goes beyond the teaching of the *Benjamin minor*. The task ahead is to understand accurately what this earlier treatise has to say about imaginative activity.

We need to know a little about the *Benjamin minor* as a whole. The precise subject matter of the treatise is not contemplation but the preparation of the rational soul (*animus*) for contemplation.[4] Hence, its subtitle: *de praeparatione animi ad contemplationem*.[5] Richard indicates that the treatise is directed primarily, if not exclusively, to young men.[6] And, apparently, what they must realize is that, for anyone who desires to receive the grace of contemplation, there comes first a necessary and specific development of reason (*ratio*) and what Richard calls affection (*affectio*). The specific development required constitutes the *praeparatio*.

The architectonic conception governing the whole treatise is that man is a rational spirit who is given a twofold power by God.

To every rational spirit a certain twin power is given from that Father of Lights from whom is every best gift, every perfect gift. One is reason, the other is affection: reason by which we may discern, affection, by which we may love; reason, with respect to truth; affection, with respect to virtue.[7]

Viewing man in a way both theological and psychological, Richard explains how reason and affection, through their specific activities and subtle interaction, lead one toward contemplation. But in this enterprise, two other and subsidiary powers of man fall into Richard's purview. Associated with affection is sensory appetite (*sensualitas*), and with reason, imagination (*imaginatio*). How imagination serves reason will be our primary interest.

Richard's method of exposition is tropological or moral interpretation of Scripture. The object of his exegetical reflections is the Genesis story relating the generation of Jacob's children. The persons and deeds in the story symbolize the progress toward contemplation. Jacob, man as a rational spirit, takes two wives, first Lia (inspired affection) and then Rachel (illumined reason). Upon these women and their handmaidens Zelpha (sensory appetite) and Bala (imagination), Jacob begets thirteen children. The last of them is Benjamin, whom Scripture calls "a youth in ecstasy of mind" (Ps. 67:28). He personifies the grace of contemplative ecstasy. In giving birth to him, his mother Rachel dies. The death of Rachel and the ecstasy of Benjamin suggest two kinds (*genera*) of contemplation. They are the term of the entire *praeparatio*.

These, therefore, are the two kinds of contemplation, one of which pertains to the death of Rachel, the other to the ecstasy of Benjamin. In the first, Benjamin kills his mother, where he goes above all reason; in the second, however, he even exceeds himself, where, in that which is known from divine revelation, he transcends the manner of human understanding.[8]

Other formulations clarify the difference.[9] Rachel's death symbolizes contemplation "above reason but not excluding it" (*supra rationem sed non praeter rationem*). In this kind of contemplation reason grants that certain things exist but cannot investigate them or prove them. The ecstasy of Benjamin symbolizes contemplation "above reason and excluding it" (*supra rationem et praeter rationem*). In such contemplation one looks to things believed about the unity of the Trinity and to many other things concerning the body of Christ that are held on the indubitable authority of faith. Richard never formally defines contemplation in the *Benjamin minor*. In the *Benjamin major*, he defines it as "a free perspicacity of mind, suspended in wonder, into things exhibiting wisdom."[10] Perhaps the inexperienced audience of the *Benjamin minor* may have made him content to describe contemplation from various viewpoints suggested by Scripture. He utilizes not only the death of Rachel and the ecstasy of Benjamin. He also avails his audience of the insights into contemplation provided by the biblical account of the transfiguration of Christ and of the rapture of St. Paul.[11]

The order in which the children of Jacob are born is an important part of Richard's whole doctrine. For the order symbolizes the specific phases of the general preparatory movement of the rational soul toward contemplation. The schema below depicts the order of generation and the tropological significance of each member of Jacob's household.

Jacob

Lia	Rachel
1. Ruben (fear)	•
2. Simeon (sorrow)	•
3. Levi (hope)	•
4. Judah (love)	•
•	. . . . by Bala (imagination)
•	5. Dan (imagination disposed by reason)
•	6. Nephtalim (imagination mixed with understanding)
. . . . by Zelpha (sensory appetite)	•
7. Gad (temperance)	•
8. Asher (patience)	•
9. Issachar (joy)	•
10. Zabulon (hatred of vice)	•
11. Dinah (shame—Jacob's only daughter)	•
	12. Joseph (grace of discretion, self-knowledge)
	13. Benjamin (grace of comtemplation)

In order to understand how the soul utilizes imagination in its progress toward contemplation, we must first learn some important things about Rachel and her sister Lia.

RACHEL AND LIA

Jacob, who represents the rational soul or the human person, desires a wife. Of Laban's two daughters, Lia and Rachel, Jacob immediately desires Rachel. She is the more beautiful. In desiring her, Jacob longs for the "teaching of truth" (*doctrina veritatis*), or the "zeal for wisdom" (*studium sapientae*).[12] Jacob burns for Rachel as did he who wrote, "Her have I loved and sought from my youth and have striven to take for my spouse, and I have been made a lover of her form" (Sap. 8:2). Intense and constant is the desire for Rachel in Jacob.

Let us not mistake Jacob's desire for Rachel. We know that the Greeks called the desire for wisdom "philosophy." But Jacob's desire for Rachel is not the philosophy of the Greek sages. They desired, according to Richard, not Rachel but one who followed in her footsteps, her servant or *pedissequa*, the wisdom of the world, *sapientia mundi*. "It does not surprise you now," he says, "that Rachel is so much desired, when even her servant is sought after, as we realize, with so much love by the philosophers of the world—I am speaking of the wisdom of the world that,

in comparison to her mistress, is thought to be foolishness." [13] The echo of St. Paul's words to the Greeks of Corinth is clear (I Cor. 1:18). To the pagan Greeks, belief in Christ crucified seemed foolishness (*stultitia*). Such foolishness has for Richard become the wisdom which the Greek philosophers foolishly sought in the world.

Rachel is, accordingly, said to symbolize *ratio*, one of the major powers of man, but not *ratio* simply. "Reason," says Richard, "is indubitably called Rachel when it is illumined by the light of the highest and true wisdom." [14] Rachel's name means "seeing the beginning" or "sheep." [15] In order to be worthy of the name, reason must fulfill what is written in Scripture: "Think of the Lord in goodness, and in the simplicity of heart seek him" (Sap. 1:2): God is the beginning of all things. To see Him requires the "eye of faith" and the simplicity suggested by a sheep. Richard is presenting us with a view of human reason opened by faith and simplicity of heart to illuminating revelation—the revelation, as we will see, both of grace and Scripture. Thus, Rachel is called "reason illumined by divine revelation." [16]

Though Jacob desires Rachel, he is not able immediately to take her as his wife. We will recall that by the ruse of Laban, Lia instead of Rachel comes to Jacob in the night, and Lia he must keep for many years before Rachel can be his. Lia represents the desire for justice (*desiderium justitiae*), or affection (*affectio*) inflamed by divine inspiration. [17] Like reason, affection, the second principal power of man, is conceived as being affected by divine action—by *divina inspiratione*. By Rachel do we meditate, contemplate, discern, understand; by Lia we weep, groan, sorrow, and sigh. [18] Lia is called "blear-eyed" (*lippa*) in Genesis. Her name means "laborious" (*laboriosa*). [19] Though she will prove more fecund than Rachel, she is not as beautiful as her sister, and, therefore, not as attractive to Jacob or to men in general. All men desire wisdom, but very few expect or are willing to undergo a prior and necessary moral formation in justice. Perfect justice, explains Richard, requires us to love our enemies, to relinquish readily whatever belongs to us. "But what is thought by the lovers of this world to be more foolish and more laborious?" [20] Jacob will have to take Lia as his first wife, and she will bear him many children. But it is Rachel whom Jacob desires from the first.

In this interpretation of Jacob's wives, we can recognize the stamp of the Christian spirituality first shaped by St. Augustine and St. Gregory the Great, and, for Richard, given its most immediate organization in the teachings of his master, Hugh of St. Victor. [21] Augustinian by intellectual filiation as well as by vocation as a canon regular of St. Victor, Richard conceives Scripture to be the place where the desire for Rachel can be fulfilled. This is where Jacob, fully expecting the connubial embrace of Rachel, finds himself, however, in the arms of Lia.

What do we say Sacred Scripture is but the bedchamber of Rachel, in which we do not doubt that divine wisdom lies hidden beneath the comely veil of allegories. Rachel is sought after in such a bedchamber as often as spiritual understanding is pursued in sacred reading. But as long as we are still very inadequate in penetrating sublime things, we will not yet find the long-desired, diligently sought-for Rachel. We begin, therefore, to groan, to sigh, and not only to bemoan but even to feel shame for our blindness. Then, while sorrowing and questioning why we deserve this blindness, there occur to us the evil things we have done . . . As often as we find compunction instead of contemplation in sacred reading, let us not doubt that we have found in the bedchamber of Rachel not her but Lia.[22]

Jacob's desire for Rachel leads him to her bedchamber. That is, in divine reading (*lectio divina*) the rational soul seeks spiritual understanding of the divine wisdom allegorically veiled in Scripture. But it does not find wisdom. It finds rather its own evil and experiences compunction, not contemplation. Jacob finds Lia; and, before he can beget children upon Rachel, he will have to beget them upon Lia. In Richard's thinking the desire for wisdom cannot be fruitfully consummated until a necessary moral reformation occurs. The children of Lia and Jacob will be those ordered and moderated affections that must arise in the rational soul when, still unfit for contemplation, it seeks to see the sublime things that constitute the highest wisdom. Affection is ordered when directed to the right thing (*ad quod debet*), moderated when possessing the right degree (*tantus est quantus esse debet*).[23] This is virtue—nothing other than the soul's affection, ordered and moderated.[24]

RACHEL AND BALA

Rachel, now married to Jacob, but afflicted by sterility, is jealous: Lia has given birth to four sons—Ruben, Simeon, Levi and Judah. They personify fear of punishment (*timor poenae*—the beginning of wisdom), sorrow of repentence (*dolor poenitentiae*), the hope for forgiveness (*spes veniae*), and the love of justice (*amor justitiae*).[25] These are the precise moral affections that arise in the soul stricken in the beginning with desire for Rachel but having first to conceive these children of moral reformation upon Lia. And Rachel? What else does she feel, seeing her sister's fertility, but a deep grief? What, then, does she say to her husband? "Give me children, or else I will die" (Gen. 30:1 *Da mihi liberos, alioquin moriar*).[26]

Why is it, asks Richard, that Rachel burningly longs for children just after the birth of Lia's fourth son Judah? Richard reminds us that Lia is affection. To love (*diligere*) pertains to her. To know (*cognoscere*) pertains to

Rachel. What else could Judah represent but the ordered love, heavenly love, the love of God, love of the highest good?

With Judah born, that is, with the desire for invisible goods surging up and growing ardent, Rachel begins to burn with desire for offspring because she begins to want to know. Where there is love, there vision is. Gladly do we look upon one we love much. No one doubts that he who is able to love invisible things surely wants to know right away and through understanding to see; and the more Judah grows (the affection of loving, that is) so much the more in Rachel does the desire to give birth burn, that is, the zeal for knowing.[27]

Ubi amor, ibi oculus: here is the principle of transition from Lia back to Rachel. Affection causes reason to grow ardent in the desire to produce what it can, having seen the products of affection. But in the beginning, Jacob's love for Rachel leads unexpectedly to children through Lia. Now, with Judah born, with love rectified, Rachel feels that she will die unless she gives birth to children of her own. But she cannot.

There now occurs in the progress of the rational soul toward contemplation an important moment. Who does not know, asks Richard, how hard it is, how nearly impossible it is for the carnal mind, still rude in spiritual studies, to rise toward understanding of invisible things and to fix on them the eye of contemplation? Rachel is still rude in spiritual studies. What is she, then, to do, burning with an obscure desire to see by the eye of contemplation—she being barren, unable to bring forth spiritual understanding because she is dependent upon carnal sense? Rachel, then, turns to Bala for help. If she cannot have children, she can nevertheless arrange the next best thing: she can send Bala to Jacob. Through Bala, Rachel will get children.

It [the mind, *mens*] does what it can and looks to [invisible things] in the way it can. It cogitates through the imagination because it cannot yet see through the purity of understanding. I think this is why Rachel has children through her handmaiden before giving birth herself, for it is sweet for her, at least by imagining, to retain the memory of those things the understanding of which she cannot yet apprehend through reasoning. For just as by Rachel we understand reason, so through her handmaiden we understand imagination. Therefore, reason feels that it is more suitable for one to cogitate true goods in some way and to rouse the rational soul to the desire of those things by at least a certain imaginative beauty than to fix cogitation upon false and deceptive goods. And this is why Rachel would wish to give her handmaiden to her own husband. That this is the first way for everyone proceeding toward the contemplation of invisible things no one is ignorant, except, perhaps, one whom experience does not yet instruct with respect to this knowledge.[28]

This text indicates a form of knowing (*cogitatio*) through the imagination, through Bala.[29] Such knowing is the first way of the rational soul proceeding toward contemplation. Contrasted with knowing through the purity of understanding (*intelligentia*), this first way appears imperfect.[30] It is, however, easier. Bala works in the service of Rachel's desire to see invisible things. But Rachel's barrenness points to the difficulty of seeing invisible things by reasoning alone.

Bala, the handmaiden of Rachel, is imagination. Zelpha, who serves Lia, is sensory appetite. Their service is indispensable in directing reason and affection toward the external world. "For without imagination, reason would perceive nothing; without sensory appetite affection would feel nothing."[31] Richard observes that Bala's service as a handmaiden is to be an intermediary between her mistress and the slave of "carnal sense" (*sensus carnis*). Carnal sense (the bodily senses) looks only to exterior visible things. Reason, like a tender, delicate, and beautiful young woman, ought not to go about in the streets. Nor ought the slave of sense rudely to burst into reason's private chambers. Imagination is the means of concourse between sense and reason. "Whatever [imagination] draws from outside through the sense of the flesh, she represents on the inside for service to reason."[32] Indeed, even when the bodily senses are inoperative, imagination continues to serve. "For placed in darkness," says Richard, "I see nothing, but, if I wish, I can imagine there anything at all."[33] Bala, whose name means "one having grown old," is not an old woman, but often acts like one when she garrulously repeats to Rachel the sights and sounds of carnal sense.[34] However, now that Rachel wants children, Bala will have to attend more to Rachel's plans than to the report of sense.

When Richard introduces us to Bala in the *Benjamin minor*, he cites St. Paul's words in Romans 1:20. Because visible things have been created by God, imagination, by presenting to reason the appearances of visible things, can truly aid it in the attempt to see invisible things. For *reason will make similitudes from the appearances of things* in order to rise to the acquaintance of things beyond the senses.

Again, since it has been written that, from the creature of the world, the invisible things of God are seen, understood through the things that have been made, one clearly gathers that reason cannot rise to the acquaintance [*cognitionem*] of invisible things unless her handmaiden, namely imagination, represents to her the form of visible things. For through the appearance of visible things, reason rises to the acquaintance of invisible things as often as from these [visible] things reason draws a certain similitude with respect to that acquaintance.[35]

Rachel's own designs will guide the service of her handmaiden now. If Rachel cannot have children of her own, she will adopt those of Bala and

Jacob, namely, the boys Dan and Nephtalim. Richard prepares us to understand the tropological meaning of the brothers by distinguishing the rational from the bestial imagination.

DAN AND NEPHTALIM

Making an image of something not in the experience of carnal sense is the work of the rational, not the bestial imagination. The rational imagination is poetic, in the root sense of the word. It is not ruled by the report of the senses. They provide only the looks or appearances out of which the rational imagination makes images.

There is bestial imagination, therefore, when we scurry here and there in inconstant mind, without deliberation and without any utility, through things we have seen or done a little while ago. Surely this is bestial, for a beast can also do this. That imagination is rational, however, when we imaginatively fashion something out of the things we have come to know through bodily sense. For example, we see gold; we see a house; but we never see a gold house. We can, however, if we wish, imagine a gold house. A beast cannot do this; it is possible only for a rational creature.[36]

We use rational imagination, Richard explains, when we "search into the goods or the evils of the future life."[37] In life here, things good and evil mix together. Never are they found here separate. But in the future life they exist without being mixed. Nor do the highest good and evil things exist here. There, however, in the next life, they do exist.

Therefore, as often as, out of the many goods and evils that corporeal sense experiences in this life, we gather what sort and how great that highest good or evil of the future life can be, and from the imagining of these things a certain image of future things is fashioned, we are indeed easily convinced that such imagination is rational and seems to pertain both to Bala and Rachel. It pertains to Bala inasmuch as it is imagination, but to Rachel inasmuch as it is rational. Such offspring is of the imagination by birth and of reason by adoption. An offspring of this kind one generates, but the other educates. From Bala it is born, but by Rachel it is moderated.[38]

The distinction between rational and bestial imagination prepares for another within rational imagination itself. There are two kinds of rational imagination.

Rational imagination is one thing disposed through reason, another thing mixed with understanding. We use the former when, according to the known appearance of visible things, we bring to mind some other visible thing, and yet from that we do not think of something invisible. But then we use the latter when, through the appearance of visible things, we try to ascend to an acquaintance with invisible things. In the former there is imagination not without reason; in the latter there is understanding not apart from imagination.[39]

The first sort of rational imagination is Dan. Nephtalim is the second. Richard here uses the word *consideratio* to name Dan's activity, and for Nephtalim's, *speculatio*. The words express differences both in the things imagined—the evils and the goods of the future life—and in the ways reason cooperates with imagination. Dan is disposed (arranged) through reason. Nephtalim is mixed with understanding (*intelligentia*).

A few words about *intelligentia* are necessary at this point. In the *Benjamin major*, it is the highest of the three cognitive powers of the rational soul, the other two being *ratio* and *imaginatio*.[40] *Intelligentia* is suited to the apprehension of divine things beyond the grasp of both reason and imagination. For it is capable of receiving the illumination of God's grace. When it is called pure, as it is in the higher genres of contemplation (four, five, and six), *intelligentia* works either by itself or with reason, but in either case it works apart from imagination. When it does cooperate with reason and imagination, it endows them with a wondrous agility, acumen, and comprehensiveness.[41] Whenever the soul contemplates, in whatever genre of contemplation, *intelligentia* is involved: "There can be no comtemplation," says Richard, "without a certain liveliness of understanding" (*Numquam enim contemplatio potest esse sine quadam vivacitate intelligentiae*).[42] But in the *Benjamin minor*, *intelligentia* receives no special emphasis as the rational soul's highest power. Rather, it is viewed from the perspective of *ratio* (Rachel) illumined by grace. The verb, *intelligere*, signifies an act of reason: "By Rachel (*ratio*) do we meditate, contemplate, discern, understand (*intelligere*)."[43] The noun, *intelligentia*, signifies an understanding of invisible, spiritual things outside the ordinary range of reason. Thus, Benjamin's ecstasy is called "pure understanding," because it is not involved with imagination and passes beyond reason (Rachel, who has died).[44] Richard distinguishes Dan from Nephtalim by associating *intelligentia* with the latter and *ratio* with the former. Both Dan and Nephtalim, however, personify imaginative activity that is rationally controlled, for both are sons adopted by Rachel. Richard's subsequent discussion of Dan and Nephtalim concerns the sort of representations they make.

Dan, observes Richard, "knows nothing but corporeal things." Nevertheless, "he seeks out things which are far removed from corporeal sense."[45] The torments of hell, for example, are far removed from corporeal sense. No one sees where hell is and what sort of torments exist in hell. Yet Dan, as often as we wish, can bring them in images before the eye of the heart.

> No one of the faithful, when he reads in Sacred Scripture about the inferno, the flame in Gehenna, the darkness outside, believes these things have been said figuratively, but he does not disbelieve that these very things truly and bodily exist somewhere. Hence, it is not surprising that, although someone through imagination places these things before the eye of the heart, he does not right away seek their signification through spiritual understanding, because he does not doubt that they have been said not so much figuratively as historically.[46]

Richard is trying to explain the specific way in which the images of Dan, when set before the eye of the heart, affect the contemplator. He introduces the notion of signification and the terms of biblical exegesis to explain the nature and effect of an image when disposed by reason. We note that the image *signifies*, that it brings other visible things to mind, the fire of hell, for example. Hell, the place where the damned suffer torments, is not in our experience; but the corporeal things by which the torment of hell is signified—the depths of the earth (*infernum*), flame, darkness—these things are in our experience. And nothing *in an image* arranged by reason according to these things compels us to understand it figuratively. Its spiritual significance (the torment of hell) is to be taken according to the letter, or, as Richard says, "historically." We can, therefore, bring the torment of hell before the eye of the heart and come to an acquaintance with it by way of an image-sign that does not distort the reports of corporeal sense.

Nephtalim represents a higher and better kind of rational imagination. He also produces images that have the power of a sign. They signify the joys of the blessed. But these images often (not always) represent things *in such a way* that they demand figurative interpretation. They compel the contemplator to seek spiritual understanding.

> But when one reads of a land flowing with milk and honey, walls of precious stones in the heavenly Jerusalem, gates of pearls, streets of gold, what man of sound sense will want to accept these things according to the letter? Wherefore he makes recourse at once to spiritual understanding and inquires what mystical things is contained there.[47]

The image of land flowing with milk and honey does not correspond to anything in sense experience. It so mixes together the things of sense that a reasonable man cannot entertain it without trying to find in it something signified mystically, something that does not in any way correspond to the visible things of experience. Richard concedes that there are many things written about the torments of the damned that must be accepted "mystically" and, likewise, that there are many things about the life of the blessed that, although described corporeally, are to be understood simply as described.[48]

Richard epitomizes the difference between Dan and Nephtalim in a neat formula: "Through a true image of things present, Dan represents a fictive image of future things; but Nephtalim often raises a fictive image of a thing described to true understanding."[49] The image made by Dan represents present things truly. Reason, we know, has a part in the making of the image; and, apparently, reason uses present things to apprehend other things, far removed from the things of this world—the torment of the damned, for example—but remaining things that are visible. The image of these things is called fictive because it does not show them as they are in the future but only as they are judged to be according to the things of the present life. The name "Dan" means "judgment."[50] Richard observes that "one will describe these torments for the sake of the mind's judgment by figuring [in images] not what sort of torments they are, but what sort of torments he knows how to fashion."[51] And what Dan knows how to fashion are images made according to rational judgment of present things.

The language Richard uses to distinguish Nephtalim from Dan emphasizes the role of understanding (*intelligentia*). Nephtalim is not at all ruled by present visible things. He may make a true representation of visible things just as Dan does, but he may also make a fictive representation of them. Such an image will compel one who looks upon it to seek true understanding of the invisible goods of the future life. It will compel one to do so because the image presents us with a picture of something not found among the visible things in this world.

Richard does not explain at length why images that are true to present things befit the representation of hell's evils but not heaven's joys. He merely states that "it is not right to contrive through spiritual understanding something false about future invisible goods, although it is free from fault to perceive the torments of the damned much otherwise than they are."[52] His point seems to be one of practical morality. For Dan and Nephtalim have a moral office.[53] Dan's images, brought before the eye of the heart, check the swelling of wicked desires. Nephtalim's inflame the soul with desires for heavenly joys. The implied reasoning seems to be that there is less moral danger in imagining the evils of hell other than they are. Falsely to imagine the joys of heaven may lead to wicked desires. How Nephtalim represents heavenly goods will be our final point of consideration.

NEPHTALIM

There are two ways, Richard explains, by which Nephtalim raises our rational souls to ardent desire of heavenly goods. One way is by "comparison" (*comparatio*), and the other by "translation" (*translatio*): "Nephtalim uses comparison when, from the number and magnitude of present goods, he infers how many and how great can be the joys of the future life." [54] Richard asks that we consider the light of the sun, which is a corporeal light. If sunlight, which we have in common with the beasts of the world, is so great and so wonderful, how great, he asks, will the light be that we will share in common with the angels? Consider, in addition, the vast number of good things found in this present life. Who can number the goods of the future life? How many will there be? "If there are so many delights of bodies, how many delights of spirits will there be? If we possess so many good things in time, how many are there which we await in eternity?" [55] The technique called comparison shows us just how, in one way, Nephtalim practices the program for seeing the *invisibilia Dei* according to St. Paul's words in Romans 1:20. From the number and greatness of the goods we possess *in tempore*, we can ascend, with the help of imagination, to acquaintance with the immeasurable goods we will possess *in aeternitate*.

Richard returns to the example of light to illustrate how Nephtalim practices translation. By this technique, Nephtalim "carries over a description of visible things to the signification of invisible things." [56]

In Scripture one hears of light, as of God it is written "that He dwells in inaccessible light" (1 Timothy 6:16). He asks, then, what is that incorporeal light that the invisible and incorporeal nature of God inhabits, and he discovers that this light is the very wisdom of God, because this is true light. [57]

In this instance, one's spiritual understanding of the image of light does not result from a comparison according to quantity, whether understood as magnitude or number. It results from a transfer from one thing to another, from the light in which we dwell to that in which God dwells, that is, God's own wisdom. The understanding rises to an acquaintance of spiritual light by making a movement of metaphor, by leaping from sunlight to God's wisdom. [58] Nephtalim's name means either "comparison" (*comparatio*) or "conversion" (*conversio*, understood by Richard to be synonymous with *translatio*). [59] By both methods, Nephtalim rises to acquaintance with invisible, spiritual things.

Richard claims that there is "something distinctive and particularly notable" about the activity of rational imagination that Nephtalim personifies. To those still unschooled and untrained, it is "easier to understand" and "more delightful to hear" than contemplation through pure understanding—that is, unmixed with any images.[60] Richard finds the reasons for the relative ease and delight of "vision" (*speculatio*) through images in the description of Nephtalim that his father Jacob made: he called his son "a deer sent off, uttering words of beauty" (*cervus emissus, dans eloquia pulcritudinis*). Richard's commentary on these words falls into two parts, the first of them dealing with the image of the deer, and the second with its speech. Let us listen first to what he says about Nephtalim as a deer.

Unless I am deceived, Nephtalim is rightly called "a deer sent off" because, *through the grace of contemplation*, it pleases him greatly to run. For in such great speed does this Nephtalim raise up the contemplator's rational soul (yet only a little practiced in this sort of activity), now to the highest things, now sets it down to the lowest things, now takes it through countless things; and this very rational soul, which undergoes these things, often marvels at itself, having learned by happy instruction how fittingly our Nephtalim is called "a deer sent off."[61]

Continuing his commentary on the text, Richard remarks that Nephtalim is not compared to a flying bird. In its flight, a bird is suspended far above the earth and must return to it. Though Nephtalim leaps when he seeks invisible things, even at the highest point of his leaping, he does not fly. He carries with him the shade of corporeal things in images and never deserts the earth.

The image of the bounding deer is not, however, as noteworthy as the assertion Richard makes that the grace of contemplation, the *gratia contemplationis*, assists Nephtalim in his activity. The full range of bounding and running comes from the grace of contemplation. Up to this point, Richard has spoken of Nephtalim's activity as a kind of seeing (*speculatio*) through images. In this way, we seek to rise up through the appearance of visible things to an acquaintance with spiritual and invisible things: *Nephtalim utimur, quando per visibilium rerum speciem ad cognitionem ascendere nitimur.*[62] Ours is the effort to rise up. In Richard's language generally, what we do by our natural powers to see divine things is metaphorically described as "ascent." What God does by grace or revelation to enable us to ascend is spoken of as "descent." Richard says, for example, that the Sacred Scriptures "condescend" (*condescendant*) to our infirmity by using images to signify divine things.[63]

In the text above, Richard speaks of the rational soul as "undergoing" the activity of Nephtalim—*ipse anius, qui haec patitur*—as if the soul were not acting of itself. The indication is clear. Grace is at work in the rational soul. We may also infer that the images that Nephtalim forms do not result from the powers of the human soul alone, that they also spring from the *gratia contemplationis*.

The speech of Nephtalim is Richard's final point of consideration. Nephtalim is not only a deer sent off; he is also one "uttering words of beauty."

See how Nephtalim is a deer sent off. But how he is one "uttering words of beauty"? If perhaps we can show this more plainly through examples, we will persuade more fully. You wish to hear words of beauty, words of sweetness, full of decorousness, full of pleasantness, words such as Nephtalim is accustomed to form or such as it befits him to form: "Let him kiss me, with the kiss of his mouth" (Cant. 1:1). "Support me with blossoms, surround me with apples, for I languish with love" (Cant. 2:5). "Your lips wet with honey, honey and milk beneath your tongue, and the fragrance of your vestments like the fragrance of frankincense" (Cant. 4:11).[64]

Nephtalim speaks the very poetical language of Canticles. We are clearly meant to understand that such speech illustrates Nephtalim's distinctive vision of spiritual things. And it is a vision causing much sweetness and delight. For, as Richard says, "Nephtalim knows how to mix carnal with spiritual things and to describe incorporeal things through the corporeal."[65] The significance of such a mixture is very great. According to Richard, the union in the image of spiritual and corporeal things allows man to discover "whence he may wondrously remake himself, who consists in a nature corporeal and incorporeal."[66] Man discovers in such images not only the invisible things there figured but the model for refashioning himself, who is a union of the corporeal and the incorporeal.

Nephtalim's words (images) delight particularly when the image makes no literal sense.

"Your hair is like a flock of goats which arise from the mount of Galaad. Your teeth are like a flock of ewes which arise from the wash" (Cant. 4:1-2). "Your nose is as the towers of Lebanon which looks toward Damascus, your head, like Carmel" (Cant. 7:5). When these and things of this sort are read or heard, they seem especially delightful, and yet in all these things, if we follow the literal sense alone, we find nothing in them which we worthily admire. But perhaps in words of this kind, this is what we so willingly embrace—that because of a certain delightful foolishness, so to speak, of the letter, we are compelled to have recourse to spiritual understanding.[67]

Once again, Richard explains response to the image in terms of exegesis. In the presence of an image making no sense according to the letter of the words expressing it, the reader or listener, far from being disturbed, freely takes it in and, being compelled by the fatuity of what is said, seeks out some spiritual understanding of it. Seeing (*speculatio*) through this sort of image is particularly pleasing.

Let us summarize the main points of Richard's teaching on imaginative activity. When the human rational soul, illumined by Scripture, desires to see the highest wisdom in faith and simplicity of heart, reason turns, after a required moral development, to the imagination (Bala) for help in becoming acquainted with invisible things. This turn to imagination by reason, still unschooled in spiritual matters, is the *prima via* for anyone aspiring to receive the grace of contemplation and corresponds to St. Paul's teaching in Romans 1:20. From the appearance of things visible, reason can fashion similitudes of images of things invisible. The rational imagination accomplishes this work in two ways. Disposed by reason, it (Dan) makes images that represent present things as they are but that signify things far removed from the bodily senses—the fire of hell, for example. Such images require spiritual understanding "according to the letter" or "historically." Mixed with understanding, rational imagination (Nephtalim) can fashion images that do not represent things as they are. Present things are so combined in the image that it compels one to search for spiritual understanding of invisible things—a land flowing with milk and honey, for example. In the composition of such images, the grace of contemplation affects the rational imagination. Interpreting these images is particularly pleasing to man because he, like such an image, is a mixture of the spiritual and corporeal. Both forms of rational imagination have a moral office because the things brought into view for the ratinal soul's acquaintance are the torments (by Dan) and joys (by Nephtalim) of the future life beyond death. Wicked desires are thereby checked. Good desires are thereby encouraged.

NOTES

1. The *Benjamin* treatises are found in vol. 196 of the *Patrologia latina*, ed. J.-P. Migne (Paris, 1855), cols. 1-64A (*Minor*) and 63B-192C (*Major*). Hereafter, the *Minor*, will be cited according to chapter, and the *Major* according to book and chapter. Numbers in parentheses refer to the *PL*. All translations of Latin texts are mine. I follow Richard's wording of Scripture and his spelling of Biblical names. English translations of extracts from both treatises appear in Clare Kirchberger, *Richard of St. Victor: Selected Writings on Contemplation* (London, 1957). The *Minor* has been three times fully translated in English: *Benjamin Minor*, trans. S. V. Jankowski (Ansbach, 1960); and *The Benjamin*

Minor, or the Preparation of the Mind for Contemplation, trans. Anne Chamberlain Garrison (Unpublished dissertation, Michigan State University, 1957); and *Richard of St. Victor: The Twelve Patriarchs, The Mystical Ark, Book Three of the Trinity*, trans. with introduction by Grover A. Zinn, in *Classics of Western Spirituality*, ed. Richard J. Payne (New York, Ramsey, Toronto: Paulist Press, 1979). The dating of the *Benjamin* treatises cannot be precisely fixed, but the *Minor* appears to be the earlier of the two. Both were probably composed between 1153 and 1165. Richard died in 1173. For attempts at dating, see Kirchberger, *Selected Writings*, pp. 20–25; and Gervais Dumiège, *Richard de Saint-Victor et l'idée chrétienne de l'amour* (Paris, 1952), pp. 168–170. The texts of Richard's works, their dating and classification, and all the pertinent literature are discussed in Hugh Bernard Feiss, O.S.B., *Ubi amor ibi oculus: The Ascent to God in the Writings of Richard of St. Victor*, 2 vols. (Unpublished dissertation, Pontificium Athenaeum Anselmianum: Facultas Theologica, Rome, 1976), I, 187–192.

2. For attempts at a comprehensive treatment of Richard's works, see Feiss, *Ubi amor ibi oculus* and Carmelo Ottaviano, *Riccardo di S. Vittore, la vita, le opere, il pensiero*, Atti della Reale Accademia Nazionale dei Lincei, scienze morali, storiche, e filologiche, vol. 4, fasc. 4 (Rome, 1933), pp. 411–541. For studies of the imagination that treat Richard's doctrines, see Murray Wright Bundy, *The Theory of the Imagination in Classical and Medieval Thought*, University of Illinois Studies in Language and Literature, 12, 2–3 (Urbana, 1928), pp. 199–224; Edgar de Bruyne, *Études d'esthétique médiévale*, 2 (1946; repr. Geneva, 1975), 205–54, 334–43; M. D. Chenu, "Imaginatio: Note de lexicographie philosophique médiévale," *Studi e testi: Miscellenea Giovanni Mercati*, vol. 122, 1946, pp. 593–602; and Robert Javelet, *Image et ressemblance au douzième siècle de Saint Anselme à Alain de Lille* (Paris, 1967), 371–374.

3. Useful general surveys of Richard's theory of contemplation appear in Jean-Marie Dechanet, "Contemplation au XIIe siècle," *Dictionnaire de spiritualité* II, cols. 1961–1966; and F. Cayré, *Manual of Patrology*, trans. H. Howitt (Paris, 1940) II, 452–456; and G. Zinn, *Richard of St. Victor*, pp. 1–49. For Richard's conception of the *genera contemplationis*, see J.-A. Robilliard, "Les six genre de contemplation chez Richard de Saint Victor et leur origine platonicienne," *Revue des sciences philosophiques et théologiques*, vol. 28, 1939, pp. 229–232; Kirchberger, pp. 37–47; Joseph Ebner, *Die Erkenntnislehre Richards von Saint Viktor*, Beiträge zur Geschichte der Philosophie und Theologie des Mittlealters 19,4 (Münster, 1917), pp. 111–121; Feiss I, 282–286; and J. Chatillon, "Les trois modes de la contemplation selon Richard de Saint Victor," *Bulletin de littérature ecclésiastique*, vol. 41, 1940, pp. 3–26.

4. Richard uses *animus* rather than *anima* in the treatise. I translate it throughout as "rational soul." Nowhere does Richard explain his usage, but he may think that *animus* more immediately denotes the human, rational soul, endowed by God with both *ratio* and *affectio*, than does *anima*, which often denotes the soul as the principle of life found in all living things, including man. *Animus*, furthermore, seems synonymous with *mens*, "mind," though the term is not

frequently used in the treatise. I suspect Richard's use of *animus* (rather than *anima*) and of *mens* reflects Augustine's usage: see *De trinitate* 15.1.1.

5. It ought to be mentioned here that the *Benjamin* treatises have had different and more appropriate titles. The *Minor* was sometimes called *De duodecim patriarchis*, sometimes *De praeparatione animi ad contemplationem*. The *Major*, which has nothing at all to do with Benjamin or the house of Jacob, was also entitled *De gratia contemplationis*.

6. See Ch. 1 (1A).

7. Ch. 3 (3B): Omni spiritui rationali gemina quaedam vis data est ab illo Patre luminum, a quo est omne datum optimum, et omne donum perfectum. Una est ratio, altera est affectio: ratio, qua discernamus, affectio, qua diligamus; ratio, ad veritatem, affectio, ad virtutem. See James 1:17.

8. Ch. 86 (62A): Haec sunt itaque duo genera illa contemplationum, quorum unum ad mortem Rachel, alterum pertinet ad Benjamin excessum. In primo Benjamin interficit matrem, ubi omnem supergreditur rationem; in secundo autem etiam seipsum excedit, ubi in eo, quod ex divina revelatione cognoscitur, humanae intelligentiae modum transcendit.

9. Ch. 86 (61D–62A).

10. *Ben. maj.* 1,4(670): Contemplatio est libera mentis perspicacia in sapientiae spectacula cum admiratione suspensa.

11. For Richard's discussion of St. Paul's ecstasy, see chs. 74–75 (52D–54C), and for the discussion of the transfiguration, chs. 74–82 (52D–58A).

12. See Ch. 1 (1B–2A).

13. Ch. 3 (3D): Jam, ut arbitror, non miraris quod Rachel tantum diligitur, cum ejus etiam pedissequa (sapientia mundi loquor, quae in dominae suae comparatione, stultitia reputatur), tanto, ut cernimus, amore a mundi philosophis requiratur.

14. Ch. 3 (3B): Et ratio Rachel esse indubitanter asseritur, quando illius summae et verae sapientiae luce illustratur.

15. Ch. 3 (3C): Rachel *videns principium* vel *ovis* interpretatur.

16. Ch. 3 (4C): Rachel est ratio divina revelatione illuminata. On Richard's notions about *revelatio*, see Feiss I, pp. 299–302. On p. 299, a useful summary is made: "Richard's notions about revelation, and even his vocabulary, center more on the subject who receives the grace than on the content of revelation or the Giver of the grace. In this way, his concept of revelation is narrower than later definitions of revelation. However, his idea of revelation is also very broad, since it embraces any grace given by God whereby fallen man is enabled to understand, and especially to contemplate, spiritual realities." In this broader sense of *revelatio* we must understand both the illumination given to Rachel (*ratio*) and the inspiration made in Lia (*affectio*). However, Scripture must certainly be a part of Richard's notion of *revelatio* here.

17. Ch. 1 (1B): Lia desiderium justitiae; ch. 3 (4B): Lia . . . affectio est divina inspiratione inflammata.

18. Ch. 4 (4C): Nam sicut Rachelis est meditari, contemplari, discernere, intelligere, sic profecto pertinet ad Liam flere, gemere, dolere, suspirare.

19. Ch. 2 (2C): Lia . . . laboriosa interpretatur.

20. Ch. 2 (2C): Sed ab hujus mundi amatoribus, quid stultius, quid laboriosius esse reputatur.
21. Richard's discussion of Rachel and Lia owes much to those of St. Augustine and St. Gregory the Great. See Augustine's *Contra Faustum Manichaeum* 22.51–58 (*PL* 42:432–437), and Gregory's *Homiliae in Hiezechihelam prophetam* 2.2.10–11 (*CCSL* 142:231–232; *PL* 76:954). The writings of Hugh of St. Victor were certainly well-known to Richard.
22. Ch. 4 (4A): Quid enim Scripturam sacram, nisi Rachel cubiculum dicimus, in qua sapientiam divinam sub decenti allegoriarum velamine latitare non dubitamus? In tali cubiculo, Rachel toties quaeritur, quoties in lectione sacra spiritualis intelligentia indagatur. Sed quamdiu adhuc ad sublimia penetranda minime sufficimus, diu cupitam, diligenter quaesitam Rachel nondum invenimus. Incipimus ergo gemere, suspirare, nostram caecitatem non solum plangere, sed et erubescere. Dolentibus ergo nobis et quaerentibus unde hanc meruimus, occurrunt mala quae fecimus. . . . Quoties ergo in divina lectione, pro contemplatione, compunctionem reperimus, in cubiculo Rachel, non ipsam, sed Liam nos invenisse non dubitemus.
23. Ch. 7 (5B): Ordinatus [affectus] quidem, quando illud est ad quod esse debet; moderatus, quando tantus est quantus esse debet.
24. Ch. 7 (5B): Siquidem nihil aliud est virtus quam animi affectus ordinatus et moderatus.
25. See chs. 7–12 (6B–9C).
26. Ch. 13 (9D).
27. Ch. 13 (10A–B): Nato itaque Juda, id est, bonorum invisibilium desiderio exsurgente atque fervente, incipit Rachel amore prolos aestuare, quia incipit velle cognoscere. Ubi amor, ibi oculus. Libenter aspicimus quem multum diligimus. Nulli dubium quia qui potuit invisibilia diligere, quin velit statim cognoscere, et per intelligentiam videre, et quanto plus crescit Juda (affectus videlicet diligendi), tanto amplius in Rachel fervet desiderium pariendi, hoc est studium cognoscendi.
28. Ch. 14 (10C–D): Facit tamen quod potest, intuetur ea quomodo potest. Cogitat per imaginationem, quia necdum videre valet per intelligentiae puritatem. Haec, ut arbitror, est causa cur Rachel prius liberos habeat de ancilla, quam generet de seipsa; quia dulce est ei saltem imaginando eorum memoriam retinere, quorum intelligentiam nondum valet ratiocinando apprehendere. . . . Suadet ergo ratio commodius esse qualicunque modo vera bona cogitare, et imaginaria quadam saltem pulcritudine ad eorum desiderium animum accendere, quam in falsis et deceptoriis bonis cogitationem figere: et haec est ratio cur Rachel voluerit ancillam suam viro suo tradere. Hanc esse primam viam omni ingredienti ad invisibilium contemplationem nemo ignorat, nisi forte, quem ad hanc scientiam necdum experientia informat.
29. *Cogitatio* is always associated with imagination in Richard's usage. For an explicit description of it, see *Benjamin major* I,3 (66D–67A). See also Feiss I, 226: "Seldom . . . does Richard use the word *cogitatio* without some connotation of a directionless wandering of mind . . . *Cogitatio* needs to be moderated and directed by reason."

30. On *intelligentia*, see p. 86.
31. Ch. 5 (4C): Nam sine imaginatione, ratio nihil sciret; sine sensualitate, affectio nil saperet.
32. Ch. 5 (5A): quidquid extrinsecus haurit per sensum carnis, intus representat ad obsequium rationis.
33. Ch. 5 (5B): Nam in tenebris positus, nihil video, sed quaelibet illic imaginari possum, si volo.
34. Ch. 6 (6A): Bala (hoc est *inveterata*). Her chief vice is *garrulitas*, talkativeness.
35. Ch. 5 (4D): Item, cum scriptum sit: Quia invisibilia Dei a creatura mundi per ea, quae facta sunt, intellecta conspiciuntur, inde manifeste colligitur quia ad invisibilium cognitionem numquam ratio assurgeret, nisi ei ancilla sua, imaginatio videlicet, rerum visibilium formam repraesentaret. Per rerum enim visibilium speciem surgit ad rerum invisibilium cognitionem, quoties ex his ad illam quamdam trahit similitudinem.
36. Ch. 16 (11B–C): Bestialis itaque imaginatio est, quando per ea quae paulo ante vidimus, vel fecimus, sine ulla utilitate, absque omni deliberatione huc illucque vaga mente discurrimus. Haec utique bestialis est: nam et hoc bestia facere potest. Rationalis autem est illa, quando ex his quae per sensum corporeum novimus, aliquid imaginabiliter fingimus. Verbi gratia: Aurum vidimus, domum vidimus, auream autem domum numquam vidimus. Auream tamen domum imaginari possumus si volumus. Hoc utique bestia facere non potest, soli rationabili creaturae possibile.
37. Ch. 16 (11C): Hujusmodi imaginatione saepe utimur, cum quae sint futurae vitae bona, vel mala diligentius rimamur.
38. Ch. 16 (11D): Quoties igitur ex multis bonis, vel malis quae in hac vita sensus corporeus experitur, quale, vel quantum esse possit illum futurae vitae summum bonum sive malum colligitur, et ex horum imaginatione, quaedam futurorum imago figuratur, talis utique imaginatio rationlis esse facile convincitur, et ad Balam, et ad Rachel pertinere videtur. Ad Balam pertinet, in quantum imaginatio est; ad Rachel autem, in quantum rationalis est. Talis itaque proles, et imaginationis est per nativitatem, et rationis est per adoptionem. Hujusmodi enim prolem una generat, sed altera educit. Ex Bala namque nascitur, sed per Rachel moderatur.
39. Ch. 18 (12C): Sed rationalis imaginatio alia est per rationem disposita, alia intelligentia permista. Illa utimur, quando secundum visibilium rerum cognitam speciem visibile aliud aliquid mente disponimus, nec tamen ex eo invisible aliquid cogitamus. Ista vero tunc utimur, quando per visibilium rerum speciem ad invisibilium cognitionem ascendere nitimur. In illa est imaginatio non sine ratione, in ista intelligentia non absque imaginatione.
40. *Ben. maj.* I, 3 (67A): Ecce tria ista, imaginatio, ratio, intelligentia. Intelligentia obtinet supremum locum, imaginatio infimum, ratio medium.

Richard's conception of *intelligentia* probably can be traced back to St. Augustine's. See Etienne Gilson, *The Christian Philosophy of Saint Augustine*, trans. L. E. M. Lynch (New York, 1960), p. 270: "The two terms *intellectus* and *intelligentia* were imposed on Augustine by Scripture (*Epist.* 147, 18, 45; *PL* 33, 617). Both signify a faculty above reason (*ratio*). *Intelligentia* is that which is most eminent in man and, consequently, in *mens* (*De Lib. Arbit.* I, 1, 3; *PL* 32, 1223)."

41. See *Ben. maj.* I,3 (67B–C).
42. *Ben. maj.* I,3 (67B).
43. See above n. 18.
44. Ch. 87 (62C–D): . . . per Benjamin designatus intelligentia pura . . . Intelligentiam puram dicimus, quae est sine admistione imaginationis.
45. Ch. 18 (12D): Dan nihil novit nisi corporalia, sed ea tamen rimatur quae longe sunt a sensu corporeo remota.
46. Ch. 18 (12D): Nemo fidelium cum infernum, flammam gehennae, tenebras exteriores in Scripturis sanctis legit, haec figuraliter dicta credit, sed ista veraciter et corporaliter alicubi esse non diffidit. Unde fit nimirum et, quamvis quispiam haec ante oculos cordis per imaginationem ponat, non statim eorum significationem per spiritalem intelligentiam quaerat, quia haec non tam figuraliter quam historialiter dicta, non dubitat.
47. Ch. 18 (13A): Sed cum terram lacte et melle manantem, coelestis Hierusalem muros ex lapidibus pretiosis, portas ex margaritis, plateas ex auro legerit, quis sani sensus homo haec juxta litteram accipere velit? Unde statim ad spiritualem intelligentiam recurrit, et quid ibi mysticum contineatur, inquirit.
48. See Ch. 18 (13B).
49. Ch. 19 (13C): . . . quod Dan scilicet per praesentium rerum imaginationem veram repraesentat rerum futurarum imaginationem fictam. Nephtalim vero saepe descriptae rei imaginationem fictam surgit ad intelligentiam veram.
50. Ch. 19 (13C): . . . hic talis filius Dan, id est judicium vocatur. . . .
51. Ch. 19 (13C): Sed quisque ea pro arbitrio mentis non qualia sunt, sed qualia fingere novit, figurando describit.
52. Ch. 19 (13C): Neque enim licet de futuris et invisibilibus bonis per spiritualem intelligentiam aliquid falsum fingere, quamvis absque culpa sit, tormenta malorum multo aliter quam sunt per imaginationem cernere.
53. For the moral *officia* of Dan and Nephtalim, the two kinds of rational imagination, see Chs. 20–22. The basic point made there is that control of desires depends upon imagination. See also chs. 27, 21–33 for further details on the moral office of imagination. The basic point remains the same.
54. Ch. 22 (15B): Utitur namque aliquando translatione, aliquando autem comparatione. Comparatione, quando ex praesentium bonorum multitudine colligit illa futurae vitae gaudia, quot vel quanta esse possint.
55. Ch. 22 (15C): Si ergo tot sunt deliciae corporum, quot erunt deliciae spirituum? Si tanta possidemus in tempore, quanta sunt quae exspectamus in aeternitate?
56. Ch. 22 (15D): . . . rerum visibilium descriptionem transfert ad rerum invisibilium significationem.
57. Ch. 22 (15D): Audit in Scripturis nominari lucem, sicut de Deo scriptum est: Quia habitat lucem inaccessibilem. Quaerit ergo quae sit lux ista incorporea quam inhabitat invisibilis et incorporea Dei natura, invenit quia lux ista est ipsa Dei sapientia, quia ipsa est lux vera.
58. The distinction between *comparatio* and *translatio* or *conversio* is not easy to

grasp. For two interpretations see Grover Zinn, "Personification Allegory and Visions of Light," *University of Toronto Quarterly*, vol. 46, 1977, p. 195, and Robert Javelet, *Image et resemblance*, p. 373. Neither of these commentators reproduces Richard's thought here precisely as given in the text. Richard is speaking of two ways by which Nephtalim rises to invisible, spiritual things. The soul starts with an image of visible things. It then surges up by *comparison* when it questions according to quantity: how much greater, how many more? It rises *by translation* when, having questioned the image, it makes a transfer from a visible to an invisible thing.

59. Ch. 22 (16A): Nephtalim namque comparatio vel conversio interpretatur.

60. Ch. 23 (16B): Habet tamen hujusmodi speculatio aliquid singulare valdeque notabile. Est enim prae caeteris rudibus quidem adhuc mentibus, minusque exercitatis, et ad intelligendum facilior, et ad audiendum juncundior.

61. Ch. 23 (16B–C): Recte ergo, nisi fallor, Nephtalim, cervus emissus dicitur, quia per contemplationis gratiam multa percurrere valet, et propter contemplationis dulcedinem, multum ei currere placet. In tanta enim velocitate Nephtalim iste contemplantis animum (in hujusmodi tamen negotio aliquantulum exercitatum) nunc ad summa erigit, nunc ad ima deponit, nunc per innumera rapit, et ipse animus, qui haec patitur, semetipsum saepe miretur felici magisterio edoctus quam convenienter Nephtalim noster cervus emissus dicatur.

62. Ch. 18 (12C).

63. See Ch. 15 (10D–11A).

64. Ch. 24 (16D–17A): Ecce quomodo sit cervus emissus. Sed quomodo dans eloquia pulcritudinis, fortassis hoc per exempla evidentius ostendemus, persuadebimus plenius. Vultis audire eloquia pulcritudinis, eloquia suavitatis, plena decore, plena dulcedine, qualia Nephtalim formare consuevit, vel qualia eum formare convenit; *Osculetur me, inquit, osculo oris sui. Fulcite me floribus, stipate me malis, quia amore langueo. Favus distillans labia tua mel et lac sub lingua tua, et odor vestimentorum turoum sicut odor thuris.*

65. Ch. 24 (17A): Sic novit Nephtalim carnalia cum spiritualibus permiscere, et per corporalia incorporea describere.

66. Ch. 24 (17A): . . . ut utraque hominis natura in ejus [Nephtalim's] dictis inveniat unde se mirabiliter reficiat qui ex corporea et incorporea natura constat.

67. Ch. 24 (17B–C): *Capilli tui sicut greges caprarum quae ascenderunt de monte Galaad. Dentes tui sicut greges tonsarum quae ascenderunt de lavacro* (Cant. 4:1–2). *Nasus tuus sicut turris Libani quae respicit contra Damascum, caput tuum, sicut Carmelus* (Cant. 7:5). Haec et hujusmodi alia cum audiuntur, vel leguntur, jucunda valde esse videntur, et tamen in his omnibus, si solum litterae sensum sequimur, nil in eis invenimus quod digne miremur. Sed forte in hujusmodi dictis hoc est quod tam libenter amplectimur, quod ex jucunda quadam, ut ita dicam, litterae fatuitate ad spiritualem intelligentiam confugere coarctamur. Compare St. Augustine's famous remarks on the pleasing enigma of poetical figures in *De doctrina christiana* 2.6.7–8.

Six Hexameral Blessings:
A Curiosity in the Benedictional of Archbishop Robert

KATHERINE O'BRIEN O'KEEFFE

The Benedictional of Archbishop Robert presents the student of the book with a fascinating puzzle: the presence of an unusual set of benedictions in an English manuscript otherwise unremarkable in its contents.[1] Designed for use *per anni circulum* on Sunday and the succeeding ferias, these blessings, found on ff. 66–69^v immediately following the common of saints, commemorate the days of creation, Gen. 1.1–2.3. The choice of an hexameral theme for this series is in itself curious, because such material does not figure prominently in episcopal benedictions. While the complex nature of the relationships among liturgical manuscripts and the enormous number of as yet inedited texts make a final pronouncement on the uniqueness of this hexameral series impossible, an examination of the blessings both demonstrates their indebtedness to the common patristic reading of the first chapter of Genesis and suggests a connection between their presence in the Benedictional of Archbishop Robert and the liturgical developments of the Monastic Reform in England. This inquiry, then, will divide itself into three sections: the first considers the blessings in themselves and evaluates their content against the allegorical and moral interpretations of the six days of creation; the second examines the use of hexameral material in the Roman and Gallican benedictionals; the third considers the influence of the New Hymnal on the Benedictional of Archbishop Robert.

Despite its title, *Robert* is more correctly called a pontifical, a book containing the offices proper to a bishop, although in this case one which also contains a benedictional.[2] The generally accepted date for its composition is the latter portion of the tenth century, probably between 980 and 990.[3] Commemorations for the feasts of Sts. Grimbald and Judoc, both venerated in the New Minster of Winchester, suggest that the book was made for that see. The degree of latitude in the make-up of the English pontifical of this period makes it possible that we owe the inclusion of

Medievalia et Humanistica, New Series, Number 11 (Paul Maurice Clogan, ed.). Rowman and Littlefield, Totowa, NJ, 1982.

these benedictions and the hexameral set to the taste of the bishop who commissioned the manuscript. However, an examination of its contents reveals that there is little which is idiosyncratic about the book.

Contents:

According to Wilson, the only features "unusual" about the book are the blessings for Grimbald and Judoc and the hexameral series. Yet, while the mention of Grimbald (ff. 52^v–53^r) and Judoc (f. 62^{rv}) is peculiar to *Robert,* the wording of their blessings is common to several other manuscripts.[5] The Benedictional of Archbishop Robert is not at all remarkable in its pontifical offices nor in its blessings, with the exception of the hexameral set.[6]

Some account of the content and treatment of these blessings is necessary at this point before we can proceed to examine the patristic background of the benedictions. Eight blessings appear on ff. 65^v–69^v between the "Benedictio in natale plurimarum uirginum" and "Benedictio in monasterio." The first of these, "Benedictio dominicis diebus per anni circulum," a blessing in five parts addressed to the Trinity, is of a very different character from the following hexameral blessings and is found in several other English manuscripts.[7] Following it are an alia for Sunday and six blessings for the ferias: "Deus lumen uerum" ("Item alia benedictio dominicis diebus"); "Deus principium omnium creaturarum" ("Benedictio in secunda feria"); "Omnipotens deus rerum omnium formator" ("Benedictio in tertia feria"); "Benedicat et inluminet omnipotens deus" ("Benedictio in quarta feria dicenda"); "Deus aeternae bonitatis origo" ("Benedictio in feria quinta"); "Benedicat uos dei patris clementia" ("Benedictio feria sexta. de cruce"); "Deus qui sex diebus opera" ("Sabbato benedictio"). All of these share the tripartite structure punctuated by "Amen," which is common to the blessings in *Robert*, although they tend to be somewhat longer than the average blessing in the collection. The blessing for Saturday stands apart somewhat from the series: while sharing the triple structure, it is markedly briefer and can be found in several other English manuscripts.[8] Each of these blessings commemorates the work of one day of creation. Although the formulas of invocation vary between the second and third person forms of address, in the first element of each blessing God is invoked as "Deus" and a *qui* clause follows outlining his work on that day. Some moral connection is then made, and the following two elements develop the invocation of the blessing from the association made in the first.

A reading of these blessings against the most frequent allegorical interpretation of Gen. 1–2.3 explains their choice of material from Genesis and their connections between commemoration made and blessings sought. Isidore's *Quaestiones in Vetus Testamentum: In Genesin* is extremely useful for this purpose because it amalgamates the work of earlier fathers, especially of Augustine, and is in turn drawn on heavily by later commentators on Genesis.[9] In his commentary on the work of the first day, Isidore identifies Christ as the referent of "in principio" and further makes an allegorical connection between "caelum" and "terram," interpreting them as "spirituales" and "carnales." Such a reading probably stands behind the distinction in the first blessing between the "terrenarum . . . sordium" and the inheritance of perpetual life. This Sunday blessing addressing God as "lumen uerum" asks that the congregation, having thrown off the things of this world, be admitted to life with the saints. Isidore draws on Augustine when he identifies the firmament as the "solidamentum sanctarum Scripturarum" (*PL* 83:210), but his further explanation of the firmament illustrates more clearly the development of the benediction for Monday. He writes: "Sed superposuit ipsum firmamentum legis suae super infirmitatem inferiorum populorum, ut ibi suscipientes cognoscant qualiter discernant inter carnalia et spiritualia, quasi inter aquas superiores et inferiores" (*PL* 83:210). This second blessing, commemorating the creation of the "firmamenti stabilitatem" in a similar vein, asks that man be surrounded by the "stabilitate" of God's goodness. In the following element of this blessing, the bishop prays that the congregation be separated from evil as the waters were separated from the waters.

The Tuesday benediction makes an especially careful connection between the works of the third day (the limitation of the waters and the flowering of the earth) and the blessing sought. A common reading for the waters is found in Isidore's *Quaestiones* where they signify "homines infideles, qui cupiditatum tempestate et tentationum carnalium fluctibus quatiuntur." Here the soul is dry land that God allows to produce good works: "germinare bonorum operum fructus secundum genus suum" (*PL* 83:210). The third blessing asks protection against the shipwrecks of this world ("huius mundi periculosa . . . naufragia") and in a parallel clause begs help against temptation. The second element of this blessing then shifts its focus from temptation to virtues and in a moral interpretation similar to Isidore's asks that God "inmittat . . . in cordibus uestris bonarum florentia uirtutum germina." [10]

The invocations of the Wednesday benediction ask two blessings: that God fill the minds of the congregation with virtues and grant them a place among the saints. Both are connected to the works of the fourth day by references to light and the heavens. "Inluminet," "inflammet," "inradiet," "inlustret" all describe the process of infusing what are described as "stellatis . . . uirtutibus." This connection is firmly within the traditional moral reading of Gen. 1.14–19 illustrated by Isidore's explanation that God "protulit etiam et caeteram micantium siderum turbam, id est, diversarum uirtutum in Ecclesia numerositatem" (*PL* 83:211).

The blessings of the fifth and sixth days work less clearly within the line of interpretation represented by Isidore. In the *Quaestiones* the life produced by the waters on the fifth day signified men renewed by baptism (*PL* 83:211). The connection made between the act of creation on the fifth day and the blessing sought in *Robert* is more oblique. The blessing for Thursday asks pardon for sins but more particularly asks God's mercy to produce in man "saluberrima conpunctionis fluenta." While Isidore focuses on the spiritual significance of the creation of animals and the creation of man in God's image, the Friday benediction is more particular. Its focus, as indicated by its rubric "de cruce," is on the redemptive act, connecting creation with redemption in the tradition of liturgical calendars. [11]

The benediction for Saturday recalls God's rest on the sabbath and asks that the people receive eternal rest in the next life. Such a connection is solidly founded in the standard interpretation of the correspondence of the ages of man with the days of creation. The significance of the seventh day and the seventh age is simply stated in Bede's treatise on Genesis, *Libri Quatuor in Principium Genesis usque ad Nativitatem Isaac et Eiectionem Ismah-*

elis Adnotationum.[12] As the seventh day was one of rest, Bede writes, the seventh age is "aetas perpetuae quietis in alia uita, in qua requiescit Deus cum sanctis suis in aeternum post opera bona, quae operatur in eis per sex huius seculi aetates" (*CC* 118A:39, *PL* 91:38). Similarly, the Saturday blessing in *Robert* asks that God grant that the people "ad requiem post labores seculi . . . peruenire."

A consideration of common patristic exegesis demonstrates that the hexameral series in *Robert* is rooted firmly in a traditional understanding of the first chapter of Genesis. What is now necessary is an examination of the occasions where hexameral material appears in the blessings of the Roman and Gallican benedictionals.[13] Such a task cannot hope to be exhaustive, owing to the vastness of the materials to be searched. It is possible, however, thanks to the painstaking work of the Henry Bradshaw Society and, most recently, of Dom Moeller, editor of the pontifical benedictions for the Corpus Christianorum, to draw some conclusions about the ordinary incorporation of hexameral material in episcopal blessings. Against these conclusions, the individuality of this series of benedictions in *Robert* will be even clearer.

The use of hexameral themes in the Roman and Gallican benedictionals is fairly limited. The most common occasions for their incorporation of this material are nuptial blessings whose text is usually Gen. 1.27–28.[14] There are a few other liturgical commemorations of creation: the blessings of Pentecost may recall the action of the Holy Spirit in Gen. 1.2; some blessings for Advent and Christmas allude to the creation of light, Gen. 1.3–4.[15] One series of benedictions that deserves mention in connection with the hexameral blessings in *Robert* occurs in Benedictional B of the *Benedictionals of Freising* and incorporates hexameral themes in the daily blessings for Easter week.[16] This collection, copied around 900, perhaps at the episcopal scriptorium at Freising, represents one version of the Gallican benedictional.[17] For each day during the octave of Easter, Benedictional B provides a blessing which commemorates a day of creation. For Sunday the work is the creation of light; for Monday it is the separation of the waters by the firmament. Tuesday mentions the creation of the sun, moon, and stars; Wednesday commemorates the appearance of dry land and the growth of plants. The creation of man is the theme for both Thursday's and Friday's blessings, and Saturday celebrates God's rest. The treatment of Genesis in these blessings is markedly different from the handling of the text in the series in *Robert*. Most significant about the use of hexameral material in Freising Benedictional B is its firm rooting of any mention of Genesis in the liturgical associations of Easter week. The invocation of the third ferial blessing illustrates the characteristic connections made in Freising Benedictional B. After commemorating the creation of the sun, moon, and stars, the blessing asks:

Presta quesumus omnipotens populo pascha celebrante mysteria tuo ful-
gore circumdato. uitare tetri hostis incursum. amen.
Ne ducantur aduersarii iugo captiui. baptismi sacramento redempti.
amen.
Sed inimici liberati de laqueo. creatoris sui perducantur in regnum
(Amiet, p. 89)

The blessing asked here is carefully united with Easter, baptism, and
redemption.

Despite their allusions to the works of creation, the Freising blessings
have no connection to those in *Robert*.[18] Apart from its different exegetical
associations, the Freising B series does not include all six days of creation,
and the references to the creation of man are duplicated in blessings five
and six. One might note as well the order of blessings is reversed for days
three and four.[19] A further argument against a connection with Freising B
is stylistic. Its blessings are not triple in form and show a degree of cursus
and assonance not seen in the hexameral series in *Robert*.[20]

The remaining area to be explored in this inquiry into the nature of the
hexameral blessings in the Benedictional of Archbishop Robert is a liturgical development associated with the tenth century monastic reform in
England: the adoption of a new series of Vespers hymns in the Divine
Office for the Ordinarium de Tempore. Traditionally, scholars have recognized two hymnals in the medieval church, an early one with roots in
the hymns of Ambrose and some later writers, and a later hymnal associated with the monastic reform which began on the continent in the
ninth century.[21] According to Gneuss, in England the Old Hymnal was
used through the ninth century, but in the tenth century, the New Hymnal was adopted with the introduction of the Benedictine Reform. The
Regularis Concordia (970) assumes its use.[22] Both of these hymnals limit
their use of Genesis to hexameral material, but their emphases and organi-
zations are very different.

In the older hymnal, the hymns using Genesis material praised and
entreated God as the creator of light and the governor of night and day.
Hymns with this theme were distributed over Nocturns, Lauds, Vespers,
and Compline. For example, the Vespers hymn, "Deus creator omnium,"
begins by praising God as the author of light:

Deus creator omnium,
polique rector, uestiens
diem decoro lumine,
noctem soporis gratia
(Walpole, p. 46)

Changing from attribution to invocation, it then begs God to preserve the singers from the dangers of the night. The other hymns in this collection focus chiefly on Christ as the true Light.[23]

There is a profound difference in the use of Genesis material in the New Hymnal, for here hexameral material is the focus of a set of Vespers hymns designed for use in the Ordinarium de Tempore. Walpole accurately notes the correspondence of the Vespers hymns from Sunday through Friday (Saturday was excluded) to the verses in Genesis describing creation.[24] A closer look at the way these hymns develop their hexameral themes throughout the week will reveal their impressive cohesiveness as a set. Each of these hymns is four stanzas in length, not counting the doxology, and (excepting Wednesday) is broadly structured with two verses of attribution and two of supplication. The supplications in these hymns focus almost uniformly on the needs of the interior man, and four of the hymns (Sunday, Tuesday, Wednesday, Thursday) ask God's help in correcting the mind (*mens*) of the singer. Although the supplications are at times loosely related to the creative work commemorated in each hymn, as a group the hymns establish some verbal connections between the works of each day and the people's spiritual needs.

The hymn for Sunday Vespers, "Lucis creator optime" (Gen. 1.1–5), commemorates in the first two stanzas God's creation of light and naming of morning and evening. In the third and fourth stanzas, it begs that the mind of the singer neither be weighted down by guilt nor lose the gift of eternal life. Except that the latter two stanzas recall the distinction between earthly and heavenly things, there is little to connect their invocation with the spiritual interpretation of the first day found in *Robert*. Such is not the case with the hymn for Monday Vespers, "Inmense caeli conditor" (Gen. 1.6–10). Here the separation of the waters by the firmament is celebrated, and apparently recalling the patristic interpretation of this act as the separation of faithful from unfaithful men (cf. *PL* 83:210), the hymn asks that "hanc falsa nulla conprimant." [25] The hymn for Tuesday, "Telluris ingens conditor" (Gen. 1.11–13), commemorates the creation of dry land and the flowering of the earth, entreating God to cleanse with his grace ("viroris gratia") the wounds of the mind so that it may ultimately rejoice to be filled with good things ("bonis repleri gaudeat").[26] "Caeli deus sanctissime," the hymn for Wednesday, devotes its first three stanzas to the creation of the sun, moon, and stars (Gen. 1.14–19). It connects attribution and intercession by a play on "lumen," by asking God to enlighten the hearts of men ("inlumina cor hominum" [Walpole, p. 285]). The Wednesday benediction in *Robert* makes a similar connection.

The Thursday hymn, "Magnae deus potentiae" (Gen. 1.20–23), in praising God for the creation of living things from the waters, alludes to baptism by invoking God's blessing on those cleansed by water and blood ("quos mundat unda, sanguinis").[27] Friday's hymn, "Plasmator hominis deus" (Gen. 1.24–31), by comparison, interprets more loosely the work of the sixth day. This hymn commemorates man's dominion over animals and extends the idea of dominion to the third and fourth stanzas where God is asked to preserve his servants from whatever uncleanness ("inmunditiam") threatens (cf. *PL* 83:211).

It should be clear from this summary that there is only minimal verbal agreement between these Vespers hymns and the hexameral blessings in *Robert*, although the moral readings of Genesis in the two are similar. Nevertheless, the Vespers series of the New Hymnal casts some helpful light on the presence of the hexameral series of blessings in the Benedictional of Archbishop Robert. There are two indications that the New Hymnal may have influenced the adoption of the hexameral series of blessings in *Robert*. The first of these is the striking shift in the use of hexameral material from the Old to the New Hymnal. In the New Hymnal, the creation story is commemorated in a connected series and is presented at a liturgical hour not only celebrated by monks but often attended by the laity as well. Because these hymns were assigned to the Ordinarium de Tempore, they were used for a considerable portion of the year. The second indication of the possible impact of the New Vespers hymns on *Robert* is the date for the English adoption of the New Hymnal. Although this hymnal was in use on the continent since the ninth century, Gneuss has argued that it is unlikely the hymnal had reached England by the early tenth century.[28] Indeed, the two earliest witnesses of the New Hymnal in England are the Bosworth Psalter and the Durham Ritual (ca. 970). The probable date for the writing of *Robert*, between 980 and 990, and its provenance from Winchester, a prominent center of the Reform, suggest strongly that the Vespers series influenced the adoption of the hexameral blessings as a series for the Ordinarium de Tempore.

These hexameral blessings for Sundays and succeeding ferias are unusual in their use and sequential development of material from Gen. 1.1– 2.3. Of the seven, only the benediction for Saturday is attested in other manuscripts. But the peculiar character of these blessings does not extend to their mode of interpreting Genesis, which falls well within the common line of interpretation. In the absence of sources or parallels from the Roman or Gallican benedictionals, the hexameral series of Vespers hymns in the New Hymnal is useful for explaining the presence of these blessings and their serial development. The latitude possible in the composition of pontificals, the date of the book's composition, its origin in Winchester, a center of reform which very early used the New Hymnal together suggest that it is to the impact of these Vespers hymns that the hexameral series of blessings in the Benedictional of Archbishop Robert owes its existence.[29]

NOTES

1. H. A. Wilson, ed., *The Benedictional of Archbishop Robert*, Henry Bradshaw Society, vol. 24 (London, 1903 [for 1902]), demonstrates the considerable agreement of the contents of *Robert* with several other important and early English pontificals, pp. xvi–xxi. For a more recent treatment of its agreement, see D. H. Turner, ed., *The Claudius Pontificals*, Henry Bradshaw Society, vol. 97 (London, 1971 [for 1964]), pp. xvi–xxxix.

2. Wilson, *Robert*, p. x–xi. Cf. J. Brückmann, "Latin Manuscript Pontificals and Benedictionals in England and Wales," *Traditio*, vol. 29, 1973, pp. 396–97.

3. See Elzbieta Temple, *Anglo-Saxon Manuscripts, 900–1066*, vol. 2 of *A Survey of Manuscripts Illuminated in the British Isles*, ed. J. J. G. Alexander (London, 1976), p. 53, and Wilson, *Robert*, p. xii. The manuscript, Rouen, Bibl. Munic., ms. 369 (Y. 7), was brought to France probably by Archbishop Robert when he was expelled from Canterbury late in 1051.

4. Omitted from this list are rites and blessings added to blank folios during the eleventh and twelfth centuries.

5. Cf. Dom Edmond (Eugène) Moeller, O.S.B., *Corpus Benedictionum Pontificalium*, 4 vols., Corpus Christianorum Series Latina, vols. 162, 162A, 162B, 162C (Turnhout, 1971–1979), items 1254 and 97.

6. For the similarity of *Robert* to other liturgical books including, for the period before the Conquest: London, B. L. Cod. Add. 49598 (the Benedictional of Aethelwold); London, B. L. Harl. ms. 2892 (the Canterbury Benedictional); Oxford, Bodl. ms. Bodley 579 (the Leofric Missal); Paris, B. N. ms. lat. 10575 (the Pontifical of Egbert); Paris, B. N. ms. lat. 943 (the Pontifical of St. Dunstan); Paris B. N. ms. lat. 987 (a benedictional from Ramsey); Rouen, Bibl. Munic. ms. 368 (A.27) (Pontificale Lanaletense, originally from St. Germans, Cornwall), see Moeller, *Corpus Benedictionum*, vol. 162C, pp. xxxvii–xxxviii and p. 71.

7. These are the Pontifical of Egbert, the Pontifical of St. Dunstan, and Pontificale Lanaletense. Cf. Moeller (*Corpus Benedictionum*, vol. 162, item 350) who cites this blessing in its four-part version as "Benedictio de sancta Trinitate." The six hexameral blessings which follow in *Robert* appear in Moeller, *Corpus Benedictionum*, as items: 731 (Sun.); 767 (Mon.); 1686 (Tues.); 126 (Wed.); 644 (Thurs.); 214 (Fri.); 1136 (Sat.).

8. These are the Canterbury Benedictional, the Pontifical of St. Dunstan, and several later manuscripts. Cf. Moeller, *Corpus Benedictionum*, vol. 162A, item 1136.

9. *PL* 83:209 ff. Isidore acknowledges, among others, Ambrose, Jerome, and Augustine, but in this portion of his work on Genesis he is most derivative of Augustine, *Confessiones* 13.3–13.34, which provides a short summary of Augustine's allegorical and moral treatment of hexamera in Book 13. Later commentators who drew on Isidore, often verbatim, are Pseudo-Eucherius (*PL* 50:897–900), Rabanus Maurus (*PL* 107:466–68), Remigius of Auxerre (*PL* 131:57–58). On the availability of these authors in pre-Conquest England see

J. D. A. Ogilvy, *Books Known to the English, 597–1066* (Cambridge, Mass., 1967).

10. The first element of this blessing may echo Ambrose, *Hexameron* 3.5, "tentamenta nescire, fidei ignorare naufragia." Christ calming the waters is mentioned in connection with this (*PL* 14:178).

11. The Canterbury Benedictional (B. L. Harl. ms. 2892) has a set of ferial benedictions at the end of the Temporale. The days are dedicated variously, for example, "De angelis," "De apostolis." The blessing for Friday is headed "De sancta cruce" but bears no other similarity to *Robert*. See Reginald Maxwell Woolley, ed., *The Canterbury Benedictional*, Henry Bradshaw Society, vol. 51 (London, 1917 [for 1916]), p. 74.

12. Charles W. Jones, ed., *Libri Quatuor in Principium Genesis usque ad Nativitatem Isaac et Eiectionem Ismahelis Adnotationum*, Corpus Christianorum Series Latina, vol. 118A (Turnhout, 1967).

13. On the two traditions of benedictionals, see Turner, *Claudius*, pp. xi–xii. The major lines of both traditions are reflected in Moeller, *Corpus Benedictionum*, vols. 162–162C.

14. Cf. Wilson, *Robert*, pp. 55 and 150.

15. Cf. Moeller, *Corpus Benedictionum*, items 1251, 1072, 883.

16. Robert Amiet, ed., *The Benedictionals of Freising*, Henry Bradshaw Society, vol. 88 (London, 1974 [for 1951–52]), pp. 88–90.

17. Amiet, *Freising*, p. 36. On the version of the Gallican benedictional represented by Freising Benedictional B, see pp. 49–55. See also Moeller, *Corpus Benedictionum*, vol. 162B, pp. xxiv–xxviii.

18. However, one of these blessings does appear in *Robert*. Feria IV, the shortest of the benedictions, appears in triple form as the blessing for the Saturday within the Octave of Easter (Wilson, *Robert*, p. 18).

19. "Deus qui inter orbis" (Feria. IIII. in Pascha) which commemorates Gen. 1.11–13 should precede "Deus qui olim hac die solem" (Feria. III. in Pascha) which uses Gen. 1.14–19 (Amiet, *Freising*, pp. 88–89).

20. The subject of the cursus in these blessings is a complicated one and unfortunately is beyond the scope of the present study.

21. The most commonly used text of the hymns of the medieval church is G. M. Dreves, C. Blume, H. M. Bannister, *Analecta Hymnica Medii Aevi*, 55 vols. (1886–1922; rpt. New York, 1961). A. S. Walpole, *Early Latin Hymns* (Cambridge, 1922), provides extremely useful annotations, although his theory about the Old Hymnal is outdated. The most recent works to examine the medieval hymns and hymnals are Josef Szövérffy, *Die Annalen der lateinischen Hymnendichtung: Ein Handbuch*, vol. 1, *Die lateinischen Hymnen bis zum Ende des 11. Jahrhunderts* (Berlin, 1964) and Helmut Gneuss, *Hymnar und Hymnen im englischen Mittelalter* (Tübingen, 1968). Szövérffy covers the entire Western hymn tradition although devoting little attention to the Anglo-Saxon tradition. Gneuss devotes his work to the hymnals in England alone and prints a diplomatic edition of the Latin hymns of London, B. L. ms. Cotton Julius A. VI supplemented by hymns from London, B. L. Cotton Vespasian D. XII. In a later essay, "Latin Hymns in Medieval England: Future Research" (*Chaucer*

and Middle English Studies in Honour of Rossell Hope Robbins, ed. Beryl Rowland [n.p.: Kent State Univ. Press, 1974], pp. 407–24) Gneuss corrects his discussion of "Type II" of the Old Hymnal.

22. The New Hymnal was of continental, probably Frankish, origin. Gneuss isolates two versions of the New Hymnal in Anglo-Saxon England according to manuscript groupings: a Canterbury Group and a Winchester-Worcester Group (*Hymnar*, p. 70 ff.). The differences between the two are in the Proprium de Tempore and so do not affect the hymns of the Ordinarium de Tempore considered in this study.

23. A hymn which, in its use of hexameral material, stands apart from both the Old and New Hymnals is Bede's "Primo deus caeli globum," most recently edited by J. Fraipont, *Bedae Venerabilis Liber Hymnorum Rhythmi Variae Preces*, Corpus Christianorum Series Latina, vol. 122 (Turnhout, 1955). Though composed during the time the Old Hymnal was in use, Bede's hymn focuses not on light but on the days of creation and the ages of the world. In stanzas three through eighteen, Bede links each pair of stanzas by repeating the opening line of the first paired stanza in the closing line of the second (epanalepsis) and thus reinforces the similarity between day and age. In this way, recalling his treatment of the theme in *In Genesim* (Jones, *In Genesim*, CCSL, vol. 118A, pp. 35–39), Bede links the creation of light on the first day with the giving of light to the new race of men in the first age; the placing of a firmament among the waters on the second day with the placing of the ark in the waters in the second age, and so on. While this hymn might appear closer to the New Hymnal than the Old because of its full use of the days of creation, actually its use of this material is quite different from that in the New Hymnal. Bede compresses his treatment of creation into one hymn, and he makes only general moral applications after the stanzas on the days and ages are complete. His subject is the figural interpretation of creation, while the hymns in the New Hymnal focus on the works of the days themselves. On the question of the authenticity of the final stanzas, see Walther Bulst, "Bedae Opera Rhythmica?" *Zeitschrift für deutsches Altertum and Deutsche Literatur*, vol. 89, 1959, pp. 83–91.

24. Walpole, *Early Latin Hymns*, pp. 280–88.

25. Walpole, *Early Latin Hymns* (p. 282n) indicates that the neuter for "vana" in the line preceding this is "partly contemptuous" and the word refers to emissaries of the devil. This explanation can probably be extended to the parallel "falsa" cited here. See also Gneuss, *Hymnar*, p. 283.

26. Walpole, *Early Latin Hymns*, pp. 283–84. Gneuss, *Hymnar*, p. 286, reads "virore gratie" and "gaudeat repleri bonis virtutibus." Cf. Isidore, *PL* 83:211.

27. Walpole, *Early Latin Hymns*, p. 286 and Gneuss, *Hymnar*, p. 292. On the grammatical difficulty of this line, see Walpole, pp. 286–87. The allegorical connection with baptism is made by Isidore, *PL* 83:211.

28. Gneuss, "Latin Hymns," p. 413.

29. I wish to thank David Dumville, K. D. Hartzell, and Chrysogonus Waddell, O. C. S. O., consultant to the editorial board of *Medievalia et Humanistica*, for their patient reading of the manuscript and useful suggestions.

The Moment of Resurrection in the Corpus Christi Plays

PAMELA SHEINGORN

That the Resurrection of Christ is the central tenet of the Christian faith has never been in question. Paul's words state this centrality clearly: "If Christ be not risen again, your faith is in vain" (I Cor. 15:17). The doctrine was one of the most problematic for potential converts to Christianity in the late Roman world and was therefore a focal point for Early Christian apologists. It is the basis of the feast of Easter around which the liturgical year revolves. In early Christian and medieval art, Resurrection imagery is of central importance.[1] Even in a series of only four scenes summarizing the life of Christ, an image referring to Resurrection is usually present. It is, therefore, not surprising that the earliest medieval drama is the *Visitatio*, a para-liturgical play in which the Holy Women, by witnessing the empty tomb, verify the fact of the Resurrection. The *Visitatio* was widespread in medieval Europe, with numerous surviving texts attesting to its popularity.[2]

The Resurrection plays in later medieval drama, specifically the Middle English and Cornish cycle plays, all include this *Visitatio* scene in language that reflects a derivation from the Latin plays. The inclusion in these vernacular plays of a scene dramatizing the actual moment of Resurrection was a significant change in content from the Latin plays. It underscored the theme of triumph which is an inseparable part of the celebration of the Resurrection. But at the same moment Christ is given a speech of complaint and lament that seems to undercut entirely the victorious mood.

It is perhaps this air of unresolved conflict that fostered scholarly neglect of the Resurrection plays. Although the appearance of this new scene has been noted, its role in the plays or in the cycles as a whole has not been carefully considered. Scholars have not seen the Resurrection plays as important moments in the cycles, certainly not as having the central role that the Resurrection itself has in Christian theology.[3] Nor have they fully considered the evidence provided by the visual arts, a source that can add significantly to our understanding and appreciation of their visual elements. It is the purpose of this paper to present and interpret these elements. First I would like to mention some of the reasons that the Resurrec-

Medievalia et Humanistica, New Series, Number 11 (Paul Maurice Clogan, ed.). Rowman and Littlefield, Totowa, NJ, 1982.

tion plays in the Corpus Christi cycles have not been seen as very important within the cycles. Then I will investigate the venerable tradition, both dramatic and artistic, which lies behind the plays in order to describe a theoretical reconstruction of the staging of the Resurrection scene based on artistic tradition. Perhaps we can thus recover something close to its original impact.

For the relative scholarly neglect the Resurrection plays have suffered, a number of possible explanations come to mind. First the Resurrection itself suffered neglect in late medieval piety. The triumphal theme of Resurrection was not in keeping with the prevailing religious mood of the times and thus did not find widespread cultural expression. It was devotion to the Passion, as expressed in sermons, literature, and art, that dominated religious thought. The cycles display the same preoccupation with the Passion as evidenced by the number and length of the pageants devoted to it. Lawrence Clopper has concluded that ". . . the sparse evidence of the fifteenth century suggests that the [Chester] Corpus Christi play was more a Passion play than a cycle."[4]

In terms of the structure of the cycles, the moment of Resurrection does not function as the most significant event, either in the life of Christ or in the Christian view of the history of the world. Scholars have suggested that this dual role belongs to the Harrowing of Hell,[5] a scene with thrilling action and dialogue, sources for which lay near at hand in the well-known *Gospel of Nicodemus*, and which Byzantine art substituted for the Resurrection. Not only does Christ or *Anima Christi* visibly defeat Satan and his demons in these plays, but he also releases mankind from the bondage of death. Obviously this scene evokes an emotional response in the viewer.[6] In each cycle, it is the Harrowing of Hell, coming before the moment of Resurrection, which shows the audience a Christ exercising his supernatural powers on behalf of man. In terms of world history and the dramatic structure of the cycles, the presence of Adam and Eve, representing the first parents, in combination with references to the coming Last Judgment, reinforces this moment as pivotal.

When we turn to the Resurrection plays themselves, we see that the moment of Christ's Resurrection does not bring about a shift from sorrow to joy for the characters in the play, since they cannot be allowed to witness the Resurrection. It is only in subsequent scenes, those traditionally enacted in the para-liturgical plays, that we see the joy of Mary Magdalene, the Holy Women, and the apostles as they gradually discover and are convinced by the truth of the Resurrection. The impact of the Resurrection plays is further diminished by the many short scenes that move quickly from Pilate to guards, to sepulchre before the Resurrection, and include appearances of Christ and the reporting and bribing of the guards thereafter. Perhaps readers of the plays have not seen the moment of Resurrection as powerful enough to hold these numerous scenes in orbit around it. Those actions immediately framing the Resurrection are especially problematic. They feature the braggart guards: "And sone we schall crake his croune/ Whoso comes here" (York, ll. 185–6).[7] After the Resurrection, even though they believe it actually happened, the guards are at first amusing in their cowardice and then venal in accepting Pilate's bribe. It is difficult to judge the impact of these touches of realism on the medieval audience. They have, however, succeeded in diverting scholarly attention away from the scene to which they are pendant.

These seem to be reasons sufficient to explain why the moment of Resurrection, and the plays in which it is found, are not perceived as central in the cycle plays. And when Rosemary Woolf adds that although "doctrinally important," such a moment is "awkward to dramatise," the explanation seems complete.[8] The plays themselves, however, deserve closer attention.

The ways Early Christians alluded to the doctrine of Resurrection underlie much of what we find in the mystery cycles. The Gospels do not describe the Resurrection, an event that took place without witnesses. It is handled in the Gospels as it was experienced by the followers of Christ, as a mysterious moment, proofs for which were offered after the fact. The Holy Women, the angels, the empty tomb itself, spoke to the truth of the event.

Some writers, however, supplied a description of the actual scene. In the second century *Gospel of Peter* the narrator relates how two young men come down from heaven,

in a great brightness and draw nigh to the sepulchre. That stone which had been laid against the entrance to the sepulchre started of itself to roll and gave way to the side, and the sepulchre was opened, and both the young men entered in. . . . [T]hey saw again three men come out from the sepulchre, and two of them sustaining the other, and a cross following them, and the heads of the two reaching to heaven, but that of him who was led of them by the hand overpassing the heavens.[9]

Although this account satisfies a need for detail, it is in a noncanonical gospel that seems to have reached only a small Syrian audience.

The most vivid description of the Resurrection is in a sermon by Ephraem Syrus written in the fourth century: "Neither a candle nor a lamp was there but the tomb was radiant with splendor. There was no one who left and no one who entered but within praises were resounding. There was no one who shut or opened but within a crowd of angels was standing." The body stirred, beginning with one foot, and Jesus stood, casting aside his winding sheet and clothing himself in his own glory. He left the tomb as a ray of light without disturbing the seals.[10] Neither of these imaginative re-creations had any impact on Early Christian art. Without the authority of scripture, no artist dared go so far.

Instead, Early Christian artists referred to the Resurrection indirectly.[11] They used symbols of resurrection and life familiar from the Graeco-Roman world—the peacock, phoenix, olive, and ankh—relying on the individual believer to understand their specifically Christian implications.[12] First illustrated on the walls of the catacombs, typological scenes, such as the Old Testament stories of Daniel in the lions' den, Noah and the ark, Jonah and the whale, reminded the faithful of Christ's Resurrection as well as the promise of their own. Yet another way of referring to the Resurrection was offered by a new scene, with its roots in Roman triumphal art, which showed two soldiers flanking a large cross crowned with a wreath.[13] This scene is, of course, totally lacking in narrative content, yet it effectively evokes the idea of Christ's Resurrection.

A need for a narrative scene referring to the Resurrection arose when visual cycles of the life of Christ developed in the Early Christian period. Not until the eighth century did the Byzantine East create its narrative Resurrection image, the Harrowing of Hell.[14] Drawing on Roman imperial iconography for the composition of the scene and on the apocryphal *Gospel of Nicodemus* for its content, Byzantine artists developed an image that took its place in the cycle of the life of Christ and was labelled Anastasis (Resurrection).

Like the Early Christian imagery created in the West, the Harrowing of Hell combined the idea of the resurrection of the faithful with Christ's Resurrection. By showing Christ rescuing Adam and Eve from Hell, the scene of Harrowing established the redemption of man through the defeat of Satan. Rather than illustrating the actual Resurrection, Byzantine artists substituted the consequences of that event for mankind. In western art the narrative image that referred to the Resurrection developed during the fourth century. It represents an immediate post-Resurrection event from the Gospels: the encounter, at the tomb, of the Holy Women with one or more angels. Sleeping soldiers are present as attributes of the tomb, which is often modeled on the Holy Sepulchre in Jerusalem. In this scene the fact of the Resurrection is verified by the witnesses to the empty tomb. This subject held a similar place in the church's celebration of the Resurrection. It is the main episode in the gospel pericopes that were incorporated into the Easter liturgy. Selections from an Easter homily of Gregory the Great, which concentrates on the Holy Women, formed the readings for Easter matins. Furthermore, many medieval Easter sermons embellish and enliven this simple story of followers whose faith was rewarded, emphasizing the experience of the human participants in these events. Drama also found inspiration in this Easter narrative. Of the three para-liturgical rites enacting the burial and Resurrection of Christ, as well as the visit of the Holy Women to the tomb, only the latter, the *Visitatio*, evolved into drama. The other rites, the *Depositio* and *Elevatio*, remained liturgical in character; the latter, a ritual Resurrection, was frequently performed in secret by a few clergy, as if to protect the mystery of this moment. Thus, both in liturgical celebration and in artistic expression, the Resurrection, the central mystery of Christianity, was left a mystery.

A student of the English and Cornish Resurrection plays should, then, be aware of the deep conservatism Christianity had displayed in presenting this moment. For centuries the Holy Women's witness had successfully carried the entire Resurrection message. Other post-Resurrection scenes, such as the appearances to Thomas and to the pilgrims on the road to Emmaus were added, both in art and in the para-liturgical drama. But the Latin drama of the church did not venture to dramatize the moment of Resurrection itself. Only in the vernacular was this scene, the physical passage from death to life, actually enacted. Art, which offered some examples of the scene by the twelfth century, provided a useful model. But the older scenes could not be ignored. The *Visitatio* was played until the Easter Sepulchre was suppressed, and its influence on the Corpus Christi plays is evident. The visual arts continued to represent the Holy Women at the tomb as well as the moment of Resurrection. Thus the new scene of Resurrection had to vie with powerful traditional material.

The moment of Resurrection in the English mystery cycles and in the Cornish Ordinalia passes without much in the way of descriptive language or rubrics to help visualize the scene. The soldiers' subsequent discussion of the event among themselves, however, and their reports to the authorities provide additional information that aids the reader in reconstructing the stage imagery. In all of these plays the action on earth moves in a logical narrative sequence that begins with the discussion between Pilate and his counselors who usually include Caiphas and Annas. They fear that the body of Christ will be stolen in order falsely to encourage belief in a Resurrection. Pilate responds by calling in knights "that ar of dedys dughty" (Towneley, l. 190), "the best men of kynne and blood" (Chester, l. 76), to prevent such a scandal. The knights assert their invincibility, not only if an attempt is made to steal the corpse, but even if that supernatural event, a Resurrection, should take place. As the soldiers in Chester boast:

> Yea, lett him ryse yf that him dare;

> Yea, lett him quicken! Hardlye,
> whiles my fellowes here and I
> may awake and stand him by,
> he scapeth not uncaught.
>
> (l. 106; ll. 114–7)

One of the guards in the Cornish Ordinalia is equally confident: "I'm not a bit afraid of him, not me, and even if it just might happen that he rises up, I'll hit him so hard it'll ram him right back into his shroud" (pp. 189–90). As the guards take their places surrounding the sepulchre, their boasting continues and becomes comic in its exaggeration. In N-Town, Pilate, accompanied by Annas and Caiphas, comes to the tomb to set his seal "on every corner" (l. 1272). The soldiers fall asleep, an action either directly stated by the rubrics or implicit through their later speeches. It is, however, no ordinary sleep, as they are able to describe what ensues in great detail.

The moment of Resurrection had a musical accompaniment in the Cornish Ordinalia, and in the Chester, Towneley, and York cycles: "Tunc cantabunt angeli, 'Christus resurgens' " (Towneley, l. 225.1). This liturgical antiphon was often sung during the *Elevatio* or *Visitatio* rites of Easter morning. Its triumphant tone is characteristic of the liturgical celebration of Easter: "Christus resurgens ex mortuis, jam non moritur; mors illi ultra non dominabitur; quod enim vivit, vivit Deo, alleluia, alleluia." Although the plays are ultimately related to para-liturgical Latin plays, this piece is the only liturgical selection in Latin retained in the cycles' treatment of this subject. In Theo. Stemmler's view it is proximity to the center of salvation history that motivated the retention of the Latin antiphon.[15] Such inertia is indicative of the conservative handling of the moment of Resurrection in English medieval drama.

Evidence of Christ's appearance and actions is sufficient to reconstruct the scene of Resurrection. The knights, on first awakening, seem not to know what has transpired:

> What! oute allas! what schall I saie
> Where is þe corse þat here in laye?
> (York, ll. 288–9)

> Owt, alas! Where am I?
> (Chester, l. 186)

Having verified that the tomb is empty, the soldiers in York and Towneley consider lying, claiming that the body was stolen by force of arms, but then decide to go to Pilate with the truth. In the Cornish Ordinalia the soldiers first discuss what they have seen and, realizing that they must report to Pilate, they see lying as a possible defense from his anger. Their initial interchange is filled with visual imagery:

First Soldier: Faith but I've slept heavy and've had me a nasty jolt. In my sleep it seemed like I saw that dead one in the tomb come to life again with a crowd of angels singing.

Second Soldier: The fact is I was dreaming too, and I felt his foot on my back as he came out of his grave. If he's gotten away, we're in trouble! because as of now I see the big stone sitting mighty high on the edge of the tomb.

Third Soldier: You two must really have been pounding your ear for fair. Now me, I was wide awake and saw him pass by, and I know in what style. He had a banner with a cross on it, which right away he unfurled.

Fourth Soldier: With my own eyes I saw him rise up, I'm positive I did. Fierce and monstrous huge he was as he came out of the tomb. I was too scared of him to hold my head up, and that's the truth. Besides, the light he gave off was awfully bright, I'm telling you.

First Soldier: So get a move on. Find out if he's hiding in some bush or pitchblack nook. If we can discover him, I'll truss him up like a bale of hay till he can't put hand to mouth.

Second Soldier: By God's blood, I'll capture the rascal, never mind how wild he is or how tall he stands. For I'm not afraid of his ruddy banner and his cross, by my hood I'm not, or that we won't be able to bring him in to Pilate.

Third Soldier: Well, we're not going to find him, my life on it, though we run around forever searching in every hole there is. I saw him riding the air with many followers dressed all in white.

(pp. 192–3)

The actions of Christ are vividly described: He rises from the grave in a blinding light, unfurls his victory banner and steps on a soldier as he leaves the tomb. These motifs are described in the dialogue of other plays as well, though none is as clearly detailed as the Cornish Ordinalia. The dazzling light is emphasized in Chester, where it is apparently caused by the radiance of the angel:

> Alas, what ys thys great light
> shyninge here in my sight?
>
> ---
>
> These two beastes that are so bright
> (ll. 210–1; l. 214)

Chester also underscores the motif of stepping both in the rubric ("Jesus resurgens et pede eos milites quatiat," l. 153.3) and in the first soldier's subsequent description:

> He sett his foote upon my backe
> that everye lythe beganne to cracke.
> I would not abyde such another shacke
> for all Jerusalem.
> (Chester, ll. 274–7)

The soldiers confess their great fear, not just of the return from death, but also of the force with which it took place:

Ffor whan þe body toke aȝen þe gost
he wold a frayd many An ost
kynge knyght and knave

(N-Town, ll. 1553–5)

þe prophete Jesu þat ȝe wele knawe
Is resen and gone, for all oure awe
With mayne and myght.

(York, 11. 360–2;
similar in Towneley,
ll. 505–7)

The testimony of the plays as examined so far evokes with precise clarity an image that would have been quite familiar to the audience: the Resurrection as represented in northern European art of the thirteenth to early sixteenth centuries. The main stream of Resurrection imagery in this period is fairly uniform in iconography and in expressive content. Two main features should be noted. First there is a basic concern with the physical implementation of the event. Christ is an active figure, stepping over the side of the sarcophagus.[16] He often uses the staff of the Resurrection banner as a support and plants his foot on one of the sleeping soldiers as a stepping stone. He sometimes pauses to bless the beholder, but just as frequently his entire body is involved in the motion of climbing out of the tomb. Second these illustrations stress the mood of triumph. The action of stepping from the grave is itself indicative of triumph over death, but the mood of triumph is made graphic by Christ's relationship to the soldiers, who had long been a basic element in representations of the Holy Women at the tomb. They are clearly subsidiary figures, one of their roles being simply to help identify the Holy Sepulchre. They are not participants in the interaction between the angel and the Holy Women and therefore remain secondary elements in the composition. In the representations of the moment of Resurrection, however, the soldiers take an additional role: They seem to personify some of the evil that Christ has overcome. They are defeated, as Christ's stepping gesture indicates. The theme of treading on one's enemies occurs repeatedly in the Old Testament and is associated with Christ in the New. In the new Resurrection iconography Christ has literally "made his enemies his footstool." He is the victor, triumphant over death.

Christian theology provided the triumphal interpretation of the Resurrection that motivates this kind of image. The triumphant Christ expresses the classic doctrine of the Atonement that has been called the "abuse-of-power" theory of Redemption.[17] Formulated in patristic writing and most fully expressed by St. Augustine, this theory enjoyed great popularity until the later Middle Ages. Briefly, the "abuse-of-power" theory refers to the power over human life that Satan won justly when in the Garden of Eden Adam and Eve succumbed to temptation. However, when Satan went beyond his legitimate power by bringing about the death of Christ, the blameless God—man, he "abused" his power and lost it. Thus God, through the device of the Incarnation, tricked Satan, or, in St. Augustine's formulation, "the cross of the Lord was the devil's mousetrap." The concept of a struggle between two great powers led to the corresponding ideas of victory and defeat and it is this concept, developed by the Fathers, which found its way into the Easter liturgy. "[T]he Easter festival has always been the central stronghold of the classic view of the Atonement." [18]

In early medieval art, this view was embodied in the image of a Christ triumphant on the cross rather than defeated. Like the doctrine of Atonement itself, played out on a cosmic stage, this image does not directly engage the emotions of the individual Christian. As Rosemary Woolf notes, "The scene is a self-sufficient expression of a dogmatic truth, complete within itself, and demanding no specific response from those who look at it." [19] But the crucifixion image changed during the course of the twelfth century from *Christus triumphans* to *Christus patiens*, the suffering Christ. The image of Christ's Resurrection from the tomb, which was developing during the same century, would have been a logical recipient of both the triumphant mood and the consonant impersonal nature of the *Christus triumphans* Crucifixion.

Clearly the writers of these plays were familiar with representations of the Resurrection in art, and, through the soldiers' language, deliberately evoke those representations. [20] The descriptions suggest that the moment of Resurrection in these plays appeared on the stage as a dramatic version of a late medieval figural representation. The calculated evocation of a work of art is further suggested by the soldiers' testimony that the scene was frozen for a time:

> we quoke for fear, and durst styr none
> (Towneley, l. 516)

> There came noe power him to fett,
> but such a sleepe he on us sett
> that none of us might him lett
> to ryse and goe his waye.
> (Chester, ll. 246–9)

The image is of a tableau vivant: The soldiers rest on the ground in a trancelike state, Christ stands with one foot resting on the back of a soldier and displays his red banner, while angels, kneeling to either side, sing the liturgical antiphon of triumph. The audience was thus provided with a familiar image come to life, a memory to take home with them.

But there are other aspects—verbal and visual—to this scene of Resurrection. Surviving in three of these plays, and apparently once a part of a fourth, is a lengthy monologue delivered by Christ.[21] Scholars have shown that this monologue was drawn from a popular late medieval tradition and interpolated into the plays fairly late in their history.[22] It is called "Christ's Testament" or "Christ's Complaint." In the Towneley Resurrection, Christ delivers a lyric of 108 lines that had a separate existence as a poem entitled, "The Dollorus complant of oure lorde Apoune þe croce Crucifyit."[23] In one manuscript this poem is illustrated with a crucifixion image. The speech in Chester is also interpolated and is a complaint:

> Earthlye man that I have wrought,
> awake out of thy sleepe.
> Earthly man that I have bought,
> of me thou take noe keepe.
>
> From heaven mans soule I sought
> into a dungeon deepe;
> my deare lemmon from thence I brought,
> for ruth of her I weepe.
>
> (ll. 156–61)

Although N-Town is unusual in that the Resurrection is accomplished by *Anima Christi* returning to his body, the lyric spoken at this moment is similar in tone:

> harde gatys haue I gon
> And peynes sofryd many one
> Stomblyd at stake and at stone
> ny3 thre and thretty 3ere
> I lyght out of my faderys trone
> ffor to Amende mannys mone
> my flesch was betyn to þe bon
> my blood I bledde clere
> Ffor mannys loue I tholyd dede
> and for mannys loue I am rysyn up rede
> ffor man I haue mad my body in brede
> his sowle for to fede
> Man and þou lete me þus gone
> and wylt not folwyn me a-none
> such a frende fyndst þou nevyr none
> to help þe at þi nede.
>
> (ll. 1416–31)

This is apparently also an adaptation of preexisting lyric.

As with the triumphal moment already described, there is created here a complete visual image. Speaking in the present tense, Christ avows, "My woundys ar weytt and all blody" (Towneley, l. 233). Significantly he steps outside historical time to engage the audience:

> Thou synfull man that by me gase
> Tytt vnto me thou turne thi face;
> Behold my body, in ilka place
>   how it was dight;
> All to-rent and all to-shent,
>   Man, for thy plight.
>   (Towneley, ll. 244–9)

In each of these complaint speeches, Christ draws the parallel between his body and the Eucharist.

The lyric of complaint has a visual counterpart: the Man of Sorrows or Image of Pity.[24] This is an image of the wounded, suffering Christ, directly confronting the audience with his pain. Christ often stands in front of his cross with the instruments of the Passion arrayed around him and angels at the sides supporting his tortured body. In front of him is the tomb, waiting to receive his flesh. Like other scenes (such as the Crowning with Thorns) this Image of Pity is a product of heightened interest in the Passion. But the Man of Sorrows differs from other such images in that it is outside historical time. Christ is "dead as man and living as God," "for it [the Man of Sorrows] contains both the nonrecurrent anguish as defined in the biblical story of the Passion, in its totality, and the supernatural suffering that the risen Christ must endure daily. . . . New emotional qualities characterize the western Man of Sorrows; they are intimacy, compassion, exhortation and intercession."[25]

Thus both lyric and art exhibit a general shift towards viewing Christ as the sacrificial offering for unworthy man, not as the triumphant king. This shift reflected a new theory of Atonement that by the later Middle Ages had virtually supplanted the older "abuse-of-power" theory except in the Easter liturgy.[26] St. Anselm presents an especially clear formulation of the new theory of Atonement in *Cur Deus Homo?* He answers the question, why did God become man, by showing that only a God-*man* could through self-sacrifice offer God satisfaction for original sin, thus redeeming mankind. This shift from emphasizing Christ's divine nature and Satan's abuse of power in slaying the divine to emphasizing Christ's human nature led to a preoccupation with Christ's physical suffering that was expressed both in literature and in art. Most late medieval literature dealing with the Passion creates a unified solemn mood of meditative sorrow by cutting off the narrative thread before the Resurrection. In art, scenes such as the Buffeting of Christ, the Road to Calvary, the Descent from the Cross, Lamentation, Pieta, and Entombment "seem to make each of Christ's sufferings stand alone and appeal to human sentiment and personal devotion with an intensified expression of sorrow."[27] Even sermons on the Resurrection from the later Middle Ages avoid the theme of triumph and focus instead on the Eucharist, a theme of sacrifice.

How, then, are we to reconstruct the staging of the lyric speech? Because the lyric of complaint is given to the risen Christ, both Rosemary Woolf and J. W. Robinson have argued that in the Resurrection plays of the Corpus Christi cycles Christ appears as the Man of Sorrows.[28] This assertion ignores the plays in which the lyrics are imbedded, which, as we have seen, call for a Christ triumphant. It is, however, responsive to the visual imagery in the lyric, and therefore demands serious consideration.

If we try to attach all of the visual imagery that is evoked by the play to one scene, we seem to create contradiction and confusion, or at best a scene that is overly replete with significant content. This is what happens in art when elements of the Passion begin to invade the Resurrection scene. Christ is constrained to step on the soldier, display the banner, bless the audience, and describe his suffering all in one image.[29]

However, the dramatist is not confined to one image. Indeed the moment of Resurrection in the English and Cornish cycle plays might have lasted much longer than a moment. Evidence from the texts themselves and from art suggests that the audience may have seen these two sides of Christ's nature sequentially, not simultaneously. First they may have seen a *Christus triumphans* and heard his victory sung by angels; then, perhaps with a simple motion of pulling aside his cloak and opening out his hands, Christ revealed his wounds and became the *Christus patiens* who suffered and continues to suffer for mankind. This break in the narrative thread, not without precedent in the cycle plays, could have had an especially deep and dramatic impact on the medieval audience.

At the conclusion of the *Christus patiens* scene, narrative continuity is restored, and the triumphant mood reasserts itself, but, as the late Middle Ages preferred, with a touching reminder of Christ's human nature through his appearance to his mother. There is ample precedent for this scene in devotional literature and in art; it owes its existence to the immensely popular cult of Mary. As both Christ and Mary were viewed in increasingly human terms, it seemed evident that a perfect son would immediately relieve his mother's grief by appearing to her first. In the Cornish Ordinalia, the presence of this encounter may partially substitute for the lack of a complaint speech, to the extent that both remind the audience of the human Christ immediately after his superhuman Resurrection. Mary is concerned with her son's suffering and asks:

But you, do you still have pain, do you still suffer? Are your nail and spear wounds healed, those I saw tear and defile your dear flesh? Tell me now, Beloved; give me word of how it is with you.

Jesus replies:

May honor, reverence and blissful happiness be yours, treasured Mother. No pain touches me nor can I ever again be harmed by it. I have overcome sorrow, anguish, and death and am made whole in the perfection of well-being.

(p. 192)

Similarly in N-Town, but immediately following the complaint, Christ appears to Mary and assures her that she need no longer be sorrowful:

> Salue Sancta Parens/ my modyr dere
> All heyl modyr with glad chere
> Ffor now is A-resyn with body clere
> þi sone þat was dolve depe
> þis is þe thrydde day þat I ʒow tolde
> I xuld a-rysyn out of þe cley so colde
> now am I here with brest ful bolde
> þerfore no more ʒe wepe.
>
> (ll. 1432–9)

This scene completes the movement from the mortal to the immortal Christ. Yet while human suffering is behind him, human love of a son for his mother remains.

One of the persistent difficulties with the Resurrection scene in the cycles has been that, when read rather than seen, it appears flat and uninteresting; the moment seems exceedingly brief as well as confusing in content. But a visual reading of this scene has shown that the dramatist, drawing on two distinct artistic traditions, created two distinct aspects of Christ as he appeared at his Resurrection.[30] Although it is possible that they were fused, it seems more likely that the plays displayed them sequentially so that the audience could grasp both the theological and the human significance of the event. The audience would thus be brought to full cognizance of the ultimate truth that *Christus triumphans* and *Christus patiens* co-exist, for to God historical sequential time has no meaning. Paradoxically, only by presenting the audience with a sequence of images could that theological message be fully expressed, a message that, because of its conservatism in preserving the triumphant tone of the Easter liturgy, the moment of Resurrection was best prepared to present.[31]

Figure 1. *The Resurrection*, from a Sarum Missal printed in 1512 by Richard Pynson (New York, the Pierpont Morgan Library).

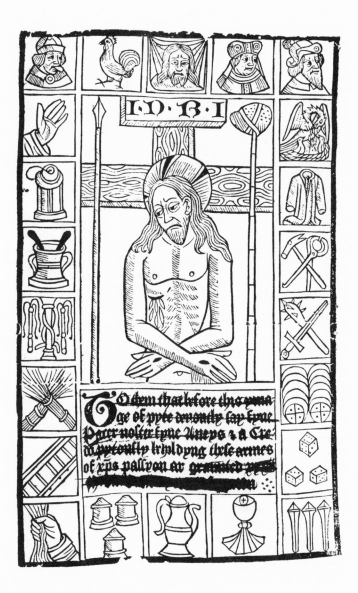

Figure 2. *Image of Pity*, English Woodcut, 1490–1500 (Oxford, Bodleian Library).

NOTES

1. In this paper contemporary visual evidence is brought to bear on a specific moment in the Corpus Christi plays, the moment of Christ's Resurrection. Because visual representations of this scene were ubiquitous, and because they antedate its dramatic representation, medieval playwrights must have been aware of and influenced by the visual tradition. I do not wish to imply that in general the direction of influence is from art to drama. Rather I see a complicated interplay in the visual and literary arts of the Middle Ages in which the treatment of a subject in one medium may elucidate problems of interpretation of that subject in another. For a discussion of methodology in studies relating medieval art and drama, see my forthcoming paper in vol. 22 of *Research Opportunities in Renaissance Drama.*

2. All known texts of the para-liturgical Easter rites have recently been re-edited by Walther Lipphardt in his *Lateinische Osterfeiern und Osterspiele,* 5 vols. (Berlin and New York, 1975–6). Volumes 6 and 7 of additional texts, bibliography, and commentary have not yet appeared. The para-liturgical plays, and especially the *Visitatio,* have been the subject of intense scholarly activity in the last fifteen years. See C. Clifford Flanigan, "The Liturgical Drama and Its Tradition: A Review of Scholarship 1965–1975," *Research Opportunities in Renaissance Drama,* vol. 18, 1975, pp. 81–102 and vol. 19, 1976, pp. 109–136.

3. Glynne Wickham has most clearly perceived this difference: "Theologically, the centre or core of Christianity is the double mystery of the Nativity and Resurrection, since acceptance of these miracles is the gateway to belief. Dramatically, however, the centre or 'middle' is the Crucifixion: for this is the climactic event after which relationships, and the situation arising from them, can never be quite as they were before." *Early English Stages 1300–1660,* vol. 1, 1300–1576 (London and New York, 1959; rpt. with corrections, 1963), p. 316.

   Other scholars who have written on the Resurrection in the cycles include Robert A. Brawer, "The Middle English Resurrection Play and Its Dramatic Antecedents," *Comparative Drama,* vol. 8, 1974, pp. 77–100; Brawer is primarily concerned with the *Visitatio Sepulchri* in Orleans 201, *La Seinte Resurrection,* and two thirteenth century Latin Easter plays from Klosterneuberg and Tours. Brawer also suggests some parallels to the Towneley and York Resurrection plays, specifically "in the assimilation of what has been termed a Pilate-action into the traditional play of the resurrection" (p. 92). V. A. Kolve, *The Play Called Corpus Christi* (Stanford, 1966), pp. 196–7, discusses the Resurrection as game. Rosemary Woolf, *The English Mystery Plays* (Berkeley, 1972), pp. 274–80, has a penetrating though brief discussion of Resurrection plays in her chapter "Triumphal and Eschatological Plays" in which she suggests some of the relationships between art and drama that are more fully explored in this essay. J. W. Robinson has examined the "static, non-narrative scene" in which Christ delivers a monologue to the audience, and has linked the monologue to the Image of Pity in art. His purpose is to understand "the religious (and social) contexts of the *performances* (especially the rationale of the presence of the audience)," "The Late Medieval Cult of Jesus and the Mystery Plays," *PMLA*, vol. 80, 1965, pp. 508–14.

4. "The History and Development of the Chester Cycle," *MP*, vol. 75, 1978, p. 219.

5. "Dramatically, the binding of Satan marks the end of the drama, for now the long conflict has been resolved in the victory of Christ over Satan," Timothy Fry, "The Unity of the *Ludus Coventriae*," *SP*, vol. 48, 1951, p. 563. This argument is extended to all of the cycles by Peter Stuart Macaulay, "The Play of the Harrowing of Hell as a Climax in the English Mystery Cycles," *Studia Germania Gandensia*, vol. 8, 1966, pp. 115–134.

6. Clifford Dividson sees in the Harrowing of Hell plays in the York and Towneley cycles a "movement from *tristia* to *gaudium* which traditionally characterized the Lenten liturgy and which is particularly accentuated in the services for Holy Saturday," "From *Tristia* to *Gaudium*: Iconography and the York-Towneley *Harrowing of Hell*," *American Benedictine Review*, vol. 28, 1977, p. 261.

7. All quotations from the cycle plays are taken from the following editions: K. S. Block, ed., *Ludus Coventriae, or the Plaie Called Corpus Christi*, E.E.T.S. E.S. 120 (London, 1922, rpt. 1960), cited herein as N-Town; George England and Alfred W. Pollard, eds., *The Towneley Plays*, E.E.T.S. E.S. 71 (London, 1897, rpt. 1973); Markham Harris, trans., *The Cornish Ordinalia* (Washington, D.C., 1969); Lucy Toulmin Smith, ed., *York Plays* (Oxford, 1885, rpt. 1963); R. M. Lumiansky and David Mills, eds., *The Chester Mystery Cycle*, E.E.T.S. S.S. 3 (London, 1974).

8. Woolf, *Plays*, p. 274.

9. Edgar Hennecke and Wilhelm Schneemelcher, eds., *New Testament Apocrypha*, trans. ed. R. McL. Wilson (Philadelphia, 1963), vol. 1, pp. 185–6.

10. Ephraem Syrus, *Sancti Ephraem Syri Hymni et Sermones*, ed. Thomas J. Lamy (Mechlin, 1882), vol. 1, p. 524 ff. John Wyatt, Beloit College, provided valuable assistance in the translation of Ephraem's sermon.

11. Gertrud Schiller, *Ikonographie der christlichen Kunst*, vol. 3, *Die Auferstehung Christi* (Gütersloh, 1972), supersedes other studies on Resurrection iconography. Still useful is Hubert Schrade, *Ikonographie der christlichen Kunst*, vol. 1, *Die Auferstehung Christi* (Berlin, 1932).

12. Schiller, *Auferstehung*, pp. 120–35. For the ankh and the olive see also Harry Bober, "On the Illumination of the Glazier Codex; A Contribution to Early Coptic Art and its Relation to Hiberno-Saxon Interlace," *Homage to a Bookman: Essays written for Hans P. Kraus on his Sixtieth Birthday*, ed. Hellmut Lehmann-Haupt (Berlin, 1967), pp. 31–49.

13. Andre Grabar, *Christian Iconography: A Study of its Origins* (Princeton, 1968), p. 125. See also plates 297–9.

14. Schiller, *Auferstehung*, pp. 47–56. See also Ellen C. Schwartz, "A New Source for the Byzantine Anastasis," *Marsyas*, vol. 16, 1972–3, pp. 29–34.

15. Theo. Stemmler, *Liturgische Feier und geistliche Spiele* (Tübingen, 1970), p. 244.

16. In England, this is especially true of those artistic media which reached a wide audience: woodcuts, alabasters, sculpture, and brasses. There was a concern with Christ's supernatural nature that was also expressed in iconography of the Resurrection. One group, which originated in Italy, shows Christ hovering in the air above the tomb, and another depicts him stepping through the sealed sarcophagus lid.

17. Gustaf Aulén, *Christus Victor: An Historical Study of the Three Main Types of the Idea of Atonement*, trans. A. G. Herbert from 1st Swedish ed. (1930; rpt, New York, 1967); Fry, "Unity," pp. 527–32.

18. Aulén, *Christus*, p. 98.

19. Rosemary Woolf, *The English Religious Lyric in the Middle Ages* (Oxford, 1968), p. 21.

20. Both Kolve, *Play*, p. 196, and Woolf, *Plays*, p. 274, refer to the visual arts in discussing the plays of the Resurrection.

21. Such a speech exists in the Chester, N-Town, and Towneley cycles; W. W. Greg and Alfred Pollard agree that it was once a part of the York cycle as well. W. W. Greg, "Bibliographical and Textual Problems of the English Miracle Cycles," *The Library*, Ser. 3, vol. 5, 1914, p. 285. Rosemary Woolf says that Greg "wrongly inferred" the presence of a complaint although she agrees that "the form of the York stage direction shows that it was accompanied by something" (Woolf, *Plays*, n. 15, p. 406). For Woolf, this is accounted for by the marginal note in the manuscript directing the singing of "Christus resurgens." The Cornish Ordinalia does not contain this monologue.

22. These monologues are drawn from pre-existing lyric. For the literature on this relationship see Robinson, "Cult of Jesus."

23. Woolf, *Lyric*, pp. 203–4.

24. Gertrud Schiller, *Iconography of Christian Art*, vol. 2, *The Passion of Christ*, trans. from 1968 German ed. by Janet Seligman (Greenwich, 1972), pp. 197–224. See also Erwin Panofsky, " 'Imago Pietatis' Ein Beitrag zur Typengeschichte des 'Schmerzenmanns' und der 'Maria Mediatrix,' " in *Festschrift für Max J. Friedländer* (Leipzig, 1927), pp. 262–308.

25. Schiller, *Passion*, p. 198.

26. Aulén, *Christus*, p. 98, concludes that "Finally it is to be noted that this Devotion to the Passion co-operated with the Latin theory [of the Atonement] in banishing what remained of the classic idea of the Atonement. . . . What was lost was the note of triumph."

27. Schiller, *Passion*, p. 16.

28. Woolf, *Lyric*, pp. 202–5. See also Robinson, "Cult of Jesus."

29. Woolf, *Plays*, p. 275, says that it might have been images of the type, "according to which Christ, with his wounds strongly marked, motionlessly confronts the beholder as if demanding a devotional response, that must have suggested both the propriety and the possibility of placing a complaint at this point." However, this type is rare in late medieval English iconography, in which the active, physical Resurrection is commonly found.

30. It is, of course, an oversimplification to generalize about all of the plays. Each is a unique mixture of *Christus triumphans* and *Christus patiens* imagery. In the Cornish Ordinalia, for example, the triumphal imagery is most vividly

evoked, but Christ is not given a lyric of complaint. The Towneley play, which contains the longest and most moving lyric, has relatively little triumph imagery. These playwrights, perhaps aware of a potential conflict in mood, chose to emphasize clearly one image over the other. Yet in each play elements of both are present.

31. This essay originated in a presentation to an NEH Summer Seminar, "Medieval Origins of Modern Drama," directed by Professor Jerome Taylor, University of Wisconsin, Madison. I owe Professor Taylor an enormous debt for his patience in introducing me, an art historian, to the field of medieval drama. The ideas expressed in the essay underwent considerable revision as a result of discussion with Professor David Bevington and my colleagues in his NEH Seminar, "The Drama of Medieval and Renaissance England, 950–1616," at the University of Chicago. To Professor Bevington and my colleagues I wish to express here my gratitude for their gracious interest in my work. Errors are, of course, my own.

Scientia *and* Sapientia *in the* Chanson de Roland

JUNE HALL MARTIN McCASH

A careful reading of the Digby 23 version of the *Chanson de Roland* makes it apparent that Charlemagne has a strong premonition of the treachery of Ganelon and the impending disaster of Roncevaux and yet, he does nothing to stop it. One of the long-standing problems of the text has been his apparent inability "to stay the onrushing catastrophe."[1] Just as Christ perceived the impending treachery of Judas, so Charles perceives *per speculum in aenigmate* what is to befall his rearguard. And both must suffer the very human anguish they foresee but take no steps to prevent.

Like Christ in iconographic representations of the 11th and 12th centuries, Charles stands at the juncture of the secular and the anagogic, where time and the eternal converge.[2] As *rex dei*, he functions on the vertical axis of *anagogia*. As *rex mundi*, he functions on the horizontal axis of *historia*, and it is precisely the tension between the two that creates the anguish that the emperor must suffer. As a feudal lord, he is obligated to seek *consilium* from his vassals. Marc Bloch tells us that "Selon le code de bon gouvernement alors universellement admis, aucun chef, quel qu'il fût, ne pouvait rien décider de grave sans avoir pris conseil."[3] Charles, obeying the precepts of the secular society in which he functions, does indeed take counsel at every point of narrative bifurcation. The Arab emir, Usama ibn Munqidh, writing his autobiography at roughly the same time the *Chanson de Roland* was composed, comments with some interest on Frankish customs and the obligations inherent in counsel and judgment: "Once the knights have given their judgment neither the King nor any other commander can alter or annul it, so great an influence do their knights have in their society."[4] Counsel given by wise and loyal vassals would seem, on the face of things, to work to the best advantage of any king. Charles's position as leader of a holy cause, however, places a special burden upon his counselors to see beyond the immediate implications of their advice and to perceive its ramifications in terms of the sacred—something they are not always capable of doing. As a consequence, a conflict between the *lex mundi*, by which the emperor seems unalterably bound, and the demands of the holy cause is developed and must be resolved in the character of Charlemagne.

131

Medievalia et Humanistica, New Series, Number 11 (Paul Maurice Clogan, ed.). Rowman and Littlefield, Totowa, NJ, 1982.

The matter of counsel is clearly crucial in the *Chanson de Roland*, for it is by means of counsel that decisions are made and the action is propelled. The poem is structured around a series of questions: (1) Shall Charles accept the peace offer from Marsile or shall the war continue? (2) Who will carry the message of Charles's decision to Marsile? (3) Who will command the rearguard? (4) Should Roland sound his horn? (5) Should Charles return to aid the rearguard or is Roland only blowing his horn for sport? (6) Is Ganelon guilty of treason? All of these crucial questions, save one, are posed by the emperor himself. While he listens to the advice of a variety of counselors, it is inevitably that of the loyal Duke Naimes whom he considers a "saives hom"[5] that most often determines the path he chooses to follow. The author, however, has given us early clues that the words *saives* and *sages* must be viewed with considerable caution. The first time one of the words is spoken in the poem, it comes from the lips of the pagan Marsile as he asks his counselors to recommend a plan of action that will save him from shame and death:

> "Cunseilez mei cume mi saive hume,
> Si me guarisez e de mort e de hunte!"
>
> (ll. 20–1)

But their flawed advice, especially that of Blancandrin, who is described as "des plus saives paiens" (l. 24), will lead ultimately to that very fate that Marsile seeks to avoid.

The next character who speaks of wisdom is Ganelon. Charles, who has been offered a handsome bribe by Marsile to leave Spain, takes counsel with his barons on whether to accept or not. It is the first major decision in the poem. From Roland comes the uncompromising negative response, "Ja mar crerez Marsilie" (l. 196), and then its parody in the words of Ganelon, "Ja mar crerez bricun" (l. 220). Ganelon advises accommodation and the acceptance of Marsile's offer, denigrating Roland's advice with a parting remark: "Laissun les fols, as sages nus tenuns!"

The lines of opposition have been clearly drawn by Ganelon, as he places Roland on the side of the "fols" and himself on the side of the "sages." It is at this point that Duke Naimes steps into the narrative for the first time to counsel and to conciliate in the quarrel between the two. Eugene Vance has distinguished between the two positions by suggesting that Roland's idealism is founded upon "a rectitude of memory" while Ganelon indulges in "a willful forgetting."[6] He suggests that Duke Naimes who is "ordinarily a paragon of good sense among the Franks" is seduced at this point by Ganelon's logic.[7] It is, however, far from being an isolated incident in the poem, for Duke Naimes sides consistently with

Ganelon until, finally, the recognition of Ganelon's treachery is forced upon his logical and rational mind. From a structural perspective Naimes is one of the most important characters in the poem, for it is he who, at points of narrative bifurcation, will most frequently determine the direction the story will take. Naimes is old and reputedly wise, but unfortunately his wisdom, far from the *sapientia* that leads to knowledge of God, is rather the *scientia* which Augustine describes as "the cognition of things temporal and changeable."[8]

Naimes is clearly loyal to Charles, and it is with every good intention that he urges him to accept Ganelon's judgment. He points out to the emperor that Ganelon's words demonstrate his "saveir." One must only understand his logic:

> "Ben l'avez entendud,
> Guenes li quens ço vus ad respondud;
> Saveir i ad, mais qu'il seit entendud."
> (ll. 232–4)

He goes on to suggest that Marsile is, in effect, already defeated in the Holy War, and that refusing mercy to a vanquished foe is a sin. The war, he states quite firmly, should not go on: "Ceste grant guerre ne deit munter a plus" (l. 242). Naimes's counsel has tipped the balance in favor of Ganelon, and the French all assent: "Ben ad parlet li dux" (l. 243). Charles, following this advice, which stands in opposition to that of Roland, sets in motion the events that will demand the Christological sacrifice that Roland must make.

The second question of the poem centers upon the selection of Charles's emissary to Marsile. When Roland names Ganelon, the French, in what will prove to be an ironic reminder of Ganelon's earlier words, "Laissun les fols, as sages nus tenuns," approve the appointment, saying:

> "Car il le poet ben faire!
> Se lui lessez, n'i trametrez plus saive."
> (ll. 278–9)

Ganelon is enraged, and Roland mocks him, throwing back at him his own words:

> "Orgoill oi e folage,
> Ço set hom ben, n'ai cure de manace.
> Mai saives hom, il deit faire message:
> Si li reis voelt, prez sui por vus le face."
> (ll. 292–5)

The conflict between *saveir* and *folage*, underscored earlier by Ganelon himself, becomes still more complex at this point, for we are clearly dealing with dual concepts—two sets of *saveir* and two sets of *folage* that stand in binary opposition. To Ganelon *saveir* is Augustinian *scientia*, whereas *folage* is the rashness and pride of which Ganelon and Olivier will accuse Roland. For Roland, on the other hand, *saveir* is the *sapientia* that keeps one's eye firmly fixed on the immutable. Although it may appear to be *folage* to those whose wisdom is rooted in matter,[9] to Roland it is the only wisdom. From this perspective, *folage* is that which distracts man from God, from a singleness of purpose characteristic of the Christian martyr. We are confronted with a situation in which "what appears as error or falsehood in one theory of culture or society appears as truth or fact in another."[10]

Ganelon, the only one of the Christians to enter both literally and symbolically into the pagan camp, carries with him his inverted sense of *saveir*, where he finds it well received and totally compatible with the pagans' own idea of *saveir*. He counsels Marsile in almost the same words he has used in advising Charles: "Lessez la folie, tenez vos al saveir" (l. 569). The *saveir* in question is the recognition of the importance of killing Roland. If the inverted and ironic concept of *saveir* by Ganelon is not already obvious, it is forced into the reader's consciousness by the words of the pagan king, who compliments Ganelon, lauding his "wisdom": "Mult par ies ber e sage" (l. 648). The pact between them is appropriately sealed as the Saracens bestow rich gifts upon their Judas.

After Ganelon's return to the Christian camp, Charles is confronted with the third major choice upon which the action of the poem is predicated: Who will lead the rearguard? Ganelon, bent upon expediting his treacherous plot, quickly names Roland. Charles clearly recognizes the dangers of the position; the decision, however, is not his, but that of his vassals. Again it is Duke Naimes who steps forward to side with Ganelon and confirm the appointment of Roland:

> "Ben l'avez entendut,
> Li quens Rollant, il est mult irascut.
> La rereguarde est jugee sur lui,
> N'avez baron ki jamais la remut."
> (ll. 776–9)

Volunteers to accompany Roland are many, but none is more enthusiastic than Archbishop Turpin.

From this point in the narrative there is a dual line of action that must be followed, that of the main army and that of the rearguard. As the main army moves through the mountain pass toward Gascony, "la tere lur seignur" (l. 819), the men are overcome with emotion, and none moreso than Charles. Their feelings are described as "pitet," his more powerfully as "anguissus."

> Sur tuz le altres est Carles anguissus,
> As porz d'Espaigne ad lesset sun nevold.
> Pitet l'en prent, ne poet muër n'en plurt.   AOI.
>
> (ll. 823–5)

Charles's overwhelming emotion at this point in the text seems quite clearly to result from his understanding of the full implications of the course of action that Ganelon has recommended and that Duke Naimes had approved. His awareness of Ganelon's treachery has become increasingly evident as the poem progresses. Ganelon's *défi* before the council, his naming of Roland to the rearguard, and the visions sent to the emperor in a dream have provoked in Charles a reaction that reflects his growing recognition of what is about to happen on the plane of *historia*. His choice of words to Ganelon, "Vos estes vifs diables" (l. 746), when he hears the nomination of Roland to the rearguard suggests his cognition both of Ganelon's treason and of its theological implications, and Charles withholds the bow, symbol of the appointed office, until Naimes, as we have already seen, steps in to confirm the appointment. Only once, however, does Charles direct his helpless anger and frustration at the duke, and it occurs precisely as the main army moves through the pass toward its homeland. Duke Naimes, noticing the emperor's tears, rides up to him and inquires, "De quei avez pesance?" (l. 832). Charles turns on him angrily and seems, if only for a moment, to consciously place the blame for what is happening upon the loyal but misguided duke:

> "Tort fait kil me demandet!
> Si grant doel ai ne puis muër nel pleigne.
> Par Guenelun serat destruite France.
> Enoit m'avint un avisiun d'angele
> Que entre mes puinz me depeçout ma hanste,
> Chi ad juget mis nes a rereguarde."
>
> (ll. 833–8)

The verb form of the phrase "Chi ad juget. . ." is singular, and Charles falls short of openly blaming Naimes, but the reader is well aware of the duke's unwitting complicity in Ganelon's plot.

Charles's weakness at this moment in the poem is underscored. Despite his efforts to obey God, he has placed the *lex mundi* before his obedience to divine commands, and he stands both literally and figuratively poised between two directions. To continue on toward la "dulce France" is to choose the way of *scientia;* to return against the advice of his counselors and complete his holy mission in Spain is to choose the way of *sapientia.*

With the rearguard itself, *scientia* is still represented in the person of Olivier. The famous line, "Rolland est proz et Oliver est sage," must be examined within the context of the normal usage of the words *sage* and *proz* within the poem. Forms of the adjective *sage,* its variant *saive,* and the noun *saveir* are used twenty times in the *Chanson de Roland.* Seven references are made about or by pagans, and seven are made about or by Ganelon. The word *sage* is used once to refer to Olivier, *saives* once to refer to Naimes, and on one occasion, *sage* is used in conjunction with *proz* to refer to Archbishop Turpin. A form of the word *saive* is used twice to refer to Christians in an essentially neutral context and once by Roland, as we have seen, as an ironic echo of Ganelon's words (1. 294). It is significant to note that none of the three terms is ever used by the poet or another character in the poem with reference to either Charles or Roland.[11]

Proz, on the other hand, is used twenty-two times. Four times it refers to Roland and six times to Olivier, although one must be cautious of the references to Olivier since three of them appear as the words of Ganelon and one occurs in a statement of Baligant. *Proz* is used twice to refer to Charles, once to Turpin, once to Naimes (and the context of this usage, which we shall examine in a moment, is particularly interesting), and four times to other Christians. With reference to pagans, it is used twice in a negative context ("Cunseill n'est proz . . . ," l. 604, and "Cil ne sunt proz . . . ," l. 1514 [1557]). It is used once by Baligant to refer to Jangleu, the judgment of a pagan by a pagan. Only once does it appear in a truly problematic context. The author seems to have used the word fairly consistently as the highest form of praise until line 3915, when he says, "Mult par est proz Pinabel de Sorence." The noun form *prouesse* appears only twice—once to refer to Roland and once to refer to Turpin.

Gerard Brault, in his article "*Sapientia* dans la *Chanson de Roland,*" contends that "le champ sémantique du mot *sage* dans la *Chanson de Roland* comprend assez souvent la notion de courage."[12] He argues further, both in that article and in his recent commemorative edition of the *Chanson de Roland,* for attributing to the word *proz* the meaning, among other meanings, of "wise." "When a knight in the *Song of Roland* is *prod,* he is worthy; that is, he is brave, loyal, pious, trustworthy, or wise, depending on the circumstances, but usually he possesses *all* these qualities."[13] He goes on to say that ". . . a man could hardly be considered excellent without being intelligent, so *prod,* in the *Song of Roland,* comes naturally to refer to a person's wisdom."[14] Brault's reasoning leads him to conclude, erroneously in my opinion, that *prod* and *sage* in the *Chanson de Roland* "are plainly synonymous."[15] Although both may, as he suggests, mean "wise," their use in the Digby 23 seems to indicate a clear hierarchy of meaning, with *sage* and *saives* taking on a limited, almost negative connotation, and *proz* a higher, more elevated significance.[16] We are, needless to say, far from the usual *sapientia-fortitudo* topos.

The line in the *Chanson de Roland*, "Rollant est proz et Oliver est sage," viewed in this context, takes on a new importance. It explains quite clearly the position of the two men concerning the sounding of the olifant. Olivier has seen the empirical evidence of impending danger—the pagans with their helmets blazing in the sun and their gonfanons waving in the breeze, so many pagans that it is impossible to count them. The horn, he insists, must be sounded to call back the army of Charles. We are confronted here with the fourth narrative bifurcation. Shall Roland sound the olifant or not? Roland, in contrast to Olivier, understands instinctively that it is his function to rectify the compromise with *scientia* that Charles has made. His own reputation, his family, his country, his God, are all at stake. Nowhere does Roland stand more firmly in a Christological position, for it falls his lot to expiate another's sin. If Charles by his adherence to the *lex mundi* has disobeyed his mission to rid Spain of the Saracens, Roland must reestablish the boundaries of obedience to God and the army's purity of purpose.

The quarrel between Roland and Olivier is put to an end by the sermon of Archbishop Turpin, who has rarely been mentioned up to this point. From this moment on, he will become a crucial factor in determining the direction of the action. For him, as for Roland, there is no question of blowing the horn. That he perceives the battle in pure ideological terms is unmistakable. He rides to a hilltop and preaches a sermon to the soldiers, explaining the full implications of their role in *historia:*

> "Seugnurs baruns, Carles nus laissat ci,
> Pur nostre rei devum nus ben murir:
> Chrestïentet aidez a sustenir!"
>
> (ll. 1127–9)

The archbishop aids Roland in his purpose throughout the battle, striking mighty blows and, above all, encouraging the soldiers to stand and fight although the instincts of the flesh may tell them to flee:

> "Seignors barons, n'en alez mespensant!
> Pur Deu vos pri que ne seiez fuiant,
> Que nuls prozdom malvaisement n'en chant.
> Asez est mielz que moerjum cumbatant."
>
> (ll. 1472–5 [1515–18])

When the battle seems hopeless, with only sixty Christian knights remaining, Roland announces to Olivier his intention to sound the horn. Olivier's reaction is one of self-righteous anger. He reminds Roland of the reputation he must uphold, of himself and his family, but he mentions neither the reputation of "la dulce France" nor God, both of which have been significant in Roland's earlier decision. Now, however, Charles must be brought back to finish the task that his pragmatic advisors had urged him to abandon. The necessary sacrifice to faith has been made. Charles, purified by the shedding of Roland's blood, must once again take up the task. But Olivier the "sage" is incapable of understanding the pure and certain logic of martyrdom. At this point in the quarrel Archbishop Turpin steps in to make his most important conciliatory gesture. The two friends must not die with such a dispute between them. The simplicity of his explanation is designed to take Roland's side in the quarrel at the same time he explains the need for sounding the olifant in terms that the simple-hearted but valiant soldier, Olivier, can comprehend. He agrees with Olivier that sounding the horn will not save them, but then it is not intended to. It will bring back the king, who can avenge their deaths and bury their bodies so they will not be eaten by wolves, dogs, or wild pigs:

> "Venget li reis, si nus purrat venger,
> Ja cil d'Espaigne ne s'en deivent turner liez.
> Nostre Franceis i descendrunt a pied,
> Truverunt nos e morz e detrenchez.
> Leverunt nos en bieres sur sumers,
> Si nus plurrunt de doel e de pitet.
> Enfuërunt en aitres de musters,
> N'en mangerunt ne lu ne porc ne chen."
>
> (ll. 1744–51)

Olivier makes no further objection, and the two friends seem reconciled as the mournful sound of the horn echoes across the mountains to the place where, thirty leagues away, the Franks continue their homeward march.

Charles, hearing the horn, announces: "Bataille funt nostre hume!" (l. 1758). Ganelon responds with a sense of mockery, the first open disrespect that he has shown for the emperor: "S'altre le desist, ja semblast grant mençunge!" (l. 1760). In the second of the *laisses similaires*, the sound of the horn is a cry of "dulor," as Roland, by his superhuman effort, ruptures his temple. This time we are told that the sound of the horn is also heard by Duke Naimes and the Franks:

> Karles l'entent, ki est as porz passant.
> Naimes li duc l'oïd, si l'escultent li Franc.
> Ce dist li reis: "Jo oi le corn Rollant!"
>> (ll. 1766–8)

Again Ganelon rebukes the emperor. During his interviews with Marsile, Ganelon had scrupulously defended his king against any disparagement, and especially against the Saracen's accusation that Charles was "mult vielz." (l. 523). Now he flings these very words at Charles:

> "Ja estes veilz e fluriz e blancs,
> Par tels paroles vus resemblez enfant."
>> (ll. 1771–2)

His lies are not a mere absence of truth. They take on the tone of cold-blooded deception, and like the serpent, "the satanic mediator of the fall of man," [17] Ganelon tempts the Franks with the certain knowledge of the joys that lie ahead in their homeland:

> "Car chevalcez! Pur qu'alez arestant?
> Tere Major mult est loinz ça devant." AOI.
>> (ll. 1783–4)

We stand at the fifth narrative bifurcation. Should Charles return or ride on? Again the horn is heard, and its mournful appeal prompts Duke Naimes, for the first time in the poem, to contradict Ganelon:

> "Baron i fait la peine!
> Bataille i ad, par le men escïentre.
> Cil l'at traït ki vos en roevet feindre."
>> (ll. 1790–2)

Naimes is a loyal vassal and a sincere Christian seeking to do what is right. His limited perceptions in time and space are not the "willful forgetting" of Ganelon. They are, rather, the simple perspective of the "little ones," as Augustine calls the literal-minded. [18] The duke's virtue is *bonum in saeculo* and, hence, subject to error, particularly when viewed from Roland's and Turpin's clearer perspective *sub specie aeternitatis*. While Naimes is unalterably bound to the empirical, he is not a stupid man. He has seen his mistake and attempts to rectify it by advising Charles to turn back. They will, of course, arrive too late to save the lives they value so highly.

Albert Pauphilet, in his trenchant study of the *Chanson de Roland*, has discussed in some detail the order and manner of deaths of the three hero-martyrs of Roncevaux—Olivier, Turpin, and Roland. [19] Concerning the order of deaths, Olivier and Turpin may be said to represent two aspects of the Roland figure. The part that must die first is the earthly vassal, who falls "en obscur et quelconque soldat"[20] among the thousands of other dead at Roncevaux. He does not even have the honor of being the last of the simple soldiers to die, for Gautier de l'Hum, returning from his own disaster in the mountains, outlives him. Turpin, on the other hand, might be said to represent the element of Roland that is, like his sword Durendal, "seintisme." When Charles finds him, his wounded and broken body will be surrounded by four hundred dead pagans. The poet invokes at this point the authority of Saint Gilles, who supposedly observed the battle in a vision and wrote a charter which he placed in the monastery of Laon. The invocation of the martyr Saint Gilles emphasizes the vertical axis of Turpin. For a priest, especially an archbishop, anagogy is a given, which is stressed even more strongly in other Roland texts. The *Pseudo-Turpin*, for example, allows the archbishop to survive the battle of Roncevaux and gives him special visions foretelling the death of Charles.[21] Throughout the Digby 23, however, the poet has sought to some extent to balance the vertical with the horizontal. Turpin is the only character in the poem who is described in a single line as "sages e proz" (l. 3691). He is, as Edmond Faral has depicted him, "le symbole de la foi agissante, riche de ses oeuvres, qui établit sur la terre la royauté de Dieu en y servant la royauté Chrétienne."[22] At the moment of his death, it is his sacerdotal rather than his secular function that is stressed, and in terms of narrative emphasis, his martyrdom is of far greater importance than that of Olivier. His death is no mere fall on the field of battle. He stands with Roland until the end to put the Saracens, who have suddenly realized that they are dealing with no ordinary *chevalier*, to flight.

When their mission for Charles is accomplished, their mission for God is not yet done. Roland musters enough strength to lay the dead peers before the archbishop who, even while he weeps in recognition of their earthly sacrifice, rejoices in their heavenly blessing. As Roland places the body of Olivier before the archbishop, he is overwhelmed by grief, but his *planctus* for his friend emphasizes his secular function.

> "Bels cumpainz Oliver,
> Vos fustes filz al duc Reiner
> Ki tint la marche del Val de Runers.
> Pur hanste freindre e pur escuz peceier,
> Pur orgoillos veintre e esmaier
> E pur prozdomes tenir e cunseiller
> E pur glutun veintre e esmaier,
> En nule tere n'ad meillor chevaler!"
>
> (ll. 2207–14)

Olivier is a youthful reflection of Duke Naimes, a "little one" limited to the perspective of *historia*.

Roland swoons with grief for his friend, and Turpin, despite his multiple wounds, rushes to fill the olifant, whose sound has been called a symbol of Roland's "undying spirit," [23] with water. Only on the most literal level is this act the gesture of a soldier on the battlefield bringing water to a dying comrade. On the level of *anagogia*, it is the gesture of a priest, God's earthly *figura*, bringing the spiritual water of life eternal to a martyr, and it is in this final, self-sacrificial act that Archbishop Turpin meets his death. Unlike Olivier, whose fate can only be inferred by his association with the other martyrs of Roncevaux, Turpin's place in Paradise is made explicit:

> Deus li otreit seinte beneïçun!   AOI
> (l. 2245)

Roland's *planctus* for the archbishop befits his cruciform function in this world.

> "E! gentilz hom, chevaler de bon aire,
> Hoi te cumant al Glorius celeste!
> Jamais n'ert hume plus volenters le serve.
> Des les apostles ne fut hom tel prophete
> Pur lei tenir e pur humes atraire.
> Ja la vostre anme nen ait sufrait!
> De pareïs li seit la porte uverte!"
> (ll. 2252–8)

Nothing could be in sharper contrast with his lament for Olivier. For Archbishop Turpin, while he is depicted as a "chevaler de bon aire," it is the vertical axis that is emphasized by Roland as he commends the body to the "Glorius celeste." He compares Turpin to the apostles in keeping God's law and attracting other men to it, and finally exhorts the gates of Paradise to be opened to him. No one is more important to a full understanding of Count Roland than the archbishop, for he is the only character in the poem who unswervingly sides with Roland on every issue. Only he has completely shared the *sapientia* with which the count is imbued.

The return of Charles's army to the field of battle at Roncevaux brings certain grief. Duke Naimes, despite his "mult grant pitet" (l. 2417) is the first to recover his composure and speak to the emperor, urging him at last to do precisely what Roland had advised from the beginning—to pursue the pagan army and avenge the wrong they have done. For the first time in the poem, Duke Naimes is described not as *sages* or *saives* but as *proz*

("Naimes li dux d'iço ad fait que proz," l. 2423) as he counsels the emperor:

> "Car chevalchez! Vengez ceste dulor!"
> (l. 2428)

It is interesting to note that Naimes's words "Car chevalchez!" stand in direct opposition to the "Car chevalcez" of Ganelon in line 1783. Ganelon was urging Charles and his men to ride on toward France, while Naimes, taking now the stance of Roland, urges that the army turn its horses and swords once more toward the Saracens in Spain. It is the last advice that Naimes will give in the poem. From this moment on, he renews his value to the king in purely earthly terms, through his consolation and his military skills. Just as Duke Naimes has, through Roland's sacrifice, become *proz*, so has Charles become *fols*. For the first time the word is used to refer to the emperor, as we are told in the words of the Saracen emir:

> "Karles de France chevalchet cume fols."
> (l. 3234)

It is with the *folie de Dieu* in his heart that Charles completes his mission, overcoming not only all the Saracens in Spain, but the Babylonian emir himself. It is interesting to note that the course of action recommended at the outset by Roland has been accomplished, but only the ultimate sacrifice of Roland has allowed the emperor to complete his task. Roland's death has restored the harmony between *lex mundi* and *lex dei*.

There remains one final question to be resolved in the poem. Does Ganelon's act of vengeance against Roland constitute treason? Given the context, Ganelon's trial becomes more than a mere trial by combat on the plane of *historia*. It is an act of judgment between two views of life—one of which would invert *sapientia* by calling it *folie* and would consider *scientia* the only true *saveir*, and another which recognizes *sapientia* quite rightly as the highest form of wisdom and *scientia* as, at best, human weakness and, if it aspires to higher pretentions, human folly.

At Ganelon's trial, Duke Naimes is conspicuously silent. He stands among the shadows as others, still audacious in their earthly judgments, try once again to convince Charles that compromise is the best solution. Knowing that Ganelon's champion is the strong and brave Pinabel, they rationalize their own fears by asserting that

"Morz est Rollant, jamais nel revereiz,

. . .

Mult sereit fols ki . . . se cumbatreit."

(ll. 3802–4)

The question of *folie* reintroduced into the poem, Charles suffers his familiar anguish, until there steps forth from among the group a neo-Roland, Thierry d'Anjou, who is *fols* enough to undertake this foolhardy but right action, who trusts in God beyond the scope of human logic. He refuses the compromise urged by the Franks and makes a judgment of treason against Ganelon. His victory against Pinabel despite overwhelming odds is seen as a miracle, and it symbolizes the ultimate victory of *folie* over *saveir*, unveiling what the Saracens and Ganelon call *folie* as being, after all, the highest form of wisdom, the *sapientia* that comes only from God.

As one considers the opposition between the two concepts of *folie* and *saveir*, one becomes aware that the *scientia* of Duke Naimes and Olivier, carried to logical extremes, can lead to the pagan perspective. In the *Couronnement de Louis*, in a debate between Guillaume and Corsolt similar to that between Roland and Ferracutus in the *Pseudo-Turpin*, Corsolt articulates the pagan notion that Christianity is "toz fuleiemenz."

"Di va, Guillelmes, molt as fol escient,
Quant celui creiz qui ne te valt neient.
Deus est la sus, desor le firmament;
Ca jus de terre n'ot il onques arpent.
Ainz est Mahom et son comandement.
Totes vos messes ne toz vos sacremenz,
Vos mariages ne vos exposemenz
Ne pris je mie ne qu'un trespas de vent,
Crestiienté est toz foleiemenz."[24]

Certainly the Christian pragmatists, Naimes and Olivier, or even Ganelon, would not go so far in their views, but the words of Corsolt reflect the theological dangers of their position. What we are dealing with in the Digby 23 is, essentially, an Augustinian hierarchy of wisdom:[25]

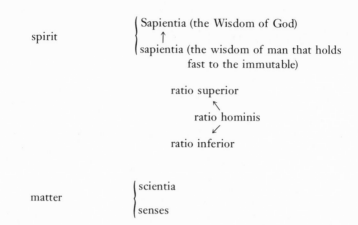

No human but Christ himself can attain the *Sapientia* which is co-equal and co-eternal with God, but man is capable of attaining some semblance of *sapientia*. Of the characters in the Digby 23 who exhibit the wisdom that reflects the *consilium dei*, there are only three: Charles, Roland, and Turpin.

Within the epistemological hierarchy, Duke Naimes and Olivier fall below the level of *sapientia* to that of *scientia*. According to Augustine, *scientia* is not inherently evil. It is necessary and legitimate for the management of the affairs of this life and becomes folly only when it refuses to acknowledge its own limitations. Johannes Scotus Erigena would agree with this essential position. He perceives faith, action, and *scientia*, all of which clearly characterize Naimes and Olivier, as the first three steps of spiritual ascent.[26] But there are no guarantees that one can achieve the fourth and most difficult step, variously identified with *sapientia, theologica, contemplatio*, and *speculatio*. *Scientia*, he contends, is concerned with matters of this world with its temporal and spatial limitations, while *sapientia* has a clearly vertical axis, centering itself upon that which is "divina, aeterna et incommutabilia."[27] In instances of conflict between the higher and lower reason of man, *scientia* must clearly yield to *sapientia*, for according to Augustine, the former is subject to error, whereas the latter is not. Olivier and Naimes, despite their fundamental goodness and best of human intentions, err in depending so utterly on *scientia*, for, as the book of *Wisdom* suggests: "The reasoning of man is feeble, and our plans are fallible; because a perishable body weighs down the soul, and its frame of clay burdens the mind so full of thoughts."[28] While Naimes and Olivier both aim, despite their error, toward the good, man's path, Erigena tells us, is not immutably fixed toward good or evil. Just as Bramimonde can be saved, so Naimes and Olivier can, through the burden of their earthly perceptions, stray from the vertical path.[29]

Below Naimes and Olivier in the gradualistic schema and still further removed from *sapientia* are Ganelon and the pagans. For Ganelon, as for Baligant, his physical beauty is underscored in the text. Gerard Brault sees Roland's sword as "literally a reflection of the hero's virtues."[30] The same may be said of Ganelon's sword. When one compares the two weapons, the differing ethos of the men are thrown into sharp relief. Durendal is described by Roland in triple *laisses similaires* as "bone . . . bele e clere e blanche . . . e seintisme" (lines 2304, 2316, 2344). The sword of Ganelon, on the other hand, is described by its owner as "bele e clere" (l. 445). Conspicuously absent are precisely those attributes that would allow Ganelon to relate to the spiritual dimension to which Roland seems so attuned. Ganelon's sword is neither "bone" nor "blanche" (i.e., pure) nor "seintisme." The emphasis is clearly on its handsome exterior, mirroring the material values of Ganelon as they are emphasized throughout the poem.

Charles's role would be less burdensome if all characters were as clear-cut and categorical as Ganelon and Roland. Unfortunately, however, such is not the case. Just as Ganelon is rooted in matter, so, as we have seen, are such "wise" counselors as Naimes and Olivier. They have placed their confidence in *scientia*, which is taken to task throughout the *Chanson de Roland*. Roland, on the other hand, with Turpin, the personification of Erigena's *theologica*, at his side, is touched by *la folie de Dieu* and allowed to glimpse *sapientia*. Charles is, quite clearly, the pivotal point between these two epistemological concepts. He serves as the nuclear figure in whom the conflict between them must be resolved and for whom the two concepts must ultimately conjoin and function as co-implicates. Caught between the two ways of knowing to which man can aspire and which often contradict one another, it is little wonder that he weeps and tugs at his long, white beard as he plays out eternally his temporal role of *seigneur* in this world and his figural role of *Seigneur* in the next.

NOTES

1. Gerald J. Brault, *The Song of Roland: An Analytical Edition* (University Park and London, 1978), vol. I, p. 96. This article was first written in connection with the 1978 NEH Summer Seminar at Dartmouth College on "The Spirit of Truth: Interaction of Myth and Culture in Medieval Narrative Literature," conducted by Stephen G. Nichols, Jr. of the editorial board of *Medievalia et Humanistica*. It was presented, in a somewhat shorter version, at the Kentucky

Foreign Language Conference, April 26–28, 1979. I am grateful to Professor Nichols for his helpful suggestions.

2. This idea has been well expressed by Stephen G. Nichols, Jr., "Brightest and Best of the Signs of Mourning: A Poetics of the Passion in Romanesque Art and Epic," *Modern Approaches to Medieval Literature*, Douglas Butturff, ed. (Conway, Arkansas, 1980), in press. The concept of the hero as "cruciform model" is further explored by Nichols in his recent article, "Sign as (Hi) story in the *Couronnement de Louis*," *Romanic Review*, vol. 71, 1980, pp. 1–9. See especially pp. 5–8.

3. Marc Bloch, *La Société féodale* (Paris, 1968), vol. II, pp. 565–6.

4. *Arab Historians of the Crusades*, selected and translated from the Arabic sources by Francesco Gabrielli; translated from the Italian by J. Costello (Berkeley and Los Angeles, 1969), p. 74.

5. Brault, *The Song of Roland*, vol. II, p. 16, l. 248. All subsequent line references are to this edition and are cited within the text.

6. Eugene Vance, "Roland and the Poetics of Memory," *Textual Strategies: Perspectives in Post-Structuralist Criticism*, Josué V. Harari, ed. (Ithaca, 1979), p. 387.

7. Ibid.

8. *De Trin.* 12.11.16.

9. One may, as Gerard Brault has done, describe it as "la folie de la Croix." See "*Sapientia* dans la *Chanson de Roland*," *French Forum*, vol. 1, 1976, p. 108. Larry Crist uses the term "la Folie de Dieu." See "A propos de la desmesure dans la *Chanson de Roland:* Quelques propos (démesurés?)," *Olifant*, vol. 1, 1974, pp. 10–20. See also Norman R. Cartier, "La Sagesse de Roland," *Aquila: Chestnut Hill Studies in Modern Languages and Literature*, vol. 1, 1968, pp. 33–63.

10. Hayden White, "Ethnological 'Lie' and Mythical 'Truth,' " *Diacritics: A Review of Contemporary Criticism*, vol. 8, 1978, p. 8.

11. See Jean Misrahi and William L. Hendrickson, "Roland and Oliver: Prowess and Wisdom, the Ideal of the Epic Hero," *Romance Philology*, vol. 33, 1980, p. 366, which contains a similar statistical analysis of the *sage-proz* opposition. At the time this article was first written and submitted for publication, the Misrahi-Hendrickson article had not yet appeared, and I was unaware of their work. I am, however, somewhat puzzled by their suggestion that *sage* or a variant is used once to refer to Baligant and once to refer to Emir, as though they were different characters. Lines 3174 and 3279 both refer, of course, to Baligant, the pagan emir. I have considered line 369 along with the references to pagans, whereas Misrahi and Hendrickson have considered it with reference to Ganelon. The line refers, in fact, as they have pointed out, to both.

12. Brault, "*Sapientia*," p. 111.

13. Brault, *The Song of Roland*, vol. 1, p. 182.

14. Ibid.

15. Ibid.

16. See Misrahi and Hendrickson, p. 364, concerning the moral value of *proz*. They go on to suggest that the related "foolhardy" attitude of Roland, which

modern critics have labelled *demesure* and which Olivier calls *estultie*, "is much closer to the Celtic, the Germanic, the Deuteronomic, and the Pauline views of heroic excess, which may seem to be *stultitia*, than to our own, or the Greek, position," p. 371.

17. Augustine, *De Trin.* 12.12.17. See *A Companion to the Study of St. Augustine*, Roy Battenhouse, ed. (New York, 1955), p. 306.

18. *The Confessions*, 12.27.

19. Albert Pauphilet, *Les Legs du moyen âge: Etudes de littérature médiévale* (Melun, 1950), pp. 65–89.

20. Ibid., p. 76.

21. See *The Pseudo-Turpin*, H. M. Smyser, ed. (Cambridge, Mass., 1937), Ch. XXV, pp. 94–5.

22. Edmond Faral, *La Chanson de Roland* (Paris, 1948), p. 227.

23. Brault, *The Song of Roland*, vol. I, p. 93.

24. *Le Couronnement de Louis*, Ernest Langlois, ed. (Paris, 1920), p. 27, ll. 836–44.

25. See Ronald H. Nash, *The Light of the Mind: Saint Augustine's Theory of Knowledge* (Lexington, 1969), p. 81, for another epistemological schema.

26. See Jean Scot, *Commentaire sur l'Evangile de Jean*, Edouard Jeauneau, ed. and trans. (Paris, 1972), p. 112, n. 8. See also p. 160, I, 28, ll. 25–34.

27. Joannis Scoti, *De Divisione Naturae*, Liber III, 3, *Patrologiae Cursus Completus*, series Latina, J.-P. Migne, ed., t. 122, col 629AB: Sapientia namque proprie dicitur virtus illa, qua contemplativus animus, sive humanus, sive angelicus, divina, aeterna et incommutabilia considerat; sive circa primam omnium causam versetur, sive circa primordiales rerum causas, quas Pater in Verbo suo semel simulque condidit, quae species rationis a sapientibus theologia vocitatur. Scientia vero est virtus, qua theoreticus animus, sive humanus, sive angelicus, de natura rerum, ex primordialibus causis procedentium per generationem, inque genera ac species divisarum, per differentias, et proprie-tates tractat, sive accidentibus succumbat, sive eis careat, sive corporibus adjucta, sive penitus ab eis libera, sive locis et temporibus distributa, sive ultra loca et tempora sui simplicitate unita atque inseparabilis.

28. *Wisdom* 9:15.

29. Joannis Scoti, *De Divisione Naturae*, cols. 917–18. Misrahi and Hendrickson suggest that Olivier represents "practical, prudent *sapientia*" (p. 371), a curious contradiction of terms. Their article fails to address the fundamental distinc-tion between *scientia* and *sapientia*.

30. Brault, *The Song of Roland*, vol. I, p. 92.

Structural Transpositions and Intertextuality:
Chrétien's Cligés

MICHELLE A. FREEMAN

Contemporary research in "intertextuality" and medieval French romance composition do not make strange bedfellows, despite, apparently, their finding themselves at opposite ends of a chronological spectrum. This is because intertextuality, known, it might be argued, under the alternate rubric of *translatio studii* in the twelfth and thirteenth centuries, was a poetic principle practiced consistently within the genre of romance, as well as within other art forms of the time. Indeed, for a literary discourse that conceived of itself (1) as born of a process of textual imitation, and (2) as perpetuating this process while (3) renewing an ever-widening canon of (mostly vernacular) texts in recombination, intertextuality was an integral part of its poetics. The written (and *read*-aloud) romance text was itself a *reading*, or *re-writing*, of previous texts, and, in turn, it invited both reading and re-writing, so that the two activities of reading and writing invariably remained inseparable.

Every Old French romance, then, deliberately constructed itself by fusing other textual fragments together in order to demonstrate itself as a gloss, commentary, imitation, and renewal that attempted to complete and perfect the text—or texts—as process. In a very real sense, no medieval romance ever has a determinate place of beginning or of ending—hence, the episodic character of the *genre*, whether we consider, e.g., one episode in the life, say, of the *Chevalier de la Charrette* or the romance of Lancelot as, itself, an episode in the history of Guenevere and Lancelot, and/or their history as an episode in the (larger) account of the Kings of Britain, etc. Each romance, instead of being merely a reperformance of a model or paradigm, constitutes a *link* in a chain of texts—a textuality—that absorbs and rearticulates its predecessors together with articulating a reading or an interpretation of them. Each one represents an "episode" in the on-going dialogue—or symposium—of texts, with each one proffering an invitation for a new gloss, transformation, or continuation to be affected by the reader who sees the romance in a new context or places it, either literally or figuratively, in a new codex.

149

Medievalia et Humanistica, New Series, Number 11 (Paul Maurice Clogan, ed.). Rowman and Littlefield, Totowa, NJ, 1982.

Folio 29 v° of MS 126 in Princeton University's Garrett Collection [1] contains a miniature, a text from the *Roman de la Rose*, and a new heading in rubrics. An enterprising Jehan de Meun is presented by scribe and illuminator as engaged in the activity to *parfaire* the open-ended text of his predecessor, Guillaume de Lorris. By incorporating other segments of discourse into itself, a romance seeks to complete these segments by adding what is construed as "missing"—*le surplus mettre*, as Marie de France put it. By "translating" and conjoining these earlier segments, i.e., by carrying them over and on to a new point of perfection or completion, each romance sets itself up as a point of transition and transformation, a point of intersection for a number of texts as well as a point of intersection between a lineage of poems and a reader. In this way it represents a point of *conjointure* and *aventure* that leads to succeeding episodes, new open-ended paths, and other "interlacings" (*entrelacements*).

In the following pages, I propose to examine an episode in Chrétien's *Cligés* [2] that implements intertextuality so as to transpose an episode from Thomas' *Tristan* [3] in a manner that glosses the poetics of both texts, in dialogue. The procedure is one whereby one text results from reading another text through yet a third text. In this case, the *Tristan* is read through the *Cligés*, and this in such a fashion as to define, with precision, the poetics of the *Tristan* as a single textual phenomenon. Concomitantly, the *Cligés* works itself out similarly as an essentially intertextual operation in which the second part of the narrative derives poetically from the first part. This "reading" leads to the third manifestation of text in dialogue, to the "translation" of the first two operations into a metatext that comments on the poetics of *Cligés*, affording, then, an example of romance as a self-referential *genre* based on what we should call the poetics of intertextuality. This practice of reading one text *through* another in medieval romance often involves, as it does here in *Cligés*, a cyclical movement from metonymy to metaphor worked out within the confines of a description—a description seen as a digression, i.e., as a *locus* that is particularly appropriate for clerkly commentary, a place of explanation, of translation, of saying anew. [4]

One of the famous motifs of the *Tristan* legend is the single strand of golden blond hair carried by a swallow to Mark who decides to marry the woman from whom it was removed, provided she can be found. This vow prompts Tristan to seek her out and to bring her on a fateful voyage to her husband-to-be. As far as one can judge, Thomas excludes this detail. Meanwhile, Chrétien puts it back into his text; but he introduces it in such as way as to work in as many twists and reversals as possible.

Soredamor, Gauvain's sister and lady-in-waiting to Queen Guenevere, has fashioned a shirt out of fine white silk; she has sewn the seams and attached the collar and cuffs with gold threads.[5] She has also woven into the stitching strands of her own golden blond hair together with the gilded threads, as a test. She hopes to locate the knight who will take notice of this artifice, who will discern the comparison, detect the origin of the second thread and, by judging the two components simultaneously, will prefer the merits of her naturally golden hair used, here, however, in an original context of craft. Consequently, the shirt as shirt, though delicate and beautiful—sufficiently so as to be chosen by the Queen as a fitting gift to mark the occasion of Alexandre's being dubbed a knight by King Arthur himself—is not interesting primarily as an example of the perfect *chemise*. These secondary characteristics, presented as primary only superficially, permit the garment to figure in the story, to take its place among the events that tie the characters together. Just as the finest gift Guenevere could locate from among the contents of her coffers, though meant as a token of homage to *chevalerie*, finally plays a key role in a very different domain, so the text Chrétien "found" while in the library at the cathedral of Beauvais [6]—where he was presumably looking for his subject—seemingly starts out as a salute to our chivalrous ancestors only to finish by serving quite a different purpose.[7]

The *chemise* is primarily valuable as an example of artifice and as a test. The processes and the materials that went into its fabrication as well as their detection by an interested outsider constitute its value. The shirt subtly calls attention to the devices and the ulterior purposes of its fabrication by means of the very direct connection between artificer and artifact—Soredamor's strand of hair and the stitching—and by means of the carefully chosen strategic points on the shirt where the creative devices are displayed. Fashioned by Soredamor, the shirt can consequently be viewed as analogous to a text—to a text, indeed, that poeticizes its intertextuality. Like Soredamor, Chrétien also works in at strategic moments of his romance clues to his own identity as romancer. The *conjointure* of the two sorts of strands that figure in the structuring of the various segments of the garment, i.e., in that part of the putting-together of a piece of clothing most usually taken from granted, here is the very part of the garment that would call attention to itself. Similarly, at structurally important moments that bind the romance together, Chrétien combines a thread of his own peculiar discourse of commentary along with *Tristan* motifs intertwined in a new context—a new con-"texture"—of artifice.

Naturally, Alexandre fails the test. He notices only the superficial elegance of the Queen's gift and fails to recognize the deeper significance for him. Only later, when the Queen recalls by chance that it was Soredamor who made the shirt, does she take advantage of this fact. She has her lady-in-waiting describe her handiwork to Alexandre, once she has finally realized that the two are in love. In this way, the Queen becomes a kind of reader of the signals of the shirt, though not through an original discovery. Rather, she reads through memory, through an accidentally perceived intertextual relationship, as what she recalls becomes functional in a new context. In this instance the shirt serves to initiate a process of mediation whereby the slow but nevertheless observant Guenevere, in two separate stages, prompts the young lovers to agree to wed. By doing so, the string of events the silk shirt triggers intersects with another, equally famous, Tristan motif (as well as with its evocation in an earlier scene of *Cligés*).

When Guenevere notices the lovers turning pale before her, Alexandre wearing his new silk finery and Soredamor sitting shyly next to him, it dawns on her that they alternately blush and turn pale because they are in love. This recognition makes up for her previous failure to ascribe to love the same symptoms she noted before during the Channel crossing. Guenevere fails to read the *Tristan* intertext into the first episode; the audience of course cannot fail to seize the opportunity, something which Chrétien assures by repeating the famous pun on *l'amer* 'loving', *la mer* 'the sea', and *l'amer* 'bitterness' [8] that, given Gottfried's adaptation of Thomas, was in his model's poem. In the *Tristan* the pun is introduced by Iseut in order to reveal, with subtlety, what she thinks: her feelings for Tristan. Her lover is somewhat hesitant to accept the implication, so Iseut spells it out for him, making sure which one of the homonyms is responsible for her turning green. In *Cligés* Chrétien separates what seems inseparable: the similar appearances between the three above-quoted words *and* the function to which that bit of paranomasia is put, reserving this function for the scenes in which the *chemise* figures. In this fashion, a *conjointure* of stellar *Tristan* motifs occurs, wherein resemblances and what they can mask have been dissociated and rearranged in order to show off their components and their roles in the composition, or "text-ure."

The audience, in a sense, also fails to pass Soredamor's test, or, rather, it is not given an opportunity to do so, since it never sees the shirt. The audience is only afforded the explanatory description by the poet-narrator, presumably akin to the one Soredamor eventually gives to Alexandre but which the audience never hears. The narrator's description preëmpts what Soredamor will reveal and undercuts its possible significance for the audience, dissociating its reactions from those of the principal characters. But the narrator's description parallels Soredamor's in another way, and justly preëmpts it, since it enables him to comment *par moz coverz* on his own creative devices in the suturing of the intertextual plays in his own text, so as to test those who gaze upon his handiwork, as received perhaps through the hands of Marie de Champagne. In this way, the seemingly gratuitous description of the shirt, performed as it were out of sequence, serves two purposes at once. It introduces an object that will act in conjunction with the cup bestowed by Arthur,[9] to bring the first story to a close, and, by playing on *Tristan* patterns and motifs, it functions as a self-referential commentary on the poetic discourse that is unfolding.

Additional relationships to the *Tristan* are involved in the reworking of the strands of hair motif. These play hinge on Chrétien's connecting the motif to a comparison: the metaphorical value of Iseut's hair—hair of spun gold—is exploited here quite literally in the metonymic comparison between two types of gold: one inferior, one superior. A comparison between the two objects made of gold(s) of differing qualities becomes a device in a typical *Tristan* scene where two levels of discourse are carried on simultaneously, thanks to disguise and thanks to an object functioning as a sign of something other than itself, i.e., thanks to its *poetic* value. The object in question can do these things since it has developed a secondary meaning by playing a role in a history—in a sequence of events lived by Tristan and Iseut, unbeknownst to Mark, that leads to this specific event. In other words, a previous narrative context is introduced into a seemingly banal and unrelated context, where no other meaning for the object or the words spoken would rightfully be suspected unless the item is recalled and recognized in terms of its previous history. Consequently, the natural—or the conventional—in *Tristan* can become a vehicle for a staged artifice, for a hidden dialogue; the scene depends on a built-in bit of intertextuality in order to function successfully and completely. Its intertextuality seems to originate with the characters and is demonstrated consistently to the audience by the narrator but revealed only gradually to some of the characters and never to others. The drama of *Tristan* depends on both factors. Chrétien imitates this but even outdoes it by transposing the audience's interest away from a character's reading of the object to the reading of the object in a dialogue between the reader and the poet-narrator.

At the end of Thomas' poem Kaherdin makes the trip from Brittany to Cornwall, from Tristan to Iseut, in order to fetch Iseut who alone can minister to the dying Tristan.[10] Kaherdin appears upon Tristan's instigation as a merchant who sells rich silks and the like at Mark's court. He gives the king a cup as a present and as a free sample of his wares; he encourages the queen to purchase a gold brooch. In order to extol the merits of the ornaments, he pulls out his own ring so as to show, by comparison, the superiority of the gold worked into the brooch. But the ring is actually Iseut's own, the one she gave Tristan when they parted. Upon seeing the ring, Iseut recognizes Kaherdin, discovers the ploy, and arranges secretly to make the return journey to Tristan. It is interesting that once Iseut recalls an object out of the present context and in its former context, she sees through the disguise, or persona, of the individual addressing her and returns to the one who devised the disguise and who introduced the device that triggers the intertextual reading of the scene.

Chrétien recombined and inverted many of these elements in *Cligés*. Firstly, the cup and the gold comparison no longer figure at the end of the story but in the first part of the romance. They are no longer together, rather they have been split up so as to figure in separate scenes that orient the two separate strands of the themes of *chevalerie* and *amour*: arms and love. They do not preface the dénouement of the romance and the death of the protagonists; instead, they serve to introduce the birth of its principal protagonist, Cligés himself. Secondly, Chrétien has borrowed the presence of silks and the comparison of golds (which had functioned merely as props, or distractions, in the theatrical setting) and made of them integral parts of the object he describes. He also transposes the technique of extolling the merits of the object, not by invoking a comparison that camouflages, as was done in the *Tristan* model, but in order to point out a comparison that itself was artfully camouflaged and, consequently, difficult to see. It is as if the givens that went into the staging of this penultimate *Tristan* scene are rendered into abstractions, in such a way that they operate metaphorically and intertextually with reference to the creative processes of that particular scene. What was metonymic and compared in the one scene served to introduce a third function, the alternate, or poetic, identity of the ring. I repeat: Metonymy in the *Tristan* example serves as a camouflage, as a vehicle for the introduction of functional intertextuality and for the reorientation of Iseut's reading of the signs placed before her. In the second scene, from *Cligés*, what is not so clearly metonymic and blatantly comparative, when finally revealed as such, takes on a metaphorical value. The scene uses the intertext of *Tristan*, borrowing and blending motifs that were originally distinct there, and but latently metonymic, in order to create a new kind of intertextuality—a translation of itself by means of this digression into description read, finally, as metaphor.

Lastly, the audience witnesses Tristan planning the scene, as he invents and directs the characters, their stage props, and their actions, wherein Kaherdin will stand in for Tristan, acting like him and for him by meeting Iseut in the open but in disguise. In *Cligés*, Soredamor functions as a stand-in for, or as a transposed projection of, the poet-narrator, acting for him and like him in the romance as she *devises* the test of the shirt. The shirt's natural, or obvious, meaning is accepted by Alexandre just as Mark accepts the comparison of the ring and the brooch at face value. The alternate connotation, the device as sign, is apprehended by Iseut on the one hand and by the audience on the other; the audience, like Iseut, is returned to the one who devised the system initially, i.e., to Tristan (in Thomas) and to the poet-narrator (or Chrétien) in *Cligés*. In this fashion Chrétien manages to provide in his description both narrative and commentary, *simultaneously*.

Chrétien is able to communicate in this dual manner in part because this usage to which he puts description has a history of similar usage which he developed himself in his first romance, *Érec et Énide*. He provides there an example of the elaboration of what has been termed "intertextualité restreinte."[11] We observe this in his description of the saddle given to Énide after she and her husband have become reconciled.[12] The saddle portrays, in ivory and gold—note the reappearance of the white and gold motif—, the exemplary failure of Dido and Énéas on one side, and, on the other side, it depicts the triumph of Lavinia and the hero. This explicit intertextual reference emblematizes the various stages through which the development of the romance's *single* couple takes place. The description introduces an intertextual note into the narrative—once more in a digression—just as the workmanship of the saddle introduces another kind of artistry, of a representational sort, into its display. But in *Érec et Énide* the description afforded a commentary on the themes elaborated and on the events narrated; in *Cligés* the working in of intertextuality is less obvious—names are not mentioned, the story of Tristan has not as yet been retold (and will not be referred to until Fénice enlists the help of Thessala), though decidely *Tristan* motifs are everywhere present. The commentary afforded by the description-digression now concerns the workmanship or the art of romance; Chrétien can proceed this much further because in *Érec et Énide* he prepared his audience for the interpretation of description as intertextual commentary anchored within the confines of the narrative itself.

The description of the *chemise* understood in the context of self-referential commentary begins a pattern of similar descriptions to which the audience becomes progressively more attuned, thus assuring it of a new orientation in its reaction to the poet-narrator's discourse. The characters in *Cligés* try at times to duplicate similar arrangements; they try to emulate the brilliant deceptions of a Tristan and an Iseut, but their efforts usually fail. Alexandre, e.g., gains admittance into the traitor's castle by means of disguising himself as one of the enemy. His ruse succeeds; he defeats the enemy, taking them by surprise, and so wins back Windsor Castle for Arthur. However, he succeeds at the expense of a fair amount of grieving and despair on the part of his companions and in particular on the part of his lady-love Soredamor. They have not been informed of his plan and therefore do not read the signs of deception properly, i.e., any differently from those who are deliberately being deceived. The disguise works only one way. Similarly, Fénice pretends to be dead and deceives her husband and the entire court, so that she might eventually escape to a secret hide-away with her lover, but not without first tricking him as well. Cligés believes Fénice to be truly beyond his grasp and is about to enact a death-scene like that of Piramus and Thisbe from which he is spared only in the nick of time. Fénice and Thessala somehow overlook informing Cligés of the second potion—or the first one for that matter—for some time.[13] Therefore, he too can only read the signs of feigned death, of disguise, one way.

The backfiring of Fénice's plan is brought about interestingly by means of the interference of a third party, by a trio of third parties, in fact, who read the signs correctly, who are aware of the trick of duping one's husband by playing dead. Fénice's plan comes close to utter failure, i.e., Cligés and Fénice almost suffer the tragic fate of Tristan and Iseut, though this time this fate is played out in reverse with Fénice at death's door and Cligés ready to expire over her corpse, because three learned Doctors of Salerno stroll unexpectedly into the situation. Because these men perceive the scene intertextually when it is retold to them as a narrative by the townspeople, they grasp the double significance of the signs before them immediately. Their interpretation serves of course to underscore rather amusingly the way the romance calls attention to itself at every turn in the mosaic-like composition it derived from various textual fragments like the *Tristan*. But this exercise of intertextual reading is clearly performed within the story—not, then, as a digression, but, rather, as an integral part of the plot. The kind of activity so far suited to the system of commentary communicated by the poet-narrator to the audience, that takes place on a level distinct from narrative events, is with this episode located right at the heart of the romance. The metalanguage that operated so well between Tristan and Iseut, and that was transferred from their counterparts in *Cligés* in order to be conferred on the dialogue between poet-narrator and audience, has now, with the Doctors of Salerno episode, been restored to work among characters, but only accidentally and not between the right ones.

If the audience succumbs to the fictional argument that Chrétien is transmitting an historical account concerning the Greek grand-nephew of Arthur, then the Salerno Doctors' intertextual exercise, performed, of course, with the story of Solomon's wife as intertext, is history; on the other hand, such a reading practice constitutes the underpinnings of the way Chrétien's fiction is put together. Whereas Tristan's staging of events, that deliberately calls for intertextual perceptions, is portrayed as historical fact and therefore as authorization of the document that bears witness to the couple, a similar application of causality in *Cligés*, though apparently practiced, leads to absurdities. Fénice, in trying to avoid a repetition of Iseut's example,[14] thereby basing her conduct on intertextual decisions, does not escape becoming a notorious example in her own right. The narrator informs the audience at the close of his tale, that as a result of her subterfuge and its eventual coming to light, forever after—even to the present day of Chrétien's writing—Emperors of Constantinople have kept close watch over their wives, making of them prisoners guarded by eunuchs.[15] An exotic and bizarre custom is, as it were, explained by this lengthy romance, the way an explanation of the origin of the flower seems to be the point of Ovid's presentation of Narcissus. It would seem that the text of *Cligés* itself is authorized and validated by Fénice's decision and example and is therefore based in turn on the example of Tristan and Iseut—thus providing us with a third lineage for *Cligés*—since her story has been told and kept alive through the ages, presumably in texts like the one Chrétien "found" at Beauvais and which he "translates" for us. Chrétien imitates the pattern that underlies the verisimilitude of a *Tristan*, as portrayed for example by Béroul, in imitation of epic and hagiography, in a way that makes that delicately laid plan look foolish in a romance, though, to be sure, interesting and amusing as a contrivance. The principle of an intertextual reading is not, on the other hand, portrayed as a principle of authorization when we find it in the central episode. Rather, this principle that the reader has been practicing steadily up to this point finds a blatant confirmation at the same time that it affords a source of comedy when transposed from a technique of composition to a narrative event.

There continues to be, therefore, a structural inversion in *Cligés* of the *Tristan* events inclusive of the principles that generate that text. This inversion is designed in such a way as to confuse quite differently what is seemingly natural but false from what is artificial but real. Perhaps the most striking example of this reversal is suggested by Anthime Fourrier's[16] presentation of historical events of the twelfth century that Chrétien draws upon in his text for purposes of parody. Unlike the *Tristan* which portrays romance fiction as history, *Cligés* draws upon historical events, transforming them into fictional material.

The *Tristan*, essentially an episodic piece, reperforms its principles of deception in virtually every scene. It recalls itself by reperforming these patterns of textual generation, and specifically by reëchoing previous scenes and motifs in new settings. The text is constantly repeating itself, in other words, and deriving a margin of verisimilitude from this repetition and reënactment, not of a paradigm or model extraneous to it, but of itself. The *Tristan*, therefore, applies the principles of reënactment and variation within a tradition that makes epic and hagiography work, i.e., that allows them to evince responses of belief in the audience, and has applied them to romance material, to a tangential episode in the history of Arthur and the Kings of Britain. This is, of course, the genius of the *Tristan*; this is what makes it so powerful.

Chrétien's *Cligés* has demonstrated the *Tristan*'s ability to cloak artifice under the cover of conventionality by first divorcing what is inseparable in the working-out of certain *Tristan* motifs—by dissociating similarities between elements—from what the similarity serves simultaneously to hide and to reveal. Ultimately the *Cligés* transforms the creative process of intertextuality as it applied in the *Tristan* so that the text no longer echoes or repeats itself but rather translates itself within a context of a canon of texts including the maverick *Tristan*. It thus initiates a novel dialogue of intertextual commentary, claiming—in opposition to the *Tristan* example, which it has absorbed and transposed—this very commentary as a new path for subsequent romance composition to follow.[17]

NOTES

1. This text is depicted by the emblem for the program and brochures of the Columbia-Princeton Symposium on Intertextuality and Medieval French Romance (where the original version of the present paper was delivered, on 8 December 1979; the proceedings of the Symposium will be published, in French, in a forthcoming issue of *Littérature*). The rubrics read, in my transcription: "Ci commence li romans maistre Jehan de Meuin et le parfist tout jusques en la fin . . ." The text beneath the miniature continues: "Et si lai je perdu espoir/ a pou que je ne men despoir/ Despoir laz et je non ferai/ ja ne men des espeirrai/ Sesperance mestoit faillanz/ Je ne seroie pas vaillanz/ En li me doi reconforter/ Quamors por miex mes maus porter/ Me dist quil me garantiroit."

2. All quotations from *Cligés* will be taken from *Les Romans de Chrétien de Troyes édités d'après la copie de Guiot (B.N. f.fr. 794) II, Cligés*, Alexandre Micha, ed. (Paris: Champion, 1970).

3. All passages cited from Thomas's *Tristan* are taken from Thomas, *Les Fragments du Roman de Tristan, Poème du XIIᵉ siècle*, Bartina H. Wind, ed. (Geneva and Paris: Droz and Minard, 1960). The Thomas text as I refer to it is a construction, because we only have a number of fragments from various manuscripts and do not possess one or more completed versions of the whole as is the case with *Cligés*.

4. For another example of this kind of textual process, see my "Problems in Romance Composition: Ovid, Chrétien de Troyes, and the *Romance of the Rose*," *Romance Philology*, Jean Frappier Memorial Issue. XXX, No. 1 (August, 1976) pp. 158–168.

5.   La reïne la chose set,
              Qui Alixandre pas ne het,
              Einz l'aimme molt et loe et prise.
              Feire li vialt un bel servise,
              Molt est plus granz qu'ele ne cuide.
              Trestoz ses escrins cerche et vuide,
              Tant c'une chemise en a treite;
              De soie fu, blanche et bien feite,
              Molt delïee et molt soutil.
              Es costures n'avoit un fil
              Ne fust d'or ou d'argent au mains.
              Au queudre avoit mises les mains
              Soredamors, de leus an leus;
              S'avoit antrecosu par leus
              Lez l 'or de son chief un chevol,
              Et as deus manches et au col,
              Por savoir et por esprover
              Se ja porroit home trover
              Qui l 'un de l 'autre devisast,
              Tant cleremant i avisast:
              Car autant ou plus con li ors
              Estoit li chevox clers et sors.
              Soredamors [La reïne?] prant la chemise,
              Si l 'a Alixandre tramise.
              Et, Dex! con grant joie an eüst
              Alixandres, s'il le seüst
              Que la reïne li anvoie!
              Molt an reüst cele grant joie
              Qui son chevol i avoit mis,
              S'ele seüst que ses amis
              La deüst avoir ne porter.
              Molt s'an deüst reconforter,
              Car ele n'amast mie tant
              De ses chevox le remenant
              Come celui qu'Alixandre ot.
              Mes cil ne cele ne le sot:
              C'est granz enuiz que il nel sevent
                            (*Cligés*, vv. 1139ff.).

6.   Ceste estoire trovons escrite,
              Que conter vos vuel et retraire,
              En un des livres de l 'aumaire
              Mon seignor saint Pere a Biauvez;
              De la fu li contes estrez (*Cligés*, vv. 18ff.).

7. See my *The Poetics of* TRANSLATIO STUDII *and* CONJOINTURE: *Chrétien de Troyes's* CLIGÉS (Lexington, Ky.: French Forum, Publishers, 1979) for a discussion of how Chrétien lauds *clergie* at the expense of *chevalerie* in his second romance.

8.   La reïne garde s'an prant,
      Qui l 'un et l 'autre voit sovant
      Descolorer et anpalir;
      Ne set don ce puet avenir,
      Ne set por coi il le font
      Fors que por la mer ou il sont.
      Espoir bien s'an aparceüst,
      Se la mers ne la deceüst;
      Mes la mers l'angingne et deçoit
      Si qu'an la mer l'amor ne voit;
      An la mer sont, et d'amer vient,
      Et d'amors vient li max ques tient.
      Et de ces trois ne set blasmer
      La reïne fors que la mer,
      Car li dui le tierz li ancusent
      Et por le tierz li dui s'escusent
      Qui del forfet sont antechié (*Cligés*, vv. 533ff.).

9. The cup the narrator describes presents another similar commentary on Chrétien's romance. For further remarks on this additional description-commentary see my *The Poetics of* TRANSLATIO STUDII *and* CONJOINTURE . . ., pp. 150ff. and these remarks by Jean Frappier: "On dirait que Chrétien, dans cette brève description, a songé à enclore et cherché à suggérer son esthétique du roman; la hiérarchie des trois éléments qui constituent la beauté de la coupe ne correspond-elle pas à celle de la *matière* (il faut savoir rencontrer un sujet riche en possibilités), de l'*art* ou du *passage au style* sans lequel il n'est pas de création véritable, du *sens* enfin, qui illumine l'oeuvre entière, comme les pierres précieuses donnent son éclat suprême à la coupe? Si je ne m'abuse, Chrétien, sans en avoir l'air, mettait tout un enseignement à l'intention de certains de ses confrères, dans cette coupe du roi Arthur" (*Le Roman breton, Chrétien de Troyes:* CLIGÉS [Paris: Centre de Documentation Universitaire, 1951], p. 92).

10.   Tristran respunt: "Vostre merci!
      Ore entendez que jo vus di.
      Pernez cest anel ov vus.
      Co sunt enseingnes entre nus,
      E quant en la terre vendrez,
      En curt marcheant vus frez,
      E porterez bons dras de seie.
      Feites qu'ele cest anel veie,
      Car des qu'ele l'avrad veü
      E de vus s'iert aparceü
      Art e engin apres querra
      Qu'a leiser i parlera.

      _____

      Venuz i est dan Kaherdin
      Ove ses dras, a ses oisels,
      Dunt il ad de bons e de bels.

En sun pung prent un grant ostur
E un drap d'estrange culur
E une cupe ben ovree:
Entaillee e neelee.
Al rei Markes en fait present
E li dit raisnablement
Qu'od sun aveir vent en sa terre
Pur altre guanier e conquerre:
Pais li doinst en sa regiun
Que pris n'i seit a achaisun,
Ne damage n'i ait ne hunte
Par chamberlens ne par vescunte.
Li reis li dune ferme pes,
Oiant tuz iceus del pales.
A la reïne vait parler,
De ses avers li volt mustrer.
Un afiçail ovré de or fin
Li porte en sa main Kaherdin,
Ne qui qu'el secle melliur seit:
Present a la reïne em fait.
"Li ors est mult bons", ce dit;
Unques Ysolt melliur ne vit;
L'anel Tristran de sun dei oste,
Juste l'altre le met encoste,
E dit: "Reïne, ore veiez:
Icest or est plus colurez
Que n'est li ors de cest anel;
Nequedent cestu tenc a bel."
Cum la reïne l'anel veit,
De Kaherdin tost s'aperceit;
Li quers le change e la colur
E suspire de grant dolur
(Thomas, *Tristan*, vv. 1183f. and 1392f.).

11. On *intertextualité générale* and *intertextualité restreinte*, defined respectively as "rapports intertextuels entre textes d'auteurs différents" and "rapports intertextuels entre textes du même auteur" by Lucien Dällenbach, see his "Intertexte et autotexte," *Poétique*, 27 (1976) p. 282; see also *Claude Simon* Colloque de Cerisy, dirigé par Jean Ricardou. (Paris: Union Générale d'Éditions, Coll. "10/18", 1975), pp. 17ff., cited by Dällenbach.

12.
li arçon estoient d'ivoire,
s'i fu antailliee l'estoire
comant Eneas vint de Troye,
comant a Cartaige a grant joie
Dido an son leu le reçut,
comant Eneas la deçut,
comant ele por lui s'ocist,
comant Eneas puis conquist

Laurente et tote Lonbardie,
dom il fu rois tote sa vie.
Soutix fu l'uevre et bien tailliee,
tote a fin or apareilliee.
Uns brez taillierres, qui la fist,
au taillier plus de set anz mist,
qu'a nule autre oevre n'antandi;
ce ne sai ge qu'il la vandi,
mes avoir an dut grant desserte.
(*Les Romans de Chrétien de Troyes, édités d'après la copie de
    Guiot, I, Érec et Énide*, Mario Roques, ed. [Paris:
    Champion, 1970], vv. 5289f.)

13.   Et Cligés qui rien ne savoit
De la poison que ele avoit
Dedanz le cors, qui la fet mue
Et tele qu'el ne se remue,
Por ce cuide qu'ele soit morte;
Si s'an despoire, et desconforte,
Et sopire formant, et plore (*Cligés*, vv. 6139f.).

14.   Mialz voldroie estre desmanbree
Que de nos deus fust remanbree
L'amors d'Ysolt et de Tristan,
Don mainte folie dit an,
Et honte en est a reconter.
Ja ne m'i porroie acorder
A la vie qu'Isolz mena.
Amors en li trop vilena,
Que ses cuers fu a un entiers,
Et ses cors fu a deus rentiers.
Ensi tote sa vie usa
N'onques les deus ne refusa.
Ceste amors ne fu pas resnable,
Mes la moie iert toz jorz estable,
Car de mon cors et de mon cuer
N'iert ja fet partie a nul fuer.
Ja mes cors n'iert voir garçoniers.
N'il n'i avra deus parçoniers.
Qui a le cuer, cil a le cors,
Toz les autres an met defors (*Cligés*, vv. 3105f.).

In his "Cligés et Tristan" (*Romania*, XXXIII [1904] pp. 465–89), A. G. Van
Hamel concludes that in this passage Fénice is concerned with her reputation
as a character. Critics have been known on occasion to run to Fénice's rescue by
concentrating precisely on the above passage in order to defend her honor and
virtue especially when she is compared to Iseut. Exceptionally, Van Hamel, I
think, puts his finger on the other side of the problem when he deems Fénice

to be interested in her future as a literary character. Nevertheless, the ambiguity between the two stances persists in the text of Chrétien's romance, and this ambiguity could well be deliberate on the poet's part.

15.   Einz puis n'i ot empereor
             N'eüst de sa fame peor
             Qu'ele nel deüst decevoir,
             Se il oï ramantevoir
             Comant Fenice Alis deçut,
             Primes par la poison qu'il but,
             Et puis par l'autre traïson.
             Por ce einsi com an prison
             Est gardee an Constantinoble,
             Ja n'iert tant haute ne tant noble,
             L'empererriz, quex qu'ele soit:
             L'empereres point ne s'i croit,
             Tant con de celi li remanbre;
             Toz jorz la fet garder en chanbre
             Plus por peor que por le hasle,
             Ne ja avoec li n'avra masle
             Qui ne soit chastrez en anfance.
             De ce n'est criemme ne dotance
             Qu'Amors les lit an son lïen (*Cligés*, vv. 6645f.).

16. Cf., "Chrétien de Troyes," in Anthime Fourrier, *Le Courant réaliste dans le roman courtois en France au moyen-âge*, I, *Les Débuts (XII*[e] *siècle)* (Paris: Nizet, 1960).

17. In addition to the well-known studies devoted to the *Tristan-Cligés* problematics written by G. Paris, A. Franz, A. Micha, A. G. Van Hamel, A. Fourrier, H. Hauvette, F. Lyons, J. Frappier and more recently P. Haidu and Karl. D. Uitti, one might also refer to the article "Mythopoetic Evolution: Chrétien de Troyes's *Erec et Enide*, *Cligés* and *Yvain*" wherein E. P. Nolan declares that in *Cligés*, Chrétien "is beginning to explore far subtler ways of using literature as a tool of social criticism than are possible in the monistic poetics of the *Erec*" (p. 149) (*Symposium* [Summer 1971], pp. 139–161).

Of Arthurian Bondage:
Thematic Patterning in the Vulgate Romances
E. JANE BURNS

The digressive form of the Vulgate romances has long troubled medievalists, most notably among them Ferdinand Lot. In his monumental study of 1918, *Etude sur le Lancelot en Prose*, Lot sought to resolve the ambiguous nature of these Arthurian narratives by revealing "une unité de conception et de plan certaine" [1] hidden beneath the disparate textual surface. Lot's case is argued, however, from a retrospective hypothesis, as he compares the medieval texts to works by Beaumarchais, Scribe, and Sardou, and claims that they are as rigorously constructed as "une tragédie en cinq actes." [2] Despite substantial evidence drawn from the *Lancelot Propre* to support his theories of single authorship, *entrelacement*, and consistent chronology, Lot is unable to document an equally tight narrative structure in the other romances included in his study: *L'Estoire du Saint Graal*, *La Queste du Saint Graal*, and *La Mort le roi Artu*.[3] He concludes reluctantly that the cycle's abundant repetitions and incongruities are "d'une monotonie presque offensante pour le lecteur." [4]

This problematic gap between modern reader and medieval text finds a more viable solution in Vinaver's notion of decorative textual flourish. Explaining that the digressive adventures of thirteenth-century romance should not be viewed in dramatic terms for they are dramatic superfluities, he suggests that we read them in pictorial terms, or as patterned embellishments.[5] In his firm commitment to the theory of *entrelacement*, however, Vinaver defers ultimately to the search for narrative unity, stating that in the Vulgate romances, "nothing is left to chance." [6] The prose texts only appear to be frought with fragmentary episodes which, if unravelled by the able critic or trained reader, can be seen to serve a logical, coherent plan.[7]

Neither the case for narrative coherence nor the concept of textual ornament offers a convincing explanation for the most glaring esthetic anomaly of the Vulgate romances: the text's characteristics *ressorts*, or events which occur in slightly varied forms at random intervals, not generally linked through relationships of cause, consequence, or subordination. Why, for example, are the prisoners of the Doloreuse Garde liberated twice in succession without any mention of their immediate recapture

Medievalia et Humanistica, New Series, Number 11 (Paul Maurice Clogan, ed.). Rowman and Littlefield, Totowa, NJ, 1982.

(*Lancelot* III: 151, 152, 192)? Or why does Perceval purposefully wound himself after his encounter with the island temptress in the *Queste* (VI: 79)? What is the motivation for such spectacular occurrences as the closing of all the doors and windows before the Grail appears at Camalot (*Queste* VI: 7), or the rationale behind the flying lances which attack Hector and Gawain in the Wasteland cemetery (*Lancelot* IV: 339–41)?

These textual incongruities can perhaps be explained best by a process that Vinaver suggests but does not develop. In discussing Romanesque ornament, he states that "the artist's problem . . . is primarily one of design." [8] Vegetal and animal shapes are transformed into ornamental motifs, stylized, and adapted to fit the pattern of the page or initial. These decorative elements are, however, not independent of one another, nor are they disconnected from the composition as a whole. They are made to cohere on a formal basis, according to the dictates of the overall pattern. Is it possible, then, that those elements which are not neatly interwoven with one another, not "entwined, latticed, knotted, or plaited" [9] into the logical story line of the Vulgate romances, are related by a kind of formal or patterned coherence, a second kind of interlace that carries meaning while remaining independent of linear narrative logic?

Close analysis of the most widely repeated images found throughout the Vulgate Cycle reveals that they are linked on the basis of common function. If we take the phenomenon of imprisonment, for example, it becomes clear that description of the prison in realistic terms as castle, tower, or dungeon is often accompanied by a secondary, more abstract evocation of captivity. This second narrative layer, which appears to be a repetition of unlinked motifs, is actually a controlled proliferation of thematic allomorphs. The imprisonment of Arthur's men at the Doloreuse Garde, for example, is rendered through a double motif. The fortified castle, an obvious prison topos that appears frequently throughout the Vulgate corpus, is accompanied in this case by its functional equivalent, the graveyard. The prison of the Doloreuse Garde is described both as an island with a castle at its center, and a cemetery with a tombstone at its center.

Et tan tost vient deuant la porte lors esgarda le castel si uoit quil siet trop orguelleusement & trop bel. Car toute la fortereche siet en une haute roche naie & si nest mie petite . . . (*Lancelot* III: 143)

Si mainent le cheualier en une chimentiere moult merueilleus qui estoit dehors les murs. si sen meruella moult quant il le uit. (*Lancelot* III: 152) [10]

It soon becomes clear, however, that this cemetery is not a resting place for dead bodies, but a second version of the multi-faceted prison locale.

The inscription on the central tombstone establishes the link between castle and cemetery because it states that the stone will be lifted by him who conquers the castle and frees it inhabitants.

& el milieu de la chimentiere si auoit vne grande lame de metal tres merueilleuse-ment ouuree a or & a pieres & a esmax. Et si i auoit lettres qui disoient ceste lame niert ia leuee par main domme ne par esfors. se par chelui non qui conquerra cest doleros castel. (*Lancelot* III: 152)

As Gawain later discovers, none of Arthur's knights whose tombstones appear in the cemetery of the Doloreuse Garde is dead: they are, however, imprisoned in the nearby dungeon called the Doloreuse Chartre.[11] Thus the tombstone does not signify death but a temporary withdrawal from active life, an in-between existence characterized by internment and im-mobility. Both castle and cemetery function here as sites of imprisonment.

The analogical relationship between these two motifs explains the otherwise illogical connection between lifting the tombstone in the graveyard and freeing the distant castle inhabitants. It accounts as well for the two-fold liberation of prisoners. In the first instance, Lancelot van-quishes several guards and lifts the central tombstone allowing the cap-tives to escape, "Lors le saisist a .ij. mains par deuers le plus [gros]. si la tant leuee quele est plus haute que sa teste .j. pie." (*Lancelot* III: 152).[12] In the second liberation, however, the prison described initially as both castle and cemetery undergoes a thematic modulation to become a cave with a pillar at its center.[13] Lancelot turns the key in the central pillar which, in addition to freeing the captives, causes the cemetery to disappear.

Li cheualiers desferme le piler a le cleif grosse . . . Et il se regarde si voit le piler fondre tot ius quen terre. & la demoisele de creure autresi. & les .ij. cheualier qui lui gardoient tous debrisies. Et il vient hors a tous les cles. si voit toutes les gens del castel qui vienent a lencontre. Et com il vint en la chimentiere si ne voit nule des tombes ne des hiaumes qui sor les creniax soloient estre. (*Lancelot* III: 192)

This second liberation is not a superfluous repetition but a retelling of the initial event in an altered version, a version that corresponds to the ceme-tery aspect of the prison locale. Rather than two successive liberations, the text presents a single incident of releasing prisoners through two thematic allomorphs. Imprisonment is depicted as a kind of false death and en-tombment is presented as a form of captivity. The second freeing of the prisoners at the Doloreuse Garde is thus a necessary echo of the prison's double nature.

Although the two versions of the prison motif at the Doloreuse Garde are not linked sequentially or causally, their relationship is signaled through juxtaposition. There are however many other variants of this same imprisonment motif scattered without apparent link through the Vulgate romances. Spatially distant and materially different from one another, these images often seem illogical and misplaced. They can be seen to cohere nevertheless through a kind of generic coherence, or as thematic analogues.[14]

The cemetery motif reappears for example in the *Estoire* where Symeu and Cahan await liberation from the tombstones under which they are imprisoned (I: 267). Similar to the prisoners of the Doloreuse Garde, the captivity of these men is rendered twice but with slightly different motifs. The tombstone in this case is doubled not by a castle, but by the immobile sword lodged in the stone, ". . . & il lor dist metes sor chascune tombe lespee de celui qui desous gist. & ie quit que nus ni vendra qui les puisse oster . . ." (*Estoire* I: 267). The curious presence of the immobile sword has no logical explanation. It serves throughout the narrative, however, as an indication of captivity. Galahad must pull the sword from the stone in the *Queste* to become the liberator of the Arthurian realm, "lors met le main a lespee & la traist del person au(s)si legierement comme sele ni tenist point." (VI: 11). Joseph of Arimathea is freed from a temporary captive state when he pulls the sword from his wounded thigh in the *Estoire*, "puis [ioseph] traist hors de sa cuisse le piece de lespee qui dedens estoit . . ." (I: 256). However, when Bohort refuses to lift the sword from the wounded knight's body in the *Lancelot*, the latter is relegated to perpetual infirmity and immobility.

Lors apele bohort si li dist Sire or y poes vous assaier quar cils autres y a failli Biaus sire fait bohors saues vous bien que nus ne vous y puet aidier sil nest li mieldres cheualiers del monde. Oil fait li ie le sai certainement enon dieu fait bohort. dont ni meterai iou ia le main. (*Lancelot* IV: 260)

Despite the variance in agents and circumstances, the hero changes from Galahad to Joseph to Bohort, and the object enclosing the sword alternates from tombstone or simple stone to the human body, all these incidents evoke the same function, the function of lifting the sword from an enclosure, of extracting it from a fixed milieu, of transforming the uselessly static sword into a tool of liberation.[15] Although they share no causal rapport, this series of motifs can be considered thematic variants of one another, much in the same manner that successive incidents of releasing prisoners at the Doloreuse Garde form two versions of a single act of liberation.

If we pursue the search for thematic analogues of captivity, it becomes clear that the wound serves alone in many cases to depict prisoners awaiting liberation. The incident of the sword lodged in Joseph of Arimathea's thigh is elaborated further in the scene where the Roi Méhaignié and Nascien suffer bodily paralysis as a result of sword wounds, and when the Grail King is maimed by Solomon's sword.

Et einsi quil aloient de lune en lautre si fu nascienjns ferus dune espee parmi lesepaule (senestre) si durement quil chai en la neif (adens). (*Queste* VI: 149)

Mais maintenant fu ferus dune lanche tres parmi les quisses si durement quil en remist mehaignies si comme il peirt encore. (*Queste* VI: 150)

. . . lors uns hons en flammes laisse courre un glaiue quil tenoit & le fiert parmi les cuisses ambes ij. si q il parut tout oltre si dist al roy. (*Estoire* I: 289)

The wounds incurred by these kings cannot be read in realistic terms, for they are neither moral nor curable. Immobilized by their infirmity, these kings await physical release much in the same manner as the entombed Symeu and Cahan. Rather than simple battle scars, their wounds serve to indicate a perpetual state of inactivity analogous to captivity.

Thus we can see how the single motif of the sword in the stone is surrounded by a network of images that denote both wounding and captivity. The sword caught in the stone has the same function as the sword trapped in the gravestone, or the sword lodged in the wounded man's flesh. Although the specifics vary, a thematic pattern clearly emerges in which the sword in the stone is implicitly likened to the sword in the man, and captivity is likened to the wound. The captive whose internment is signaled by tombstone, sword, or wound can vary from an individual knight to a group of victims. Yet this repetition of individual cases through variant motifs serves ultimately to reflect the general captive state of the entire Arthurian realm. The release of Joseph, Symeu, Cahan, or the wounded knight who addresses Bohort constitute microcosmic versions of the ultimate liberation of the Arthurian universe that Galahad is slated to procure.

The inherent link between wounding and imprisonment can explain the otherwise incongruous punishment of Hector and Gawain in the scene of the Wasteland cemetery in the *Lancelot*. After reading the tombstone inscription that prohibits entry to anyone but Lancelot, "gardes que ia ne metes le pie en cheste chimentiere, por [col] accomplit les aventures qui y sont, quar chou serait paine gastee. Si tu nes li chaitis chevaliers qui par sa luxure a perdu a achiever les aventures del saint graal" (*Lancelot* IV: 339), the two knights defy the warning and attempt the adventure of the tomb.

They are immediately attacked and wounded by twelve lances that detach themselves from twelve tombs (*Lancelot* IV: 339–41). This scene makes use of the same elements found in the scene of liberation at the Doloreuse Garde but employs them to reverse effect. Whereas lifting the tombstone procured the freedom of prisoners at the castle-cemetery of the Doloreuse Garde, failure at the same task in this scene results in wounding, the functional equivalent of captivity.

On one level of the narrative, then, the tale of the Vulgate Cycle is told through the use of associational patterned images whose coherence is not logical but analogical. In these instances, cumulative thematic development takes precedence over linear narrative sequence.[16] This type of compositional process results in clusters of motifs that are used simultaneously to render a single thought. The notion of imprisonment can thus be evoked by a combination of its thematic allomorphs, which need not include description of an actual physical enclosure.

The motif of the wound, for example, often occurs in conjunction with its sensory counterpart: blindness. The victims who suffer paralysis and immobility as a result of sword wounds are frequently characterized by limited vision as well. In the *Queste*, the wounded corpse-like Mordrain has suffered a total loss of physical faculties including sight, "Et maintenant descendi vne nue deuant lui qui li tolt la veue des iex & le pooir del cors en tel maniere quil ne (uit goute ne que il ne) se pot aidier se poi non" (*Queste* VI: 62). In the *Queste*, Lancelot loses the power of movement and sight while attempting to see the Grail at Corbenic, "lors na pooir daler auant come cil qui a perdu le poo(i)r del cors & loir & la veue. ne na membre dont li aidier se puisse" (*Queste* VI: 180).[17]

The association between the wound and blindness is particularly clear in the *Estoire* when Joseph or Arimathea is wounded in the thigh by a lance and Nascien is blinded when trying to see the Grail. The two wounds are healed simultaneously when the angel withdraws the spear from Joseph's thigh, thereby causing the would to close, and then drips the resultant blood on Nascien's eyes, restoring his sight.

.j. angele qui issi del arce uestu dune blanche robe si tenoit en sa main la lanche dont iosephes auoit este ferus . . . & quant il retraist la lance a lui [iosephe] si uirent que li fers en issi auec la lance . . . et en commenchierent a caior goutes de sanc & li angeles . . . uint a iosephe & li enoinst sa plaie del sanc meisme & a nascien les iex. & si tost comme il estoient enoint si uit ausi cleir com il auoit onques fait . . . (*Estoire* I: 80)

Whereas the wound initially signified loss of motor control, it is here extended to include the loss of sensory control as well. The captivity of the wounded men is rendered once through the concrete image of the wound, and reinforced through its perceptual counterpart, blindness.

It is this phenomenon of layered storytelling that can explain Perceval's surprising self-inflicted wound in the *Queste*, "lors traist sespee [del fuerre] & sen fiert si durement en sa senestre quisse qui li sans en issoit de toutes pars" (*Queste* VI: 79). Faced with the illusion of luxurious bed and lavish table setting created by the island temptress, Perceval is seduced for a moment into accepting these mirages as real. His failure to see clearly parallels the blindness of the wounded men. It resembles as well the impaired sight of the young Melian who also encounters a lavish table and a gold crown. Failing to discern the deceptive nature of the sumptuous objects before him, Melian attempts to take the crown, and is consequently wounded by a rival knight, "& cil vient maintenant (quanquil pot del cheual traire) vers melian & le fiert si durement que parmi lescu & parmi li hauberc li met le glaiue el coste senestre a tot le fust . . . & li cheualiers saproche de lui & li oste la corone del brasch" (*Queste* VI: 31). In Perceval's case, the rival knight who inflicts the wound is absent, but the double-layered story motif remains. As in the case of the wounded knights in the preceding examples, Perceval's captivity at the temptress's isle is evoked through twin allomorphs of impaired vision and corporeal wound. Despite its lack of rational motivation, Perceval's self-inflicted wound is not a careless narrative oversight. It forms an integral part of a pattern network based on connotative and plural signification rather than denotative precision. In addition to the moral explanation given for Perceval's action,[18] the motif of wounding carries a generic meaning of imprisonment which is context-free. The latent meaning of captivity inherent in images of the wound throughout the Vulgate Cycle is brought out, in this case, through association with the blindness motif.

We have seen thus far how the notion of captivity is presented in the Vulgate romances through a series of thematic allomorphs. The motifs of tombstone, wound, and blindness can be used in conjunction with the traditional prison topos of castle or dungeon, as in the case of the Doloreuse Garde. They can also serve to indicate imprisonment in the absence of an actual fortified enclosure, as in the scene of the island temptress where blindness and wound are combined to indicate Perceval's captive state. Once the associational web of latent meanings is established, a single allomorph can evoke imprisonment, as in Joseph's wounded thigh, or many allomorphs can be combined in one scene.

The incident of the *lis aventureus* at Corbenic provides an example in which captivity is rendered through a three-fold motif incorporating the allomorphs of wound, blindness, and physical enclosure. Submitted to the test of the *lis aventureus*, Gawain and Bohort are both temporarily wounded and blinded when they become trapped by the spell of the bed.

Mais moult se sent durement naures. Si y demora en tel maniere tan que il fu anuitie einsi auint a monseignour gauuain kil ne uit goute. (*Lancelot* IV: 345).

si issi de vne cambre vne lance grant & longe dont li fers sambloit aussi comme vns cierges ardans si vint uers bohort au(s)si durement comme vns foudres & le feri. (*Lancelot* V: 298)

During their respective trials, both these knights are also physically constrained within the castle. Gawain discovers that all the doors are locked making exit impossible, "& si ne pot de laiens issir quar li huis furent bien ferme . . ." (*Lancelot* IV: 344). Bohort notices that all the windows in his room are closed, "Quant li quarrel orent laissiet a uenir si reclosent les fenestres toutes . . ." (*Lancelot* V: 299).

A less complex version of this same mechanism can explain the miraculous closing of the doors and windows when the Grail appears at Arthur's castle at the outset of the *Queste*, "Quant il orent eu le premier mes si lor auint vne si merueilleuse auenture que tot li huis et les fenestres del palais ou il mangoient closent sans ce que nus i mist main" (*Queste* VI: 7). Although the inhabitants of Arthur's castle suffer no wounds, Gawain explains that when the Grail appeared on a previous occasion at the Roi Méhaignié's castle, its observers suffered impaired vision and, as a result, could not see the Grail clearly, "& ce nauint onques mais en cort se ne fust cies le roi mahaignie. Mais de ce furent il engignie quil ne le virent apertement. ains le(u)r fu couerte la veue par semblance" (*Queste* VI: 13). The blindness of these untrained Grail observers is rendered in a concrete form by the closing of the doors and windows in the fabled room at Camalot before the Grail enters. Comparison with the imprisonment of Gawain and Bohort at the *lis aventureus* where the doors and windows are locked, clarifies the otherwise incongruous mention of the mysterious window slamming at Camalot. Rather than a miraculous occurrence associated with the Holy Vessel, this incident is a clear and direct evocation of the captive state of Camalot's residents. They await liberation from the Chosen Hero who will pull the sword from the stone.

A final layer of thematic patterning used in the Vulgate romances to develop the notion of captivity is found in the allied motifs of disguise and anonymity. Many of the wounded victims are marked by a physical covering which accompanies their corporeal infirmity. When Perceval views the corpse-like king Mordrain at the hermitage in the *Queste*, the wounded king is covered, "Et Perceval regarde le lit & auise tant quil voit que dedens gist ou hons ou feme mais il ne set lequel. Car li vis estoit couers dune touaille blance & delie si quil nel pooit mie veoir apertement" (VI:

59). Gawain, when approaching the bed where the ailing Agravain lies immobile, must pull back the cover to see the wounded knight, "Gauuain vait iuscal lit & lieue le couertoir. si voit desous .j. des plus biax cheualiers del monde" (*Lancelot* III: 313). Yvain uncovers the wounded knight pierced by two lances and a sword outside the castle of Trahans li Gai, "Et mesire ywain descent & soslieue le drap, et uoit le cheualier naure moult durement de .lj. gla[i]ues parmi le cors (*Lancelot* IV: 92,93).

The physical covering accompanying the wounds of these three victims is modulated slightly in the case of the knight who seeks a defender at Arthur's court at the outset of the Lancelot. Similar to the wounded man encountered by Yvain, this knight is impaled by two swords and a lance. Although his body is not concealed by a physical covering, his identity is unknown and thus hidden, "Li cheualiers fu grans & gens & bien taillies. mais son non ne noume pas li contes chi endroit" (*Lancelot* III: 119–20). He lacks the physical properties of disguise worn by the other knights, but enjoys the resultant anonymity. The wounded Lancelot shares a similar anonymity when he is transported on a litter past Gawain who fails to recognize his companion.

lors demande as valles que chou est. Sire font il .j. cheualier naure. & li cheualier naures fait hauchier le drap. & demande a monsignor Gauuain qui il est. Et il dist quil est vns cheualier de la maison le roi artu. Et quant il lo[i]t si a paor quil ne le conna[i]sse si se recueure. & mesire Gauuain li demande qui il est. & il dist quil est vns cheualiers qui vait en vn sien affaire (*Lancelot* III: 175).

In like manner, no one recognizes Lancelot in his comatose "pseudo-wounded" state which results from viewing the Grail at Corbenic, "Einsi disoient maintes fois cil de laiens de lancelot & ploroeint. ne il ne le povent connoistre" (*Queste* VI: 181). Thus the wounded knight cloaked in anonymity or covered by bedclothes and curtains exists in a veiled state. His wound, which causes a physical transformation into a death-like stasis, affects as well the way he is perceived.

Liberation of these knights can take many forms in accord with the plural motifs used to indicate captivity. The wounded victim is partially freed by removal of the sword from his ailing body. The knights who, in addition to their physical infirmity, are unnamed and unknown, approach liberation when the curtain is parted or the covers withdrawn revealing their physical characteristics and establishing their identity.

The acts of revelation and liberation are established as functional equivalents throughout the Vulgate texts. When Lancelor lifts the cemetery slab at the Doloreuse Garde, he not only frees the captives from the twin prisons of tower and cemetery, but discovers his own identity as well. The raised tombstone reveals for the first time Lancelot's name and the identity of the future liberator, "ceste lame niert ia leuee par main domme ni par esfors. se par chelui non qui conquerra cest doleros castel. & de chelui est li nons escris desous" (*Lancelot* III: 151). Galahad's heroic identity is similarly unveiled at Arthur's court when the cloth is removed from the Siege Perilleux and an inscription bearing Galahad's name is uncovered, "Et li rois meismes vint al siege [perilleus] & leua le drap de soie si troua le non de galaad quil desiroit moult a sauoir" (*Queste* VI: 10). The literal revealing of the hero's identity is accompanied by a reference to future liberation in the most general sense in the well-known motif of the sword in the stone. The inhabitants of Arthur's troubled realm will be freed when Galahad pulls the sword from the stone and establishes thereby his reputation as the Chosen Quester. Releasing the quester from his hidden identity and releasing prisoners from captive existence are posited as thematic analogues that can be drawn in variant motifs. The act of pulling the sword from the stone, withdrawing the covers from a wounded man, and lifting the tombstone or cloth over a hidden name are all acts of extraction that affect liberation. The announcement of the romance hero is thus rendered in terms appropriate to his task as liberator. The process by which his identity is freed is also that which will enable the future liberation of victims trapped by tomb, wound, blindness, and disguise.

The thematic patterning of the Vulgate romances is certainly incompatible with the Aristotelian concept of unity through linear development. The pattern structure creates rather a kind of unity through multiplicity in which associative resonance replaces logical cohesion. Northrop Frye delineates the difference between Aristotelian (realistic) and romance narrative in spatial terms, stating that realism attempts normally to keep the action horizontal through the technique of causality while romance abandons and even avoids the line of direct action to emphasize the vertical dimension. Whereas the realist creates a "hence" narrative, which leads us to the end of the story, the romancer builds an episodic "and then" structure, which he attempts to surmount, trying seemingly to get to the top of the narrative.[19] Romance then has a third dimension which allows episodic "digressions" of a nondevelopmental nature. The criticism that many romance narratives lack unity actually constitutes, according to Frye, a judgement against their lack of "hence" or causal structure.[20]

The same holds true for the Vulgate romances where events are often linked through functional similarity rather than causal progression. In these instances, episodes are justifiable not as being necessary or indispensable, as Lot thought, but as being appropriate, as analogues to other patterned episodes.[21] Although many images in the Vulgate corpus have no specific denotative meaning, they draw connotative signification from their participation in the overall pattern of imprisonment and liberation that governs the production of narrative repetitions. In this manner, the form of the Vulgate romances can be seen to have a semantic movement of its own, an underlying content which is neither historical nor symbolic. The result of the layered patterns is to create a third dimension in the romance text, a dimension which provides the possibility of a new reading balanced between strict representation and meaningless decorative flourish. If we accept the organizing principle of thematic patterning, the abundant textual incongruities in the Vulgate romances make sense according to an internal narrative logic. For these troublesome *ressorts*, the meaning is in the pattern.

NOTES

1. Ferdinand Lot, *Etude sur le Lancelot en Prose*, 2nd ed. (1918; rpt. Paris: Librairie Ancienne Honoré Champion, 1954), p. 8.
2. Ibid., pp. 28, 74.
3. Ibid., p. 63. *La Mort le roi Artu* differs substantially from the other romances of the Vulgate Cycle (*Lestoire de Merlin, Lestoire del Saint Graal, Le Livre de Lancelot del Lac, Les aventures ou la queste del Saint Graal*) as it is ordered along more logical and discursive lines, and depends to a great degree upon hierarchical and causal relationships which are de-emphasized in the other romances. Although it shares certain important characteristics with the other Vulgate texts, *La Mort le roi Artu* requires special consideration which is beyond the scope of this study.
4. Ibid., p. 263. See also Pauphilet's disparraging but accurate comment in his *Etudes sur la Queste del Saint Graal* (Paris: Librairie Honoré Champion, 1921), "les mêmes epithètes, trop générales et peu topiques y reviennent constamment: 'tournoi grand et merveilleux, mêlée grande et merveilleuse' . . .", p. 187.
5. Eugene Vinaver, "From Motif to Ornament," *Medieval Literature and Folklore Studies: Essays in Honor of Francis Lee Utley*, ed. Jerome Mandel and Bruce Rosenberg (New Brunswick, New Jersey: Rutgers University Press, 1970), p. 153.
6. Vinaver, *The Rise of Romance* (Oxford: Clarendon Press, 1971), p. 80.
7. Ibid., p. 128. It is difficult to reconcile Vinaver's notion of the decorative logic in thirteenth-century romance with his apparent preference for linear narrative perspective. He explains how in the *Suite de Merlin* Morgan's adventures are inessential to the development of the narrative, but understandable as decorative flourishes ("Motif," p. 152). Yet in his analysis of the Balin episode, each version is described as a necessary elaboration that contributes to the subtle development of theme, "several faint visions superimposed one upon another served to illumine the last and greatest of them" (*Rise of Romance*, p. 110). In this case, each element is considered indispensable to the creation of a coherent whole.

8. Vinaver, "Motif," p. 153.

9. Vinaver, *Rise of Romance*, p. 82.

10. All quotations are from the edition by H. Oskar Sommer, *The Vulgate Version of the Arthurian Romances* (Washington: The Carnegie Institute, 1909–13).

11. "Et quant mesire Gauuain ot quil sont einsi mort si en pleure moult durement. Car il quide bien & tout li autre que che soit voirs. & si estoit il de tex i auoit & de tex i auoit menchoigne dont les lettres estoient faites la nut deuant." (*Lancelot* III: 155); "Et sachies que le plus de che que vos aues veu la sus nest se menchoigne non & enchantemens. Mais ie vous monstrerai verite. Car ie vous ferai veoir des compaignons le roi vne partie tous sains & tous vis. de tex que les lettres de la sus tesmoignent a estre mors." (*Lancelot* III: 158); "La doloreuse chartre einsi auoit non li castiax ou mesire Gauuain estoit en prison . . ." (Lancelot III: 162).

12. See also *Lancelot* IV: 175 Galahad's tomb, and *Lancelot* IV: 279 Galehot's tomb.

13. "De le chimentiere extrent en vne capele qui estoit el chief deuers la tout. Et quant il sont ens si li mostrent lentree dune caue deso(u)s terre. & dient que laiens est la cles des enchantemens . . . puis vient au pilier de coiure qui est en milieu de chele cambre." (*Lancelot* III: 190–91).

14. On the concept of generic coherence see Eugene Falk, *Types of Thematic Structures* (Chicago: University of Chicago Press, 1967), and "Stylistic Forces in the Narrative," *Patterns of Literary Style*, ed. Joseph Strelka (University Park: Pennsylvania State University Press, 1971).

15. In the cases of Bohort, Symeu, and Cahan, the function of liberation is potential only. The principle use of the sword motif is these scenes is to indicate captivity.

16. For a discussion of cumulative construction in epic narrative see Berkeley Peabody, *The Winged Word* (Albany: State University of New York Press, 1975), p. 207.

17. In Lancelot's case the physical wound is replaced entirely by blindness and immobility as sole markers of the knight's captivity.

18. "biax sire cest en amende de ce que ie (me) aui mesfais enuers uous." (*Queste* VI: 79).

19. Frye, *Secular Scripture: A Study in the Structure of Romance* (Cambridge, Massachusetts: Harvard University Press), 1976, pp. 47–48.

20. Ibid., p. 51.

21. On generic unity and thematic analogy in Chrétien de Troyes see Norris Lacy, "Spatial Form in Medieval Romance," *Yale French Studies*, 51 (1974), 160–70, "Thematic Structure in the *Charrette*," *L'Esprit Créateur*, 12, No. 1 (Spring 1972), 13–18.

Beowulf and the Danish Succession:

Gift Giving as an Occasion for Complex Gesture

JOHN M. HILL

Fifty years ago L. L. Schücking noticed that Wealhþeow's speeches in Heorot, during the great banquet scene, in part express her worry that Hroðgar might adopt Beowulf more in fact than spirit. He might designate Beowulf as heir or successor to the Danish kingship.[1] Schücking's comment has since been unelaborated, although noticed. It implications, however, require exploration. If we credit Wealhþeow's worry, we need to reexamine her speeches to Hroðgar and Beowulf, as well as the scene of gift giving following Hroðgar's adoption speech. That in turn leads to a general reassessment of the banquet scenes, both in Heorot and in Hygelac's hall. Those scenes, in consequence, become much more portentous than *Beowulf* scholars have suspected: especially if understood as occasions for complex gestures revolving around the giving of gifts. As we shall see, Hroðgar does more than fulfill his promise to reward Beowulf; implicitly he offers Beowulf the leading place in the Danish succession. Wealhþeow also seizes the occasion, fulfilling her role but doing more than is customary: gold-adorned, the gracious queen counters Hroðgar's offer. And Beowulf, although silent during the banquet scene, apparently understands the significance of gestures made toward him and around him. When he returns to Hygelac's hall, he does more than reaffirm his proper relationship to Hygelac: he clears himself of any suspicion that he may have compromised himself while in Hroðgar's service.

The common issue for those gestures is dynastic succession; the common vehicle used by all principals is the giving of gifts. Each character uses that vehicle—minimally a proper gesture in each case—for special purposes. To see that best requires a review of attitudes toward gift giving in Germanic culture generally and then an explication of speeches accompanying gifts in *Beowulf*.

Commentators long have noted the commonplace functions of gift giving in *Beowulf*. Gift giving establishes an important reciprocity: gifts, trust and honor on the lord's part for service, honor and loyalty on the retainer's

Medievalia et Humanistica, New Series, Number 11 (Paul Maurice Clogan, ed.). Rowman and Littlefield, Totowa, NJ, 1982.

part. In turn the lord rewards or repays service by gifts, through which he ever affirms the heroic contract (his relationship between himself and his retainers).[2] More than a bond, that affirmation underlines an entire system of reciprocal relationships between equals and unequals.[3] Moreover, the lord's generosity may indicate either the value of services performed or the quality of service looked for.

Marcel Maus has given us a "global" view of exchange in archaic societies, such that we can invest the system of gift-exchange and gifts for services, insofar as we can glimpse that through *Beowulf* and other Germanic texts, with an anthropological reality.[4] Similar systems exist in archaic societies today. Furthermore, Mauss briefly reviews Germanic societies—asserting that, although few meaningful traces survive, ancient Germanic systems of gift-exchange appear typical.[5]

Germanic exchange could approach "potlatch"—a premonetary system of exchange between families and between clans in which one must give, receive and return gifts. The system is competitive and gifts carry their owner's mana (his power and identity). It is also a system within which a giver and receiver affirm a relationship.[6] Some of Mauss's observations were anticipated by earlier scholars, especially Vilhelm Grønbech— whose discussion of the gift owes much to *Hávamál*, a poem also cited by Mauss.[7] But neither Grønbech nor Mauss examines the scenes of gift giving in *Beowulf*. Had Mauss done so, he might have concluded that meaningful traces of Germanic gift giving in fact survive, and he might have expanded his sense of the extra purposes gift giving can serve.

The *Hávamál* is an invaluable, but not an all-purpose, source for Germanic attitudes toward the gift. It focuses on gift giving between equals, essentially between folk and friends. Friendship requires an exchange of gifts, which forms the bond for a relationship—the identification of friend to friend. A gift always looks for a return.[8] The advice in *Hávamál* is general, even gnomic in its formulation (although some of it is manipulative). Doubtless it would resonate well in any Germanic context. But it is neither particularly Anglo-Saxon nor aristocratic. As evident in different themes woven through and around gifts, Germanic literature does not exploit the gift all in one way; different cultures and different audiences must have responded to different aspects of gift giving and the gift. Old Icelandic poetry, for example, often focuses on the darkly portentous or tainted gift—this especially in the Sigurth cycle—and on sardonic liberality (in the Atli cycle).[9]

When commenting on gifts, the Old English *Maxims I* and *II* focus on aristocratic liberality as an unalloyed good—a necessary and proper state of things.[10] Elsewhere, munificence in a king is also praiseworthy— whether the king is important to Bede for his humility or to the *Widsith* poet for his patronage.[11] Exchange between a superior and an inferior, as a good and wonderful affair testifying to the inferior's deserts, is reported in *Widsith* in the narrator's account of his exchange with his lord—he gave a magnificent ring because his lord had given him land. The land was the poet's father's. In that passage we learn also that the queen, queens are noted in the Maxims as good if generous, deserves praise for her liberality.[12] Out of all that, we can conclude that liberality is expected of Anglo-Saxon kings and queens. Liberality is good and natural, a part of their role—in the exercise of which they confirm their worthiness. Against that background, gift giving in *Beowulf* comes into focus, both for its commonplace and its unusual features.

Something approaching total exchange (or potlatch) may occur in the poem—referred to by Hroðgar and reflected in the adjective *gemæne* ('in common,' 'mutual,' 'shared'). Significant usages of the word appear in lines 1857a and 1860a.[13] There Hroðgar says that Beowulf has brought to pass a bond of peace (or 'kinship,' *sib*), such that Danes and Geats will share that and gifts. Otherwise, unless we see the *comitatus* as a continuing exchange of gifts for services, potlatch does not appear fully in *Beowulf*. But relatively brief acts of giving in the poem clearly have commonplace purposes—apparent in the intentions of the giver and in the immediate social context. They also suggest something beyond either establishing a relationship or acting in a properly generous role.

The giver's intentions appear either in the nature of the object given or in the effect attributable to the giving. Marcel Mauss notes the former for all archaic exchanges, whereas the *Beowulf* poet makes the latter clear.[14] The first mention of gift giving occurs in the Exordium, in a hortatory passage. It establishes a familiar function for giving: a young warrior works good, the poet says, by a 'splendid' dispensing of treasure (*fromum feohgiftum*, l. 21a) so that later on, when war comes, dear retainers in turn will stay with him.[15] His generosity has a purpose: "I give so that you will stand by me in time of war" might express that. The effect of giving reveals the purpose. Therefore, the functional meaning of *fromum feohgiftum* is not 'splendid' dispensing of treasure—that, essentially, is an editorial comment—but a 'martial' or warriorly one (from *from*, meaning 'strenuous,' 'bold,' 'brave'). The next mention of gift giving involves Hroðgar's munificence. He would share (*gedælan*) all that God gave him among young and old alike (excluding the people's land and the lives of men). His sharing, however, will occur in a great hall, which he will build. Hroðgar's munificence, then, complements the fame of the great hall and justifies it. Here we can see sharing as the consummate gesture of one possessing power, honor and fame: munificence redounds upon the stature of the giver. Hroðgar says he will share, and he does. But articulated with mention of his sharing is a suggestive statement that the hall towered, high and horn-gabled (ll. 80–82). This completes several connections in the passage between Hroðgar's intentions and his deeds: in his glory as a war-band leader and king, he would build a world famous hall, in which he would share magnificently. His sharing would become as famous as his hall, and both would testify to his power, fame and stature. Hroðgar's munificence enhances both himself and the hall he creates and names. What Hroðgar's gesture in part says is that "I give because I can give all this."

Those two instances of gift giving show that either practical or prestige-enhancing purposes can control the act. Indeed, gift giving may encompass both purposes simultaneously. The merely practical function fits Hroðgar's undescribed gifts to Beowulf following the fight with Grendel's mother, but both functions appear in Beowulf's giving of a sword to the coastguard. Beowulf rewards the coastguard for watching over the Geats' ship, thus enhancing the guard's prestige in the hall. That effect necessarily is one of Beowulf's intentions, indicating his newly won stature. Only those with prestige can confer it.

The instances noted above, however, remain simple when compared to dramatized gift giving. The poet does more than enumerate the gifts. He reports on the particular gifts, describes them and the manner of giving, and reports the words spoken. When all of that happens, we can expect that more is at stake than we have believed before. The heroical scenes of gift giving are not just practical or even prestige enhancing.[16] They contain special acts controlled by special purposes. Moreover, the scenes are related, which indicates that special acts of giving can acquire a narrative interest extending over a thousand lines or more. That extension also testifies to the portentousness of Hroðgar's generosity.

The prelude to Hroðgar's giving of magnificent treasures, going back to Beowulf's arrival among the Danes, is important for our understanding of what he does. After Wulfgar announces Beowulf's arrival, Hroðgar says he will 'offer,' 'tender' or give treasures (*madmas beodan*) to that good one for his *modþræce* (l. 385a), for Beowulf's impetuous courage. He will do that because God, out of a kindness or favor (*arstafas*) requiring reciprocity, has given him cause for hope against Grendel. *Ar* comes from the ethical vocabulary of the *comitatus*, indicating favor from the superior, requiring gifts from the inferior.[17] Hroðgar cannot give gifts to God, but he can and must reward the warrior God sends. All of this comes after mention of gifts already passing from Danes to Geats (ll. 378–79a).

Earlier Hroðgar mentions Beowulf's father, Ecgþeow, and speaks of knowing Beowulf the boy. Mention of the father mainly identifies Beowulf's noble lineage here: Hreðel of the Geats gave his daughter to Ecgþeow in marriage. Hroðgar implies that Beowulf brings a noble courage the Danes can graciously reward, especially as Hroðgar now expects help against Grendel's terror. Presumably he will encourage Beowulf, should Beowulf announce a willingness to fight Grendel. Later he says that Beowulf will lack nothing desirable or good (*wilna gad*) if he survives that brave work (ll. 660–661). He seems to expand his intentions by expanding the largesse of his promises of reward. The giving he enacts eventually is a *feohgyft* (l. 1025)—which, in the Exordium, the poet says Beow performed (that 'martial' dispensing of treasures). Thus Hroðgar's initial intentions may have been to arrange for martial support only, although they were vague in their extent. *Feohgyft* occurs elsewhere only in the Finn episode, as part of the arrangement binding both parties to each other. Would Hroðgar especially bind Beowulf in some way, especially include him in his *comitatus?* Although initially Hroðgar's promises are vague, it seems he would sound Beowulf's character and intentions before committing himself to particular rewards; eventually he appears to invite Beowulf into his war-band—as both an honored retainer and a possible successor.

As indicated by Hroðgar's sharing in Heorot, he can share almost anything desirable or good—especially if that completes a great act. Building Heorot is one such act; purging it is another, one that spurs Hroðgar to an extraordinary generosity. Does that generosity include an implicit offer of the kingship? Can Hroðgar in effect give the kingdom away by appointing a successor? I think the great banquet scene indicates that Hroðgar can: in what we may read as an attempt to tie Beowulf to himself, Hroðgar first spiritually adopts Beowulf and then seems to offer the right of succession. If so, we will see that gift giving can involve quite different intentions when anticipated and when enacted. Intervening events can bring the giver to revise his intentions dramatically.

The great banquet scene is a victory celebration, a feast of song and gift giving. In his narration the poet includes an account of the treasures Hroðgar gives Beowulf and closes on Wealhþeow's speech to Beowulf. Usually readers understand that scene as a complex affair beginning with grand gestures of reward and ending on the poignancy of Wealhþeow's futile peace weaving. Commentators also stress the uncertain duration of hall joy among kinsmen, recalled for us through the Finn digression. But insufficient attention has been paid to the poet's comments on the unparalleled qualities of the banquet, to the particular gifts given and what they might signify, and to Wealhþeow's concern first to address Hroðgar and then Beowulf—ending with her famous lines about earls true to each other doing as she bids.

Obviously Hroðgar makes good on his promises of reward. Moreover, he would express his gratitude, and he would honor this superlative warrior. But his purposes have broadened, now encompassing more than he intended initially. Beowulf has become especially dear through his behavior in Heorot, his victory over Grendel and his demeanor in general.

Hroðgar has already taken this best of warriors as a "son":

> 'Nu ic, Beowulf, þec,
> secg betsta, me for sunu wylle
> freogan on ferhþe; heald forð tela
> niwe sibbe. Ne bið þe [n]ænigre gad
> worolde wilna, þe ic geweald hæbbe.'
>
> (ll. 946b–950)

Hroðgar has pronounced Beowulf's achievement as unparalleled—an achievement he attributes to God's power, and which he admits exceeds any deed the Danes had the skill or wit to perform. And he has said that Beowulf's mother was blest in Beowulf's birth: God the Old Governor or Ruler showed favor toward her in her child bearing. The thought of Beowulf's parent, his mother only, may have led Hroðgar to offer himself as a "father." For if she were blest in the birth of a son become mighty beyond all warriors, Hroðgar must feel blest now in Beowulf's presence: he has given effusive thanks to God for the sight of Grendel's hand, and he has praised God, the Guardian of Glory—may He always work wonder after wonder. In his ecstasy Hroðgar feels the glory of the moment and of his own incredible good fortune. For all of that he is piously thankful, and he would appropriate the human agent of it—by extending a spiritual paternity to Beowulf. He would love Beowulf, perhaps feeling as blest as he imagines Beowulf's mother must have been. But that he means this as more than a figure of speech and as more than a momentary effusion is clear in his command—'*heald forð tela / niwe sibbe*'—and implied in the social situation. By what better means than adoption can an ecstatic Hroðgar tie this magnificent warrior to himself? [18]

He hopes this new kinship will be mutual, especially in its feeling; indeed, he commands its mutuality. In return for holding well this kinship, Beowulf will lack nothing in Hroðgar's power to give. Such a remark exceeds a notion of mere gifts in exchange for good services, no matter how great the services or how splendid the gifts. Hroðgar would not withhold any good thing of the world, anything at all in his power to grant. His verb is *gewealdan* ('control,' 'wield'), and I think implicitly he differentiates it from the normal purview of reward: '*Ful oft ic for læssan lean teohhode*' (l. 951—'often I assigned reward for less'). Indeed, simple reward is not enough by all past measures. And when repayment becomes a function attributed to God—'*Alwalda þec / gode forgylde, swa he nu gyt dyde!*' (ll. 955b–956)—it is out of Hroðgar's hands entirely. No, mere repayment cannot do justice to Beowulf's deed or Hroðgar's desire.

If "king" etymologically suggests "kin-right," then Hroðgar proceeds properly in making the gesture I think he makes, in implicitly offering the right of succession to Beowulf.[19] Through spiritual adoption, he first raises Beowulf before all the Danes to something like kindred status. Beowulf has already demonstrated throne worthiness, evident in God's favor and his own noble prowess. In looking to Beowulf, Hroðgar can satisfy the criterion of suitability and, having adopted Beowulf in some sense, he can satisfy the demands of kindred. Moreover, youth makes unsuitable his own sons by Wealhþeow. Of course offering the succession to Beowulf, if that is what he does, is not election in itself. Beowulf must first agree, then the *witan* and the folk must elect him—or so it seems. The entire business of choosing a successor—which it seems that a king can do—and the subsequent election remain largely mysterious.[20]

We do know, from the poem itself, that a direct offer of the kingship, made by Hygelac's widow, can come by way of an offer of the tribal hoard and gift-seat or throne. Moreover, Beowulf is a kinsman, Hygelac's nephew, and a subking himself—having been given vast lands and a gift-seat of his own. Hygelac also gave Beowulf Hreþel's heirloom, perhaps betokening Beowulf's fitness to succeed to the kingship. But what about the possibility of an indirect offer—one that exists if openly acknowledged, but not if ignored (this is touchy diplomatic ground)? I think the poet calls attention to just such an offer, initially by way of backhanded statements, and finally by revealing the dynastic history of Hroðgar's gifts.

Hroðgar gives Beowulf a splendid battle-standard, a helmet, a corselet and a renowned sword—all gold-adorned. Gifts of horses and Hroðgar's war-seat follow those kingly gifts. The first four are among the most precious gifts the poet has heard of. Moreover, he has never heard of four gold-adorned treasures given in a more friendly fashion to a warrior (*freondlicor* and *for sc[e]oten[d]um*)—who need not in any way feel ashamed of them.[21] In narrating the initial phase of the banquet, the poet uses two 'I have never heard' constructions. Doubtless he would indicate the unparalleled splendor of the event, its conviviality and its wealth. One construction concerns the amiable behavior of the company, the other concerns Hroðgar's gift giving. Why especially should one note its friendliness, and that this is just to a warrior? Surely other kings have given equally expensive gifts—as Hygelac later does to Beowulf. Yet no special mention describes the manner of Hygelac's giving, and Hygelac gives something splendid—a subkingship and his father's heirloom. In the moment before us, however, the poet emphasizes the preciousness of the sword and the unparalleled friendliness of Hroðgar's gestures. More seems meant than a simple notation about good cheer. The famous prince so generously repays Beowulf, the poet insists, that no man will ever find fault with Hroðgar's gifts—not he who will speak truth according to what is right. These rather broad, if oblique, remarks seem to hint at something. Indeed, why should Beowulf even think that this gift giving might fall short somehow. Why should we? Shall we say, then, that the poet would suggest such magnificence both in those gifts and in the giver's intentions that Hroðgar's gesture transcends all possibility of shame or fault; that, just the converse, Hroðgar offers the greatest honor imaginable? The poet remains broadly suggestive only. But his backhanded suggestiveness becomes especially notable when we look forward and see that here he withholds identifying information about the treasures. The effect of that, which reinforces his suggestiveness, is an accord between Hroðgar's indirection and his own—a nice correspondence between the gesture dramatized and his own narrative manner at this point. He would indicate the indirection of Hroðgar's gestures partly by means of his own.

Hroðgar gives kingly objects—a clue to his intentions. His treasures, moreover, are heirlooms but, more than that, they are probably dynastic treasures—as confirmed by a later reference to Heorogar's corselet (l. 2158)—for *yrfelaf* or 'heirloom' applies in general to gifts given to Geats. At the least Hroðgar opens his personal treasure chest and gives items signifying both his warrior heritage and his past role as kingly war-band leader. By passing on those tokens to Beowulf, Hroðgar invites Beowulf to those roles for the Danes. But because he is a king and the last of a line on his father's side, he implicates the dynastic succession when he gives dynastic gifts. He does not give Beowulf the high-seat because that would require abdication, would make his gestures overt, and would exceed choosing a successor. And if, as in Anglo-Saxon laws, *freond* denotes legal responsibility, then Hroðgar also takes full responsibility for his implicit offer.[22] *Freond* usually means something like 'comrade' in *Beowulf*, but it can mean 'someone who supports or protects' (ll. 1838a, 2393a). In compound forms *freond* occurs only a few times: as supportive or protective counsel (*freondlar*, l. 2377), friendship as a bond of peace (l. 2069), and a friendly invitation (*freondlaþu*, l. 1192). Something special is meant in each case. The emphasis on friendliness in the passage in question, then, requires attention. That a king is so friendly is cause for thought.

Having given gifts, described and commented on by the poet, Hroðgar commands that Beowulf use them well—a command probably applying beyond the horses and saddle to all of the gifts. Beowulf uses the same injunction when passing on his armor, and war-band leadership, to Wiglaf. He uses it on a third occasion when giving Hroðgar's gifts to Hygelac, after telling the dynastic history of that 'war-dress' Hroðgar gave him, and after the poet tells us that the victory standard is a boar banner and the helmet one that towers in battle—information indicating the royal, dynastic character of those gifts.[23] The reference in line 2155a to Heorogar's 'war-dress' includes the sword, helmet, corselet and banner. Heorogar is the king and brother Hroðgar succeeded. And the poet elsewhere associates victory banners, gold-adorned, exclusively with dead kings. Therefore the command to 'use them well,' given its contexts in *Beowulf*, seems more than a formula accompanying all gift giving—if only because it does not accompany all such instances.[24] Its use may verbally seal Hroðgar's circumspect offer of the succession. That Beowulf uses it for Hygelac suggests that he both understands the phrase's significance and that of the gifts. He would transfer the place of honor thereby conferred to Hygelac. His use of it when speaking to Wiglaf indicates that it is a highly formal phrase that accompanies the passing on of roles.

Beowulf in Heorot, however, accepts Hroðgar's gifts without comment. It is as though they signify nothing more than the proper munificence of a ring-lord good to his word and good in his gifts. Beowulf does not even acknowledge their status as part of Hroðgar's royal patrimony. In Heorot he always ignores any suggestion that he has or will have anything but a high-minded relationship to Hroðgar and the Danes. Throughout he insists on his kinship with and retainer relationship to Hygelac. He intends no close connection with the Danes: he came to Heorot simply out of good will and performed a daring deed, with God's assistance. Only twice does he acknowledge Hroðgar's special attentions, once indirectly and once directly: his reply to Hroðgar's "adoption" speech includes the phrase, *estum miclum* (l. 958b)—a term of good will usually associated with kinship (cf. ll. 2149a, 2165b, 2378a); before meeting Grendel's mother he asks that Hroðgar act in a father's place toward him and protect his retainers, should death take him. Beowulf would acknowledge Hroðgar's gestures to that extent and in that extremity only.[25] He never acknowledges a closer tie than that of friendly fosterage. Beowulf would hold well the kinship Hroðgar offers, but only in spirit: prior to meeting Grendel's mother he would still, should she win, have his treasures and armor sent to Hygelac (as heriot, no doubt). And he would still see Hroðgar primarily as a ring-giver good in his gifts. He responds consistently only to the conventional aspects of Hroðgar's munificence. Beowulf effectively defends himself against Hroðgar's gesture by reducing it to its vehicle, by acknowledging only that.

But lest we suppose that Beowulf's later account of Heorogar's war-dress is a fortuitous invention, and that the poet means nothing special by his odd remarks or by the particular treasures given, we have Wealhþeow's responses to consider. Essentially she underlines the significance of Hroðgar's gestures: first by worrying about the adoption and Hroðgar's intentions, and then by turning graciously to Beowulf with gifts and words. Her gifts given in good will (*est*) indicate that she approaches Beowulf approvingly, but outside *comitatus* reciprocity. In her speech, moreover, she would define clearly his best relationship to the Danes generally and to her sons particularly. What she envisions is much less than Hroðgar's adoption and gifts invite. In her speech to Hroðgar she focuses first on gifts, discretely, then on the adoption. Because she would urge Hroðgar not to give Beowulf the kingdom, she avoids reference to the nature of the gifts—as though to undo the invitation. As Irving notes, there is an element of incantation in her speeches, but not for the purpose he suggests. Wealhþeow worries about the here and now, not about a possibly treacherous future involving Hroðulf.[26]

Turning to Hroðgar, Wealhþeow approves of his kindness toward the Geats:

> 'Onfoh þissum fulle, freodrihten min,
> sinces brytta! þu on sælum wes,
> goldwine gumena, ond to Geatum spræc
> mildum wordum, swa sceal man don!
> Beo wið Geatas glæd, geofena gemyndig,
> nean ond feorran þu nu hafast.
> Me man sægde, þæt þu ðe for sunu wolde
> hereri[n]c habban. Heorot is gefælsod,
> beahsele beorhta; bruc þenden þu mote
> manigra medo, ond þinum magum læf
> folc ond rice, þonne ðu forð scyle,
> metodsceaft seon.'
>
> (ll. 1169–1180)

['Receive this full cup, my lord and king, / dispenser of treasure! Thou in gladness be, / gold-friend of warriors, and to the Geats speak / with generous words, so shall a man do! / Be gracious with the Geats, mindful of gifts / that you now have from near and far. / A man said to me, that you would for a son / the warrior have. Heorot is purged, / the ringhall bright; make use of while you may / the many rewards, and to your kinsmen leave / folk and kingdom, when you forth shall go, / to look at the decree of fate.']

Gladness, generosity and graciousness are fine; Hroðgar should fulfill the titles attributed to him (*since brytta, goldwine gumena*). But Wealhþeow is disturbed. Hroðgar certainly should 'be gracious with the Geats, mindful of gifts.' But those gifts should be ones he has now from far and near.[27] Such gifts would be tribute, splendid no doubt, but ordinary. Emphatically they would not be dynastic treasures inherited from his royal predecessors. She then says that someone has told her that Hroðgar would have the warrior (Beowulf) for a son, thereby making him likely heir to folk and kingdom. She must have been on Heorot's steps when Hroðgar "adopted" Beowulf and urged that he hold well that new kinship. She does not, apparently, understand Hroðgar's intentions as other than serious. Perhaps Hroðgar's gifts leave no doubt in her mind. But, interestingly, she does not attribute the words about Beowulf as a son to Hroðgar himself. Perhaps she would separate him from his words and, instead, have him respond to Beowulf and the Geats only in a commonplace way. She especially urges him to enjoy what he has, now that Heorot is purged and Beowulf, presumably, no longer needed.

I think we can understand Wealhþeow as urging that Hroðgar not give away what, strictly considered, is not part of his function as dispenser of treasures and gold-lord of warriors, his patrimony, his kingdom and his people. Apparently to give those away, which Hroðgar may do (otherwise her worries are moot), would involve another function of his—the power to choose a successor. Wealhþeow would not have Heorot become a ceremonial hall in which a successor is chosen. It should remain simply a bright ring-hall, in which Hroðgar distributes tribute from surrounding tribes.

Wealhþeow worries so much about this that she would even offer Hroþulf in preference to Beowulf. She knows her sons are in their minority, that they could not suitably succeed Hroðgar should he die soon. She says that she knows Hroþulf will honor them. She expects that he will repay them with good if he remembers all that 'we two' previously performed to his pleasure and honor when he was a child (ll. 1180b–1187). Her qualifying remark, 'if he remembers,' indicates an awareness that Hroþulf might not do as she hopes, but I do not think she attempts here to weave peace or, with Beowulf, a defense against a future of possible treachery (the nearly universal interpretation of her remarks). Indeed, given the present reading of the gift giving scenes, it is more fitting to think of Hroðgar as attempting, in his move toward Beowulf, to forestall some future action by Hroþulf. But in any case, I think foremost in Wealhþeow's mind, whatever else she may hope for, is an intense desire to forestall Hroðgar's moves toward Beowulf. In doing so, she offers Hroþulf as an acceptable guardian should Hroðgar die soon.[28] In short, perhaps against her better sense concerning Hroþulf, she would say that Hroðgar does not need Beowulf. Perhaps the problem she knows seems better to her than one she knows nothing about.

Without waiting for a reply from Hroðgar, Wealhþeow turns to Beowulf. This is the second time in the poem that she approaches him. Previously she apparently utters what is on her mind: she thanks God that her wish has come to pass, that she can count on a warrior for help against wicked deeds (ll. 625b–628). On that occasion Beowulf responds high mindedly, iteratively. After taking the cup Wealhþeow properly offers, he asserts again that he will perform a brave deed or else see his last day alive. But prior to that remark he offers, for the first time since arriving among the Danes, the information that he resolved, while still at sea, to do the will of the Danes in the Grendel affair. Wealhþeow well likes Beowulf's words, perhaps especially for the commitment they carry on the Danes' behalf. All that she says in that meeting is paraphrased, however—as though to indicate the ordinary if sincere quality of her speech. But when we confront direct speech in *Beowulf*, the exact wording becomes especially significant. In replying to Wealhþeow on that first occasion, Beowulf speaks precisely and says something not said before. Perhaps now, during the great banquet scene, Wealhþeow will again draw out Beowulf's exact resolve in relation to the Danes—this especially given her worries.

As Beowulf sits between her two sons, Wealhþeow approaches and gives him gold rings, arm ornaments, a mail-shirt, gracious words and the largest of necklaces the poet has heard of on earth—second only to the splendor of the legendary Brosing necklace. Obviously, adorned in gold, Wealhþeow expresses her gratitude in a conventional role, one befitting her position and nobility. But she approaches Beowulf in a particular way, not as a superior in a reciprocal relationship, but in kindly good will, making a friendly invitation. She bestows the necklace upon Beowulf, implying free largesse, but to what would she invite him? Using her proper role as a peace weaver and a generous queen, she would counter Hroðgar's offer. After all, there Beowulf sits, on the bench beside her two boys: an unusual place for a guest Hroðgar perceives and honors as an exceedingly powerful man, a noble warrior. Having placed Beowulf on that bench, Hroðgar may now think of Beowulf as equal in kinship to his own boys, if only Beowulf would have it so. Thus in approaching Beowulf, especially where he is, Wealhþeow would especially seek a redefinition of the relationship between Beowulf and her boys and between Beowulf and the Danes. This becomes apparent in what she says and in the gifts she gives.

Beginning with the necklace, I think the poet's commentary, down to its 'I have heard' construction, is an attempt to convey Wealhþeow's intentions. Her queenly necklace is a splendid gesture and something like a going away gift, which is what she would have Beowulf do. She might be thought of as saying: "Here, take this as an expression of my gratitude; it should more than satisfy your desire. Take it and leave." We do not know which legends of the Brosing necklace the poet knows, but it is a necklace tainted by lasciviousness, theft, deceit and a cruel bargain or two.[29] The poet only emphasizes that Hama took it to his bright city, fleeing Eormenric's enmity (did he steal it? in what legend? is the bright city home? a monastery?). Whatever the poet refers to here, the general point suggests a pattern Wealhþeow would have Beowulf adopt. The poet also notes that Hygelac wears Wealhþeow's necklace on his death day—a comment that frames the given moment. Wealhþeow's necklace—between past and future, legend and history, happy outcome and bad—poses this question: How will Beowulf fare? Will he take the necklace and go happily or will he accept it and undertake a foolhardy venture? Thus without moving to interior thought, the poet can suggest intention and doubt on the giver's behalf, as well as contemplate contrasting fates.[30]

Having given gifts, Wealhþeow bids that Beowulf use them with good luck (perhaps may bad luck befall him otherwise):

> 'Bruc ðisses beages, Beowulf leofa,
> hyse, mid hæle, ond þisses hrægles neot,
> þeo[d]gestreona, ond geþeoh tela,
> cen þec mid cræfte, ond þyssum cnyhtum wes
> lara liðe! Ic þe þæs lean geman.'
>
> (ll. 1216–1220)

['Use this necklace, beloved Beowulf, / young man, with prosperity, and use this mail shirt, / from the people's storehouse, and flourish properly; / show thyself with strength, and to these boys be kind of counsel; I to you for that reward bear in mind.']

She has not asked him to use those gifts well. She calls him dear Beowulf as a token of her gratitude and esteem; but she also calls him a young man. She would, I think, keep a distance between Beowulf and herself, as well as between Beowulf and her people. The mail shirt is from the people's storehouse, she says. By stressing the origin of the gift, she would indicate where Beowulf should place his loyalty. Perhaps she hopes he will resolve again to work the will of the Danes, in this case especially her own. On her sons' behalf she urges that Beowulf be strong and kind of counsel, by which she means that he should relate to her boys only as a kind counsellor. For doing so she will bear rewards in mind. Here she may imply that it would be weak of Beowulf to assume more in relation to her sons. And she clearly offers her powers of reward as an incentive for the behavior she urges. Apparently Beowulf might behave otherwise; he might accept Hroðgar's offer.

Having offered a continuing reciprocal arrangement—reward for kind counsel to her boys—Wealhþeow speaks of Beowulf's stature and again wishes him prosperity. Her earlier phrase, *geteoh tela*, can be translated as 'flourish properly.' Her phrase now, *æþeling, eadig!* (l. 1225a), comes simply and after a statement that Beowulf's deeds have earned him great, wide praise from men, far and near, as wide as the sea surrounds the shore. Be satisfied with that great renown, she seems to say, and prosper in your life. Above all she would not have Beowulf prosper or flourish at her sons' expense (hence 'flourish properly' can imply an admonition). She ends her speech with what have become her most famous lines:

'Beo þu suna minum
dædum gedefe, dreamhealdende!
Her is æghwylc eorl oþrum getrywe,
modes milde, mandrihtne hol[d],
þegnas syndon geþwære, þeod ealgearo,
druncne dryhtguman doð swa ic bidde.'

(ll. 1226b–1231)

She seems to imply that Beowulf, much favored, might be unkind to her sons, that he might commit deeds against their interest and against his own present fame. Having noted his favored state, she seems bent on stating under what conditions joy shall continue. The qualities she notes as binding one earl to another, and all to Hroðgar their *mondryhten*, are ethical qualities central to reciprocity within the *comitatus*. D. H. Green has indicated the vertical reciprocity of terms such as *milde*, *hold* and *trywe* drawn from the ethical vocabulary of the *comitatus*.[31] The case for reciprocity is stronger for *hold* and *trywe* than for *mylde* ('kind,' 'generous'). However, Green cites this passage in *Beowulf* and understands the relationships proposed as both reciprocal and horizontal on the one hand and vertical on the other: the earls are *trwye* and *milde* toward each other and *hold* toward Hroðgar.[32] That at least is as Wealhþeow would have it. Because *trwye* and *milde* denote a vertical relationship, Wealhþeow's use of them in a horizontal connection indicates a special gesture: especially she would bind each earl to all others, including Beowulf, in a horizontal reciprocity in which kindness and good favor would be returned in kind. And she would separate everyone from the king, though bound to him by a vertical reciprocity. She would have Beowulf remain a much honored retainer among retainers, in a system of relationships that emphasizes an unusually horizontal reciprocity. She would not have some earls set above others.

Her appeals for kindness toward her sons are not couched in a specifically reciprocal vocabulary. *Liðe* and *gedefe* concern courteous manner and behavior only. That is why she has said that she would reward Beowulf for kind counsels. She would establish direct reciprocity between Beowulf and herself, rather than have Beowulf take on a formal relationship of any kind toward her sons. Were she to couch her invitation in a reciprocal vocabulary, thereby asking for a commitment from Beowulf (against future uncertainty, say), the only proper invitation would have Beowulf take a superior position in the relationship. He would have to assume the role of protector, a role she has assigned already to Hroþulf (if needed): she knows that gracious Hroþulf will hold her sons in honor (*arum healdan*). *Ar* implies reciprocity: reverence and obligation on the part of an inferior; gifts and favor on the part of the superior.[33] That she does not specify just which role Hroþulf will assume may indicate her attempt to finesse this dangerous situation. Perhaps Hroþulf will both protect and revere her sons. If he does either, they stand a chance of coming into their rightful inheritance. But in Beowulf's case no such reciprocity, however construed, is offered or anticipated. She would have the bench where he sits remain a place for companions, among whom the stronger and more famous shall be courteous to the others.

Following her speech, she walks to her seat. No reply is given, nor is it easy to imagine what Beowulf could say. He accepts gifts and says nothing. The poet tells us that 'There was the best of feasts, warriors drank wine.' Perhaps Beowulf's manner settles everything: he chooses by not choosing; rather he remains magnificently courteous and convivial. Having no new intention to state, he remains silent. Apparently that is the ethically pure choice, the best way out of a dilemma. Saying anything at all might raise hints that untoward thoughts have indeed crossed his mind. A denial or a rejection of some kind might not close the matter. By his silence Beowulf remains unimpeachably loyal to Hygelac and noble toward the Danes—this even when committing his life (possibly) in the service of the Danes. Yet what Beowulf says in Hygelac's hall confirms that he understands the implications of those gifts. That, I think, is clear in the distorted account he gives of banqueting and gift giving in Heorot. By that account, I think, he would avert any suspicions Hygelac has.

Beowulf arrives home in the glory of his deeds and in the splendor of his plated gold, but he emphasizes his utter loyalty to Hygelac. By his actions and speech, he would forestall any thought that now he is something other than Hygelac's beloved retainer. He even works in a reference to Hygelac on Hroðgar's behalf: that Hroðgar asked Beowulf, in Hygelac's name, to seek the dam (something Hroðgar does not do). The importance of this, I think, concerns the implications of continuing service. Beowulf only went to the West Danes and Hroðgar to help in the feud against Grendel. That he continues to help the Danes, first avenging Grendel's crimes and then avenging Æschere's death, could raise the thought that he has become more than a one time adventurer willing to help a foreign king. Beowulf continually forestalls such thinking, however; he transposes details from the two banquet scenes, perhaps to render his relationship to Hroðgar as innocent as possible. Instead of speaking about his seat with Hroðgar's sons as one given after the Grendel fight, he speaks of it as given when Hroðgar first learns of Beowulf's purpose. He moves Hroðgar's melancholy moods back, to the first victory celebration. He says that by avenging Grendel's crimes, he did honor to Hygelac's people and, as already noted, he tells Hygelac that Hroðgar asked him, by Hygelac's life, to seek the mother. How, then, could he refuse? When Beowulf introduces the treasure, he says that it was given to him after each fight, into his own use at his discretion—as though to indicate that none of it ties him to Hroðgar. Also he emphasizes treasure given to him on each occasion almost equally, hence minimizing the first occasion and making it unclear just what was given when.

He culminates his show of good will be bringing all of the magnificent treasure to Hygelac, adding the remark that on Hygelac's kindness all *still* depends. Beowulf has not become someone else's retainer. He commands that the battle standard, the helmet, the corselet and the sword be brought in. According to his recounting of Hroðgar's gift giving, it is not clear that these four were given at once. Perhaps Beowulf wishes to appear as having selected from his many treasures the very best, the most kingly, to give first. But interestingly, he has them brought in exactly in the same order they were given to him. And the poet elaborates upon them in telltale ways. Such care would not, I think, be necessary if Beowulf were not aware of their purport. They were originally presented to him as follows: the boar-adorned battle standard, suggesting that Beowulf take up the standard as kingly war-band leader; then the high helmet, the corselet and the sword. Despite his minimizing account of the first giving of treasure in Heorot, Beowulf may still feel the pull of those gifts; he may still be taking care to undo any obligation they might carry—hence the precise order in which he has them given to Hygelac (bestowed upon, or given unto) may be important. Beowulf also says that Hroðgar told him to tell the ancestry of 'this war-gear' (l. 2155): it belonged to Heorogar, who passed it on to Hroðgar, thereby passing over Heoroweard and marking succession in the dynasty. By reporting what did not happen, Beowulf indicates tactfully that he understands the significance of those gifts and that he would pass the honor they pose on to Hygelac. He ends with the phrase, 'use all well.' Essentially he deflects all to Hygelac, having it reflect Hygelac's glory and stature, not his own. He has, finally, behaved well—exactly as befits a kinsman and loyal retainer. He is absolutely true and faithful to his uncle. That is what the giving of gifts to Hygelac finally tells us: Beowulf has not compromised his loyalty to Hygelac in helping the Danes and in accepting dynastic gifts. He bestows them all upon Hygelac—*geywan*, 'bestow,' not *gyfan*, 'give'—as befits a loyal kinsman and retainer bringing tribute to his lord (only the superior in a relationship can *give* gifts).[34]

In return for Beowulf's gestures, and doubtless in recognition of what he has done, Hygelac rewards Beowulf with a subkingship. He gives Hreðel's heirloom, seven thousand hides of land, a hall and a gift-seat. He gives all he can consonant with his status: this for a prodigious warrior who would not be king of the Danes because of his loyalty to Hygelac. Moreover, giving Hreðel's heirloom—significantly, the most magnificent of all Geatish treasure swords—implicates the succession. Perhaps this is one of the gestures a king makes in designating his successor. Later, after Hygelac's death in battle, Hygd offers the kingdom to Beowulf. He chooses instead to champion Hygelac's son. He would not become

Heardred's king anymore than he would become successor to Hroðgar over Wealhþeow's sons. Rather, he would hold Heardred in friendly counsel, kindness with favor (*estum mid are*, l. 2378)—as befits an older kinsman and eventual subordinate.

By his various remarks, Beowulf has not so much affirmed his relationship to Hygelac as insisted on its continuing, uncompromised integrity. The gifts were given with no strings attached, he insists. Beowulf's actions, then, constitute a third instance of unusual gift giving in *Beowulf*. When dramatized, gift giving in *Beowulf* is not typical. Usually several intentions operate: A giver may offer a new relationship, counter an impending possibility, or clear an established relationship of possible suspicion. According to *Beowulf*, aristocratic gift giving is a highly manipulable affair, adaptable in surprising ways to unusual circumstances: to Hroðgar's desires, Wealhþeow's fears and Beowulf's probity. Gift giving is not confined to the affirmation of relationships within the *comitatus*. Thus *Widsith* and the *Maxims I* and *II* do not give a misleading picture of what is proper and good: Kings and queens should be generous, gifts returned and services rewarded. But *Beowulf* fills in that picture in surprising and complex ways. In this connection it is fair to say that *Beowulf*, in part, is a drama of gift giving, a drama involving revised intentions, startling gestures, counter gestures and a dispelling of possible implications.[35] Once we appreciate this, the formal speeches during hall celebrations suddenly become more than they have seemed. We begin to appreciate the poet for his skill as a subtle delineator of complex gestures, and we may glimpse something of the likely scope actual Anglo-Saxon gift giving had in aristocratic contexts.

NOTES

1. Schücking's comment appears in "Heldenstolz und Würde im Angelsächsischen, mit einem Anhang: Zur Charakterisierungstechnik im Beowulfepos," *Abhandlungen der Philologisch-historischen Klasse der sächsischen Akademie der Wissenschaften*, vol. 42, no. 5 (Leipzig, 1933). See especially page 41.
2. The outline of this is familiar to *Beowulf* scholars. But a few wrinkles have appeared recently. Arthur Gilchrist Brodeur, *The Art of* Beowulf (Berkeley, 1959), thinks of the gifts given in Heorot as "appropriate rewards . . . and the material pledge of Beowulf's adoption" (pp. 118–19). Edward B. Irving, Jr., *A Reading of* Beowulf (New Haven, 1968), emphasizes the necessity that gift giving be entirely public (p. 131), whereas Margaret Goldsmith, *The Mode and Meaning of* Beowulf (London, 1968), emphasizes Hroðgar's splendid gifts as symbols of social relationships that "signal the munificence of the royal giver" as well as the worth of the receiver (p. 90). Charles Donohue, "Potlatch and Charity: Notes on the Heroic in *Beowulf*" in *Anglo-Saxon Poetry: Essays in*

Appreciation (Notre Dame, 1975), pp. 23–40, thinks of Hroðgar's rewards for Beowulf's service as a "counter-gift," a potlatch (p. 26). Although intersting, none of these views is accurate. Hroðgar's gifts are not pledge gifts; gift giving does not have to be public, as is clear by Beowulf's gifts of weapons to Wiglaf; Hroðgar's splendid gifts imply an invitation rather than mainly assert his munificence; and the idea of potlatch—a system of obligatory giving and receiving—does not apply because Hroðgar would both reward Beowulf and invite a new relationship, rather than exchange within an established relationship.

3. E. Talbot Donaldson, *Beowulf* (New York, 1966), stresses treasure given as "a kind of visible proof" of a bond between lord and retainer (ix). See also Vilhelm Grønbech, *Vor Folkeæt i Oldtiden* (1909, 1912), translated into German as *Kultur und Religion der Germanen*, 2 vol. (Hamburg, 1937). Grønbech stresses the function of gifts as a bond, a concomitant of friendship. Gifts possess a kind of magic that identifies the parties, each to and with the other; gifts carry the giver's identity (*Religion der Germanen*, vol 2, pp. 47–59). For reference to this work I am indebted to Richard N. Ringler.

4. Ideas of affirmed relationship have anthropological justification in Marcel Mauss's *The Gift: Forms and Functions of Exchange in Archaic Societies*, Ian Cunnison, trns. (New York, 1967). Mauss wrote his study in 1925.

5. Mauss, *The Gift*, pp. 59–62.

6. In *Beowulf* the simple function of repayment or reward for services and services for gifts takes us away from total potlatch or at least is a variation. A reward can end a relationship; although the gifts for services arrangement of the *comitatus* approaches a total exchange: a continuing relationship in which both parties must return something for the other's gift (or service).

7. Mauss, *The Gift*, quotes *Hávamál*, verses 39, 41–2, 44–6, 48 and 145.

8. *Hávamál*, verses 41 and 42 are notable: *Vin sínom scal maðr vinr vera / oc gialda giǫf við giǫf; / blátr viðblátri scyli hǫlðar taca, / enn lausung viðlygi.* Verse 42, *Edda: Die Lieder Des Codex Regius* (Heidelberg, 1962). Verse 41 emphasizes the good of friends gladdening each other with gifts, for the friendship of gift givers lasts the longest, fate willing.

9. Gudrun's liberality comes to mind, both with Atli's treasury and his boys' lives.

10. In *Maxims I* both the king and queen shall *ærest / geofum god wesan* and the woman *rumheort beon / mearum ond maþmum, meodorædenne / for gesiðmægen symle æghwær / eodor æþelinga ærest gegretan / forman fulle to frean hond / ricene geræcan, ond him ræd witan / boldagendum bæm ætsomne* (ll. 86b–92). These lines are quoted from *The Anglo-Saxon Poetic Records*, III, *The Exeter Book*, eds. G. P. Krapp and Elliott Van Kirk Dobbie (New York, 1936, 1966). All citations from Anglo-Saxon poetry, outside of *Beowulf*, will be from the ASPR, indicated by the acronym, volume, poem and line (ASPR III, *Maxims I*, ll. 86b–92). *Maxims II* tells us, in a section on what should be or what should dwell where, that *Cyning sceal on healle/beagas dælan* (ASPR VI, *Maxims II*, ll. 28b–29a).

11. Bede, *Ecclesiastical History of the English People*, III, 14, pp. 256–58 in the dual language edition edited by Bertram Colgrave and R. A. B. Mynors (Oxford,

1969). The king in question is Oswine, bounteous to nobles and commoners. Noblemen come from every kingdom to serve him. Widsið's exchange is a gold ring given to his lord, for his lord's gift of lands. But Widsið refers to his giving as '*on æht sealde, / minum hleodryhtne*' (ASPR III, *Widsith*, ll. 93b–94a): he 'gave,' but somehow the ring came into the lord's possession also. Ordinarily *sellan* is reserved for the superior in a gift giving relationship.

12. Widsið's queen, gold-adorned and a giver of treasure, is better than any other he knows about. One of Wealhþeow's characteristics is that she is gold-adorned. And, according to *Maxims I*, Wealhþeow behaves as a queen should.

13. All citations from *Beowulf* are to the text as edited by FR Klaeber, 3d edition (Boston, 1950). However, vowel length is not indicated nor are Klaeber's carrots indicating loss of 'h.'

14. Mauss, *The Gift*, p. 59: "The nature and intention of the contracting parties and the nature of the thing given are indivisible."

15. The poet makes this clear elsewhere, as when Beowulf gives the Danish coastguard a sword—as a consequence the guard has prestige in the hall.

16. The vocabulary of gift giving suggests this as well. In *Beowulf* it is richly varied, reporting that gifts are given (*sellan*, *gifan*) or indicating the nature of particular acts: *feohgift*, *gedælan*, *beodan*, *teohhian*, *geteon*, *forgyldan*, *forgifan*, *geywan*, *leanian* and *gemæne*. *Gedælan* means 'to share' or 'distribute,' which distinguishes it from *feohgift*, an act within a martial or *comitatus* context (reward usually, or a gift for expected services). *Forgyldan*, 'to repay,' suggests a definitive (usually deadly) paying back; it is not mere reward or compensation—*leanian*. The common word for 'give,' *gyfan*, appears repeatedly as something a superior does—this in *Beowulf* and elsewhere in Old English poetry. In distinctly Christian poetry a noun form becomes God's gift or Grace. The especially interesting items in *Beowulf* concern the inferior's giving of gifts to a superior or a giving of gifts outside of a lord to retainer relationship. The key items are *geteon*, 'to confer,' 'grant,' 'bestow' and *geywan*, 'to show,' 'bestow.' Bosworth and Toller, *An Anglo-Saxon Dictionary*, give a definition for *geteon* as 'to bring as an offering or gift, contribute, bestow, give.' In this sense Beowulf has the sword hilt given unto Hrothgar, as though it were tribute already due him. *Geywan* usually means 'to show, manifest, reveal' in Old English poetry and prose. In *Beowulf* it accompanies a phrase indicating that kindness is shown, this when Wealhþeow gives gifts to Beowulf and when Beowulf gives gifts to Hygelac. It shares a sense of 'bestow' with *geteon*.

17. For a remarkable study of that vocabulary, see D. H. Green, *The Carolingian Lord: Semantic Studies on Old High German* 'Balder,' 'Fro,' 'Truhtin,' and 'Herro' (Cambridge, 1965), pp. 115–357.

18. The idea of binding in some social sense is strikingly argued, not for these lines, but in general for the poem. See Harry Berger, Jr., and H. Marshall Leicester, Jr., "Social Structure as Doom: The Limits of Heroism in *Beowulf*" in *Old English Studies in Honour of John C. Pope* (Toronty, 1974), pp. 37–79.

19. For comments on kin-right and succession, see Fritz Kern, *Kingship and Law in the Middle Ages*, trns. S. B. Chrimes (New York, 1970), pp. 12–13, especially

n. 3. On the etymology of OHG *kuning*, D. H. Green offers the following summary discussion: "Whichever of the rival etymological explanations we accept (derived from **kunjam* in the sense of *stirps regia* or in the sense of the tribe as a whole, or derived from **kunjaz*), it is clear that the basic element is nowhere that of the kinship as an institution, but instead the extended idea of 'tribe' or the idea of 'stock, lineage' (p. 317, n. 4). Fritz Kern is in essential agreement only with the idea of lineage, focusing on kin-right as belonging to *any* member of the royal family. Clearly the issue is not precise, tending toward extension and ambiguity. But close blood ties within the royal family are not necessary, nor is natural membership within a particular kinship necessary. Hrothgar offers something that falls between legal adoption and mere fraternal spirit.

20. Peter Hunter Blair, *An Introduction to Anglo-Saxon England* (Cambridge, 1956, 1959), p. 198, thinks that Bede implies that a king can choose his successor. But nowhere does Bede clearly say so. D. A. Binchy finds that an agreeable suggestion and points to designation of a successor in Welsh law from the Tenth Century. See *Celtic and Anglo-Saxon Kingship*, The O'Donnell Lectures for 1967–8 (Oxford, 1970), pp. 29–30. The Irish also chose a successor while the reigning king lived. Spenser, Binchy notes, says it is done at the inauguration of the king. But when in fact it was done for the ancient Irish, for the Welsh (who in the Tenth Century borrow *æðeling* to indicate the heir designate—Binchy, p. 29) or for the Anglo-Saxons is not known. Nor do we have any historical evidence for how it was done: the words said, the things done. Tacitus mentions that among the Germans a successor might be carried about on a shield. Gregory of Tours tells of this for Sigibert of Cologne's successor, Clovis, for Sigibert, the son of Chlothar, and also for Gundobald Ballomer. The shield probably betokens the successor's crucial function as war-band leader and defender of the folk. In each case he is not in the direct line of descent.

21. If Hroðgar sees Beowulf as king material, he is not alone (cf. ll. 860–861).

22. *Freond* is often associated with one's lord. See *The Wanderer*, ASPR III, l. 28; *The Dream of the Rood*, ASPR II, ll. 132, 144. Toller's *Supplement* to *An Anglo-Saxon Dictionary* lists a domain for *freond* as 'one who wishes well to another, favours, supports, helps.' Under that, in the laws, a *freond* is 'one who undertakes responsibility on behalf of another.'

23. For commentary on royal cult objects, particularly banners and helmets, see William A. Chaney, *The Cult of Kingship in Anglo-Saxon England* (Berkeley, 1970), pp. 121–156.

24. Notably Wealhþeow's giving does not use it. We might understand *wel* in this phrase as meaning 'rightly,' according to right.

25. For an account of *est*, drawn from the vocabulary of relationships between kinsmen, see Green, *Carolingian Lord*, pp. 248–50.

26. Irving, *Reading*, sees Wealhþeow as worried about the adoption, an action she fears will make Beowulf a rival to her sons (p. 140). But Irving mainly thinks of Wealhþeow as casting "brave fragile hopes" out "over the uncontrollable future" (p. 141). For Irving on incantation, see *Reading*, pp. 141–144. Editors

often assume a missing line somewhere around line 1174. But awkward syntax aside, Wealhðeow makes good sense.

27. *Nean ond feorran* implies tribes who pay tribute. Scyld received tribute (*gombe*, l. 10a) and apparently had many treasures from far lands (*or feorwegum*, l. 37a). Also, Hrothgar summons tribes from all over middle earth to adorn Heorot (ll. 74b–76a).

28. We can argue for dramatic irony at Wealhþeow's expense, then, but see Irving, *Reading*, pp. 141–144.

29. For a convenient summary, see G. N. Garmonsway and Jacqueline Simpson, trns., Beowulf *and its Analogues* (New York, 1971).

30. Perhaps by using stories we do not know (Hama and the necklace), or by conflating stories (Hama's flight with Brosing legends), the poet would suggest the ambiguous promise of the event. Will gifts redound or not to the good luck of the possessor?

31. Green, *Carolingian Lord*, pp. 115–215.

32. Ibid., p. 166.

33. Ibid., pp. 186–87. Neither here nor elsewhere in *Beowulf* does *ar* mean Christian mercy (cf. *arstafum*, ll. 317, 382, 485). Before Green's study, we did not well understand the ethical vocabulary of the *comitatus*, which the poet uses carefully. Usually we overinterpret that vocabulary in Christian directions, especially when applied to God: this because we draw on reformed usages in later Christian texts.

34. See notes 11 and 16.

35. *Beowulf* may be a poem about exchanges, both positive, fruitful ones and negative, destructive ones. A kind of negative exchange characterizes feuds in which life is exchanged for life (*forgyldan*) or in which life is taken without a *wergild* paid—a refusal to exchange that characterizes the greedy and niggardly.

Literary Genres in a Medieval Textbook

PAUL M. CLOGAN

Medieval attitudes toward literary genres were neither those that we find in Aristotle's *Poetics*, which had been completely neglected by medieval writers though it had actually been translated in the thirteenth century, nor those which have been elaborated since the Renaissance. The exact meaning and classification of tragedy, comedy, epic, elegy, lyric was gradually forgotten; and there was complete confusion of ancient classification in the Middle Ages. Dante considered the *Aeneid* a tragedy and his own poem a comedy because his poem ended with happiness in Paradise and was composed in the "middle" style and not in the "noble" style which was reserved for tragedy and epic or in the "humble" style which was reserved for "elegy." Also, the theoretical basis for medieval aesthetics emphasized the intellectual value of poetry and not emotion as does modern aesthetic theory. Indeed the Middle Ages developed literary genres of their own, but no Aristotle to attempt a definition or classification of them.

Yet the educators of the twelfth and thirteenth centuries, in particular Conrad of Hirsau, Alexander Neckham, and Eberhard the German developed lists of "curriculum authors" which they considered to be suitable for study in the schools.[1] They assumed the student had a solid foundation in Latin from the famous grammar of Donatus, and they compiled lists of Latin authors, including pagan and Christian writers, on the basis of their educational as well as moral value. Although there is some variation in their lists regarding the selection of advanced authors, there was general agreement on the primary texts. That young students were instructed in the same literary genres is evidenced by an examination of thirteenth and fourteenth century manuscripts of one of the textbooks containing the introductory authors. The manuscripts are as follows.

Cambridge, Peterhouse, MS. 2.1.0 (James 207), (saec. xiii–xiv).
Cambridge, Peterhouse, MS. 2.1.8 (James 215), (saec. xiii).
Lincoln, Cathedral Library, MS. 132 (C.5.8.), (saec. xiii–xiv).
London, British Library, MS. Additional 21213, (saec. xiii).
London, British Library, MS. Royal 15. A. vii, (saec. xiii).

Medievalia et Humanistica, New Series, Number 11 (Paul Maurice Clogan, ed.). Rowman and Littlefield, Totowa, NJ, 1982.

Munich, Bayerische Staatsbibliothek, MS. Monacensis 391, (saec. xiv).
Oxford, Bodleian Library, MS. Auct. F. 5. 6 (SC 2195), (saec. xiii).
Oxford, Bodleian Library, MS. Canonici Class. Lat. 72, (an. 1274).
Vatican City, Bibl. Apostolica Vaticana, MS. Barb. lat. 41 (saec. xiii).
Vatican City, Bibl. Apostolica Vaticana, MS. Pal. lat. 1573, (saec. xiv).
Vatican City, Bibl. Apostolica Vaticana, MS. Reg. lat. 1556, (saec. xiii–xiv).
Vatican City, Bibl. Apostolica Vaticana, MS. Vat. lat. 1663, (saec. xiii–siv).
Worcester, Cathedral Library, MS. F. 147, (saec. xiv).

The history and composition of this textbook, known as the *Liber Catonianus*,[2] was described briefly in 1914 in an article by Marcus Boas, the author of the standard edition of the *Disticha Catonis*. Since then there have been studies on some individual authors in this collection, but as far as I know, no study on the work as a whole. The *Liber Catonianus* became a standard medieval school reader which was used in a curriculum of instruction in grammar in the thirteenth and fourteenth centuries. This textbook originated in the ninth century and comprised only the Distichs of Cato and the Fables of Avianus. By degrees other works were included: the Latin Iliad, the Eclogues of Theodolus, the Elegies of Maximianus, the *Achilleid* of Statius, and the *De Raptu Proserpinae* of Claudian. The addition of Statius and Claudian eventually forced out the Iliad. The final structure, which first appears in the manuscripts of the thirteenth century but may have originated in the twelfth century, comprised Cato, Theodolus, Avianus, Maximianus, Statius and Claudian. These six authors remain standard into the fourteenth century with little change except that sometimes Claudian precedes Statius. In the fifteenth century this group of Latin authors evolved into *Auctores Octo*, which was printed in Lyon, by John de Prato, 31 December 1488.

In the thirteenth and fourteenth century manuscripts of the *Liber Catonianus*, which I have so far examined, the texts of the six *auctores* are frequently glossed, some more extensively than others.[3] The standardized glosses and commentaries, some of which originated in the ninth century and grew by accretion, reveal the pedagogic uses of this important textbook. The medieval glosses show the way in which the author was read and studied in the schools. Both what is and is not glossed are significant. What is necessary to point out to students reading Cato, Theodolus, Avianus, Maximianus, Statius and Claudian perhaps for the first time and the way in which it is done tells us something concrete about medieval education and medieval ideas of literary genres. Like their present-day counterparts, the commentaries preserve the transcription of the text of the author and the commentary of the medieval lecturer. When the commentaries came into the possession of university, cathedral, and monastic schools, the nature of the commentary underwent allegorical and exegetical influences. The textual and manuscript traditions of the glosses and commentaries in the *Liber Catonianus* vary, those of Claudian, Statius, and Theodolus have been examined in detail, and the influence of some of the authors has been studied.[4]

Philippe Delhaye has shown how the study of the *artes* as a study of ethics was central to the ethical pedagogy of the twelfth century.[5] At the heart of grammar, the language and literature course seems to have made room for ethical lessons collected by the *grammaticus* in the *auctores*. This combination of grammar and morality was an ancient tradition revived by medieval education and applied to pagan poets the technique of allegorical and moral explication to justify the serious study of classical authors. What Delhaye has shown about the pedagogy of the *moralis scientia* of the twelfth century seems, in the light of the thirteenth and fourteenth century manuscripts of the *Liber Catonianus* I have studied, to apply to the later period also. This medieval textbook reveals pedagogic use of poetry in the grammar lessons of the *auctores* and the continuity of this teaching technique from the ninth to the fifteenth century. Of the six *auctores*, Cato is, in terms of *grammaticus*, the one whose poetry has the greatest edifying value. The glosses, the *accessus*, and the *Dialogue super auctores* of Conrad of Hirsau invariably remind us to what part of philosophy the *Disticha Catonis* pertain: "Ethice subponitur quia ad utilitatem morum nititur."[6] Cato as an *acutores scholastici* is in effect a professor of morality.

Composed in the third century by an unknown author,[7] the Distichs of Cato offered easy and practical wisdom in a collection of philosophical maxims put in distichs or couplets. They preached proverbial wisdom— diligence in work, avoidance of quarrels, loyalty to friends, bravery in misfortune, respect of the lessons of book and of life. As a literary genre of practical ethics, the Distichs were an early and safe schoolbook in the educational training of the Middle Ages. From Remigius of Auxere's glosses in the ninth century to Erasmus' commentary in the sixteenth, the commentaries of Cato developed by degrees. In the thirteenth century the character of the teaching of Cato in the schools is represented in the relatively standardized set of glosses in the manuscripts of the *Liber Catonianus*. Richard Hazelton, who has studied these Cato glosses, notes that they "not only Christianized the pagan precepts but also established them within the system referred to as the *moralis sciencia*, a system founded on the four cardinal virtues, which the Christian culture of the Middle Ages also inherited from the pagan world and made its own."[8]

In addition to the materials of *rhetorica* and *poetria*, the Cato glosses provide patristic and scriptural quotations and allusions, definitions and classifications of the cardinal virtues, quotations from the Roman poets, and popular proverbs. Moreover, two supplements to Cato are found in some of these manuscripts: the *Facetus* and the *Cato Novus* of Martinus.[9]

The genre of the eclogue is represented by the *Ecloga* of Theodolus, a 344 line pastoral debate written for the most part in hexameters with a simple leonine rime or assonance (Leonine hexameters) in the style of Vergil's third Eclogue. The pastoral conventions of the classical eclogue are preserved: the two debators are shepherds who engage in a singing contest for a prize; a third shepherd acts as judge; and the contest ends with the coming of night. The debate is between Pseutis (or Falsehoood) who hails from Athens and Alithia (or Truth) a maiden shepherdess of the lineage of David, with Fronesis (or Prudence) the sister of Alithia as their judge. They conduct their poetical contest in quatrains, concerning the heroes of antique mythology and the Old Testament. Pseutis praises the story of Saturn and the Golden Age, and Alithia the story of Adam and Eve in the Garden of Eden; Pseutis describes Deucalion and Pyrrha and the Flood, and Alithia recounts the history of Noah and his family.

Written in the ninth or tenth century, the poem has occasionally been attributed to Godescalc or Gottschalk of Orbasis.[10] According to this theory the name Theodolus (or Theodulus) is a Greek translation of Gottschalk, slave of God. The commentaries on the *Ecloga* and the biographical dictionaries in the eleventh century assumed Theodolus to be an ancient author who had studied and written his poem in Athens before 529. In the fourteenth century, commentators considered Theodolus to be a pseudonym used by St. John Chrysostom for this work. In the sixteenth century Theodolus was associated with the fifth-century author Theodulus of Coelesyrian, and finally in the eighteenth century Theodolus was recognized as medieval Western author.

Bernard of Utrecht wrote his commentary on the *Ecloga* between 1076 and 1099 and dedicated it to Bishop Conard of Utrecht. Bernard of Utrecht is an obscure schoolmaster of the eleventh century and has sometimes been confused with Bernardus Silvestris of Tours. Little is known about the commentator except that he was a humble and modest schoolteacher in the diocese of Utrecht and that he wrote the commentary at the request of his students. It is chiefly concerned with grammatical explanations, understanding the text, and careful narration of the Biblical story or myth.

In the schools of England and Europe in the twelfth and thirteenth centuries the commentary ascribed to Alexander Neckham supplanted Bernard of Utrecht's. It is ascribed to him in two Paris manuscripts (B. N. lat. 1862 and B. N. lat. 2638), and he is identified in nine of the forty-seven manuscripts of this commentary as the source for the amazing defi-

nition of a distich. This commentary is known for its Euhemeristic interpretations of the pagan myths; Biblical stories are chiefly viewed as prefig-
urations of Christian doctrine. The commentator defines a distich (*dystigii*)
as derived from *dys-* and *stix, -igis* and refers to Ennius's book on the rivers
of the underworld.

The genre of the fable is represented by the forty-two Fables[11] in the
collection ascribed to Avianus, which were composed around the year 400
A.D. Little is known of the author except that he was a Roman fabulist
who dedicated his Fables in elegiac metre to the distinguished grammarian
Ambrosius Theodosius Macrobius. His main source was the Greek
fabulist Babrius, or probably a Latin prose version of Babrius which
Avianus expanded and versified. The style of the Fables is picturesque;
Avianus develops his models by expanding the descriptive elements; but
his copious employment of Ovidian and Vergilian phrases creates at times
a mock-heroic effect. The edificatory subject matter and the pretentious-
ness of the style of the Fables made them immensely popular in medieval
schools. They were introduced into the schools during the Carolingian
epoch, perhaps by Alcuin, who may have written a commentary upon
them. They were imitated, expanded, rendered in prose, translated and
accompanied by commentaries and introductions. The *promythia* or
epimythia, rhetorical exercises attached to the beginning or end of some of
the Fables to point the moral, were composed during the Middle Ages,
although some *epimythia* may have come from Avianus himself. Verse
paraphrases of Avianus were composed by Alexander Neckham who entitled his work *Novus Avianus*. Most of the 115 manuscripts of Avianus
contain some scholia, indicating the assiduity with which the Fables were
studied in the schools.

The fourth genre in the *Liber Catonianus* is represented by the *Elegiae* of
Maximian.[12] Written in the sixth century by a man who was of Estruscan
origin and a contemporary of Boethius, the six Latin elegies form a loosely
connected cycle in which the main theme is complaints about old age. The
dismal picture of the painfulness and weakness of old age without the
delights of youth painted by an old man expressing his own disenchant-
ment is not easy to justify as appropriate reading for a young student.
Either the author was developing an elaborate conceit after the manner of
the Roman elegiac poets or he was painting his own depressing portrait.
As a cruel *Memento mori* the elegies would indeed seem quite unsuitable for
a school text. In particular the controversial meaning of the third elegy, in
which the young poet is in love with the young girl Aquilina, involves the
role played by Boethius and Maximian's relationship to him. The elegy
states that Boethius tried to corrupt the morals of both Aquilina and the
"innocent Maximian."

Writing around 1200 Alexander de Villedieu in his *Doctrinale* (lines 3–4) objected to Maximian's elegies as trifling verses and as unsuitable as a school text, but his condemnation was not general. In 1280 Hugo of Trimberg praised the verses and sentiments of the elegies,[13] and the author of *Accessus ad auctores* noted that the intention of the elegies was to expose and warn against the foolishness of old age.[14] The subject, of course, was not new and is found in both Greek and Roman poetry. Recent studies[15] of the text suggest that the elegies contain many satirical elements directed against the sensuous character of women and that the autobiographical character of the elegies is, apart from a few minor details, far from being assured. Moreover, the antifeminist tendency in two of the satires (second and fifth elegies), which is noted in the glosses to the text in the *Liber Catonianus*, may account for Maximian's popularity in the medieval schools.

The genre of the epic is exemplified in the medieval textbook by the work of Caludianus Claudian, a Greek-speaking Alexandrian who came to Italy before A.D. 395 and became court poet under Emperor Honorius.[16] Claudian was the last notable representative of the classical tradition of Latin poetry. His unfinished epic, *De Raptu Proserpinae* (3 books), is one of two examples of that literary genre in the *Liber Catonianus*. His diction and technique bear comparison with the best Silver Age work. His gift of invective, description and epigram are offset by a tendency to over-elaboration. As early as the ninth century, Claudian was included among school authors, as shown in Ceronensis 163. The circulation of *De Raptu Proserpinae* was given great impetus from its inclusion in the *Libri Catoniani* in the twelfth and thirteenth century. It probably continued to be studied in the schools in the sixteenth and early seventeenth century. There are more than 130 manuscripts of the poem, and fifty were written before the mid-fourteenth century. The study of *De Raptu Proserpinae* in the schools created the need for a commentary to help the master in his exposition and the student in his comprehension of the poem. This need was supplied by the commentary of Geoffrey of Vitry, written not later than the twelfth century and preserved fully in a thirteenth or fourteenth century manuscript (Oxford, Bodl. lat. class. c. 12) and in abbreviated form in nine manuscripts from the twelfth to the fourteenth century. Four of these manuscripts are *Libri Catoniani* (Cambridge, Peterhouse, 2.1.8, 13th cent.; Munich, Bayrische Staatsbibliothek 391, 14th cent.; Oxford, Bodleian Library ms. Auct. F.5.6, 13th cent.; Vatican City, Barberinianus lat. 41, 13th cent.).

The commentary was composed by Geoffrey, a master at Vitry, probably near Cluny, where there was a strong teaching center in the twelfth century.[17] It begins with the usual classified introduction or *accessus*, comprising a brief biographical sketch of Claudian and general comments on the purpose and subject-matter of the poem (*vita, causa, materia, intentio, utilitas, cui parti philosophiae supponitur, titulus*). Commenting on the poem itself, Geoffrey makes the conventional division into *propositio, invocatio,* and *narratio*. Mythological allusions are fully explained, and quotations from classical authors are abundant.

Geoffrey's treatment of the poem is straightforward and is suited to a poem which was included among primary texts in a school reader. There is little treatment of philosophical matters and of critical appreciation of the unfinished epic. Claudian's poem is narrated in not too difficult Latin and was of appropriate length for a class text. Some of the variant readings in Claudian's text may indeed be simplifications designed to assist the beginning student. Geoffrey's commentary is concerned to please and interest as well as instruct. Together the poem and commentary offer a splendid example of a "school edition" and provide a glimpse into the master's schoolroom and the techniques he employed. This has special value not only for medieval and classical scholars but for all who are interested in education.

A second example of the genre of an epic in the *Liber Catonianus* is the *Achilleid* of Statius. Born in Naples, Statius learned much of his poetic technique from his father, who was himself a poet and a schoolmaster. In the writing of Statius, who flourished under the Flavian emperors, the self-conscious artistry of Silver Latin reached its peak. In many ways he is a typical product of his age and reflects the prevalent literary fashions: excessive use of hyberbole, highly colored and rhetorical episodes, lively descriptive, narrative, and "pathetic" passages. Throughout the Middle Ages, Statius was much admired and was considered as a Christian by Dante, who made him an important character in the *Purgatorio*.

Although Statius planned the *Achilleid* as an epic to cover the entire life of Achilles from his childhood in Scyros through the Trojan War, it remains incomplete, probably cut short in book two by the poet's death in September 96. One of the striking features of the text of the *Achilleid* as found in the *Liber Catonianus*, and in certain late manuscripts of the poem, is that the incomplete epic is divided into not two but five books, apparently an attempt to make the unfinished epic into a complete work.[18] As the glosses point out, Book I treats the education of Achilles by the Centaur Chiron in his cave in Thessaly; Book II his disguise in feminine garb by his solicitous mother Thetis during his sojourn at the court of Lycomedes in Scyros; Book III his infatuation with Deidameia at Scyros while the Greeks clamored for his valor at Troy; Book IV his detection by Ulysses and Diomedes when he chose armor instead of a feminine gift; and Book V his departure for Troy.

The glosses to the *Achilleid* of Statius appear to be of ancient origin, but are not connected with the commentary of Lactantius Placidus.[19] In addition to grammatical explanations, the Statian glosses also point out the ethical themes of the poem. The *accessus* notes that the author's intention is "non tantum de illis agere que Achilles egit circa Troiam, sed quomodo eum Chiron nutrivit et mater sua Thetis in aula Licomedis eum abscondidit"; *utilitas* of the epic is to know and understand the story of Achilles; and the *moralitas* is to be found in the mother's solicitude for her son and in the son's obedience to his mother.

In short, the *Liber Catonianus* was designed and used for more than mere language training. The pedagogic techniques as found in the selection of and commentaries on the six *auctores*, representing five literary genres, show the combination of grammar and morality, the study of the *artes* as a study of ethics, and the integration of the *ethica* in the *Septennium* of the liberal arts in the thirteenth and fourteenth centuries. The *Liber Catonianus* provided students of this period with not only training in Latin, but also an introduction to ethics. It is reasonable to assume that in this sourcebook of ethical precepts we have nothing more than the standard authors and literary genres which formed part of the regular course of study in the schools. In the collection of these authors and genres as well as in the type of commentary made on them, we may learn something about the character or technique of teaching ancient language and literature in the schools of the thirteenth and fourteenth centuries. An examination of the manuscripts of this standardized textbook of Latin authors suggests that literary genres were used to embody and to teach young boys the process of making moral decisions.[20]

NOTES

1. For the Latin text of the systematic list of Eberhard the German, see his *Laborintus* edited by Edmond Faral, *Les arts poetiques du XIIe et du XIIIe siècles* (Paris, 1924), pp. 358–377. On the lists of Conrad of Hirsau, Alexander Neckham, and Hugo of Trimberg as well as a discussion of the "curriculum authors," see Ernst R. Curtius, *European Literature and the Latin Middle Ages* (New York, 1953), pp. 48–54; and M. L. W. Laistner, *Speculum*, XXIV (1949), 260ff. On the educational system and texts used in medieval schools, see, for example, Astrik L. Gabriel, "The College System in the Fourteenth Century Universities," in Francis L. Utley, *The Forward Movement of the Fourteenth Century* (Columbus: Ohio State Univ. Press, 1961), pp. 79–124; Louis J. Paetow, *The Arts Course at Medieval Universities with Special Reference to Grammar and Rhetoric (University of Illinois Studies in Language and Literature)*, 3 (Urbana, Illinois, 1910), 497–628; Charles H. Haskins, "List of Text-Books from the

Close of the Twelfth Century," *Harvard Studies in Classical Philology*, 20 (1909), 76–94; ibib., *The Renaissance of the Twelfth Century* (Cambridge, Mass. 1927); H. J. Thomson, "Lucan, Statius, and Juvenal in the Early Centuries," *Classical Quarterly*, 22 (1928), 24–27; Hastings Rashdall, *The Universities of Europe in the Middle Ages*, eds. F. M. Powicke and A. B. Emden, 3 vols. (Oxford, 1936), passim; H. R. Mead, "Fifteenth Century Schoolbooks," *Huntington Library Quarterly*, 3 (1939), 37–42, P. Kibre, *The Nations in the Mediaeval Universities* (Cambridge, Mass. 1948), passim; Pierre Riché, "Recherches sur l'instruction des laics du IXe siècle," *Cahiers civil, mediév.*, V (1962), 175–182.

2. On the *Liber Catonianus*, see Marcus Boas, "De Librorum Catonianorum historia atque compositione," *Mnemosyne*, 42 (1914), 17–46; Eva M. Sanford, "The Use of Classical Latin Authors in the Libri Manuales," *Transactions of the American Philological Association*, 55 (1924), 190–248; R. Avesani, "Il ritmo per la morte del grammatico Ambrogio e il cosidetto 'Liber Catonianus,' " *Studi Medievali*, 3rd sér. 6 (1965), 475–485; P. M. Clogan, ed., *The Medieval Achilleid of Statius* (Leiden: E. J. Brill, 1968), pp. 2–17; Y. F. Riou, "Quelques Aspects de la Tradition Manuscrite des *Carmina* d'Eugène Tolède: du *Liber Catonianus* aux *Auctores Octo Morales*," *Revue d'Histoire des Textes*, Tome Deuxieme (1972), 11–44.

3. For a list of the glossed manuscripts of the *Liber Catonianus*, see P. M. Clogan, *ibid.*, pp. 11–15.

4. See Amy K. Clarke and Harry L. Levy, "Claudius Claudianus," *Translationum et Commentariorum*, Vol. 3 (Washington, 1976), pp. 141–171; ibid., *The Commentary of Geoffrey of Vitry on Claudian's De Raptu Proserpine* (Leiden: E. J. Brill, 1973); J. B. Hall, ed., *De Raptu Proserpinae* (Cambridge, 1969); Betty N. Quinn, "ps. Theodolus," *Catalogus Translationum et Commentariorum*, Vol. 2 (Washington, 1971), pp. 383–408; Arpad P. Orban, "Anonymi Teutonici Commentum in *Theoduli Eclogam* e Codice Utrecht, U. B. 292 editum (1)," *Vivarium*, 11 (1973), 1–42; (2) *Vivarium*, 12 (1974); (3) *Vivarium*, 13 (1975), 77–88; (4) *Vivarium*, 14 (1976), 50–61; and Christian Schmitt, "Zum Kanon eines bisher unedierten Theodul-Kommentars," *Germanisch-romanische Monatsschrift, Neue Folge*, 24 (1974), 1–12; R. A. Pratt, "Chaucer's Claudian," *Speculum*, 22 (1947), 419–429; R. Hazelton, "Chaucer and Cato," *Speculum*, 35 (1960), 357–380; P. M. Clogan, *The Medieval Achilleid of Statius*, pp. 1–9; ibid., "An Argument of Book I of the *Thebaid*," *Manuscripta*, 7 (1963), 30–32; ibid., "The Manuscripts of the *Achilleid*," *Manuscripta*, 8 (1964), 175–179; ibid., "Chaucer and the *Thebaid* Scholia," *Studies in Philology*, 61 (1964), 599–615; ibid., "Medieval Glossed Manuscripts of the *Achilleid*," *Manuscripta*, 9 (1965), 104–109; ibid., "Chaucer's Use of the *Thebaid*," *English Miscellany*, 18 (1967), 9–31; ibid., "Medieval Glossed Manuscripts of the *Thebaid*," *Manuscripta*, 11 (1967), 102–112; ibid., "The Manuscripts of Lactantius Placidus' Commentary on the *Thebaid*," *Scriptorium*, 22 (1968), 87–91; ibid., "The Latin Commentaries to Statius: A Bibliographic Project," *Acta Conventus Neolatini Loveniensis*, eds. J. Ijsweijn and E. Kessler, (Leuven: Leuven Univ. Press, 1973), pp. 149–157; and A. E. Hartung, "The Non-Comic Merchant's Tale, Maximianus and the Sources," *Medieval Studies*, 29 (1967), 1–25.

5. "L'enseignement de la philosophie morale au XIIe siècle," *Mediaeval Studies*, 11 (1949), 77–99; and Delhaye, "Grammatica et Ethica au XIIe siecle," *Recherches de théologie ancienne et mediévale*, 25 (1958), 59–110.

6. See Delhaye, "Grammatica et Ethica," p. 73.

7. See Marcus Boas, ed., *Disticha Catonis recensuit et apparatu critico instruit Marcus Boas: Opus post Marci Boas mortem edendum curavit H. J. Botschuyver* (Amsterdam, 1952). On the fiction of "Dionysius Cato," see, in addition to Ferdinand Hauthal, *Catonis Philosophi Liber* (Berlin, 1869), pp. xxii–xxiii, Marcus Boas, "Woher stammt der Name Dionysius Cato?" *Philogische Wochenschrift*, L (1930), no. 21, pp. 649–656, "Nachträgliches zu den Titeln Dionysius Cato und Disticha Catonis," ibid., LIII (1933), 956–960. "Medieval men called the book *Cato*, or *Caton*, or *Liber Catonis* or *ethica Catonis*."

8. See R. Hazelton, "The Christianization of 'Cato': The *Disticha Catonis* in the Light of Late Medieval Commentaries," *Mediaeval Studies*, 19 (1957), 164–167.

9. See M. Boas, *Mnemosyne*, N. S. XLII (1914), 43; and Sanford, pp. 230–240.

10. See Max Manitius, *Geschichte der lateinischen Literatur des Mittelalters*, I (1911), p. 573; J. Osternacher, "Die Uberlieferung Der Ecloga Theoduli," *Neues Archiv*, xl (1915), 331ff; Karl Strecker, "Ist Gottschalk der Dichter der Ecloga Theoduli?" *Neues Archiv* xlv (1923), 18; F. J. E. Raby, *A History of Secular Latin Poetry in the Middle Ages* (Oxford, 1957), I, 228; and Quinn, "ps Theodolos," pp. 383–408.

11. See A. Guaglianone, ed., *Aviani Fabulae* (*Corpus scriptorum latinorum Paravianum*), Turin, 1958, p. xviii; K. McKenzie and W. A. Oldfather eds. *Ysopet-Avionnet: The Latin and French Texts* (U. of Illinois Studies in Language and Literature, Vol. 5, No. 4, Urbana, 1921); and Avianus, *Oeuvres*, edited by L. Herrmann (Brussells, 1968), pp. 26–29.

12. Emil Baehrens, *Poetae Latini Minores*, 5 (Teubner, 1883), p. 316; W. Schetter, *Studien zur Überlieferung und Kritik des Elegikers Maximian* (Klassische-Philol. Studien, 36, Wiesbaden, 1970); Maximianus, *Elegie* a cura di T. Agozzino (Bologna: Silva, 1970); Maximianus, *Elegiae*, edited by R. Webster (New York, 1900); and F. Raby, *Secular Latin*, I, 124–5.

13. *Registrum multorum auctorum*, edited by K. Longosch (Darmstadt, 1942), I. 612.

14. See R. B. C. Huygens, *Accessus ad auctores, Bernard d'Utrecht, Conrad d'Hirsau, Dialogus super auctores* (Leiden, 1970), p. 25.

15. See J. Szoverffy, "Maximianus a satirist?" *Harvard Studies in Classical Philology*, 72 (1967), 351–67.

16. See Alan Cameron, "Claudian," in *Latin Literature of the Fourth Century*, edited by J. W. Binns (London, 1974), pp. 134–159; ibid., *Claudian: Poetry and Propaganda at the Court of Honorius* (Oxford, 1970); Claudian, *De Raptu Proserpinae*, edited by J. B. Hall (Cambridge, 1969); and Clarke and Levy, "Claudius Claudianus," pp. 141–171.

17. Gaufridus Vitreacensis, *The Commentary of Geoffrey of Vitry on Claudian's De Raptu Proserpine*, edited by A. K. Clarke and P. M. Giles (Leiden: E. J. Brill, 1973); and Clarke and Levy, "Claudius Claudianus," pp. 161–162.

18. See Clogan, *The Medieval Achilleid of Statius*, pp. 1–17; and ibid., "The Manuscripts of the *Achilleid*," pp. 175–179.

19. See Clogan, "The Manuscripts of Lactantius Placidus' Commentary on the *Thebaid*," pp. 87–91; and ibid., "Medieval Glossed Manuscripts of the *Achilleid*," pp. 104–109.

20. An earlier version of this article was presented at the 15th International Congress of Historical Sciences held in Bucharest in August, 1980. I am grateful to Professor A. L. Gabriel, President of the International Commission for the History of Universities, for his helpful suggestions and comments.

Medieval Tragedy and the Genre of Troilus and Criseyde

ANDREA CLOUGH

The biggest obstacle for critics in their discussions of medieval tragedy has been the limitations of medieval theorising on the subject. Attention to theory at the expense of practice has created two related problems: the impoverishment of our notions of medieval tragedy—some critics have questioned the validity of Chaucer's own description of *Troilus and Criseyde* as a "tragedye"—and a failure to trace the relationship between such tragic narratives and Renaissance dramatic tragedy.[1] Until recently, most critics were unwilling to dignify such narratives with the title of tragedy, invoking the authority of Aristotle, tacitly or otherwise.[2]

However, medieval tragedy is now becoming accepted as a genre in its own right, and the task of analysis has begun.[3] The pronouncements of medieval theorists are undoubtedly useful in this respect, particularly because they characterise the genre according to its formal elements (the conventions of social rank, subject matter, plot structure, style, and so on).

The medieval rhetoricians derived their definition of tragedy from late antiquity and the Aristotelian school.[4] But as these theorists had no knowledge of Greek drama, nor of Aristotle's *Poetics*, tragedy was transformed from a dramatic to a narrative mode, as in the definition of Donatus.[5] The term was extended to classical narratives of suffering and misfortune. Jerome refers to the *Iliad* as a tragedy, Dante's Virgil calls his *Aeneid* a tragedy, and Chaucer cites Virgil, Homer, Ovid, Statius, and Lucan as tragic writers in the envoy to *Troilus*.[6]

Such definitions undoubtedly opened up the possibility of treating medieval narratives of misfortune as formal tragedy, but there is an interval of some 800 years between these formulations of an obsolete classical genre and the fourteenth-century narratives ascribed to their influence.[7] They cannot account for the spontaneous birth of narrative tragedy in the later Middle Ages.

The major discrepancy is that medieval theory is limited to the *de casibus*, or Fall of Princes, tragedy, whereas medieval narrative is often concerned with romantic love.[8] On the theoretical side, for example,

Medievalia et Humanistica, New Series, Number 11 (Paul Maurice Clogan, ed.). Rowman and Littlefield, Totowa, NJ, 1982.

Diomedes is quite explicit: "comoedia a tragoedia differt, quod in tragoedia introducuntur . . . luctus exilia caedes, in comoedia amores, virginum raptus . . ." ("comedy differs from tragedy in that in tragedy, sorrow, exile, and ruin are represented, but in comedy, love affairs and seductions." McMahon, "Seven Questions," p. 102). So it is often denied that *Troilus* is an authentic medieval tragedy on the grounds that the subject of love is incongruous with tragedy.[9] *De casibus* narrative has little time for sexual love, but it has played a vital part within the genre as a whole, from Greek tragedy, right through into the Elizabethan and Jacobean periods. Although it is alien to the theoretical prescriptions of Aristotle, and the medieval and neo-classical authorities alike, sexual love has always been used as a subject for tragedy, as Ovid makes clear:

> omne genus scripti gravitate tragoedia vincit:
>   haec quoque materiam semper amoris habet.
> num quid in Hippolyto, nisi caecae flamma novercae?
>   nobilis est Canace fratris amore sui. . . .
> tempore deficiar, tragicos si persequar ignes,
>   vixque meus capiet nomina nuda liber.

(*Tristia*, II, 381–4 and 407–8. "Every kind of writing is surpassed in seriousness by tragedy, but this also constantly deals with the theme of love. Is there aught in the *Hippolytus* except the blind passion of a stepmother? Canace's fame is due to her love for her brother. . . . Time will fail if I tell all the loves of tragedy, and my book will scarce hold the bare names.")[10]

Ovid classifies such tales of unfortunate love as tragedies when cast in dramatic form, and his interest in them was clearly narrative rather than dramatic. If, then, tragic theory in the Middle Ages fails to account adequately for such major works as Chaucer's *Troilus* and Malory's *Morte Darthur;* if such theories are "petrified by restatement . . . devoid of vivifying inspiration," is it not possible that the interest in formal tragedy first shown by writers of the fourteenth century was stimulated rather by the tales of ill-fated love, inspired by Ovid, which enjoyed considerable popularity throughout the period?[11] Is it not possible, in fact, that the reemergence of formal tragedy, albeit in the narrative mode, was as spontaneous as that of drama, and that the critical interest of scholars like Boccaccio and Chaucer in the theory and formal conventions of the genre was one stage in the transition from tragic love tale to full-blown dramatic tragedy?

Boccaccio treated the theme of ill-fated love many times in both romance and novella form; all of these tales precede his handling of formal *de casibus* tragedy in his *De casibus virorum illustrium* and *De claris mulieribus.* [12] There is ample evidence of Chaucer's own interest in the Ovidian type of tragic love tale, from the *Book of the Duchess* on. By the fourteenth century, at least one classical tale of unhappy lovers had already been formally classified as tragedy—the story of Dido and Aeneas in Virgil's "alta tragedia." [13]

With the authority of Virgil and Dante behind him, Chaucer needed no apology for the inspiration that led him to label *Troilus* as a formal tragedy. I would like to show how Chaucer's generic labeling is useful, and not misleading, as an indication of the poet's handling of his material and his relation to a specific literary tradition. At the same time, I hope to show that this tradition of the medieval tragic narrative is more varied in type and complex in origin than has hitherto been recognised.

This revival of interest in formal tragedy in the fourteenth century, when applied to very different types of narrative, gave rise to at least three closely connected but distinct categories of medieval tragedy: the Fall of Princes, the Ovidian tale of the deserted heroine, and the romance tragedy. Boccaccio may have initiated this interest, and developed the Fall of Princes narrative under the direct influence of the scholarly definitions. His *De claris mulieribus* represents a wider range of experimentation, including: *de casibus* tragedy as applied to a female ruler, as in the tale of Zenobia (already an unconventional application of the type, which is otherwise overtly anti-feminist); the combination of *de casibus* tragedy with the Ovidian tale of the deserted heroine, as in stories of Dido and Cleopatra; and, more rarely, short tales of ill-fated lovers such as Piramus and Thisbe.

Chaucer experimented with the *de casibus* tradition in the *Monk's Tale*, and the mixed type of the *de claris mulieribus* in the *Legend of Good Women*, but in *Troilus* he developed a third type, only hinted at in Boccaccio's work: the combination of formal tragedy with full-length tragic romance. For it was Chaucer's unique achievement to perceive the analogy between the fall of lovers and the Fall of Princes, and by applying the conventions of formal tragedy to the subject of ill-fated love, he created a new type, a hybrid form, which I label "romance tragedy."

There is good evidence in the literature that medieval authors thought of the tale of tragic lovers as a literary type in its own right. For example, Chaucer grouped together classical and medieval tales of unfortunate lovers in the *Parliament of Fowls;* Boccaccio grouped his tragic love tales together into one day in the *Decameron*, and drew attention to the unity of subject matter. [14] Both recognise and comment on the type of story they are categorising in this way. It is scarcely possible to indicate here the full scope of this type or its historical development in the two centuries before Chaucer. The area is vast, much work remains to be done, and besides, a very brief introduction to the medieval tale of tragic lovers will, I hope, be sufficient for my purpose.

The theme of ill-fated love dates back to the very beginnings of the literary expression of courtly love. Indeed there was a preoccupation with suffering in love and "les récits d'amours contrariées" in twelfth-century French culture so uniform that it has been attributed to the influence of one woman, Eleanor of Aquitaine, the wife first of Louis VII of France, later of Henry II of England.[15] These tales make their appearance in romance, lay, and later in novella and ballad, and the sources are equally diverse. In brief, three groups emerge: those with classical sources (Virgil and Ovid), the Arthurian tales of Breton lays of Celtic origin, and a third, more heterogeneous group, which remains distinct from the other two by being non-legendary in material.[16]

Setting aside for the moment the Ovidian tradition of the deserted heroine, we are left with the tale of ill-fated lovers. As F. Whitehead has observed, this type of narrative as found in medieval romance shows three clear characteristics.[17] Firstly, it is based on a mutual, self-absorbing and fatal passion; the story of Tristan and Isolt is a classic example, with its symbol of the love potion (glanced at by Chaucer in *Troilus*, II, 651). Life is meaningless to the lovers without each other, and loyalty is of paramount importance:

> D'euls deus fu il [tut] autresi
> Cume del chevrefoil esteit
> Ki a la codre se perneit:
> Quant il s'i est laciez e pris
> E tut entur le fust s'est mis,
> Ensemble poënt bien durer;
> Mes ki puis les volt desevrer,
> Li codres muert hastivement
> E li chevrefoil ensement.
> 'Bele amie, si est de nus:
> Ne vus sanz mei, ne mei sanz vus!'[18]

This true love is thematically contrasted to false love, which is ephemeral.

Secondly, the love is illicit though innocent, forbidden by the patriarchal authority of husband (Lancelot and Guinevere) or father (Piramus and Thisbe). It exists in opposition to society, and to fortune, as in the *Lais* of Marie de France. As a result, secrecy is essential, whether motivated by the conventions of *amour courtois*, as in *La Chastelaine de Vergi*, fear of patriarchal authority, as in *Romeo and Juliet*, or simply demanded by the fairy lover, as in *Yonec*.

Thirdly, the most outstanding characteristic is the *Liebestod*, the double death by mischance; this convention recurs from the incident of the black sails in the Tristan story to the fatal delay of the Friar's message in *Romeo and Juliet*. The nature of their passion causes the lovers to prefer death to separation, and there are strong hints of the transcendence of death by love in the union of the lovers at death, symbolised by burial in a common tomb, or by the entwining of plants that grow from their separate graves.

The stories of Tristan and Isolt, of Lancelot and Guinevere, express the medieval sense of the tragic in simple but powerful form, in the emotional pattern of union and subsequent separation or death of the lovers. The simplest element of the tragic romance is the evocation of pity at the irrevocable ending of a love affair: the celebration of joy in love and the elegiac lament for its destruction captured in quintessential form in Marie's *Laüstic*.

Boccaccio had written tragic tales of unhappy love in the Ovidian manner; he had also applied the prescriptions of classical tragedy as understood by the medieval tradition to narratives of the Fall of Princes type. But Chaucer was the first artist to apply the pyramidal structure and philosophical colouring of formal tragedy to tragic romance. He perceived the analogy between the rise-and-fall structure of objective events in *de casibus* tragedy and the subjective movement from joy to sorrow, the pattern of union and separation, of the episodic tragic romance. Chaucer used the conventions of formal tragedy to give concentrated dramatic structure to this medieval sense of the tragic, while reinterpreting the pyramidal tragic structure as a pattern of psychological significance. It is this dual structure—subjective and objective—which Shakespeare and the Elizabethans inherited.

In analysis, then, three distinct types of medieval tragedy appear: the *de casibus*, the Ovidian tale of the deserted heroine, and the romance tragedy; but in practice there was much cross-fertilisation, which guaranteed the continuing fertility of tragic narrative in later periods. Malory's *Morte Darthur*, for example, combines the *de casibus* theme of the fall of Arthur with the romance tragedy of Lancelot and Guinevere. Henryson's *Testament of Cresseid*, on the other hand, further complicates the ironies of the Troilus story by applying to Cresseid techniques, such as the complaint, characteristic of the Ovidian tale of the deserted heroine. Experimentation continued into the Elizabethan period, with Marlowe's *Hero and Leander*, and Shakespeare's *Venus and Adonis* and the *Rape of Lucrece*. The transition to drama, with Marlowe's *Dido, Queen of Carthage* and Shakespeare's *Romeo and Juliet*, already appears less daunting, and the close links between *Romeo and Juliet* and *Troilus and Criseyde* noted by several critics bridge that gap even more closely.[19]

However, I now wish to turn to romance tragedy, and Chaucer's *Troilus* in particular, to indicate the significance of its departure from the *de casibus* concept of tragedy. Both *de casibus* and the romance tragedy show the influence of the traditional requirements of formal tragedy, and as a result, they share certain characteristics of style, plot, and philosophical tone. The plot is historical, and exhibits a distinctive pyramidal structure of ascent, apex, and descent; the peripety is usually ascribed to the agency of fortune, and (less systematically) to moral factors. The style is elevated; the narrative is felt to express the tragic philosophy of rejection of life, in the *contemptus mundi* tradition.[20]

The differences between the two are subtle but crucial variations of emphasis within this broad convention. The characters in both are of high rank, but the hero of the Fall of Princes is the king or conqueror, that of the romance tragedy the knight and lover. In the Fall of Princes, the sphere of action is public, and largely political; its major theme is the overthrow of kingdoms, as Chaucer's Monk makes clear:

> Tragediës noon oother maner thyng
> Ne kan in syngyng crie ne biwaille
> But that Fortune alwey wole assaille
> With unwar strook the regnes that been proude. . . .
>   (*Mk.T.* VII, 2761–4).[21]

The heroes of his tales are all, with the exception of Lucifer and Adam, rulers, or conquerors and men of physical prowess. In romance tragedy, on the other hand, the hero appears as knight and lover, and the sphere of action is more private, even domestic, though the events may well have public consequences. Troilus appears primarily as a lover, and Chaucer explicitly omits the presentation of him in his more public roles as prince and defender of the city; however, the fate of the city retains great importance as the background against which the more intimate drama is set.

In *de casibus* narrative, the fatal outcome is characterised as the fall from prosperity into adversity, whereas that of the love tragedy is the fall from joy into sorrow. This distinction may appear slight on first scrutiny, but its consequences are significant, for the distinction is that between public ruin and the loss of power and rank on the one hand, and private and emotional ruin, the loss of the beloved, on the other. The one concentrates primarily on external effects: physical torture, sudden death, the loss of power; to the other, the emotional effects are primary: passionate grief and despair. The gross physical horrors undergone by Antiochus and Hercules in the *Monk's Tale*, the humiliation of pride to which Zenobia is subjected, are of a very different nature from the passionate spiritual suffering of Troilus.

The greater emotional power of the romance tragedy is no doubt due to the nature of the romance itself: to the more refined psychological analysis of romance, and to its subject, which is romantic love. It is perhaps unfair to compare the *Monk's Tale* with *Troilus* in this regard, as the moral and philosophical inadequacy of the former may be intended simply as an ironic reflection on the Monk himself, but it is hard to avoid the impression that Chaucer's critique is literary as well as personal.[22] It may be significant that the Knight's strictures in his interruption of the Monk (VII, 2767–79) concern the fall from prosperity into adversity, rather than the loss of the beloved, which is more characteristic of romance tragedy; and this distinction would remove the inconsistency of his remarks in relation to his own tale, where one knight progresses from sorrow to joy, but the fate of the other is death and the irrevocable loss of the lady.[23]

The fact remains, however, that the Troilus represents an enormous gain in moral and emotional power in comparison with *de casibus* tragedy, and this must be ascribed in great measure to Chaucer's conception of the tragic lover. The protagonists of the *de casibus* are men of action, their chief attributes either physical prowess or pride and ambition. Troilus' martial achievements are greatly played down in Chaucer's retelling of the story;[24] if he is a hero, he is heroic in the quality of his passion and his capacity for suffering rather than in his deeds. Whether or not this underplaying of physical prowess had any direct influence on the Shakespearean preference for passionate and sensitive protagonists rather than the merely ambitious, romance tragedy made original contributions to the creation of narratives, as opposed to lyrical images, of passion and suffering.

The diversity in tone is due to the differences between love and ambition. Both are forms of human desire, but there is a wide discrepancy— and this is a point Robertson overlooks in applying his definition of medieval tragedy to *Troilus*—in the moral status of the objects of these desires: the Monk's protagonists lose health, position, and power; Troilus loses a lover.[25] Chaucer's romance tragedy takes over from the tragic romance one crucial element that is quite alien to the Fall of Princes theme: the centrality to the plot of human relationships.

The heroines of romance tragedy exist as moral agents in their own right, and their presence was to reshape formal tragedy as the rhetoricians understood it. To Boccaccio may be attributed the introduction of women into the male preserve of the Fall of Princes narrative, but I would argue that Chaucer was the first to realise the moral significance of this development.

Robertson's theory of *Troilus* as just another Boethian tragedy is inadequate because, for Chaucer, working from within the tradition of the tragic romance, women are not just one more worldy possession. Love of

Criseyde, or of Guinevere, cannot be reduced to mere avarice. Romance heroines are moral agents with responsibility for themselves, and to their lovers. The objects of ambition in a *de casibus* narrative lack this peculiar burden of responsibility.

Working from within the romance tradition, Chaucer inevitably brought new moral and psychological subtleties to the tragic plot, initiating a movement away from the mechanical devices of plot motivation such as fate and fortune, toward a more conscious search for human explanations. In *Troilus*, the responsibility for the tragic demise of the relationship is placed squarely on the shoulders of its participants. Criseyde is responsible for deserting Troilus, but surely Troilus is also responsible for allowing Pandarus to pressurise her into the relationship in the first place.

In integrating tragedy with romance, Chaucer set out to combine psychological causation with the external causes of downfall of *de casibus* narrative. Our awareness of the human drama coexists with our sense of fate, but is not destroyed by it. Our perception of Criseyde is modified by Troilus's final ironic reduction of her to a mere symbol of the transience of worldly possessions, but she began the narrative as an independent woman with full moral autonomy. She gradually surrenders this independence, as she yields to the blandishments first of Pandarus, then of Diomede. Nevertheless, Criseyde herself is responsible for her loss of moral individuality; in this she surely lies far beyond the scope of a figure such as Emily in the *Knight's Tale*, who must remain innocent of all the suffering she causes.

Thus Chaucer modifies the crude anti-feminism of the *de casibus* tradition, because within a love relationship both the suffering and the moral responsibility for it are shared. As romance writers, both Chaucer and Malory went against the powerful tradition of their sources, refusing to put all the blame on their heroines. Boccaccio's moral at the end of *Il Filostrato* is simply the folly of trusting women; Chaucer, on the other hand, refuses to put total responsibility for the evil she has caused onto Criseyde's shoulders, because she too suffers.

The psychological theme of suffering in love had been a common concern from the twelfth century on, but in fourteenth-century literature generally, writers explored with heightened philosophical interest the question of the relation of suffering to divine justice and the moral questions of guilt and personal failure. In *Troilus*, Chaucer complicates and deepens the subjective emotional response to suffering encouraged by tragic romance by raising such metaphysical questions about his love story. In doing so he adds one element which we now consider indispensable for great tragedy. He confronts the problem of the role of suffering in human life and in the whole cosmic scheme within the simple frame of a tale of courtship, and he does so on the authority of the *de casibus* tradition, which claimed for itself (though rarely with conviction) great philosophical seriousness in the expression of the *contemptus mundi* moral. Chaucer's chief concern is to evaluate the fate of the lovers with objectivity as well as sympathy; it is arguably the highest achievement of romance tragedy that in retelling tales of unhappy love, it brought both the imaginative empathy of romance and the moral objectivity of *de casibus* to the exploration of human suffering.

The hybrid nature of romance tragedy may perhaps throw new light on other critical problems. Chaucer does not try to hide this hybrid form in *Troilus:* he places formal *de casibus* tragedy and tragic romance in ironic relation to each other, juxtaposing the emphasis on romance in the first three books to the tragic emphasis of the last two, to create a new form which criticises both tragic romance and *de casibus* tragedy in order to present a more profound critique of human life than either had yet been capable of. Chaucer used the psychological and emotional depth of tragic romance to criticise *de casibus* tragedy, but he was equally capable of showing up the limits of tragic romance in the context of the greater philosophical austerity of the *de casibus* tradition.

For example, Chaucer plays with the convention of the double death by mischance, in *Troilus*, IV, 1184–97. The lovers are to be parted, and in their mutual commiserations, Criseyde is so overcome with grief that she faints. Troilus is unable to bring her back to consciousness, and leaps to the conclusion that she is dead. He lays out her body, and prays for her soul, then without a second thought draws his sword and prepares to follow her. At this moment he could well be Romeo or some other tragic lover, grimly resolute to die, defiant of the power of fortune to do him further hurt. Her "death" brings him to the calm beyond despair that we associate with later tragedy; but irony casts its shadow over this moment: Criseyde revives, assures him that if she had woken to find him dead she would have killed herself rather than endure life without him, and then proceeds to wheedle him back into bed.

This subtle mingling and opposing of the two types has created some confusion: *Troilus* patently does not fit the standard *de casibus* definitions of tragedy, but there is a general feeling that the poem is "tragic," if not a tragedy, and even tragic according to some "modern" understanding of the word.[26] Nevertheless, the current orthodoxy states that *Troilus* is a tragicomedy—a tragic story that is somehow transformed into a divine comedy by Troilus's transcendence of this life. Yet in the Middle Ages tragedy and comedy were incompatible—they were always defined as antithetical and mutually exclusive categories.[27] In any case, *Troilus* is not a poem where tragic catastrophe is averted, and the protagonist restored to happiness and good fortune at the end. More relevant is the convention of tragic romance, where the lovers are rewarded in death for their fidelity to love and to each other, and, in a sense, Troilus receives this reward, no less than Malory's Guinevere, of whom he tells us that "whyle she lyved she was a trew lover, and therefor she had a good ende." [28]

But the ending of *Troilus* gives a deeply ironic twist to this romantic tradition. In Chaucer's poem, the destruction of love is brought about by internal as well as external causes. It was conventional to present love in opposition to society, to fate, or fortune, but its gradual attrition by time and human weakness is rare. The *Liebestod* of the tragic romance is replaced by Criseyde's betrayal of Troilus, and his angry seeking out of death. The thematic opposition of true love to false, with its concomitant stress on secrecy and loyalty to the death, is typical of the tragic romance: how ironic that this opposition should manifest itself in the contrast between Troilus's *troube* and Criseyde's infidelity, and ultimately between divine love and all human love.

Yet the effect is anti-romantic rather than anti-tragic, since it allows Chaucer to widen the tragic implications. In tragic romance, absolute value is placed on human love: love is eternal and transcends death. In his romance tragedy, Chaucer shows the collapse of Troilus's faith in love as a metaphysical value, together with the fallacy of building such hopes on fallen human nature. Criseyde's love barely survives separation, but even Troilus's love for Criseyde does not survive his death. His laughter from the eighth sphere at the end of the poem suggests that human love is unable to sustain idealisation into a metaphysical absolute.

The poet uses a variety of techniques to map the limitations of human love—the use of comic material, especially the expanded role of the go-between; the mock-defence against the charge of anti-feminism, which plays off the idealisation of the heroine in tragic romance against the anti-feminism of *de casibus* narrative, where betrayal of the hero by his mistress was often the cause of his fall; the frustration of Troilus's wish to die for love, and the hiatus between Criseyde's desertion of him and his death on the battlefield. All these cast an ironic light on the romantic tendencies of the tragic romance, and of Troilus's own attitudes.

However, Chaucer's irony is ambivalent. In the Prologue to the *Legend of Good Women* (G. 248–72, in Robinson, pp. 489–90), the God of Love castigates *Troilus and Criseyde* as a transgression against his law; yet C. S. Lewis hailed it as a "great poem in praise of love," and his opinion has been echoed by many later critics. [29] That the celebration of love is an important element in the final meaning of the poem is virtually indisputable. Moreover, the romance tragedy retained and broadened the concept of love. Malory widens his conception of love to embrace the chivalric ideal of fraternal love, and the social bonds of feudal love between a knight and his king. Beyond the Middle Ages, Shakespeare utilises the tragedy of love in its most inclusive sense, not just in the relation of man to woman, or to fellow knights of one's own class, but the love of one human being for another. The destruction of love in its widest sense is the essence of tragedy in *Romeo and Juliet*, in *Othello*, and *King Lear*, as much as in the *Morte Darthur*.[30] Nevertheless, simultaneous with elegiac celebration of love, *Troilus* offers a stringent criticism of the romantic ideal; this is the central paradox of the poem, giving it a unique position within the tradition. The poem invites us to separate human love from its religification, to see it stripped of its metaphysical pretensions, as a beautiful ideal that is nevertheless flawed, and, by its very nature, subject to time and to death.

The final significant innovation of romance tragedy is in its presentation of the tragic philosophy of death.[31] *De casibus* tragedy often gives the impression that it is not altogether successful in subordinating its emotional involvement in worldy values to the tragic philosophy of the rejection of life: Chaucer criticises this unselfconscious naivety in his characterisation of the worldly Monk. The root of this impression lies in its treatment of death.

In *de casibus* narrative, death is usually violent, frequently unexpected, always terrible (Lydgate, *Troy Book*, I, 170, ll. 887–90). It is the final degradation in a series of humiliations,[32] and so the narrative ends in disorder—of the soul, and of the body politic—as the theorists required. Romance tragedy initiated the important change in the tragic denouement from disorder to order. As in tragic romance, death is not just expected but longed for. It becomes an attitude of the soul, a consummation devoutly to be wished.

In *de casibus* tragedy, the reader reacts either with moral condemnation of the ambition, in the spirit of pure *contemptus mundi*, or with rejection of that attitude in horror at the humiliation inflicted. But romance tragedy evokes a more ambivalent attitude toward the protagonist: both *Troilus* and the *Morte Darthur* celebrate the paradoxical nature of love as spiritual and carnal, a force for both inspiration and corruption. The effect is altogether more complex, balancing the beauty of the lover's ideal against his discovery of its inevitable degeneration in a fallen world.

The moralistic statement of the *de casibus* author is replaced by the dramatic development of the protagonist's personal disgust with life resulting from the failure of his romantic ideal. It is Troilus, Lancelot, and Arthur who express the folly of trusting to the things of this world, for they have learnt this lesson for themselves.

Their resignation to death elevates them beyond the reach of *de casibus* protagonists, to that calm rejection of life that is the philosophical colouring of tragedy. The protagonist attains spiritual tranquility and new insight; his story ends in the ordering of the soul at death, and, from Malory on, the restoration of order in the public sphere too. This element of self-transcendence is Chaucer's contribution to the genre. But where Troilus's transcendence is external and eschatological, the process becomes increasingly internalised and secularised as a part of human experience in this life. In this way, medieval tragedies include and go beyond tragedy as it is usually defined today, though it has been argued that this tendency toward apotheosis and affirmation is inherent in all tragedy: it is not alien to Aeschylean, or even Shakespearean tragedy.[33]

Romance tragedy contributes to the tradition on which the Elizabethans drew for the depiction of the experience of suffering, and the creation of human meaning out of that experience. Farnham asserts: "consciously artistic tragedy . . . does not begin until man in all seriousness brings intellectual curiosity, critical ability and, what is paradoxical and most important, even creative pleasure to the dramatic imitation of life's destructive forces" (*Medieval Heritage*, p. 2). He points out the importance of *de casibus* narrative, particularly as a significant prepartion for Elizabethan tragedy, yet he merely notes in passing the incongruity of the *Troilus* with the *de casibus* tradition. He and others have failed to discern the relevance of the popularity of *Troilus* in the sixteenth century. It provides the clue to the even greater importance of romance tragedy, not merely for its significant contributions to the concept of tragedy, but as an intellectual exploration of tragic experience that was to flower into an artistic genre in its own right.

NOTES

1. *Troilus and Criseyde*, V, 1786, in *The Works of Geoffrey Chaucer*, ed. F. N. Robinson, 2nd. ed. (Boston, 1957). I use this edition of Chaucer's works throughout. This ascription was questioned by Willard Farnham, *The Medieval Heritage of Elizabethan Tragedy* (1936; rpt. Oxford, 1956), pp. 154–9. Amongst modern critics, William Provost, in "The Structure of Chaucer's *Troilus and Criseyde*," *Anglistica*, vol. 20, 1974, finds Chaucer's term "suspect" and "confusing" (p. 18). June H. Martin, in *Love's Fools: Aucassin, Troilus, Callisto and the Parody of the Courtly Lover* (London, 1972), pronounces *Troilus* to be more comedy than tragedy (see pp. 37–70). See also n. 9.
2. Aristotle's definition of tragedy in the *Poetics* is of limited application to Greek tragedy, and should be used with even greater caution in reference to post-classical literature. A plea for a broader sense of tragedy than that of Aristotle is voiced by Paul Ruggiers, "Notes Towards a Theory of Tragedy in Chaucer," *Chaucer Review*, vol. 8, 1973, pp. 89–99 (on p. 95). Tragic narra-

tives have been denied the status of tragedy on the grounds that they are not dramatic; see the comments by Ian Robinson on the *Knight's Tale*, in *Chaucer and the English Tradition* (Cambridge, 1972), pp. 144–5. An additional argument is the assumed incompatibility of tragedy with medieval Christianity; see, e.g., John M. Steadman, *Disembodied Laughter. Troilus and the Apotheosis Tradition* (Berkeley, 1972), pp. 96–7; Donald W. Rowe, *O Love, O Charite! Contraries Harmonized in Chaucer's Troilus* (Carbondale, Illinois, 1976), esp. Ch. IV, pp. 121–51; Monica E. McAlpine, *The Genre of Troilus and Criseyde* (Ithaca, New York, 1978), who stresses throughout that the tragic qualities of the poem are limited by the fact that it is essentially comic and religious; Paul Ruggiers, "Theory of Tragedy."

3. Some of the more important discussions include: J. W. H. Atkins, *English Literary Criticism: the Medieval Phase* (Cambridge, 1943), pp. 159–61; Farnham, *Medieval Heritage*; John F. Mahoney, "Chaucerian Tragedy and the Christian Tradition," *Annuale Medievale*, vol. 3, 1962, pp. 81–99; McAlpine, *The Genre of Troilus*; D. W. Robertson, Jr., "Chaucerian Tragedy," *ELH*, vol. 9, 1952, pp. 1–37; Ruggiers, "Theory of Tragedy."

4. The continuity of late classical theories of tragedy into the Middle Ages and up to the Romantic Movement is asserted by Philip McMahon, "Seven Questions on Aristotelian Definitions of Tragedy," *Harvard Studies in Classical Philology*, vol. 40, 1929, pp. 97–198. He defends the authentic Peripatetic origin of the definitions, and their possible derivation from a lost dialogue of Aristotle, "On Poets." He denies that their evolution is due simply to ignorance of classical drama on the part of medieval writers, and argues that this tradition was more influential even on Renaissance practice than the more academic theories of the *Poetics*.

5. See McMahon, "Seven Questions," p. 102 for the definition of Donatus, and many others.

6. See McMahon, ibid., p. 128, n. 2, for Jerome; for Dante, *Inferno*, XX, 112–13, quoted in McMahon, p. 140; for Chaucer, *Troilus*, V, 1791–2. See also the definition of Boethius in *De Consolatione Philosophiae*, Book II, Prose 2, quoted in McMahon, p. 132; Chaucer's translation in Robinson, p. 331, ll. 67–72. Dante himself defines both comedy and tragedy as "genus quoddam poeticae narrationis"—"a certain kind of poetic narrative;" see Paget Toynbee, "Dante's Letter to Can Grande (Epist. X), Emended Text," *MLR*, vol. 14, 1919, pp. 278–302 (the quotation is on p. 286). Cf. the Monk's definition in the prologue to his tale (VII, 1973–82).

7. A similar conclusion is reached by Monica McAlpine, *The Genre of Troilus*, see esp. pp. 15–46.

8. Works in the *de casibus* tradition include *De casibus virorum illustrium by Giovanni Boccaccio*, ed. L. B. Hall (Gainesville, 1962); Chaucer's *Monk's Tale*, in Robinson, pp. 188–98; *Lydgate's Fall of Princes*, ed. Henry Bergen, EETS (E.S.) 121–4, 4 vols. (London, 1924–7).

9. The same doubts are often cast on *Romeo and Juliet*. Both Steadman and McAlpine are aware of the problem of the genre appropriate to secular love in

medieval literature, and the failure of the rhetoricians to discuss the serious treatment of noble lovers. See Steadman, *Disembodied Laughter*, pp. 90 ff.; McAlpine, *The Genre of Troilus*, pp. 116–19. Yet both Steadman and McAlpine conclude that love and tragedy are incompatible in literature. For McAlpine, *Troilus* falls into two "mutually exclusive" halves: Books I to III tell a love story, Books IV and V, a tragedy (p. 119). Consequently, for her there is a conflict throughout the poem between the love poet and the tragedian. Similarly, for Steadman, the historical background to *Troilus*—the fall of Troy—would have furnished legitimate material for a tragedy, whereas the erotic theme should be treated as romance, or even as comedy (pp. 89–90).

10. Both quotation and translation are taken from *Ovid with an English Translation: Tristia: Ex Ponto*, by Arthur Leslie Wheeler, in the Loeb Classical Library (New York, 1924), pp. 82–5. I am grateful to Paul Ruggiers for this reference; see "Theory of Tragedy," n. 10, p. 98. The whole passage (ll. 381–408) lists many other examples of tragedies of love. It is not improbable that Chaucer knew the *Tristia*; it is thought, e.g., that the line "For pitee renneth sone in gentil herte" (*Knight's Tale*, A, 1761) is based on *Tristia*, III, v, 31–2. See the discussion of this ascription in R. L. Hoffman, *Ovid and the Canterbury Tales* (Philadelphia, 1966), pp. 68–71.

11. Quotation from McAlpine, *The Genre of Troilus*, p. 89.

12. Boccaccio's major romances on the subject of unhappy love are: *Il Filostrato* (c. 1339), *Il Teseida* (c. 1340–2), *Fiametta* (c. 1344–6), and the *Ninfale Fiesolano* (c. 1346–9). The theme is treated in novella form in the *Decameron* (c. 1350–5) on Day IV: see esp. Tales 1, 3, and 5 to 9. The two Latin works, of course, belong to the last period of Boccaccio's life, from c. 1355 on, when he immersed himself in classical scholarship.

13. By Dante, in the *Inferno*, Canto XX, l. 113, in the *Divine Comedy*, tr. Charles Singleton, Bollingen Series LXXX (1970; rpt. London, 1971), I, 210.

14. *Parliament of Fowls*, ll. 284–94 in Robinson, p. 313, and see the relevant note on p. 794; the list includes Troilus, interestingly enough. See the introduction and tales of Day IV, esp. Tales 1, and 3 to 9, in the *Decameron*, tr. G. H. McWilliam (1972; rpt. Harmondsworth, 1978), pp. 325–42, 353–91.

15. See Rita Lejeune, "Le Rôle littéraire d'Aliénor d'Aquitaine et de sa famille," *Cultura Neolatina*, vol. 14, 1954, pp. 5–57. The reference is to p. 41.

16. The first group, deriving from classical sources, mainly from the *Aeneid*, the *Metamorphoses*, and the *Heroides*, includes: in the twelfth century, *Piramus et Tisbé*, *Narcissus*, Chrétien de Troyes's *Philomena*, the Ovidian elaboration of tales as separate episodes within the longer *romans d' antiquité*, such as the love of Dido and Aeneas in the *Roman d'Eneas* and that of Troilus and Briseide in the *Roman de Troie*; not to mention later adaptations of these, such as the retelling of the Dido and Aeneas story in Chaucer's *House of Fame* and the *Legend of Good Women*, and the *Troilus* itself. The second group, of Celtic origin, includes: several Breton lays by Marie de France, e.g., *Laüstic*, *Yonec*, *Chevrefoil*; the story of Tristan and Isolt in all its many versions, including those by Thomas of Britain and Béroul, together with its offshoot, the story of

Lancelot and Guinevere, which also passed through numerous rehandlings, including the prose *Lancelot* of the French Vulgate Cycle and Malory's *Morte Darthur*. The third group has its roots in folk oral tradition, and some examples may even be based on historical fact. It occurs in three literary forms: 1) The non-legendary lay or romance: the "Lai de Guiron," which does not survive, but is referred to in *Tristan*. See ll. 833–46 of *Le Roman de Tristan par Thomas. Poème du XIIe siècle*, ed. Joseph Bédier (Paris, 1902), I, 295. The *Lai d'Ignaure* (end of the twelfth century). *La Chastelaine de Vergi* (c. 1250). The *Chastelain de Coucy*, by Jakemon le Vinier (end of the thirteenth century).
2) The tragic ballad: for example, see the versions of "Willie and Lady Margerie" (no. 35), "Fair Janet" (no. 45), "Lord Thomas and Fair Annet" (no. 46), and "Fair Margaret and Sweet William" (no. 58), in the *Oxford Book of Ballads*, ed. James Kinsley (1969; rpt. Oxford, 1970). The latter two include the motif of the intertwining of the plants on the graves of the lovers, which may have originated from the analogy of Tristan and Isolt to the intertwining honeysuckle and hazel tree in *Chevrefoil:* see n. 18.
3) The Italianate novel: examples may be found in Boccaccio's *Decameron* (Day IV), see n. 14, Marguerite de Navarre's *Heptameron* (e.g. Tale 70, which is a version of the "coeur mangé" motif to be found in the *Lai d'Ignaure* and the *Chastelain de Coucy*), and Bandello's *Novelle* (e.g. I, 33, the Tale of Livio and Camilla; II, 9, the Tale of Romeo and Giulietta). The novella forms a direct link between this tradition and the Elizabethan drama.

17. I am greatly indebted at this point to Whitehead's observations in *La Chastelaine de Vergi*, whose account this is based on. See the introduction to *La Chastelaine*, ed. F. Whitehead (Manchester, 1961), esp. pp. xl–xlii.

18. "These two were just like the honeysuckle clinging to the hazel tree: when it has entwined itself around the tree, clinging to it and embracing the whole trunk, together they can survive; but if they are separated, the hazel tree soon dies, and the honeysuckle likewise. 'Fair love, it is the same with us: you cannot live without me, nor I without you!' " *Chevrefoil*, ll. 68–78, in *Marie de France: Lais*, ed. Alfred Ewert (1940; rpt. Oxford, 1976), p. 125. Chaucer echoes this image in *Troilus*, III, 1230–2.

19. The links between *Troilus* and *Romeo* were noted by Nevil Coghill (amongst others) in *The Tragedy of Romeo and Juliet* (London, 1950): "the most pervasive influence, one which gave Shakespeare the definable form of tragedy that we see in *Romeo and Juliet*, came from *Trolius and Criseyde*" (p. 8). Shakespeare's immediate source, Arthur Brooke's poem, is also part of the narrative tradition, and derives from Bandello's novella (II, 9). Both of Shakespeare's tragic narratives are variations on the theme of the abandoned heroine. The *Rape of Lucrece* is written in the Troilian stanza form, rhyme royal, attesting the great popularity of *Troilus* in the Elizabethan period, and the coninuity of its conventions; it may also be indebted to Chaucer's treatment of Lucretia in the *Legend of Good Women*.

20. McMahon, "Seven Questions," pp. 101–4. For discussion of the pyramidal structure, see Farnham, *Medieval Heritage*, pp. 99–101.

21. Cf. *Boece*, II, ii, 67–72, in Robinson, p. 331. See also *Lydgate's Troy Book. A.D. 1412–1420*, ed. Henry Bergen, EETS (E.S.) 97, 4 vols. (London, 1906–1935), I, 169, ll. 852–9.

22. For this theory of the tale, see Robert Kaske, "The Knight's Interruption of the *Monk's Tale*," *ELH*, vol. 24, 1957, pp. 249–68, and Mahoney, "Chaucerian Tragedy."

23. For a general discussion of the Knight's comments, see Kaske, "The Knight's Interruption."

24. Chaucer's alteration of his sources for this precise purpose are outlined by C. S. Lewis, "What Chaucer really did to *Il Filostrato*," *Essays and Studies*, vol. 17, 1932, pp. 56–75, and Farnham, *Medieval Heritage*, pp. 139 ff.

25. D. W. Robertson, Jr., "Chaucerian Tragedy."

26. See Stanley S. Hussey, *Chaucer: An Introduction* (London, 1971), p. 91. Robert Burlin finds *Troilus* "a tragedy far more universal in its resonance than would seem possible to the fragile rhetoric of medieval romance," in *Chaucerian Fiction* (Princeton, 1977), p. 126. If the *de casibus* formula has failed to explain *Troilus*, critics have been too ready to turn to medieval philosophy to fill the gap. The most popular theory is that *Troilus* is a "Boethian tragedy," despite recent demonstrations that Boethian philosophy is anti-tragic. See Theodore Stroud, "Genres and Themes: A Reaction to Two Views of Chaucer," *MP*, vol. 72, 1974–5, pp. 60–70; he also points out that Boethius deals with carnal love "briefly and contemptuously" (p. 68). McAlpine, for example, extrapolates from the *De Consolatione Philosophiae* a concept of tragedy which she claims is compatible with Boethius's philosophical system, but applies it only to Criseyde. She points out that love is incompatible with *de casibus* tragedy, that the *de casibus* concept of tragedy is reductive and shallow with respect to *Troilus*, and that Boethius is anti-tragic, but fails to challenge the old concept of medieval tragedy based on the *de casibus* formulations. She offers an unconvincing solution, splitting *Troilus* into two plots, a Boethian tragedy of moral degeneration, whose protagonist is Criseyde, and a Boethian comedy of moral improvement, whose protagonist is Troilus.

27. The use of comic (i.e. humorous) material in *Troilus* does not make the poem a comedy in the structural, or formal, sense. The inclusion of comic material in *Troilus*, or in *Tristan*, or the *Morte Darthur*, or *Romeo and Juliet*, is rather a Gothic mixing of materials than a shift of genre from tragedy to comedy.

28. *The Works of Sir Thomas Malory*, ed. Eugène Vinaver, 2nd. ed. (Oxford, 1967), III, 1120.

29. C. S. Lewis, in *The Allegory of Love. A Study in Medieval Tradition* (1936; rpt. Oxford, 1958), p. 197. Critics who concur with this judgment, by and large, include Dorothy Everett, "*Troilus and Criseyde*," in *Essays on Medieval Literature*, ed. P. M. Kean (Oxford, 1955), Ch. 5, pp. 115–38; E. T. Donaldson, "The Ending of Chaucer's *Troilus*," in *Early English and Norse Studies Presented to Hugh Smith*, ed. A. Brown and P. Foote (London, 1963), pp. 26–45; Peter Dronke, "The Conclusion of *Troilus and Criseyde*," *MÆ*, vol. 33, 1964, pp. 47–52; the view is challenged by Robertson, "Chaucerian Tragedy," and

Rober Sharrock, "Second Thoughts: C. S. Lewis on Chaucer's *Troilus*," *EIC*, vol. 8, 1958, pp. 123–37.

30. Cf. Helen Gardner, *Religion and Literature* (London, 1971), pp. 75–9.
31. For Shakespeare and the Elizabethans, violent death was the defining characteristic of tragedy. See J. V. Cunningham, *Woe or Wonder. The Emotional Effect of Shakespearean Tragedy* (1951; rpt. Denver, 1964), pp. 52–9; cf. Theodore Spencer, *Death and Elizabethan Tragedy* (Cambridge, Mass., 1936), pp. 231–40.
32. It is quite likely that the Monk's rather sadistic delight in the humiliation of his protagonists has a dramatic function as part of the characterisation, but is is also an exaggeration of the theme of the protagonist's loss of dignity central to the Fall of Princes narrative.
33. See Hegel, *The Philosophy of Fine Art*, tr. F. P. B. Osmaston (London, 1920), IV, pp. 293 ff.; Walter Kerr, *Tragedy and Comedy* (London, 1968); Gardner, *Religion and Literature*, esp. pp. 87–8.

Natural Law and John Gower's Confessio Amantis

KURT OLSSON

John Gower's frequent use of the concept of natural law in the *Confessio Amantis* provides a rich example of the adaptation of legal topoi to the literary concerns of writers in late medieval England. In his sources Gower finds various, sometimes opposed ideas about the *jus naturae*, and in the ambiguity of the term and the multiple meanings assigned to it he finds a means to organize material he has gathered for this vast encyclopedic work. That the poet knew so much about so complex a subject perhaps will not surprise us, for his knowledge of law has been a common topic in writings about him from the Renaissance to the present. But the range of his knowledge of this concept has never been adequately shown. Recent critics, though they note the importance of natural law in the *Confessio*, commonly assume that the term meant only one or two things to Gower. Such is not the case. In order to enlarge our sense of what the concept for him includes, in the first part of this inquiry I shall identify five separate meanings of the *jus naturae* that he inherited from others and introduced in his poem.

There is value in seeing the scope of Gower's knowledge of natural law, for it offers one more proof of his gift as an encyclopedic poet. But there are other reasons for examining his treatment of the subject. Gower is not content merely to collect and present ideas he has found in legal texts. He also seeks to unify them in a full, coherent statement, and this, though complicating his task, also makes the outcome more noteworthy. Some of his ideas were, even when isolated, a source of controversy in medieval legal history; when combined, they often gave rise to extended debate and increasingly complex and intricate arguments. Gower restates the problem of the *jus naturae* in the *Confessio*, and despite the range of meanings he introduces, he seeks simplicity of argument as well as richness. His fiction demands simplicity especially because its main character, the pupil Amans, is a slow and reluctant learner. But the fiction also allows Gower to enrich his statement about *jus naturale* because the education that fiction recounts is both intensive and extensive.

Medievalia et Humanistica, New Series, Number 11 (Paul Maurice Clogan, ed.). Rowman and Littlefield, Totowa, NJ, 1982.

In the frame narrative, we may recall, a frustrated Amans asks Venus to bestow on him "som wele" in his amorous suit, but the goddess insists that he first confess his sins to her priest, Genius. Through the ensuing dialogue, which occupies virtually all eight books of the poem, Genius defines the sins, tells illustrative tales, offers Amans "lore" on a wide variety of subjects, and hears the confession. On certain topics in the priest's instruction, more is offered than Amans seems to need, but on other subjects less is said than seems appropriate in a compendium of narrative and lore. The *Confessio* is not merely a fiction about a confession, not merely a collection of tales and ideas. Its various elements coalesce in the poet's sustained argument involving *jus naturale*. Little by little Genius ties together the various meanings of the *jus naturae* he has introduced, and, as slowly as Amans seems to require, he adopts in his statement other terms and concepts with equally impressive medieval ancestries: his many references to charity, grace, Fortune, and "honeste" (*honestum* or *honestas*), to name but a few of these concepts, add clarity and depth to his argument concerning the *jus naturae*. Thus, in looking at Gower particularly, we may see how the concept of natural law can affect the shaping of a long medieval poem, and how a poem can enrich the history of a major concept. After introducing the five meanings Gower assigns to the *jus naturae*, I shall describe in a second part of this paper some of the basic features of the argument of the *Confessio*.

1. The *jus naturae* as the law of animal nature. As defined by the Roman jurist Ulpian and codified by Justinian in the *Corpus iuris civilis*,

Natural law is what nature has taught all animals, for this law is not proper to the human race, but to all living beings. . . . From it descends the union of male and female, which we call marriage; from it the begetting and rearing of offspring.[1]

Natural law in this sense governs or affects every aspect of sentient life, and in the course of his poem Gower will note the extent of its influence. His first concern, however, is with sexual desire or the love that "every kinde hath upon honde" (I.11).[2] In a marginal gloss he announces this as the theme of his work and uses terms reminiscent of Ulpian to describe it: "The author intends in his present book, called the *Confessio Amantis*, to write concerning that love by which not only the human race, but also animals of whatever kind are naturally subjected."[3]

Among late medieval poets Gower is certainly not unique in applying the law of animal nature to love—Jean de Meun, for example, had done so in the *Roman de la Rose*[4]—but Gower goes beyond such writers in exploring issues raised by glossators, decretists, and theologians who comment on Ulpian's definition. One such issue was the controversy generated by

Ulpian's statement that "hinc descendit maris atque feminae coniugatio, quam nos matrimonium appellamus." How can marriage be judged a part of the *jus naturae* when the latter is what Nature has taught all animals? Gower, like writers before him who also take Ulpian's idea seriously, answers this question by a refinement. Near the end of the poem he is concerned with *conjugatio*, sexual desire, and marriage when he writes,

> The Madle is mad for the femele,
> Bot where as on desireth fele,
> That nedeth noght be weie of kinde.
>
> (7.4215–17)

In the large context of this passage—a section of the work explaining chastity—the poet resolves the specific problem of whether "habere plures est contra naturam" by making a distinction between nature as animal nature and nature as reason. Reason identifies what is fitting or "honeste" for mankind: it promotes married love and teaches a man to perceive his wife as "to him wel more honeste / Than other thing which is unknowe" (7.4224–25). The term "honeste" is basic to the developing argument of the *Confessio*. As J. A. W. Bennett has shown, Gower frequently applies it to love in marriage.[5] In a large context, however, the poet uses it to reinforce his distinction between the laws of sentient and rational nature. Thus, sexual love is a "lawe of kinde"—a law of animal nature—that must be modified to become "honeste" for mankind. This idea had been anticipated in medieval legal tradition: "Natural law of this kind has been modified through the order of distinguished and worthy [honesti] custom, namely that only certain persons, and only under the lofty celebration of marriage, may be joined." [6]

Given his knowledge of that tradition, Gower could have altered Ulpian's definition by championing "reson" and "love honeste" early in the *Confessio*. But he did not. What is unusual about his treatment of natural law is that he devotes so much space to exploring nuances of Ulpian's sense of the term. And in the fiction, what compels him to dwell on a love common to all nature instead of one proper to mankind is Amans, who seems to follow the laws of nature "al at large." Thus, on the matter of *procreatio*, for Ulpian simply a law of animal nature, Amans seems to take a firm "theological" stand, introducing a Biblical text to challenge the priest's defense of virginity:

> god to man be weie of kinde
> Hath set the world to multeplie;
> And who that wol him justefie,
> It is ynouh to do the lawe.
>
> (5.6422–25)

In legal writings the divine command—"crescite et multiplicamini"—can be treated with considerable sophistication as a law of nature, but in poetry it is often humorously misinterpreted by characters who embody *sensualitas*.[7] Such is the case in the *Confessio:* the "lawe" has little to do with Amans' specific love; it has much to do with an attitude based in animal "kinde." Gower's own stance is markedly different from that of his persona. Again it is revealed late in the poem when, through the priest Genius, he expressly accommodates natural law to reason and a generic moral probity (*honestum*), as well as to the special honesty of marriage and chastity. Genius praises Apollonius of Tyre because

> he hath ferst his love founded
> Honesteliche as forto wedde,
> Honesteliche his love he spedde
> And hadde children with his wif.
>
> 8.1994–97

Bennett, recalling the priest's "original role, in the *Roman* [*de la Rose*], as sponsor of reproduction," does not find it surprising "that Genius should link 'honest' marriage with child-bearing."[8] To the extent that Gower's priest is modeled on the Genius of the *Roman*, however, it is indeed surprising that he should celebrate honest marriage at all. In fact, the connection he makes is more adequately explained by a medieval theory of natural law that accommodates both reason and "honesty": "Procreation can be taken in two ways: according as it is an act delighting in touch, or according to the effect, namely offspring. If in the second way, . . . then it will be through reason welcoming it on account of the honor ["honestatem"] of marriage, and it will be according to natural law so defined."[9] This idea anticipates Gower's own view. In the fiction, however, Amans cannot distinguish between the two senses of procreation. In Book 5 he comically admits his desire for a "lusti touch"—*actus delectans in tactu*—and such desire, for him, is the law. Kind love is a compulsion, and he is content to follow where it leads. He certainly is not yet prepared to modify "kinde" into something "honeste."

Amans' sense that he is constrained to love by nature is a focal concern of the confession, and the priest frequently agrees that it is not in Amans' power to reject the *leges naturae:*

> kinde assaileth the corage
> With love and doth him forto bowe,
> That he no reson can allowe,
> Bot halt the lawes of nature.
>
> (3.154–57)

But this is a controversial point. Henry Kelly, in commenting on a like statement of it (3.342–59), contends that "Gower has once again let his confessor run away with himself" and suggests, following a marginal gloss in another context, that "Genius is not speaking the truth but merely the opinion of lovers."[10] The matter, unfortunately, is not so simple, for though this indeed might be the opinion of lovers, it is not therefore necessarily false or handled by Gower ironically. Whether a person "may . . . fordon the lawe of kynde"[11] is a question that late medieval poets often take seriously. In the *Roman de la Rose*, for example, Raison, without a trace of irony or humor, makes the same point as Gower's priest: natural love is irresistible in the sense that Nature forces creatures—"ausinc li home com les bestes"—to it.[12] And this power in nature was also a concern for writers other than the poets. According to some legal authorities, for example, the law of animal nature, a *motus sensualitatis*, is an instinct that, in its first impulses, is involuntary: "primi motus non sunt in nostra potestate."[13] On grounds such as these Genius is justified in excusing or showing compassion toward those who love "be weie of kinde."

But neither Gower nor his priest in the fiction is content merely to exonerate the impulses of animalic "kinde." The poet sees in man a twofold nature, a nature divided according to a principle made popular by Peter Lombard: "What may not be in common with the beasts pertains to reason; what you find in this common with the beasts, however, pertains to sensuality."[14] Gower sees those things described by the term *sensualitas*—a term he replaces with "kinde" or the "lawe of kinde"—as more ambiguous than writers like Peter would have them. A suggestion about that ambiguity that might help us in reading the *Confessio* is provided by William of Auxerre. William separates sensuality into two kinds. The first he identifies as "brute sensuality or what is moved through the manner of nature: it is irrational, and it is not subject to free will." The second he describes as

human sensuality, that is, the inferior part of the concupiscible power. The human concupiscible power indeed has two parts, the superior by which it desires eternal things, and the inferior by which it desires temporal things. And according to each part it is moved voluntarily, and therefore in it is sin and in it are the first impulses by which, in an improper manner, we desire temporal things prior to the judgment of reason.[15]

In contrast to Peter Lombard, William therefore argues that sensuality in us "non est communis cum brutis."

Genius in fact takes a double stance toward Amans that reflects ideas represented by these two writers. On the one hand, he recognizes that "kinde" may cancel choice and the judgment of reason, and in this sense Amans' love "be weie of kinde" or his sensuality is of the sort identified by Peter Lombard: it involves "quod [est] commune cum beluis." On the other hand, the priest, late in the confession especially, insists on the lover's powers of reason and choice, even in matters of love. In this sense, Amans' sensuality is of the second type identified by William: it is human sensuality, and therefore it is subject to free will. Occasionally in one statement, Genius reveals the paradox in his position, in Amans' sensuality, and finally in the animalic "lawe of kinde" itself:

> love is of so gret a miht,
> His lawe mai noman refuse,
> So miht thou thee the betre excuse.
> And natheles thou schalt be lerned
> That will scholde evere be governed
> Of reson more than of kinde.
>
> (3.1194–99)

2. The *jus naturae* as an instinct leading to charity. The "lawe of kinde" is sometimes an impulse to be tolerated or condemned, but it also can become, in Genius' view, a source of good. In a second meaning, it is a social instinct that is extended first to those related by blood—as in the *educatio* of offspring—and then to other members of the same species. Ulpian did not elaborate on this instinct as a law of animal nature, but some of his commentators did. One such author is the decretist Huguccio:

Natural law is called an instinct and order of nature by which like are propagated from like, by which like rejoice in like, by which they agree among themselves, by which they nurture their offspring, desire peace, avoid injuries, and do the other things which must be done according to sensuality, that is, natural appetite: this law seems to be nothing other than sensuality. Concerning it one learned in the law has said: natural law is what nature has taught all animals.[16]

Gower also sees this instinct as a common law that is not distinctive to mankind. He might argue, for example, that "Men schal noght finde upon his liche / A beste forto take his preie" (3.2588–89) in order to show that a "lawe of kinde" as well as reason should keep man from injuring others. In other contexts he might find in nature a principle to guide us to such virtues as gratitude and pity. "Kinde" in these contexts complements but is not identified with reason. Gower ultimately subscribes to the ancient and medieval commonplace that man is uniquely a social animal because he is endowed with powers of reason and speech, but in evolving this second meaning of natural law, he does not stress these differentiae of man. His emphasis rather falls on a law, common to sentient "kinde," that like is naturally drawn to its like and by nature is inclined to support, nurture, and protect it. Thus in the poem a number of virtues—compassion, trust, patience, and benevolence—are implicitly or explicitly presented as originating in a basic recognition of and sensitivity to a nature shared.

The poet also uses topoi concerning things naturally "set to the co-mune" or beings naturally like to promote that affection he describes in the Prologue:

> Forthi good is, whil a man may,
> Echon to sette pes with other
> And loven as his oghne brother.
> (P. 1048–50)

Gower's statement about how such love is generated out of the "lawe of kinde" develops gradually over the course of the entire *Confessio*, but many of the ideas involved had been briefly catalogued by Alain de Lille:

Consult nature: she will teach you to love your neighbor as yourself. For indeed, she has made all things common and has made a single origin for all things, because 'All mankind descends from a like beginning.' If you deny to another what you wish done to yourself, you attack nature and weaken a common law.

Impose on no one what you yourself cannot endure; offer those things to others that you wish offered to you. How can you despise your nature in another, who embrace the same thing in yourself? Every animal loves its like, so every man ought to love his neighbor. All flesh is joined to its like company.[17]

Alain's assertion, "If you deny to another what you wish done to your-self, you attack nature," is drawn from a topos also familiar to Gower. Indeed, Genius' single most important statement about the "lawe of kinde" in its second, expanded meaning is taken from it:

> he that made lawe of kinde
> Wolde every man to lawe binde,
> And bad a man, such as he wolde
> Toward himself, riht such he scholde
> Toward an other don also.
> (2.3275–79)

This divine command appeared frequently in medieval interpretations of the *jus naturae*, sometimes as a gloss on Romans 2:14: "the gentiles, who have no law, do by nature what the law prescribes."[18] When Gower introduces it, he is interested in how the emperor Constantine, before his conversion, is moved to pity, and the very context of this passage is therefore reminiscent of the text in Romans. Much later in the poem the association of this law with the *gentes* is confirmed by Gower's version of a tale he found in the *Secretum Secretorum*, where a pagan—a *magus orientalis* in the original—states his creed:

> be the lawe which I use
> I schal noght in mi feith refuse
> To loven alle men aliche,
>
> ---
>
> So schal I live in unite
> With every man in his degre.
> For riht as to miself I wolde,
> Riht so toward alle othre I scholde
> Be gracious and debonaire.
>   (7.3223–25*, 3229–33*)

The "lawe of kinde" described in the tale of Constantine is therefore not restricted to those who accept a "newe lawe" of "Cristes lore," but applies to all mankind.

Gower is also interested in how this law guides man to charity, and there is precedent for the connection he sees. Some medieval writers argue, in fact, that natural law is nothing other than charity. Peter Abelard associates the two terms, and he introduces as a link between them the divine command that also appears in Gower's narrative:

The words of natural law are those that commend the love of God and neighbor, such as these: 'What you do not wish done to you, do not do to another' (Tob. 4:16); and: 'What you wish men would do to you, do also to them' (Matt. 7:12).[19]

The tale of Constantine is an exemplum of this virtue: after the emperor enacts the law, "ferforth he was overcome / With charite" (3301–02), and "Thurgh charite thus he despendeth / His good" (3311–12).

But there is something about the natural goodness of Constantine that causes uneasiness, forcing us to ask whether Gower at this point in the poem meant by charity what a writer like Abelard meant. The emperor's *caritas* lacks some of the qualities we have come to associate with the theological virtue, and even as the virtue of a pagan, it cannot be identified with that love of God which Langland perceived in the Saracens:

Hit may be that Sarrasyns hauen • a suche manere charite,
Louye, as by lawe of kynde • oure lord god al-myghty.[20]

In Gower's poem it would appear that the "charite" treated in Book 2 as a
specific antidote for envy is distinct from the higher charity mentioned in
the Prologue and expounded in later books. By the conclusion of the work
we have a much clearer sense that love "confermed of charite" is the end of
human action and desire, and that charity is, in fact, "the vertu sovereine."
Moreover, we have a clearer sense that man's charitable deeds reflect a
fullness of his nature, including the clear judgment of his "reson."

The outcome of the tale of Constantine provides the most important
evidence that we have not yet achieved this higher love. Although the
emperor is virtuous, Genius proceeds to expose the "venym" of the famous donation: the gift betrays Constantine's confusion over goods, "of
temporal, / Which medleth with the spirital" (3491–92). This confusion
has its origin in natural law itself, as we shall discover when we advance to
a third sense of the term, developed by Gower during his treatment of
avarice in Book 5 of the poem.

3. The *jus naturae* as primitive nature. At the outset of Book 5, Gower
describes the world shortly after its creation:

> Ferst whan the hyhe god began
> This world, and that the kinde of man
> Was falle into no gret encress,
> For worldes good tho was no press,
> Bot al was set to the comune.
>
> (5.1–5)

Because of avarice, however,

> werre cam on every side,
> Which alle love leide aside
> And of comun his propre made.
>
> (13–15)

As his source for this discussion contrasting a primitive state of nature
when all goods were shared with a subsequent state marked by greed,
violence, and division, Gower could have used any of a number of authors
who developed the topos of the golden age. He could have found this
commonplace in ancient writers, of course, or in writers such as Boethius
or Jean de Meun:

riche estoient tuit egaument
et s'entramoient loiaument.
Ausinc pesiblement vivoient,
car naturelment s'entramoient,
les simple genz de bone vie.[21]

The idea of natural love among those equally rich—an idea also implied in the second meaning of the *jus naturae*—underlies Gower's statement in the opening distich of Book 5: "Obstat auaricia nature legibus."

In connecting the notion of all things possessed in common with the concept of *jus naturale*, Gower follows writers who explore the literary topos of the golden age, but he also draws upon others who share his interest in natural law. This larger tradition included the Fathers, Isidore and medieval grammarians, Gratian and the decretists, and later theologians.[22] Some of these authors, while explaining "omnium quaedam communis possessio," raise serious questions about natural law itself: either it is prescriptive and unchangeable, or it is merely descriptive of an original "state of nature." Thus, following the familiar distinction between nature *ante peccatum*—that time, to use the words of Chaucer's Parson, "er that synne bigan, whan natureel lawe was in his right poynt in paradys" [23]— and nature *post peccatum*, an author could argue that a law ordering the common possession of all things belonged to instituted nature, but it was necessarily replaced in a fallen world by laws of acquisition and restitution.[24]

Gower, in presenting the *jus naturae*, often seems to imply that it is an immutable good even in a postlapsarian world, a world "out of reule and mesure." He sometimes treats it in its second meaning as a remedy for *natura lapsa* without accounting for the fact that it has itself been vitiated by mankind. In Book 5, however, he explores this problem through an excursus which implies as background a commonplace division of man's history into three periods. As briefly stated by Hugh of St. Victor, "There are three periods through which the course of the present world runs. The first is the period of natural law; the second the period of written law; the third the period of grace. The first age extends from Adam to Moses." [25] In this framework, natural law was seen as the first remedy for original sin. The written law was then given, as one author expresses it, "to repair natural law, corrupted through sin." [26]

Gower incorporates this history in his review of the world's religions. His account begins with the worship of the pagan gods, an appropriate topic in Book 5 because avarice "est simulacrorum servitus." [27] Such idolatry is concentrated in a first period, a time after the flood when "al was torned to likinge / After the fleissh" (1616–17) and when men "the high god ne knewe, / Bot maden othre goddes newe" (1621–22). The second period begins with Abraham, who "fond out the rihte weie," proceeds through Moses, to whom God "yaf the lawe," and ends with the "baptesme of the newe lawe, / Of which Crist lord is and felawe" (1779–80), which begins the third period.

All three periods are relevant in the evolving argument of the *Confessio*, but the first period is especially appropriate in showing the weakness of natural law and the inability of man naturally to recover "thastat of Innocence." The first age is a time of worshiping nature—the stars, the elements, various beasts—and it is marked by a shifting of "thonour / Which due is to the creatour / . . . to the creature" (777–79). This age passes in a confusion over goods—which are little and which great, which are proper and which common. In a perverse way, all things are "set to the comune," and because of this, the first age provides an important lesson for Gower's contemporaries, who live at a time, as Genius remarks, when avarice has become the chief vice.[28] But this natural or fleshly age also provides a lesson for Amans because its confusion over goods is most memorably exemplified in those who serve Venus.

Rather startlingly, Genius in Book 5 attacks the goddess he serves, but there is good reason for this attack in the stance he here takes toward natural law. If in one perspective Venus, or the natural love she sponsors, might be thought generous and kind, now, in another perspective, she or that love appears prodigal, lacking in "mesure," and foolish. The goddess is condemned for committing incest with her lecherous son, for teaching "That wommen scholde here bodi selle" (1431), and for making love common:

> Sche made comun that desport,
> And sette a lawe of such a port,
> That every womman mihte take
> What man hire liste, and noght forsake
> To ben als comun as sche wolde.[29]
>
> (5.1425–29)

As good as natural law in its second meaning may be, it must be enlarged to accommodate man's proper nature, a capacity to separate good and evil, to identify virtue as a mean, to weigh goods according to their worth, and to distinguish between mere possession and love. Amans is unquestionably "kinde": he can even be said to act towards his lady as he would have her act toward him. But his love lacks measure, and it is, at last, a kind of avarice. His confusion over goods is exemplified in his comical admission of sacrilege: he ogles at his mistress in church—"al mi

contemplacion / . . . / Is only set on hire ymage" (7126–28)—and he tries
to lead her when "sche wolde gon offre" in order to "winne . . . therby / A
lusti touch, a good word eke" (7140, 7146–47). This humorous confession
of idolatry, especially because it is preceded by Genius' excursus on a
primitive law of nature and on man's enduring confusion about the value
of things, points a need not only for grace, but for discrimination and a
higher natural law than the "kinde" Amans represents. And as the historical excursus in Book 5 points the way to that law—a law of "reson"—a
cosmological excursus in Book 7 takes the reader to its threshold.

4. The *jus naturae* as cosmic order. In Book 7, where Gower treats the
education of Alexander in its three parts of Theorique, Rhetorique, and
Practique, we are introduced to images of *justitia naturalis* in the created
universe. Gower does not, in this book, introduce the goddess Nature,
present a myth of creation, use formulae such as *natura naturans* and *natura
id est deus*, or address the large cosmological issues that engaged the attention of writers on nature during centuries immediately preceding his own.
He writes literally about God as the first cause "Of which that every
creature / Hath his beinge and his nature" (7.89–90), but he devotes much
less space to theology than to those sciences that help explain the interdependence of physical things in the universe. His argument about that
universe rests on a definition of the *jus naturae* originating in writers such
as William of Auxerre, Hugh of St. Cher, and Roland of Cremona: this is
the law which is present

in the concord of all things; Plato treats such natural justice in the *Timaeus:* one
element cannot be without another; whence, as Augustine says, the judgment of
divine liberality is that a creature, of whatever kind, is compelled to offer itself.[30]

A number of assumptions underlie Gower's implied use of this definition. In the Prologue of the *Confessio* the poet introduces the principle that
whatever is, exists so long as it is one, and there he explores its negative
implication: Sin is "moder of divisioun," and because of the sin that "ferst
began in Paradis," man suffers division in his "complexioun," his body
and soul, his language, and his relationship with other men and with
nature (P.849–1052). Book 7 develops an idea of man the microcosm
reunified in himself, and it does so, first, by observing unity in the macro-
cosm. A view of the interdependence of all things in the larger universe
becomes a means of identifying what the whole man should be.

The concord of all things, in contrast to that love based on the likeness
of specific natures, assumes unlikeness. Each creature has a proper nature
that allows it to contribute to the whole, and yet, because of its natural
limitation, that creature is dependent on others whose nature differs from

its own. But this interdependence implies an element of determinism in the universe. Not only is each creature bound or ruled by its own nature, but, because it is assigned a place in the larger universe, it is also to some extent restricted by what surrounds it.[31] For Gower, the external powers which especially affect men are the "constellacion" and Fortune, and in Book 7 these are treated, respectively, in the sections devoted to Theorique and Practique.

In evolving the section on Theorique, Gower selects from his primary source—the *Trésor* of Brunetto Latini—those passages that serve to emphasize man's limitation according to "kinde." [32] Because all things are interdependent, man does not seem to be the cause of what he does. He is directed by the planets, natural things in his world, his place of origin, the elements, his complexion. This idea of the "grete world" affecting the "litel" also relates to a premise of earlier books of the poem: it would seem to reinforce Amans' sense that he is not free, that he is driven by "kinde" and natural love to do what he does. Now the coercion of "kinde"— Amans' sensuality—appears all the more unavoidable because of the powers in the external, physical world that also influence him.

But Book 7 ascends through powers. Genius also shows how man is distinct from the beasts with which he shares the "lawes of nature":

> Alle othre bestes that men finde
> Thei serve unto here oghne kinde,
> Bot to reson the Soule serveth.
>
>   515–17

And this leads the priest finally to a consideration of Rhetorique and Practique. Man is unique because of his power of speech, a power "noghwhere elles sene / Of kinde with non other beste" (1514–15). But though in one sense man by this faculty is able to transcend physical nature and its influence because language is more powerful than "alle erthli thinges" (1547–49), in another sense he is not necessarily freed by language from the bondage of his own sensuality or indeed from the potentially harmful effects of rhetoric itself, since language can be used "to evele or goode." For Genius, what is essential for man is the highest art—Practique—an art "Which stant in disposicion / Of mannes free eleccion" (45–46). And in dealing with the practical art, Gower articulates the *jus naturae* in its fifth sense—the law of "reson"—a law that provides a wholly new outlook on sensuality or the "lawe or kinde": the latter now becomes an instinct or appetite that is distinctive to man in the sense that he possesses the reason and free will to accept or reject its impulses.

5. The *jus naturae* as natural reason, the judgment of reason, free will, or the power to choose good over evil.[33] This sense of the *jus naturae* is discussed in a variety of contexts in medieval legal tradition, but the most relevant inquiries for our purposes are those that comment on Ulpian's law of animal nature even while they examine man's proper nature. Some writers who identify the law of nature with reason or powers unique to man do so by reducing Ulpian's law to the status of mere *sensualitas* or natural appetite: thus, for one author, "Certainly the beasts copulate, but they are moved by the appetite of natural impulse alone, not by natural law." [34] Other writers preserve a sense of a "law" of animal nature, but at the same time argue that this law is altered in mankind by *ratio naturalis*.[35] The two groups differ in their terminology and often in the ideas their terminology implies, but their common field of interest encourages dialogue between them, and it is against the background of such dialogue that Gower occasionally uses "kinde" to refer alternatively to natural appetite and reason:

> It sit a man be weie of kinde
> To love, bot it is noght kinde
> A man for love his wit to lese.
>   (7.4297–99)

But the difference between the groups is also important to Gower's poem. The poet prefers the distinction between an *animalic* law of nature and reason to the distinction between a *rational* law of nature and sensuality. He applies the former distinction to his treatment of marriage, for example, and thus follows a tradition of glossators who make the same distinction when they argue that marriage is ordained not by the law of nature but by reason.[36] More largely, Gower is inclined to see the good (and not merely the danger) in what others might identify as sensuality, and he can perceive more by working through the sometimes more neutral and sometimes more positive terms or concepts of "kinde" and the "lawe of kinde." This is not to disregard what we have already observed: the poet knows the limitation of the "lawe of kinde," especially in its first meaning. This law would be wholly restrictive and inviolable—a law in the narrowest sense—were it not for reason. Reason offers choices, and its laws provide a means of liberation from the constraints of "kinde." Gower's use of the distinction between an animalic law of nature and reason nevertheless gives his argument point and direction. His emphasis shifts from what binds to what frees man, and this means, at last, that the law of animal nature must be modified in the human species:

> For god the lawes hath assissed
> Als wel to reson as to kinde,
> Bot he the bestes wolde binde
> Only to lawes of nature,
> Bot to the mannes creature
> God yaf him reson forth withal,
> Wherof that he nature schal
> Upon the causes modefie,
> That he schal do no lecherie,
> And yit he schal hise lustes have.
>
> (7.5372–81)

"Reson" obviously applies to the issue of greatest concecn to Amans: if love can overturn the heart from "reson in to lawe of kynde" (8.3146), reason in its turn can order love, letting man have his pleasure, yet keeping him from lechery. But it is also clear in the last books of the poem that Gower is concerned with more than Amans' pleasure and the insight of conscience that might regulate it. The laws of "reson" influence all human behavior, and in referring to them in various contexts near the end of the poem, the poet seeks to show how man is guided in his proper nature to a happiness unknown to the "bestes."

The richness of Gower's allusions to the law of nature illustrates the extent of his encyclopedic knowledge, and it is a temptation to argue that his treatment of the *jus naturae* can explain all things in the *Confessio*. But it cannot. It cannot explain all the nuances of Gower's varied assortment of tales and excursus, all the details of the confessional dialogue, or all facets of the "vices dedly" that Genius introduces. But his treatment, nevertheless, can illumine elements in the structure of the poem that have hitherto eluded the most determined critics. It can begin to explain the rationale for the work—the large contours of the priest's argument, his varied stances, the placement of specific excursus, and the occasionally unusual choice of topics to govern the dialogue within particular books.

It is natural to assume that an inquiry into the whole of the *Confessio* should begin with its major topics, the seven capital vices. As means of discovery, they will obviously help Genius perceive the nature and extent of Amans' guilt. They will show why the lover is divided in himself, why he cannot his "wittes gete." But Genius' insights into the lover's condition are isolated, discrete perceptions framed by the species of the vices; they are not unified in a single, coherent view of Amans' inner "querele" or his history as a lover. And that, I think, is because a psychology of moral sickness, though important, is ultimately less important to the priest than Amans' cure. Through the topoi of the vices, the priest comes to present an ideal of the remade man, *homo renovatus*, and the unity of his argument and the poem rests not so much on the sins as on a psychology of regeneration.

Genius does not wholly succeed in "remaking" Amans, for the lover recovers his wits only through acts of "grace" by Cupid and Venus, but nevertheless the priest prepares Amans for conversion, and later his teaching sustains "Gower," the sometime lover:

> Homward a softe pas y wente,
> Wher that with al myn hol entente
> Uppon the point that y am schryve
> I thenke bidde whil y live.
>
> (8.2967–70)

To the end of presenting the psychology of a man made whole, Genius defines specific remedial virtues such as humility, mercy, and largess; he champions virtue in tales illustrating the vices—in good characters who are the victims of misdeeds of others. But most importantly, he proceeds in stages of the confession to identify and expound higher and higher capacities in man, and he uses his various meanings of natural law to sharpen his auditor's perception of what man, ideally, can become.

With the exception of Book 7, each of the eight books of the *Confessio* treats one of the deadly sins. The sins introduced in Books 1, 2, and 3 are the most unnatural of the seven—pride is "unkynde" (1.2565), envy "hath kinde put aweie" (2.3140), and wrath does "to kinde no plesance" (3.8)— and the person who succumbs to them variously shows his contempt for natural "lawes." Nature encourages "felaschipe," but he is self-centered and, much like a figure later introduced, "Unto non other man is frend, / Bot al toward himself al one" (5.5492–93). Men are made equal and "franchised" by a common nature (2.3263), but he scorns natural equality.[37] In nature malice is unknown (3.386–87), but he acts maliciously, exhibiting ill-will or practicing deceit. Nature "in hir lawe" commends peace (3.2264), but he, given to impatience and wrath, injures others.

In opposition to his exemplars of these sins, Genius introduces characters in Books 1–3 who are guided by the "lawe of kinde," characters who by nature display good-will toward others and seek their company. In nature, like perceives and is attracted to like. Obviously, such kindness is first manifested in the family, where it is based as much on instinct as on a formal recognition of connection by blood. In Gower's version of the legend of Constance, for example, the priest offers as a foil to the monstrous unkindness—the hatred, envy, and "bacbitinge"—of the tale's two wicked mothers, the goodness of Alle, a king drawn by natural affection to the child he has not yet recognized as his son:

> The king was moeved in his thoght
> Of that he seth, and knoweth it noght;
> This child he loveth kindely,
> And yit he wot no cause why.
>
> (2.1379–82)

On the basis of a perceived resemblance, Alle loves instinctively.

Genius returns to scenes such as these elsewhere in the *Confessio* to illumine the *jus naturae* in its second meaning: among those closest in nature we should see the greatest accord. But far more important to the priest's statement about this law is man's natural capacity to extend such love to the rest of mankind. Every man "in the balance / Of kinde [is] formed to be liche" (2.3244–45), and each should be moved by "kinde" to respond to that likeness—a shared humanity—in others. Such a response is the origin of virtue in a number of Genius' exemplars in the early books, including that of the king in Book 1 who leaps out of his carriage to embrace two very old pilgrims, and who then explains his action:

> I behield tofore my sihte
> In hem that were of so gret age
> Min oghne deth thurgh here ymage,
> Which god hath set be lawe of kynde,
> Wherof I mai no bote finde.
>
> (1.2228–32)

Such natural humility is also displayed by the emperor Constantine, for this exemplar is led to perform his acts of "charite" partly out of a recognition that "Mai non eschuie that fortune / Which kinde hath in hire lawe set" (2.3250–51). But his virtue, like that of others who observe the "lawe of kinde," also grows out of the related natural impulse "to loven alle men aliche." Genius notes a similar impulse in exemplars of compassion, trust, patience, generosity, and mercy, and he thereby shows that such virtues are interconnected "be weie of kinde." In building a case for their common origin in the *jus naturae*, Genius makes it apparent that he hopes to do more in these early books than merely identify separate remedies for the malicious sins. In Books 1–3, he reveals how men are led by nature to gather in peaceful "compaignie," establish relationships of good-will and trust, and practice not only one but many related virtues that directly benefit others.

The priest does not limit his perception of the good in "kinde" to the first three books. The *jus naturae* in its second meaning forbids treachery, malice, and violence wherever they occur, and in the later books scenes of such unkindness are common enough. Nevertheless. Genius also makes it increasingly apparent that "kinde" as a law is insufficient for man. The last sins introduced in the confession are the most difficult to moderate by "kinde" because they are in us by nature. Although a measure of what is needed to satisfy physical wants has been established in "kinde," [38] it is incapable of keeping man from loving temporal or corporal goods too much, indeed from injuring others to obtain them. What is worse, in a world of immoderate loves, "kinde" is only partially successful in teaching man benevolence. By nature man should be inclined to graciousness, trust, and a liberality modeled on the "fre largesse" of Nature herself, but as Genius points out in his excursus on religion in Book 5, this is a fallen world where man's longings "after the fleissh" often lead to mistrust and deception. To the extent that a nature remains innocent, it becomes prey to those who are "unkinde." Earlier in the poem one exemplar might well assert to another:

> For hou so this fortune falle,
> Yit stant mi trust aboven alle,
> For the mercy which I now finde,
> That thou wolt after this be kinde.
>   (3.2703–06)

But in Book 5 the priest enlarges on what he only hints at earlier, that those who are "kinde" are vulnerable either to their own sensuality or to the unkindness of others.

The poet finally sees man released from the bondage of vitiated nature by grace, but in the last three confessional books—Books 5, 6, and 8—he also focuses our attention on "reson" (the *jus naturae* in its fifth meaning) as a key element in man's regeneration. Genius suggests in many places, and not only near the end of the confession, that "reson" must complement "kinde" as a law for the human species. In the later books, however, he stresses the effects of reason in tempering man's sensual appetite, and given the nature of avarice, gluttony, and lechery—the last three sins—it is only appropriate that he should do so. By these sins man not only falls prey to fleshly desire, but also loses what his proper nature should provide: through avarice, he rejects "the stiere / Of resonable governance" (5.2226–27); through gluttony, he forgets "Or he be man, or he be beste" (6.47); and through lechery, he finally descends to the likeness of a beast, indulging his appetite as a "Stalon in the Fennes" (8.160). Reason and its "lawes" clearly supply natural remedies for these sins.

Genius also sees other powers in reason. As in Books 1, 2, and 3 he discovered a good in the "lawe of kinde" independent of its power to offset the sins of malice, so in Books 5, 6, and 8, he identifies a good in "reson" independent of its power to remedy the sins of "nature." Not only through these later books, but through Books 4 and 7 as well, he hopes to show what man can achieve by "reson" once he is freed from the worst elements in his sensual "kinde." This prospect appears in the last three confessional books; it is offered in its greatest breadth in Book 7, a book devoted in its entirety to Alexander's education in Philosophie; but it begins to appear in Book 4.

Book 4, the middle confessional book, provides a significant transition in Genius' argument. Whereas in the course of treating the seven vices, the confessor gradually shifts his emphasis from remedies grounded in a "lawe of kinde" to remedies grounded in "reson," in handling sloth in Book 4, he applies both laws to Amans' condition and offers as his judgment what seems to be, at first glance, a contradiction. On the one hand, he commends Amans' busyness as a lover: he is not one of the slothful who deny their amorous nature (the *jus naturae* in its first meaning). On the other hand, the priest suggests that in another way Amans is slow: drawn to his mistress by "kinde," he neglects great goods, loving them too little. These are goods that "reson" can identify, and the priest, now starting to describe them, initiates a phase of his argument that leads eventually into Book 7.

First Genius repeats his earlier claim that all men are equal at birth:

> Of mannes berthe the mesure,
> It is so comun to nature,
> That it yifth every man aliche.
> (4.2231–33)

But now the priest is also interested in what distinguishes men, and that, he notes, is a function of labor: virtue makes man "gentil," and "studie" makes him wise. In a digression on inventors, Genius introduces the founders of "mechanical" arts such as cookery, wool-making, and hunting, as well as the founders of portraiture, music, and the science of physiognomy. He devotes most of this excursus, however, to the inventors of alchemy and the verbal arts. These two regions of human knowing represent fields more fully expounded in the later description of Alexander's education: the introduction of the "craft" of alchemy, "wroght be weie of kinde" (4.2508), anticipates the emphasis on corporeal things in Theorique, and the introduction of the verbal arts obviously foreshadows the later treatment of Rhetorique. What is conspicuous by its absence is a counterpart to Practique: instead of showing how inventors apply reason to deeds, as they have applied it to "kinde" and words, Genius introduces as his sole instance of the practical art the *ars amatoria*, specifically the "remedies" described by Ovid; Amans, who still has much to learn, will read Ovid's books "if thei mihte spede / Mi love" (2675–76). In Book 7, this practical art will be displaced by another which is more clearly grounded in the law of "reson" and which, to use Ciceronian terms adopted by Genius, is more profitable because more honest.

Elsewhere in Book 4, however, Genius begins to separate loves by the criterion of honesty, which for him means something quite unlike that introduced in a courtly "ars honeste amandi." The tale of Rosiphelee, one of the best in the entire collection, reveals the unkindness of a woman who defies love, but this story is followed by the tale of Jephthah's daughter, a woman who scorns marriage. This juxtaposition of tales allows Genius to contrast marriage—"ilke feste, / Wherof the love is al honeste" (1483–84)—with love of "paramours" or love by "Cupides lawe," which is full "Of janglinge and of fals Envie, / Fulofte medlid with disese" (1474–75). In Book 4, more largely, charity (a sidenote identifies it: "Nota de amore caritatis") takes on its fuller meaning as a love that

> above alle othre is hed,
> Which hath the vertus forto lede,
> Of al that unto mannes dede
> Belongeth.
>
> (2326–29)

Amans' labor, according to which, he tells us, "I serve, I bowe, I loke, I loute" (1169), contrasts with deeds issuing from this higher love, and his repeated failure leads him to the final point of sloth, Tristesce.

Book 4 is important not only because it begins to reveal what "reson" can discover, but because its defense of reason is juxtaposed with a defense of sensual "kinde": the conflict between these two positions gives rise to a key question about Genius' treatment of Amans that must be answered before the confession ends. Although the priest here commends "reson" and charity, he also tells Amans not to yield to despair by giving up his suit too quickly: the lover cannot know "what chance schal betyde" (1779) or when "love his grace wol . . . sende" (3504). How can Genius attack "Cupides lawe" when he also defends it by encouraging Amans to place his trust in chance or the grace of Love? To be sure, he here has the dual obligation of keeping Amans from despair and at the same time showing him that in "reson," charity, and grace—even the grace of Love—he may discover his escape from "kinde" and the ill-fate he finds so difficult to bear. But the problem is a deeper one: it originates in the *jus naturae*, and in the *jus naturae* Genius finds its solution.

As a servant of Venus, Genius accepts Amans' love as natural because it follows the *jus naturae* in its first sense. As a priest inclined to virtue and reason, however, he judges that same love in Amans to be unnatural because it violates the *jus naturae* in its fifth sense. So long as we assume a logic of exclusion, this is a contradiction: Genius cannot have it both ways. But the logic of his argument is inclusive. Even after he has finished presenting his case for "reson," Genius still judges the law of animal nature to be a good in the human species provided it is adapted to and ordered by higher laws. Late in the poem the priest rejects Amans' *claim* of kindness because the lover identifies nature exclusively with sensual appetite and pleasure and thus divorces it from the *jus naturae* in all its other senses. It is not Genius' intent to reject "kinde" love itself, but to enlarge Amans' perception of it. By gradually adding new meanings to "nature," he shows that such love can be something more than the mere observance of "Cupides lawe," and in enlarging the concept of natural law to its fullest meaning, he shows how love "be weie of kinde" can become most natural for man.

This instruction in love follows the pattern of the confession as a whole, where the priest, we have noted, bases remedies for the principal vices on progressively larger and more complex senses of nature. In that process of transforming perception, he often lifts terms to higher meanings, and this is what he does with those words of encouragement he utters in Book 4. In later books the priest still consoles Amans: "Mi Sone, bot abyd thin ende, / Per cas al mai to goode wende" (5.4565–66), he states in Book 5, and in his encouragement, he mixes terms of chance or Fortune with terms of grace: "Of time which thou hast despended, / It mai with grace been amended" (5.7813–14), and a few lines later, he finds an analogy in the sudden change from "Wynter wast and bare" to summer:

> And soudeinliche ayein his floures
> The Somer hapneth and is riche:
> And so per cas thi graces liche.
> (7830–32)

Amans is likely to think of sudden change as success in love's cause, but the confessor perceives change differently, and this becomes more and more apparent as the argument proceeds. In Book 6, while sustaining Amans' hope, he shifts his focus from the grace of Fortune and the deities of love to grace of another kind. Cupid the "blinde Boteler" has given Amans a drink: it will remain bitter, Genius tells the lover, "til god the sende / Such grace that thou miht amende" (6.389–90).[39]

If Amans is to be fit for this divine gift of amendment, he must understand more clearly the extent of his bondage to "kinde," the heavens,

Fortune, and the apparent whims of his mistress and Venus; obviously, he must also reperceive the extent of his own power to choose. Genius' treatment in the last books, roughly analogous to that applied by Boethius' physician in the *Consolation*, involves turning his patient's attention to an internal source of freedom.

In Book 6 the confessor still suggests that Amans is destined to a specific natural love, the premise being that "ther is no wyht / That mai withstonde loves miht" (6.317–18). By Book 8, however, he will insist that Amans has a choice and will urge him to leave love that is a "Sinne" and "Tak love where it mai noght faile" (8.2086). That final insistence on Amans' freedom is justified by the perception offered in Book 7, a perception of man restored to his own nature and rightly placed in the universe. As the topics of this didascalic book shift from Theorique to Practique, from natural destiny (the *jus naturae* in its fourth meaning) to practical "reson" and the points of kingship, so too does Genius' perspective on Amans' bondage to "kinde." The introduction of Practique which is based upon "mannes free eleccion" follows in its distinction from "kinde" and natural destiny treated under Theorique that distinction between human sensuality and brute sensuality that concerned medieval writers such as William of Auxerre. In the full perspective on man's nature that Book 7 offers, Genius can now show that the "lawe of kinde" or sensuality in man, because it is subject to reason and free will, is distinct from that nature in the "bestes." This distinction is more important than the fact that all sentient beings commonly endure an external "fortune" and a natural destiny. Man, unlike the beast, can order his love of temporal goods, and this power becomes a focal concern in the priest's discussion of Practique and the five essential virtues of a king.

Gower's choice of those virtues or "pointz" has vexed scholars. The group of five has no strict counterpart in the *Secretum Secretorum* or any other treatise *de regimine principum*.[40] But Gower did have a source. Having advanced beyond animalic "kinde" as well as the "constellacion" that so strongly influences it, he seeks a way to treat those things that seem to bind or inhibit man's power to choose or act, things that seem to represent a natural destiny, but which, in fact, are irresistible because man has failed by reason to recognize them as things he has chosen for himself. Gower found what he sought, I believe, not only in other storehouses of tales or other "kinges bokes," but in the *Consolation of Philosophy*. The five points of Policie, not in some absolute sense, but in the sense in which Gower defines and embodies them in exposition and narrative, are devised as remedies for the human desire for the five great *temporalia*, the gifts of Fortune. As each virtue, supported by the others, displaces a gift— Truth-power, Largess-fame, Justice-wealth, Pity-office, Chastity-sensual pleasure—so the virtues together order man's lower nature and become interdependent strengths in the remade man which liberate him from the compulsions of "kinde."

Man is *homo renovatus* when he achieves the five virtues, but the last temporal good (the pleasure of the senses) and the last virtue (Chastete) present a special problem. Man cannot achieve felicity if he practices four of the virtues but lacks the fifth; chastity is an especially difficult virtue to maintain, however, because man is natural or fleshly and "schal hise lustes have." In a passage of Book 5 that appears in only some manuscripts of the *Confessio*, Genius observes:

> Out of his flessh a man to live
> Gregoire hath this ensample yive,
> And seith it schal rather be told
> Lich to an Angel manyfold,
> Than to the lif of mannes kinde.
> Ther is no reson forto finde,
> Bot only thurgh the grace above,
> In flessh withoute flesshly love,
> A man to live chaste hiere.
>
> (5.6395*–6403*)

In all manuscripts of the poem, however, Gower makes the same point while discussing chastity in Book 7:

> And natheles, bot it be grace
> Above alle othre in special
> Is non that chaste mai ben all.
>
> (4242–44)

The human dilemma—that man cannot live "out of his flessh"—will make grace a necessity, especially for Amans, an exemplar of "flesshly love." And Genius, by juxtaposing the topics of incest and "love honeste" in Book 8, will prepare for the intervention of grace by taking his argument to its limit—to a perception of what "reson" finally demands of the lover.

The reader turning to Book 8 expecting a collection of stories and sayings about lechery, much as he had found six of the earlier books to treat the six other vices, will be surprised to find that the poet here deals exclusively with incest, tells few stories, and seems to limit his argument to a history and defense of laws of consanguinity. Nowhere, not even at the end of Book 7, where he presents chastity as the virtue counterposed to lust, does Gower justify his choice of incest as the chief exemplary species of the last of the "vices dedly." The relevance of his choice becomes apparent, however, in the setting of medieval legal thought. His argument grows out of a view of history and the *primordia nature* that had appeared, rather more starkly, among the Schoolmen:

All that is contrary to natural law always is and has been culpable; but the union of brother and sister has not always been culpable, as, for instance, in the beginning; therefore it is not according to natural law that brother and sister are excepted.[41]

The final book of the *Confessio* begins with an account of creation—"The myhti god, which unbegunne / Stant of himself and hath begunne / Alle othre thinges" (8.1–3)—and in this the poem seems imitative of another, more famous medieval work of confession. But the account quickly becomes a history involving perspectives on the issue of *cognatio* or blood relationship and marriage; these perspectives are ordered first by the *primordia nature* and later by the *racionis arbitrium* and *ecclesie legum imposicio.*[42] In the earliest times, Genius argues,

> it was no Sinne
> The Soster forto take hire brother,
> Whan that ther was of chois non other.
> (68–70)

This argument, as it progresses, focuses the concerns of the poem in a rather remarkable way. The terms of man's earliest history, we recall from Book 5, are fixed in Amans' head: when the priest defends virginity, the lover observes that he understands better the divine command to increase and multiply. In Book 8, incest represents an analogous issue. Just as some legal authorities observe that the command "crescite et multiplicamini" was a natural law especially appropriate before the earth was replenished,[43] so Genius notes that incest was permissible until the time of Abraham, when "The nede tho was overrunne, / For ther was poeple ynouh in londe" (100–01). But just because incest was permissible once or because it is encouraged in nature, that does not mean that "nou aday" we are permitted to follow those "That taken wher thei take may" (152). Again, this excursus into history is important to Gower because it identifies a psychological issue. By natural law like things are drawn together. Clearly there can be no greater likeness in nature than likeness by blood, and incest therefore manifests physically that natural law "quo similia similibus gaudent." History gives Gower a further insight into this law. It is obviously no longer the case that the incestuous can claim "ther was of chois non other": the only justification for that claim is brute appetite.

Incest is an especially powerful exemplary species of lechery in the priest's argument because it reveals what it is like for man to live without choice, as a "beste" limited to momentary sensual pleasure with those who live in closest proximity:

> For love, which is unbesein
> Of alle reson, as men sein,
> Thurgh sotie and thurgh nycete,
> Of his voluptuosite
> He spareth no condicion
> Of ken ne yit religion,
> Bot as a cock among the Hennes
> Or as a Stalon in the Fennes,
> Which goth amonges al the Stod,
> Riht so can he nomore good,
> Bot takth what thing comth next to honde.
>
> (153–63)

Honest love stands in opposition in this bestial appetite. Gower's use of the term "honeste" in an argument where he is concerned as well with issues of primordial nature, marriage, incest, and nature multiplied, has a clear precedent in legal tradition.[44] But two senses of "honeste," not often distinguished in the *honestum* or *honestas* of legal texts, have been introduced by Gower in the poem, and both senses apply to his discussion of honest love.

In one sense, "honeste" is derived from the *honestas* that became, in ancient and medieval treatises on the cardinal virtues, a species of temperance. Thus in Book 7 the *honestas* of chastity is set against *voluptas:* "honesty, attending to the impulses of unchasteness, more especially preserves the cleanness of body and soul." [45] Honest love can mean chaste love, and consequently, when the priest contrasts honest love and incest, as in the powerful, concluding tale of the *Confessio*—the tale of Apollonius of Tyre—his implied statement about the latter reflects a traditional idea: those related by blood are to be kept from union "either for the seemliness of nature or for the increase of chastity." [46]

In another, much larger sense, Gower perceives "honesty" as the genus of all virtue. It is the moral good unique to the human species; the "honesty" of chastity and other virtues are but aspects of it. Honesty in this generic sense—Gower's "honeste" as upright and "honestete" as moral probity—may be identified with the *honestum* that Cicero defined as moral worth "commended in and for itself, apart from any profit or reward." [47] For Cicero, men are capable of this good—they can do things which are proper, right, and "honest"—because nature has endowed them with reason. Gower, similarly, sees something as honest when it is suited to man's proper nature, to "reson" and not merely to "kinde." Genius uses the term in this larger sense in earlier passages of the poem (see, for example, 3.2596–98), and he also uses it in this sense in Book 8. He insists that

> love and reson wolde acorde.
> For elles, if that thou descorde,
> And take lust as doth a beste,
> Thi love mai noght ben honeste.
> (8.2023–26)

Undoubtedly, "honeste" here still carries the meaning of shamefast or chaste, but it also conveys a meaning of reasonable. Obviously, what is needed to ensure that "love and reson wolde acorde" is a power of discrimination, reason itself. Reason identifies what is "honeste," and what is honest is consistent with "reson."

In the last books of the poem, as the "lawe of kinde" is limited to its most restricted sense—the brute appetite so vividly exemplified by incest—the law of "reson" expands to encompass all human knowledge and virtue. The discussion of "love honeste" in Book 8 is anticipated in the preceding book, but there Genius also refers to a much larger field for "reson" and "honestete." Alexander is taught

> *Noght only upon chastete,*
> *But upon alle honestete;*
> Wherof a king himself mai taste,
> Hou trewe, hou large, hou joust, hou chaste
> Him oghte of reson forto be,
> Forth with the vertu of Pite,
> Thurgh which he mai gret thonk deserve
> Toward his godd.
> (7.5387–94) [emphasis added]

This larger meaning of honesty, introduced early in the *Confessio* and elaborated at its close, reflects a rich medieval literature dealing with the Ciceronian terms *honestum* and *utile* and sometimes also a third term— *delectabile*. It is appropriate for the final judgment of Amans' love that all three terms should have appeared in medieval works on confession. Among the questions a priest is to ask in the confessional, one involves the end sought by the sinning, and in the Statutes of Coventry, the possible answers are explored:

Why: because of what end. One is accustomed to distinguish a three-fold end: the profitable, the honest, and the delightful. Many commit sins because of expediency, many because of pleasure; no one can commit a sin because of honesty.[48]

This test of ends applies to all actions, and it is in this framework that Genius finally comes to judge Amans' limited desire by the standard of honesty. We have been told earlier in the poem that "love honeste in sondri weie / Profiteth" (4.2297–98) and that marriage "should be moderated by the rule of honest pleasure." [49] Now, in Book 8, the concluding argument about Amans' case concentrates not only on honest love, but on "lust" and "profit." It is clear that Amans, though he seeks "lust," gains little pleasure from his quarrel, and in Book 8 the priest shows him what he already fears, that his love is useless: in the lover's sin, Genius says, "I not what profit myhte availe" (8.2091). And by presenting a new end—an honest one—to Amans, the confessor takes his treatment of the *jus naturae* to its limit, for "honestete" is the all-encompassing end of the highest natural law he knows, the law of "reson."

Genius has done his job admirably: by his argument he has restored the power of reason in his pupil, and he has taught him about the most profitable love, a love that cannot fail (8.2070–2148). To be sure, he has not changed him in the most important sense, as Amans himself knows:

> Mi resoun understod him wel,
> And knew it was soth everydel
> That he hath seid, bot noght forthi
> Mi will hath nothing set therby.
> (2191–94)

Nevertheless, he has prepared him for a dream, a dream in which Cupid, by his grace, removes the lancegay from his heart. When Amans wakens from that dream, he sees himself transformed: "I was mad sobre and hol ynowh" (2869).

In the largest sense, then, the fiction of the *Confessio* traces the psychological recovery of Amans. And we have seen how terms associated with the *jus naturae* have been modified and expanded in the course of the argument conducing to that change. The "lawe of kinde" as sensual appetite shifts from something irresistible to something chosen. Natural law as the attraction between beings naturally like expands to virtuous fellowship and "charite." Charity becomes less a *motus naturae* and more a *motus gratiae* through which man achieves the fullness of his proper nature. Grace means less the compliance of the mistress and more that divine gift which makes man's amendment possible. Reason extends beyond the "in-sihte of conscience" that judges sexual desire to an "honestete" that not only ensures chaste love, but also guides man in all his choices and actions.

How then, in summary, might we describe the role of natural law in Amans' recovery? The lover's health is restored by a process involving the application of the "lawe of kinde," reason, and grace to his condition. In a general sense, the model—the rationale—for this process is suggested by Hugh Ripelin of Strassburg when he identifies three things that incite us to good works. Hugh's statement is relevant not as a direct source for Gower's developing argument, but as a useful brief description of the elements in the law of nature, reason, and grace that the poet ultimately celebrates:

Three things incite us to good works, namely the law of nature, which is written in the heart of man, saying: 'Whatever you wish men to do to you do also to them,' etc. Reason, which calls these things delightful, profitable, and honest. Grace, which says that God is to be served because he is supremely good; that one's neighbor is to be succored, because he is a son of God, an image of God, and a partner in beatitude. Grace is not given to him, who does not make himself fit for grace.[50]

Grace, for Amans, is a necessity, and natural law—including both "kinde" and "reson"—has been the primary means of making Amans fit to receive it. Moreover, natural law has been a primary reference point in teaching Amans how to act, once he is empowered to act freely: from it he learns what natural love *in corde hominis* should be, and from it he learns how honesty, profit, and delight can be united meaningfully in human experience. In a work so devoted to remaking the man, however, it is proper also that we be shown the limitation of nature and reason and that we be asked to shift our attention at last to a higher power. And thus, as the tale of Amans ends with a gift given to him, so Gower, the former lover, ends his poem by praying for a gift for his readers and himself, a gift that transcends natural law and encyclopedic knowledge about it:

> Bot thilke love which that is
> Withinne a mannes herte affermed,
> And stant of charite confermed,

> The hyhe god such love ous sende
> Forthwith the remenant of grace;
> So that above in thilke place
> Wher resteth love and alle pes,
> Oure joie mai ben endeles.
>
> (8.3162–64, 3168–72)

NOTES

1. "Ius naturale est, quod natura omnia animalia docuit. nam ius istud non humani generis proprium est, sed omnium animalium. . . . hinc descendit maris atque feminae coniugatio, quam nos matrimonium appellamus, hinc liberorum procreatio et educatio." *Inst.* 1.2, ed. P. Krueger (Berlin, 1872), p. 3; cf. *Dig.* 1.1.1.3.

2. Quotations of Gower's works are from the edition of G. C. Macaulay, 4 vols. (Oxford, 1899–1902).

3. ". . . intendit auctor ad presens suum libellum, cuius nomen Confessio Amantis nuncupatur, componere de illo amore, a quo non solum humanum genus, sed eciam cuncta animancia naturaliter subiciuntur." *Works*, 2:35.

4. Guillaume de Lorris and Jean de Meun, *Le Roman de la Rose*, 5733–36, ed. Félix Lecoy (Paris, 1974), 1:176.

5. "Gower's 'Honest Love,' " in *Patterns of Love and Courtesy*, ed. John Lawlor (London, 1966), pp. 107–21.

6. "Lex huiusmodi naturalis modificata est per ordinem discreti et honesti moris, scilicet ut non nisi tales persone et sub tanta celebritate coniugii iungerentur." Rufinus, *Summa Decretorum*, ed. Heinrich Singer (Paderborn, 1902), p. 7.

7. Most notably Chaucer's Wife of Bath, *Canterbury Tales*, 3.26–29, ed. F. N. Robinson, *The Works of Geoffrey Chaucer*, 2nd ed. (Boston, 1957), p. 76.

8. Bennett, pp. 117–18.

9. "Procreatio potest duobus modis accipi: prout est actus delectans in tactu; uel secundum effectum, scilicet prolis. Si secundo modo, . . . tunc erit per rationem excipientem ipsam per honestatem nuptiarum et erit de iure naturali sic dicto." Albertus Magnus, *Summa de bono*, in the selection edited by Odon Lottin, *Le droit naturel chez Saint Thomas d'Aquin et ses prédécesseurs*, 2nd ed. (Bruges, 1931), p. 43.

10. *Love and Marriage in the Age of Chaucer* (Ithaca and London, 1975), p. 144.

11. Chaucer, *Troilus and Criseyde*, 1.238 (*ed. cit.*, p. 392).

12. *Roman*, 5745–54 (*ed. cit.*, 1:177)

13. Azo, *Summa Institutionum* 1.2, ed. F. W. Maitland, *Select Passages from the Works of Bracton and Azo*, Selden Society, 8 (1895), 32, 34; repeated by Bracton, *De Legibus et Consuetudinibus Angliae*, more recently edited by George E. Woodbine (Cambridge, Mass., 1968), 2:26.

14. "Quod non sit commune cum bestiis, ad rationem pertinet: quod autem in ea reperis commune cum beluis, ad sensualitatem pertinet." *Sententiae in IV libris distinctae* 2. dist. 24. cap. 5.2, 3rd ed. (Quaracchi, 1971), 1:454; cf. Augustine, *De Trinitate* 12.12.17 (*PL* 42:1007); Alain de Lille, *De planctu Naturae* (*PL* 210:443) and *Distinctiones dictionum theologicalium*, "ratio" (*PL* 210:922).

15. ". . . sensualitas brutalis vel que mouetur per modum nature: et est irrationabilis, nec subest libero arbitrio. . . . sensualitas humana que est inferior pars vis concupiscibilis. Uis enim concupiscibilis humana habet duas partes, superiorem qua concupiscit eterna, et inferiorem qua concupiscit temporalia. Et secundum vtramque partem mouetur voluntarie, et ideo in ea est

peccatum et in ea sunt primi motus quibus indebito modo concupiscimus temporalia ante iudicium rationis." *Summa aurea in quattuor libros sententiarum* (Paris, 1500–01; reprt. Frankfurt-Main, 1964), fol. 131ra.

16. "Dicitur ius naturale instinctus et ordo nature quo similia de similibus propagantur, quo similia similibus gaudent, quo inter se conueniunt, quo partus nutriunt, quietem appetunt, molestias fugiunt et cetera faciunt que secundum sensualitatem id est naturalem appetitum habent fieri: hoc ius nil aliud uidetur esse quam sensualitas. De hoc iure dicitur a legisperito: ius naturale est quod natura omnia animalia docuit." *Summa Decretorum* (Lottin, p. 109).

17. "Consule naturam, illa te docebit diligere proximum tuum sicut te ipsum. Ipsa etenim fecit omnia communia, unum fecit omnibus ortum, quia *Omne genus hominum simili descendit ab ortu.* Si alii negas quod tibi vis fieri naturam impugnas, jus commune enervas.

"Nulli imponas quod ipse pati non possis; haec exhibe aliis, quae tibi optas exhiberi. Quomodo in alio tuam potes aspernari naturam, qui in te ipso eamdem amplecteris? Omne animal sibi simile diligit, sic omni homo diligere deberet proximum suum. Omnis caro conjungitur ad sui similem societatem." *Summa de arte praedicatoria (PL* 210:154).

18. See Alain de Lille, *Distinctiones,* "natura" *(PL* 210:871); Peter Lombard, *In Epistolam ad Romanos (PL* 191:1345); for other views of the connection between God's command and the *jus naturae,* see *Sententie Anselmi,* ed. F. Bliemetzrieder, *Anselms von Laon Systematische Sentenzen* (Münster, 1919), p. 79; Hugh of St. Victor, *De sacramentis* 1.11.7 *(PL* 176:347–48); Gratian, *Concordia discordantium canonum,* ed. A. Friedberg, 2nd ed. (Leipzig, 1879), 1. dist.1.

19. "Verba autem legis naturalis illa sunt, quae Dei et proximi charitatem commendant, sicuti ista: *Quod tibi fieri non vis, alteri ne feceris (Tob.* IV, 16); et: *Quod vultis ut faciant vobis homines et vos facite illis (Matth.* VII, 12)." *Expositio in Epist. Pauli ad Rom.* 1 *(PL* 178:814).

20. *The Vision of William Concerning Piers the Plowman,* C.18.151–52, ed. W. W. Skeat (Oxford, 1886), 1:463.

21. *Roman de la Rose,* 9491–95 *(ed. cit.,* 2:39); see also *Consolation of Philosophy,* 2. m.5; Chaucer, "The Former Age" *(ed. cit.,* p. 534 and note, p. 859).

22. See, for example, Ambrose, *De officiis* 1.28.132 *(PL* 16:62); Isidore, *Etymologiae* 5.4; Gratian, 1. dist.8, pt.1, C.1; Johannes Teutonicus, *Glossa ordinaria* (Lottin, p. 23); William of Ockham, *Dialogus* 2.3.6.

23. *Canterbury Tales,* 10.920 *(ed. cit.,* p. 258).

24. See, for example, John of la Rochelle's contribution to the *Summa fratris Alexandri* 248 (Quaracchi, 1948), 4.2:350.

25. "Tria enim sunt tempora per quae praesentis saeculi spatium decurrit. Primum est tempus naturalis legis; secundum tempus scriptae legis; tertium tempus gratiae. Primum ab Adam usque ad Moysen." *De sacramentis* 1.8.11 *(PL* 176:312); see also Anselm, *Sententie diuine pagine* 5, and *Sententie Anselmi* (ed. Bliemetzrieder, pp. 35, 78–79).

26. ". . . ut legem naturalem per peccatum corruptam repararet." *Ysagoge in theologiam* 2, ed. Artur Landgraf, *Écrits théologiques de l'école d'Abelard* (Louvain, 1934), p. 132; see also *Summa sententiarum* 4.2 *(PL* 176:120).

27. See Macaulay's note on 5.1952 (*Works*, 2:519).
28. 5.7610; see Lester K. Little, "Pride Goes Before Avarice: Social Change and the Vices in Latin Christendom," *American Historical Review*, 76 (1971), 16–49.
29. Cf. *Roman de la Rose*, 13845–68 (*ed. cit.*, 2:171–72).
30. ". . . in concordia omnium rerum; et de tali iustitia naturali agit Plato in Thimeo: unum elementum non potest esse sine alio: unde, ut dicit Augustinus, iudicium divine largitatis est quod quelibet creatura compellitur dare seipsam." William of Auxerre, *Summa aurea* (Lottin, pp. 33–34); for Roland of Cremona and Hugh of St. Cher, see also Lottin, pp. 115–16.
31. The assumptions underlying Gower's sense of universal harmony are topoi quite variously formulated in writers such as Boethius, *Consolation*, 3. pr.11; John of Salisbury, *Metalogicon* 1.1, ed. Clemens C. I. Webb (Oxford, 1929), p. 6; and Chalcidius, *Timaeus a Calcidio translatus commentarioque instructus*, ed. J. H. Waszink, *Plato Latinus*, ed. R. Klibansky (London, 1975), 4:206.
32. In concentrating on bodily or "erthli" things in his treatment of Theorique, Genius describes what the elemental order of the universe contributes to the human constitution, and how the planets, the signs of the zodiac, and the stars bear special influence over geographical place, the human complexions, time, and other physical things. In *Li Livres dou Tresor*, Brunetto Latini likewise devotes little space to theology and writes extensively on the world of nature while discussing the theoretical arts, and he shirks none of the things the English poet considers—the complexions, the heavens, the *mapamounde*. But Brunetto incorporates more: he traces the history of mankind through its ages, describes great men of the past, writes at length on natural history, and even introduces architecture as a theoretical art. Because Gower is concerned in treating Theorique with topics that contribute to a clear image of how nature "determines" the course of human affairs, he avoids Brunetto's catalogue of beasts, for example, and shifts his emphasis to Astronomie, reminding us that without it, "All othre science is in vein / Toward the scole of erthli thinges" (628–29).
33. These meanings are conveniently catalogued by the decretists. Among the six meanings of *jus naturale* listed in the *Summa Lipsiensis*, for example, one may discover three of the above possibilities; see Lottin, p. 108.
34. "Pecora quidem coeunt, non tamen iure naturali, sed solo naturalis motus appetitu mouentur." Simon of Bisignano, in the selection edited by Lottin, pp. 106–07.
35. See Azo, *ed. cit.*, p. 34; Accursius, *In Institutiones* 1.2 (Venice, 1499), fol. 3vb; *Summa Vindobonensis*, ed. J. B. Palmerius (Bonn, 1913–14), p. 6; *Summa Institutionum 'Iustiniani est in hoc opere,'* ed. Pierre Legendre (Frankfurt-Main, 1973), p. 27; on the tendency of the civilians to accept Ulpian's definition and of the decretists to prefer those meanings where the law of nature is identified with reason, see the post-glossator Cinus of Pistoia, *In Digesti Veteris libros*, 1.1.1.
36. See, for example, Johannes Faber: "Non videtur quod sit de instinctu naturae matrimonium: sed coniunctio corporum sic quia natura adeo prona est ad

fornicationem, sicut ad matrimonium. . . . Ratio enim naturalis sic dictat, quod liberi per utrumque parentem, simul educari debeant, et erudiri, et ideo ne parentes incerti sint, ratio naturalis, et necessaria, dictat matrimonium." *In Institutiones commentarii* 1.2 (Lyon, 1557, reprt. Frankfurt-Main, 1969), 6v; W. Onclin cites other instances of this position in Accursius, Jacobus de Arena, and Albericus de Rosate, in "Le droit naturel selon les Romanistes des XIIe et XIIIe siècles," *Miscellanea Moralia in Honorem Arthur Janssen* (Louvain, 1949), pp. 336–37; see also Ennio Cortese, *La Norma Giuridica* (Milan, 1962–64), pt. 1:69–71.

37. One guilty of presumption, for example, "Nec sibi consimilem quem putat esse parem." *Works*, 2:86.

38. See, for example, 5.121–24, 6.1152–58, and 7.4215–17.

39. For a brief discussion of the development of the concept of grace in later books of the *Confessio*, see Patrick J. Gallacher, *Love, the Word, and Mercury* (Albuquerque, 1975), pp. 60–63.

40. Allan Gilbert, for example, found no source, though he suggested that "such a conception as Gower's five points . . . would probably have been derived from some treatise rather than devised by the poet himself." "Notes on the Influence of the *Secretum Secretorum*," *Speculum*, 3 (1928), 85–86.

41. "Omne quod est contra legem naturalem semper est et fuit culpabile; sed non semper fuit culpabilis coitus fratris cum sorore, sicut in principio; ergo non ex lege naturali est quod excipiatur [sic] frater et soror." John of la Rochelle, *Summa fratris Alexandri* 254 (*ed. cit.*, 4.2: 359).

42. These terms are taken from Gower's marginal gloss at 8.1 (*Works*, 3:386).

43. See Philip the Chancellor, *Summa de bono*, and John of la Rochelle, *Summa de preceptis*, in the selections edited by Lottin, pp. 112–13, 120.

44. ". . . lex naturalis quoddam dictat quia debitum, quoddam vero quia decens et honestum. Lex ergo naturalis a matrimonio excepit fratrem et sororem, non quia debitum, sed quia honestum et decens, maxime in natura multiplicata, quia lex etiam, licet hoc in statu naturae non mulitiplicatae concederet, non tamen in statu naturae multiplicatae." John of la Rochelle, *Summa fratris Alexandri* 254 (*ed. cit.*, 4.2:360).

45. ". . . honestas impudicicie motus obtemperans tam corporis quam anime mundiciam specialius preseruat." *Works*, 3:353.

46. ". . . sive ad decorem naturae, sive ad pudicitiae argumentum [sic]." Hugh of St. Victor, *De sacramentis* 2.11.4 (*PL* 176:483).

47. *De finibus* 2.14.45, trans. H. Rackham, Loeb Classical Library (New York, 1914), p. 133.

48. "Cur: propter quem finem. Solet autem triplex distingui finis, utile, honestum, delectabile. Multi committunt peccata propter utilitatem, multi propter delectationem; nullus potest committere peccatum propter honestatem." "Statutes of Bishop Alexander of Stavensby for the Diocese of Coventry and Lichfield (1229–37)," ed. F. M. Powicke and C. R. Cheney, *Councils and Synods* (Oxford, 1964), 2.1:224.

49. ". . . honeste delectacionis regimine moderari debet." *Works*, 3:382.

50. "Ad opera bona tria nos incitant, scilicet lex naturae, quae scripta est in corde hominis, dicens: *Quaecumque vultis ut faciant vobis homines, et vos facite illis*, etc. Ratio, quae dicit ea esse delectabilia, utilia et honesta. Gratia, quae dicit serviendum esse Deo, quia summe bonus: subveniendum proximo, quia Dei filius, quia imago Dei, quia in beatitudine socius. Gratia non datur ei, qui se non habilitat ad gratiam." *Compendium theologicae veritatis* 5.2, in Albertus Magnus, *Opera Omnia*, ed. A. Borgnet (Paris, 1890–98), 34:154.

I am grateful to Professor Siegfried Wenzel and the editorial board of *Medievalia et Humanistica* for reading this essay and offering many helpful suggestions; I also wish to thank the National Endowment for the Humanities and the University of Idaho Research Council for their financial support of this project.

Awaiting an End:
Research in Medieval Apocalypticism, 1974–1981

BERNARD McGINN

At the outset the reader deserves at least a minor revelation regarding the chronological and substantive parameters of the following bibliographic essay. I have restricted myself to materials that have appeared during the past seven years, first, because three bibliographical pieces have recently surveyed aspects of medieval apocalypticism up to roughly 1974,[1] and second, because the wealth of material that has appeared over the seven years 1974–81 provides an argument even more potent than the apocalyptic propriety of the number for such a limitation. The substantive principles underlying the essay are more important. This is a bibliographical essay, not a bibliography.[2] It makes no pretense to completeness, especially where European materials are concerned, but represents the fruits of my own attempts to keep up with the expanding literature on medieval apocalypticism.

The principles governing the selection of materials deemed in some way apocalyptic are based upon those put forth most fully in my book *Visions of the End. Apocalyptic Traditions in the Middle Ages,* and to a lesser extent in my other book, *Apocalyptic Spirituality.*[3] In attempting to provide what I called a "textual history" of medieval apocalypticism in the former work, it was necessary to confront the thorny issues of the meaning of apocalypticism and the range of its functions. Such a task is complicated not only by the different ways in which historians and social scientists use such terms as apocalypticism, eschatology, millenarianism, and messianism, but also by the debates on the origin and nature of apocalypticism among biblical scholars. Despite a certain overlapping range shared by the two terms, I have argued that there is good reason for distinguishing between eschatology and apocalypticism,[4] and that apocalypticism has an understanding related to, but separate from, millenarianism and messianism as well.[5] In the following essay "eschatology" is understood to include every view that sees historical process as fundamentally teleological, whereas "apocalypticism" will be taken as a particular kind of Christian eschatology that holds

Medievalia et Humanistica, New Series, Number 11 (Paul Maurice Clogan, ed.). Rowman and Littlefield, Totowa, NJ, 1982.

not only that history is given meaning by its end, but that that end is proximate as the last act in a divinely determined structure of history. Apocalyptic views of history are always compounds of pessimism about the present evil state of the world and optimism about the coming vindication of the just, either in a better state in this world or in the world to come. The understanding of history and history's relation to eternity that grounds this mixture of optimism and pessimism can vary somewhat from author to author so that it is preferable to speak of apocalyptic traditions, theories, and attitudes in the plural. Similarly varied are the religious affections shared by apocalypticists. These form a series of variations on the common themes of illumination, consolation, moral exhortation and condemnation, and finally the hope for vindication.[6]

I. GENERAL WORKS

Our concern is medieval apocalypticism, that is, with the literature about materials and movements dating from roughly 300 to 1500 A.D. Nevertheless, the origins of apocalypticism in the Intertestamental Period remain of such vital importance for all subsequent studies, that it may be worthwhile to list just two books on early apocalypticism that can introduce the medievalist to the questions currently under debate among scripture scholars.

Walter Schmithals, *The Apocalyptic Movement. Introduction and Interpretation* (New York and Nashville, 1975) is a good illustration of one typical approach to the problem of apocalypticism, namely, the attempt to determine the inner *Geist* of *the* apocalyptic understanding of existence (see pp. 147–50). This approach, in which discernment of this inner nature is used as the yardstick for measuring what texts may be judged to be properly apocalyptic (see pp. 188–212) forms a striking contrast to approaches that begin with the study of texts that describe themselves as apocalypses, that is, "revelations." A good example of the latter is to be found in the studies gathered in *Apocalypse. Morphology of a Genre* (*Semeia* 14. Missoula, Montana, 1979) edited by John Collins. These papers move from detailed analyses of the themes found in all the relevant early apocalypses (Jewish, Christian, Gnostic, Greek and Latin, Rabbinic, and Persian) to construct a model of the genre and its types. The results are impressive, but one wonders if greater "weighting" of elements that appear to be given more attention and centrality when they do appear would effect any significant changes in the picture of the genre that is presented. In any case, I believe it imperative that students of the later history of apocalypticism have some acquaintance with the rich biblical literature on the subject.

General works on the history of medieval apocalypticism have become more rare as the range of our knowledge of the complexity of the topic has expanded. Still, several important books and papers of the past seven years fit into the general category. The most recent of these is Richard K. Emmerson's *Antichrist in the Middle Ages. A Study in Medieval Apocalypticism, Art, and Literature* (Seattle, 1981). Professor Emmerson has had unusual courage in taking on such a vast topic; given the available material, the book must be judged to be only an introduction. Nevertheless, it is a very useful introduction (despite some problems), and can rightly be called necessary reading for all interested in medieval apocalypticism. Emmerson's basic purpose is to trace the continuity of the standard view of the Antichrist from its formation in biblical exegesis through the apocalyptic writings, as well as the literature and art of the Middle Ages. He closes with a long section on "Antichrist in the Renaissance" that also treats of Reformation views. The author does admit variety in medieval views of the Final Enemy, and he studies the late medieval development which identified specific figures, especially popes, with the Antichrist. I am inclined to question, however, if there is not more variety to Antichrist traditions in the Middle Ages than this introduction suggests, especially in the continuity of "double Antichrist" views (not invented by Joachim of Fiore) and in the great complexity of the corporate views, especially those influenced by Tyconius (an important writer neglected by Emmerson).[7]

The name of Marjorie Reeves needs no introduction to students of the history of medieval apocalypticism. In July of 1974 a Symposium was held at St. John's College, Oxford, in honor of Miss Reeves. The papers of this gathering have now been published under the title *Prophecy and Millenarianism. Essays in Honour of Marjorie Reeves* (London, 1980) edited by Ann Williams. The sixteen essays included range widely, both chronologically and in other senses. Among the more general essays, I would especially like to single out the paper of the late Paul J. Alexander on "The Diffusion of Byzantine Apocalypses in the Medieval West and the Beginnings of Joachimism," a masterful survey of the influence of Byzantine apocalyptic in Latin lands that includes a convincing new theory on the date and context of the Joachite section of the Erythraean Sibyl.[8] This is certainly among the most important contributions to the study of medieval apocalyptic of the past seven years.

Among broad general accounts there should also be noted the treatment of apocalyptic thought in works on medieval heresy. This is not an area that has contributed much that is original recently. Malcolm Lambert's *Medieval Heresy. Popular Movements from Bogomil to Hus* (New York, 1976), justly praised for its inclusiveness, treats apocalypticism under two headings. The account of the "Spiritual Franciscans and Heretical Joachimites" (pp. 182–206) is one of the weakest parts of the book, derivative and at times in error; the treatment of the Hussites in two long sections (pp.

288–334) is much better and is a valuable and judicious survey. Very few articles are sufficiently broad in scope to be included under our general heading. One of the few that covers the whole period of medieval apocalypticism is Robert E. Lerner's "Refreshment of the Saints: The Time after Antichrist as a Station for Earthly Progress in Medieval Thought."[9] Lerner is interested in showing the continuity of inherited Patristic traditions in the Middle Ages, in this case the remarkable history of the brief period of repentance (forty or forty-five days in most accounts) after the defeat of the Antichrist that Jerome argued for as a way to reconcile exegetical inconsistencies in Daniel. In tracing the story of this theme, Lerner has demonstrated the importance of a largely unstudied non-Joachite optimistic hope in medieval apocalypticism.

II. EARLY MEDIEVAL APOCALYPTICISM (300–1200 A.D.)

The division between the early and late medieval periods as used here centers on the career of Joachim of Fiore (died 1202) to whom a separate section will be given.

The early period has been rather neglected in recent scholarship in comparison with the wealth of material on Joachim and on the later Middle Ages. An area that has been productive, fortunately, has been the editing of texts. Pride of place must be given to D. Verhelst's edition of Adso of Montier-en-Der's *De Ortu et Tempore Antichristi* (Turnhout, 1976. *Corpus Christianorum. Continuatio Mediaevalis* XLV), a model of what a text edition should be. For the first time we have been given detailed knowledge of the full history of one of the most important medieval apocalyptic writings.[10] In the same year a critical edition of four versions of the Greek text of the Pseudo-Methodius was published in Germany, one vastly improving on V. Istrin's old edition of 1897.[11] Much work still remains before we shall be in possession of a more adequate picture of the transmutations of this text, "the jewel of Byzantine apocalyptic." The most pressing need is for a critical edition of the Syriac original.

A number of other texts from the period before 1200 published over the past seven years have significance for our topic, though I should not want to label them all apocalyptic in the full sense of the term. In the *Corpus Christianorum* Series, among the *Continuatio Mediaevalis*, we have the splendid but costly edition of the *Scivias* of Hildegard of Bingen,[12] and also that of Ambrosius Autpertus's commentary on the Apocalypse.[13] In the Sibylline tradition, we have an edition of an Anglo-Norman poetic version of the *Sibylla Tiburtina* that seems to date from about 1140.[14]

The report sheet on secondary literature on early medieval apocalypticism is more limited. I can point to no single monographic study devoted solely to this period during the past seven years, though at least one recent book has given much space to the analysis of the apocalyptic beliefs of two Anglo-Saxon authors.[15] Several articles are of interest, particularly those that have advanced controversial theses. In his paper "The Medieval Legend of the Last Roman Emperor and its Messianic Origin,"[16] Paul J. Alexander argued that the creation of the myth of the Last World Emperor by the Pseudo-Methodius in the seventh century took place under the influence of Jewish messianism. I find the evidence advanced too hypothetical to be convincing, and I would suggest that the question cannot be considered apart from the debate over whether or not the lost fourth-century translation of the Tiburtine Sibyl already contained a Last Emperor figure.[17] Even more challenging is the study by David Flusser of the Hebrew University entitled "An Early Jewish-Christian Document in the Tiburtine Sibyl."[18] Through an analysis of the many versions of this crucial text, Prof. Flusser argues that the original dream of the nine suns was a Jewish-Christian text of the time of Domitian. Much of the evidence presented, however, involves a series of speculative interlocking hypotheses that I do not find probative. Flusser has certainly demonstrated the importance of some ancient Jewish-Christian elements in the Tiburtine Sibyl, but further research is needed before we need be convinced that the *Sibylla Tiburtina* is the contemporary of the John of the Apocalypse. A third article worthy of further discussion is Guntram Bischoff's "Early Premonstratensian Eschatology: the Apocalyptic Myth,"[19] which argues that certain twelfth-century Premonstratensian authors, especially Eberwin of Steinfeld, were immediate predecessors of Joachim of Fiore in their rejection of traditional Augustinian theology of history for a form of chiliastic vision in which optimism about the future was possible. The argument is suggestive, but further research, as well as a discussion of Bischoff's dense theoretical structure is needed. A number of other recent articles have also made contributions to the study of individual early medieval apocalyptic texts.[20]

III. JOACHIM OF FIORE

Though several scholars have recently reminded us that the influence of Joachim may have been exaggerated in recent years, the abbot of Fiore remains the most important medieval apocalyptic author. Even within the restricted limits of our apocalyptic seven years, there has been an impressive literature devoted to the Calabrian.

To begin with texts of Joachim, Marjorie Reeves and John V. Fleming produced a handsome edition of two poems attributed to the abbot,[21] and E. Randolph Daniel edited and studied one of the minor works, the *De*

Ultimis Tribulationibus in the Reeves *Festschrift*.[22] Prof. Daniel has also been at work on an edition of the first four books of the *Liber Concordie* which he defends as Joachim's exegetical introduction to his great trilogy of works.[23] This edition has been accepted for publication in the Proceedings of the American Philosophical Association. In addition, Y.-D.Gélinas has announced an edition of the lengthy *Expositio in Apocalypsim* to be completed about 1985.[24] Good versions of these major works will undoubtedly do much to stimulate further research on Joachim and will contribute to the solution of a number of disputed questions.

In 1975 Delno C. West edited a two-volume collection entitled *Joachim of Fiore in Christian Thought. Essays on the Influence of the Calabrian Prophet* (New York, 1975). This valuable gathering of material reprints twenty essays dealing with aspects of Joachim and his influence written between 1885 and 1971. Prof. West also includes a bibliography of Joachim studies between 1954 and c. 1973. Two of the essays in West's collection are by the much lamented Herbert Grundmann, whose 1927 *Studien über Joachim von Floris* (reprinted in 1966) marked a decisive stage in modern critical study of Joachim. We are fortunate that the second volume of Grundmann's posthumous *Ausgewählte Aufsätze* (*Schriften der Monumenta Germaniae Historica*. Band 25.2 Stuttgart, 1977) collects eleven of his papers on Joachim that appeared between 1928 and 1969. These essays are classics that rank among the most important contributions to Joachim scholarship of any era.

Several monographs devoted to Joachim have appeared during these years. Marjorie Reeves's *Joachim and the Prophetic Future* (London, 1976; New York, 1977) is not so much a new work, as a modified "student version" of her massive *The Influence of Prophecy in the Later Middle Ages* (Oxford, 1969). Like the earlier book, only the first chapter is devoted to Joachim; the substance of the work concentrates on the later influence of the abbot's ideas. There is some new material here, most notably on Joachim's role in Reformation and modern thought, but the interpretive viewpoint and contents are basically the same as in the earlier study.[25] A second introductory book treats Joachim more directly and from a rather different point of view. Gert Wendelborn's *Gott und Geschichte. Joachim von Fiore und die Hoffnung der Christenheit* (Vienna-Cologne, 1974) is a nuanced presentation of what might be described as the traditional German view of Joachim, stressing the more radical implications of the abbot's theory of the three *status* of history.[26] The book is divided into two parts, an extended consideration of Joachim's thought in six sections,[27] and a second brief and weaker treatment that compares Joachim with thinkers from Augustine to twentieth-century savants. Wendelborn provides good summaries of many of the major lines of the abbot's thought;[28] and, for reasons that I have argued in a number of places, I am much in sympathy with an approach that recognizes the radical implications, if not intentions, of Joachim's theory of history; but I am inclined to suspect that Wendelborn has presented an exaggerated view of Joachim's third *status*, not least of all in the way in which he deals with the abbot's hopes for the future of the papacy.[29]

Also stressing the radical features of Joachim's thought have been two important French studies of recent years. The first is the stimulating work of Henri Mottu, *La manifestation de l'Esprit selon Joachim de Fiore* (Neuchatel-Paris, 1977). Despite some debatable theses, this book must certainly be judged to be among the most important contributions to Joachim studies in recent years.[30] The Genevan theologian concentrates on the abbot's teaching on the Holy Spirit's role in history, especially as presented in the *Tractatus super Quatuor Evangelia*. What is particularly noteworthy about Mottu's approach is not only his splendid analysis of Joachim's exegesis, which he rightly sees as the basis for the Calabrian's radical revival of an apocalyptic view of history, but also the broad range of the theological perspective from which he seeks to interpret Joachim's significance in Western thought. Mottu is also prescient in seeing the relation between Pneumatology and Christology as a major area for further work in Joachim studies. If the abbot of Fiore remains in some way a resource for contemporary theology, the kinds of issues raised by Prof. Mottu are in need of further investigation.

The recent study of Henri de Lubac, *La postérité spirituelle de Joachim de Flore. tome I. de Joachim à Schelling* (Paris, 1978), is also a contribution to the wider issues raised by Joachim's thought. Like Mottu, whom de Lubac frequently cites,[31] the French Jesuit scholar stresses the radical character of the third *status* of history. All students of Joachim have learned much from Fr. de Lubac's noted discussion of Joachim's exegesis in *Exégèse médiévale*, where despite his insistence on the dangers of the notion of the third *status*, he paid compliments to the religious genius of the Calabrian.[32] In the more recent work the lines have hardened, for *La postérité spirituelle de Joachim de Flore* is the story of the delusions of all those who have looked forward to a coming third age that would surpass the era of the church of the New Testament, however tenuous their connection with Joachim.[33] The abbot of Fiore is reduced to a prophet of the third status (e.g., pp. 38, 49–65), and those who would emphasize the variety of Joachim's views of the future are given short shrift. This is not the place to investigate in detail the theological premises upon which de Lubac's judgments are based; what can be questioned in an historiographical review is whether or not the picture of Joachim is an adequate one, and whether the principles upon which later thinkers are included in Joachim's "postérité spirituelle" are coherent. I think the answer must be no on both counts. Joachim is much more than a prophet of the third age, however central this may be to his thought, and the picture that is presented of his posterity is far too broad. De Lubac distinguishes between two currents of Joachimism— those dependent on the abbot's exegesis and those which follow the dangerous three-age theory. No one would question his decision to stick with the latter tradition (by far the more influential in Western history), but the criteria for the inclusion of figures in his account, that is, the nature of their relation to Joachim, remain obscure. Some were directly influenced, others indirectly, and some had no contact at all. In what sense can they be said to form one posterity?

In turning to other recent literature on Joachim, a pessimist might be inclined to conclude that the past seven years provide a counter-example to the abbot's claims, if not for progress in history, at least for progress in historiography. The division between German and French students who tend to stress the more revolutionary, radical, or heretical features of the abbot's thought and some Italian scholars anxious at any cost to defend Joachim's orthodoxy seems as strong today as ever before.[34] The radical interpretations of Wendelborn, Mottu, and de Lubac are present, if in muted fashion, in C. Baraut's article "Joachim de Flore" in the *Dictionnaire de spiritualité*.[35] This piece is rich in bibliography and provides a useful introduction to the abbot's life and writings, but the treatment of his doctrine concentrates on the three-*status* theory to such an extent that it neglects many other important elements of his thought. On the Italian side the recent work of Professor Giovanni di Napoli of the University of Rome represents a rather strident return to the case for Joachim's complete orthodoxy advanced earlier by such scholars as Tondelli, Foberti, and Crocco.[36] Two of di Napoli's articles are doctrinal summaries, one of the abbot's ecclesiology, the other of his doctrine of the Trinity.[37] In each of these, the argument is based upon a selection of texts that many scholars would be inclined to see as one-sided. In the article on ecclesiology, for instance, Prof. di Napoli rigorously avoids texts which speak of any real transformation in the church of the third *status*. It would be an instructive exercise on the current divisions in Joachim studies to see how many of the texts that are central for the interpretations of Mottu and de Lubac are not even mentioned by di Napoli.

Of greater importance is di Napoli's lengthy polemical article, "Gioacchino da Fiore e Pietro Lombardo,"[38] where the author revives Foberti's thesis that the *De Unitate Trinitatis*, the work of Joachim condemned at the Fourth Lateran Council, was really a falsified summary of Book I of the *Psalterium decem chordarum*, probably drawn up by Cistercian enemies to besmirch the abbot's reputation. Because this document has never been found, the explanation cannot be ruled out; indeed, the idea that a version of Book I of the *Psalterium* was used has some degree of plausibility, but it is largely supposition that it was the work of a Cistercian cabal. Di Napoli insists that Joachim's condemnation was really a misunderstanding, his Trinitarian doctrine being perfectly orthodox.[39] But the evidence presented shows that the Council knew quite well what it was about. The abbot had misunderstood the Lombard quite severely (di Napoli admits this); and, despite Joachim's orthodox admission of the one divine essence, he had used language regarding the unity of the three divine Persons that taken in itself could be interpreted as indicating a merely collective oneness.

Prof. di Napoli expends considerable effort to show how Thomas Aquinas misjudged Joachim, if partly through ignorance.[40] Other scholars have recently pursued the relation between the abbot and the Angelic Doctor and come up with quite different findings. Besides the treatments found in the works of Mottu and de Lubac, mention should be made of an important article of Y.-D. Gélinas showing how Thomas's criticism of Joachim's hermeneutics is far more basic to his opposition to the Calabrian than earlier investigators, including myself, had been inclined to admit.[41] An article of Peter Meinhold also emphasizes the contrast between the views of history of Joachim and Thomas, but this account is marred by an inadequate picture of Joachim that stresses only the most radical elements in his theology of history.[42] Gianni Baget-Bozzo has also probed the relation between the historical theories of the two men in recent years, but without breaking any new ground.[43]

These studies of the contrast between the abbot and the Dominican doctor indicate that the central issue in current Joachim research remains the abbot's apocalyptic theology of history. Several articles of the past seven years have made notable contributions to our understanding of this element in Joachim.

Marjorie Reeves contributed three important pieces. In "The Abbot Joachim's Theology of History"[44] the dean of Joachim scholars cast new light on the relations between the Trinity and history by analyzing the meaning of the various *figurae* through which the abbot presented the processions and missions of the trinitarian Persons.[45] The second part of the article discussed the relation between Joachim's number symbolism of five and seven and his hermeneutics of five kinds of *intelligentiae* of scripture and seven *species* of *sensus typicus*, a theory that is also tied to a trinitarian view of history. An earlier more detailed essay studied how history came to be seen as prophecy in some twelfth-century circles, so that the structure of past events could serve as a clue for what was still to come.[46]

The new insights present in these two essays culminate in the third, most recent, offering, certainly one of the most significant papers on the study of medieval apocalyptic of the past seven years. In this substantial study on "The Originality and Influence of Joachim of Fiore"[47] Miss Reeves takes on three difficult questions—". . . to examine the

background of ideas out of which Joachim's theology of history was generated, to pinpoint the original aspects of his thought, if any, and thence to
define and apply criteria for claiming later individuals, groups or writings
as 'Joachite' or 'Joachimist'." [48] The first question is resolved by claiming
that although Joachim's thought has affinities with some developments in
the twelfth century, it is basically a new departure in Christian theology of
history. In answering the second question Miss Reeves takes a decisive
step beyond her earlier formulations, for she now boldly claims that
Joachim's originality ". . . lies in the great imaginative step which he took
when he threw the full manifestation of the Third Person of the Trinity
forward into the period ahead" (p. 288). This creation of a second turning
point in history, which Reeves views as more in the line of "originality"
than of "revolution," [49] is now affirmed to be Joachim's boldest and most
vital contribution to Western thought (pp. 292, 293, 297). Although Miss
Reeves is thus prepared to admit a more radical character to the coming
age of the Spirit than she did in her earlier writings, she is still resolutely
opposed to the simplifications of those who would reduce Joachim to
simply a prophet of a coming age of the Spirit which will supersede the
activity of the Second Person of the Trinity. [50] In the third section Reeves
takes on the delicate question of what constitutes a Joachite, that is, how
far can those thinkers who do not hold to an explicit three-*status* theory of
history, but who still look forward to some better coming period on earth,
be placed in the Joachite camp? Her judgments here are subtle and well
argued, however, I tend to think that they are not final answers, but only
contributions to ongoing discussion, especially when dealing with such
complicated cases as those of Bonaventure and Peter Olivi.

The only other recent paper that ranks along with these offerings of
Miss Reeves in importance is the stimulating article of E. Randolph
Daniel, "The Double Procession of the Holy Spirit in Joachim of Fiore's
Understanding of History." [51] Reeves was the first to show that along with
the pattern of three *status* Joachim gives equal attention to the pattern of
the two eras of world history. Prof. Daniel now takes the argument a step
further by showing that "The double procession of the Holy Spirit is the
central clue needed to comprehend both of Joachim's schemes of history
. . . In the light of the double procession . . . they become complements
. . . Neither can be understood without the other." [52] This key overlooked
element in the abbot's thought shows that Joachim's strict adherence to the
Latin *filioque* is far more central to his thought than the anti-Lombard
polemic. What the demonstration does not fully answer, at least at this
stage of Prof. Daniel's work, is how radical a coming change in history this
complementarity of the two patterns suggests. Daniel stresses an organic
growth where more is still expected in the future (pp. 481–2), but I am
inclined to ask "How much more?" The third *status* may not be a period of

doubt that at least in the *Collationes* Bonaventure adopted a number of Joachite themes concerning exegesis, the role of the *viri spirituales*, etc. Whether these are judged to be secondary excrescences or crucial elements of his thought seems largely dependent more on how each critic views the enigmatic Calabrian than on anything else.

A prime source for the history of Joachite influence among the Franciscans is Salimbene of Parma's *Cronica*. There has been considerable interest in Salimbene in recent years. Delno C. West has emphasized the importance of a moderate Joachite element, both in his education and even late in life when he wrote his great work,[78] though some of the themes that West stresses are common to all medieval apocalyptic and not distinctive of the Joachite variety. Jacques Paul has given us a good critical survey of the evidence that the friar presents about the earliest days of Franciscan Joachimism,[79] and M. da Alatri has contributed to the Italian literature on the subject.[80] The first great crisis caused by the infiltration of Joachite ideas into the mendicants, the "Scandal of the Eternal Gospel" of 1254–5, has been the subject of a wide-ranging if idiosyncratic essay by M.-M. Dufeil comparing the views of history found in Gerard of Borgo San Donnino, William of St. Amour, and Thomas Aquinas.[81]

The three great Spiritual leaders, Peter Olivi, Ubertino of Casale, and Angelo Clareno, have not lacked for recent attention.[82] No scholar has done more to stress Olivi's importance than Raoul Manselli, who, since his 1955 book *La "Lectura super Apocalypsim" di Pietro di Giovanni Olivi*, has poured out a flood of articles devoted to the great Provençal thinker and spiritual leader. In these studies Manselli has continued to stress his thesis that Olivi's use of Joachim is real but also quite critical, a position for which he has been criticized by those who would see a more direct and positive appropriation of Joachim by the Franciscan. During the past seven years, Prof. Manselli has announced a major forthcoming study on Olivi and contributed at least five articles to the study of his thought.[83]

The year 1976 saw a major addition to the Olivi literature in the monograph on *The Persecution of Peter Olivi* by David Burr (Philadelphia. Transactions of the American Philosophical Society. N.S. Vol. 66, Part 5). Prof. Burr, the author of numerous articles on Olivi's theology, provides a judicious account of the troubles that Olivi encountered in life and posthumously. Not least of the contributions of this volume is an excellent summary of the Provençal's view of history (pp. 17–24).

Ubertino of Casale has been the subject of a fine bibliographical article by G. L. Potestà,[84] and a paper by Charles T. Davis.[85] R. Manselli's "L'Anticristo mistico: Pietro Giovanni Olivi, Ubertino da Casale e i papi del loro tempo" investigates the identification of specific popes as Antichrist on the part of the later Spirituals, concentrating on Ubertino's *Arbor vitae crucifixae Jesu*.[86] The third Spiritual leader, Angelo of Clareno, has been especially prominent of late as the work of Lydia von Auw, long a recognized scholar on Angelo, culminated in several new papers,[87] as well as her book *Angelo Clareno et les spirituels* (Rome, 1979). This work is the fruit of a lifetime of research begun in 1929 at the suggestion of Ernesto Buonaiuti. As the first major monograph devoted solely to the life and works of Angelo it will be the starting point for all subsequent research. The same author's edition of Angelo's letters is proximate to publication.

Research on the Fraticelli groups, the fourteenth and fifteenth-century descendents of the Spirituals, has not been as rich in the past seven years as in earlier periods, although a long article by the late Decima L. Douie should be noted.[88] Finally, although neither of the following authors was a Franciscan or properly a Spiritual, both have connections with the movement and can be included here. Arnald of Vilanova was a great friend and defender of the Spiritual cause. Harold Lee has traced the influence of Joachimist themes and *figurae* on his early writings.[89] The relation of Dante to both Joachim of Fiore and to the Joachite Spirituals has been the subject of an extensive literature. Although some noted Dante scholars, such as Bruno Nardi and Michele Barbi either totally denied or severely restricted any connection of Dante with Joachim or the Joachites, and although it would be an exaggeration to speak of Dante as a Joachite, most scholars today would admit that Dante knew something of Joachim (at least the *figura* of the three Trinitarian Circles), more of the Spirituals (especially Ubertino's *Arbor vitae*), and was deeply interested in history and its end. Prof. Manselli has written a summary study of the relation between the poet and Joachim and his followers, stressing connections with the ecclesiology of the Spirituals.[90] R. K. Emmerson and R. B. Herzman have recently studied Dante's relation to the Antichrist—Simon Magus tradition in a rich paper that also surveys Joachite influences.[91] In a non-Joachite vein, Charles T. Davis has written a survey piece on "Dante's Vision of History" in which he plausibly holds that the mysterious Veltro who destroys the rapacious Wolf is none other than the Last World Emperor.[92]

B. Other Aspects of Late Medieval Apocalyptic

It is obviously impossible to draw a sharp line between the activity of the Spirituals and the topics to be considered here, since the Spirituals contributed to a number of these themes and movements. However, the focus of the books and articles surveyed here is not exhausted by the Franciscan movement.

There have been only a few broad articles on the late medieval period in recent years. Robert E. Lerner's "Medieval Prophecy and Religious Dissent" studied a number of late medieval prophecies according to a fourfold typology (visionary, biblical, astrological, and pseudonymous); among the texts treated was the "Tripoli prophecy" on which Lerner has a book forthcoming.[93] On the basis of his analysis of the origin and function of these documents, Lerner criticized the "disaster theory" of the origins of medieval apocalypticism which Norman Cohn had done so much to propagate in *The Pursuit of the Millennium* (London, 1957. Most recent edition, Oxford, 1970).[94] My own paper on "Angel Pope and Papal Antichrist" attempted to show that the growing role of the papacy in late medieval apocalypticism must be seen ". . . from a dialectical point of view, an antithesis between hope for a coming papal messiah and dread of a pope who would be man's final enemy."[95] The dialectical scenario, which I believe developed out of a reaction to the papacy's failure as an instrument of reform, dissolved in the sixteenth century with the Reformers appropriating the negative pole and the Catholics being left with the positive, a point taken up in more detail in R. K. Emmerson's *Antichrist in the Middle Ages*.

One of the major difficulties in dealing with late medieval apocalypticism is the inaccessibility of much of the texts. The many short prophecies that circulated widely are imperfectly known and rarely listed in standard manuscript catalogues, important texts are available only in scarce and imperfect early printings, and many key authors (e.g., Jean de Roquetaillade) are virtually unedited. The past seven years have seen one major addition to critical text editions, Angela Crucitti's edition of Savonarola's *Compendium revelationum*, the central prophetic work of the Dominican reformer;[96] but much remains to be done. Various important projects are underway, including an edition of the pseudo-Joachim *Vaticinia de summis pontificibus*. One can only hope that this and other texts soon see the light of day.

Detailed treatments of particular periods, problems and personalities have been fairly numerous. Among the substantial contributions is Roberto Rusconi's *L'Attesa della Fine. Crisi della società, profesia ed Apocalisse in Italia al tempo del grande scisma d'Occidente (1378–1417)* (Rome, 1979). Despite its limitation to Italy and lack of a clear perspective on the broad significance of the Schism in the history of medieval apocalypticism, this is a richly detailed book in which even experts in the field will find new information and judicious evaluations.[97] Rusconi's evidence tends to confirm the continuity of traditional apocalyptic patterns in the face of the new Joachite scenario of the end. For an apocalyptic reaction to the Schism outside Italy, see Louis Pascoe's "Pierre d'Ailly: Histoire, Schisme et Antéchrist."[98] Another period recently studied is the era of the Black Death in Robert Lerner's "The Black Death and Western European Eschatological Mentalities."[99] Prof. Lerner's consideration of "post-Antichrist" and "pre-Antichrist" varieties of chiliasm, valuable as it is, suggests that the impact that the plague (arguably the greatest disaster of the Middle Ages) had upon apocalyptic expectations was less than might be expected,[100] another observation that tends to cast doubt on a one-sided disaster theory of apocalypticism. Another crisis recently studied is the Fall of Constantinople. G. Podskalsky surveys the effects of the event on Byzantine eschatology, especially on Returning Emperor myths, and gives a valuable summary of the major themes of Byzantine "Reichseschatologie" which remained virtually unchanged even after the Turkish capture of the city.[101]

Along with the study of periods and events, there have also been treatments of individual texts, writers, and themes. Michael Thomas has argued for a Franciscan background and possible knowledge of the *Liber figurarum* in the author of the well-known *Speculum humanae salvationis*.[102] Several studies have looked at aspects of late medieval uses of the Last World Emperor myths. Tilman Struve's article is less broad than its title indicates (it excludes French and Italian examples, except for Jean de Roquetaillade), but the rich evidence he summarizes supports his thesis that in late medieval Germany the Last Emperor myth took on a tone increasingly critical of the religious, political, and economic conditions of the day.[103] Klaus Schreiner's piece on the Hohenstaufen comes up with no new information, but is a useful summary.[104] Also in the area of political prophecies, we have the article of Erwin Herrmann on "Spätmittelalterliche englische Pseudoprophetien,"[105] a subject little treated since R. Taylor's pioneer work of 1911.

One marked feature of the period 1200 to 1500 was the increase in the use of apocalyptic ideas in the service of heretical and revolutionary (or proto-revolutionary) causes. Studies have been devoted to a number of these individuals[106] and groups in recent years, among them the fascinating Apostolic Brethren and their leader Fra Dolcino, arguably the first real revolutionary apocalyptic movement of the Middle Ages.[107] The literature both from Eastern and Western Europe on the Hussite movement has continued to grow during our seven years.[108] I claim no mastery over it, but do wish to list a number of articles I have seen that deal with Hussite views on eschatology and apocalypticism and which would repay the interest of students.[109] Finally, the appearance of a critical edition of the *Book of a Hundred Chapters* of the enigmatic "Revolutionary of the Upper Rhine" in 1967 has sparked some interest in the identification of the author.[110]

One final area of late medieval apocalypticism that deserves at least a notice is the use of apocalyptic themes in literature, especially in Middle English literature. I make no claims to exhaustive reading in this area, nor do I pretend to be expert in the critical background to the texts under discussion; but it is obvious that there is considerable interest in investigating the eschatological and apocalyptic dimensions of many literary texts. A word of caution may be helpful. Almost any medieval text, if it touches on history to any extent, is bound to be at least eschatological, if not apocalyptic. What we need to be shown is what particular apocalyptic currents were used in a text and for what purposes. Vagueness here seems to me to defeat the ends of literary criticism, and yet frequently the poet or dramatist has so transformed his sources that it may be almost impossible to trace the process of assimilation. Thus a number of the arguments that I have seen concerning the relation between specific literary texts and apocalyptic sources seem either too general or too dubious to be convincing,[111] and one general thesis recently advanced concerning the role of Apocalypse exegesis on late medieval literature lacks precision in dealing with the intricate history of the exegesis of the Apocalypse and rigor in setting forth the lines of connection to the literary texts.[112] Still, there are a number of studies that are as informative for the student of apocalyptic literature as I hope they are for the scholars of Middle English literature.[113]

V. CONCLUSION

At the risk of boredom, to the author as well as to the reader, this bibliographical essay has reached its term. Dull as the genre is, it has some useful functions. Landscape paintings are usually more pleasing things than maps, but maps have their uses too. This essay has been designed to give the reader a sense of direction through the rich terrain of recent literature on medieval apocalypticism. Most maps must exaggerate the salient features at the expense of details, and hence I have had to summarize intricate arguments in a few words and to express critiques in a sentence that should have been detailed at length in the leisure of a book review. A map, after all, is only a preliminary guide for a journey. The real goal of this essay is to invite the reader to become personally acquainted with the literature—and to reach, if need be, rather different evaluations from those of the guide.

Living with the prophets of the Middle Ages off and on during the past ten years has been a salutary lesson in the folly of prediction. I have tried to express some judgments about areas I believe are in need of further research to get beyond impasses in current debates. Whether others will agree, or, more importantly, whether anyone is willing to take on these tasks, is not within my power to predict.

NOTES

1. Bernard McGinn, "Apocalypticism in the Middle Ages: An Historiographical Sketch," *Mediaeval Studies*, vol. 37, 1975, pp. 252–86, surveys literature through c. 1973. Morton Bloomfield updated his noted 1957 bibliographical essay on Joachim of Fiore in "Recent Scholarship on Joachim of Fiore and his Influence" in *Prophecy and Millenarianism: Essays in Honour of Marjorie Reeves* (London, 1980), pp. 21–52. This covers literature up to c. 1974. See also the more general essay of Hillel Schwartz, "The End of the Beginning: Millenarian Studies, 1969–75," *Religious Studies Review*, vol. 2, 1976, pp. 1–15.
2. A bibliography that has been helpful in compiling this essay is the recent work of Carl T. Berkhout and Jeffrey B. Russell, *Medieval Heresies. A Bibliography 1960–1979* (Toronto, 1981), especially section 8 on "Joachim and Millenarianism."
3. B. McGinn, *Visions of the End* (New York, 1979), Introduction, pp. 1–36; and B. McGinn, *Apocalyptic Spirituality* (New York, 1979), Introduction, pp. 1–16.
4. *Visions of the End*, pp. 2–4. In her review of the book, Marjorie Reeves has questioned aspects of this distinction, see *The Journal of Theological Studies*, N.S., vol. 31, 1980, p. 637.
5. *Visions of the End*, pp. 28–9.
6. *Apocalyptic Spirituality*, pp. 7–13.
7. Also to be noted in continuing work on the Antichrist is Klaus Aichele, *Das Antichristdrama des Mittelalters, der Reformation und Gegenreformation* (The Hague, 1974), a handy summary of information on forty-three plays devoted to the Antichrist. See also the same author's "The Glorification of Antichrist in the 'Ludus de Antichristo'," *Modern Language Notes*, vol. 91, 1976, pp. 424–36.
8. *Prophecy and Millenarianism*, pp. 53–106.
9. *Traditio*, vol. 32, 1976, pp. 97–144.
10. For a translation of the new critical text, see McGinn, *Apocalyptic Spirituality*, pp. 89–96.
11. *Die Apokalypse des Ps.-Methodius*, Anastasios Lalos, ed. (Meisenheim am Glan, 1976. *Beiträge zur klassischen Philologie*, Heft 83).
12. *Hildegardis Scivias*, A. Führkötter and A. Carlevaris, edd. (Turnhout, 1978. *Corpus Christianorum. Continuatio Mediaevalis* XLIII–XLIIIA).
13. *Ambrosii Autperti Opera. Expositionis in Apocalypsim*, Robert Weber, ed. (Turnhout, 1975. *Corpus Christianorum. Continuatio Mediaevalis* XXVII–XXVIIA). A minor early medieval commentary on the Apocalypse has just been edited by E. Ann Matter, "The Pseudo-Alcuinian *De septem sigillis:* An Early Latin Apocalypse Exegesis," *Traditio*, vol. 36, 1980, pp. 111–38.

14. *Anglo-Norman Texts. Le Livre de Sibile by Philippe de Thaon*, Hugh Shields, ed. (London, 1979. Anglo-Norman Text Society). The ascription of this text to Philippe de Thaon (see pp. 24–6) appears doubtful to me.

15. Milton McC. Gatch, *Preaching and Theology in Anglo-Saxon England* (Toronto, 1977), discusses eschatological and apocalyptic themes in the preaching of Aelfric and Wulfstan on pp. 60–116. See also Emmerson, *Antichrist in the Middle Ages*, pp. 150–5.

16. *Journal of the Warburg and Coutauld Institutes*, vol. 41, 1978, pp. 1–15.

17. A position that Alexander had earlier rejected, but which under the influence of M. Ranghieri's arguments he left open in his last article, "The Diffusion of Byzantine Apocalypses," in *Prophecy and Millenarianism*, p. 58.

18. In *Paganisme, Judaisme, Christianisme. Mélanges offerts à Marcel Simon* (Paris, 1978), pp. 153–83.

19. In *The Spirituality of Western Christendom*, E. Rozanne Elder, ed. (Kalamazoo, 1976), pp. 41–71.

20. E.g., I. Shahid, "The *Kebra Nagast* in Recent Scholarship," *Le Muséon*, vol. 89, 1976, pp. 133–78, gives a summary of work on the Ethiopian national epic, a text which may have bearing on the origins of the Pseudo-Methodius. R. K. Emmerson, "Antichrist as Anti-Saint," *American Benedictine Review*, vol. 30, 1979, pp. 175–90, discusses the hagiographic background to Adso's *De Ortu et Tempore Antichristi*. A. R. Bell, "Muspilli: Apocalypse as Political Threat," *Studies in the Literary Imagination*, vol. 8, 1975, pp. 75–104, gives an unconvincing political interpretation of this ninth-century vernacular apocalyptic poem.

21. Marjorie Reeves and John V. Fleming, *Two Poems attributed to Joachim of Fiore* (Philadelphia, 1978).

22. E. R. Daniel, "Abbot Joachim of Fiore: The *De Ultimis Tribulationibus*," in *Prophecy and Millenarianism*, pp. 165–89.

23. Prof. Daniel translated an important section of Book II of the *Liber Concordie* in B. McGinn, *Apocalyptic Spirituality*, pp. 120–34. In addition, I have translated other selections from Joachim both in *Apocalyptic Spirituality*, pp. 113–9, 136–48; and *Visions of the End*, pp. 130–41.

24. As reported in L. Goia, "Bibliography of Editions and Translations in Progress," *Speculum*, vol. 55, 1980, p. 199.

25. For my critique of *Prophecy in the Later Middle Ages*, see McGinn, "Apocalypticism in the Middle Ages," pp. 276–83.

26. Wendelborn lists only German scholars in his bibliography (pp. 293–8). For his thesis on Joachim's radicalism, see pp. 38–48, 88, and 154–63.

27. The six sections treat: I. Divisions of History; II. Concordances; III. *Initiatio-Fructificatio* Schema; IV. The Unity of the Trinity and its Implication for History; V. The Call-Fall-Return of the Jews and Greeks; and VI. Church Structure in the Third *Status*.

28. The book lacks a detailed treatment of Joachim's exegesis, but Wendelborn has provided this in his article, "Die Hermeneutik des kalabresischen Abtes Joachim von Fiore," *Communio Viatorum*, vol. 17, 1974, pp. 63–91.

29. E.g., on pp. 105–6 and 166, where he plays down the role of the "spiritualis pater" in the third *status*.

30. I have reviewed the book at greater length in *The Journal of Religion*, vol. 59, 1979, pp. 240–2.

31. De Lubac also wrote a review article of Mottu's book, "L'énigmatique actualitè de Joachim de Fiore: A propos d'un ouvrage récent," *Revue de théologie et de philosophie*, vol. 111, 1979, pp. 35–46.

32. *Exègése médiévale* (Paris, 1959–63), vol. 2.1, pp. 437–558.

33. De Lubac also studies some of Joachim's most noted opponents, especially Thomas Aquinas and Bonaventure, whom he judges as radically different from the abbot despite some borrowings, see Chapter three, pp. 123–60. This chapter resumes material de Lubac put forth in "Joachim de Flore jugé par S. Bonaventure et S. Thomas," in *Pluralisme et Oecumenisme en recherches théologiques* (Paris, 1976), pp. 37–49.

34. See McGinn, "Apocalypticism in the Middle Ages," pp. 268–70, 280–1.

35. *Dictionnaire de spiritualité* (Paris, 1974), vol. VIII, cc. 1179–1201. On the radical character of the third *status*, see cc. 1190–3.

36. A less noteworthy example of the same tendency is V. Ferrara, "Gioacchino da Fiore come esponente della vocazione del popolo di Dio dell'Italia meridionale alla speculazione teologica ed il Concilio Ecumenico Vaticano Secondo," *Monitor ecclesiasticus*, vol. 102, 1977, pp. 116–43.

37. "L'ecclesiologia di Gioacchino da Fiore," *Doctor Communis*, vol. 32, 1979, pp. 302–26; and "La teologia trinitaria di Gioacchino da Fiore," *Divinitas*, vol. 23, 1979, pp. 281–312.

38. *Rivista di Filosofia Neo-Scolastica*, vol. 71, 1979, pp. 621–85.

39. Part of di Napoli's argument for Joachim's orthodoxy is his suggested correction of the anti-Lombard *figurae* from *Liber figurarum* (see pp. 648–9). The arbitrary character of his reading can be seen by a comparison with the study of Harold Lee, "The Anti-Lombard Figures of Joachim of Fiore: A Reinterpretation," *Prophecy and Millenarianism*, pp. 127–42, who provides a far more convincing reading of these difficult and enigmatic images without indulging in arbitrary manuscript emendations.

40. "Gioacchino da Fiore e Pietro Lombardo," pp. 663–9. Bonaventure gets slightly higher marks on pp. 670–2.

41. Y.-D. Gélinas, "La critique de Thomas d'Aquin sur l'exégèse de Joachim de Flore," in *Tommaso d'Aquino nel suo settimo centenario. Atti del Congresso Internazionale* (Rome-Naples, 1974), vol. 1, pp. 368–75. This piece contains an extended discussion of B. McGinn, "The Abbot and the Doctors: Scholastic Reactions to the Radical Eschatology of Joachim of Fiore," *Church History*, vol. 40, 1971, pp. 30–47.

42. P. Meinhold, "Thomas von Aquin und Joachim von Fiore und ihre Deutung der Geschichte," *Saeculum*, vol. 27, 1976, pp. 66–76. Meinhold's emphasis is on the thought of Thomas where he provides a provoking analysis of the main lines of a Thomistic theology of history, though without distinguishing between explicit and implicit elements in the text of Thomas.

43. G. Baget-Bozzo, "Modello trinitario e modello cristologico nella teologia della storia: Gioacchino da Fiore e Tommaso d'Aquino," *Renovatio*, vol. 9, 1974, pp. 39–50.

44. In *1274 Année charnière. Mutations et continuités* (Paris, 1977), pp. 781–96.

45. "In applying his Trinitarian doctrine to the process of history Joachim conceives his 'threes' clearly in the relationship of Two sent by One, and One proceeding from Two. Thus the second *status* of the Son must have its beginning away back in the first *status* of the Father . . . But equally the third *status* of the Holy Spirit must have a double origin, proceeding not only from the Son, but also the Father" (p. 785).
46. M. Reeves, "History and Prophecy in Medieval Thought," *Mediaevalia et Humanistica*, N.S., vol. 5, 1974, pp. 51–75.
47. *Traditio*, vol. 36, 1980, pp. 269–316.
48. *Ibid.*, p. 269.
49. See her evaluation of the positions of B. McGinn and H. Mottu in *ibid.*, pp. 294–7.
50. See the remarks on the importance of Christology in *ibid.*, pp. 290–1.
51. *Speculum*, vol. 55, 1980, pp. 469–83.
52. *Ibid.*, p. 471.
53. In *Septième centenaire de la mort de Saint Louis. Actes des Colloques de Royaumont et de Paris* (Paris, 1976), pp. 291–301. Manselli explains the purpose of the article in a "Note additionnelle" which gives a listing of the articles contributed by the Italian scholar to this area of study between 1970 and 1975.
54. In *Geschichtsschreibung und Geistiges Leben im Mittelalter. Festschrift zum 65. Geburtstag von Heinz Löwe* (Cologne, 1978), pp. 427–49.
55. F. Seibt, "*Liber Figurarum XII* and the Classical Idea of Utopia," in *Prophecy and Millenarianism*, pp. 257–66, resuming points developed in "Utopie im Mittelalter," *Historische Zeitschrift*, vol. 208, 1969, pp. 550–94.
56. For a translation of the text accompanying this *figura*, see McGinn, *Apocalyptic Spirituality*, pp. 142–8.
57. See especially F. Seibt, *Utopica. Modelle totale Sozialplannung* (Dusseldorf, 1972).
58. In *Prophecy and Millenarianism*, pp. 143–64.
59. R. Manselli, "Testimonianze minore sulle eresie: Gioacchino da Fiore di fronte a catari e valdesi," *Studi medievali*, 3a serie, vol. 18, 1977, pp. 7–17.
60. R. Lerner, "Joachim of Fiore as a Link between St. Bernard and Innocent III on the Figural Significance of Melchisedech," *Mediaeval Studies*, vol. 42, 1980, pp. 471–6.
61. S. Wessley, " 'Bonum est Benedicto mutare locum': The Role of the 'Life of Benedict' in Joachim of Fiore's Monastic Reform," *Revue Benedictine*, vol. 90, 1980, pp. 314–28.
62. L. Clucas, "Eschatological Theory in Byzantine Hesychasm: A Parallel to Joachim of Fiore?" *Byzantinische Zeitschrift*, vol. 70, 1977, pp. 324–46. Clucas admits that there is no evidence for direct contact between Joachim's ideas and the Hesychast movement.
63. "L'énigmatique actualitè de Joachim de Fiore," pp. 40, 45.
64. For more detail, see the reviews of C. Schmitt in *Archivum Franciscanum Historicum*, vols. 69 and 71, 1976 and 78, pp. 521–5, and 221–6.
65. E.g., D. Maselli, ed., *Eretici e ribelli del XIII e XIV sec. Saggi sullo spiritualismo francescano in Toscana* (Pistoia, 1974); and Cahiers de Fanjeaux 11, *La religion populaire en Languedoc du XIIIe siècle à la moitie du XIVe siècle* (Toulouse, 1976).

66. Especially, E. R. Daniel, "St. Bonaventure: A Faithful Disciple of Saint Francis? A Reexamination of the Question," and "St. Bonaventure: Defender of Franciscan Eschatology," both in *San Bonaventura 1274–1974* (Grottaferrata-Rome, 1973–4), respectively vol. II, pp. 170–87, and vol. IV, pp. 793–806.

67. W. Kölmel, "Franziskus in der Geschichtstheologie," *Franziskanische Studien*, vol. 60, 1978, pp. 67–89 (pp. 76–83 discuss the Joachite Spiritual view).

68. G. Leff, "The Franciscan Concept of Man," in *Prophecy and Millenarianism*, pp. 217–37.

69. B. McGinn, "The Abbot and the Doctors," pp. 41–5.

70. N. Falbel, "Sao Boaventura e a Teologia da História de Joaquim de Fiore. Un Resumo Crítico," *San Bonaventura*, vol. II. pp. 571–84.

71. A Gerken, "Besass Bonaventura eine Hermeneutik zur Intepretation der Geschichte?" *Wissenschaft und Weisheit*, vol. 37, 1974, pp. 19–39.

72. W. Schachten, "Die Trinitätslehre Bonaventuras als Explikation der Offenbarung vom personalen Gott," *Franziskanische Studien*, vol. 56, 1974, pp. 191–214. On the relation of Bonaventure to Joachim, see pp. 195–7, 202–3, and 213, which stress the Franciscan's corrections of Joachim's failure to emphasize the role of Christ. To the best of my knowledge Schachten's 1974 Freiburg dissertation on Joachim, *Trinitas et Tempora. Trinitätsdenken und Geschichtslehre Joachims von Fiore* has not yet been published.

73. R. Manselli, "San Bonaventura e la storia francescana," in *1274 Année charnière*, pp. 863–72.

74. In *San Bonaventura Maestro di Vita Francescana e di Sapienza Christiana, Miscellanea Francescana*, vol. 75, 1975, pp. 409–27. The same collection contains a survey article by Enrique Rivera de Ventosa, "Tres visiones de la historia: Joaquín de Fiore, san Bonaventura y Hegel. Estudio comparativo," pp. 779–808.

75. B. McGinn, "The Significance of Bonaventure's Theology of History," in *Celebrating the Medieval Heritage. A Colloquy on the Thought of Aquinas and Bonaventure. The Journal of Religion*, vol. 58, 1978, Supplement, pp. S64–S81.

76. S. Otto, "Bonaventuras Christologische Einwand gegen die Geschichtslehre des Joachim von Fiore," in *Miscellanea Mediaevalia 11. Die Mächte des Guten und Bösen* (Berlin, 1977), pp. 113–30.

77. H. de Lubac, *La postérité spirituelle*, pp. 125–39.

78. D. C. West, "Between Flesh and Spirit: Joachite Pattern and Meaning in the *Cronica* of Fra Salimbene," *Journal of Medieval History*, vol. 3, 1977, pp. 339–52; and "The Education of Fra Salimbene of Parma: The Joachite Influence," in *Prophecy and Millenarianism*, pp. 191–215.

79. J. Paul, "Le Joachimisme et les Joachimites au mileau du XIIIe siècle d'après le témoignage de Fra Salimbene," in *1274 Année charnière*, pp. 797–813.

80. M. da Alatri, "Predicazione e predicatori nella Cronica di Fra Salimbene," *Collectanea Francescana*, vol. 46, 1976, pp. 63–91; and "Presenza di San Francesco nella Cronica di Salimbene da Parma," *Archivum Franciscanum Historicum*, vol. 69, 1976, pp. 321–35.

81. M.-M. Dufeil, "Trois 'Sens de l'histoire' affrontés vers 1250–60," in *1274 Année charnière*, pp. 815–48. The article contains translations and analyses of

the key documents in an appended dossier. The same volume contains an introductory account by B. Guillemain, "Le sens de l'histoire au XIIIe siècle," pp. 881–6, and a discussion of this theme by the participants in this section (pp. 887–97).

82. For translations of texts from the three Spirituals, see McGinn, *Visions of the End*, pp. 208–16. Olivi's "Letter to the Sons of Charles II" is translated in McGinn, *Apocalyptic Spirituality*, pp. 173–81; and Angelo's "Letter of Defense" on pp. 159–72 of the same volume.

83. Particularly note "L'ideal du spirituel selon Pierre Jean-Olivi," in *Franciscains d'Oc*, pp. 99–126; and "Pietro di Giovanni Olivi spirituale," in *Chi erano gli Spirituali?*, pp. 181–204.

84. G. L. Potestà, "Un secolo di studi sull' 'Arbor vitae': Chiesa ed escatologia in Ubertino da Casale," *Collectanea Francescana*, vol. 47, 1977, pp. 217–67. After an exhaustive survey of the literature, the author offers a survey of Ubertino's apocalyptic ideas (pp. 252–66).

85. C. T. Davis, "Le Pape Jean XXII et les Spirituels, Ubertin de Casale," in *Franciscains d'Oc*, pp. 262–83.

86. *Collectanea Francescana*, vol. 47, 1977, pp. 5–25.

87. E.g., "Angelo Clareno et les spirituels du midi," in *Franciscains d'Oc*, pp. 243–62.

88. D. Douie, "Some Treatises against the Fraticelli in the Vatican Library," *Franciscan Studies*, vol. 38, 1978, pp. 10–80.

89. H. Lee, "*Scrutamini Scripturas:* Joachimist Themes and *Figurae* in the Early Religious Writing of Arnold of Vilanova," *Journal of the Warburg and Courtauld Institutes*, vol. 37, 1974, pp. 33–56.

90. R. Manselli, "A proposito del Cristianesimo di Dante: Gioacchino da Fiore, Gioachimismo, Spiritualismo Francescano," *Letteratura e Critica. Studi in Onore di Natalino Sapegno* (Rome, 1975), vol. II, pp. 163–92.

91. R. Emmerson and R. Herzman, "Antichrist, Simon Magus and Dante's Inferno XIX," *Traditio*, vol. 36, 1980, pp. 373–98.

92. *Dante Studies*, vol. 93, 1975, pp. 143–60.

93. *Past and Present*, vol. 72, 1976, pp. 3–24.

94. *Ibid.*, p. 19. See also my own criticism of Cohn in *Visions of the End*, pp. 28–32.

95. *Church History*, vol. 47, 1978, pp. 155–73. The quotation is from p. 155.

96. Girolamo Savonarola, *Compendio di Rivelazioni. Testo volgare et latino e Dialogus de veritate prophetica*, A. Crucitti, ed. (Rome, 1974). The text of the *Compendium* has been translated in *Apocalyptic Spirituality*, pp. 192–275.

97. Rusconi has also written an article on the role of Jerusalem in fifteenth-century thought that overlaps in part with material in Chap. VI of this book; see "Gerusalemme nella predicazione populare quattrocentesca tra millenio, ricordi di viaggi e luogo sacro," *Bullettino dell'Istituto Storico Italiano per il Medio Evo e Archivio Muratoriano*, vol. 87, 1978, pp. 229–47.

98. In *Genèse et dèbuts du grande schisme d'Occident* (Paris, 1980), pp. 615–22.

99. *American Historical Review*, vol. 86, 1981, pp. 533–52.

100. *Ibid.*, p. 551, n.43: ". . . the Black Death itself seems to have inspired fewer prophecies than one might have expected, but as yet this is only an impres-

sion . . ."

101. G. Podskalsky, "Der Fall Konstantinopels in der Sicht der Reichs-eschatologie und der Klagelieder. Vorahnungen und Reaktionen," *Archiv für Kulturgeschichte*, vol. 57, 1975, pp. 71–86. The same author's "Marginalien zur byzantinischen Reichseschatologie," *Byzantinische Zeitschrift*, vol. 67, 1974, pp. 351–8, should also be noted.

102. M. Thomas, "Lo *Speculum humanae salvationis* e l'idea occidentale della reden-zione," *Nuova Rivista Storica*, vol. 58, 1974, pp. 379–97.

103. T. Struve, "Utopie und Gesellschaftliche Wirklichkeit. Zur Bedeutung der Friedenskaisers im späten Mittelalter," *Historische Zeitschrift*, vol. 225, 1977, pp. 65–95.

104. K. Schreiner, "Die Staufer in Sage, Legende und Prophetie," in *Die Zeit der Staufer. Geschichte-Kunst-Kultur* (Stuttgart, 1977), vol. III, pp. 249–62.

105. *Archiv für Kulturgeschichte*, vol. 57, 1975, pp. 87–116.

106. For one little-known condemned apocalyptic prophet, see R. E. Lerner, "An 'Angel of Philadelphia' in the Reign of Philip the Fair: The Case of Giuard of Cressonessart," in *Order and Innovation in the Middle Ages*, W. C. Jordan et al., edd., (Philadelphia, 1976), pp. 346–64, including an edition of the relevant Inquisition documents.

107. See S. D. Skazkin and V. V. Samarkin, "Dolchino i bibliia," *Srednie veka*, vol. 38, 1975, pp. 84–99 (with Italian summary, p. 99); and R. Olioli, *L'Eresia a Bologna fra XIII e XIV secoli. II. L'eresia dolciniana* (Rome, 1975).

108. C. Berkhout and J. Russell, *Medieval Heresies. A Bibliography*, list 294 items in their section on the Hussites, second only to the number of pieces on the Cathars.

109. J. Schwarz, "Chiliasmus als christliche Utopie," in *Bohemia Sacra: das Christentum in Bohemia 973–1973*, F. Seibt, ed., (Dusseldorf, 1974), pp. 209–21; R. Cegna, "Fonti escatologiche del rivoluzionarismo ussita," *Rivista di Storia e Letteratura Religiosa*, vol. 15, 1979, pp. 349–71; A. Molnar, "Taboritisches Schrifftum," *Communio Viatorum*, vol. 22, 1979, pp. 105–22; and R. Gladstein, "Eschatological Trends in Bohemian Jewry during the Hussite Period," in *Prophecy and Millenarianism*, pp. 239–56.

110. See J. Bücking, "Der 'Oberrheinische Revolutionär' heisst Conrad Stürtzel, seines Zeichens kgl. Hofkanzler," *Archiv für Kulturgeschichte*, vol. 56, 1974, pp. 177–97. See the critical remarks of H. Boockmann in *Deutsches Archiv*, vol. 31, 1975, pp. 291–2.

111. E.g., D. Jeffrey's discussion of the apocalyptic Franciscan background for some Middle English lyrics in *The Early English Lyric and Franciscan Spiritual-ity* (Lincoln, 1975), pp. 69–72, 238–9. Also the articles of T. P. Campbell, "Eschatology and the Nativity in English Mystery Plays," *American Benedic-tine Review*, vol. 27, 1976, pp. 297–320; and M. Vaughan, "The Three Advents in the *Secunda Pastorum*," *Speculum*, vol. 55, 1980, pp. 484–504.

112. See B. Nolan, *The Gothic Visionary Perspective* (Princeton, 1977).

113. E.g., P. R. Szittya, "The Antifraternal Tradition in Middle English Litera-ture," *Speculum*, vol. 52, 1977, pp. 287–313; and (despite some reservations) R. Adams, "The Nature of Need in 'Piers Plowman' XX," *Traditio*, vol. 34, 1978, pp. 273–301.

Addendum

This essay was intended to include a section on medieval apocalyptic art, but as the limited scope of my own reading became more evident to me, and as the essay grew in length, this section had to be dropped. I can only hope that an art historian may soon give us an extended analysis of what strikes me as a particularly rich outpouring of literature on apocalyptic themes in medieval art in recent years. I feel constrained, however, to mention a few key items. First and most important, because it studies the interaction between exegetical and iconographical traditions, is *L'Apocalypse de Jean. Traditions exégètiques et iconographiques IIIe–XIII siècles* (Geneva, 1979. Colloque du Fondation Hardt). In second place should be noted Frederick van der Meer's *Apocalypse: Visions from the Book of Relevation in Western Art* (London, 1978; but published simultaneously in several European languages), an expensive and flawed study, but important for its scope and splendid color illustrations. In addition, a number of facsimile editions and studies of noted illustrated apocalyptic texts have recently appeared, from the Trier Apocalypse (1975), through various Beatus manuscripts (Gerona in 1975, and a Madrid manuscript in 1976), to the earliest typographic version of the vernacular *Der Antichrist und die fünfzehn Zeichen* (1979). I make no attempt here to deal with other secondary literature, either monographs or articles.

"Less Than I Was Born To":
Two Studies of King Henry VI

MICHAEL ALTSCHUL

Bertram Wolffe, *Henry VI*. (English Monarchs Series). London: Eyre Methuen, 1981. Pp. xii, 400; 3 maps, 24 plates. £19.95.

Ralph A. Griffiths, *The Reign of King Henry VI*. Berkeley and Los Angeles: University of California Press, 1981. Pp. xxiv, 968; 5 maps, 39 plates. $35.00.

In scene (i) of Act III of *3 Henry VI*, two gamekeepers come upon Henry of Lancaster—alone, disguised, prayer book in hand. Overhearing him, and knowing him to be the deposed king, the keepers resolve to deliver him over to Edward IV. The second keeper interrupts Henry's soliloquy and receives this initial reply:

> *keeper* Say, what art thou that talk'st of kings and queens?
> *Henry* More than I seem, and less than I was born to.
> $$\text{(III.i.}55\text{--}56)$$

Shakespeare's meaning is clear: Henry is more than, or other than, a mere shepherd; but also now less than the regal figure, the bearer of the Lancastrian inheritance, that was his birthright. Shakespeare's Henry, of course, is also the well-meaning, long-suffering, political and moral innocent: part cause, part victim (and by extension symbolic of England as victim) of the "Wars of the Roses." Historians have long regretted that Shakespeare's image, which owes at least something to the (unsuccessful) Tudor efforts at canonization, dominates popular perception; but until now Henry and his reign have not received the kind of full, critical attention by scholars to counter this tradition. The two books under consideration here, by happy coincidence of simultaneous publication, do at last provide a comprehensive, and complementary, view of the last Lancastrian king, his kingship and his kingdom. They fill, singly and together, an enormous gap in the literature, and they fill it admirably.

Dr. Wolffe's book, prefigured in a paper published in 1972,[1] is an altogether worthy addition to the English Monarchs series. His task is doubly daunting: not merely to write a biography of a medieval figure, but of one so "insubstantial and unsuccessful" (p. x) as Henry VI. Dr. Griffiths, by contrast, consciously eschews a biographical approach (cf. p.

291

Medievalia et Humanistica, New Series, Number 11 (Paul Maurice Clogan, ed.). Rowman and Littlefield, Totowa, NJ, 1982.

vii), preferring a combination of analytical and narrative chapters that by their length and wealth of detail come close to the character of an encyclopedic reference work. Both approaches work; each stands independently, and each nicely complements the other. Additionally, both authors bring special orientations and expertise to their respective tasks: Wolffe, the fiscal and financial history of the crown lands, Griffiths, an almost unrivalled knowledge of Wales and the marches.[2] Along with scholars such as J. R. Lander, R. L. Storey, and Charles Ross, Wolffe and Griffiths are bringing to fruition the vision of mentors and historians like Chrimes and McFarlane: the rehabilitation and the study, on its own terms and within its own frame of reference, of 15th-century England as a whole.[3]

Wolffe's ability to sustain a narrative biography is grounded in both a skillful writing style and an unrelentingly negative view of Henry as king. Griffiths successfully controls the massive dimensions of his work by a carefully nuanced analytical framework and the inclusion of narrative chapters. But by being twice as long, and organizationally more complex, it runs the dangers, as it were, of twice as many pitfalls, not always avoided. For example, a partial analysis of Cade's rebellion is given on pp. 304–10, while the narrative and a fuller analysis are found only some 300 pages later. Similarly, there are three quite brief sections on xenophobia and the treatment of aliens, chronologically separate and widely scattered in terms of pagination (pp. 167–71, 551–61, 790–95); a single integrated discussion might have been more effective. No organizational scheme in a work of this magnitude and scope can be perfect; the point is simply that, by taking a "simpler," more straightforward approach, Wolffe's book avoids this sort of commentary on organization.

Each book falls naturally into three broad, slightly overlapping sections: the period of conciliar rule, 1422–1437; the age of "personal rule," 1436–1453; and the emergence of Richard of York and civil wars, 1450–1460/61 (with brief epilogues, more significantly treated by Wolffe because of his biographical framework, taking the story to Henry's death in 1471). Both authors are in substantial agreement on the major issues: the breakdown of the earlier Lancastrian achievement and consensus; an alarming proliferation of lawless, violent factions; and the utter lack of credibility to any later (posthumous) claims for Henry's saintliness. Some significant differences of emphasis, however, warrant detailed examination.

The conciliar period and the minority. Wolffe argues that the councilors fulfilled a near-impossible task both reasonably and effectively; their regime bore witness to the substantial Lancastrian inheritance and the political "maturity" of the age: "it was to prove easier for the kingdom to flourish under a minor than under a weak and ineffective adult king who failed to harness its powerful energies, or misdirected them" (p. 27). The feuds of Gloucester anf Beaufort were for the most part nullified by the timely interventions of Bedford, the one man who truly showed the "qualities of kingship" (p. 79). More than the death of Bedford, it was the assumption of personal rule by Henry that quickly blasted the substantial achievements of the previous decade and a half.

Griffiths takes a less favorable view, emphasizing the scramble for preferment and a basic ineffectiveness in sustaining consistency and order. He is harshest on Gloucester, dubbing him "imperious" (p. 75) and unwilling to work in concert with others. Griffiths shrewdly argues a paradox: the personal rivalries among Gloucester, Beaufort, and Bedford simultaneously undermined the corporate effectiveness of conciliar rule but also made it possible, since they prevented any one man from assuming a permanent and consistent domination of policy and resources. He stresses, even more than Wolffe, the murky constitutional significance of conciliar rule, in the long run unworkable in principle because of the theory of answerability to the person of the monarch. Both authors agree that when Henry did assume personal rule, the council returned to its normal character as an advisory body, but one that now bore within it an added theatre (beyond the household and the local networks) for frictions and personal rivalries.

The period of personal rule. Wolffe's judgment is clear, mordant, and important: an unmitigated disaster in every respect. Henry *created* faction and factionalism; he capriciously destroyed Gloucester; he lavished patronage and titles on the unworthy, above all Suffolk and Fiennes; he was consistently out-thought and outmaneuvered by Charles VII of France (yet *another* uncle!). His regime let loose an "undignified scramble for grants" (p. 110); his style betrayed a "dangerous combination of forcefulness and weakness" (p. 133). The period culminated in a series of disasters in 1449–1453, for all of which Henry must take not merely theoretical, but actual and direct personal responsibility: the parliamentary complaints and impeachments, bankruptcy, the legitimate grievances in Cade's rebellion, the final loss of Normandy and Gascony. To Wolffe, these are the fruits of Henry's rule and simultaneously a series of damning indictments of that rule. Worst of all, Henry learned nothing: the fall of Suffolk was immediately followed by the ascendancy of Somerset.

Griffiths disagrees, yet perhaps more in degree than in kind. He views Henry as schooled in dependence (a line from Gloucester and Bedford, through Suffold and Somerset, ultimately to Queen Margaret); neglectful, overly generous, but well-intentioned (p. 253). Overly credulous, too easily led and manipulated, his indulgence promoted instability and a ready recourse to violent self-help. Griffiths detects less of Henry's direct hand in policy and decision-making than does Wolffe; clearly, however, he does not deny it. The difficulties of raising adequate resources for prosecution of the French wars, the lack of abilities of certain commanders, the wilfulness of faction (above all the almost self-generating Suffolk "covin," p. 588)—all lend a certain cover to his direct rule. Henry *stimulated*, but did not necessarily directly create, difficulties and disasters; and perhaps *no* king could have prevented or mastered or overcome them all.

Clearly, historians have in Henry what should be termed an "under-mighty" king. Both Wolffe and Griffiths, taken together, have more in common than otherwise. They substantially modify, and should altogether replace, the hitherto dominant characterizations of K. B. McFarlane, who dubbed Henry's reign as one of "inanity" (with its shrewdly designed half-echo of "insanity") and perpetual childishness, for does not a Shakespearean *persona* lurk behind McFarlane's terms? [4]

Richard of York and the civil wars. In the summer of 1453 Henry suffered a total mental collapse. He recovered by late 1454 or early 1455, then seems to have had a partial relapse in 1455–1456, and was thereafter, for the remainder of his life, now truly a cipher, a puppet in others' hands. His illnesses witnessed the two protectorates of Richard, duke of York, intertwined with the ascendancy and fall of Somerset, and finally the all-out Yorkist challenge to the Lancastrian throne, by now dominated by Queen Margaret on behalf of her son Prince Edward. Wolffe sees in Richard of York a more attractive, and more competent, figure than most other historians would allow. In his view, Richard's military abilities were consistently undermined by Henry and Somerset, as were his support and (self-interested) sympathies for the reforms espoused in the 1449–1453 period. Richard, in short, was forced into open opposition, an opposition made more acute and urgent because of well-grounded fears for his lineage (both before, and after, the birth of Prince Edward with its impact on his possible rights of succession). The removal of the court to Coventry in 1456 erased the last vestiges of normal government and made open warfare inevitable. York overplayed his hand in 1455 after St. Albans, and again in 1460 after Northampton: his supporters did not view him as a replacement for King Henry. But Wolffe is firmly on the Yorkist side: if not Richard, then at least Richard's son replaced Henry VI. The reign of Edward IV is not Wolffe's concern; the point is that Richard of York's ambitions were not entirely without merit or value: *anyone* would have been preferable to Henry as king!

Perhaps predictably, Griffiths takes a far less sympathetic view. He discounts Richard's military effectiveness, save for the important defense of Calais in the 1450s, particularly when it was used, along with Wales and Ireland, for the Yorkist assault in 1459–1460. In fact, he sees Richard as Wolffe sees Henry: consistently outmaneuvered, in France and in England, by his adversaries. In 1450, and again during his protectorates, Richard operated more as a factionalist than as a reformer; his concerns were his lineage, recouping his loans, and personal ascendancy, and he was as avaricious in his way as Suffolk or Somerset were in theirs. He consistently failed to realize how narrow, and how limited, his base of support was; his "fall" in 1456 was because he did not truly dominate his own protectorate (p. 748), and his actions in October 1460 recklessly threw away all the otherwise legitimate gains that Northampton had earlier secured. The judgment is harsh: Wakefield may have blasted, but also culminated, the "aspirations of a decade" (p. 854); and Richard, more than the Queen, certainly more than the by now almost invisible King Henry, bears primary responsibility for the murderous battles of 1460–1461 (p. 867).

Do the differences of opinion about Richard of York generalize into fundamental disagreements about the nature and quality of Lancastrian rule, and about the true scope and meaning of the "Wars of the Roses"? Neither writer directly confronts such questions in so many words; my own impression, however, is that they would not. Both agree that the reign of the last Lancastrian witnessed the emergence of a spectacular and ultimately deadly factionalism; Wolffe would simply assign more personal responsibility for that to Henry himself than would Griffiths. Both would also agree, I believe, that the phrase "Wars of the Roses" has little beyond a certain shorthand convenience to commend itself to historians. The battles were few, no more and no less murderous than some earlier—and some later—periods in English history, and the essential flavor of public and local life remained remarkably the same after as before them. Factionalism, local interests, and self-help were hardly unique to mid-15th-century England. If the wars were fought over no great "national" cause, they were certainly understandable as an *enhanced* and *concentrated* episode within a framework of values stretching back to the eleventh and twelfth centuries, and forward to the seventeenth and even eighteenth centuries: property, local power, patronage, lineage, clientage. The fact that the crown itself was now at issue is again not unique to this period. In the long perspective, in one important sense, the "Wars of the Roses" are but one phase or stage in the *longue durée* of aristocratic domination of English politics and society. In a more strictly fifteenth-century context, Wolffe and Griffiths have shown us—and this is their most impressive and enduring contribution—the reign of Henry VI in its own right, not as a mere prelude to or precondition for "The Wars of the Roses." [5]

Finally, historians of the fifteenth century cannot entirely wish away Shakespeare—or more precisely, burden themselves with the interpretation of Shakespeare associated with Tillyard and his followers.[6] Wolffe and Griffiths treat the plays cooly, briefly, and for the most part appropriately; I would enter the lists on Shakespeare's side to make one specific point. Clearly, Henry VI was no saint; and if he was a fool, it was in the sense of incompetence rather than of simple-mindedness or of childish innocence. Henry *was* more than he seemed—he was a king with, at least for a time, a mind of his own. And he was also less than he had been born to—he was, in a word, an "undermighty" king. "More than I seem, and less than I was born to": might it not be that in this line Shakespeare, perhaps without fully realizing it, was a better historian than Henry was a king, and might it be hoped that neither Dr. Wolffe nor Dr. Griffiths, whom I have remorselessly yoked together throughout this essay, will begrudge or disdain this association of a third name with their own?

NOTES

1. B. P. Wolffe, "The Personal Rule of Henry VI," in S. B. Chrimes, C. D. Ross and R. A. Griffiths, eds., *Fifteenth Century England* (Manchester, 1972), pp. 29–48.
2. Wolffe's major studies are: "Acts of Resumption in the Lancastrian Parliaments, 1399–1456," *English Historical Review*, LXXIII (1958), pp. 583–613; *The Crown Lands, 1461–1536* (London, 1970); *The Royal Demesne in English History from the Conquest to 1509* (London, 1971). Apart from numerous important articles in such journals as the *Welsh History Review* and the *Bulletin of the Board of Celtic Studies*, *Speculum* and the *Journal of Medieval History*, and others, Griffiths's major work has been *The Principality of Wales in the Later Middle Ages*, of which vol. 1, *South Wales, 1277–1536*, has thus far appeared (Cardiff, 1972). "Almost unrivalled" in the text because he must share pride of place with two other scholars, T. B. Pugh and R. R. Davies. I have discussed Davies's work in my article, "Conquests and Cultures, Norman and Non-Norman," *Medievalia et Humanistica*, new series, no. X (1981), pp. 219–22.
3. J. R. Lander, *Government and Community: England, 1450–1509* (Cambridge, Massachusetts, 1980), a summary and distillation of innumerable specialized studies on aristocratic politics; R. L. Storey, *The End of the House of Lancaster* (London, 1966), a seminal and pioneering work based on the judicial records of the 1450s; Charles Ross, *Edward IV* (Berkeley, 1974), the only comprehensive modern biography. Ross is also preparing a much-needed biography of Richard III, to appear in the English Monarchs series. Chrimes's major books are *English Constitutional Ideas in the Fifteenth Century* (Cambridge, 1936) and *Henry VII* (Berkeley, 1972); McFarlane's work is accessible to two major collections, *Lancastrian Kings and Lollard Knights* (Oxford, 1972) and *The Nobility of Later Medieval England* (Oxford, 1973), both posthumously edited.
4. K. B. McFarlane, "The Wars of the Roses," *Proceedings of the British Academy*, L (1964), p. 97: "the war was fought because the nobility was unable to rescue the kingdom from the consequences of Henry VI's inanity by any other means"; *idem*, "Crown and Parliament in the Later Middle Ages," in *The Nobility of Later Medieval England*, p. 284: "in Henry VI second childhood succeeded first without the usual interval and under him the medieval kingship was in abeyance."

5. The entire cluster of associations, images, and implications of the phrase "The Wars of the Roses" has been subject to more than one withering criticism by modern historians, in particular McFarlane and Lander: McFarlane, "The Wars of the Roses," pp. 87–119, is a brilliantly written critique; for Lander, see his collected articles, *Crown and Nobility, 1450–1509* (London, 1976), *passim*. A good, brief, summary statement is provided by Wolffe himself in his paper "The Personal Rule of Henry VI" (above, note 1), p 44.

6. Most fifteenth-century social and political historians seem to feel that E. M. W. Tillyard's *Shakespeare's History Plays* (New York, 1946) still dominates the Shakespearean scholars' conceptions of what the history plays were all about. But Tillyard no longer commands universal, perhaps not even majority, support among literary critics; see, for example, Robert Ornstein, *A Kingdom for a Stage: the Achievement of Shakespeare's History Plays* (Cambridge, Massachusetts, 1972), and the collected studies in W. A. Armstrong, ed., *Shakespeare's Histories* (London, 1972).

Books Received

Aers, Davis. *Chaucer, Langland and the Creative Imagination.* Boston: Routledge and Kegan Paul, 1980. Pp. 236. $25.00.

Allen, Judson B. and Theresa A. Mortiz. *A Distinction of Stories: The Medieval Unity of Chaucer's Fair Chain of Narratives for Canterbury.* Columbus: Ohio State Univ. Press, 1981. Pp. 258. $20.00.

Anderson, William. *Dante the Maker.* Boston: Routledge and Kegan Paul, 1980. Pp. 497. $45.00.

Barney, Stephen A., ed. *Chaucer's Troilus: Essays in Criticism.* Hamden, CT: Archon Books, 1980. Pp. 216. $22.95.

Barron, W. R. J. *Trawthe and Treason: The Sin of Gawain Reconsidered: A Thematic Study of Sir Gawain and the Green Knight.* Manchester: Manchester Univ. Press, 1980. Pp. 150. $23.00.

Batra, Ravi. *Muslim Civilization and the Crisis in Iran.* Dallas: Venus Books, 1980. Pp. 218. $8.00.

Beers, Jesse, Jr. *Pendragon: The Lost Book of Tyneclif.* New York. Vantage Press, 1980. Pp. 249. $9.95.

Bernardo, Aldo S., ed. *Francesco Petrarca: Citizen of the World.* (Proceedings of the World Petrarch Congress, Washington, D.C., April 6–13, 1974.) Albany: State Univ. of New York Press, 1980. Pp. 313. $35.00 paper.

Blayney, Margaret S., ed. *Fifteenth-Century English Translations of Alain Chartier's le Traite de l'Esperance and Le Quadrilougue Invectif.* Oxford: Oxford Univ. Press, 1980. Pp. 259. $23.50.

Bolton, J. L. *The Medieval English Economy: 1150–1500.* Totowa, NJ: Rowman and Littlefield, 1980. Pp. 400. $25.00.

Bony, Jean. *The English Decorated Style: Gothic Architecture Transformed, 1250–1350.* Ithaca: Cornell Univ. Press, 1979, Pp. 315. $38.50.

Brown, Peter. *The Cult of the Saints: Its Rise and Function in Latin Christianity.* Chicago: Univ. of Chicago Press, 1980. Pp. 187. $15.00.

Bruckner, Matilda Tomaryn. *Narrative Invention in Twelfth-Century French Romance: The Convention of Hospitality (1160–1200).* Lexington, KY: French Forum Publishers, 1980. Pp. 230. $11.50.

Bullough, Vern L. *Sexual Variance in Society and History.* Chicago: Univ. of Chicago Press, 1980. Pp. 715. $9.95.

Carr, Francis. *Ivan the Terrible.* Totowa, NJ: Barnes & Noble Books, 1981. Pp. 220. $18.50.

Champanella, Tommaso. *A Poetical Dialogue (La Citta del Sole: Dialogo Poetico).* Trans. Daniel J. Donno. Los Angeles: Univ. of California Press, 1981. Pp. 152. $14.50.

Chancellor, John. *The Life and Times of Edward I*. Totowa NJ: Weidenfeld and Nicolson, 1981. Pp. 224. $17.50.

Chapman, Paul H. *The Norse Discovery of America*. Atlanta: One Candle Press, 1981. Pp. 120. $5.95 paper.

Cole, Douglas, ed. *Renaissance Drama*. Evanston, IL: Northwestern Univ. Press, 1980. Pp. 204. $22.95.

Collinson, Patrick. *Archbishop Grindal, 1519–1583: The Struggle for a Reformed Church*. Los Angeles: Univ. of California Press, 1979. Pp. 368. $27.50.

Cook, Albert. *Myth and Languages*. Bloomington: Indiana Univ. Press, 1980. Pp. 332. $22.50.

Coudert, Allison. *Alchemy: The Philosopher's Stone*. Boulder: Shambhala Publications, 1980. Pp. 239. $8.95.

Dawson, Christopher. *Mission to Asia*. Toronto: Univ. of Toronto Press, 1980. Pp. 247. $6.00.

Dennis, Andrew, P. Foote and R. Perkins, eds. *Laws of Early Iceland: Grágás I*. Manitoba: Univ. of Manitoba Press, 1980. Pp. 279. $27.50.

Dillon, Janette. *Shakespeare and the Solitary Man*. Totowa, NJ: Rowman and Littlefield, 1981. Pp. 182. $26.50.

Duby, Georges. *The Three Orders: Feudal Society Imagined*. Chicago: Univ. of Chicago Press, 1980. Pp. 381. $25.00.

Dunning, T. P. *Piers Plowman: An Interpretation of the A Text*. Rev. and ed. by T. P. Dolan. Oxford: Clarendon Press, 1980. Pp. 178. $34.95.

Eaker, Helen Lanneau, ed. *Giovannie de Conversino da Ravenna: Dragmalogia de Eligibili Vite Genere*. Lewisburg, PA: Bucknell Univ. Press, 1980. Pp. 291. $24.50.

Endres, Clifford W. *Joannes Secundus: The Latin Love Elegy in the Renaissance*. Hamden, CT: The Shoe String Press, 1981. Pp. 239. $25.00.

Fonternrose, Joseph. *Python: A Study of Delphic Myth and Its Origins*. Los Angeles: Univ. of California Press, 1980. Pp. 626. $8.95.

Foster, Kenelm. *The Two Dantes and Other Studies*. Los Angeles: Univ. of California Press, 1978. Pp. 260. $16.00.

Fowlie, Wallace. *A Reading of Dante's Inferno*. Chicago: Univ. of Chicago Press, 1981. Pp. 237. $18.00 (cloth); $6.50 (paper).

Fox, Denton, ed. *The Poems of Robert Henryson*. New York: Oxford Univ. Press, 1981. Pp. 596. $98.00.

Francis, Anne F. *Hieronimus Bosch: The Temptation of Saint Anthony*. Hickville, NY: Exposition Press, 1980. Pp. 61. $15.00.

Freddoso, Alfred J. and Henry Schuurman, trans. *Ockham's Theory of Propositions: Part II of the Summa Logicae*. Notre Dame: Univ. of Notre Dame Press, 1980. Pp. 212. $20.00.

Freeman, James A. *Milton and the Martial Muse*. Princeton: Princeton Univ. Press, 1981. Pp. 253. $17.50.

Freeman, Michelle A. *The Poetics of Translatio Studii and Conjointure: Chrétien de Troyes's Cligés*. Lexington, KY: French Forum Publishers, 1979. Pp. 199.

Gibaldi, Joseph, ed. *Approaches to Teaching Chaucer's Canterbury Tales*. New York: Modern Language Association of America, 1980. Pp. 175. $13.50 (cloth); $6.50 (paper).

Gibaldi, Joseph, ed. *Introduction to Scholarship in Modern Languages and Literatures.* New York: Modern Language Association, 1981. Pp. xii, 143. $6.25 paper.

Ginzburg, Carlo. *The Cheese and The Worms: The Cosmos of a Sixteenth-Century Miller.* Baltimore: Johns Hopkins Univ. Press, 1980. Pp. 177. $14.00.

Giroux, Farrar Straus, comp. *The Pilgrimage of Peace: The Collected Speeches of John Paul II in Ireland and the United States.* New York: Romano and William Collins Sons and Co., 1980. Pp. 175. $17.50.

Goffart, Walter. *Barbarians and Romans.* Princeton: Princeton Univ. Press, 1981. Pp. 279. $25.00.

Gower, John. *Confessio Amantis.* Ed. Russell Peck. 1966. Toronto: Univ. of Toronto Press, rpt., 1980. Pp. 525. $7.95.

Hamilton, Bernard. *The Medieval Inquisition.* New York: Holmes & Meier Publishers, Inc., 1981. Pp. 111. $13.50.

Harland, John. *Word Controlled Humans.* Rochester: Sovereign Press, 1980. Pp. 117. $8.95 (cloth); $5.00 (paper).

Hartung, Albert E., ed. *A Manual of the Writings in Middle English, 1051–1500.* Vol. 6. Hamden, CT: The Shoe String Press, 1980. Pp. 1743–2194. $17.50.

Haveley, N.R., ed. *Chaucer's Boccaccio: Sources of Troilus and the Knight's and Franklin's Tales.* Totowa, NJ: Rowman and Littlefield, 1980. Pp. 225. $31.50.

Heisserer A. J. *Alexander the Great and the Greeks: The Epigraphic Evidence.* Norman: Univ. of Oklahoma Press, 1980. Pp. 252. $29.95.

Held, Julius S. *The Oil Sketches of Peter Paul Rubens: A Critical Catalogue.* Princeton: Princeton Univ. Press, 1980. Pp. 698. $125.00.

Hibbard, G. R. ed. *The Elizabethan Theatre VII.* Hamden, CT: Shoe String Press, 1981. Pp. 204. $18.50.

Hollander, Robert. *Studies in Dante.* Ravenna, Italy: Longo Publisher, 1980. Pp. 222. L. 10.000.

Howard, Donald R. *Writers and Pilgrims: Medieval Pilgrimage Narratives and Their Posterity.* Los Angeles: Univ. of California Press, 1980. Pp. 133. $10.95.

Hughes, Andres. *Medieval Music: The Sixth Liberal Art.* Toronto: Univ. of Toronto Press, 1974. Pp. 360. $25.00.

Hughes, Gwylyn Rees and A.O.H. Jarman, eds. *A Guide to Welsh Literature.* Volume 2. Atlantic Highlands, NJ: Humanities Press, 1980. Pp. 400. $22.50.

Kaminsky, Alice R., ed. *Chaucer's "Troilus and Criseyde" and the Critics.* Athens, OH: Ohio Univ. Press, 1980. Pp. 245. $15.00.

Keohane, Nannerl O. *Philosophy and the State in France: The Renaissance to the Enlightenment.* Princeton: Princeton Univ. Press, 1980. Pp. 501. $30.00.

Labarge, Margaret Wade. *A Baronial Household of the Thirteenth Century.* Totowa, NJ: Rowman and Littlefield, 1980, Pp. 235. $9.95.

Labarge, Margaret Wade. *Gascony: England's First Colony, 1204–1453.* London: Hamish Hamilton, 1980. Pp. 275. $23.50.

Ladurie, LeRoy. *Carnival in Romans.* New York: George Braziller, 1980. Pp. 426. $8.95.

Lawler, Traugott. *The One and the Many in the Canterbury Tales.* Hamden, CT: Shoe String Press, 1980, Pp. 209. $17.50.

LeGoff, Jacques. *Time, Work and Culture in the Middle Ages.* Trans. by Arthur Godhammer, Chicago: Univ. Chicago Press, 1980. Pp. 384. $22.50.

Little, Lester K. *Religous Poverty and the Profit Economy in Medieval Europe.* Ithaca: Cornell Univ. Press, 1978. Pp. 267. $29.50.

McFarland, Thomas. *Romanticism and the Forms of Ruin.* Princeton, NJ: Princeton Univ. Press, 1981. Pp. 432. $30.00 (cloth); $9.50 (paper).

Mandelbaum, Allen, trans. *Inferno.* Los Angeles: Univ. of California Press, 1980. Pp. 307. $19.95.

Manley, Lawrence. *Convention, 1500–1750.* Cambridge: Harvard Univ. Press, 1980. Pp. 355. $17.50.

Márquez-Sterling, Manuel. *Fernán González, First Count of Castile: The Man and the Legend.* University, MI: Romance Monographs, Inc., 1980. Pp. 155. $16.00.

Mellinkoff, Ruth. *The Mark of Cain.* Los Angeles: Univ. of California Press, 1980. Pp. 151. $12.95.

Milella, Edizioni. *Universita Degli Studi di Lecce, Bollettino di Storia Della Filsofia.* Ufficio, Cambi: Universita Degli Studi, 1977. Pp. 408.

Mullett, Michale. *Radical Religious Moements in Early Modern Europe.* Boston: Allen & Unwin, Inc. 1980. Pp. 193. $19.50.

Myers, A. R. *London in the Age of Chaucer.* Norman, OK: Univ. of Oklahoma Press, 1972. Pp. 239. $6.95.

Newton, Stella Mary. *Fashion in the Age of the Black Prince.* Totowa, NJ: Rowman and Littlefield, 1981. Pp. 151. $37.50.

Nohrnberg, James. *The Analogy of the Faerie Queene.* Princeton: Princeton Univ. Press, 1980. Pp. 870. $15.00.

Oakley, Francis. *The Western Church in the Later Middle Ages.* Ithaca: Cornell Univ. Press, 1979. Pp. 345. $19.50.

Ogilvie, R. M. *Roman Literature and Society.* Totowa, NJ: Barnes and Noble Books, 1980. Pp. 303. $22.50.

Paetow, Louis John. *A Guide to the Study of Medieval History.* Revised and Corrected Edition. NY: Kraus Reprint, 1980. Pp. 643. $55.00.

Percy, Christine G., ed. *Studies in the Age of Chaucer.* Norman: Univ. of Oklahoma Press, 1978. Pp. 296.

Pesce, Luigi. *La Visita Pastorale di Sebastiano Soldati della Diocesi di Treviso.* Roma: Edizioni di Storia e Letteratura, 1975. Pp. 179. L. 25.000.

Piltz, Anders. *The World of Medieval Learning.* trans. David Jones. Totowa, NJ: Barnes & Noble Books, 1981. Pp. 299. $30.00.

Pullan, Brian. *Sources for the History of Medieval Europe from the Mid-Eighth to the Mid-Thirteenth Century.* Totowa, NJ: Basil Blackwell, 1981. Pp. 277. $7.95.

Riehle, Wolfgang. *The Middle English Mystics.* London: Routledge & Kegan Paul, 1981. Pp. 244. $32.50.

Robertson, D. W., Jr. *Essays in Medieval Culture.* Princeton: Princeton Univ. Press, 1980. Pp. 404. $35.00 (cloth); $12.95 (paper).

Rous, John. *The Ruos Roll.* Atlantic Highlands, NJ: Humanities Press, 1980. $30.00.

Rowland, Beryl. *Medieval Woman's Guide to Health: The First English Gynecological Handbook.* Kent, OH: The Kent State Univ. Press, 1981. Pp. 192. $17.50.

Rowley, Trevor, ed. *The Origins of Open Field Agriculture.* Totowa, NJ: Barnes & Noble Books, 1981. Pp. 258. $26.50.

Ruggiero, Guido. *Violence in Early Renaissance Venice*. New Brunswick: Rutgers Univ. Press, 1980. Pp. 235. $18.50.

Ruiz, Juan. *The Book of True Love*. Trans. by Saralyn R. Daly. University Park: Pennsylvania State Univ. Press, 1978. Pp. 454. $7.95.

Scherman, Katharine. *The Flowering of Ireland: Saints, Scholars and Kings*. Boston: Little, Brown and Co. Pp. 368. $16.95.

Scott, A. F. *The Saxon Age: Commentaries of an Era*. London: Croom Helm, 1979. Pp. 192. $20.00.

Scott, Margaret. *The History of Dress Series: Late Gothic Europe, 1400–1500*. Atlantic Highlands, NJ: Humanities Press, 1981. Pp. 256. $62.50.

Searle, Eleanor, ed. *The Chronicle of Battle Abbey*. Oxford: Clarendon Press, 1980. Pp. 357. $55.00.

Siraisi, Nancy G. *Taddeo Alderotti and His Pupils: Two Generations of Italian Medical Learning*. Princeton: Princeton Univ. Press, 1981. Pp. 461. $32.00.

Slights, Camille W. *The Casuistical Tradition in Shakespeare, Donne, Herbert, and Milton*. Princeton: Princeton Univ. Press, 1981. Pp. 307. $21.00.

Sorrell, Mark, ed. *Reconstructing the Past*. Totowa, NJ: Barnes & Noble Books, 1981. Pp. 168. $19.50.

Strayer, Joseph R. *The Reign of Philip the Fair*. Princeton: Princeton Univ. Press, 1980. Pp. 450. $35.00 (cloth); $13.50 (paper).

Strem, George G. *The Life and Teaching of Lucius Annaeus Seneca*. New York. Vantage Press, 1981. Pp. 175. $10.00.

Takamiya T. and D. Brewer, eds. *Aspects of Malory* (*Arthurian Studies 1*). Totowa, NJ: Rowman and Littlefield, 1981. Pp. 232. $35.00.

Thomson, John A. F. *Popes and Princes 1417–1517*. Boston: Allen & Unwin, 1980. Pp. 252. $19.50.

Ullman, Berthold Louis. *Ancient Writing and Its Influence*. 1932. Toronto: Univ. of Toronto Press, rpt. 1980. Pp. 240. $7.50.

Unterkircher, F., comp. *King Rene's Book of Love*. New York: George Braziller, 1980. Pp. 48. $9.95.

Vaillancourt, Jean-Guy. *Papal Power: A Study of Vatican Control Over Lay Catholic Elites*. Los Angeles: Univ. of California Press, 1980. Pp. 375. $16.95.

Vaughan, Sally N. *The Abbey of Bec and the Anglo-Norman State 1034–1136*. Totowa, NJ: Boydell & Brewer Ltd., 1981. Pp. 168. $40.00.

Violante, Cinzio. *Economica societa stituzioni a Pisa nel Medioevo*. Bari: Dedalo Libri, 1980. Pp. 398.

Walker, D. P. *Unclean Spirits*. Philadelphia: Univ. of Pennsylvania Press, 1981. Pp. 116. $15.00.

Walsh, William. *F.R. Leavis*. Bloomington: Indiana Univ. Press, 1980. Pp. 189. $15.00.

Whigham, Peter, ed. *The Music of the Troubadours*. Santa Barbara: Ross-Erikson, 1979. Pp. 203. $35.00.

Willman, Daniel. *Bibliothéques Ecclésiastiques au Temps de la Papauté D'Avignon: Inventaires de Bibliothéques et Mentions de Livres dans les Archives du Vatican (1287–1420)*. Paris: Editions du Centre National de la Recherche Scientifique, 1980. Pp. 382.

Williams, Miller, ed. *A Roman Collection: Stories, Poems, and Other Good Pieces by the Writing Residents of the American Academy in Rome*. Columbia: Univ. of Missouri Press, 1980. Pp. 309. $12.50.

Wolpers, Theodor. *Burgerliches bei Chaucer*. Gottingen: Vandenhoeck and Ruprecht, 1981. Pp. 288. DM 12.

Wunderli, Richard M. *London Church Courts*. Cambridge, ma; The Medieval Academy of America, 1981. Pp. 162. $5.00 (paper); $12.50 (cloth).

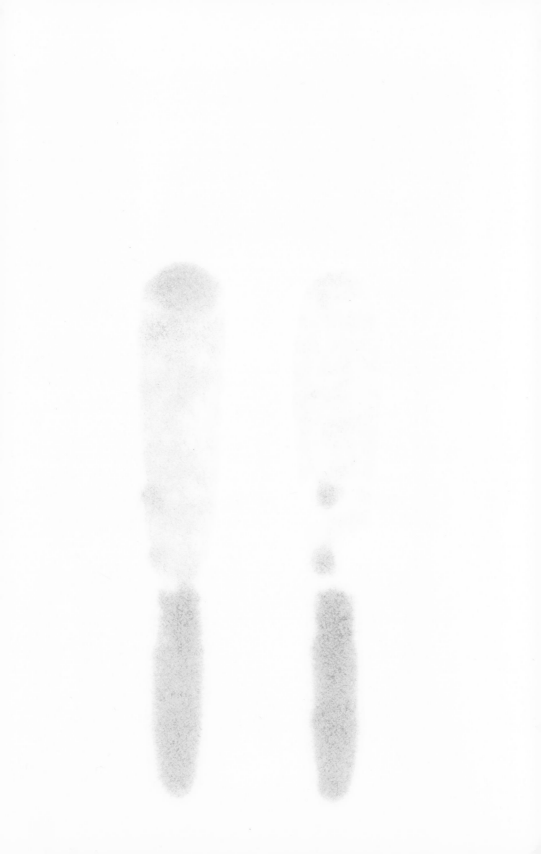

DATE DUE

GAYLORD   PRINTED IN U.S.A.

THE
BATTLE
FOR
CRETE,
1941

BY G. C.
KIRIAKOPOULOS

TEN DAYS
TO
DESTINY

FRANKLIN WATTS 1985 NEW YORK TORONTO

Maps by Vantage Art, Inc.

Library of Congress Cataloging in Publication Data

Kiriakopoulos, G. C.
Ten days to destiny.

Bibliography: p.
Includes index.
1. World War, 1939–1945—Campaigns—Greece—Crete.
2. Crete—History—20th century. I. Title. II. Title:
10 days to destiny.
D766.7.C7K57 1985   940.54'21   85-700
ISBN 0-531-09785-4

CONTENTS

TEN DAYS
TO
DESTINY

O Passer-by, Tell the Lacedaemonians
That We Lie Here Obeying Their Orders.

Simonides' epitaph at
Thermopylae, 480 B.C.

PREFACE

What follows is the documented story of one of the most important yet least acknowledged battles of the Second World War. *Ten Days to Destiny* describes the audacity and horror of Operation Mercury, which involved thousands of soldiers and civilians in the first airborne invasion of an island-fortress in the military history of mankind. It is the tale of a battle that had a decisive effect upon the outcome of World War II.

The germinal idea for the writing of the historic and dramatic events depicted in this narrative began almost a decade ago.

While visiting the land of my ancestors, I decided to include the island of Crete in my itinerary. For many years I had heard of its primitive natural beauty, of the genial hospitality of its proud inhabitants, and of the glorious antiquities of the Minoan civilization that once flourished there.

As I stood in line at Athens' Hellenikon Airport waiting to purchase my ticket for the flight to Crete, I could not help noticing a tall, well-built man several places behind me. He towered over six feet, impressive in appearance, and stood as erect as a granite monument. I eyed his apparel—the costume of his native Crete—a black kerchief with a fringed border adorned his head, and a black vest covered a billowing white long-sleeved shirt. His black pantaloons tapered below his knees and disappeared into his shin-high boots. But it was in his eyes that the pride of the Cretan people could be discerned. I stared at him, trying not to be too obvious. This was my first encounter with a Cretan.

When I arrived in Khaniá, the administrative capital of Crete, I took a taxi to my destination. A few miles westward, on the main northern highway near the village of Galatas, I caught sight of a huge military monument. Later I learned that it was a war memorial built by the German invaders after the battle of Crete to honor their military dead. That this monument of a defeated enemy still stood more than three decades later intrigued me.

By inquiring about the German war memorial at Galatas, I opened the door on a little-known vista in the saga of the Second World War. As my questions prodded their memories, the elders of the many villages I visited began to reminisce about the terrible time in May 1941 when the German parachutists invaded Crete.

In the days that followed, I traveled widely across the length and breadth of the large island, enjoying its natural beauty. I found Crete to be a land steeped in history, and I found its people to be proud yet courteous, cordial, and friendly. I made many friends very quickly, and they were all willing to tell me about their struggle against the German invaders.

Little by little, the more I heard, I began to realize that here was a dramatic tale of heroic human endeavor to resist oppression, and that it was a story well worth telling.

When I returned to Athens, I browsed through the bookstores and bookstalls searching for material related to the battle of Crete. Much had been written by the Germans and the British. It was all objective, informative, yet indifferent. Nowhere, I felt, had the subjectively stark reality of the conflict among the determined German paratroopers, the resolute, gallant British Commonwealth soldiers, or the heroic Cretan civilians been captured. Little had been written and even less was known in the United States of the events that took place in Crete in May 1941; the battle of Crete was a British affair, when Pearl Harbor was still seven months away.

To fill this void, I decided to write *Ten Days to Destiny*.

In the course of the years that it took me to research this book, I traveled an estimated 100,000 miles to England, Germany, Austria, Switzerland, Greece, and, of course, Crete seeking material. I interviewed countless hundreds of people who were directly or indirectly involved. The dialogue is real: it comes from texts, transcripts, stenographic notes, and from the memories of the people I interviewed. (Occasionally, I have taken the liberty of altering the tense to suit the action.) I also read and reviewed hundreds of primary sources, after-action reports, staff journals, published and unpublished monographs, and diaries.

To familiarize myself with the battlefield sites on Crete, I took many trips to the island, trekking over the fields, hills, valleys, and mountains of that beautiful land of Minos.

PROLOGUE

This is the story of a battle that took place during the early years of the Second World War on an island in the middle of the Mediterranean. For ten dramatic and bitterly fought days, Crete served as a battlefield in the struggle between German paratroopers and free-spirited Cretan civilians fighting side by side with their gallant British Commonwealth allies.

The battle of Crete has been referred to as the Thermopylae of the Second World War. Herodotus tells us in his *History of the Persian Wars* that King Xerxes of Persia invaded Greece in 480 B.C. with a vast army. Most of the Greek city-states put aside their differences and banded together to fight the Persian invader.

The Greek armies attempted to defend Thessaly at the site of Mount Olympus. Defeated, they withdrew southward, leaving only a small army to block the Persian advance. This army decided to fight at a narrow pass between the mountains and the sea, a position that offered some possibility of success. The pass was called Thermopylae.

The whole civilized world has read of the heroic defense that King Leonidas and his 300 Spartans, together with their allies, made at Thermopylae. The defenders fought valiantly until they were betrayed, whereupon they were overcome by the Persian hordes. Leonidas and his Spartans sacrificed themselves in order to delay the Persians.

After Thermopylae the Persians swept onward. They sacked Athens and eventually reached Salamis, where the Athenian fleet was waiting for them. In the sea battle that followed, the Persian fleet was virtually destroyed. Unable to sustain his army, Xerxes was forced to return to Persia. He had won the battle at Thermopylae, but the delay had lost him the war at Salamis.

In World War II, Adolf Hitler did not intend to invade Greece or Crete. Mussolini's failure to conquer Greece, however, caused Hitler to come to his aid, and to put off his plan to invade Russia. Once in Greece, Hitler was persuaded to seize Crete to protect the oil fields in Rumania from Crete-based aerial bombing. This occupied precious weeks of a very tight military timetable, and the delay represented a period of time Hitler would have required to bring Russia to its knees. The campaign in Greece and in Crete forced Hitler to postpone the invasion of Russia until June 1941.

At first the German armies rolled victoriously across the Russian plains, reaching Leningrad and Moscow. However, Hitler never captured Leningrad, and although within sight of the Kremlin towers, he never took Moscow. Then the Russian winter hit with all its ferocity, bringing Hitler's war machine to a standstill.

Stalemated at Leningrad and Moscow, Hitler ordered his southern armies to attack toward Stalingrad. What happened there is history. One million Germans were lost in the military debacle that followed. It was to be the farthest point of the German advance—and the turning point of the war. After Stalingrad the German armies were to travel a downhill road to eventual defeat.

Like Xerxes in 480 B.C., whose delay at the battle of Thermopylae granted the Athenian fleet time to gather and defeat him at Salamis, Adolf Hitler in 1941 was so delayed in Greece and in Crete that he was forced to fight a winter campaign in Russia. Hitler won *his* "battle of Thermopylae" in Crete, but it was a pyrrhic victory. The delay lost him the war in Russia.

If the events that culminated in the battle of Stalingrad marked the beginning of the end for Adolf Hitler, then the events that took place on Crete in May 1941 marked the end of the beginning.

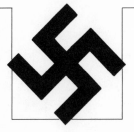

THE
ADVENT

YUGOSLAVIA

BULGARIA

ALBANIA

GREECE

Salonika

Athens

PELOPONNESUS

CRETE

CRETE

SANTORINI

Rodopos
Peninsula

CRETAN

SEA

GULF OF KHANIA

Akrotiri

Kastelli

Khania

Suda

WHITE MOUNTAINS

Rethimnon

Iraklion

Ag.
Nicholas

Sfakia

CRETE

"NO, IT IS WAR!"

OCTOBER 28, 1940

During the early morning hours of October 28, 1940, in the quiet Athens suburb of Kephisia, a huge black limousine drove up to the private residence of Ioannis Metaxas, prime minister of Greece.

The Metaxas household was awakened by the persistent ringing of the front doorbell. It was 2:15 A.M. The maid who answered the door was informed that the predawn visitor was Emmanuele Grazzi, the Italian ambassador, and that it was urgent he see the prime minister. Still half-asleep, the maid misunderstood the announcement. She thought he said he was the French ambassador. She mistook the word *Italia* for *Gallia*.

"The French ambassador is here with an important message from his government," were the first words uttered by the prime minister's personal secretary.

"The French ambassador, at this hour?" grumbled Metaxas. "Haven't the French done enough harm to the world by surrendering to the Germans so easily, without bothering us at such an ungodly hour?"[1]

Metaxas agreed to see the French representative, but he was not going to rush. He took his time washing his face, and sipped a hot cup of coffee to awaken his senses. Throwing a kimono over his pajamas, he decided that enough time had elapsed. He slowly descended the stairs to the drawing room as the clock chimed.

It was 3:00 A.M.

When he entered the room with his secretary-bodyguard, he hesitated momentarily at the entrance. At the sight of the dark, rotund Italian ambassador, he realized the error that had occurred. His heart skipped a beat. A visit from this man at such an undiplomatic hour meant that trouble was afoot.

"Well, what brings you here at this hour, Signore Grazzi? Could you not have waited until the light of day?" [2]

"I have an important message from my government which requires an immediate reply," [3] answered Grazzi, handing the prime minister a large envelope.

Metaxas was now fully awake. He took the document, put on his spectacles, and began to read.

He read through it once in startled disbelief. Removing his glasses, he glared at the Italian ambassador, who looked away. Metaxas replaced his spectacles and read through the document a second time. The silence was so profound one could almost hear the heartbeats of the three men in the room.

The document was an ultimatum. It demanded that Greece open its borders to the passage of Italian troops. Greece was to cede all its major seaports on the mainland and in the Ionian and Aegean islands to the Italian army. All strategic army and air bases were to be turned over to the Italians. In effect, Greece was to be occupied by Italy. All this was to be agreed upon by 6:00 A.M.—in just three hours.

As the Greek prime minister read through the ultimatum once more, he realized he had only two choices: to accede to the demands, or to fight.

Count Galeazzo Ciano, the Italian foreign minister, had forecast the meaning of this ultimatum. "Naturally," he commented in his instructions to Grazzi, "it is a document that allows no way out for Greece. Either she accepts, or she will be attacked."[4]

Grazzi waited for Metaxas to make some response. Finally Metaxas broke the silence. "This note does not give me much time to consider these proposals. I could not set my own house in order—much less surrender my country—in three hours."[5]

Flipping the ultimatum carelessly onto the coffee table in the center of the room, he again removed his spectacles and glared at the Italian ambassador. "The answer is no."

With that curt reply, Metaxas turned and left the room. Grazzi stood alone, mouth agape and speechless. At the door, with tears welling in his eyes, Metaxas repeated his answer to his secretary. "No. It is war!"[6]

The Italian ultimatum to the Greek prime minister was scheduled to expire at 6:00 A.M. on October 28, 1940. However, Mussolini's army did not wait for the set hour to arrive. By 5:30 A.M., 125,000 troops crossed the Greek frontier. Only two Greek divisions stood in defense against the invader, and they were outnumbered six to one. The Greek General Staff had not mobilized its other sixteen divisions earlier, for fear of giving Mussolini some cause for provocation.

The Italian army crept over the rugged mountains of the northern Greek provinces of Epirus and Macedonia in a three-pronged attack. The eastern prong headed from Kónitsa through Florina to Thessaloniki; the central spearhead climbed through the Pindus Mountains toward Metsovon; while the third prong followed the western coast road. The invaders moved southward slowly against light opposition, at a pace of some six miles a day.[7]

It was not a blitzkrieg in the German sense of the word, but it was an advance.

Back in Rome, Mussolini had a huge billboard constructed in the Piazza Venezia. On it was a huge map of Greece, with large red arrows indicating the victorious advance of the Italian

army. The public watched and cheered each southerly movement of the arrows.

The newly mobilized Greek army began counterattacking in
the Kalamas River area, and the Italians were soon thrown back.
By November 2, just six days after the Italian attack began, there
was an amazing communiqué that read: "Greek forces had
counterattacked in the central region and had captured Mount
Pissoderri. . . ."[8] The Greek forces had penetrated three-and-
a-half miles inside the Italian border.

This was the beginning of many victories for the small, brave
Greek army. Fighting in the rugged, cold, windswept mountains
of Epirus amid deep snowdrifts, the Greeks succeeded in decimating the Italian Third Alpine Division—the crack "Julia" division—capturing more than 5,000 prisoners and tons of Italian
supplies.

When Greek neutrality was violated by the Italian invasion,
Great Britain came to Greece's assistance. On the day following
the Italian invasion, British naval forces sailed for Crete from
Alexandria with supply ships and auxiliary craft. The Second
Battalion of the York and Lancaster Regiment landed on Crete
as the first element of a defense garrison.[9]

The Greeks continued to fight the Italian invaders, chasing
them over the rugged mountains of northern Greece into Albania. Victory followed victory. Church bells rang continuously
and untiringly throughout Greece with the announcement of each
Greek victory. The battles for towns such as Kónitsa, Pogradec,
St. Ostrovitz, Sarande, Tepeleně, Klissura, and Argyrokastron
resulted in smashing victories for the Greeks.

Back in Rome, the billboard with the huge map of Greece
was taken down. One official commented that it interfered with
the flow of traffic in the plaza.

By November 22, less than one month after Mussolini's
troops had invaded Greece, the Italians were in full retreat on
the whole front. As 1941 began, not a single Italian soldier was
left on Greek soil, unless he was dead or a prisoner of war. The
Greeks had chased the Italians eighty miles back into Albania.

Mussolini's attempt to conquer the Greeks left 20,000 Italian soldiers dead on Greek soil, and as many as 40,000 wounded, 26,000 prisoners, and 18,000 men crippled with frostbite from the hard winter of northern Greece.[10] Worst of all, the Greeks had made Mussolini the laughingstock of the entire world. He stood humiliated in the eyes not only of his enemies but also of his Axis ally, Adolf Hitler.

Now it was obvious to Hitler that he would have to invade and occupy Greece, so he could once again push the British off the continent of Europe and bring peace and security to his southern flank.

So it was that on December 13, 1940, Hitler issued War Directive Number 20—Operation Marita—for the invasion of Greece.[11] This meant that Hitler had to postpone the preliminary date set for the German invasion of Russia until the Greek campaign was concluded.

A fateful decision that was destined to alter the course of the Second World War, it spelled doom for the Axis alliance.

On April 6, 1941, Operation Marita went into effect. The German army launched a simultaneous attack against Greece and Yugoslavia.

Through the mountain passes at Monastir and over the mountains into the Vardar Valley came the German legions. Their armored units sped forward over the rough terrain in multiple spearheads across the Greek peninsula.

Outnumbered in masses of troops, outweighed in armor, and continuously harassed by the Luftwaffe's onslaught from the sky, the Greeks gave ground. By April 30 it was all over. What Mussolini could not do in six months, Hitler accomplished in twenty-four days. And now the German soldiers stood on the southern shores of Greece—just 168 air miles from Crete.

The island of Crete lies like a huge barrier reef in the middle of the Mediterranean.

To the Greeks, the island of Crete is known as Megalonisos, meaning "great island." It is the fifth-largest island in the Mediterranean and lies between three continents: Europe to the north, Asia to the east, and Africa to the south. Because of this geographically strategic position, Crete has played a principal role in the history of the Mediterranean.

It is an island where shadows of artistic giants lurk everywhere. Great artists painted the walls and fashioned the vessels of the Minoan palaces. It is the birthplace of Theophanis, of Georgis, of Michael Damaskinos, and of Doménikos Theotokópoulos, better known as El Greco. It is the Crete of poets and authors—of the idyllic *Erotocritos Erofylli, Vascopoula,* and *Abraham's Sacrifice.* It gave us Nikos Kazantzakis, author of *Zorba the Greek* (among hundreds of other works), one of the great literary figures of our century. From Crete, too, came Eleftherios Venizelos, to whom John Gunther referred as the great statesman of modern Europe.

Legends from Crete fill the pages of mythology. It was to the land of the Minotaur—the monster with the body of a man and the head of a bull—that Theseus, prince of Athens, came to slaughter this predator of Athenian youth. Theseus followed the silken thread that led him out of the labyrinth. And it was the builder of the labyrinth, Daedalus, and his son, Icarus, who attached wings to their shoulders and soared skyward.

Beyond the realm of mythology, ancient and modern Crete throughout the centuries has been involved in a continuous struggle among the many peoples that have coursed the surface of this inland body of water. These forces met and clashed on this island, crushing each other through the ages, leaving vivid traces of their existence on the stark face of the land that had been the cradle of the first European civilization.

Crete was first inhabited about 7000 B.C., during the Neolithic period, by tribes from the northern mainland and from the depths of Syria. With the passage of time, Crete developed the illustrious Minoan civilization that became the forerunner of present-day European civilization. The heart of this Minoan culture was Knossos, the strongest and greatest city in Crete. Minoan civilization became preeminent in the Mediterranean, spreading the shadow of its wings across the waters as far west as Gibraltar and as far north as the Black Sea.

According to the natural law of life, every civilization is subject to destruction. To Crete came the natural calamity of earthquakes and the man-made force of war, weakening and dispersing its people and causing the great Minoan civilization to totter and fall.

Then there arrived from the Grecian mainland a new people, ferociously aggressive and better armed, who overwhelmed the weakened and dispersed inhabitants of the Minoan empire. These first invaders of Crete were the Dorians.

They were a crude and rustic horde, ignorant of art or handicraft, and in their ignorance, they destroyed everything that was beautiful or of significance. Their own artifacts were inferior to the wonderful craftsmanship of the classical Minoan civilization. Crete fell into an unexalted existence, a slumbering and neutral state, during the Persian and Peloponnesian wars that racked the ancient city-states on the Greek mainland. In the end Dorian Crete also succumbed to the law of destruction; in 69 B.C. the Romans arrived to add their name to the list of invaders.

The Roman legions, under Consul Quintus Caesilius Metellus, sought to capture the island because of its critical position regarding Roman supremacy in the East. It took three years for Metellus to conquer the island. But with the eventual division of the Roman Empire into Eastern and Western states, Crete became a part of the Byzantine, or Eastern, half of the dual empire.

After the Romans came the Saracen Arabs who built the city of Handox on what is now the site of Iráklion. The Arabs, held Crete for more than 130 years until General Nikiforos Fokas, who later became the emperor of Byzantium, liberated the island and made it a province of the Byzantine Empire.

The Crusaders who seized Constantinople in the thirteenth century A.D. divided the conquered provinces of Byzantium among themselves. Crete was taken by Bonifatius, marquis of Monferate, who promptly sold it to the Venetians. The Genoese, not to be left out, overran the Venetians and took possession of the island. After a bitter war, the Venetians succeeded in recapturing Crete in A.D. 1212. Crete was now divided into feudal fiefdoms constantly at war with each other. The Venetians threw out the Greek Orthodox bishops, installed Roman Catholics, and forced the Cretan inhabitants into serfdom. The Cretans, tired of these foreign incursions, finally rose in rebellion. During the 450 years of the Venetian presence, the Cretan population revolted some twenty-five different times to regain their liberty. There was a constant struggle against the great strength of Venetian arms.

In A.D. 1669 Iráklion was captured by the Turks after a bitterly fought war that lasted twenty years. If the Venetians were oppressive, the Turks were cruel beyond all human calculation. For more than two centuries, the Turks treated the people of Crete as subhuman slaves. The decades passed with years of struggle, sacrifice, heroism, and savage torture that embittered the people. It caused the Cretans to revolt against these latest conquerors countless times during the years 1692, 1770, 1821, 1841, 1855, 1866, 1868–69, 1886–87, and 1896–97.

The great Cretan revolt of 1866 was the eruption that shook the very foundation of the might of the sultan ruling the Ottoman Empire. The heroic drama of the rebellious Cretans and the unimaginable torment they suffered at the hands of the Turkish armies of occupation reached such a peak that it stirred the conscience of all free Greeks and of Europeans as well.

The massacre of Christians by the Turks at Khaniá in 1897 forced the Greek government to send an army of 1,500 men under Colonel Timoleon Vassos to Crete. He landed with his troops at Khaniá and took possession of Crete in the name of the king of Greece. Crete then proclaimed itself free of the Ottoman Turks, uniting herself with Greece. Turkey declared war, defeating Greece the same year. However, Crete was able to preserve its autonomy.

In 1898 the Turks again resorted to their inhuman treatment. They massacred both Greek and English subjects at Iráklion. In the furor that followed, the Turkish army was forced to leave Crete, and Prince George of Greece was appointed high commissioner of Crete. With his arrival at Suda Bay on December 9, 1898, the first step in Crete's union with Greece had been achieved.

On October 5, 1912, the prime minister of Greece, Eleftherios Venizelos, a native son of Crete, declared that Crete had been united with Greece. Crete was free at last.[12]

After centuries of foreign invasions and domination, Crete settled into a peaceful existence through the decades that followed, only to be confronted by a new danger—another foreigner was threatening to invade the beautiful island.

The Cretans remembered the Dorians and Romans of ancient times, and the Franks, Venetians, Genoese, Saracens, and Turks of modern times. To this list would now be added the Germans.

2

WAR COMES TO
THE LAND OF MINOS

MARCH 26, 1941

The quiet waters slapped the steel sides of the huge warship that was anchored in the middle of Suda Bay in Crete. Not too far away, four freighters were moored closer to the shore. There was not a glimmer of light from the ships, nor from the farmhouses dotting the hills that surrounded the harbor on three sides. Only the blinking stars above marked the sky from the inky blackness of the shore.

The warship was the majestic eight-inch-gun cruiser, HMS *York*. This 10,000-ton ship of the line had escorted a convoy of freighters into Suda Bay the previous day, bringing supplies to the storage depots on shore. The *York* was scheduled to depart the following morning, returning to her home base at Alexandria, where she was to lend the might of her six eight-inch guns to Admiral Andrew Cunningham's ships of the Mediterranean Fleet.[1]

The first alarm came from the lookout astern. He reported a low hum of motors from the direction of the outer harbor. The duty officer checked with the man monitoring the Low Angle Direction Control—or LADCT, as they called it—who confirmed that his detection apparatus had picked up the sound of multiple motors of unknown identity approaching, and gave the bearing. Considering the possibility that the disturbances might be aircraft, the duty officer turned to the ship's newly-installed Air Warning Radio Direction Finder, an early type of radar. If they were aircraft, however, they were too low for radar to pick them up.

A second lookout on the after-superstructure, using infrared glasses, reported the appearance of white disturbances in the water, aft of the port side, which appeared as wakes of small craft. The officer on deck ordered a flare to be fired, then called the captain.

The brilliance of the flare illuminated the whole harbor like daylight, and on the outer fringe of that light there appeared a flotilla of eight motor torpedo boats heading for the freighters near the shore.

The *York*'s captain was still buttoning his jacket when he stepped onto the bridge, to hear a deafening roar accompanied by a fiery red ball. Two fingers of flame reached high into the dark sky from the stricken freighter *Pericles,* sending shadows dancing across the waters and silhouetting the other ships anchored nearby.[2]

The alarm for action stations was sounded aboard the *York,* and the ship's crew of 623 officers and men hurried to their assigned stations and prepared for action. The anchors were raised and the boilers fired to increase power. Slowly the huge turbines began to throb as the ship was prepared for any eventuality. The skipper did not intend to be caught like a sitting duck.

The crew stood ready at their four-inch antiaircraft guns, mounted at the break of the forecastle, abreast of the forward funnel. Other gunners cleared the multiple 20-mm antiaircraft guns and, like the men on the four-inch guns, waited for orders to open fire.

From the bridge the captain and his executive officer followed the course of the speedy little boats with their glasses. Both men, veterans of years of service, were familiar with the German E-type motor torpedo boats, which depended on speed and torpedoes to attack shipping. But these motorboats were smaller, faster, and—more surprising—carried no torpedoes. Yet the flames billowing from the heavily listing freighter gave strong evidence that they were craft to be reckoned with.

"How did they get past the boom of the inner harbor?" asked the *York*'s executive officer.[3]

Both men watched another motorboat veer sharply and head for a second freighter. Racing on a straight course, it plowed into the hapless ship. A few seconds elapsed, and then a huge fiery blast lifted the freighter out of the water, broke her apart, and left her to settle quickly to the bottom of the bay.

"That explains it," said the surprised skipper of the *York*. "The whole bloody boat is a torpedo!"[4]

The explosive motorboats, designated EMBs, were Italy's newest weapon, manned by groups of volunteers who attacked with courage and speed. Each craft had a single crewman, who selected a target and then steered at full speed on an impact course. The forward part of the motorboat contained a warhead of some 6,600 pounds of explosives that would detonate on contact. If the crewman chose, he could alter the explosive setting, allowing the prow with the warhead to separate, sink below the target's waterline, and by hydrostatic detonation, explode with the effect of a depth charge.

The EMBs were difficult to hit because they were so low in the water, and when at full throttle, they sped at thirty knots, driven by powerful Alfa-Romeo outboard motors.[5]

The *York*'s captain ordered all secondary batteries to open fire. The four-inch and 20-mm antiaircraft guns were lowered to zero depression, many of them firing over open sights at the small motorboats dodging and weaving in the waters of the harbor. A curtain of hot metal spouted tall geysers and churned the black waters into foam. One motorboat was hit, exploding in a single brilliant flash.

From the starboard side of the *York,* an EMB spotted the cruiser, now well silhouetted against the flames of the two burning freighters. The EMB zigzagged across the waters as the starboard batteries concentrated their fire on this immediate threat. The motorboat shot forward at thirty knots, knifing through the water and closing fast. It slipped through the ring of shells without being struck.

The single crewman set his controls on a collision course, aiming the prow of his boat to strike the cruiser amidships. With the throttle open to maximum, he locked the rudder controls on target. From his position at the rear of the craft, he pressed a release and was ejected backward into the water, together with his seat. The seat rose to the surface and just as quickly the crewman unfolded it—transforming it into a raft—and climbed aboard. When the warhead exploded against the cruiser's outer plates, the underwater force of the detonation would have little effect on the sailor, now sitting securely on the bobbing raft.

The motorboat churned through the remaining distance to its target while the starboard crew watched helplessly. Orders came from the bridge for a full right rudder, but it was too late. The motorboat with its 6,600-pound warhead struck the cruiser just aft of amidships, with a deafening roar.

A geyser of water shot skyward carrying with it pieces of steel, causing the cruiser to rise slightly out of the water from the force of the explosion. When it settled down again, amid hissing steam and heavy smoke, the *York* had a slight list to starboard.

The men of the *York* picked themselves off the tilting deck. Some had been flung into the water, and lines were thrown to pull them in. Others stood dazed and momentarily frozen by the force of the blast.

Damage control reported that the explosion had pierced the *York*'s four-inch armor below the waterline, opening her to the sea and flooding the forward boilers. The captain ordered ballast to be altered to correct the ship's list and to begin the pumps. However, the pumps could not work fast enough to remove the torrents of water pouring in from the huge hole in the cruiser's side, and she began to settle by the stern. There was no alternative but to beach her.

As the cruiser slowly drifted toward the western end of the bay, the captain remarked that the situation could have been much more tragic. Before her recent refitting, the *York*'s high-angle magazine had been located exactly where she was struck. Since the modification, the magazine had been moved forward of the boilers. This change had saved the *York* from a disastrous explosion that would have torn her apart. Beaching the ship now would keep her from foundering, and repairs could be made.[6]

Less than a quarter mile from the western shore of Suda Bay, the *York* shuddered to a halt. Her bottom had gently come to rest on a sandbar.

Only twenty minutes had elapsed from the moment the first report announced the approach of the EMBs until they disappeared again into the night. They had done their work well, leaving two freighters burning and sinking, and an eight-inch-gun cruiser severely damaged and beached. Of the eight motorboats in the flotilla, three had been destroyed but their crewmen had been picked up.

As the first light of dawn began to streak across the eastern sky, Cretans gathered on the shores surrounding the bay. From their positions on the heights, they could see the awesome results of the previous night. Before them appallingly thick, black smoke rose skyward from the now partially submerged and burning freighters, flames still licking hungrily at their superstructures.

Not too far away lay the sleek cruiser *York,* her afterdeck low and awash in the swirling waters.

The events of the night of March 26, 1941, had rent the tranquility of Suda Bay. Slowly, the conflagration that had already engulfed the millions of people on the European continent would extend itself southward across the Aegean to this peaceful, beautiful island of Crete.

3

MERCURY IS BORN

APRIL 25, 1941

Within two weeks of the torpedoing of HMS *York* in Suda Bay, the Cretan people heard the news of the German invasion of Greece. No matter how the news reached them, most Cretans stubbornly clung to the belief that war was still far away across the northern waters that separated Crete from the Greek mainland like a great moat.

In the days that followed the German invasion of Greece, plans were formulated that would overcome that watery defensive barrier. Like the Mycenaean invaders of ancient times, who came to destroy the land of Minos, this invader would also come—not by sea this time, but over it.

On April 15, 1941, Colonel General Alexander Löhr, the commanding general of the German Fourth Air Fleet, requested a special conference with his immediate superior—the commander in chief of the Luftwaffe.

It was General Löhr's air fleet, striking from bases in Austria and Bulgaria, that had struck the first blow in the invasion of Greece and Yugoslavia. In the morning hours of Palm Sunday, April 6, 1941, his aircraft pounded into submission the cities and the defenses of those two nations. By punishing and unmerciful bombing, high-level bombers and Stuka dive-bombers from his command completely devastated the city of Belgrade. At the end of that first day's air attack, 17,000 defenseless Yugoslavian civilians lay dead in the rubble of the capital city. By April 15, Yugoslavian resistance had been broken by the air fleet's persistent attacks.

Satisfied that his air command had played a major role in clearing the path for the advance of the German invasion army, General Löhr felt that the time was at hand to discuss further air operations in the Mediterranean.

For several weeks the Luftwaffe General Staff had been considering a tactical plan for the seizure of Crete. The plan could be put into effect immediately after the successful completion of the military operations in Greece, but it first had to gain the approval of the commander in chief of the Luftwaffe.[1]

Hermann Goering first gained fame as a World War I pilot, and after a downhill postwar trek, he rose once again to become the number-two man in the hierarchy of the German Reich.

When the Second World War erupted in 1939, the Luftwaffe soon became its most respected and feared weapon. The Luftwaffe's support of the German armies advancing into Poland, Norway, Denmark, the Low Countries, and France made German victory inevitable. With each Luftwaffe success, Goering's prestige reached greater heights.

Hitler was most grateful. He promoted Goering to the new and special military rank of Reichsmarschall. Greater still was his appointment as deputy Fuehrer of the Third Reich—number-two man and heir to the leadership of Germany. Goering had now fulfilled his dream: both wealthy and famous, his star was at its zenith.

As the commander in chief of the Luftwaffe, he was a law unto himself. Yet, with all his power, Goering feared competition. He was afraid that someone else would displace him in Hitler's favor. Because of this fear, the Reichsmarschall developed a distrustful hatred for the generals of the Oberkommando der Wehrmacht, or OKW (the high command of the armed forces), of the army high command (the Oberkommando des Heeres), and of the Oberkommando der Kriegsmarine (the naval high command). They, in turn, looked upon him as a pompous, arrogant egomaniac interested only in self-aggrandizement. Hitler alone acted as a buffer in the friction between Goering and the commanders of the armed services.

When, in 1940, Goering heard that the retreating British and French armies were fighting with their backs to the sea at Dunkirk, he pompously proclaimed that his Luftwaffe could prevent their successful evacuation. But the Luftwaffe failed. The British survived the evacuation from Dunkirk and came back to fight another day. And the brightness of Goering's star dimmed slightly.

Hitler's next plan was the invasion of England. To succeed in this operation, he first had to gain control of the skies over Britain. Goering's Luftwaffe was given this task.

The Battle of Britain was the first major British victory over Germany. Goering's much-vaunted air force suffered its greatest defeat. The skies over England remained British, and the planned invasion of England—Operation Sea Lion—had to be canceled. It was a crushing blow to Hermann Goering's prestige.

By 1941 Reichsmarschall Goering's credibility and position, relative to his Fuehrer, had waned to their lowest ebb.[2] He would have done anything within his power to be restored to Hitler's favor. It was at this juncture that Colonel General Alexander Löhr arrived with the plan for the seizure of Crete.

Löhr proposed the use of the armed might of the Luftwaffe—and only the Luftwaffe—in an air attack upon Crete. In a sustained program of continuous bombing, aircraft of all types would pound the island into submission. This would be followed by an airborne invasion of the island carried out by glider troops and parachutists. Once the strategic points had been captured, reinforcements would be ferried to the island by air transport. The whole operation was estimated to be completed within a period of three to ten days.

Here was the solution to Goering's dilemma. He realized that this would be the first airborne attack in the history of the world to seize an objective without the assistance of an army moving overland.

The next day, April 16, 1941, Reichsmarschall Goering arrived at Hitler's daily staff conference, a little after 2:00 P.M. The meeting was already in progress, and his tardy entrance disrupted the proceedings. He entered noisily and, with a broad smile, nodded his greetings to Hitler. The other members of the conference received a wave of his baton as their salutation. Hitler responded to his Luftwaffe chief's greeting with a cold, fixed glare. His coolness was obvious to all present.

Resplendent in the full-dress uniform of a Luftwaffe field marshal, Hermann Goering had come to the conference directly from an air force ceremony. His tunic glittering with medals and decorations, around his neck sparkled the Collar of the Annunziata, a gift from the king of Italy.[3]

"Mein Fuehrer!" interrupted Goering. With a quick stride, the Reichsmarschall placed on Hitler's desk a map of Crete. "I have a proposal to make! Now that Greece is finished, I offer you a plan by which my Luftwaffe forces would seize the island of Crete."[4]

"Goering! Are you not aware of the great plans already in preparation regarding Operation Barbarossa?" Hitler snapped angrily. "Perhaps you should attend these conferences punctually and more often!"[5]

Goering blushed, then mumbled a few words in his defense: "This plan involves only the airborne units of my Luftwaffe. . . ."

At this point, Field Marshal Keitel saw his opportunity to embarrass Goering further. "Mein Fuehrer," he interjected, "the airborne units of the Luftwaffe are inexperienced for such an operation alone. Suppose we put this plan into effect, are we certain that it can succeed? If the airborne units fail to gain their objectives, can we spare the additional men that would be needed to make the attack successful? Time is against us!"[6]

The flush left Goering's cheeks. His eyes flickered in anger. He would take insults from the Fuehrer but not from this lackey, posing as the head of the German High Command.

"My Luftwaffe has proven itself equal to any of the other armed services! My paratroopers are the best trained men in the whole German army. They are second to no one! Look at what they did in Norway and in the Low Countries!"[7]

"Yes," retorted Keitel, "we have seen. You promised that your Luftwaffe alone would destroy the enemy ships evacuating the British from Dunkirk. They failed to do so! Did your Luftwaffe fulfill your promise to clear the skies over England?" Rising to face Goering, Keitel concluded, "And your well-trained paratroopers still are untried for an operation such as as the one you propose for Crete."

Hitler broke the suspenseful silence. Much to everyone's surprise, he came to Goering's defense: "Goering, you know how I feel about *our* parachute troops. I have always considered them to be men of iron—ruthless men—who would float down from the skies loaded with death."[8]

Hitler continued, "You know that this operation in the Balkans has delayed our time schedule for Barbarossa, yet, with this knowledge you ask me to delay even more and get further involved with an attack upon Crete?"

Goering finally saw the opportunity to defend his proposal. "That is the reason why this operation becomes necessary. Shall Crete remain a *Pfahl im Fleisch*—a thorn in our flesh—in our lifeline to the eastern Mediterranean and to the Suez Canal? We had hoped that the Italians would have taken that problem from our shoulders, but they failed. Their failure would be our success."[9]

Goering was himself again. This was the Goering of the early years, displaying an energetic, clear mind, persuasive and refreshing in his argument. All eyes were upon him. "Certainly, you cannot equate the heroic professionalism of the German soldier to that of the Italian. Where the Italian has failed, the German has succeeded.'' He added, ''The seizure and subjugation of Crete would be the crowning glory of our Balkan campaign.''[10]

The Reichsmarschall had finished his argument. It was now for Adolf Hitler to accept or reject the proposal. Alfred Jodl, OKW Chief of Operations, spoke up.

''Mein Fuehrer, may I emphasize one point that I had mentioned in my report.'' Hitler signaled him to continue.

''In that report, I had stressed the fact that the seizure of Crete would keep the enemy from using the island as an air base from which they could bomb the Ploesti oil fields.''[11]

The Ploesti oil fields, in Rumania, were just four hours' flying time from Crete. Hitler needed their oil for his tanks and for his airplanes. He could not jeopardize the security of those oil reserves.

Hitler nodded as Jodl's comment struck a warning bell in his brain. His army chief of operations was right. Hitler walked pensively to his desk, head bowed, hands clasped behind him. ''Your point is well taken, Jodl,'' he said. Then, turning inquiringly to Goering, ''Who, may I ask, is the creator of this proposal for the airborne operation on Crete?''

Again it was the chief of operations who responded: ''Lieutenant General Kurt Student, Mein Fuehrer.''[12]

''Ah, yes, of course, Student! I shall give your proposal careful consideration, Goering.''

With that, Hitler left the room. The meeting was over.

On April 20, 1941, a well-built, square-faced Luftwaffe officer of average height was ushered into the hallway of Hermann Goering's hunting lodge in Rominten. He was met by Robert Kropp, Goering's personal valet since 1933. Kropp informed the officer that the Reichsmarschall would see him shortly.

This was the first time the visitor had ever seen the interior of this renowned hunting lodge. Seated in a corner in a straight, high-backed chair, he was impressed with the plush, rich decor of the huge room. His eyes feasted themselves upon the paneled ceilings whose crystal chandeliers cast shimmering light upon the huge tapestries that adorned the four walls. Centered before a 400-year-old French tapestry was a long, highly polished table, with one tall bronze lamp at each end. On one side of the table were two large straight-backed armchairs, separated by a coffee table. On the other side, facing the straight-backed chairs, was a huge thronelike armchair. Obviously, this was Hermann Goering's official reception room where he held audience with his visitors.

The visitor had traveled widely in his long military career, but never had he seen such opulence and grandeur. "The Reichsmarschall lives like an emperor," he thought to himself.[13]

Dressed in the uniform of a lieutenant general, the visitor's appearance epitomized the upright, immaculately attired Prussian officer, a member of the Luftwaffe General Staff.

He wore an open-collared tunic with pegged trousers, all in the familiar shade of Luftwaffe blue. The piping cords and insignia of his uniform were in gold, and his breeches bore the white stripes indicating the rank of a general officer. His waist was adorned with a brocade belt of silver interwoven with threads of black and red. It was centered by a gold general officer's buckle with a silver eagle motif.

Over his right breast pocket was a Luftwaffe eagle woven in metallic gold thread. His left breast bore a small silver eagle symbolizing the 1939 bar to the Iron Cross issued to him in the First World War. Below this was pinned a Maltese cross designating the award of the Iron Cross of 1939, First Class. Attached in a circle around this Iron Cross were a silver wound badge and the paratrooper qualification medal. Above his left breast pocket were attached varicolored ribbons representing campaign and service medals of his long career. Perhaps the most impressive medal worn by this much-decorated officer was the black-red-black ribbon that passed under the collar of his white shirt, and from which was suspended the Ritterkreuz—the Knight's Cross.[14]

This handsome, well-dressed general was, in fact, the commanding general of the Eleventh Air Corps—the XI Fliegerkorps. Under his command were all the paratroopers and airborne soldiers of the German Army. It was only proper that he should be their commander. This selected, specially trained group of men had been the brainchild of his fertile imagination. Some officers in the higher echelons of command appreciated his genius. But many veteran officers of the German General Staff looked upon his work as too experimental to be successful in actual warfare. In the course of military events, his "too experimental" plans bore fruit.

With the bold use of his paratroop and glider units in the invasions of Belgium and the Netherlands in 1940, and in the rapid capture of the impregnable Belgian fortress of Eban Emael, this ingenious general had proved that his plans could work. The airborne units had become an important component in the German military scheme of surprise and lightning warfare, and their successful operations brought much fame to their commander. There were few officers in the Third Reich who had not heard of the exploits of Lieutenant General Kurt Student.

Kurt Student was not a "Johnny-come-lately" officer who had received his rank because of loyalty to Adolf Hitler or to the Nazi party. All his life, from early youth, he had been devoted to the military in the service of his beloved Germany.

In 1901, at the age of ten, he had entered an army preparatory school as a cadet, beginning his career as an officer candidate. He wore a uniform for the first time and he did not remove it until the end of World War II. In 1911 he received his commission as an officer, making him a member of the German officer corps.

In November 1933 Student had been promoted to lieutenant colonel and appointed director of the technical training schools for the air services. His work dealt with the technical study and construction of airframes, engines, weapons systems, and parachutes. He labored many long hours on the multiple problems posed by this work.

There was a great deal of politics in those early days of Hitler's rise to power. Student knew little of politics and liked them less. He was a member of the German officer corps—an elite group—who wished only to continue serving the fatherland. Because he was not a party member, he was repeatedly passed over for promotion. But he was not discouraged. All he wished was to be instrumental in the development of German air power.

It was not until his forty-eighth birthday, in 1938, that he was promoted to major general. With this rank, he was given command of the Seventh Air Division. Now Student, known in the higher army echelons as the "little adventurer," had been given a command that was an adventure in itself, carte blanche to form an airborne division. It would be his duty to organize, train, and develop an elite group of volunteers to become an exclusive fighting arm of the newly developed Luftwaffe. (In addition, he was appointed an inspector general of the airborne forces.) Student's early experiences with gliders suggested to him the idea of developing glider troops as an adjunct to the paratroopers.

When World War II began in 1939, he sought to put his units into action in support of the Wehrmacht. But the General Staff did not feel that his units had proved themselves. The paratroopers were not used in the blitzkrieg attack upon Poland. But when they were used in the invasion of the Low Countries, they finally had their chance to prove their military value.

On May 14, 1940, during the final hours of the successful campaign in the Netherlands, Kurt Student was struck by a sniper's bullet. Wounded severely in the head, he hung precariously between life and death for many days. In the weeks that followed, he lay in bed half-paralyzed, unable to speak or to recognize anyone. It was a long, arduous path to recovery. His spirit and determination to recover overcame his illness. In September of the same year, he was finally considered fully recovered and returned to duty.[15]

Now a lieutenant general, he was made commanding general of the XI Fliegerkorps and commander of all the German airborne forces. Kurt Student, "the Father of the German Paratrooper," was back.

General Student waited patiently for the conference with his commander in chief. It was known that Goering always kept his visitors waiting; perhaps it added to his image of importance. This did not disturb Student. While he waited he fingered the briefcase resting on his lap. In it were two sets of plans for airborne operations that he wanted to present personally to the Reichsmarschall.

A sound on the step announced the Reichsmarschall's approach. "I am glad you are here, Student," was his opening greeting. "I am leaving for a hunt in an hour. I understand that you wish to discuss the Corinth project."

As Hermann Goering settled his corpulent body into his thronelike armchair, General Student unrolled a huge map upon the table.

"I plan to land the Second Parachute Regiment right at the Corinth Canal. They will secure the bridge and thus sever the Peloponnesus from the rest of Greece. Its success will trap and cut off the British forces." The plan was to go into operation in the morning hours of April 26.[16]

The time was approaching for Goering to leave for his scheduled hunt. He rose to leave.

"Herr Reichsmarschall, has any decision been made regarding our proposed plan for Crete?"

Four days had elapsed since Goering first proposed the plan to Hitler. "I do not think the Fuehrer plans any further campaign in the Mediterranean, once Greece is occupied," he replied.

Student rolled up the maps, seemingly undisturbed by the Luftwaffe chief's remarks. "That is unfortunate. It looks like our Luftwaffe will always play a secondary role in this war!"[17]

Goering's head jerked to attention. He sat down again. Student's remark had a telling effect upon him. Student pressed his point: "This would be strictly a Luftwaffe operation. It need not require assistance from the Wehrmacht nor the Kriegsmarine. We can take Crete with the sole use of our airborne forces. Why should the German Air Force play second fiddle to the army and navy?''

Goering, whose enthusiasm was easy to arouse, fell prey to Student's argument. "Nothing is impossible for the parachutists!" [18]

The Luftwaffe chief was convinced that Student was right. Goering longed to find the opportunity to press his airborne soldiers into action. He believed that Hitler had been misled by the generals of the OKW into relegating the Luftwaffe to a secondary role. "They never would give our Luftwaffe a major vital place in an important battle," Goering muttered dejectedly. We are always second—but our airmen are worthy of better things!"

"Yes, Herr Reichsmarschall, and this operation for Crete would add great glory for our Luftwaffe and even greater glory for you."

"You are right, Student. I shall go to see the Fuehrer today. He must give his approval!" [19]

The Reichsmarschall was true to his word. He cut short his hunting plans and flew to Hitler's headquarters in time to attend that afternoon's situation conference. He was determined to press for approval of the attack upon Crete.

Much to the Reichsmarschall's surprise, Hitler received the renewed proposal with calm. His only reply to Goering was: "Let me talk with Student tomorrow."

Early the next morning, Kurt Student received a telephone call from the Reichsmarschall.

"The Fuehrer is willing to see you today regarding the plan for Crete." Student's pulse beat faster. He would now have the opportunity to present his plan to Hitler personally. Perhaps he would succeed in getting approval to seize Crete with his paratroopers. It would be a dream fulfilled.

Goering continued, "I will meet you at three this afternoon, immediately following the Fuehrer's daily staff conference. Bring Jeschonnek with you." [20] (General Hans Jeschonnek was the

Luftwaffe chief of staff. As an *Oberleutnant*—Lieutenant—he had been Student's assistant in earlier years at the German Air Mission.)

Student and Jeschonnek arrived at Hitler's field headquarters at Münchenkirchen early in the afternoon. They were admitted into the anteroom, an austere, simply furnished chamber. In the adjoining conference room, Adolf Hitler was holding court with the members of the German General Staff. The German leader was elated, for earlier in the day he had received the news that the Greek Army had capitulated to Field Marshal List's Twelfth Army. The operations in Greece were virtually complete. His southern flank was now once more secure.

A military aide appeared at the door of the conference room and beckoned to the two Luftwaffe officers to enter. Goering greeted them at the entrance and escorted them to Adolf Hitler. The Fuehrer stood at his desk acknowledging the Deutsche Gruss—the German salute—tendered by Student and Jeschonnek.

"I have reviewed your plan for Crete, Student," Hitler remarked as the meeting convened. "It seems all right, but I do not think it is practical." [21]

Student was not going to be discouraged by this opening comment. He countered, "Mein Fuehrer, I strongly believe that the conquest of Crete from the air is not only possible, but certain."

Hitler mumbled something to Jodl. Student, undisturbed by the Fuehrer's inattentiveness, continued more firmly, "What I propose is a limited airborne operation of short duration. It would involve only the Luftwaffe forces. The plan is economical in its scope and it will succeed, if given the opportunity! Besides, mein Fuehrer, we have learned from experience that it is harmful for the paratroop units to remain inactive too long." [22]

Hitler faced his airborne commander. With a fleeting glance at Goering, he posed a question tinged with sarcasm: "Are you aware, General Student, that the General Staff has operational plans of greater importance?"

Of course, Hitler was referring again to Operation Barbarossa—the planned attack on Russia. Already the Oberkommando der Wehrmacht was committed to the deployment of one hundred thirty-seven divisions along the eastern front.

"I am aware of those plans, mein Fuehrer. Our proposal for Crete need not disturb the Wehrmacht from their program."[23]

"Why have you not considered the seizure of Malta instead of Crete?" asked Hitler. Field Marshal Wilhelm Keitel, chief of the German General Staff, had repeatedly suggested that Student's paratroopers should be used in the seizure of Malta.[24]

At this point Goering threw in an unexpected question: "Crete or Malta?"

Hitler made a nervous gesture to him to be silent. He knew that Malta had been a hornet's nest. The little island, located sixty miles south of Sicily, stood like a bastion against repeated air attacks. The Aeronautica Regina—the Italian air force—had bombed it day after day. Later reinforced by the German Tenth Air Corps, the bombing continued with even greater vehemence. The island was bombed until clouds of pulverized dust obscured it. Yet, when the dust settled, Malta was still operable. Its aircraft would rise to attack the Axis sea convoys sailing from Italy to North Africa. Not a single convoy carrying supplies to General Rommel and his Afrika Korps escaped damage.

"Mein Fuehrer," answered Student, "I feel that Crete, with its long northern coastline and with those airbases located on the north coast, would be a better objective to seize. An air drop upon Malta might jeopardize our attacking forces, because the island is small and the British could easily transfer their reserve forces from point to point. It would be too risky for our paratroopers."[25]

The Fuehrer nodded his head in agreement. He could not dare risk this elite group of men in an operation that might exhaust their number and destroy their potential.

Student pressed his argument further: "Crete could be the stepping stone to the mastery of the Mediterranean."

Not a single thought or a single plan existed in the German

war scheme to extend the battle lines into the eastern Mediterranean. All of Adolf Hitler's thoughts since November 1940 had been centered on the attack upon Russia.

"And the next step?" Hitler asked.

"Cyprus! From there to the Suez, through the back door," replied Student with a self-assurance that startled even Hitler. At that moment new glory for the Luftwaffe, somewhere in the eastern Mediterranean, was conceived.[26]

Hitler now regarded Student closely; a look of interest had crossed the Fuehrer's face. Goering smiled, for he also saw the familiar glitter in Hitler's eyes. Student felt victory within his grasp. It was time to show his trump card.

"The seizure of Crete, mein Fuehrer, would deprive the British of those airfields located on the northern coast of the island. If the British retain those airfields, they could pose a constant threat of bombing, at will, the Ploesti oil fields in Romania. That would be disastrous to our overall war effort."[27]

Hitler rose and walked to the map table. He gazed at Student's campaign map of Crete. He remembered the memoranda about Crete submitted by the chief of staff of the German army, General Franz Halder, and by Grand Admiral Karl Raeder, chief of the Kriegsmarine. Both had mentioned the necessity for the occupation of Crete. Even his chief of operations, Alfred Jodl, had concurred in such an operation. Hitler slowly realized that the seizure of Crete could become a springboard for future operations against North Africa, the Suez Canal, and the whole of the eastern Mediterranean—after Russia had been brought to her knees.

"How much time would you need for this operation?" the Fuehrer inquired.

"The island could be captured within three days!"

"That's impossible!" Hitler countered Student's boast. "I shall give you five days! You would, in any case, have to move with great speed. That is necessary in the interests of the other fronts. Every day lost needlessly is paid for dearly."

Goering and Student exchanged triumphant glances.

"Mein Fuehrer, do your words mean that you approve of the attack upon Crete?" asked Student excitedly.

"I don't know," replied Hitler vaguely, bending once more over the maps on the table before him. "I'll think it over!" [28]

For some reason, Adolf Hitler took four days to "think it over." It was not until April 25 that he finally arrived at the decision to attack Crete. [29]

During those four days, he wrote a letter to his Italian ally, Benito Mussolini. He mentioned to him the proposed plan concerning the seizure of Crete. Since this was in Mussolini's sphere of influence, Hitler felt it was proper to consult him.

General Jodl, however, thought it unusual that the Fuehrer took time now to inform Mussolini of this pending military operation. It was the first time that the younger member of the Axis alliance had ever bothered to take the Italian dictator into his confidence.

It also seemed paradoxical to the generals of the high command that the Fuehrer—who had raged in anger at Mussolini's military failures, and with the date for Operation Barbarossa rapidly approaching—would delay his decision in order to write to this discredited man.

On April 25 the decision was made: Germany would attack Crete. On that date the Fuehrer's headquarters issued a military order bearing Hitler's signature:

DIRECTIVE NO. 28: Order for the seizure of Crete as a base for air warfare against Great Britain in the eastern Mediterranean. [30]

Hitler had imposed two limitations on this operation. The first restriction was that it involve only the units of the Luftwaffe. The second dictated that it should start no later than the middle of May and that it was to be concluded by May 25, just ten days later. The operation was assigned the code name *Merkur*.

Operation Mercury—the plan for the attack upon Crete—was born.

4

"DETERMINE THE NEXT GERMAN OBJECTIVE"

APRIL 21, 1941

On the same day that Lieutenant General Kurt Student was meeting with the Fuehrer to discuss the proposed plans for an airborne attack on Crete, another meeting was taking place across the English Channel.

The British chiefs of staff, and the service ministers of the coalition government that directed Great Britain's war effort against Nazi Germany, had been summoned to an important conference scheduled for noon, April 21, at the official residence of the prime minister, Ten Downing Street.[1]

As the men who led Britain arrived for the conference, the skies above grew dark with the threat of imminent rain. It was a gloomy Monday; everything seemed bleak and depressing.

The problems that faced these men were harrowing. At sea, the toll of ships sunk by German U-boats was still dangerously high, in spite of efforts to counter the menace. On land, Yugoslavia had capitulated and was almost completely overrun by the German army. British and Greek forces were in full retreat in the face of persistent attacks by overwhelming German armor in Greece. But perhaps the most crucial and startling news came from North Africa.

In February 1941 Hitler had sent General Erwin Rommel to Libya with the first elements of the German troops that were to become the nucleus of the Afrika Korps.[2]

Winston Churchill realized that General Sir Archibald Wavell, Commander in Chief, Mediterranean, had to be reinforced immediately. To accomplish this, Churchill had formulated a daring plan. He had summoned his military leaders to this conference to present it to them.

Churchill proposed that a special convoy be prepared, comprised of fast motor-transport ships. "Let these ships be filled with all available artillery, tanks, and aircraft, and let them be rushed *through the Mediterranean* to Alexandria instead of going around the Cape!"[3]

To remarks concerning the risk involved, he retorted that it *was* risky, "but we must accept the risk." The chiefs of staff still had to be convinced.

"Of course, secrecy is of vital importance, and no one outside the highest circle of command need know of our intention to turn off, eastward, at Gibraltar. Even those aboard the convoy must think they are going around the Cape of Good Hope!"[4]

The conference members stirred, yet not one offered any encouraging word of acceptance. Undismayed, Churchill pressed forward. "The fate of the war in the Middle East is at hand. Let us not forget," he reminded them, "that the loss of the Suez Canal would have a calamitous result for our interests in that area. The loss of this vital waterway would end all prospects of future American cooperation through the Red Sea. Yet, gentlemen, all this may hinge upon a few hundred armored vehicles reaching Wavell on time."[5]

"It is obvious that our operations in Greece will end shortly. We are rapidly approaching the need for the withdrawal of our troops from the Greek mainland." Churchill went on to say that it would again be up to the Royal Navy to help evacuate the troops. The majority of these men were to be taken to the island of Crete. There, they would be rearmed and amply supplied for the defense of that Mediterranean island. "I have made repeated injunctions these past six months," Churchill emphasized, "that Suda Bay be fortified. We must have a strong, well-armed garrison there, with a strong air force as a protective cover. The island must be stubbornly defended! *I strongly feel that the Germans will strike next at Crete!"* [6]

"We do not agree, Prime Minister!" the chief of the Imperial General Staff demurred. Churchill raised his head, and with his eyeglasses resting halfway down his short nose, he frowned at General Sir John Dill.

In the light of the events then taking place in Iraq and in the western sands of North Africa, General Dill continued, "We feel that the next German objective would *not be Crete, but Iraq!"* [7]

Pointing to the map with a long unlit cigar, Churchill queried, "If the German plans to occupy Iraq, why is he even now concentrating his bombing efforts upon our defence positions in Crete?"

"It is possible that the German wants us to *think* that he is planning to attack and occupy Crete," was Dill's unhesitating reply. "His air attacks upon Crete would be a feint to divert our attention, while his real plan would be directed at Iraq. I might say that General Wavell concurs with me that Crete might be a coverup'!" [8]

Churchill's frown had been replaced by a pensive expression. "If Hitler follows the strategy that Dill set forth," he thought to himself, "then we might well be in dire straits." What gave Churchill consolation, however, was that Dill's strategy was too logical; Hitler did not always follow sound military logic.

Admiral Dudley Pound, the First Sea Lord, raised his hand to speak. "[British] air attacks have been staged from our air bases on *Malta*. The German knows this, and he also realizes that he must have a supply line free from attack if he is to succeed in North Africa. The German must get rid of Malta!" Now everyone in the room stirred. Admiral Pound continued, "This is the reason we feel that Hitler's next objective in the Mediterranean is neither Crete nor Iraq, but rather the island of Malta!" [9]

"I know only too well of Malta's strategic value to our Mediterranean war effort," Churchill replied, "but what makes you think that the German would attempt to seize Malta *now* that she stands like a bastion of defence when he did not do so last year when she lay as naked of defence as a newborn babe?" [10]

Winston Churchill remained unconvinced. He admitted to himself that each argument was strategically sound. However, there were also plausible arguments against each theory. The innate ingenuity that made him a great leader still argued that the next German goal was Crete.

Though undaunted in his conviction, Churchill did not wish to counter the professional expertise of his military leaders. He would still press for Crete's defensive buildup.

"Gentlemen," concluded the prime minister before adjourning the meeting, "we have a distinct difference of opinion which must be resolved immediately. I shall recommend that our intelligence people find out for us in what direction Hitler will march next!" [11]

That same afternoon orders were dispatched to all British intelligence sections, to the effect that every effort should be made to determine the next German objective in the Mediterranean.

Thus, on the afternoon of April 21, following the meeting at Ten Downing Street, W. Cavendish-Bentick, director of the Joint Intelligence Board, received a memorandum from Winston Churchill, asking him ". . . *to determine the next German objective in the Mediterranean.*" [author's italics] [12] Would it be Malta, Iraq, or Crete?

5

"ANY DAY AFTER THE SEVENTEENTH"

MAY 14, 1941

On the morning of April 7, a man in his early thirties arrived at the Athens railroad station. The dirty, wrinkled appearance of his clothes and the streaks of dust on his round face told of the ordeal that he and his fellow passengers had undergone during this particular trip.

The train, one of the last to leave Saloniki, had departed just ahead of the advancing German columns. Twice it had been bombed and strafed by German Messerschmitts, the second attack causing several casualties among the passengers. Only the darkness of night protected the train and its passengers from total disaster.

The young man did not resemble the average Greek, for he was taller and lighter complexioned than most, blue-eyed, and had a tousle of light brown, almost blondish hair.

As he passed through the exit gate, his height and Nordic appearance raised the suspicion of two officers of the National Security Police. An alert had been issued for them to be wary. It was not unlike the Germans to sneak an espionage agent into a swarm of arriving refugees. The two officers following the tall young man felt that he was suspect; they decided to detain him.

Searching him from head to toe, rummaging through his valise, and carefully scrutinizing his identity papers, they found nothing extraordinary. The papers identified him as one John Drakopoulos, a teacher from Thessaloniki. Inasmuch as his name did not appear on the secret police wanted list, and finding nothing else to substantiate their suspicions, they reluctantly released him.

John Drakopoulos walked along Delighianni Street, past Platia Kariskaki, and down St. Constantine Avenue to Omonia Square. He took a room in a second-rate hotel and rested from the ordeal of his trip.

For the next few days, he did not leave his room except to eat or to buy the latest editions of the Athens newspapers. Back in his room, he ignored the headlines that reported defeat in Thrace, Thessaly, and Attica. Instead, he thumbed through the pages of each newspaper searching for one particular item. This became a daily practice, and when he did not find it, he threw down the papers in dismay. It was only a matter of days before Athens would fall to the invader. The Greek government already advised evacuation. King George II had left for the safety of Crete, while Athens had been declared an open city.

On April 25, eighteen days after his arrival in Athens, John Drakopoulos finally found the item he had been anxiously looking for. It was a five-line insert in the classified section of the Acropolis newspaper:

WANTED

CIVILIAN MAINTENANCE ENGINEER
GRANDE BRETAGNE HOTEL
MUST HAVE APPROPRIATE CREDENTIALS
APPLY IN PERSON

The time had arrived for Drakopoulos to go into action. Leaving his hotel, he stopped momentarily on the corner of Athena Street and looked up its length to the distant Acropolis, glowing majestically in the morning sunshine. He walked quickly past the milling throngs of Athenians, who had gathered on each corner reading the latest headlines, and turned up Panepistimiou, or University, Street, toward Constitution, or Syntagma, Square. As he hastened past the National Library and the neoclassical buildings of Athens University, the crowds thickened noticeably. He finally reached the corner of Kriezotou Street, where the density of the crowds made his passage almost impossible and the echoes of their voices had risen to a steep crescendo. Pushing to the corner of Queen Sofia Avenue, Drakopoulos saw the cause of the uproar.

There in the middle of Syntagma Square, in front of the Parliament building, was a long armored column of Royal Artillery. The battered, exhausted men clearly demonstrated the pitiful signs of soldiers who had fought hard in continuous, futile battle. The Athenians were swarming all about them, cheering, clapping, and shouting words of encouragement.

This unit belonged to Major General Harold Eric Barrowclough's brigade—possibly the last defending unit between Athens and the advancing Germans. The column could not proceed in its southward retreat to the ports of evacuation because of the crowds that had gathered around them. The Athenian men and women jumped onto the running boards of the vehicles. The girls kissed and hugged the startled, smiling soldiers, while the men shook their hands with a heartfelt gratitude. They did not know how to thank these gallant soldiers who had traveled halfway around the world to fight on Hellenic soil in order to save the Greeks from German conquest.

One woman ran up to the staff car, which led the convoy, and gave a bouquet of flowers to an officer. Lieutenant Colonel R. Waller smiled in embarrassment as another woman kissed him on both cheeks. Other women threw bouquets at the vehicles, shouting in Greek: *"Ef haristo"*—"Thank you." [1]

The column finally resumed its movement through the streets of Athens. These soldiers would never forget the kindness, affection, and expressions of goodwill that the Athenians bestowed upon them. Some of these soldiers were to gain even greater glory and everlasting affection in Greek hearts by their heroic deeds in the battle that would soon follow on the island of Crete.

Just opposite from where John Drakopoulos stood was his destination. The Grande Bretagne had long been, and even at that time remained, the most luxurious and renowned hotel in Athens. It was also British headquarters. When the British forces arrived in October 1940 to aid the Greeks in their war against the Italian invaders, they converted this hotel into the General Headquarters of the British Expeditionary Forces in Greece under the command of General Henry Maitland Wilson.

Darting between the vehicles of a British armored column, and struggling through the crowds, Drakopoulos reached the entrance of the hotel.

The main lobby was bustling with activity; soldiers of all ranks were racing to their assigned duties. Drakopoulos stopped a sergeant and in precise English asked for the civilian personnel officer. The young captain who was the personnel officer listened patiently and glanced briefly at the classified advertisement that Drakopoulos showed him. "We really have nothing to do with this anymore, old chap," he replied, handing him back the folded newspaper. "As you can see," he continued, "we are in the midst of departing. This is no longer our concern." Then he suggested that Drakopoulos apply to the civilian directors of the hotel for employment.

In 1941 there were two associate directors of the Grande Bretagne Hotel: One was a Swiss named Walter Schmidt; the other was a Greek, George Canellos. It was Canellos who interviewed Drakopoulos for the vacancy, and since no one else had applied, Drakopoulos was given the position of maintenance engineer for the hotel.[2]

By the evening of April 26, all British troops had left Athens. In their wake there remained a suspenseful vacuum—a void of silent anxiety. In the early morning hours of April 27, the first elements of Field Marshal Wilhelm List's Twelfth Army entered Athens. The Athenians glared at them from street corners and from behind shuttered windows. A silence of imminent doom prevailed. All that was audible was the grinding squeal of tanks and the tramp of hobnailed boots beating a harsh tempo on the city pavements. Athens, the birthplace of democracy, had lost its freedom as the Greek flag on the Acropolis was replaced by the Nazi swastika.

Shortly after the Germans entered the capital, a Volkswagen jeep followed by four armored personnel carriers drove up to the entrance of the Grande Bretagne. This advance headquarters billeting party lost no time in taking over the hotel. All vestigial reminders of the British presence were quickly removed. In their place appeared German eagles and a host of swastika banners. On the pavement outside, two tanks took up positions as guardians of the entrance. In no time at all, the beautiful, plush, Victorian-style hotel had assumed a Germanic flavor. What had been the headquarters of the British Expeditionary Army the previous day now became German headquarters in Greece.

A few hours after the Germans commandeered the Grande Bretagne, a sleek, black Mercedes limousine drew up before the hotel, followed closely by another vehicle filled with black-uniformed soldiers. These troops belonged to the Schutzstaffel— the dreaded SS.

The tall, lean officer who got out of the limousine was dressed in the black duty uniform of an SS colonel. He was the commanding officer of this headquarters security unit, Standartenfuehrer Heinz Gellermann. Under his command, the SS set up its own headquarters within that of the Wehrmacht.

The German military organization was unique in that it held within its fold two distinct armies. One was the regular army— the Wehrmacht—under the Oberkommando des Heeres, as the army high command was called. The other army was composed of selected units collectively called the Schutzstaffel, or the SS.

Perhaps the most important subgroup of the Schutzstaffel was the National Central Security Office—the Reichssicherheitshauptamt, or RSHA for short. In 1941, Reinhard Heydrich, whose assassination in Czechoslovakia led to the terror of the town of Lidice, was the director of the RSHA.

This National Central Security group had within its body several departments: Bureau III with the SD (Sicher Dienst) was a security service inside Germany; Bureau IV, the Gestapo, was the State Security Police; Bureau V, the criminal police; and Bureau VI dealt with foreign intelligence.[3]

Standartenfuehrer Heinz Gellermann was a member of the Gestapo, or Bureau IV.

It was the duty of the SS unit to enforce security in the Greek capital and to establish even tighter security at German headquarters. To begin with, SS Colonel Gellermann ordered the immediate investigation of all civilian personnel employed at the Grande Bretagne.

John Drakopoulos was in the first group of hotel personnel to be interviewed by Colonel Gellermann's Gestapo staff. Afterward, Gellermann read the dossiers very carefully and found Drakopoulos' background to be the most interesting of all. What he read about Drakopoulos pleased him.

It appeared that John Drakopoulos had spent the last ten years of his life in Germany. He had received his engineering degree at Kiel University. His student days had been spent amidst the political turmoil preceding Adolf Hitler's rise to power.

When Germany went to war, the young student from Greece returned to his home city of Saloniki. In this second-largest city in Greece, he obtained employment as a high school German teacher. When Germany invaded Greece, Drakopoulos fled before the tide of battle with countless thousands of other refugees—arriving in Athens in the morning hours of April 7.

It was obvious to the SS colonel and his Gestapo staff that this young Greek engineer was a Germanophile. There was something Germanic about his appearance. It would be advantageous to have Drakopoulos working for the German occupation forces. But Standartenfuehrer Gellermann was an officer in the hated Gestapo. A member of an organization that from its inception was nurtured on suspicion and raised on deceit, the SS colonel was not going to accept the young engineer's statements at face value. The validity of Drakopoulos' dossier would have to be confirmed. Gellermann wired Gestapo headquarters on Prinz Albrechtstrasse in Berlin requesting all available information on John Drakopoulos, the former student at Kiel University.

Within thirty-six hours the colonel had his reply. It confirmed everything in the Drakopoulos dossier. The Gestapo report added that on several occasions Drakopoulos had participated in pro-Hitler student rallies. The information was enough to satisfy Colonel Gellermann.

The next day John Drakopoulos was summoned to Gellermann's office. It was a nerve-racking moment when the two burly SS guards pushed him gruffly through the door. Standing before the colonel, watching his pen scratch across a page, Drakopoulos did not know what to expect. The silence became ominous. Finally Gellermann closed the file before him, looked up, and smiled.

"I congratulate you, Herr Drakopoulos," Gellermann remarked, rising from his chair. "It is obvious from your record that you are one of us! We shall be pleased to have you work with us."

Drakopoulos released an inaudible sigh of relief.

Without further word, Colonel Gellermann handed Drakopoulos his pass. This passport-size document carried more authority than any other similar permit issued by the German occupation forces. It gave Drakopoulos permission to go anywhere in Athens and its environs. It also indicated that he was in the good graces of the Gestapo.

The tall Greek glanced quickly at this vital permit. There was his picture with his vital statistics on the right side, while the left bore the imprint of the German eagle with Reichsfuehrer Heinrich Himmler's signature. Below the eagle there appeared the Gestapo seal, signed by the SS commandant in Athens.

When Drakopoulos left Gellermann's office, a broad smile slowly crossed his face as a feeling of elation welled up within him. He had fooled the Germans. Not only had he fooled them, he had also fooled the *Gestapo*—and seldom did anyone succeed at that.

In reality, John Drakopoulos was a Greek working for the British, with the rank of major in British military intelligence. He had been planted in the Grande Bretagne as an employee and his orders were specific: Find out if the Germans planned to invade Iraq, Malta, or Crete?

During the first week in May, John Drakopoulos noticed an increase in Luftwaffe personnel at the Grande Bretagne. The Luftwaffe command had taken over the entire second floor of the hotel. The largest room on the floor had been converted into a carefully guarded war room, with access granted only to members of the Luftwaffe General Staff and their aides. From photographs, Drakopoulos easily recognized Colonel General Alexander Löhr, who commanded the Fourth Air Fleet in the Balkans; and General Wolfram von Richthofen, cousin of the famous "Red Baron" of World War I fame, who was the commander of the Eighth Air Force in Greece. What impressed Drakopoulos most of all was the continuous presence of Lieutenant General Wilhelm Suessmann, a parachute commander; and that of the commanding general of all German parachute units, Lieutenant General Kurt Student, who had set up residence in the hotel. Their constant presence in the war room gave clear evidence that the pending operation would involve the entire parachute corps.

Drakopoulos knew the answers he sought were in the war room. However, with tight Luftwaffe security, and the ubiquitous Gestapo always present to scrutinize the identity of each person entering the inner sanctum, gaining access would be the most difficult part of his assignment. Drakopoulos asked the cleaning women to bring him all war-room refuse. Perhaps, he thought, he could piece together some clues of what went on there daily. This plan, however, failed, for all refuse was personally dealt with by the SS. Attempts at planting listening devices also proved futile. Drakopoulos was stymied. Then he got lucky.

On a clear, hot, humid morning in the second week of May, the Grande Bretagne was inundated with Luftwaffe officers of all ranks arriving en masse. John Drakopoulos observed the ranks—generals, colonels, majors, captains, even a few Ober-leutnants—as they were quickly ushered into a huge salon at the rear of the hotel's first floor. As each officer entered the heavily draped, hermetically sealed meeting room, he was handed a writing pad. It was evident to Drakopoulos—who made mental notes of the proceedings—that the simultaneous arrival of pre-dominantly general and field-grade officers, with only a smat-tering of company-graders, meant that the major briefing of the planned operation was about to take place.

Throughout the meeting John Drakopoulos positioned him-self behind the main reception desk, helping a young commu-nications corporal wire a switchboard. He worked slowly, hop-ing that the meeting would adjourn before he completed the wiring. For three long hours he labored, doing and undoing the wires, until the huge double doors opened and the swarm of of-ficers emerged. Drakopoulos watched with chagrin as Gestapo personnel collected the writing pads from each officer. What-ever had happened in that room was meant to remain a secret.

The hotel lobby rapidly emptied as each officer returned to his unit. Two officers—one a major, the other an Oberleut-nant—remained in the outer foyer chatting amiably. It was ob-vious to Drakopoulos that they were renewing an acquaintance. But what caught his quick eye was that the young Oberleutnant had neglected to surrender his writing pad. The major also noted this omission and cautioned the young officer as the two finally took leave. Before exiting, the Oberleutnant turned, walked over to the main desk, and placed the writing pad on the counter—right in front of John Drakopoulos.

Drakopoulos' heart skipped a beat. He eyed the writing pad momentarily, then—pretending that the midday heat had be-come unbearable—he removed his jacket and threw it on the counter, directly over the pad. A little later, his work finally completed, Drakopoulos nonchalantly picked up his jacket, being careful to hide the writing pad within its folds, and casually left for his room.

Once in his room with the door locked, Drakopoulos examined the writing pad carefully. It was devoid of any writing, but he could make out an imprint on the top sheet. He took a piece of charcoal from a censer that stood on a corner shelf together with some icons, and crumbled it over the top sheet. He smeared it smoothly over the whole page, then blew off the excess. Removing the shade from his bedside lamp, he tore off the page and placed it against the naked light bulb. The imprint, which was previously barely discernible, now appeared clearly in white against the black background.

What appeared to Drakopoulos as a jagged, broken line, similar to a thunderbolt, streaked halfway down the page. It was obvious that the Oberleutnant had been doodling. At the end of the jagged streak appeared the letters *K,R,E,T,A*. The *K,R,E* were quite clear; the *T* was faint; and the *A* was barely distinguishable. But it was enough for Drakopoulos, for in German the word *Kreta* meant Crete!

Farther down the page there appeared another scribbled symbol. It was in the form of a huge *V* followed by the Arabic numeral 17.

Drakopoulos knew that the Fifth German Mountain Division was stationed outside Athens. The Germans designated their divisions with Roman numerals. Could this young lieutenant, who had so carelessly disposed of his writing pad, have been the commanding officer of the seventeenth company in the Fifth German Division? It was not a plausible inference, for there had not been many Oberleutnants at the briefing. It appeared that *V* 17 had a different connotation. He then gave credible weight to the thought that the letter *V* designated the Roman numeral for the fifth month of the year, while the Arabic numeral 17 denoted the day of the month. He felt that this was a more logical conclusion.

Drakopoulos left the Grande Bretagne for his prearranged "drop-off" point. At the corner he was stopped by two Gestapo troopers. When he showed them his Gestapo pass, they gave him the Nazi salute and let him proceed with a nod and a smile. The tall young engineer strode quickly down University Street until he reached a basement bookstore located directly opposite the University of Athens. He walked to the rear of the shop where the shelves were filled with out-of-print books in Greek, English, German, and French. From the top shelf, he removed a moldy, weatherbeaten volume entitled *A Popular History of Greece.* Opening the book to Chapter 7, "Characteristics of the Minoan Empire," he placed in it a piece of paper containing three digits: 17–5. He returned the book to the shelf and left.[4]

Two blocks away and parallel with University Street is an equally lengthy thoroughfare called Akademias, or Academy, Street. At a point left of where Academy curves to join Queen Sofia Avenue and Constitution Square, there is a narrow street named Canaris Street. In those dark days of the German occupation, a person walking up Canaris Street immediately encountered a barbed-wire barricade at the first street on the right. This barricade marked the beginning of Merlin Street, a two-block connection of Canaris Street with Queen Sofia Avenue. Merlin Street became a place of foreboding and nightmare for the victimized citizens of Athens—for it was the center of Gestapo terror activity. The cellars of the buildings on both sides of the street testified in blood to the tales of broken bodies, of torture, terror, and death.

At 5 Canaris Street, there was a four-story town house. On the top floor, in an apartment whose windows overlooked the Gestapo buildings on Merlin Street, the British had a wire transmitting station. It was typical of the phlegmatic British to place such an apparatus directly under the nose of the dreaded Gestapo.

An hour after Drakopoulos left his message in the book, a fourteen-year-old boy arrived at the same bookstore. Like Drakopoulos, Athanasios Tziotis was employed at the Grande Bretagne. Each day at the same hour, he would come to the bookstore and pick up several newspapers for his employer, George Canellos, the associate director of the hotel.

On certain occasions the bookstore proprietor would ask young Athanasios if he would deliver a book or a newspaper to a special customer. The thought of earning a few extra drachmas appealed to him. The person to whom he made these deliveries lived on the top floor of a town house at 5 Canaris Street. It was many months before Athanasios Tziotis became even remotely aware that he was a runner for the Greek underground in the British intelligence service.[5]

Drakopoulos' message, hidden within the pages of the newspaper *Estia*, was delivered to 5 Canaris Street the same afternoon. That night the message was transmitted across the waters to a British submarine stationed on special picket duty off the western tip of Crete. The submarine relayed the message to Gibraltar, and from there it was transmitted to Admiralty House in London.

As Winston Churchill's personal bodyguard, it was Inspector Walter Henry Thompson's official duty each morning to awaken the prime minister and to deliver a large yellow sealed box that contained all communications received during the night.

This morning Thompson left the box as usual on the little table at Churchill's bedside. As Thompson turned to leave the room, he was startled by Churchill's jubilant exclamation. In an exhilarated, almost boyish voice, Winston Churchill cried out, "I knew it, Thompson, I knew it would be Crete! Send in my secretary! I must send a message!"[6]

Within the hour the message was transmitted to the commanding general of all the British forces in the Mediterranean:

PRIME MINISTER TO GENERAL WAVELL   14 MAY 1941
ALL MY INFORMATION POINTS TO [the invasion of Crete] ANY DAY
AFTER THE SEVENTEENTH.[7]

6

SCORCHER
ON COLORADO

MAY 16, 1941

The hour of reckoning was rapidly approaching. From the day in October 1940 when Greece found itself at war with Italy, Churchill had insisted that military aid be rushed to his Balkan ally, even though this meant stripping the defenses from General Wavell's army in Egypt. Not only did Churchill insist that troops be dispatched to the Greek mainland, but he repeatedly exhorted Wavell to convert the huge natural harbor at Suda Bay in Crete into another Scapa Flow. It was difficult for Wavell to comprehend how Suda Bay could be fortified into a Scapa Flow. That famous naval base north of Scotland was well out of German bomber range, while Suda Bay lay exposed and defenseless to the might of the Luftwaffe. However, Churchill's enthusiasm for Crete's defense would not be dampened by such a reality; long before the Germans came to the aid of the Italians, Churchill had recognized Crete's strategic importance in the Mediterranean.

The responsibility of providing men for the defense of Crete fell upon the broad shoulders of the British commander in the Mediterranean, but Wavell did not have the soldiers to spare. His defenses covered a vast perimeter: In the Western Desert, his troops were defending themselves against Rommel's threatening incursions; to the south, they were fighting the Italians in Ethiopia; and now it appeared that more troops would be required to put down a rebellion in Iraq. In the face of these problems confronting his beleaguered command, Wavell gave the defense of Crete a lower priority.[1] In spite of this, Churchill insisted that steps be taken to convert Crete into an island bastion.

British Intelligence had become aware that the Germans were planning an airborne operation against Crete. As early as April 18, Churchill had informed Wavell in Cairo that an airborne invasion of Crete was to be anticipated. The British had been successful in intercepting and decoding German messages originating in the highest command echelon via an apparatus known as *Ultra*.[2] As more and more information was intercepted, the magnitude of the attack became alarmingly impressive. It was enough for Churchill to telegraph Wavell:

PRIME MINISTER TO GENERAL WAVELL   28 APRIL 1941
IT SEEMS CLEAR FROM OUR INFORMATION THAT A HEAVY AIRBORNE ATTACK BY GERMAN TROOPS AND BOMBERS WILL SOON BE MADE ON CRETE.
LET ME KNOW WHAT FORCES YOU HAVE ON THE ISLAND AND WHAT YOUR PLANS ARE. . . .
. . . IT OUGHT TO BE A FINE OPPORTUNITY FOR KILLING THE PARACHUTE TROOPS.
. . . THE ISLAND MUST BE STUBBORNLY DEFENDED.[3]

The next day, Churchill received a reply:

GENERAL WAVELL TO PRIME MINISTER   29 APRIL 1941
CRETE WAS WARNED OF POSSIBILITY OF AIRBORNE ATTACK ON APRIL 18.

He went on to describe the disposition of the troops arriving daily from the Greek mainland:

BESIDES ORIGINAL PERMANENT GARRISON . . . CRETE NOW CONTAINS AT LEAST 30,000 PERSONNEL EVACUATED FROM

GREECE. THESE ARE BEING ORGANIZED FOR THE DEFENSE OF THE
VITAL PLACES ON THE ISLAND: SUDA BAY, CANIA, RETIMO, AND
HERAKLION.

Wavell proposed to visit the island on the next day for a personal inspection. However, the final paragraph of his reply disturbed Churchill:

IT IS JUST POSSIBLE THAT PLAN FOR ATTACK ON CRETE MAY BE
A COVER FOR ATTACK ON SYRIA OR CYPRUS, AND THAT REAL
PLAN WILL ONLY BE DISCLOSED EVEN TO [their] OWN TROOPS AT
THE LAST MOMENT. THIS WOULD BE CONSISTENT WITH GER-
MAN PRACTICE.[4]

When John Drakopoulos' message was received on May 14,
confirming the date of the German airborne assault, Churchill
wondered if Wavell had done everything possible to fortify the
island.

In a seven-month period, the command of Crete had changed
hands seven times. How was it possible to build up a strong defense structure under such conditions?

Back on December 1, Churchill had forwarded a memo to
General Hastings Lionel "Pug" Ismay, his liaison with the Imperial General Staff, with a specific inquiry:

EXACTLY WHAT HAVE WE GOT DONE AT SUDA BAY . . .? I HOPE
TO BE ASSURED THAT MANY HUNDREDS OF CRETANS ARE
WORKING AT STRENGTHENING THE DEFENSES AND LENGTHEN-
ING AND IMPROVING THE AERODROMES.[5]

The response was long in coming, but when it finally arrived,
Churchill discovered that in spite of all his exhortations and suggestions, *nothing* had been done. The inhabitants of Crete, though
eager to defend their native soil, had not been mobilized to
strengthen defense positions or to improve the airfields. Nor had
a reserve division been organized into a well-trained fighting force.
All those months had gone to waste. Churchill knew the reason:
The command structure on Crete was at fault. It was time he

personally intervened again as he had had to do in the past. He would have to designate his own choice for the next commanding officer of the Cretan garrison.

The man he was going to appoint would bear the whole responsibility for the defense of Crete. For that position he chose a personal friend held in high esteem, who was also a hero of the British Empire.

Respectful of protocol and not wishing to override the echelons of military command, Churchill submitted the name of his choice to the chief of the Imperial General Staff. General Sir John Dill concurred with Churchill's recommendation and forwarded the name to General Wavell in Cairo.

The man who was appointed commanding officer of all forces on Crete was a fifty-two-year-old New Zealander, Major General Bernard Freyberg.

Although born in England, Bernard Freyberg had spent most of his early youth in New Zealand. Churchill first met him in September 1914, when Freyberg arrived as a young volunteer seeking a commission. Great Britain was at war, and Churchill, as First Lord of the Admiralty, was instrumental in organizing the Royal Navy Division. Bearing the First Lord's recommendation, Freyberg was assigned as a junior officer to a battalion in that naval division.

In the four years of trench warfare that followed, Freyberg proved himself a man of extraordinary courage. His days in the trenches were filled with legendary feats of gallantry and valor. He became a national hero and was awarded the Victoria Cross and the Distinguished Service Order with two bars in recognition of his unsurpassed service. By the end of the war, Freyberg had risen in rank from a sublieutenant to commander of a brigade.

After the war Freyberg remained in the British army but— more suited to the daring deeds of battle than the pomposity of garrison life—he was unhappy. To overcome the dull existence of a peacetime officer, he sought diversions such as attempting to swim the English Channel, a feat in which he failed by only a few hundred yards.

During that period, Freyberg also often met with his old friend and patron Winston Churchill. At one such meeting, Churchill inquired about Freyberg's war wounds. When Freyberg obligingly stripped to the waist, Churchill was able to count twenty-seven scars on his body.

As the years passed into the thirties, men of Freyberg's caliber were becoming a liability to the penny-pinching bureaucrats of the War Office. Thought was given to retiring and pensioning off the old war-horses—when war erupted again in Europe.

As early as September 1940, Winston Churchill had great plans for his old friend. The prime minister looked upon Freyberg as a man who would "fight for King and Country with an unconquerable heart anywhere he is ordered, and with whatever forces he is given by superior authorities, and he [thus] imparts his own invincible firmness of mind to all around him."[6]

These were the qualities that Churchill sought in the man who should command in Crete. They were qualities that would drive a commander to a resolute defense of the island and, in so doing, deny it to the enemy.

True to the promise given in his April 29 message, General Wavell left the next day for a visit to Crete. He arrived early on the morning of April 30, fatigued by the uncomfortable flight and weary from the many problems that burdened him. Upon his arrival, he immediately summoned a conference of all the senior officers on the island.

About the time that Wavell arrived in Crete by air, Bernard Freyberg sailed into Suda Bay aboard a warship, with troops that had been evacuated from the Greek mainland.

New Zealand had shipped its only division of three brigades to fight in the Mediterranean. With defeat in Greece and in the ensuing evacuation, the Fourth and Fifth Brigades were deposited on Crete, while the Sixth Brigade was transported directly to Egypt. As division commander, it was Freyberg's hope to reunite the three brigades in Egypt and reconstitute the whole New

Zealand Division. For that reason, he left the warship in Suda Bay just before it sailed with the rest of the convoy for Egypt. He planned to visit the two brigades of his division and make plans for their transfer to Egypt. No sooner had Freyberg stepped ashore, however, than he was handed a message summoning him to the conference with Wavell.

The meeting took place on the rooftop terrace of a villa in the village of Platanias, halfway between the airfield at Maleme and the capital at Khaniá. Under the shade of a huge awning, the people who would resolve the defense situation in Crete gathered.

Wavell immediately realized that he faced a protocol problem, for he had too many senior commanders on hand. General Henry Maitland Wilson was senior to the island's garrison commander, General Edward Weston. Any message from Wavell to Weston required, out of courtesy, that a copy be sent to Wilson. Wavell would not "order" Wilson, but would only "suggest" that he act in conjunction with Weston. To add to the problems, Freyberg was expected momentarily, and he was junior to Wilson and senior to Weston. Someone would have to be sent away.

"Henry, what is your appreciation of the problem we face in defending Crete?" Wavell asked of Wilson when they were finally alone.

Wilson thought for a moment before answering. "I consider that unless all three services are prepared to face the *strain of maintaining adequate forces up to strength,* the holding of this island is a dangerous commitment, and a decision on the matter must be taken at once."[7]

"That is what you stated in your report. Then you haven't altered your opinion," replied Wavell, referring to the report Wilson had submitted to him on April 28. To the commanding general of the Mediterranean forces, Wilson's remarks represented an abdication of responsibility.

"You realize, of course, that it would be beyond our ability of 'maintaining adequate forces,' " commented Wavell, simultaneously remembering Churchill's exhortations "that Crete be held." Obviously, Wilson's thinking—although logistically sound—was at cross-purposes with that of the prime minister. Clearly, it was Wilson who had to go. Wilson was not too displeased when Wavell said: "I want you to go to Jerusalem and relieve Baghdad. . . ."[8]

Bernard Freyberg appeared on the terrace just as Wavell and Wilson were concluding their conversation. When Wilson departed, Wavell greeted Freyberg warmly.

"I want to tell you how well I think the New Zealand division has done in Greece. I do not believe any other division would have carried out those withdrawals as well."[9]

Freyberg, though never unduly impressed by compliments, accepted these warm words. He agreed that his New Zealanders had performed well.

Wavell took Freyberg by the arm and led him to a chair in the center of the terrace.

"I want you to take command of the forces in Crete!" Wavell stated without preamble, and then he added, "We expect Crete to be attacked in a few days. . . ."[10]

Taken by surprise, Freyberg still had other thoughts on the subject: "General, I would much rather get back to Egypt and concentrate the division and train and re-equip it. Besides," he added as an afterthought, "my government would never agree to the division being split permanently."

Wavell studied the tall, husky New Zealander for a few moments. "You realize, of course, that these orders come from the highest echelon in London."[11]

Freyberg took a deep breath. Then it must have been Churchill who had proposed his name for this assignment, he thought to himself. As if reading his mind, Wavell leaned forward and touched him lightly on the knee with his riding crop.

"It is your duty to take on the job."[12]

Freyberg shrugged his shoulders, replying, "I could do nothing but accept, under the circumstances."

"Good. Now let us take a close look at the problem," Wavell said as he opened a map of Crete.

When General Wavell stretched out the map before him on the table, it was Freyberg's first opportunity to make a critical observation of the island he had been asked to defend.

A cursory glance told him that Crete lay like a huge barrier reef in the middle of the Mediterranean, controlling the sea-lanes that connected the three continents of Europe, Africa, and Asia through Asia Minor. Whoever held possession of this island *could* maintain strategic control over the fortunes of enemy armies in southern Europe, North Africa, and the Near East. Now he appreciated Churchill's demands that Crete be defended and held.

After a light lunch, Freyberg was met by Colonel Keith Stewart, his chief of staff when he had commanded the New Zealand Division in Greece. Together they drove to the capital of Crete, Khaniá, to visit Crete Force Headquarters. What they found there was complete disorganization; there *was* no headquarters. No one seemed to know anything about the new command setup. Freyberg was horrified to learn that he had no staff officers and not even a single clerk to write out a general order.

Later, when he met his predecessor, General Weston, he asked if any defense plan had ever been drawn for Crete. Weston, who had held the command of Crete for only four days, smiled and shook his head. Much to Freyberg's chagrin, it was obvious that he would have to start from the beginning.

Freyberg appointed Colonel Keith Stewart as his chief of staff on Crete and ordered him to select a complete headquarters staff. He also requested an estimation of the strength of the forces available to defend the island. In the meantime, Freyberg would make a personal study of the lay of the land.

From the beginning, he was aware of Crete's primitive existence. The first point that impressed him was that not a single railroad existed. Only a narrow, paved road ran approximately 160 miles of the island's 186-mile length. It started at the western end of the island at Kisamos Kastelli and, running parallel to the north coast, went through the capital of Khaniá to the city of Rethimnon, and beyond to Iráklion. From Iráklion it proceeded inland past the village of Neapolis to Ayios Nikolaos, and then it deteriorated into a dirt road. This was the only paved road in Crete. One narrow, rocky, dirt road was the only passable connection to the southern coast, reaching the village of Timbakion. The other secondary roads leading inland began as dirt paths but soon narrowed into trails as they ascended into the foothills of the mountains that ran along the southern face of the island like a huge monolithic barrier. The mountains rose from 6,000 to 10,000 feet and were almost always snow-covered. The trails along the foothills disappeared amid the rugged crags, only to reappear on the southern coast, where the mountains ended in cliffs that fell in a sheer drop to meet the waters of the Libyan Sea.

To a military man like Freyberg, it was obvious that only the paved main northern road could be used for vehicular transportation by an army that had to maintain communications from one end of the island to the other.

Most of Crete's inhabitants lived on the northern coast of the island. Some of those near the main road had electricity in their homes; the rest still used kerosene lamps and candles. The few telephones that were available were used only by the rich or by businessmen in the cities.

Freyberg would have to create his own telephone communications system.

He observed that the northern coast was fertile and verdant—the reason why most of the Cretans lived in that area—covered with vineyards, olive groves, and fields of grain. But the fields were intersected by deep ravines, gullies, dry riverbeds, stone walls, dense bamboo glades, and tall grass sprinkled with angry cactus. To the military eye, such terrain posed a problem for a body of men that might have to move cross-country rapidly for a counterattack. Such broken ground would make a mobile attack force almost useless.

On the western extension of the northern road lay the sleepy town of Kastelli, little bigger than a village, nestled around a deep harbor between the Gramvousa and Rodopos peninsulas. Traveling eastward, Freyberg passed through the town of Tavronites, crossed over a dry river on a three-span steel-girder bridge, and just beyond the bridge, he came to a small, single-strip airfield named after the adjacent village of Maleme.

Across the road from the airstrip, there rose a height the Cretans called Kavzakia Hill. Freyberg noted that the hill and the airfield would have to be well defended.

From Maleme, Freyberg traveled along the road passing through the village of Platanias and the other villages that lay further inland, returning to Khaniá early in the evening.

On the map the barren hills of the Akrotiri Peninsula, where Freyberg now had his headquarters, appeared as the left profile of a human skull. The capital of Khaniá was at the Adam's apple, while the huge natural harbor of Suda Bay lay at the nape of the neck. The harbor was littered with sunken hulls of freighters that had suffered at the hands of the Luftwaffe.

Farther east, the village of Georgeopolis stood near the sandy shore. The village had no significance except that its beach could be a possible landing site for a seaborne invasion.

The north coast road continued eastward beyond Rethimnon for another forty-eight miles until it entered the walled city of Iráklion, the largest city in Crete. The harbor was the best of the three cities, second only to Suda Bay. Its airfield was the largest and most modern on the island, with a double landing strip.

When Freyberg finished with the study of his map, he counted the circles he had drawn around Maleme, Khaniá, Suda Bay, Georgeopolis, Rethimnon, and Iráklion. Slowly a defense plan was forming in his mind.

In the corner of his makeshift desk several sheets of paper caught Freyberg's eye. Neatly handwritten—there were no headquarters clerk-typists—was a report on the total manpower situation on the island. Freyberg's chief of staff had done his homework.

Except for the men of the original island garrison, the majority of troops arriving in Crete were evacuees from the Greek mainland. Countless thousands poured onto the island, with few weapons and fewer supplies. Dirty and disorganized, they had just the clothing on their backs; all their personal equipment had been left behind in Greece in their haste to leave. Most of the men were unassigned, and lacking the supervision of junior officers—of which there were too few—they wandered aimlessly through the fields and villages at will, hungry and thirsty. Some resorted to stealing; some fought among themselves; there was even a report of a civilian murder. Many of them had become ill-disciplined and disrespectful of authority. It was time to bring order out of this turmoil and restore the discipline that marks a military fighting unit. Court-martials were put into effect for the malefactors, and there were field punishment centers for the incorrigibles. To a punctilious person like Bernard Freyberg, this was a bad sign of the breakdown in morale.

As far as equipment and supplies were concerned, the report continued, matters were equally bad. Many of the men who arrived unassigned had no rifles or any other infantry weapons, much less ammunition. The units that landed intact were devoid of artillery or antiaircraft weapons. There was no transport or any adequate reserves of equipment or supplies with which to arm the arrivals.

Of the meager rations and arms supplies sent from Egypt, only one-third arrived safely in Crete. Nothing entered Suda Bay during daylight, when the Luftwaffe was always present to attack the defenseless supply ships.

Attached to Colonel Stewart's summary, which painted such a grim picture of the situation in Crete, was a military appreciation dated April 29 from the War Office, which reported the extent of the expected German attack in numbers of aircraft and shipping. Freyberg thought for a moment, shocked by what he had read. Then he picked up a pencil and scribbled a message to be telegraphed to Cairo.

GENERAL FREYBERG TO GENERAL WAVELL   1 MAY 1941
FORCES AT MY DISPOSAL ARE TOTALLY INADEQUATE TO MEET
ATTACK ENVISIONED. . . .

URGE THAT QUESTION OF HOLDING CRETE SHOULD BE RECON-
SIDERED. . . .
IT IS MY DUTY TO INFORM NEW ZEALAND GOVERNMENT OF SIT-
UATION IN WHICH GREATER PART OF MY DIVISION IS NOW
PLACED.[13]

True to his threat, a few moments later Freyberg scribbled a
second message, addressed to the prime minister of New Zealand, Mr. Peter Fraser:

P.M.–N.Z.   1 MAY 1941
FEEL IT IS MY DUTY TO REPORT MILITARY SITUATION IN CRETE
. . . WOULD STRONGLY REPRESENT TO YOUR GOVERNMENT
GRAVE SITUATION IN WHICH BULK OF NEW ZEALAND DIVISION
IS PLACED, AND RECOMMEND YOU BRING PRESSURE TO BEAR
ON HIGHEST PLANE IN LONDON EITHER TO SUPPLY US WITH
SUFFICIENT MEANS TO DEFEND ISLAND OR TO REVIEW DECI-
SION [that] CRETE MUST BE HELD.[14]

Freyberg's worry about the Royal Navy was needless.
    The evacuation of the British troops from the Greek main-
land was a monumental task that was borne successfully by the
Royal Navy—despite the Luftwaffe—after many trying days of
great effort and greater courage. Churchill forwarded a message
to Admiral Andrew Cunningham, commanding the Mediterranean Fleet:

I . . . CONGRATULATE YOU UPON THE BRILLIANT AND HIGHLY
SUCCESSFUL MANNER IN WHICH THE NAVY HAS ONCE AGAIN
SUCCOURED THE ARMY AND BROUGHT OFF FOUR-FIFTHS OF THE
ENTIRE FORCE. . . .[15]

Perhaps the prime minister, with the foresight of his genius, was
priming the commanding officer of the Mediterranean fleet for
the tremendous task he would face in the days ahead.
    In the year that Admiral Cunningham held the command of
the Mediterranean fleet, he was determined to transform the vast

Mediterranean into a British lake. With Admiral James S. Somerville's fleet guarding the strait at Gibraltar, Cunningham planned to protect the sea-lanes from Malta in the west to the Suez in the east. It would be a formidable task, with the most immediate dangers being the presence of the Italian Supermarina and the German Luftwaffe.

To keep the Italian fleet in check, Cunningham ordered an all-air attack on their naval base at Taranto in November 1940. It was a successful raid, which surprised them by its audacity and shattered the aspirations of the Italian navy.

With the threat from the Italians diminished, there remained the foreboding shadow of the ever-present Luftwaffe. The only counter to that threat would be the intervention of the Royal Air Force. Unfortunately, the RAF could not spare the aircraft required to defend Crete and the waters around the island. There were not enough fighters or bombers available to protect the Western Desert, Malta, Suez, and the Near East all at the same time, particularly after the losses suffered in the Battle of Britain.

Although Freyberg raised the question of the logistics of holding Crete with the prime minister of New Zealand, Peter Fraser's silence indicated that there was no alternative but to stay and defend. Wavell's response was the proposed delivery of equipment, supplies, and men. Freyberg replied that he had ample numbers of men, but was in dire need of equipment and supplies. However, getting the supplies past the Luftwaffe to Crete still remained the major obstacle. On this problem, Freyberg was to comment humorously that the fault lay with the topography of Crete; the mountains should have been on the northern coast, with the harbors on the south, facing Egypt.

By the end of the first week in May, Freyberg's force on Crete had reached a total of 32,000 British and Commonwealth troops, to which could be added 14,000 partially armed Greeks.

Once again Freyberg referred to his map with its red circles. It was time to put his defense plan into effect.

He decided to divide the island's defense system into three major sectors, with the greatest consideration given to areas that appeared most vulnerable to air and sea invasion. The criteria used to designate a sector were the presence of an airfield and a harbor. The sector divisions were Iráklion, Rethimnon, and Maleme (the latter extended to include Suda Bay). Looking at his roster, Freyberg saw that he had ample general officers to command these sectors.

For the Iráklion sector, he appointed Brigadier General B. H. Chappel, who had been the commanding officer in Crete two months earlier, before the arrival of Weston and Freyberg. The Rethimnon sector was placed under the command of Brigadier General G. Vasey, an Australian who had fought brilliantly in Greece and now was to command the Australians again in Crete. The third sector, Maleme, was given to Brigadier General Edward Puttick to command the Fourth and Fifth New Zealand Brigades.

Because of the extensive ground covered by this third sector, Freyberg subdivided it to include Khaniá, Akrotiri, and Suda Bay. General Weston, who had been Freyberg's predecessor in Crete, was appointed to command this subdivided area, which included the commanding general's headquarters.

Freyberg left the disposition of troops to each sector commander, but he did emphasize one specific condition: He wanted the airfields to be defended during an attack by at least one-third of the troops allocated to each sector, while the rest would be available as a mobile force to counterattack and overcome any threat to the landing strip. "You must deny the airfields to the enemy at all costs!" he warned the sector commanders at a briefing.[16]

The airfield at Maleme, with its adjacent high ground, soon to become known as Hill 107 on the war map, was given to the Fifth New Zealand Brigade to defend. Its commander, Brigadier James Hargest, was a short, plump New Zealander who assigned the defense of the airfield and its Hill 107 to the Twenty-second Battalion, while two other New Zealand battalions, the Twenty-third and Twenty-first, were echeloned further east of the airfield. The Twenty-eighth Battalion, composed of Maori New Zealanders, was kept in reserve at Platanias village, where Hargest established his brigade headquarters.

Antiaircraft guns protecting the airfield at Maleme were controlled by the gun operations room at Khaniá under General Weston, the Royal Marine general.

Thus the disposition of the troops was completed. The whole system formed a straight line of defense in which each sector was linked to the others by the frail means of radio, telephone, cable, or runner—all of them vulnerable to disruption during the course of battle.

Four days after General Freyberg sent his telegrams to Wavell and the New Zealand prime minister protesting the decision to defend Crete, he regretted his impetuous action, wondering if his remarks had created an unfortunate stir in London. After all, his appointment as the commanding general in Crete had come upon the recommendation of his old friend Winston Churchill. It would be improper to cause Churchill undue embarrassment by his negative attitude toward this new command. It was time to make amends.

GENERAL FREYBERG TO PRIME MINISTER   5 MAY 1941
CANNOT UNDERSTAND NERVOUSNESS; AM NOT IN THE LEAST
ANXIOUS ABOUT AIRBORNE ATTACK; HAVE MADE MY DISPOSI-
TIONS AND FEEL CAN COPE ADEQUATELY WITH THE TROOPS AT
MY DISPOSAL. . . .[17]

But on May 5, the date of this message, Freyberg had *not* completed his dispositions. The Second Battalion of Leicesters, assigned to Brigadier Chappel at Iráklion, did not arrive in Crete until May 16.

By that date, too, Bernard Freyberg had completed his final tour of the Cretan defense system, and he was elated. His earlier doubts seemed to have been alleviated. He thought it best to inform his superior in Cairo.

FREYBERG TO GENERAL WAVELL   16 MAY 1941
HAVE COMPLETED PLAN FOR THE DEFENSE OF CRETE AND HAVE
JUST RETURNED FROM FINAL TOUR OF DEFENSES. I FEEL
GREATLY ENCOURAGED BY MY VISIT. EVERYWHERE ALL RANKS
ARE FIT AND MORALE IS HIGH. . . .[18]

The tired, heavily burdened Wavell breathed a sigh of relief. He was so pleased with the message that he forwarded a copy to Winston Churchill.

Wavell's staff in Cairo had adopted the code name Colorado for Crete, and Scorcher for the pending German attack.[19] Freyberg's headquarters on Crete was designated Creforce.[20]

Thus, while the Germans made their plans for Operation Mercury, the defenders of Crete completed their defenses and waited for Scorcher to come to Colorado.

7

"JUST A CIRCLE
ON THE MAP"

APRIL 21, 1941

One evening, the quietude that usually prevailed after sunset along the main road in the village of Pelikapina was disturbed by the approach of vehicles on the darkened highway. The sound intensified as a motorcade, traveling with dimmed lights, came down the highway from Khaniá. The vehicles turned left and proceeded up the tree-lined road, halting before the main entrance to a villa.

The neighbors in the surrounding homes peered through their shuttered windows and, in the dim shadows of early evening, saw many people enter the house. They concluded that their respected neighbor, Constantine Manos, had late visitors.

By the next morning, the grounds of the villa had undergone a great change. The beautiful grass of the front lawn had been furrowed by the tires of the many military vehicles parked in the courtyard before the main entrance. Men in uniform stood everywhere. There were guards at each entrance; at each pathway around the house; at the juncture of the main road with the path to the house; even at the shore north of the Manos home. Overnight, the once-quiet residence had become a military compound.

The fact that the military guards would not reveal the identity of the new resident, obviously for the sake of security, only whetted the neighbors' curiosity. And then, one day, they all knew.

A single villager, Peter Lazerakis, got a brief glimpse of the guest in the villa. The newcomer was standing on the front terrace in clear view. He appeared tall and regal and wore the uniform of a Greek army field marshal. Lazerakis had seen that face before. The old villager's jaw dropped as he recognized the royal profile.[1]

The presence of the king of Greece in Crete gave Freyberg added concern. The king's safety and that of his government was also considered to be the general's responsibility.

Freyberg had considered the possibility that the king might be captured by a German raiding force and held as a war prize. From London came the order that the Greek king should be exposed to no undue risk. That order made the situation quite impossible. Even with additional guards stationed at the king's residence, a clear danger existed. To this order from London, Freyberg replied tactlessly that he "would prefer to see his Royal Highness killed or wounded in battle, rather than be taken a prisoner of the Germans!"[2] The Creforce commander decided that King George must leave Crete for the safety of Egypt.

Freyberg dispatched Colonel J. S. Blount, who was liaison officer between Creforce headquarters and the British minister in Greece, to see King George, with orders to tell him that he must leave Crete for his own safety. Provisions would be made to take him to Alexandria and then to Cairo. The Greek king would not see Colonel Blount but, through his aide-de-camp, refused curtly and emphatically.

Now it fell upon Freyberg's shoulders to see the king personally in order to persuade him to leave the island. Sir Michael Palairet, the British minister in Greece, made the appointment for the interview. The commander of Creforce arrived at the Manos villa in Pelikapina promptly at the appointed hour. He was ushered into the living room, which doubled as the royal audience chamber.

King George met Freyberg at the entrance to the room. The king's lean, taut, smooth-shaved face was slightly pale with fatigue, but his keen blue eyes twinkled cordially, and the deep lines around his mouth broadened in the warmth of his greeting. Regal in appearance, he lacked the stiffness of his office.

The New Zealander quickly came to the purpose of his visit. In clipped phrases, he reviewed the dangers to the king's safety— the possibility of assassination by any pro-German agent, or kidnapping by German parachutists. The situation pointed to one solution: It was imperative that King George leave the island.

In his zeal, Freyberg had forgotten royal tact. He had not suggested that the king depart; he had ordered him to leave. The general had spoken as if he were addressing a junior officer.

King George disregarded this lack of courtesy and graciously attributed it to Freyberg's concern for the royal safety. "My dear General," interrupted the king, "we appreciate your concern for our safety, but what you ask is quite impossible."

The king stood up and walked to the large French doors that opened onto the terrace. At last Freyberg remembered royal etiquette: he also stood up. The king resumed, "As long as a single Greek soldier fights on Greek soil, my place would be at his side. Remember, General, that I am the King of the Hellenes!"[3]

The interview was over. The decision was final—King George did not intend to leave Crete. At least, not yet.

Soon Freyberg received a cable from General Wavell in Cairo, confirming "that the king and his government should remain on Crete even if the island were attacked." This was the decision formulated by Churchill, the war cabinet, and the Foreign Office in London.[4] But the responsibility of King George's safety still remained like a lead weight upon Freyberg's shoulders. It was one more problem in addition to the many already confronting the commanding general of the Cretan defenders.

A few days later, King George requested that General Freyberg attend a meeting to be held in Khaniá, the capital of Crete. The king ordered that the commanding officers of all Greek regiments serving in Crete also attend. Freyberg arrived with his chief of staff, Colonel Keith Stewart.

The Greek king and the New Zealand general mounted the stage of the large auditorium. Standing at attention before them were the commanding generals of the four Greek army commands in Crete, with their regimental, battalion, and attached unit commanders. It was a collection of brass that filled the meeting hall to capacity.

The king greeted the commanders courteously, but did not put them at ease. Then he introduced General Freyberg.

"Gentlemen," announced King George, "from this moment forward, I commit all Greek units on Crete to the command of General Freyberg."[5]

With a formal hand salute, the laconic monarch left the stage, got into his waiting automobile, and returned to his residence. Thus the commanders of all Greek units were placed under the direct command of Freyberg's Creforce headquarters. The next day a royal proclamation made this commitment official.[6]

General Freyberg was surprised but not pleased by this additional burden of command. He requested and received from the Greek General Staff the order of battle of all Greek units in Crete. Reviewing the listing, he had 350 officers, 300 officer cadets, 11,000 infantrymen, 200 airforce personnel, and 3,000 gendarmes—a total of 14,850 men.

On paper this total looked impressive. However, the figures belied the facts. Of the armed infantrymen, most had old weapons with only ten to thirty rounds per rifle. Many had no weapons at all. Of all these men, approximately 2,000 officers and other ranks were veterans of the fighting on the Greek mainland. The only other Greek units with any semblance of military training were the Cretan gendarme units—just 3,000 of the total. The rest were raw, untrained recruits.

Freyberg referred to the Greek troops as "ill-equipped, ill-trained polyglot units."[7] He strongly felt that if they were to be directly involved in the anticipated fighting, they would be a hindrance rather than an asset. He issued instructions to his sector commanders that the Greek units be assigned to areas that would not be factors in the defense of the island. In a sense, his order implied that these units be placed out of harm's way.

The First Greek Regiment was assigned to the command of Brigadier James Hargest of the Fifth New Zealand Brigade. Hargest's Fifth Brigade had the task of protecting the airfield at Maleme, the prominent height below the airfield—designated as Hill 107—the surrounding villages, and the highway bridge over the Tavronites River.

The ground west of the river was unfortified because Hargest had no men to place in those defense positions. The small port town of Kisamo Kastelli, just twenty-six miles west of Khaniá, was located on the western edge of this undefended area. With its dozen or more limestone buildings, it stood at the southern end of Kisamos Bay, formed by the fingerlike projections of the Gramvousa and Rodopos peninsulas. The town's only claim to importance lay in its unfinished airfield and its broken-down wooden wharf. Brigadier Hargest decided to place the First Greek Regiment in that undefended area west of the Tavronites River. Such an assignment would serve a twofold purpose: First, it would cover a weak spot in his defense perimeter; second, it would keep this "ill-trained, ill-equipped" Greek unit from interfering with the defense plans of his Twenty-first, Twenty-second, and Twenty-third battalions, which together with the Twenty-eighth comprised his Fifth Brigade.

The Greek regiment had a complement of approximately 900 men—a little larger than battalion strength. More than half of them were new recruits from the surrounding Cretan hills, with only a few weeks of fundamental basic training.

Approximately 300 of the new recruits had no rifles or any other weapons. Those who did have rifles had such a vast variety that bullets from one type did not fit the others. The men who possessed no firearms armed themselves with axes, curved Syrian swords, ancient shotguns, and flintlocks that had been used against the Turks early in the century. The regiment had two machine guns of World War I vintage, both of which had a sad history of multiple breakdowns.

When Hargest inspected these men, he protested to his superior, General Puttick, that they were unfit for any battle assignment. As a compromise, Puttick dispatched several New Zealand officers from his staff and a few NCOs for the purpose of training this Greek "rabble," as Hargest had referred to them. The New Zealanders brought with them the welcome additions of two Bren guns with ammunition.

This New Zealand cadre came under the command of Major Thomas Bedding. His orders were explicit: Put up a token defense if attacked, then retreat to the hills in the south and link up with any other unit. In the meantime, he was to train the men of the First Greek Regiment in the art of military defense.[8]

Bedding immediately took over advisory command of the Greek regiment, dividing it into two battalions. One battalion was deployed west of Kastelli and the other was positioned east of the town. The best-trained men of the regiment were the members of the Cretan gendarmerie. They all had the same rifles and at least thirty rounds per man. Kept as a mobile reserve between the two deployed battalions, they were situated in the center of the town where Bedding had established his headquarters.

The Greek regimental commander, Colonel Socrates Papademetrakopoulos, had an amiable smile as long as his name. He greeted Major Bedding with courtesy and warmth and ordered his two battalion commanders, Lieutenant Colonels Skordilis and Kourkoutis, to accept the military orders of the New Zealand junior officer.

"Listen to him and learn," were his instructions. "Forget your seniority in rank and your pride. When the time comes, we will show these gentlemen that it takes more than weapons and training to fight a battle."[9]

His words were to prove prophetic. In due time this "ill-trained, ill-equipped rabble," whose existence had taught them fieldcraft and mountain marksmanship—and whose past was characterized by a long history of valorous opposition to servitude—would astound their British allies with their heroism in battle.

The other Greek regiments were distributed among the other brigades of the New Zealand division. General Puttick, the division's commanding general, had assigned the Sixth and Eighth Greek Infantry Regiments to Colonel Howard Kippenberger, the commander of the Tenth New Zealand Brigade.

Kippenberger was just getting the feel of command. Although his brigade was newly formed—composed mostly of gunners and truck drivers without infantry training—he felt that he had a good core of men. He would mold them into a fine military unit, ready to meet any offense the enemy had to offer. All he needed was time to train them.

When the 900-man Eighth Greek Regiment was assigned to his brigade, Kippenberger regarded them skeptically. He felt at home with his own men, but these Greeks were a different lot. He protested their assignment to his brigade. Puttick listened patiently to Kippenberger, just as he had listened to Hargest earlier.

"Why, these men are nothing more than malaria-ridden little chaps from Macedonia, with only four weeks service," objected Kippenberger.

"I know," replied Puttick somewhat condescendingly. Then he suggested, "Put them someplace where they would not interfere with your basic defense. Put them down at the village of Alikianou." He placed his finger on the map at a village in the Prison Valley area south of the town of Galatas.

"But, General, in this position, they would only be just a circle on the map!" the brigade commander continued. "It would be murder to leave such troops in *any* position!"

General Puttick rose to leave, giving Kippenberger a parting comment, "Remember, Colonel, that in war, murder sometimes has to be done." [10]

The other Greek unit that Kippenberger reluctantly had to accept and situate within the defense perimeter of his brigade was the undermanned Sixth Greek Regiment, under the command of Lieutenant Colonel Gregoriou. Its two battalions were commanded by Major Moraites and Major Papadakis.

This was a newly formed regiment, and the men that filled its ranks were for the most part green recruits with little or no training. Their arms varied in caliber and vintage. Kippenberger was at wit's end where to position them so that they would do the least harm to his defense perimeter. He decided to assign the Greeks to the high ground—called Cemetery Hill—south of the village of Galatas. The position would not be too far forward of his own brigade headquarters, and it would conveniently sandwich the Sixth Greek Regiment between two of his own New Zealand battalions. Kippenberger felt that his dependable New Zealanders, on both flanks, would be able to offer the inexperienced Greeks some support to offset their weakness. As for Lieutenant Colonel Gregoriou, the CO of the Sixth Greek Regiment, Kippenberger had little respect for him as a regimental commander.

First Lieutenant Aristides Kritakis had been a reserve officer in the Greek army before the war. In civilian life he had been a newspaper correspondent and a free-lance writer. When war came to Greece, he returned to active duty and was assigned to Greek Army Headquarters in Athens. With Greece's capitulation, Kritakis became one of the countless thousands who were evacuated by the Royal Navy and ferried to Crete. There he reported to the headquarters of the First Greek Army Command in Khaniá, and was assigned to the newly formed Sixth Greek Regiment stationed at Galatas.

A motorcycle carried Kritakis westward out of Khaniá on

the main highway and, after a few miles, took the left turn that led south to Galatas. It was a dusty, bumpy ride over a deeply rutted dirt road, the vehicle finally stopping in front of a coffeehouse in the Galatas village square. The coffeehouse was the headquarters of the Sixth Greek Regiment.

Kritakis dusted himself off, happy to get out of that uncomfortable sidecar. The whole square bustled with Greeks, New Zealanders, trucks, jeeps, and motorcycles. The lieutenant cast a quick eye over the scene, noted the double-belfried church that dominated the square and the New Zealand Service Club in the building adjacent to the church, and then he turned and entered the regiment's headquarters.

The regimental adjutant, a young first lieutenant, greeted Kritakis and asked him to remain until the return of the regimental commander, who wished to meet him. Kritakis took a seat in the corner and waited. He watched with amusement at first, and later with impatience, as the bureaucratic complexities of a headquarters office unfurled before him. From the experience of his previous assignment in Athens, he realized that all headquarters offices were the same, except that this one was primitive compared to its plush Athens counterpart.

A tall, slender infantry captain entered and headed for the adjutant's desk. His height, ramrod bearing, and military demeanor caught Kritakis' eye immediately.

"I have come for the ammo and rations I was promised two days ago!" he rapped sharply at the young lieutenant. The adjutant rose from his seat, somewhat surprised by the captain's brusqueness, mumbling a few words of greeting.

"Look here, Lieutenant," the captain continued, ignoring the greeting, "my men are hungry and so are their rifles." Leaning over the desk, he added, "I want those supplies and I want them now!" There was anger flashing from his blue eyes.

The lieutenant stammered, "Yes, sir, they are ready for you."

"Good," smiled the captain, his anger suddenly softening. "I have a detail of men waiting outside."

Kritakis witnessed the whole episode and admired the captain's concern for his men. That is a good officer, he remarked to himself.

Colonel Gregoriou arrived a few minutes later and greeted Kritakis cordially. "I am glad to have an experienced man like yourself in my regiment, Kritakis. Most of my young officers are just out of school, with only six weeks training. I am going to send you to a good company—let's see, ah yes, here we are." He leaned over his desk and picked up a manila envelope. "The CO is tough, but he is one of my best company commanders." Lieutenant Kritakis was assigned to the Sixth Company, encamped in a valley before the village's Cemetery Hill.

Lieutenant Kritakis refused the offer of a motorcycle ride to his company. One such motorcycle trip a day was enough for him, he thought; besides, he preferred to walk the distance. Before taking the road to his new assignment, he strode across the village square and entered the Church of St. Nicholas, lit a candle and said a few prayers, ending with the sign of the cross. Though not a deeply religious man, Kritakis felt that he was now prepared for whatever was to come.

Following the posted signs, he took the left road exiting from the village square. It was a dirt road that wound past the stone houses of the village and ascended gradually to the cemetery. At the entrance to the cemetery, Kritakis passed a small chapel and followed a path among the rows of tombstones.

At the far end of the cemetery, there was a tall stone wall like a parapet, the hilly terrain beyond dropping gradually into a deep valley. Kritakis stood on the wall and scanned the breathtaking view. To his right he could see a series of flat oblong buildings, marking the location of the prison compound that gave the area its name of Filakes, or Prison Valley. Beyond lay the village of Aghia, with its glistening water reservoir. To Kritakis' extreme right were the multihued, undulating hills that bounded Galatas on the west. To his left he could discern the varicolored rooftops that marked the city of Khaniá, near the horizon, with the deep azure of the sea beyond.

In the valley below him was a tented encampment. A road,

forking at the entrance to the cemetery, descended into the valley toward the encampment. That must be the company area, Kritakis thought.

The headquarters tent for the Sixth Company was a huge square tent pitched under a group of trees. Aristides Kritakis introduced himself to two officers he found in the tent. They were Second Lieutenants Koulakis and Piperis, platoon leaders, waiting for the company commander.

"What's the CO like?" Kritakis inquired, hoping to get an opinion of his new commanding officer.

"He is a good officer, is Captain Emorfopoulos. We call him Captain 'E' for short—but with respect," replied Piperis.

"He does everything for the soldier in the field. He wouldn't ask a single man to do what he himself wouldn't do first. The men love him," continued Koulakis, adding, "I served as a sergeant under him in Albania. He is a good man!"

"His only drawback," interjected Lieutenant Piperis, lowering his voice as if to lessen the critical aspect of his remark, "is that he is often moody and too philosophical."

Both Koulakis and Piperis snapped to attention as a tall shadow fell across the entrance to the tent. Kritakis turned, and there standing before him was his new company commander. Kritakis had not forgotten the captain's bearing, his blue eyes, his smile. It was the same man he had seen in the regimental headquarters a few hours earlier. He had already drawn his own conclusions about this officer.

Captain Athanasios Emorfopoulos introduced himself to Kritakis and, ignoring military protocol, warmly shook the lieutenant's hand. A close attachment was born between the two men. It was obvious that Captain E knew how to gain the immediate respect of the men under his command.

Because of Kritakis' seniority, Captain E appointed him company executive officer.

"I need you here looking after the company's paper work while I train the men in the field. You know, my dear Kritakis," he added prophetically, standing in front of the tent looking out at his men just back from a field exercise, "we don't have too much time."

In the days that followed, Lieutenant Kritakis observed his company commander carefully. Captain E was in the field continuously from sunup to sunset, working tirelessly to train his company in the rudimentary aspects of infantry life. In the mornings he had his men undergoing manual-of-arms and short-order drill and weapons familiarization. In the afternoons he led them in target and bayonet practice and basic field defense. Hour after hour he was out there, sweating with his platoons under the hot sun. After dusk he roamed through the encampment listening to the men and their gripes, giving them inspiring pep talks. They loved him for it.

Whenever he learned, through the grapevine, that a supply of rifles or ammunition was available, he would take a few of his sergeants and sweep in like a vulture to snatch them for his ill-equipped men.

One evening, after a long day of training, Captain E sat quietly in the headquarters tent, alone with his executive officer. The captain was in one of the philosophical moods Lieutenant Piperis had mentioned. Kritakis broke the long silence.

"It looks as if the company is shaping up," he remarked, hoping that Captain E would snap out of his mood. There was no response, and he tried again: "How does it look to you?"

Suddenly Captain E realized that Kritakis was speaking to him, and his eyes cast off that distant look.

"The men will do well," he replied, "in spite of the fact that they have not completed their basic training. They will do all that is asked of them, even if they don't have enough rifles, bayonets, or ammunition. I am satisfied with them; they are not the weak link. The weakness lies in those pompous asses on the staff in regimental headquarters."

Kritakis was shocked that his company commander would criticize the regiment's leadership.

"Take our jolly good Colonel Gregoriou," Emorfopoulos continued. "He has let himself get too fat in mind and in body.

Did you notice the New Zealand officers? They are lean and hardy. Don't misunderstand, our regimental commander is an excellent soldier. Why, I've seen him throw a can five feet into the air and hit it three times with his pistol before the can fell to the ground. He is a good soldier, considerate of the officers in his command—but that is not enough in war today! His worst fault is that he lacks *initiative*. His thoughts deal with a war of a bygone era, not what we expect to hit us tomorrow or the next day."

The captain left his chair, lit a cigarette, and resumed. "Did you know that in Khaniá there is a whole warehouse filled with rifles and ammunition, just waiting to be distributed? Yet the Colonel makes no effort to requisition the rifles, even though he knows that many of our men have *no* weapons. He claims that the English will distribute them when the proper time arrives— can you imagine that? Someday the Luftwaffe will discover the warehouse's location and blow it to hell!

"He leaves everything to our allies, the British and New Zealanders. He has made no effort to set up a secondary regimental defense or make provisions for an open supply line to the frontline companies. He doesn't even allow us to distribute ammunition to our men, just in case we are attacked suddenly.

"As a matter of fact, from what I can see of the overall picture, our whole regiment presents a stagnant, walled-in defense. There are no provisions for a mobile attack force to hit the enemy at his weakest point. When he comes, we will sit here waiting for the enemy to land and to come to us—instead of us going after him and killing him before he is massed and reinforced.

"I have made my suggestions to Regimental in writing, but they have been ignored. There is an air of defeatism up at Regimental, but not here in the ranks. *My men will fight!*

"Mark my words, if they don't change their attitude at Staff, we can lose this battle even before it begins, and it will begin sooner than they think." [11]

Angered at his own words, the captain picked up his helmet and walked out of the tent, leaving his executive officer with a stark picture of the regiment's situation.

The island of Crete was now rapidly becoming a bastion of armed men. More than 46,000 troops filled the island-fortress from Kisamo Kastelli in the west to Sitia in the east.

The civilian inhabitants of Crete were aware of the existing danger. Even before the final occupation of the Greek mainland, light German air attacks had been made upon Crete. By the first week of May, the attacks had become increasingly heavy. In time, they began at sunrise and did not cease until sunset. Their fury pinpointed the defensive positions located in the hills about the airfields at Maleme, at Rethimnon, and at Iráklion. More concentrated bombing focused on the Suda Bay defenses. The waters of Suda Bay were choked with debris and submerged hulls of sunken ships. A heavy layer of black smoke rose skyward for thousands of feet from the burning ships in the bay. Even the superstructure of the beached HMS *York* had been shattered by the persistent attacks of the Stuka dive-bombers in their all-out effort to silence the antiaircraft batteries on the eight-inch-gun cruiser.

All ships arriving by daylight were trailed by a string of dive-bombers or were constantly strafed by ME-109 fighter aircraft. These persistent bombings aggravated the island's critical supply problem. Of a total of 27,000 tons of munitions sent to Crete in the first weeks of May, only 3,000 tons were landed safely.

After May 15 the scope of these air attacks was expanded to include the cities of Khaniá, Rethimnon, and Iráklion. With an earsplitting, earthshaking roar, the bombs fell upon the defenseless cities. They whistled as they plummeted to earth, erupting into flames and spewing pieces of concrete, steel, lumber, and human bodies into the air.

The first bombing raid caught most city inhabitants by surprise. They had not sought shelter—nor were there any adequate shelters available. People died like flies in the rain of explosives, as tons of steel slammed into their dwellings and into the streets. The concussion was so stupefying that those who survived that early attack would never forget it. In a matter of a few days, the cities were a mass of ruins. Skeletal, fire-blackened remnants of walls, shattered streets, and corpses became a common sight.

Below this debris and destruction lay the bodies of more dead and of the dying, pinned under timbers, fallen walls, and roofs. In the heat of day, the dead began to decompose, and the stink of death permeated the dust-filled air, making rescue work even more difficult.

Yet the German air attacks continued relentlessly on a daily schedule from sunrise until dusk.

The Cretan inhabitants took even this hardship in their stride. Most city dwellers left for the fields, the hills, and the caves of the southern mountains. Others sought refuge with relatives in distant villages. They had to alter their routines, but life went on.

While the city dwellers left their destroyed homes for the safety of villages in the hills, many other Cretans left their homes in the safe villages in order to serve in the island's defense.

Manoli Paterakis was one of these. Leaving his family and his home in the village of Koustogeriko, located high in the White Mountains of southern Crete, he descended to the northern coast. A gendarme by profession, he had come to serve in the defense of Crete. Indeed, Manoli Paterakis would fight well. In the months ahead, his heroic deeds were destined to thrill many adventurous hearts.

There were others. George Psychoundakis was twenty-one and, dressed in a typical black Cretan shirt, black trousers, and patched black boots, he was an example of the simple poverty that prevailed among the mountain people. But heroism gave no ground to poverty. He left his home in Asi Gonia, in western Crete, for the same purpose as Paterakis. A man of small stature, lithe, agile, with soft dark eyes, his timid personality belied his tremendous nervous energy. Psychoundakis, too, was destined to leave his name in the historic pages soon to be written.

Kostas Manousos, a six-foot six-inch giant, made plans to leave his home in Sfakia, a fishing village on the southern coast of Crete. His trip would take him across the White Mountains to the northern shore for the same purpose that drew Paterakis and Psychoundakis.

Manousos was typical of the Cretan warrior: tall, wiry, and virile. (The Cretan is the second-tallest Caucasian in the West— second only to the Montenegrin.) His father, Kapetan Manousos, had fought the Turks for Cretan independence in the late 1800s and early 1900s. He wanted to accompany his son to the north so that he too might join in the fight to protect the island from enemy invasion. Kostas tried to dissuade him, but to no avail. It was destined to be their last trip together.

As had been his habit for many years, Kapetan Vasili Kazantsakis began his daily task of fishing in the earliest hours of daybreak, with the rising sun still low in the eastern sky. His father and his grandfather had been fishermen before him.

Before the war, Kapetan Vasili would sail out in the company of the other fishing boats belonging to his brother Dimitri and to his two cousins Pavlos and Stelios. This small fishing fleet sailed at daybreak and returned in the early hours of the evening. Their produce—the fish caught during their daily excursions—would be brought to the agora, the central marketplace in the city of Khaniá.

The first to fall victim to the war were the fishing vessels belonging to Kapetan's cousins Pavlos and Stelios. It occurred after the Greek mainland had been occupied by the Germans. Having made a wide fishing sweep, the little fleet stopped at the island of Milos to refuel. Kapetan Vasili and his brother, Dimitri, had an extra supply of fuel aboard; thus they did not have to enter the harbor. Pavlos and Stelios went into the harbor. Before the two cousins had a chance to sail, their caïques were seized by the German port command. Although they protested the confiscation, their remonstrances proved fruitless. So intense were their objections that the German commander ordered their detention.

With the increase in the air attacks upon Crete, the Germans flew sortie after sortie of Stukas and ME-109's on their bombing and strafing attacks. This heightened enemy air activity had no effect upon Kapetan Vasili or Dimitri. They took their vessels out early each morning and returned late each evening. At those hours, the sky was empty of enemy aircraft.

One day Vasili and his brother Dimitri decided to return to their home port of Khaniá earlier than usual. Dimitri's caïque had developed engine trouble, and they hoped that by returning earlier they might make repairs before the next morning's sailing tide. A few miles outside Khaniá harbor, Dimitri's boat failed. Kapetan Vasili brought his caïque alongside to offer aid. The two fishing vessels wallowed in the trough of a rough sea. It was at this moment that a passing flight of ME-109s sighted them.

The German aircraft made four passes, as Vasili and Dimitri cowered behind the bulkheads of their boats for protection.

Finally, luck ran out. A solitary rocket struck Dimitri's fuel tank. The ensuing blast tore the craft apart. When the smoke cleared, all that remained on the frothing waters was a piece of wood—a remnant of Dimitri's boat. Dimitri had disappeared.

Kapetan Vasili recovered slowly from his shock. Then, unable to find any trace of his brother, he hastened to depart in order to salvage the sole surviving vessel of a once-proud fishing fleet. Luckily the aircraft broke off their attack and disappeared into the gathering dusk of the northern horizon.

In the days that preceded the German invasion, Kapetan Vasili continued his daily fishing trips. He would not be deterred by the ubiquitous enemy aircraft. He simply altered his routine: He left port long before sunrise and returned long after sunset.[12]

Life had to go on.

8

THE HUNTERS
FROM THE SKY

MAY 17, 1941

Lieutenant General Kurt Student, Commanding General of Fliegerkorps XI—the Eleventh Air Corps—had spent days refining
his plan for the seizure of Crete.

He studied the island's lengthy expanse carefully and observed that it possessed seven critical objectives that had to be
seized for the success of the operation. His plan was designed
to include the simultaneous capture of these seven points, all to
be taken on the first day of the assault.

Student proposed that his parachutists attack from west to
east, beginning in the western part of the island with the seizure
of the strategic village of Kisamo Kastelli; eastward to Maleme
airfield with its dominantly strategic Kavsakia hill, Hill 107; then
the Cretan capital of Khaniá, with its adjacent natural harbor of
Suda Bay; then on to the village of Georgeopolis; and the cities
of Rethimnon and Iráklion with their respective airfields and
harbors. The seventh objective would be the Askifou plateau,
which was really a valley, in the central part of Crete.

Student's immediate superior, General Alexander Löhr, the
commanding general of Luftflotte IV—the Fourth Air Fleet—
objected to this aspect of the plan. Löhr proposed instead that

the spearhead of the attack—what he called the *Schwerpunkt*—should concentrate upon one objective only—Maleme airfield and its adjacent Hill 107.[1]

Student turned a deaf ear to Löhr's modified proposal. He was adamant that all seven objectives be attacked simultaneously. Even General Hans Jeschonnek, Luftwaffe chief of the general staff, concurred with Löhr. A stalemate had been reached, and Operation Mercury was in jeopardy. Jeschonnek suggested that the conflicting proposals be placed before the Luftwaffe commander in chief for resolution.

Hermann Goering was not going to permit this plan to fall apart under any circumstances. He appreciated Löhr's conservative approach and realized that logistically the air fleet commander was correct. However, Goering did not wish to contravene Student's well-conceived plan.

Goering weighed the problem carefully, then arrived at a decision. He announced a compromise. Student's proposal that all seven objectives be attacked on the first day would stand.

Student smiled; Löhr shook his head dejectedly.

"However," Goering continued, "the attack will be undertaken in two stages."[2]

Now both generals frowned.

Goering ignored the frowns as he clarified his decision. He explained that the objectives in the western part of Crete would be attacked during the first stage of the invasion, which would take place in the early morning hours. The second stage would concentrate on the objectives in the eastern part of Crete, and would take place in the afternoon of the same day. In this way the air transports used in the morning attack could return to their respective bases in Greece to refuel. In the afternoon the same transports would ferry the rest of the troopers to the remaining objectives.

"I think that is a fair compromise," Goering commented with a satisfied sigh, knowing he had resolved the difficulty. "Now, go ahead and work out the details."[3]

For reasons of their own, neither Student nor Löhr cared much for the decision. But Goering would brook no further discussion.

Reichsmarschall Hermann Goering was proud of his paratroopers. He was almost as proud of them as was General Kurt Student—the man who had trained and developed them.

It was a paradoxical situation in the hierarchy of the Third Reich that each major personality had created autonomous formations of troops, as a means of personal insurance, personal aggrandizement, and for expansion of his personal sphere of influence in governmental circles. They all had one goal: to insure a position of strength within Adolf Hitler's inner circle. Hermann Goering had called his own police force the Landespolizeigruppe "General Goering."

When the German Fuehrer announced the official creation of the German air force in October 1935, Goering—as commander in chief of the Luftwaffe—incorporated his special police units into the air force and entitled them the "Regiment General Goering." One month later, 600 members from this regiment volunteered to serve as Germany's first airborne unit. It was designated as the IV Falschitzer Battaillon, detached from the parent unit, and placed under the command of Major Bruno Brauer. Thus the nucleus of the future German paratroopers had been created. Three years later, in 1938, this unit became the I Battaillon/Fallschirmjäger Regiment I, or the First Battalion of the First Paratroop Regiment.[4] The German high command appreciated the potential value of such troops—who could drop directly onto a target from the air—and ordered the creation of a Fallschirm Infanterie Kompanie, a company of airborne infantry under the command of Major Richard Heidrich. This unit was later augmented to battalion size and given wide recognition in public military displays. They were placed under the command of the Luftwaffe in 1939, becoming II Bataillon/Fallschirmjäger Regiment I—the Second Battalion of the First Paratroop Regiment.

These two battalions were eventually raised to regimental strength and were incorporated within the newly formed Flieger Division 7, the Seventh Airborne Division. The divisional commander was Kurt Student, at the time only a major general.

So great became its renown and so restricted was the selection of recruits that it rapidly developed into the most elite unit in the German armed forces. German civilians looked in admiration at the Fallschirmjäger, girls even swooning at sight of the badge with the golden plunging eagle—the symbol of the paratrooper. The word *Fallschirmjäger* soon became an electrifying one in the German military lexicon. It means "hunter from the sky."[5] The flower of German youth sought to join their ranks.

They were all highly trained and molded into a finely disciplined, organized unit. They were ruthless and fearless. Their skull-shaped helmets and their strange uniforms, reminiscent of something out of a Jules Verne novel, were meant to be forbidding.

German youth were not the only group to volunteer. Professional soldiers, officers of all ranks, and personnel from other branches of military service sought admission as well.

Old professional soldiers like Major General Eugen Meindl, who was admitted to the paratroopers at the age of 48 after having served many years in the Wehrmacht; or Colonel Hermann Bernhard Ramcke, a veteran of the First World War, who joined the paratroopers at the age of 51, admittedly because it offered him an opportunity for promotion to higher rank; Major Richard Heidrich, who had transferred from an instructorship at the Potsdam War College to the command of the Third Parachute Regiment of the Seventh Airborne Division.

The paratroopers also attracted men from Germany's aristocratic families. These families, with such famous names as Von Braun, Von Plessen, and Von Blücher, had always distinguished themselves in military service.

A Von Plessen had been military aide to Kaiser Wilhelm II in the First World War. The Von Blüchers' ancestor had assisted the Duke of Wellington in defeating Napoleon in the Battle of Waterloo. In the Battle of Crete, the Von Blücher family was destined to lose the last three heirs of that famous name.

Baron Friedrich August Freiherr von der Heydte was another member of Germany's aristocracy who entered the newly formed paratroop units.

Captain Friedrich von der Heydte was thought to be too scholarly to be a battalion commander. In fact this slender officer seemed out of place in a military setting. His quiet, intellectual bent added to the incongruity. At first glance, his fellow officers felt that he belonged in a university classroom rather than in command of an elite body of paratroopers. Yet not one person doubted his courage or his ability as a leader of men.

He excelled in the problems undertaken during training periods, and he went through each phase of training with his men. Nothing was asked of them that he himself would not do. The officers and enlisted men in his command realized this, and their respect for him increased.

In the Battle of Crete he was to command the First Battalion of the Third Parachute Regiment. Thus, on the eve of battle, this student of international law was to put aside his scholarly robes and textbooks and exchange them for a uniform, a pistol, and a canopy of silk. He was to lead a group of men into a battle destined to enter the pages of history.[6]

Karl Schoerner was born and raised in Linz, Austria, Hitler's favorite city. When Schoerner reached military age, he rushed to enlist in the glorified Fallschirmjäger Korps. He was sent for his basic paratrooper training to a camp at Stendal, about 100 miles from Berlin. He would be carefully tested for stability and intelligence—prime requisites for the rigorous training of a paratrooper. Those who failed this part of their indoctrination were transferred back to their original units. Schoerner successfully completed this period and entered the first phase of his "ground" Fallschirmjäger training.

In the initial weeks of this period, paratroopers were taught basic skills. From a dummy aircraft fuselage, they learned how to position themselves for jumps and how to roll on impact with the ground. Proper handling of the parachute harness and the correct methods of packing parachutes were additional skills instilled in the trainees. It was felt that no man would be careless with his parachute packing if his life depended on his work. It was good psychology.

The air phase of training involved six successful jumps. During this period, Schoerner and his classmates learned the science of falling bodies. They learned how it felt to jump into space from a moving airplane and float gently to earth.

Aside from being sick with nervousness, the paratrooper's first descent was exhilarating. He had been taught how to station himself in the open doorway of the transport plane and, with the rushing wind slapping him in the face, to assume a squatting position with his feet far apart. From this pose, he would launch himself out into space—almost like diving from the edge of a swimming pool. Jumping from a JU-52 transport, his first drop was a solo, from a height of 600 feet. During his descent, he had to master the technique of landing accurately on a given target. As he approached earth, he would twist his body and face downwind, so that he would be thrown forward onto his hands and knees to break his momentum. Many suffered wrist and knee injuries during touchdown. Schoerner was luckier than most.

The parachute descent had an initial arc of about 85 feet, in which time the chute would be fully opened. After a few seconds of oscillation, the paratrooper would float steadily downward, reaching earth in about fifteen seconds. His rate of fall would be anywhere from twelve to nineteen feet per second.

The RZ-16 parachute was made of silk, with all the shroud lines culminating in two straps attached to the *back* of the harness. There was a distinct disadvantage to this type of attachment because it limited the paratrooper's control of the drift of his descent. Ironically, the shroud lines of parachutes issued to Luftwaffe air crews terminated in two straps, one on each shoulder. This more conventional system gave the air crewmen better control of drift during descent. It was odd that the paratroopers, who required the greatest drift control, were given the RZ-16s.[7]

The next four jumps were also made from 600 feet, but they were made in groups. The sixth and final jump was made from an altitude of 400 feet, in battle groups landing under simulated combat conditions. Once the paratroop trainee had successfully completed six jumps, he became a full-fledged Fallschirmjäger.

After twelve months of hard, grueling training, Karl Schoerner received his parachutist's qualification badge. To retain it, he would have to make six jumps a year.

The third phase of training now began. The paratrooper arrived in battle with the dual advantages of surprise and mobility. However, once the objective on the ground had been reached, his success depended upon his effectiveness as a member of a combat team. So the next period of training focused on light-infantry combat tactics. The paratrooper was taught how to function in a team to disrupt enemy lines of communication, to move quickly against an enemy, to attack enemy positions, and to hold those positions once captured.

By necessity, the paratrooper was very lightly armed. When he jumped, he carried only a 9-mm Parabellum Luger automatic pistol, a few grenades, and a large, flat, gravity knife whose blade would be activated by gravity once the spring in the handle was released. One man in four carried a folding-stock MP.40 Schmeisser 9-mm submachine gun. The rest of the weapons were dropped in special supply canisters. These had to be located and opened on the battlefield and the weapons had to be distributed before the parachutists could become combat-effective. This was a disadvantage, as the paratroopers were to learn in Crete.

The cylindrical canisters carried the standard German rifle, the Mauser K.98; the rest of the MP.40 submachine guns; and the MG.34 light machine guns. Per squad the rifles outnumbered the submachine guns two to one.

To give the attacking paratroopers additional firepower, an effective airborne artillery piece was developed as early as 1940. It was a 75-mm recoilless gun resembling a bazooka, mounted on a wheeled carriage. Readily dismantled, it could be dropped in two supply canisters and easily reassembled in the field. In addition, each battalion was also issued thirteen .81-mm mortars as mobile fire support.[8]

The parachutes used during these drops were of different colors: Officers' parachutes were pink, while other ranks' were black. Arms and ammunition canisters had white canopies, and medical supply canisters floated to earth under yellow parachutes.

With the final phase of his training completed, Karl Schoerner graduated and awaited assignment to a Fallschirmjäger unit.

By 1941, like Schoerner, enough trainees had qualified for a third regiment to be formed and added to the Seventh Airborne Division. With this division fully manned and combat-ready, General Student now relinquished his command in order to concentrate on his duties as commanding general of the Eleventh Air Corps. In his place, he put Lieutenant General Walter Suessmann. He also decided to organize an additional unit.

This new unit would be a specialized assault force comprised of parachutists and glider-borne stormtroopers. It was to be called the Luftlande-Sturm-Regiment, or the Air Assault Regiment. If the paratroopers were the elite of the German army, the men of the Air Assault Regiment would be the elite of the elite.

The regular parachute division was now composed of three regiments; each regiment had three battalions; and each battalion had three companies. With attached antitank, engineer, medical, and heavy machine-gun units, this represented a force of about 12,000 men.

The assault regiment differed from the others of the Seventh Airborne Division in that it was composed of four battalions. Each battalion, in turn, had four companies. This regiment represented a total force of approximately 2,000 men.[9]

It had another special feature, too: Its First Battalion was composed of glider-borne troops—600 men to be transported into battle by seventy gliders. The gliders would prove to be unique newcomers to mobile air warfare. (After World War I, there developed among the Germans a great craze for gliders. The demand was such that gliders were being constructed privately and commercially.)

The glider was a direct outgrowth of the restrictions imposed upon Germany by the Versailles treaty. Prohibited from construction of any motorized aircraft, the Germans were later allowed to develop a transport plane for commercial use. The JU-52 air transport thus became the workhorse of the German Luftwaffe, as a troop carrier, supplier, and glider-tow.

As far back as 1932, the Rhön-Rossitten-Gesellschaft had built a newly designed widespan glider that was to be used for meteorological measurements from high altitudes. In 1933 the design of this glider was taken over by the German Institute for Glider Research, known more succinctly as the DFS, located in Darmstadt.

Ernst Udet, a veteran pilot in the German air force during the First World War, had been appointed by the Luftwaffe commander in chief as Generalluftflugmeister. This position made him the director of the Luftwaffe Experimental Unit. He was the overseer of all experimental air models that might be developed for military use.

When Udet had been advised of this glider model's existence, he requested a demonstration. He immediately realized its military potential. He likened it to "a modern-day Trojan Horse—a wooden horse which would land amidst the enemy and discharge its secreted soldiers . . . to the enemy's surprise. . . ." Udet ordered that various refinements of the original prototype model be developed in order to conform to its ultimate use as a troop carrier.[10]

This militarized glider was the size of a fighter plane of World War I vintage, weighing about 1,600 pounds. Its long, tapered wingspan was set high, well braced to the fuselage. The body was a box-shaped fuselage with a framework of steel tubes covered by a tightly drawn canvas, which had thick, translucent portals for windows. These steel tubes were built with *Sollbruchstellen*, or breaking points, which were joints of purposely weakened construction in order to allow a certain flexibility to the body of the glider once it came into contact with a hard surface.

It had a wooden floor with a central beam that ran the full length of its body. On this beam, ten armed men would sit, one behind the other, while in flight.

The undercarriage of this propellerless craft possessed a set of wheels that were released and discarded when the glider was airborne. When it returned to earth, it landed on a central skid. This central skid was often wrapped in coils of barbed wire for breakage. Some of the gliders had a barbed hook that could stop the craft within thirty-five yards of contact with the level surface.

Tests proved that this glider model was easily adaptable for towing behind a JU-52 transport or a HE-111 bomber, and that it could undergo speeds of up to 100 miles an hour. Once released, it had a descent rate of 240 feet per minute.

This militarized model performed so successfully during tests that Udet ordered its immediate production. It was designated as the DFS 230 glider.[11]

When, in 1932, General Student was apprised of these successful tests, he decided to introduce it into his scope of airborne operations. He recognized the glider's distinct advantage over parachutists. Whereas the parachutists would be betrayed by the noise of the transports as they approached the target, the gliders would slip silently upon their target, having been released at some distance from their towing aircraft. Whereas the parachutists would swing helplessly for fifteen seconds before touchdown, and whereas they would have to regroup on the ground and obtain their weapons before being ready to fight, the gliders brought the attackers within twenty yards of point zero, already armed and grouped to enter battle. The glider definitely had multiple advantages in this new form of air warfare.

The DFS-230 glider was introduced to the surprised world during the German invasion of the Low Countries in 1940. General Student had dispatched fifty-one gliders, under the command of Captain Walter Koch, with orders to seize various bridges, forts, and crossroads in Holland and Belgium, in support of the invading German army. Eleven of these gliders attacked and seized the fortress of Eben Emael on the Albert Canal in Belgium.[12] So well-constructed and so heavily fortified that it was thought to be impossible to capture either by land or by sea, it was almost impregnable—"almost" in the sense that the Belgians discounted the possibility of a landing from the sky. But that is exactly what happened.

From April 25, when Adolf Hitler gave his approval for the promulgation of Operation Mercury, General Student had less than one month to put the gears of the operation into full motion. In that short time, he had to overcome all the difficult problems of logistics and supply.

The air staff was ordered to collect all available gliders and ship them to Greece; most of them had to be dismantled and shipped by truck. The gliders could have been flown to Greece in JU-52 transports, but those planes were needed for Operation Mercury. These slow, lumbering workhorses would be needed to tow the gliders and ferry the parachutists in the attack on Crete, and they were being overhauled for that purpose. From airfields scattered all over Europe, the JU-52s were collected into one massive fleet and flown to maintenance centers at Brunswick and Cottbus in Germany, Prague and Brno in Czechoslovakia, and Aspern in Austria. By May 15, 493 transports had been overhauled and were ready for their new assignment. They were immediately flown to the Athens area.

The Athenians observed the daily arrival of these huge, trimotored square-boxed aircraft. Soon the airfields around Athens were filled with JU-52 transports. And there was another type of aircraft that confounded the curiosity of the Athenians—the propellerless planes that were lined up wing tip to wing tip at the outer perimeter of Eleusis Airfield.

To General Student's satisfaction, this phase of the logistical problem was slowly but successfully being resolved. There now arose a new difficulty.

As the days passed rapidly toward May 17, hundreds of bombers and fighters, together with the JU-52 transports, were arriving daily at the many airfields in Greece. They had to be refueled and made ready for the day of attack. However, an incident that had occurred on April 26 during the Allied defense against the German invasion now presented a critical supply problem, and it would also cause the delay of the scheduled attack on Crete.

Two brave British engineers who were trying to reach their evacuation point on mainland Greece stole a munitions truck and were inadvertently instrumental in destroying the bridge over the Corinth Canal, keeping the German tanks from rushing into the Peloponnesus in pursuit of the retreating British army. This allowed most of the British troopers to be evacuated so they could fight another day at another place. Some British troops were transported to Crete, where a month later they would fight the Germans.

However, the debris of the fallen bridge blocked the Corinth Canal so effectively that no German tankers could pass through; not a single barrel of fuel could reach Piraeus to supply the German aircraft. With plans for the attack on Crete in full force and the deadline drawing near, some 650,000 gallons of fuel were needed to supply the huge air armada scheduled to participate in the first-day assault.

The bridge had been destroyed in the morning hours of April 26, yet by May 17 not a single drop of gasoline had reached the empty tanks of the German aircraft waiting on the airfields around Athens.

The canal was not cleared of debris until the quartermaster of the Eleventh Air Corps, Lieutenant Colonel Seibt, requested that divers be sent to Corinth from the submarine base at Kiel, Germany. And not until May 17 was the first tanker able to pass through the connecting waterway.[13]

The attack on Crete, which had been scheduled to begin on May 17, had to be postponed. It was rescheduled for the morning hours of May 20.[14]

There was another meeting of the German air command at the Grande Bretagne. Staff cars and jeeps arrived all morning at the hotel entrance, discharging officers of various ranks. They were ushered into a huge salon that had been converted into a conference room. At the double-door entrance, a Gestapo officer with a squad of armed men checked credentials.

John Drakopoulos observed the entire proceedings.

No sooner were the officers assembled than General Kurt Student strode in with his staff, and the meeting began. An aide walked over to the map board and removed a sheet, revealing the huge battle plan for the island of Crete. The map was filled with arrows and punctuated by tiny colored flags representing the position of each attacking unit.

Student began to describe how the invasion would be preceded by a one-hour bombing of the objectives by Von Richthofen's Eighth Air Corps. Following this heavy bombing, the Eleventh Air Corps would send its troops into action.

Student explained that the operation would be divided into two phases. The first phase would be the assault on the western part of the island, which would take place in the morning. The attack on the eastern sector of Crete, the second phase, would follow that same afternoon.

The morning attack would consist of a center and a western Kampfgruppe, or battle group. The western group, Task Force Komet, would have three parachute battalions and one glider battalion of the assault regiment and it would attack and seize Maleme airfield and the heights around it. The center group would have two companies of gliders, and it would attack the capital of Khaniá. The Third Regiment of the Airborne Division would be landed around Galatas and Alikianou village and sweep northward to capture the capital of Khaniá from the south.

In the afternoon the second phase of the assault would attack and seize the cities of Iráklion and Rethimnon and their respective airfields.

All of these objectives were to be achieved, and the cities to be in German hands, by nightfall. A convoy of steamers carrying elements of the Fifth Mountain Division as reinforcements would land the first night of the invasion at Maleme and at Iráklion.[15]

Student was followed by the Eleventh Air Corps' intelligence officer. Briefly, he sketched a summary of the defense situation on the island of Crete. Then he gave two pieces of intelligence that sounded reasonable enough yet were grossly erroneous. First he stated that there were only 10,000 Empire troops on the island, with remnants of two Greek divisions. Second, he said that most Cretans were sympathetic to the Germans and would welcome them as allies. This group would identify itself by the code name "Major Bock."[16]

No one at the staff meeting thought to challenge these assertions, so the German commanders left the meeting with the opinion that Crete would be underdefended, and that the civilian population would be hospitable to the Germans.

9

IT IS
ONLY A RUMOR

MAY 19, 1941

King George of Greece carefully followed the defense plans for
Crete. Although he had placed the Greek regiments under overall command of the British, he studied their disposition with ex-
ceptional interest. His questions and suggestions did not endear
him to Freyberg or his staff.

Besides the defense of Crete, the king was concerned with
another matter. He felt that it was up to him, as the leader of
the Hellenes, to fan the flame of national fervor. It was important that he give courage and succor not only to the Greeks on
Crete but to the Greeks on the mainland.

On May 18 King George paid a visit to the residence of his
prime minister, Emmanuel Tsouderos. He proposed a royal proclamation to be circulated among the Greeks in Crete and in occupied Greece, reminding them of their ancestral heritage of
freedom:

> Nations that uphold their national honor and respect their
> commitments to their allies are placed upon a holy pin-
> nacle of esteem. Our honor has been written in blood
> and circumscribed by sacrifice and heroism.

> Be certain, people of Greece, that a bright new day shall
> soon dawn for the greater glory of Greece![1]

Tsouderos, who had become prime minister after the suicide of
his predecessor, Alexander Korysis, was staying in the home of
George Volanis in Malaxa, a small hamlet located high in the
foothills of the White Mountains. The house was located some
six miles south of the royal residence at the village of Pelikapina.

The Greek king arrived on Sunday afternoon, May 18. He
worked with the prime minister throughout the next day, and the
proclamation was drawn up the night of the nineteenth.

With this task completed, the king wished to return to his
own residence near the north shore. Tsouderos dissuaded him
from leaving at such a late hour. He stressed the danger of traveling in total darkness. The king reluctantly agreed to remain
another night and to depart early the next morning. He did not
know it at the time, but his decision was to save him from certain capture or even death.

General Weston, the Royal Marine general commanding the defenses around Suda Bay, had given specific orders that all antiaircraft guns remain silent during the continuous German air attacks. They were under *no* circumstances to fire at the enemy
aircraft. "Let them think that they have silenced our air defenses!" was his retort to objections raised by the antiaircraft
gun commanders. The general did not wish to reveal the well-
camouflaged defense positions to the Germans. It would be better to surprise them when the actual day of attack arrived.

Weston's orders affected the Germans exactly as he had
planned. The Luftwaffe commanders were surprised by the silence of the defense batteries; their aircraft flew over the hills of
Suda Bay without a single shell being fired at them. They reached
the conclusion that the weight of their massive and continuous
attacks had actually destroyed the defense positions. They re-

ported these conclusions to the intelligence section of Flieger-korps VIII.

General von Richthofen, the commanding general of Flie-gerkorps VIII, was not so easily deceived. He ordered that re-connaissance and photographic sorties be flown over the Suda Bay area.

Private Dimmy Rose of the Royal Marines was positioned be-hind a mounted Lewis machine gun in the hills west of Suda Bay. For days his gun had remained silent, obedient to orders, while German aircraft crossed the sky above him.

On this day, May 19, an ME-110 reconnaissance aircraft slowly and repeatedly circled the harbor in a wide sweep. It was obvious to ground observers that it was on a photographic mission.

Gunner Rose followed the low-flying aircraft in the sights of his Lewis gun, swinging it in a wide arc on its tripod. The Ger-man plane was a very tempting target. Taking courage from the lack of defensive fire, it swooped in even lower on its photo-graphic mission. Once again it flew past Rose's gun position, and once again he followed it in his sights. When the ME-110 flew past him a third time, almost at eye level to his hill posi-tion, Rose could no longer resist the temptation. He opened fire.[2]

A string of tracer bullets arched toward the German aircraft, seeming to disappear into its fuselage. The men in the other gun positions stood aghast as the low rattling sound of the machine gun echoed through the valley.

No sooner had the echoes subsided than a wisp of smoke trailed from the aircraft's port engine. The ME-110 dropped into the choppy waters of the bay.

A motor launch manned by Royal Marines of the MNBDO (Mobile Naval Base Defense Organization) raced out to the downed plane. As they cleared the island of Suda in the outer bay, they could see that a fisherman's caïque had already reached the Germans. One of the pilots was being lifted out of the water, while the second stood on the wing, clutching a map case in his arms. The fisherman pulled him off the submerged wing just as the aircraft disappeared below the waves.

As the airmen were being transferred from the fishing skiff to the marine launch, the fisherman shouted in comprehensible English, "This fellow says that the invasion will come tomorrow."[3]

When the marines landed, they took their two German prisoners to Freyberg's Creforce headquarters for interrogation. They repeated the fisherman's warning remarks to the interrogating officer, who just shrugged his shoulders. He did not know that a valuable source of information was missing from the interrogation—the map case with its contents. Earlier the German crew had boasted to the Greek fisherman that they would invade the next day, but now they both kept their silence. The fisherman had withheld the pilot's map case out of curiosity. He wanted to see if it contained anything of value for himself. All he found were a map and some typewritten papers.

When the fisherman docked his caïque in Khaniá harbor, he took the map case with its contents to Greek Army Headquarters Command. After explaining how he happened to be in possession of the German documents, the crafty fisherman waited for a reward. All he received was a curt smile of appreciation for "doing the right thing."

The map case eventually passed into the hands of Major Hector Pavlides, an officer on the staff of the Greek army commander in Crete, General Achilles Skoulas. Pavlides was curious about the contents of the map case and decided to study them. One typewritten sheet in particular caught his attention. The word *secret* was stamped across the top, with the additional precautionary admonition that it be burned and not carried into battle. His eye ran quickly down the page, and his eyebrows arched in surprise. As the meaning of the translation slowly penetrated, his excitement grew and his heart beat faster. Carefully he translated the remaining sentences, often cursing the Germans for always putting the verb at the end. When he completed the trans-

lation, he realized the enormous value of the document before
him. It was a copy of a German operational order for the pending attack upon Crete!

Specifically, the operational order was for the Third Parachute Regiment of the Seventh Airborne Division. It was dated
May 18, and briefly summarized the initial objectives of the attack:

> Group Central was to capture Khaniá and Suda Bay in
> the initial wave of attack. . . . Rethimnon was to be
> attacked in the second wave, eight hours later, capture
> its airfield, then turn west toward Suda. . . . a Western
> Group was to attack Maleme, capture its airfield for
> subsequent reinforcements by air . . . then turn east-
> ward join Group Central, and help capture Khaniá and
> Suda Bay. . . .

The document then referred to the specific objects of the Third
Parachute Regiment:

> It was to seize Prison Valley, storm Galatas . . . then
> turn northward to join the Western and Central Group
> in their sweep to capture Khaniá and Suda Bay.

All this was to be accomplished by sundown of the first day of
attack.[4]

Pavlides rushed to the office of the chief of staff of the Greek
Cretan command, Colonel I. Vachlas. The chief of staff lost no
time in taking the document to General Achilles Skoulas.

"Freyberg should know about this," said Skoulas, after he
had digested the contents of the document. Then he picked up
the phone to personally contact the Creforce commander.[5]

Pavlides was ordered to transcribe into English his Greek
translation of the German document, and was then sent immediately to Freyberg's headquarters on Akrotiri Peninsula.

Freyberg's chief of staff, Colonel Keith Stewart, did not share

Pavlides' excitement over the importance of the captured operational order, but he agreed to inform the commanding general.

"I think you should see this, sir," Colonel Stewart remarked as he handed the English copy of the translation to General Freyberg. Pavlides stood at rigid attention near the entrance of the dugout that served as the general's office.

Freyberg read the translation slowly, without the slightest change of expression on his face. "Interesting, indeed. Thank you, Major Pavlides." Pavlides did not budge. He expected the general to exhibit some degree of excitement and to issue a bevy of orders alerting the whole garrison. None were forthcoming.

Colonel Stewart glared at Pavlides, who finally took the hint. Still disappointed by the lack of reaction, Pavlides snapped to attention and, with a smart salute, wheeled and left Freyberg's headquarters.[6]

Freyberg turned to his chief of staff, "What do you think, Jock?"

"General, I believe that this is a ploy to deceive us. Why would the Germans allow such a classified document to be carried in the pilot's map case, in a reconnaissance aircraft—particularly when the danger of being shot down is so great?'

Freyberg listened attentively, then handed Stewart a single sheet of paper from the pile on his desk. It was a carbon of a letter from General Wavell that had been forwarded on April 29 to Prime Minister Churchill and to the chiefs of staff in London. The letter reported on Wavell's plans for the defense of Crete. Paragraph four of the letter had been circled in red:

[It] is just possible that the plan for attack on Crete may be cover for attack on Syria or Cyprus, and that the real plan will only be disclosed even to [their] own troops at the last moment. This would be consistent with German practice.[7]

The information given by the two captured German pilots flowed like electricity from mouth to mouth. In a matter of hours, Cretan civilians and Greek soldiers of all ranks had heard of the attack due the next day, May 20.

The news did not escape the ears of the New Zealand troops in the western zone of the Cretan defense. However, no orders of any kind were forthcoming from Freyberg's Creforce headquarters. In the absence of official confirmation, the warnings had to be taken as rumors by all officers in authority.

First Lieutenant Kritakis heard about the rumor from his company commander, Captain E. The captain stormed into his headquarters tent in Galatas as Lieutenant Kritakis was completing the company orders for the next day.

"Can you imagine," growled the captain, as he flung his helmet onto the cot, "can you imagine the idiocy of it all? It is sheer stupidity!"

The lieutenant looked up in surprise. He had never seen his CO so angry. He opened his mouth to speak, but the captain cut him off.

"That's what I meant when I said 'no initiative'—by our own general staff officers. Here we are on the eve of being attacked, and the regimental C.O. orders a *dress parade* rehearsal by the whole regiment for tomorrow. Incredible, isn't it?"

Again, the lieutenant opened his mouth to speak and again the captain cut him off.

"Look at these orders—a dress parade rehearsal in order to look well for an inspection by General Freyberg at 10:00 hours on May 23. Can you imagine that?" repeated the seething company commander. The captain stalked back and forth in the close confines of the tent, removing his field tunic and pistol belt as he did so.

"You have heard the rumors about the Germans attacking tomorrow—I believe them! And what do we do about it?" queried the captain sarcastically, "we get orders to prepare for a dress parade!"

With one final grunt of disgust, he threw himself, half-dressed, upon his cot and pulled a sheet over himself.

Lieutenant Kritakis read the written order that the angry

captain had flung on the desk. He shook his head, realizing that the captain was right. The order was illogical—but, after all, since when did any army reason logically? In the course of history, battles had been won by that army whose reasoning was less illogical than that of the army opposing it.[8]

Across the blue waters separating Crete from the Greek mainland, the Germans were completing their preparations for the attack. On the afternoon of May 19, the various detachment and battalion commanders held a final critique. It was at this conference that the last assignments were issued to the various companies and platoons.

As afternoon passed into evening, the paratroopers received special rations of beer and brandy.

Karl Schoerner from Linz, Austria, the newly trained paratrooper, had been assigned to the First Company of the First Paratroop Battalion of the Third Fallschirmjäger Regiment. Being a new face in the company, he was befriended by Gefreiter Hans Kreindler. Private First Class Kreindler was a veteran. He had already undergone the baptism of fire, making his first parachute jump in combat during the invasion of the Netherlands.[9] Schoerner looked up to Kreindler as a boy looks up to his older brother. It was a pleasant relationship.

Both of them had just spent the last few hours on special detail, assisting the ground crews fueling the transports and bombers that were to be used in the next day's attack. The blockage of the Corinth Canal had so delayed the passage of gasoline barges that, in the few remaining hours before takeoff, many aircraft had still not been fueled. Fueling was being done by hand pump, a slow and grimy task. So the call had gone out to the paratroopers for volunteers. The sergeants selected the "volunteers" for this special detail, Schoerner and Kreindler among them.

When the two returned to their encampment, they were exhausted. Karl Schoerner was too tired and nervous about tomorrow to enjoy the special rations. He slumped to the ground in the shade of a lemon tree and sniffed its fragrant scent. He decided to write to his mother:

> May in Greece is hot, but its fruit trees do give off such
> a cooling fragrant breeze. . . . Tonight I shall sleep un-
> der the stars. . . . When the war is over, I shall return
> to live here.[10]

Unlike Schoerner, the veteran Kreindler was not going to let his fatigue prevent him from enjoying his ration of beer and brandy. He remembered an old soldier's slogan: "Eat today and be merry for there may be no tomorrow."

While Schoerner wrote to his mother and Kreindler enjoyed his drinks, their battalion commander, Captain von der Heydte, was too concerned with responsibility to be as carefree as his enlisted men. After his final staff conference, the commanding officer of the First Paratroop Battalion returned to his headquarters tent, where he busied himself with the last minutiae of the pending attack.

On this same day, the British air officer commanding in Crete, Group Captain G. Beamish, requested that the remainder of his aircraft be excused from further service in Crete. The request was granted.[11]

It was a difficult decision but the problems that had confronted the RAF in Crete were insurmountable. The air battle over Britain was now in its waning stages, but there were few surplus aircraft available for transfer to the Mediterranean theater of operations. Air Marshal A. Longmore, the air commander in Cairo, had only ninety bombers and forty-three fighter aircraft to cover all of North Africa, Syria, Iraq, Cyprus, and Crete.

The remnants of four squadrons, which had been evacuated from Greece, were now based on Crete.

Aircraftman Ryder was stationed at Maleme airfield in Crete. On the morning of May 13, thirty ME-109s struck the field in an unannounced surprise attack. The air was suddenly filled with the exploding crash of their cannon shells and the rattle of their machine guns, as wave after wave attacked the field from all directions.

Unlike the Battle of Britain, the RAF in Crete had no radar stations to help them locate the enemy or to advise them of their approach. No sooner were the Germans sighted than they dove into the attack.[12]

In this morning's attack, Ryder sat behind his Lewis machine gun, firing as each airplane sped past. The sky was filled with ME-109s. There were so many of them they were difficult to count. Wherever Ryder turned his gun, a German aircraft loomed into his sights.

Momentarily, something else caught his attention. He watched anxiously, with growing apprehension, as two Hurricane fighters taxied down the runway in an attempt to take off while under attack.

Flight Sergeant Reynish raced his aircraft down the strip at full throttle, while enemy planes came at him from all directions. Miraculously, he rose into the air, banking his Hurricane sharply with three ME-109s on his tail. He skillfully looped onto the tail of a German, gave him a short burst from his machine guns, and watched as the Messerschmitt rolled over out of control. Reynish's victory was shortlived. Twelve ME-109s now raced after him as he fled for the protection of the hills.[13]

Reynish's CO, Squadron Leader Edward Howell, raced the second Hurricane with open throttle down the same runway as six Germans sped after him in pursuit. Howell was flying a Hurricane fighter plane for the first time that day, handling it superbly against great odds. That day, alone, he shot down three German planes, landing safely when the raid had ended.[14]

Again, unlike the Battle of Britain, the defenders of Crete did not possess the appropriate equipment with which to communicate to the pilots when the raid was over, or, more important, when it was safe to land and refuel.

A Hurricane fighter came in to land during an air raid. It was obvious to the pilot that the airfield was under attack, but he was out of fuel and had to land. He was followed down by a swarm of ME-109s.

He lowered his landing gear, and as he made his final approach with full flaps down, all eyes of the airfield's defenders and ground crew watched him, rooting for him to land safely. Then the Germans hit him—it was like shooting at a sitting duck. He flamed, arched upward, turned over and fell into the sea with a splash, disappearing below the waves.[15]

Flight Lieutenant Woodward had made two attempts to take off while the airfield was under attack. Each time, his aircraft was riddled by bullets from the attacking fighters, never getting off the ground. On his third attempt, with a new Hurricane, he succeeded.[16]

With the coming of dusk, the sky cleared of all German aircraft. An eerie quiet settled over the island. Soldiers and civilians alike could move about without fear of strafing bullets or falling bombs. It was hard to imagine the sense of relief that prevailed when another day of bombing had passed. In those hours of dusk, before the darkness of night cast its cover, the island came to life. Motor vehicles carried supplies to their designated units; entrenchments were repaired or modified; messengers sped on their motorcycles with the orders for the next day.

Australians and New Zealanders left their foxholes, their entrenchments, and their encampments, removed their clothes and plunged into the cool waters that lapped the shores of Crete. They swam and frolicked, forgetting the dangers of the day and those that would come tomorrow. Passing Cretans gazed at them, wondering with amazement at the love these foreigners had for the ocean.

While these men cooled themselves, others ventured to the surrounding villages to visit the homes of civilian friends or to enjoy a drink of ouzo or retsina at a village tavern.

With the sun slowly descending behind the western horizon, the crimson colors of sunset deepened as night settled over the island. Suddenly it grew dark, as if a shade had been drawn. Not a light was to be seen; not a sound was to be heard; only the fragrant scent of the island's subtropical flora floated gently on the cool evening breeze.

Around 2:00 A.M., May 20, General Kurt Student's telephone rang with a loud urgent sound and an aide answered it. Colonel Heinz Trettner, Student's personal staff officer, was calling. It was imperative that he speak to the general immediately.

Student was awakened, and he listened to Trettner's apprehensive voice. In excited tones Trettner referred to an air reconnaissance report that had sighted British warships in Khaniá Gulf.

"Could it be possible that the British Fleet knows of our scheduled attack tomorrow, Herr General? Shall we postpone the hour of the attack?"

Student considered the question. Both Goering and General Löhr had repeatedly stressed the importance of time; Student had promised Hitler that he would take Crete in three days, with May 17 as the initial target day. Already the date of attack had been postponed once; besides, all units were prepared, eager, and ready to go.

"We have to risk that danger," he replied after a long moment's silence. "I appreciate your anxiety, Trettner, but it was really unnecessary to awaken me. Let the attack go on as scheduled." [17]

The decision was final. The attack upon Crete would begin in four hours, at 6:00 A.M. Operation Mercury was ready to be launched.

In the early predawn hours of Tuesday, May 20, Kapetan Vasili Kazantsakis untied his fishing boat from its mooring post in the small harbor of Khaniá. As he left the harbor behind him, the first brilliant rays of the ascending sun scattered the shadows of night. It looked as if it would be another bright and cloudless day. A stillness prevailed over the whole expanse of the island. To the Kapetan, it was a foreboding silence—the calm that proclaimed the approach of a storm.

At 6:00 A.M. that bright, sunny morning of May 20, the storm broke over Crete.

THE
ATTACK

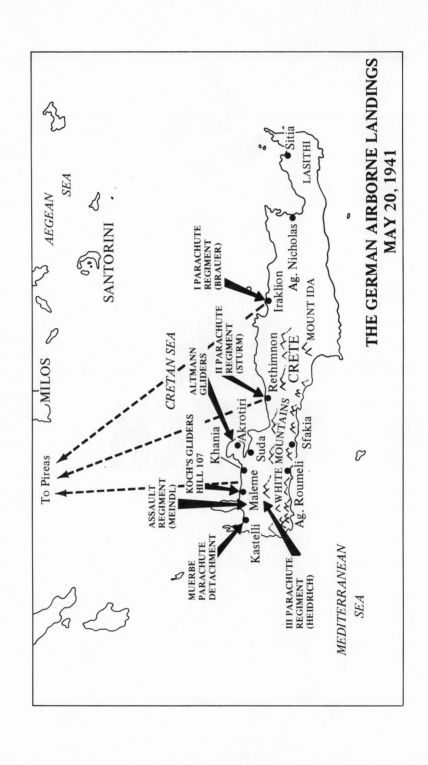

THE GERMAN AIRBORNE LANDINGS
MAY 20, 1941

10

MERCURY
IS AIRBORNE

MAY 20, 1941

In the darkness of the predawn hours, the many Germans who were to participate in the first phase of the attack upon Crete were awakened. Some of them had slept soundly after an extensive beer party. Others had been too excited even to close their eyes, much less sleep. Their moment of truth would soon arrive.

Some of the assault companies were bivouacked adjacent to the airfields. All they had to do was march to their assigned transports. Others had to be trucked across bumpy, dusty roads to their respective fields.

Captain von der Heydte, the CO of the First Battalion, Third Regiment, sat in the passenger seat of the jeep leading the convoy of trucks carrying his battalion to their assigned section of the airfield. As they approached the field, he turned to speak to his adjutant. His voice was lost in the roar that broke the silence of the night.

At that moment, 120 JU-52 trimotor transports started their engines. The sound of 360 whirring propellers was deafening. Von der Heydte could not even hear his own words in the rush of noise.[1]

His convoy left the roadway and was guided by traffic control officers to its assigned aircraft. It was very difficult for the drivers to see the traffic directors because of the darkness and the heavy dust that seemed to fill the air. Silhouettes of the nearby troop carriers would periodically emerge from the dust cloud. This fine, powdery dust, coming from the parched soil that covered the airfield, was stirred into cyclonic swirls by the spinning propellers. It rose like a red pillar almost a thousand feet into the sky, covering men and machines alike. It crept into the cylinders of the motors and into the nostrils of the men. In the dim light, the moving formations of men appeared as grotesque shadows.

Group after group, in multiples of thirteen to fifteen men per group—called a "stick" in paratrooper language—followed a beckoning pale beam from the boarding officer's flashlight. The only signal that would guide the men to their assigned aircraft, it brought order out of possible chaos.

Gefreiter Hans Kreindler walked closely behind his guide. He was followed by his squad, each man dressed in the bulky equipment of the paratrooper, from the dome-shaped steel helmet on his head to the rubberized pads on his knees to the parachute on his back. Karl Schoerner was second in the file of fifteen men, keeping in step behind Kreindler.

Slowly and patiently the men waited to enter the transport, each one holding his parachute static line in his gloved hand. As they entered the plane, they would take the white cords between their teeth, leaving both arms free to grasp the grabirons on either side of the door.

It was a slow, time-consuming process, as the men of the Third Parachute Regiment and the assault regiment boarded the troop carriers, but it was completed even against the difficulties of darkness and dust. By 4:00 A.M. the paratroopers were settled in their transports. All was in readiness, waiting for the signal to depart.

At 4:30 A.M., the first heavily laden bomber trundled down the runway and lifted itself into the sky. Other bombers taxied from their stations, taking their place in line, waiting for the signal to take off. At thirty-second intervals, each aircraft followed the one before it down the strip, slowly rising and disappearing into the deep blue sky of approaching dawn.

These bombers were the first group of aircraft scheduled to leave. They were to provide the final pulverizing destruction of the defenses on Crete—the "softening-up" phase before the actual invasion.

The Dornier, Heinkel, and Junker bomber groups were to strike their objectives from an altitude of 6,000 to 10,000 feet. They were to discharge their bombs and return to their respective airfields to refuel and rearm for the afternoon phase of the attack on the eastern half of Crete.

From airfields in the Peloponnesus and from the island of Karpathos (known during World War II as Scarpanto), located midway between Crete and Rhodes, came the "glamour boys" of the Luftwaffe. These were the pilots of the Stuka dive-bombers, who had been assigned to this mission from Dive-Bomber Group 2.

Two groups of these JU-87 dive-bombers came from airfields at Mycenae and Molaoi in the Peloponnesus, under the command of Lieutenant Colonel Oskar Dinort. A third group of Stukas, led by Captain Brücker, came from Karpathos.[2]

The JU-87 Stuka dive-bomber had established a dreaded reputation in the early part of the war. Its narrow silhouette, its large square-tailed rudder, its fixed undercarriage, and its reverse gull wings were the outstanding characteristics of this aircraft. Its shrill shriek, during its dive, struck terror into the hearts of retreating troops and fleeing refugees during the German conquests of Poland, the Low Countries, France, Yugoslavia, and Greece. It was already familiar to the defenders of Crete.

While the medium bombers performed from high altitude on a given target, the Stukas were used tactically, attacking any feasible target at random, in support of ground forces.

Finally came the aircraft of Fighter Group 77. This unit consisted of three groups of fighter planes, two of them under

Major Woldenga and the other under Captain Ihlefeld, all based on Molaoi.[3]

These groups were comprised of the famous Messerschmitt 109, the best single-seat fighter of the Luftwaffe—if not in the world—in that period of the war. A beautifully designed aircraft, its slim, sleek contours, light weight, and excellent maneuverability made it a fighter pilot's dream.

The ME-109 was used as a protective escort for bombers on short-range targets, as an attack fighter to engage in air duels, and as a tactical fighter to harass and destroy ground troops. It was perhaps the most versatile airplane in the air in 1941. In the days that preceded the battle, the defenders of Crete had come to fear this fighter more than the Stuka or any other aircraft.

In his headquarters, the commanding general of this vast air armada, Major General Wolfram Freiherr von Richthofen, was pleased with himself. He had successfully mustered 650 aircraft of all types from his Eighth Air Force for this operation. When the report arrived that his last available groups were airborne, he settled back to await the results of the attack.

Slowly the many aircraft from all the airfields in Greece rose to a point of rendezvous over the Greek mainland. It had taken them almost an hour to overcome the visibility problems caused by the huge clouds of dust blanketing the airfields. Now they were above the clouds.

In the east, the huge red ball of the sun rose slowly over the Aegean Sea. It would be another beautiful, sun-filled day with a cloudless blue sky—a perfect day for the task ahead.

At last the mighty armada was airborne and turning southward, in the direction of Crete.

At Topolia air base, Colonel Rüdiger von Heyking, the commanding officer of three bomber groups for special assignment, was studying the landing gears of the trimotor transports in his command.

"How can these machines be expected to take off with their

landing gears buried in sand almost to their axles?'' he protested. He shook his head pessimistically. ''It would take a miracle if some of these aircraft don't bog down or crack up on take-off!''

He scooped up some soil with his gloved hand and remarked disgustedly, ''These airfields are a sea of sand—they are nothing but deserts!''[4]

Von Heyking was standing outside the operations van and, half-choking in the dust, tried to determine if the transports of his group were ready to take off. He had before him 150 Junker-52 transports of Air Groups 60, 101, and 102—all half-hidden in a cloud of dust.

His remarks had been addressed to his superior officer, General Gerhard, standing beside him. Major General Gerhard was the air service commander for Operation Mercury. He was the officer responsible for the availability and serviceability of the transports and gliders to be used in this operation. He had ten groups in his command, consisting of 500 JU-52 transports and about 70 DFS-230 gliders.

''I agree, Colonel, but there was little time to lay down metal runways. I ordered that the fields be sprayed by water wagons, but it has not helped. We must do the best we can,'' said General Gerhard. ''Conditions are no better at Tanagra, Dadion, Megara, or at Corinth!''[5]

It was a fact that the other transport groups located at these airfields were also confronted with the same problems of poor visibility caused by the swirling dust. It was a situation that was to affect the whole operation.

Near the runway at Eleusis airfield rested the many gliders that were to take part in the opening phase of the assault upon Crete. This group of gliders represented the task force assigned to the capture of Khaniá. In one of these gliders, the commanding general of the Seventh Airborne Division and his whole divisional staff had taken their places.

Lieutenant General Wilhelm Suessmann, who sat in the lead glider, was not only in command of the paratroop division but also commanding officer of the central attack force, designated as Task Force Mars.

A veteran of the First World War, he had only recently joined the airborne forces. Prior to his transfer, he commanded an infantry division in the Polish campaign, and later served in the attack on Norway. Since Suessman had worked with General Student on the details of Operation Mercury, the commanding general of the Eleventh Air Corps decided to place him in charge of this elite paratroop division.

In the dim light of the canvas-bodied glider, General Suessmann glanced at his watch. It was 5:25 A.M.

Suessmann knew that the bombers of the Eighth Air Corps were already flying toward Crete. Shortly the signal would be given for the gliders to become airborne and follow the bombers to the same destination.

There was silence in the gliders and the transports as the minutes ticked by. Few noticed that the air was becoming stifling.

An Obergefreiter, acting as a starter, stood outside the operations shack, a red flag in his left hand—the signal to hold—and a white flag with a green cross in his right, indicating "all clear for takeoff." He waved the white flag. Nothing happened. The pilot of the lead transport could not see the signal for the heavy cloud of dust. The Obergefreiter dashed into the shack and returned with a flare gun.

At 5:30 A.M. a huge green flare arched into the sky. It was the signal. General Suessmann leaned forward in his seat, satisfied that they would finally depart. He had no way of knowing that fate had willed he would never reach Crete.

The pilots of the transports throttled their motors to an ear-shattering roar. The lead transport began to move slowly across the field, followed by another and then another. Behind each transport trailed a glider of the First Assault Regiment. With the added burden of a fully loaded glider in tow, the transports taxied sluggishly down the runway.

As each transport rolled forward, the tow line extending from its tail grew taut with the attachment in the nose of each glider. The gliders jerked forward slowly, bounced unevenly, then picked up speed as they rolled down the strip in the wake of the towing transports. At the end of the runway, the first transport left the ground. The glider pilot slowly pulled back the control stick. The rumbling sound of the fuselage ceased. He was airborne. In a matter of seconds, his glider lifted noiselessly and majestically over the fields and rooftops of the surrounding countryside, gaining altitude behind its towing mother transport.

In half-minute intervals, transport after transport soared into the sky. It was daylight as the many Junkers rendezvoused over the blue waters of the Saronic Gulf. All in all, 500 JU-52 transports comprised this second great armada that filled the skies in the early hours of May 20. Behind them were seventy assault gliders in tow.

Operation Mercury was airborne.

The Junker transports, carrying the paratroopers and towing the gliders, reached their proper altitudes and settled into formation for the flight to Crete. They trembled and vibrated as they struggled through periodic air turbulence over the Mediterranean. The machines carried approximately 6,000 men in the first airborne invasion ever attempted in modern history.

The elation and exuberance that each paratrooper had felt at takeoff was diminishing. Slowly they fell into a solemn silence. Each man contemplated the approaching moment when he would jump into space and descend into battle. They were all anxious for that moment to arrive, to get it over with. The new recruits had not been in combat before and were visibly apprehensive. Some tried to smile nonchalantly at their comrades sitting opposite. Others removed their skull-shaped helmets and unfastened their harness straps for comfort.

Gefreiter Hans Kreindler, the veteran of the Netherlands campaign, was the ranking noncom in his aircraft. By virtue of his rank, as prescribed in the paratroop training manual, he occupied the first seat and would be the first to leave the transport. From his position, he glanced to his right at both ranks of men sitting quietly. Although experienced in battle, he was nervous; his throat was dry to the point of choking, and his stomach was queasy. He turned his head in order to hide any expression that might betray his feelings.

If he was nervous, he wondered what his buddy Karl Schoerner was feeling. Whereas Kreindler had undergone one airdrop into combat, Schoerner had not as yet tasted battle. Schoerner kept his head bowed and his eyes closed. Kreindler hoped that his friend would remember his advice to stick close once they touched ground.[6]

As silence pervaded the aircraft, Kreindler's eyes scanned the printed cloth attached to the inner lining of his jacket. Each paratrooper had the same message sewn to the identical spot. It was the code of the German paratrooper. Kreindler's eye ran down the list of ten "commandments," remembering his training days when he had to commit them to memory.

1. You are the chosen ones of the German army. You will seek combat and train yourself to endure any manner of test.

2. Cultivate true comradeship.

3. Beware of talking.

4. Be calm and prudent, strong and resolute.

5. The most precious thing in the presence of the foe is ammunition.

6. Never surrender.

7. You can triumph only if your weapons are good.

8. Grasp the full purpose of every enterprise, so if your leader is killed you can help yourself fulfill it.

9. Against an open foe fight with chivalry, but to a guerrilla extend no quarter.

10. Keep your eyes open.[7]

In another transport, carrying the paratroopers of the Third Parachute Regiment, the commanding officer of the First Paratroop Battalion, Captain von der Heydte, removed his helmet and carefully studied his map. He was cool and collected. He closed his eyes, hoping for a few moments of relaxing sleep. Shortly, he became aware of someone standing before him.

"Herr Hauptmann, may I speak with you?"

Von der Heydte looked up at a tall, bushy-browed paratrooper. "What is the matter, soldier?"

"I feel ill to my stomach, Herr Hauptmann."

Von der Heydte recognized him. This paratrooper had achieved international fame as a boxing champion before the war. Now he was going into combat and he was pleading illness. Was he really ill or was he feigning illness because of fear?

The battalion commander gazed out through the porthole and thought, A man who was a national hero in the boxing ring certainly could not be a coward in battle. Yet fighting in the boxing ring is not quite the same as a soldier jumping into battle. A soldier who has tasted the life-or-death baptism of combat is a hero of a different stature.

Captain von der Heydte said, "My dear fellow, there is nothing I can do for you now. You may report sick when we arrive in Crete. You know that our medical staff is flying with us."[8]

The remark was not very comforting to the anguished paratrooper, but it was practical. The former heavyweight boxing champion of the world, Max Schmeling, nodded and returned to his seat.

The airborne glider troops also sat in anticipatory silence, strapped into position, astride the central beams of their aircraft. Little light penetrated into the interior of each glider, except through the thick celluloid windows on either side of the canvas-covered fuselage.

At first, the interiors of the gliders were stiflingly hot. The heavy combat uniforms they wore added to the paratroopers' discomfort, and some of them became airsick.

As the towing transports rose to higher altitudes, the air in each glider became cooler and more comfortable. A few holes in the canvas body allowed little airstreams to filter in and circulate. It was an invigorating stimulus to the men, a fair compensation for the sickly feeling of flight, as the gliders responded to the varying air currents.

Each glider carried a team of specially trained paratroopers. According to their assigned tasks, the number in each glider varied from eight to twelve men, equipped with weapons and explosives. Each paratrooper had been trained to do a specific task, and they were considered to be masters at them. These men represented the ''point of the lance'' in the attack.

The huge armada of gliders and transports moved slowly through the radiantly blue sky of early morning. Here were the gliders of Major Walter Koch, the hero of Eben Emael, assigned to capture the strategic Hill 107, which overlooked Maleme airfield. To his right were the nine gliders of Lieutenant Wulff von Plessen, whose task would be to seize the antiaircraft batteries at the edge of the airfield and then seize the airstrip itself. Behind him followed the gliders of Major Walter von Braun, ordered to seize the main bridge over the Tavronites River, thus sealing the western approach to the airfield. To the left of the huge column flew the gliders of Captain Gustav Altmann and Lieutenant Alfred Genz, whose assignment would be the capture of General Freyberg and the seizure of Creforce Headquarters.

From the lead glider General Suessmann could see a sky filled with trimotor transports and gliders. It was a stirring sight, and he was proud to be in command.

The sun had fully risen above the horizon. Below, the beautiful Mediterranean appeared a brilliant blue, glistening in the angled rays of the early morning sun. High above, Suessmann could pick out silvery specks traveling north. These were the first flights of high-level bombers returning to the mainland. They had already discharged their bombs over Crete and were returning home to refuel and reload.

The pilot of Suessmann's transport, Sergeant Franz Hausser, marveled at the vast panorama of aircraft that filled the sky around him. He was still gazing leisurely about when his eye caught a metallic speck flickering in the rays of the morning sun. In a matter of minutes, this speck loomed larger. It was another aircraft flying a course perpendicular to his transport, and it was traveling at a greater speed. He became alarmed—if the pilot of the approaching plane did not veer from his course, they would collide in midair in a matter of minutes.

The aircraft in question was a bomber. It was, in fact, an HE-111 that had been delayed in its departure from Eleusis airfield by engine trouble. Now it was racing at top speed in order to catch up. In his anxiety to reach his squadron, the pilot, Lieutenant Paul Gerfehr, did not realize that his aircraft had intersected the flight pattern of the transport-glider group.

Sergeant Hausser had only minutes to decide what to do: Should he alter his course to avoid a possible collision with the rapidly approaching bomber or should he remain on his present heading and hope that the bomber pilot would spot him in time? It was obvious that the bomber pilot was not aware of the danger—the sun's glare must have blinded him.

Others in the huge formation had also spotted the intruder. Now all eyes in the lead flight of transports were riveted to the danger ahead.

With seconds to spare, the pilot of the endangered transport took the only possible action. Sergeant Hausser pushed his controls forward, and the huge plane's nose dropped. The JU-52 went into a steep dive, giving its attached tow-rope a sudden, sharp, and vibrating yank, as it pulled its glider in its wake. Everyone held on breathlessly.[9]

In the bomber, Lieutenant Gerfehr, seeing the Junker suddenly drop into a steep dive, followed by its glider, finally realized that he had entered the flight path of another formation. Abruptly he throttled his engine, pulled back on the control stick and rose upward, above the diving transport. A midair collision had been avoided by just a few yards.

General Suessmann and the other occupants of his glider braced themselves as the glider followed the diving transport. Slowly the transport returned to level flight. The Heinkel 111 had passed over them and was already out of sight. However, the air turbulence created by the slipstream of the passing bomber now placed a great strain on the heavy hawser that linked the glider to its mother transport. The glider vibrated uncomfortably while its pilot struggled to cope with the changes in air pressure.

The glider pilot was alarmed at the new danger now presenting itself. The towline had been stretched dangerously taut. Even before he could express his concern, a dull twang was heard, not unlike the snap of a thick elastic band. The towline had parted.

Released from its mother ship, the glider now floated free.

"How, in God's name, do we reach our objective with one hundred and fifty miles remaining to Crete?" General Suessmann knew that from a height of 4,ooo feet, it would be impossible for the glider to reach the distant objective. The only possibility would be to land safely on some island or glide back to the mainland. Then, perhaps, another JU-52 would fly them directly to Crete.

Suessmann's glider soared upward, aided by the rising warm air. Soon it had risen hundreds of feet above the flight of gliders, continuing on their course. Suessmann's pilot made every effort to control his machine. He decided to attempt a landing on the island of Aegina.

As the pilot banked the glider into a wide turn, he heard a dull thud to his left. He could not at first pinpoint the source of the noise.

Even before the pilot could identify the cause of the dull sound and thus appreciate the new danger, the sharp, rasping crack of tearing metal echoed like a pistol shot through the glider's fuselage. The left wing had fallen off!

The pilot of the JU-52 transport that had towed this ill-fated glider was still following the glider's upward trajectory. So were the pilots of the other transports that passed below them. To their horror, the stricken glider now began to fall, cartwheeling downward. Then the other wing separated from the glider. Now completely wingless, the hapless craft fell earthward, toppling end over end.[10]

From the courtyard of the Convent of the Holy Trinity, the abbot and the church acolytes followed the fall of the glider as it hurtled toward earth like a stone falling from a high precipice. Only a huge puff of dust rising upward indicated that the glider had returned to earth.

There on the mountainous terrain of the beautiful island of Aegina in the Saronic Gulf, near the ancient Temple of Aphoea, General Wilhelm Suessmann and his staff were killed. The first casualties of the German assault upon Crete, they were destined to be joined by thousands more before the day ended.

II

"THEY ARE COMING!"

MAY 20, 1941

The hour was approaching 6:00 A.M. In the deep blue of the northern sky, a vast dark shadow appeared just above the horizon. The stillness of the early morning was disturbed by a continuous low hum. As the shadow loomed larger, the low hum increased in pitch to that of a drone. It was a sound that reminded the Australians and the New Zealanders who had worked in the fields back home as farmers, of approaching locusts. The Cretans likened it to a swarm of bees.

A lookout posted on a hill some 500 yards north of Creforce Headquarters also heard the distant drone. He lifted binoculars to his eyes, focused quickly, and carefully studied the ever-growing shadow on the horizon.

Captain Theodore Stephanides was a doctor attached to the British forces at Creforce Headquarters. More recently, he had been assigned as medical officer to the dock-operating companies at Suda Bay.[1]

On this brilliant morning of May 20, he stepped out of his tent and took a deep breath of the fresh early morning air. He felt that it was too beautiful a day to fight a war. He greeted a fellow officer, Captain Fenn, and together they walked toward the tent that served as the headquarters mess. While waiting for breakfast to be served, Stephanides chatted with several headquarters staff officers. They all heard the drone from the sky. It did not interrupt their breakfast, but they knew that they were in for another day of bombing.

Lieutenant Kritakis, the executive officer of the Sixth Company of the Sixth Greek Regiment, encamped in the valley before the village of Galatas, had also stepped out of the headquarters tent to bask in the sunshine of this beautiful day. He observed his commanding officer, Captain E, out in the field, instructing the platoon leaders on the procedures for the dress parade rehearsal scheduled later that day. It was obvious that he also heard the sound of the approaching bombers. The company commander decided to dismiss the formation, ordering his men to take shelter from the forthcoming attack.[2]

Just outside the cave in the quarry that served as his headquarters, the commanding general of the allied forces in Crete, Major General Bernard Freyberg, had just been handed a message from the lookout post on the Akrotiri heights. The huge dark mass on the horizon had been identified as approaching German bombers, numbering in excess of 400. Air alarms were sounded and church bells rang from east to west. It was the warning that an enemy air attack was imminent.[3]

Trucks left the road; men sought shelter in slit trenches or in the protective shadows of grape arbors and olive trees.

Flying high above Crete, the Dornier 17s, the Heinkel 111s, and the Junker 88s began their bombing runs.

All hell broke loose. The air was torn by the sounds of Bofors guns firing at the enemy aircraft. Simultaneous with the sound of the air alarms, a battery of 3.5-inch antiaircraft guns, located at the neck of Akrotiri Peninsula, opened fire on the approaching enemy. Everyone scattered except the men firing the guns. The crewmen stood bravely by their weapons, completely exposed to the aerial attack.

Captain Stephanides dashed for the foxhole that served as his air-raid shelter. He jumped in just as the first bombs whistled down on their targets.[4]

The high-level bombers released their destructive missiles in strings of twelve. In a crisscross bombing pattern, from north to south and from east to west, the Heinkels and Dorniers, under Colonel Reickhoff, and the Junker 88s under Captains Hoffman and Kollewe, left no sector of Cretan soil unscathed. Squadron after squadron of bombers passed overhead. The roar increased to an ear-shattering din. The whine of bombs filled the air as their deadly detonations blasted everything in sight.

Soon the blue sky over Crete was obscured by a thick mantle of dust—a cloud that rose from the dry ground ripped by the hailstorm of aerial bombs. A black smoky shroud hovered like a widow's veil over the transport ships burning in Suda Bay. It was the heaviest concentration of aerial bombing since that of the English cities during the Battle of Britain.

Men of the Twenty-second New Zealand Battalion, protecting Maleme airfield from their positions on the heights of Hill 107, were entirely helpless and at the mercy of these bombers. All that stood between them and the slicing shards of exploding bombs was the dry Cretan soil. The men lay in their foxholes, and as the bombs fell, each man prayed that the pattern would miss his hole. Most of the bombs did miss the earthen shelters of the New Zealand defenders, but many were covered with dirt and debris from the earthshaking concussions. They shook dirt from their ears and spat grit from their mouths. The brain-rattling detonations left many of these men temporarily deaf. Occasionally, a bomb fell into a trench, its explosive force leaving a scar in the earth where once soldiers had sought shelter.

The intensity of the attack was such that even the disdainful Cretans thought it best to seek shelter from this madness. Alabaster dust rose hundreds of feet into the air over the city of Khaniá, as the bombs tore apart buildings and their occupants.

Stephanides and the other personnel of Creforce Headquarters, who sought safety from the aerial assault in slit trenches, could hear the persistent and continuous roar of the antiaircraft guns.

Next came the Stuka dive-bombers. These slender, square-tailed demons of the sky spread devastating and demoralizing fear. They flew at 4,000 feet, stacked in grids, one above the other. At a signal from their group leader, Lieutenant Colonel Dinort, the planes moved into line astern. Each pilot switched on his bombsight, let out his dive brakes, and closed his radiator flaps. Then they nosed over into the attack.

The Stukas plunged into their seventy-degree dives, each plane following the other down to the target. The siren in the nacelle of each dive bomber screamed a familiar sound that foretold that death was coming. Plane after plane, squadron after squadron, dove down at a speed of 275 mph, peeling off at 300 feet. Their bombs, released at 1,500 feet, plummeted toward their targets. One of the first was the battery of antiaircraft guns located on Akrotiri Peninsula.

Stephanides watched the air strike in morbid fascination. When the dirt from the exploding bombs fell back to earth and the dust cloud lifted, he saw that of the four antiaircraft guns in the battery, only one remained intact and firing. The other three guns had been destroyed by the attacking Stukas. Bodies and parts of guns lay scattered in all directions on the churned-up, bomb-cratered ground.

While the dive-bombers gathered in the sky for further attacks on other targets, the air was ripped by the roar of strafing fighters. Messerschmitt 109s took up the fight. In groups of three, they flew low across the terrain, machine-gunning anything that moved.

For one hour, the intense attack continued. It seemed as if it would never end. The cacophony of antiaircraft fire, the roar of airplane motors, the whine of falling bombs, the earsplitting din of explosions, and the shriek of the dive bombers turned this peaceful countryside into a hell on earth.

Cretans knelt before their icons and prayed for safety. Soldiers, some of whom had never believed in an Almighty Being, now prayed to God for salvation.

At 7:00 A.M. the attack suddenly came to an end.

An eerie silence followed. Heads appeared above the tops of trenches. Civilians emerged from the bombed remnants of their homes.

Just then Captain Stephanides heard a low, prolonged sibilant sound. It reminded him of wind passing through telegraph wires. A huge object blocked the sun momentarily and fleetingly cast an eaglelike shadow across the ground. The men once again dove for the security of their trenches. Over them passed a square-bodied fuselage with long tapering wings, sweeping toward the heights of Akrotiri Peninsula.

Stephanides was puzzled by the aircraft's appearance, for it had no propeller. He had never seen such an aircraft before. It was the first glider of the assault regiment descending earthward toward its objective.[5]

At Creforce Headquarters, General Freyberg's aide pointed to the appearance of aircraft in the west. With his field glasses, Freyberg saw transport planes flying over the Maleme area. From these aircraft, multicolored plumes appeared, slowly drifting to earth like flower petals.[6]

All over the western part of the island, gliders and paratroopers began to drop on Crete. From the ground, soldiers and civilians alike watched the sky above Crete fill with colorful, blossoming umbrellas floating toward earth. There were thousands of them, from Maleme to Khaniá and from Suda Bay to the foothills of the White Mountains. It was a spellbinding sight.

A Cretan farmer yelled, "They are coming . . . they are coming!" gesticulating wildly at the sky. In seconds the warning was repeated, "They are coming!"

Somewhere in the distance, a single rifle shot broke the prolonged silence. The sound echoed over the western hills and valleys of the island. It was followed almost immediately by the multiple bark of rifles and the low, repetitious rattle of machine guns.

The battle had begun.

12

"IT WAS LIKE A TERRIBLE DREAM"

MAY 20, 1941

Having flown in close formation throughout their southward flight, the paratroop-glider armada began to separate into various approach patterns. The huge yellow-nosed, black-bodied, trimotor transports headed toward their assigned drop zones. As they approached the island, the pilots could see in the distance the last of the bombers returning from their missions. There, ahead of and below the lead transport, was the major objective—the airfield at Maleme.

Events occurred in rapid succession. As the transports containing the paratroopers headed for their drop zones, the transports towing the gliders released their charges.

The three-pronged attack on the Maleme area was to be carried out by the special assault regiment of the western battle group, known as Task Force Komet. While parachutists were to seize and secure the western and eastern approaches to the airfield, the glider troops would capture the airfield itself and its commanding height, Hill 107. The Schwerpunkt—the main punch—of the attack thus fell to the men being carried to the objective in fifty-three gliders.

These glider troops represented the middle prong of the attack. Their specific objective was the seizure of the bridge over the Tavronites River, with the neutralization of the Bofors anti-aircraft battery located at its mouth, and the capture of Hill 107. Capturing the hill, which rose approximately 350 feet above ground level, was particularly essential, for whoever controlled it also controlled the airstrip.

As Major Koch's detachment of thirty gliders emerged from the low-lying dust cloud lingering from the bombardment, their objective came into view. Kavsakia Hill—Hill 107—stood like a towering sentinel over the small airfield on its northern flank.

These great gliders dropped like soaring eagles from the sky. The silence that prevailed in the few moments following the termination of the aerial bombing was broken by the sibilant sound of air being cut by the enormous wingspan of each glider as it descended toward earth.

Koch had planned to attack the hill from two directions. He divided his force into two groups of fifteen gliders each. The first group would land on the northeast side of the hill, and Koch and his group would touch down on the southwestern slope. Once the 150 men of each group had landed, the two groups would advance toward the crest of the hill.

Major Koch sat behind the pilot in the lead glider of the second group. Behind him, strapped into their seats on the glider's center sill, were ten troopers of the battalion staff. They were ready to pounce upon the enemy as soon as they touched ground. The towing JU-52 transport had released them when the target hovered into view.

Koch's glider was on course, coming in from the southwest, heading for a small clearing on the slope below. Slowly the pilot pushed the controls forward, and the huge machine dipped into a gentle glide. All was still; nothing could be heard but the hissing of air streaming past the wings.

"Hold tight!" ordered Koch in a loud voice as the glider touched down. The glider careened off a stone wall, spun clockwise, and broke in two, coming to a full stop in a cloud of dust.[1]

There was a moment of stunned silence. Then the occupants emerged through the broken fuselage, their weapons at the ready. With Koch landed the headquarters staff of the First Battalion of the assault regiment. It was 7:15 A.M., fifteen minutes before zero hour.

No sooner had Walter Koch stepped out of the smashed craft than he realized that his glider had come to rest in a huge hollow. He saw the trajectory of tracer bullets from the New Zealand positions pass harmlessly overhead. The troopers from his glider immediately took defensive positions at the rim of the hollow.

Koch looked about him and was surprised at the hilly terrain surrounding the landing site. Air reconnaissance had not disclosed the existence of so many hills. This created an immediate problem. It had been planned that the glider troops land as complete fighting units ready to be led into battle. Now Koch saw the gliders of his group disappear over the summits of many hillocks, landing in other hollows. The troopers of each glider lost visual contact with each other. Koch ordered runners to be dispatched to contact the troopers of the other gliders in his group. They were to assemble at his glider, which would serve as a temporary command post. While he waited for the troopers to arrive, he followed the flight of the other gliders coming in for landings.

He winced as he saw one glider plummet to earth minus its tail section, which had been severed by a direct hit from a Bofors gun. It dropped like a rock, and not a single trooper emerged from the wreckage after it hit the crest of a nearby hill.

Some gliders came in too high. One of these banked very sharply in its descent; its wing dipped low and struck the rocky prominence of a hill. It cartwheeled several times, until the wing crumbled and the fuselage smashed itself against a grove of olive trees. The glider's occupants were strewn along the trail of its fatal path; some lay dazed, but most were killed on impact.

Another glider floated down with its nose up and tail down. It hit the rocky ground, and the fuselage split into two parts, spilling its live cargo. Despite the shock of impact, the surviving troopers quickly emerged with their weapons, ready to enter combat.

Still another glider dropped down into a clearing of the valley. Striking the ground with force, it shot forward between two olive trees, shearing off its wings. The fuselage bolted onward until it smashed into a stone wall. A few survivors emerged dazed from the broken remnants of the glider.

However, most gliders did succeed in landing intact on the rocky terrain of the lower slopes, but they were too dispersed to form a cohesive fighting unit. Koch waited impatiently while his runners sped off to guide these men to his command post.[2]

Nine gliders of eighty men together with the skeleton staff of the assault regiment dropped exactly on target into the dry riverbed of the Tavronites. This assault detachment was under the command of Major Walter von Braun. He landed at the exact moment that Koch touched down on Hill 107. While Koch waited for his men to assemble, Von Braun turned to seize his objective—the Tavronites bridge.

The paratroopers of the Von Braun group came under the immediate fire of D Company of the Twenty-second New Zealand Battalion, entrenched on the eastern bank of the river, south of the bridge. Captain T. C. Campbell, the company commander, ordered his men to concentrate a withering fire on the glider troops. The deadly stream of bullets from the defenders tore into the canvas-covered fuselages of the gliders as they attempted to land, taking a fearful toll of the attackers. Major von Braun was one of the first to be killed while still seated in his glider.[3]

The members of the assault regiment's headquarters staff withdrew under heavy fire to the western bank of the Tavronites, and sought shelter in the nearby village of Roponiana to await the outcome of the battle.

The Germans pressed their attack. Using the steep riverbank for shelter, they fought stubbornly until they reached their objective. Once the bridge was within their grasp, they attacked the few New Zealanders who held the western end. The stout resistance put up by the isolated defenders was quickly overcome. With a rush, the attackers raced across the double span, removing any demolition charges.

Lieutenant Wulff von Plessen's gliders came over the northern coast of Crete, swung in a wide semicircle, and approached the landing site from the south. That brought them in behind the New Zealand antiaircraft positions. Nevertheless, the gliders of this attack force did not escape the New Zealander's defensive fire unscathed.

One glider was hit by tracer bullets while still in flight, setting it on fire. The stricken craft fell to the ground, enveloped in flames and black smoke, roasting the troopers still inside. Some fell or jumped out, their uniforms in flames as they plummeted to their death.

As another glider came to a stop it was hit point-blank by a British Bofors gun firing at zero elevation. The glider disintegrated, flinging bodies and parts of bodies in all directions.

The rest of the gliders landed successfully, and immediately the glider troops focused their automatic fire on the crews of the antiaircraft guns. Most of the men manning these Bofors guns had only pistols with which to defend themselves, and even these weapons were short on ammunition. Their defensive fire was no match for the well-armed glider troops of Von Plessen's detachment. Those gunners who were not killed outright had no alternative but to surrender to the Germans.

Having achieved his initial objective, Von Plessen ordered his men to advance against the western perimeter of the airfield. The Bofors crews may have been ill-armed, but it was a different story with the New Zealanders defending the airfield.

Leaving the protection of the undulating sand dunes, Von Plessen's men now entered an exposed position. They immediately ran into the blistering fire of C Company of the Twenty-second New Zealand Battalion, which was covering the northwest perimeter of the airstrip. The Germans were caught in the open, in a crossfire between C Company's 15th and 13th platoons. Von Plessen's men took to ground with heavy casualties. Even the arching fire from the crest of Hill 107 found targets in Von Plessen's troops. There was no choice; he ordered a withdrawal.

He decided to follow the Tavronites riverbed upstream and make contact with Von Braun's men. As he rose to signal his men, a burst of fire tore him in two. Von Plessen fell dead. The young medical officer attached to this assault group, Oberarzt Doktor Weizel, assumed command of the detachment. He was the only surviving officer.[4]

Once again the objective had been gained, but the heavy casualties in officers and men turned it into a costly achievement.

While the Von Braun and the Von Plessen detachments were meeting their fate, on Hill 107 Major Walter Koch was still waiting for the men of his detachment to gather at his command post.

Koch looked impatiently at his watch. At 0730 hours, the Third Assault Battalion of the assault regiment was scheduled to drop in the Pirgos-Platanias area, east of the airfield and Hill 107. It was to cut off a major segment of the important northern road, thus securing the eastern approach to the airfield. According to the timetable, Koch and his detachment of glider assault troops were to have captured and secured Hill 107 by the time the Third Assault Battalion of paratroopers had gained its objective.

The minutes were passing quickly. Only twenty-five troopers had assembled at Koch's command post. Of the 150 men of his detachment, only a handful had been able to gather. The rest had been killed during the landings or had landed too far away from the target site.

At the base of the northeastern slope of Hill 107 and running south on the eastern flank of the hill, there was a dirt road called the Xamoudokori. This road ran parallel to the dried-up

Sfakoriako River, which was no wider than a stream. Across the Xamoudokori road, on its eastern side, were the gently ascending slopes of many vineyards. Called Vineyard Ridge, this was the defense position of the Twenty-first New Zealand Battalion.

The battalion's observers easily spotted the men of Koch's second group of glider troops clustered on the northeastern slope of Hill 107. They immediately concentrated a heavy barrage of mortar and machine-gun fire on that slope.

The Germans were now enfiladed, receiving fire from their front and from their flank. Within the first hour of battle, this group ceased to exist as a cohesive fighting unit: they were decimated; it was each man for himself.

On the southwestern side of the same hill, Major Koch heard the din of battle and assumed that the second group from his detachment was attacking up the northeastern slope. He could not wait any longer for the stragglers of his own group; he decided to attack with the handful of men available.

With the twenty-five men and officers of his battalion staff, he pushed off toward the summit of Hill 107. The first objective they encountered was the RAF tented encampment on their side of the slope. The attack was originally planned to be a surprise, hoping to capture the occupants in their cots. But there was no surprise—the camp was empty.

"One less problem," remarked Koch. "On toward the summit!" he ordered, enthusiastically waving his men forward. Forward and up they charged—only to be met by another wall of blistering small-arms fire from the entrenchments of the New Zealanders defending the hill.

These New Zealanders of the Twenty-second Battalion were satisfied that they had contained the German assault from the northeastern slope, and now they turned their fire on the enemy approaching from the southwest. It was a cruel concentration of machine-gun and rifle fire. Again the Germans were caught in the open; officers and men dropped along the whole slope. Some were killed; others fell badly wounded. The survivors sought to find the slightest depression in the ground for shelter. They could not move forward nor could they retreat. They were pinned down.

In a hollow behind a bush lay Major Walter Koch. Three bullets had pierced his body, severely wounding him. The hero of Eben Emael had come to Crete to receive almost mortal wounds on the rock-strewn terrain of Hill 107.[5]

The central prong of the attack had been dented. The airfield, with its commanding high ground of Hill 107, remained in the hands of the New Zealand defenders. In the first hour of battle the Germans had been dealt a serious setback.

The eastern jaw of the huge nutcracker that was to crush the defenders of Maleme airfield was represented by the Third Assault Battalion of the assault regiment under the command of Major Otto Scherber.

The six hundred paratroopers of this battalion were being flown to their target by fifty-eight transports. Their assigned objective was the capture of the area between the village of Pirgos, located east of Maleme, and the village of Platanias, a few miles farther east along the northern coast road. Once landed, the paratroopers were to consolidate, secure their objectives, and then advance against the airstrip, attacking from the east.

The enormous black transports flew over the Gulf of Kisamos, the hills of the Rodopos Peninsula, and the blue waters of the Gulf of Khaniá. They flew a west-to-east course parallel to the north coast of Crete. As they came abreast of the village of Maleme, they made a ninety-degree starboard turn and headed inland.

The transports crossed the coastline in elements of three to five aircraft per group, flying in tight formation at the low altitude of 500 feet. The air groups extended from Maleme in the west to the island of St. Theodore off Platanias village in the east. The pilots of this flight had been instructed at their briefing to release the paratroopers before crossing the coastline in order to concentrate the assault on the beaches north of the coast road. But the pilots of the lead transports feared that premature release of the paratroopers might accidentally drop them into the sea. They decided to delay the drop until the sandy beaches of the northern coast had been crossed.

As soon as the great black iron birds crossed the shoreline, all the antiaircraft guns from Pirgos to Platanias opened up. One transport blossomed into a huge orange fireball, both plane and paratroopers disappearing in the smoke and debris. Another transport swayed side to side, out of control, with only two paratroopers jumping from the plane before it tipped over into a perpendicular dive, ending in a loud explosive roar as it struck a terraced hillside.

Yet the transports continued on their flights as if nothing had happened. The fire from the defense positions increased in intensity as 20-mm and 40-mm Bofors guns barked, releasing a furious hail of incendiary and tracer bullets on the huge targets flying over them. The tight formation of transports was now scattering and rapidly losing its cohesion as a strike force.

Another transport, black smoke gushing from its port engine, tried to no avail to steady itself until the paratroopers were released. Rapidly engulfed in flames, it fell into the sea with most of its paratroopers still aboard.

The remaining transports continued onward, descending to a height of 400 feet, with all engines throttled back to reduce speed. Slowing the aircraft would allow the paratroopers to land closer together. However, this reduction in airspeed delighted the crews of the Bofors guns. The transports were like sitting ducks; and now the roar of heavy antiaircraft fire was augmented by the lighter, more rapid staccato sound of machine guns. Dropping to an altitude of 400 feet protected the transports from the devastatingly accurate fire of the three-inch antiaircraft guns, which could not be depressed to fire below 500 feet, but the Bofors guns poured a continuous stream of lead at the targets, until their barrels glowed red from overheating.

Four hundred feet was also the predetermined altitude for the paratroopers to jump. From this height, it would take a paratrooper only fifteen seconds to reach the ground.

It was obvious to the officers and NCOs that the assault battalion had passed its assigned drop zone. Major Otto Scherber, the commanding officer of the battalion, flying in the lead plane of the second group of five transports, left his seat and approached the cockpit.

"When the hell are you going to drop us?" he yelled impatiently at the pilot over the roar of the motors.

He did not know that some of his company commanders had instructed their pilots to fly farther inland in order to avoid the dense antiaircraft fire. He knew only that the paratroopers were getting uneasy with each passing moment, and that this delay in minutes seemed like hours. They were eager to jump and meet the foe face-to-face.

Finally the signal to jump was given. It was now 7:35 A.M. The battalion was five minutes behind in its time schedule.

First Lieutenant Werner Schiller made an uneventful descent from his aircraft. His transport had discharged him and his "stick" of men over a quiet sector. As he floated to earth, he studied the terrain below him. It was unfamiliar; not a single landmark resembled the objectives discussed during their briefing. He came to the realization that they had been dropped too far off course. In the distance, about four miles to the west, he noticed the smoke that hung like a low dark pall over the airfield at Maleme.

He cursed the transport pilots for deviating from the set course. They had tried to skirt the heavy antiaircraft fire that struck them as they crossed the north coast of Crete. As a result, Lieutenant Schiller and his parachutists were dropped too far to the east. In fact, his whole company had been too widely dispersed and it would be a problem to assemble them. He resigned himself to this stroke of bad luck, as his chute floated into the village of Platanias. Platanias was the headquarters of the Fifth New Zealand Brigade.[6]

Modhion, a village about one mile south of the north coast road and lying midway between Maleme and Platanias, had become the landing ground for scores of parachutists of the 10th Company of Scherber's Third Assault Battalion.

It was at this village that the New Zealanders had established a divisional Field Punishment Center for errant Creforce troopers. Apprehensively watching the approach of the German bombers earlier that morning, Lieutenant W. J. T. Roach, the CO, had ordered his sergeant to have the prisoners taken under guard to the dugouts provided for protection from air attacks.

Few bombs fell in the area of the detention camp, but tactical dive-bombers did concentrate on the bridge just outside the town on the south road. On the heights around the bridge and overlooking the flat-roofed houses of Modhion, the New Zealand engineers had established their defense positions. Into the center of this small village floated the parachutists of the 10th Company.

Almost from the first appearance of these ill-fated parachutists, a heavy concentration of small-arms fire echoed over the rooftops and into the hills and orchards of the surrounding countryside. The machine guns, dug into ground emplacements, picked off the paratroopers as they landed. Riflemen, too, took careful aim before firing. There were dead Germans wherever the eye could see.

One German fell into a grape arbor. While still struggling to get out of his parachute harness, a few rifle rounds were fired at him. He hung limply from his harness. Gunner McDonald, from the artillery battery protecting the Modhion bridge, walked up to the German. He felt that the parachutist was faking death.

"You'd look at me like that, you bastard, would you?" And he emptied his weapon into the German.[7]

Lieutenant Roach watched the paratroopers as they descended in the area south of his camp. He ordered his prisoners released and issued them all his available weapons. Then, taking his place at the head of the column of prisoners to lead them into battle, he gleefully remarked, "Let's go headhunting for bloody Huns."[8] Replenishing their arms and ammunition from the enemy dead, the men from the New Zealand prison camp celebrated their newly won freedom with a "turkey shoot." These sixty prisoners succeeded in killing over 110 Germans during the next few hours.

Many German paratroopers landed in the town square of Modhion. Before they had a chance to reach the canisters containing their weapons, they were set upon by the townspeople.

Disregarding the danger from bullets fired by the New Zealanders, Cretan civilians, both men and women, charged out of their homes and fell upon the paratroopers. Fighting furiously in defense of their homes, they struck the enemy with scythes, axes, hoes, and spades—anything they could use as a weapon.

It was an unbelievable sight to behold. One New Zealand machine-gun squad stopped firing at the Germans in order to watch a group of civilians pursuing six Germans in the town square. Only when another parachutist fell within a few feet of their machine gun did the New Zealand gunners return to the business at hand.

Four Germans racing toward a white-parachuted canister were met by a volley of fire from two old men. The four paratroopers fell victim to bullets fired by two ancient flintlocks captured from the Turks a half-century earlier.

When the two old men disappeared to reload, three other parachutists made their way to the same weapons canister. Instantly five adults and a child charged them with hoes and axes. Two women of this group fought one paratrooper; the three men quickly dispatched the other two troopers and turned to assist the women. No assistance was required, for the luckless victim lay motionless at their feet.

The Germans paid a heavy toll at Modhion. Of the total complement of the 10th Company, more than 60 percent were killed or wounded. This high casualty rate was partly due to the furious fight put up by the villagers. But these heroic people were to pay a heavy price in retribution in the days ahead.[9]

Major Otto Scherber, the commanding officer of the Third Assault Battalion, was the first man to jump from his aircraft. No sooner had his pink parachute opened and its oscillation stopped than he surveyed the many other chutes that filled the sky. In one quick dissatisfying glance, he realized that his battalion was in trouble. Scattered over a total of four miles, they would be too far apart to support each other as a concentrated attack force.

Halfway down, Scherber became aware of a greater danger. The heavy concentration of antiaircraft fire from the Bofors guns had shifted from the departing transports to the descending paratroopers. To the syncopated boom of the Bofors was now added the staccato bark of machine guns and the hollow crack of rifle fire. The sky was filled with the crisscross trajectories of tracer bullets. The German paratroopers had become the targets of another turkey shoot.

The delay in releasing the paratroopers over their original drop zones had brought them further inland—right over the defense positions of the Twenty-third New Zealand Battalion.

As the parachutists floated toward earth, they came within easy range of rifle and pistol fire. Major Scherber had only one object in mind: to land quickly and rally the men who had survived the descent.

From a height of fifty feet, he realized that he was dropping near a command post. Under some trees below him, he noticed a huge open-sided tent, men around it firing upward in all directions. Scherber removed his pistol from its holster. In the direct path of his descent, he saw a New Zealander crouching behind a half-fallen rock wall. As he dropped closer, observing the enemy to be a sergeant, Scherber raised his pistol to fire at him, but the New Zealander turned and fired in Scherber's direction. His bullets struck the German in the body and his pistol fell from his hand. Scherber struggled in the throes of death and then went limp as his body finally touched earth. He lay still where he had fallen, his parachute enveloping him like a death shroud. The commander of the Third Assault Battalion was dead.

The New Zealander, Sergeant Ray Striker, realized that he had killed a German officer.[10] He ran to Scherber's side and detached a map case from the German's belt. It might contain information of some importance. With the case neatly tucked against his chest, he turned and headed for the buff-colored, open-sided tent located in an adjacent field, headquarters of the Twenty-third New Zealand Battalion.

When Sergeant Striker reached the tent, he found the staff officers busily shooting at the paratroopers dropping all around them. At the front of the tent, the sergeant recognized the commanding officer of the Twenty-third Battalion, Lieutenant Colonel D. F. Leckie, who was firing his pistol at a group of paratroopers. The CO stood right in the open, issuing orders and firing simultaneously. In just a few minutes, he had fired his pistol five times—killing five paratroopers.[11]

It was obvious that the colonel was too busy to be bothered.

The Cretan and New Zealand defenders were exacting a heavy price from the Germans. In less than two hours after the first paratrooper of the Third Assault Battalion had touched Cretan soil, these elite German soldiers had ceased to exist as a fighting unit. Of the 600 men who comprised Major Scherber's battalion, more than 400 were killed or wounded in the first hour of battle. The remainder survived as scattered, isolated units seeking relief from the debacle. Of 126 paratroopers from one company of this battalion—which had landed between Cretan defenders on one hill and New Zealanders on the other, in the village of Gerani just north of Modhion—only fourteen survived.

When nightfall came, the remnants of the 9th Company of the Assault Battalion fought their way westward in order to reach their own lines somewhere behind the Tavronites River. They were the sole survivors of Otto Scherber's assault battalion. To the survivors of this day's battle, "it was like a terrible dream!"[12]

13

"IT WAS MAGNIFICENT, BUT IT IS NOT WAR"

MAY 20, 1941

The first group of nine gliders, commanded by Captain Gustav Altmann, swept silently toward the Akrotiri Peninsula. As they descended toward this rugged, rock-strewn terrain that resembled the profile of a human skull, they were exposed to intense antiaircraft fire. Three gliders were totally wrecked when they smashed against the rocky hills and stone walls that ran the length and breadth of the peninsula.

Captain Altmann gathered the survivors of his scattered force, and they advanced on their first objective—the nearby antiaircraft batteries.[1]

When Altmann and his men arrived, they were surprised to find the gun emplacements empty. There were no guns and no gun crews. In place of guns, there were wooden logs. The batteries were dummies—the Germans had been fooled.

General Freyberg watched these gliders during their descent. They were not too far from his headquarters. He turned to his chief of staff and issued a terse order to attack them.

The Northumberland Hussars were sent out on this search-and-destroy mission. Moving rapidly on foot and with tracked Bren-gun carriers, which resembled miniature tanks, the British rushed to meet the invader.[2]

Altmann's force was too dispersed to offer a concerted resistance in the face of the Hussars' determined counterthrust. In a matter of a few hours, half of Altmann's men were killed or wounded. The remainder were captured or had to surrender when their ammunition was spent. They never had the opportunity to undertake the second phase of their mission—the seizure of Freyberg's headquarters.[3]

South of the city of Khaniá, the second group of assault gliders landed safely and precisely on target—the gun emplacements of the 234th Heavy Antiaircraft Battery at the crossroads of the Mournies-Khaniá road. This group of five gliders was commanded by a scholarly, English-speaking officer, First Lieutenant Alfred Genz. His group originally had six gliders, but one had been lost at sea during the flight.

Once his group landed, Oberleutnant Genz led his fifty men in an attack on the crews of the antiaircraft battery. The gun crews had no weapons whatsoever with which to defend themselves; they were no match against the well-armed Germans.

Some of the gun crews were still hiding in the slit trenches that had protected them from the earlier aerial bombing. The Germans found them there and machine-gunned them where they lay. Of the 180 men comprising the battery's gun crew, 173 were killed and the surviving 7 fled to the hills.[4]

Genz and his men now turned their attention to their second objective, the powerful wireless station located to the south. At the turn of the Mournies road, they ran into stiff rifle fire from the vineyards on their left. The firing increased in strength, pinning the Germans down; their advance had come to a halt.

A small force of Royal Marines from the nearby Suda garrison was putting up a strong defense against Genz's men. In a sharp counterthrust of shouting men wielding their bayonets freely, the Royal Marines pushed Genz and his men back to their starting point—the antiaircraft battery. There the Germans remained pinned down for the rest of the day, with increasing casualties, as steady fire picked them off one by one.

It was to remain that way until nightfall, when Genz and his survivors would make an effort to escape through the encircling British lines. Lieutenant Genz's major objective—the powerful radio station—remained untouched and still in British hands.[5]

The transports carrying the First Battalion of paratroopers from the Third Regiment of the Airborne Division approached the area called Prison Valley intact.

The island's prison colony lay one mile south of the village of Galatas and three miles west of Khaniá. It was composed of several oblong one-story buildings in a huge clearing.

From the rolling hills around Galatas a broad, undulating plain swept southward five miles toward the foothills of the White Mountains, its cultivated fields intermittently broken by the darker hues of vineyards, olive groves, and orchards. The huge expanse of land was bounded on its eastern side by a dirt road that descended southward from the heights of Galatas and ended in the village of Alikianou. From Alikianou another dirt road stretched to the western side of the plain to Aghia, a village nestled on the shores of a small lake that served as the reservoir for the entire area. This whole plain was called Prison Valley.

The First Battalion of paratroopers had flown southward across the northern coast of Crete; then they circled counterclockwise, approaching their objective from the south. In this way, once the men had been dropped, the troop carriers could continue on their northern course, returning to their respective airfields on the Greek mainland to prepare for their subsequent assignments.

As the JU-52's carrying the First Battalion approached the objective, the hooters in each plane sounded the "get ready" signal. Captain Friedrich von der Heydte, the commanding officer, had awakened moments before. Now he prepared himself for his parachute jump into combat.

He placed his steel helmet on his head and gave a final check to his harness straps, casting a quick glance at the faces of the men in his transport. Only his batman and sergeant were familiar to him; the rest were all new. By their smiles, he was satisfied that they would do what was expected of them. Even Max Schmeling was smiling now.

At a given signal, the fifteen men in the transport stood up in single file facing forward and hooked their static lines to a wire that ran the length of the aircraft. The transport's low hatch was now opened, and Captain von der Heydte stood poised at the door. True to the dictates of the paratroop manual, as battalion commander he would be the first to jump. Von der Heydte felt the rush of air strike him full in the face, taking his breath away momentarily. He looked up at the blue sky above and at the green fields rushing rapidly past below. The great black shadows of the transports, fleeting across the landscape, reminded him of ominous birds of prey ready to swoop down on a victim. His thoughts were interrupted as a dispatcher shouted over the roar of the engines, "Get ready!"[6]

Von der Heydte's knuckles blanched as his hands tightened on the grabirons at each side of the open hatch. The rest of the men stood anxiously behind him. There was no talking now— just the silence of nervous tension, broken only by the roar of the engines and the whistle of the wind as it swept past the open hatch.

The dispatcher dropped his arm—the signal to jump.

The battalion commander dived into empty space. It was like diving into a swimming pool, except that instead of water, hard earth rushed up menacingly to meet him. The force of the wind tore at his face, distorting his cheeks and roaring in his ears.

Suddenly he felt a tremendous snap that pulled his harness straps backward and up. It was as if some huge hand had grabbed him by the shoulders, stopping his free fall instantaneously with a force strong enough to knock the breath out of his lungs.

Now his rapid fall was quickly replaced by a smooth, slow descent. Breathing normally again, he looked up to see a great pink silk canopy billowing above him like a protective angel.

It took Von der Heydte fifteen seconds to reach earth. He unhooked his parachute and quickly gazed into the sky, now filled with hundreds of parachutes, the pink parachutes of the officers and the black chutes of the lower ranks. Here and there he spotted the yellow parachutes bearing canisters of medical supplies. Typical of his concern for his men, Von der Heydte had the fleeting thought that now Schmeling could report to the medical officer, if he still felt ill.[7]

His battalion sergeant-major had landed nearby and immediately dispatched a group of paratroopers to a canister floating to earth below a white parachute. It contained rifles, machine guns, and ammunition.

Throughout the whole valley south of the prison complex, the men of the First Battalion landed unscathed, meeting little or no resistance.

Also in the First Battalion, Private First Class Kreindler, as the ranking noncom in his aircraft, was the first to jump. He half-squatted by the open hatch and waited for the signal. The delay in jumping added to his tension. He watched the rush of landscape below him; he saw the mirrorlike reflection of Lake Aghia on the left, and the white buildings of the prison complex below him.

"Why the delay in jumping?" he thought.

His anxiety increased when white puffs appeared in the sky before him. He could not hear the sound of the detonations over the roar of the motors, but he knew it was enemy antiaircraft fire. The transport slowed and descended to a height of 400 feet. Nearby flak bursts caused the aircraft to lurch just as the dispatcher gave the signal to jump.

Kreindler dived out into space, followed by his buddy Karl Schoerner. The thirteen other men of this "stick" followed in sequence.

When his black chute opened above him, Kreindler was jolted upright and he swayed rhythmically side to side as he descended toward earth. He looked about him and spotted his friend Schoerner floating to his left. Schoerner waved to him.

In the fifteen seconds it took Kreindler to float to earth, he became aware of yellow and orange streaks of light arching up toward him. He recognized the danger and his heart skipped with alarm. Those streaks were tracer bullets. The enemy on the ground was shooting up at him and his men. Bullets streaked past Kreindler with a snapping sound; some made a solid thump as they buried themselves in the bodies of parachutists. One or two already had been killed and hung limply in their harnesses. Kreindler was horrified at the thought that he made such a perfectly defenseless target in his slow descent. Fifteen seconds seemed like fifteen minutes. He had only 200 feet to go!

Incendiary bullets hit Schoerner's parachute, igniting it. The parachute began to smolder. If only he could reach ground before it was too late, thought Kreindler.

Schoerner began to descend at a faster rate. The rush of air fanned the smoldering silk into a flame. One by one the parachute risers began to snap. Schoerner's face was frantic; he looked to Kreindler for help. Kreindler pulled on his own risers in an effort to alter his direction. If he could swing to his left, he might put himself into position to grab Schoerner as he dropped past him.

Kreindler was still tugging at his risers, completely oblivious to the increased whip of bullets flying past him, when he glanced up to give Schoerner a hopeful sign. All he saw was the burning remnants of a chute, floating off into space; a figure dropped past him, just beyond his reach. It was Schoerner, with that look of frantic terror still in his eyes, falling 150 feet to his death.[8]

The staccato beat of gunfire echoed over the hills from the Galatas area. Von der Heydte's executive officer looked at him apprehensively, but the battalion commander smiled.

"It is a relief to hear the sound of fighting," he said. "It is at least a token that we are not alone in this hostile land."[9]

It was now 7:40 A.M.

While the battalions of Colonel Richard Heidrich's Third Parachute Regiment were still descending into Prison Valley, the remaining two units of the First Assault Regiment were being discharged in the Maleme area. Eighty-seven JU-52s had ferried 1,300 paratroopers of the Second and Fourth Assault Battalions to their objective.

In perfect formation, without a single threatening burst of antiaircraft fire, the troop carriers released the parachutists. The sky filled with the multicolored blossoms of billowing umbrellas. It was a riveting sight for the villagers from Spilia, from Voukoulies, and from Kolimvari, on the northeastern corner of the drop zone. An awesome spectacle, it was frightening, yet beautiful.[10]

Major General Eugen Meindl jumped into the Battle of Crete with the paratroopers of the Second Assault Battalion.

Once he had landed, he issued orders that contact be made with all the units of his assault regiment. It was at this time that several bedraggled officers from the regimental staff that had been ferried to Crete in Von Braun's gliders arrived at Meindl's headquarters to report the death of Major von Braun and Lieutenant von Plessen.

Meindl had further disquieting news when he was informed that not a single wireless set had survived the descent. The major radio units, 200- and 80-watt transmitters, had been shattered on impact.

"Can you repair them?" Meindl asked his communications officer.

"Yes, Herr General," Oberleutnant Göttsche replied, "I will try to reconstruct one operable wireless from an assortment of parts available from the broken sets."

"Do your best—we must have communication with the other units!"[11]

A detachment of seventy-two German paratroopers fell in two groups at the eastern end of Kastelli, into the defense positions of the First Greek Regiment's A Battalion. Right from the start, the paratroopers were in trouble in their attempt to seize the village of Kastelli.

Many paratroopers succeeded in shedding their harnesses and raced for the canisters containing their weapons. The Greeks chased after them into the high grass. Hiding in irrigation canals and behind bushes, trees, and stone walls, the men of A Battalion followed the trail of each German like hunters stalking their prey. Each time a German was found, the Greeks fell on him with any weapon at hand. Bayonets, axes, curved Syrian knives, sticks, stones, and even bare hands became weapons to kill the enemy. In those eventful moments of conflict, the only sounds audible from the battlefield were the oaths of fighting men and the screams of the dying.

As the men of A Battalion killed paratroopers, they took their weapons. In no time at all, the poorly equipped Greeks had armed themselves with German pistols and machine guns and turned to fight the rest of the parachutists with their own weapons. The combatants were now more evenly matched.[12]

Certainly untrained and ill-equipped for combat against a foe disciplined in the regimen of modern warfare, these Cretans possessed certain innate traits the paratroopers lacked. They were a hardy lot who lived a primitive day-to-day life. Toiling the fields from sunrise to sunset beneath the searing-hot Cretan sun had steeled them to the hardships of life. To these men, fieldcraft and marksmanship were as natural as the breath of life.

Above all, the Cretans held one principle more sacred than life itself—their freedom. So it was of little surprise that these civilian soldiers of the First Greek Regiment should fight so fiercely against the elite of the German army.

In a matter of an hour, most of the paratroopers had been killed or wounded. Their CO, Oberleutnant Peter Muerbe, was among the slain. The survivors gathered in confused groups as the Greeks fired on them with their own weapons. The toll was heavy. Their only chance for survival was to fortify themselves within some nearby buildings and hold out until relief arrived.[13]

Led by a noncom, the survivors raced for a cluster of four stone houses that formed a rectangle surrounded by a stone wall. At a given signal, in twos and threes they retreated to these shelters. Bullets from Major Bedding's machine guns bit the dirt at their feet, but once inside, they bolted the doors and closed the shutters of each window. From cracks in the shutters and holes in the walls, the deadly muzzles of their own weapons emerged. In every direction, MG-34 machine guns, pistols, rifles, and tommy guns spit out flames at the Greeks.

The few Greeks who chased them were now caught in the open and cut down by a few bursts of fire. The surviving pursuers sought refuge behind a stone wall 100 feet away.

In a room in one of the stone houses, the paratroopers found four frightened civilians. It was the family of Spiro Vlahakis, which included the old man, his elderly wife, and their two grandchildren. His son was somewhere out front with the men of A Battalion.[14] In a murderous disregard for human life, one of the paratroopers fired a burst at them, killing them as they huddled fearfully in a corner of the dark room. Gefreiter Walter Schuster, who led this group, scolded the paratrooper for the needless slaughter. The paratrooper only shrugged his shoulders, replying nonchalantly, "Anyway, they would have been killed in the crossfire."

It became obvious that the Germans were well positioned behind the thick walls of these farmhouses. Their field of fire made an open approach impossible. The houses had been converted into a miniature fortress.

Major Bedding was satisfied to keep it that way. He was willing to keep them surrounded until they ran out of ammunition, food, and water.

"Let us wait them out," he advised the Greek regimental commander.[15]

But the Greek colonel was not pleased with this advice. Colonel Papademetrakopoulos spoke rapidly in Greek to his battalion commander: "Remember what I had said to you in the past? Now is the time to show these gentlemen that battles are won by men with brave hearts. Give the order!"

At a signal the Greeks rose up from behind the stone wall—on all four sides. Major Bedding was shocked to see the Greeks race across the open field toward the farmhouses. It was an old-fashioned do-or-die bayonet charge.

The Germans fired at them, but the Greeks swept forward yelling at the top of their lungs.

"What is that they are yelling?" Bedding asked.

"It sounds like—'Aeria,' " replied a New Zealand sergeant.

"Aera!" corrected the Greek colonel. "It is the battle cry of the Evzones!"

"These men are not Evzones, Colonel!" Bedding said sarcastically, remembering their lack of training. Evzones were special regiments in the Greek battle for independence, known for their valor and heroism.

"No, but they are Cretans—and this is their soil," the Greek commander answered angrily.[16]

Even intense German machine-gun fire could not stem the fury of the charge, and the Cretans reached the main buildings.

It was a heroic, almost miraculous feat. The Greeks seemed to defy the wall of lead that met them as the German bullets ate at their vitals. Some of them continued their forward momentum even after bullets struck their bodies—so great was their determination—until they fell dead. The field was soon covered with dead and wounded Greeks, but still the rest came rushing.

When they reached the houses, they smashed in the bolted doors and the shuttered windows and leaped into the muzzles of the German guns. Once inside, the frenzied Greeks fell on the Germans. The air was rent with groans, screams, and shrieks as men fought hand to hand.

It was a slaughter.

One by one the German guns were silenced. Slowly the Cretans emerged from the houses into the open air—smiling.

Eighteen German survivors walked out with their hands over their heads in surrender. As they emerged, a wounded Greek, one arm hanging at his side in shreds, lunged with his bayonet at a paratrooper—killing him. Now there were only seventeen.

Another Greek picked up a German tommy gun and pulled

back the bolt. Everyone knew what he was going to do, and the Greeks stood aside.

Just then Bedding stepped forward.

"Remember, Colonel, the rules of the Geneva Convention—these men are now officially prisoners of war."

The Greek colonel nodded his head, and the prisoners were reprieved. But Bedding did not trust the Greeks. Their blood was boiling, and their thirst for revenge had not yet been slaked.

Bedding ordered the seventeen German survivors to be placed in the Kastelli town jail for their own safety. To make certain, he ordered the men of his own advisory staff to stand guard over them.

When the survivors of A Battalion stood for roll call, Major Bedding looked upon them with admiration.

"It was magnificent," he commented to the Greek regimental commander, "but it is not war!"[17]

14

"THAT THE GERMAN SHALL NOT PASS!"

MAY 20, 1941

Colonel Howard Kippenberger, the commanding officer of the Tenth New Zealand Brigade, had begun his day as usual with the first light of sunrise. He completed the morning entry in his personal diary and went downstairs to the officer's mess for breakfast.

Kippenberger wondered if the meal served the lower ranks was as bad as his, when his attention turned to the roar of two ME-109 fighters, which raced back and forth machine-gunning everything that moved along the Khaniá-Alikianou road.[1] It was strange, he thought, that these two fighters should concentrate on such close ground strafing unless it was in support of . . . He never finished the thought, for no sooner had it crossed his mind that a shout went up. There above them swished four long-spanned gliders, heading northward, casting ominous shadows over the ground. Immediately thereafter, the sky filled with scores of trimotor transports. Amidst the roar of motors came the frightened screams of civilians and the alarmed shouts of soldiers. Men jumped from these low-flying transports, and soon the sky was filled with billowing parachutes strung out in all directions.

Kippenberger jumped to his feet, shouting, "Stand to arms!" and ran into his quarters. In his room he grabbed his Lee-Enfield rifle and his binoculars.[2] As a battle-wise veteran of the Greek campaign, he knew that an officer had a better chance of survival carrying a rifle rather than the official pistol. In his haste, he neglected his diary, which lay open on his desk. He was not to see it again for four years; it was returned to him by a Cretan girl after the war.

Rifle in hand, Kippenberger raced down the main road toward his battle headquarters. To the din of roaring aircraft was added another sound—the rising crescendo of rifle and machine-gun fire. He knew that the battle had begun.

Although short in stature, he quickly outraced the two communications men who had accompanied him. When he reached the pink stone house that served as his battle headquarters, he dashed up the path toward the entrance. A burst of machine-gun fire shook him as it cut the huge bush at his side, missing him by inches. Veteran infantryman that he was, Kippenberger quickly rolled into a hollow. Slowly and carefully, foot by foot, he crawled up the path to the house. Once within the safety of his command post, he found that his staff members were out shooting Germans. He was all alone.

From the side window, he spied the German who had shot at him hiding in the protective shadow of a huge cactus bush. Kippenberger could not get a clear shot at him from this position; he had to get closer. His ankle now began to hurt, and he realized that he must have injured it when he rolled down the embankment. Pain or no pain, he was determined to kill that German. He exited from a window on the opposite side of the house and stealthily worked himself to the rear of the building. This maneuver brought him behind the German. Taking careful aim, Kippenberger fired one shot, and the German fell dead with a bullet in his head.[3]

Colonel J. R. Gray, commanding the Eighteenth New Zealand Battalion, lost no time rounding up his men and hastening off in pursuit of the invaders. The order went out to men of all ranks in all capacities—including cooks and clerks—to pick up their weapons and go after the Germans. Colonel Gray led the pursuit through olive groves, over hills, and into valleys. Accompanying the battalion commander were his batman, his sergeant-major, and one of the clerks from the orderly room, Corporal Dick Phillips. As soon as Colonel Gray and his men reached the drop zone, they went to work in the deadly game of hide-and-seek.

Gray noticed a parachute hanging from a branch and shrewdly surmised that its former wearer must be close by. He saw a movement behind a cactus and fired at it with his rifle. (Like Kippenberger, Gray also felt safer behind a rifle than an officer's pistol.) When Gray approached the spot, his prey made a dash toward a weapon-filled canister. The colonel fired again, hitting the paratrooper in midair.

From behind an olive tree, a young paratrooper aimed and fired at him. The bullet passed unnoticed through Gray's sleeve while he spun and returned the fire, wounding the German. As the battalion commander was relieving the wounded youth of his pistol, Corporal Phillips, who was standing next to him, uttered a sharp cry of pain and fell to the ground with a bullet in his knee. Off to the left, behind some bushes, two paratroopers shot at them. Colonel Gray, the sergeant-major, and Private Andrews—the colonel's batman—all fired at once in that direction. Two Germans leaped up as the avalanche of lead hit them; they fell back dead.

Andrews took aim at another cactus bush.

"Steady," cautioned the colonel. "You might be shooting at one of our chaps!"

"No bloody fear," Andrews replied. He fired once and another German fell dead.[4]

Oberleutnant Werner Schiller was one of the many paratroopers who came down far from his designated drop zone. Being one of the first to be released from his transport, he landed farthest from the target, in the western outskirts of the village of Platanias, which was the headquarters of the New Zealand Fifth Brigade.

Once he had touched ground and discarded his parachute, he raced for the protection of some tall cactus bushes. He appeared to be alone, for not a single man from his "stick" of fifteen paratroopers was anywhere in sight.

He lay there motionless, cursing the transport pilots once again for scattering the unit over such a wide area. From the sound of rifle fire in the distance, he realized that his comrades were in a firefight. Carefully and methodically, he evaluated the situation; his only choice was to follow the sound of battle and join his men.

As he rose to leave, he heard a rustle in the branches of a tree to his rear. He turned sharply, pistol at the ready, only to come face to face with a paratrooper dangling from his parachute, his feet just inches off the ground. Schiller stood momentarily in horrified shock, staring into the glassy eyes of the dead trooper, whose chute was caught in the tree's upper branches. One neat bullet hole over the heart had brought a huge red smudge seeping through the dead man's jacket.

Werner Schiller turned away from his dead comrade, more determined than ever to make contact with the other members of his unit. Crouching in the shelter of an olive tree, he had the weirdest sensation that someone was watching him. He thought he saw movement, but before he could fire his pistol, he felt a sharp pain in his arm. Simultaneously, the force of the bullet spun him around, knocking him to the ground. Holding the wound tightly, he gasped with pain as blood plowed through his fingers and down his sleeve. He almost blacked out.

When he opened his eyes, he found himself staring into the muzzle of a rifle aimed by a huge man with wild, piercing eyes. He was not dressed as a soldier, but wore instead a black jacket, black trousers, and black boots; and his weathered face sported a thick moustache. Schiller did not realize that he was confronted by the pride of Cretan manhood—the heroic Kapetan.

The Cretan leaned over, picking up Schiller's pistol and

bandolier. His keen eyes never leaving the wounded man, he stuck the weapon into his trouser belt and threw the bandolier over his shoulder. He gave a fast glance at the dangling paratrooper and a longer stare at Schiller. The Cretan then counted the bullets in his belt and shook his head, as if to say that it was not worth wasting another bullet to kill this German.

With a quick step, the tall Cretan disappeared behind some bushes just as quickly as he had appeared.[5]

In a matter of a few hours, singly or in small groups, the scattered paratroopers of the 11th and 12th Companies of Major Ludwig Heilmann's Third Parachute Battalion of the Third Regiment were hunted, found, and killed or taken prisoner.

The third company of this battalion—the 10th Company—was destined to meet a similar fate.

They had been dropped on a promontory north of the main east-west road at a point east of where it is intersected from the south by the Alikianou-Khaniá road. This high ground had been selected by General Freyberg as the site for a major hospital station for all Commonwealth forces west of Khaniá. To this area the Creforce commander assigned the Seventh General Hospital with the Sixth Field Ambulance Unit attached.[6]

The Germans felt that this installation was tactically important and should be seized in the initial attack. The 10th Company of Heilmann's battalion was assigned to its capture. Strangely, this company was the only one in the battalion to be dropped on target.

Private George Denker had been painfully wounded in the right shoulder and, as a result, had been sent to the Seventh General Hospital for treatment. Throughout the remainder of the morning's bombing, he and the thirty other men assigned to this large rectangular tent lay on their cots. Denker was hoping that "they would all go away."

From his position in the shadows of the far corner, right against a canvas wall, Denker thought he heard guttural voices speaking German. Suddenly the flap flew open and a paratrooper carrying a tommy gun stuck his head in. He entered, followed by two other Germans.

Private Denker spied the Germans moments before the paratroopers' eyes could get accustomed to the darkness inside the tent. Rolling himself carefully off his cot, he eased himself beneath it and lay there motionless, hoping to escape detection.

The Unteroffizier (sergeant) ordered the men in the tent to be marched outside. Denker remained unobserved in the shadow of his hiding place. He lay there breathless, watching through a slit in the lower part of the canvas, as the Germans rounded up a large group of wounded. All in all, about two hundred patients were gathered in a field in front of the main hospital tent.

Lieutenant Colonel Plimmer, the medical commander of the hospital installation, surrendered to the Germans in the hope of protecting his patients. It was a fruitless gesture.

From a nearby tent, a smaller group of twenty wounded prisoners had been gathered. Watching closely, George Denker paled, and his heart skipped a beat when he saw a paratrooper open fire on the hapless group, killing them in one long burst. It looked as if the Germans did not intend to take any prisoners.

Colonel Plimmer ran up to a Feldwebel (class 2 warrant officer) and protested heatedly, shouting and flailing his arms. The German NCO looked at him disdainfully, raised his pistol and shot the colonel several times. The dead doctor fell back into a slit trench.[7]

The Germans of the 10th Company collected a total of 300 walking wounded. As the paratroopers stood with their tommy guns poised to fire, it became evident that they planned to execute them. An Oberleutnant approached the Feldwebel and, after a brief discussion, the prisoners were reprieved. They were marched down the slope of the hospital promontory, across the main northern road, and up the Galatas heights toward Galatas village, where the Germans hoped to make contact with the other units of their battalion.

The hospital prisoners were used as a protective screen by the advancing paratroopers of the 10th Company. But when the

Germans reached the outskirts of the village of Efthymi, the New Zealanders of Colonel Gray's Eighteenth Battalion were waiting for them. Gray was determined to do to them what he had done to the same battalion's 11th and 12th Companies. He was outraged when he discovered that the paratroopers were holding hospital wounded as hostages. His orders were brief and to the point: "Get them!"

In the firefight that followed, the Germans were picked off one by one or in small groups. Many hospital patients were also killed, but most of them made a break for freedom, while others helped the New Zealanders seek out the hunted paratroopers. Many of the Germans surrendered; those who fought were wounded or killed.[8]

The Second Battalion of Colonel Heidrich's Parachute Regiment had been assigned to capture the hilltop village of Galatas and the surrounding area. It was strategically obvious that once Prison Valley was occupied and Galatas and its heights were taken, the gateway to the capital of Crete would be open.

Major Wulf Derpa, commanding officer of the Second Paratroop Battalion, was one of the first of his unit to land. From the start, it was obvious to him that all was not well. The battalion had been scattered in the many hills that encircled the village like a ring. Two companies had fallen south of Galatas, while the third descended into the center of town.

Stabsfeldwebel Karl Neuhoff was the first sergeant of the company that came down in Galatas. When Neuhoff and his "stick" of fifteen men received the signal to jump from the transport, they dropped into a cauldron of pistol and rifle fire.

New Zealanders and Greeks stood in the village square shooting up at the descending paratroopers. Germans fell everywhere; some were dead before they touched the ground, and others were set upon the moment they landed.[9]

Private First Class Hans Kreindler landed with a heavy thud amid cacti and lay momentarily stunned. Although Kreindler was in the First Battalion, the delay in releasing his "stick" from the transport had brought him into the zone of the Second Battalion. The noise of pistol, rifle, and machine-gun fire filled his ears, and bullets snapped through the air. Once out of his harness, Kreindler glanced about for the men of his group and for the location of the nearest weapons canister. At that moment he felt a sharp sting on the back of his left hand, followed by another. His first thought was that he had been hit. Instead of blood on his hand, there were two huge welts. A big Cretan wasp was crawling up his sleeve. In its brush with a tree, his parachute had disturbed a hive, and the wasp stings were the first shots from their patrol! In minutes he was beset by other wasps. He rose and raced across the field, while bullets chewed the earth at his heels. He finally reached shelter behind some rocks near a farmhouse, where he was immediately pinned down by sniper fire.

Kreindler grumbled to himself. His first thought on landing had been to search for Schoerner's body, but enemy fire was now too heavy. From his position, he was able to observe soldiers running about, shooting and shouting. They did not sound English, and he wondered if they were Greek. Suddenly, from behind the farmhouse, he heard a yell: "Natos o diavolos!" Still shouting "Here is the devil!" a tall soldier charged with his bayonet. Kreindler was momentarily startled, but he quickly fired his Luger from the hip.

Kreindler had scored his first kill in battle, and the very thought of it, as he pushed the corpse away with his feet, chilled him. His position now exposed, he raced for a nearby stone wall, behind which two other paratroopers had set up a machine gun.[10]

Captain Emorfopoulos—or Captain E, as he was known to his men of the 6th Company of the Sixth Greek Regiment—was stationed in the Galatas area.

The Greek regiment was composed of green troops under the command of a veteran of the Balkan Wars, Lieutenant Colonel Gregoriou. Heavily shackled by the outmoded training of bygone campaigns, Gregoriou was totally inept in the practice of modern warfare. He had given his two battalion commanders, Major K. Moraites of the First Battalion and Major P. Papadakis of the Second, a free hand in deploying the men of the regiment. They had deployed their units in the hills to the south of Galatas, while a small reserve was kept in the village near the regimental headquarters.

The men of this regiment were numerically at battalion strength; however, these newly conscripted recruits were poorly trained and equipped, with little knowledge of the fundamentals of defense, and less of attack. Colonel Gregoriou placed the whole responsibility of his regiment's defense on the battleworthiness of his flanking allies—the Tenth New Zealand Brigade. Colonel Kippenberger, the brigade commander, thought little of the battle qualities of the Sixth Regiment and even less of Gregoriou. He was soon to be pleasantly surprised.

The commanding officer of the 6th Greek Company watched as the paratroopers descended into the rolling valley below his company's positions. Although alarmed, he appeared calm as he gave rapid and precise instructions to his platoon commanders. He ordered them to deploy their men amid the olive trees and high grass on either side of the field below Cemetery Ridge.

Captain E and his first sergeant were the only combat veterans in the whole company; both had fought in Albania during the early months of the Greco-Italian war. Emorfopoulos was worried about his newly conscripted men. (Although each had a rifle, ammuniton was in short supply.) He had no fears about their spirit or their will to fight, but he was very concerned by their lack of the most basic infantry tactics.

The Greeks could not help but admire the coolness with which the German paratroopers went about their business under fire. Once they reached the ground and removed their harnesses, they helped the other men of their groups and then ran for the weapons canisters. Armed with tommy guns and rifles, they joined the battle. While their comrades fell dead all about them, they carried on their routine almost with drillfield precision. It was unnerving and heroic. "If only my men were as well trained," thought the Greek captain.

That German training eventually made a significant difference. In time, the paratroopers' concentrated fire began to tell on the Greek soldiers. Slowly but surely, Captain E's men fell victim to German pressure, and they had to retreat to the wall that formed the southern boundary of the Galatas village cemetery. The untried Greek troops suffered many casualties in this firefight, but German losses were heavier. What concerned Captain E most of all, as his men entrenched themselves on Cemetery Ridge, was that they were short of ammunition.

The other two companies of the Second Parachute Battalion, which had fallen south of Galatas, were immediately ordered to attack the village. Major Derpa, the battalion commander, was short one paratroop company; it had been retained in Greece but was to follow later by sea. In its place, Derpa had been given two attached paratrooper companies with antitank guns. He ordered one company to advance toward Galatas from the east by way of Cemetery Ridge. The other would seize the high ground named Pink Hill and attack the village from the west.

Thus, one company of paratroopers was preparing to attack Galatas from the east, and Major Derpa was leading the other—the 7th Company—to a point west of the village. This attenuated column extended in double ranks on either side of the road that bisected the rising ground above Prison Valley, and worked its way westward. It was a forced march, and the going was foul. Once the road was left behind, the men had to hike through a maze of deep gullies, rocky ridges, and boulder-strewn, dried-up watercourses. With time of great essence, there was no resting. This company had to reach its point of attack quickly in order to coordinate its advance on Galatas with the other company's from the east.

Most of the men walked as if in a trance. With each step, their boots raised dust clouds in the wavy currents of the sun-baked air. The immediate enemy confronting the paratroopers of this company was neither the Greek soldier, the New Zealander, nor the Cretan civilian, but the scorching Cretan sun. The tropical heat was an enemy to be reckoned with; it was brutal.[11]

Rising thickly, the dust compounded their misery. It became an almost palpable barrier through which they had to thrust their sweating bodies. It settled quickly on their faces and hardened into a heavy crust that even made breathing difficult.

The standard paratroop uniform added to their problems. Designed for the cold air of northern continental Europe, it proved far too heavy for the Cretan heat. Uniforms clinging to their bodies like wet tissue paper, steel helmets like hot ovens baking their brains, the well-trained, well-disciplined Fallschirmjägers took these hardships in stride as they hiked to their destination.

When the men finally reached the hill west of Galatas, they were given a few minutes' respite. Some staggered off the trail and sought the shady shelter of the olive trees; others sat in their tracks, too exhausted by the heat even to drink the warm water from their canteens or to nibble on their rations. Still others found their compact food rations impossible to eat. The hard chocolate had become a brown mushy mix; just to lick it would add to the insatiable thirst that not even the warm canteen water could quench.

Finally Major Derpa ordered his company commander to begin the advance and occupy positions atop the vital hill. As the paratroopers formed a skirmish line, waiting for the signal to attack, they momentarily forgot the natural enemies of sun, heat, and dust and concentrated instead on the human enemy entrenched on the crest of the hill before them.

Stabsfeldwebel Karl Neuhoff, the company first sergeant who had earlier witnessed the destruction of his company as it dropped into the center of Galatas village, had succeeded, with some of the survivors, in reaching this company of paratroopers. He fell into rank and prepared to take part in the forthcoming attack.

Like the attackers of Pink Hill in the west, the paratroopers of the company attacking from the east marched off in an extended skirmish line. Slowly but deliberately they advanced up the ridge. There was no enemy fire, only a silence intermittently broken by the sharp commands of German officers and non-coms.

As the Germans passed the midway point of the hill without a shot being fired in opposition, they felt increasing tension. Now they took heart and, with an exultant yell of pending victory, raced for the cemetery wall. Then it happened.

From behind the wall, the men of the Sixth Greek Regiment popped up and opened fire. The whole German company was caught in the open, and the first blasts of rifle and machine-gun fire had a devastating effect. Men fell in all positions of instant death, the hail of lead cutting through their ranks as a scythe cuts through wheat. They sought shelter behind every available rock, bush, or hollow. Attempts to rise were limited by the crossfire from the ranks of the Nineteenth New Zealand Battalion on the right. The attack had been stopped in its tracks.

Unable to advance in the face of such withering fire and unable to remain in such an exposed position, the German company was ordered to withdraw. In groups of twos and threes, the stricken paratroopers retreated slowly down the ridge. They left half their company as casualties on the slope of the ridge.[12]

While Derpa's Second Battalion was fighting for its life in the hills around Galatas, southwest of Colonel Heidrich's command post, the Fallschirmpionier Bataillon—the attached engineer battalion under Major Liebach—was meeting heavy resistance in the attempt to capture its objective.

Where the southbound Alikianou-Khaniá road junctions with the road going west to the village of Aghia and its reservoir, lies the village of Alikianou. A small, nondescript collection of ten to twelve scattered white stone farmhouses settled amid the olive groves and citrus trees covering the foothills of the White Mountains, the village never had any claim to fame. In the ensuing days, however, it would take its place next to Galatas as the most important piece of real estate in Crete. Its seizure would secure the southern boundary of Prison Valley and simultaneously cut off any escape routes into the White Mountains. Alikianou was the objective of the German engineer battalion.

Defending the village and its surrounding hills were the raw recruits of the Eighth Greek Regiment, under the command of Lieutenant Colonel Peter Karkoulas. Colonel Karkoulas had deployed his first battalion, commanded by Major John Valegrakis, in the hills to the left of the village, while his second battalion, under Major George Vamvakis, protected the right flank. The regimental command kept a reserve force in the village itself to throw in if any breach occurred in the defense line.[13] Like the Sixth Regiment at Galatas, the Eighth had a complement of 800 men—approximately the strength of a battalion. It had only a small supply of ammunition and fewer rifles than men. This was the regiment to which Colonel Kippenberger had referred as "those malaria-ridden chaps," and whose defense positions he had dismissed as "just a circle on the map." The events that followed in the next few days changed his mind.

As soon as the engineer battalion concentrated its forces after the parachute drop, it set out to capture Alikianou. When the Germans reached the foothills leading to the village, they confronted withering fire from the men of the Eighth Regiment. The paratroopers scattered at first, but soon pressed on toward their objective. The Greeks continued to shower them with bullets, causing heavy casualties. Once the Greeks had used up their ammunition, they charged with bayonets. Charge followed countercharge, the Greeks even using rifles as clubs in hand-to-hand combat in their attempts to break the German attack.

Slowly but surely the Germans were pushed back to their original assembly line. One Greek bayonet charge advanced into the German command post before it was finally stopped. The ferocity of the Greek attack was unbelievable.

As the battle swayed back and forth across the hills of Alikianou, the Greeks were solving the problem of their weapons shortage. Each time a Greek killed a paratrooper, he took his dead foe's weapon and ammunition. After a few hours of battle, the Germans were startled to hear the familiar burp of their own P-40 tommy guns and the fast rattle of their own MG-34 machine guns firing into their own ranks.

Besides the fury of the Greek counterattacks, the Germans had to contend with the wrath of the Cretan civilians. Like the civilian population at Modhion, which had rushed out to attack the paratroopers in the town square, the residents of Alikianou raced from their houses and fell upon the Germans in a blind fury. Attacking the Germans singly or in groups and using anything at hand for weapons, they left scores of dead Germans in the fields around their village.[14]

The Greek regiment suffered severe casualties during the day's battle, casualties that included the regimental commander and most of his staff. But the spirit of their determination was such that from their hearts they shouted the battle cry: "That the German shall not pass!"[15]

The German engineer battalion finally withdrew from the attack, having suffered such heavy losses that Major Liebach decided to regroup and wait for reinforcements. He informed Colonel Heidrich of his plans to stand fast, stating that Alikianou "was strongly held by at least 4,000 Greeks, partisans, and British."[16]

His pride would certainly have been broken had he known that his attack had been repulsed by only a small group of ill-trained, ill-equipped but resolutely determined men of the Eighth Greek Regiment.

15

"WITH AXES, WITH SHOVELS, AND WITH THEIR BARE HANDS"

MAY 20, 1941

Crete represented several firsts in the early history of World War II. The airborne invasion marked the first time that any such military venture was launched without the supporting assistance of ground troops. It was also the first battle in which the civilian population stood shoulder to shoulder with Greek and British Commonwealth soldiers in the defense of the island-fortress. This brave resistance set the example for the guerrilla warfare that followed in later years in all the German-occupied nations.

Nicholas Manolakakis lived on his family farm in the hills between the villages of Spilia and Voukoulies. Like his father before him, Nicholas had been born and raised on this farm, had married a woman from a nearby village, and had three sons.

With the war on the mainland over and German troops occupying Greece, he didn't know whether his sons were alive or prisoners of war. He hid his pained concern and turned his attention to his youngest son, thankful that at least he was safe at home.

Nicholas Manolakakis was a man of habit. Each morning at sunrise, he would go out to his properties and there like all farmers in his time—and his father's time before him—he pruned the fruit trees, tilled the soil, repaired the fences, and collected the fruit. By 8:00 A.M. he returned to his home, hung his pruning sickle on the kitchen door, and sat with his wife for a brief morning repast of fresh bread, white goat cheese, and homemade wine.

From 9:00 A.M. until 1:00 P.M., he was back in the fields. When the sun reached its zenith, he returned home for lunch, followed by an afternoon siesta until 4:00. The late afternoon and early evening hours found him doing chores about the house. This was his life, day in and day out. But on May 20 the man of habit became a man of action.

On this fateful morning, Manolakakis returned from the fields earlier than usual. The thunderous sound of the heavy bombing to the northeast and the constant presence of German airplanes in the sky worried him.

As he ate his breakfast, he watched his son working in the field in front of the house, bundling the long thin branches that would serve as fuel for the oven fire. He smiled to himself proudly, wrinkling his sun-hardened face. His wife was doing her morning wash in an old wooden tub just outside the kitchen door.

The shadow of a low-flying aircraft momentarily darkened a path across the fields below. Young Manolakakis looked up and stood mesmerized, his mouth agape. Then, suddenly alert, he raced across the field toward the house, pointing upward and shouting in the high-pitched voice of a thirteen-year-old, "They're here, they're here!"

His father had heard the din of the transport, but it did not disturb him, for such aircraft had passed over him in the fields from early morning. The roar of its motor drowned out his son's shouts and muffled the report of a pistol shot.

Manolakakis watched as his son stumbled and fell forward on his face. Slowly he tried to rise, only to stagger a few feet and fall forward once again. This time he lay very still.

His mother uttered a cry and rushed to the boy's side. A muffled sob escaped from her lips.

The sharp report of a pistol again echoed through the morning air—more audible this time, since the passing aircraft's roar had diminished. The mother staggered, then fell near her son. Slowly and painfully, she crawled toward him and cradled his head in her lap. Then, gently slipping to her side, she, too, lay still.

Manolakakis watched with disbelieving eyes. "It isn't true," he thought to himself. "It is a bad dream." But there, descending before his very eyes, was the killer of his wife and son. In a rustling rush of wind, a German paratrooper, a pistol still in his hand, landed not more than ten feet from the front entrance to the house, the black canopy of his parachute following behind him.

Now Manolakakis was alert to the realization that this was no dream but a cruel reality. With the wide-legged stride of his huge frame, he charged out the front door, clutching in his right hand the only weapon within reach—his sickle.

The paratrooper had no chance to turn toward the sound of footsteps behind him. The sickle buried itself deeply in his back, at the base of the neck. He stood momentarily transfixed as if hung from a nail on the wall. When the blade was withdrawn, blood gushed from the triangular wound and the soldier crumpled soundlessly to the ground.

Manolakakis stared down at the dead German. Then, with tears welling in his eyes, he started toward his stricken wife and son. Hearing the same rush and rustle of wind, he turned and saw a portion of a parachute catch on the chimney at the back of the house, its wearer struggling to disengage himself from his harness. Thirsty for revenge, his blood racing with hate, Manolakakis ran to intercept him.

At the rear corner of the house, he came face to face with the second paratrooper. The German looked up at this towering specter of a wild man with hate-filled eyes and bristling black mustache. The sight was enough to startle any man. As the trooper pulled his pistol from its holster, Manolakakis swung his sickle in an upward stroke. Still coated with the blood of its first victim, the blade streaked upward with a hiss and it caught the paratrooper in the throat. Manolakakis' wrath was still not spent. He was poised to strike again when he heard that familiar hissing sound. There was another paratrooper, this one armed with a tommy gun, just fifty feet away. Having witnessed what the maddened Cretan had done to his two comrades, the German raised his automatic weapon to fire. In his haste to shoot Manolakakis, he neglected to unhook his parachute harness. It was a fatal mistake. As the paratrooper raised his weapon to fire, a brisk breeze filled the canopy of his parachute, pulling him off his feet. His shot missed. With catlike agility, the alert Manolakakis fell upon the German, his sickle striking repeatedly.

Now the field about him was filling with other paratroopers. Manolakakis took the dead man's machine gun and continued his one-man rampage. He fired short bursts at three paratroopers, killing them instantly. With a yell of hate, he charged like a crazed bull into the south field of his farm, where five other paratroopers had just reached the ground. He fired wildly, but the spray of bullets found their targets, and the men fell dead where they landed.

Two more paratroopers were dropping to earth. Manolakakis fired at them in single-shot bursts. The Germans kicked their feet wildly in their anxiety to reach ground quickly and escape the deadly bullets. But one by one the bullets struck home, and each man, in turn, hung limply in his harness. When these last paratroopers finally reached the ground, they were dead. Their parachutes, still filled with air, dragged them across the field. Manolakakis raced after them, emptying his last bullets into their bodies. He fired again and again until the weapon fired no more. Then all was still except for the slap of a parachute here and there, fluttering in the breeze.

Nicholas Manolakakis stood there for a long time, staring at the still forms lying in the fields in the various positions in which death had come to them. Finally, he returned to the bodies of his slain wife and son. Gently, with tender care, he picked them up and carried them into the house. He laid them on the master bed, folding their arms across their chests. He placed an icon between them, and at their heads he lit a holy light.[1]

On the morning of May 20, Manoli Paterakis found himself on the lower slopes of the White Mountains, south of the village of Gerani.

When the morning bombing had begun, he had reached the outskirts of Gerani, not far past Modhion. For an hour, he hid behind the twisted trees of an olive orchard as the whole area was subjected to the opening attack of the invasion. When the bombers left, the paratroopers arrived.

From where he stood, he could observe thousands of parachutes blossoming in the sky as far as he could see. He was fascinated by the panorama that passed before his eyes. So this is modern warfare? he thought to himself.

Suddenly, Paterakis awakened to the immediate danger. Raising his rifle, he fired quickly at a paratrooper. It was a young face that kept staring at Paterakis as it came closer. When his feet finally reached the ground, he crumpled in a heap, his dark parachute falling over him. The German was dead—his first one!

Some fifty feet away, another parachutist had just touched earth. Paterakis noticed an elderly couple approaching the German from the rear. They crept forward slowly, barefooted, each carrying a huge rock. Paterakis watched, wondering what the old man and his wife were up to.

The German turned suddenly and saw them. Just as he reached for his pistol, Paterakis fired a shot and the paratrooper fell.

"Be careful, old man," Paterakis cautioned, "he may be feigning death!"

To make sure, Paterakis fired two more times at the still body of the German. Now he was certain the man was dead.

"Can I take them?" asked the old farmer.

"Take what?"

"His boots—I need his boots," responded the old man, pointing to his own bare feet as his wife started unlacing the dead man's boots.

Paterakis nodded. What do these well-fed, well-clothed soldiers from a rich land want with poverty-stricken farmers like us? he thought. He started down the trail after the rest of the paratroopers.[2]

King George II had awakened early, as was his custom, on the morning of May 20. He dressed himself casually and stepped through the French doors separating his bedroom from the vine-covered terrace of the Volanis house. Leaning over the balustrade, he surveyed the countryside.

The view was the familiar scene of orchards filled with fruit trees, of olive groves, and of green-carpeted land rising to hilltops and dropping into the valleys beyond. It was a panorama of green offset by the deep blue sky of early morning. A cool, refreshing breeze drifted in from the north. The king took a deep, invigorating breath and thought to himself, Why must the ravages of war destroy this natural beauty?

The sky to the north over Khaniá was filled by a great dust cloud. To the east of Khaniá, the town of Suda, with its huge harbor of Suda Bay, was receiving its share of Luftwaffe attention this morning.

Thick black clouds rose hundreds of feet into the sky. The vessels in the bay still smoldered from earlier attacks, but the appearance of additional black clouds indicated that a new ship had been caught in the harbor and was burning. To the west. the dust and din over Maleme showed that the airstrip was also under attack.

Captain Basil Kiriakakis, the commanding officer of the forty gendarmes who served as the bodyguard to Prime Minister Tsouderos, stood on the terrace of the Volanis house and, through his binoculars, watched the fury of the aerial attack. Few planes passed over the villages of Perivolia and Malaxa; most of them were concentrating their attack on the region to the north from Maleme to Suda Bay.

The king and his prime minister were in conference over breakfast in the main room of the Volanis home. The massive stone structure of the house plus its location, cradled as it was in the foothills of the White Mountains offered some safety for the royal entourage. Yet Captain Kiriakakis still felt a danger existed; he wanted the king to go below into the wine cellar. One errant bomb from a passing plane could deprive the Greek people of their king and of their prime minister. But King George shunned the danger as too remote a possibility, preferring to continue his conference in the main room of the Volanis residence.

Colonel Blount, British liaison officer from Creforce Headquarters to King George, was now the senior officer in charge of the detachment of Royal Marines assigned to protect the royal party.

Blount watched in particular one black trimotor aircraft as it flew low over Perivolia, to the north.

From this transport, an object seemed to fall out and trail backward. Another followed. In seconds a whole string of them trailed each other obliquely, floating gently to earth. Shifting his binoculars to the other transports, he saw that they, too, were releasing paratroopers. He lowered his binoculars momentarily, blinked his eyes, and looked back into the sky—this time without the aid of the glasses. The sky was filled with multicolored parachutes descending from all directions. Blount quickly recovered from his surprise: "Paratroopers! By God, we're under paratroop attack! The invasion is on!" In rapid-fire order, he issued instructions to his executive officer: "Make plans to leave immediately!"

Colonel Blount returned to the terrace for a last glance. With his binoculars he followed the movements of the paratroopers in the countryside around Perivolia. From his position, he could see that the village of Pelikapina was swarming with Germans. Fate had been kind to the Greek king. Had the king returned to his home in Pelikapina the previous night as he wished, he would already have been a prisoner of war.

With that chilling thought in mind, he hastened to present himself to King George.

"Your Majesty, we must depart immediately! German parachutists have landed in the valley below us. They are only a mile or so away."

Prime Minister Tsouderos was not worried. He placed his official papers in a briefcase, put on his jacket, made certain that a few personal belongings had been packed in keeping with instructions to his personal valet, and then descended to the main room. Seating himself in a comfortable armchair, he waited quietly for the moment of departure.

The Greek king seemed even less concerned. Much to Colonel Blount's anxiety, the king hurried out the front door of the Volanis house with his uncle, Prince Peter, accompanying him through the front garden. At the garden wall, they stared in disbelief at the surrounding countryside. Wherever they looked there were paratroopers.

Prince Peter, pistol in hand, stood beside the king, shaking his head. King George realized the imminent danger: "Blount was right, we must leave."[3]

King George reappeared soon after, dressed in the full regalia of a field marshal of the Greek army. On his head he wore the officer's cap with its royal crest, while his left breast was emblazoned with multiple lines of colorful decorations. Pistol at his side and baton in his hand, the king signaled that he was ready to depart.

Finally the king, his prime minister, and the whole entourage—which also included the British ambassador, Sir Michael Palairet, and his wife—began a harsh trek, amid the din of aircraft above and battle in the valley below. It was a long and arduous climb, leading them over the rough-hewn, slate-gray crags of the White Mountain range. There were no paved highways or dirt-covered secondary roads, only goat trails leading ever upward to end abruptly at a cliff's edge above a deep ravine. Continuing under a hot, blistering sun, this was the meandering, tortuous trail that would eventually lead the royal party to safety.[4]

Oberleutnant Rudolf Toschka and the survivors of his thirty-man detachment struggled to keep alive throughout the afternoon of May 20. From the moment their gliders swooped into Venizelos Plaza in the heart of Khaniá, they were in trouble.

Toschka's survivors had left their first position behind a garden wall and were now holed up in a courtyard whose high wall offered them protection from three sides. Rations were gone and their ammunition was running low. It was almost impossible for Toschka's medics to care for the wounded. Their only chance for survival was to slip through the lines under cover of darkness—if they could hold out that long.

Their most imperative need was water.[5]

A young Gefreiter volunteered to carry a few water canteens to a well in the yard of a nearby house. He had to cross an open area of the plaza and enter the house to reach the yard; Toschka ordered his men to cover him with a volley. The young corporal ran across the plaza but never got to the well. No sooner had he reached the open ground than he fell victim to a sniper's bullet.

Another soldier, desperate for water, volunteered to attempt the same run. He raced across the open ground, past the corporal's body, to the door of the house. A bullet struck the soldier as he reached the threshold.

Toschka spotted the sniper but could not believe his eyes. It was a woman!

In one final attempt, a sergeant picked up the rest of the canteens and zigzagged across the plaza to the house. Bullets picked at his heels, spurring him to run faster. In a desperate dash, he leaped through the door, but no sooner had he entered the house than he was captured and quickly disarmed. His captors were women!

"Hello, Teufel!" The greeting came from a woman who spit the word *devil* at him in heavily accented German.

The sergeant stared at her in disbelief. She was dressed in

male clothing, as were the other six women in the room. All carried rifles or German tommy guns—obviously captured from paratroopers, and all wore bandoliers across their chests.

"How do you like fighting Cretan women, Devil?"

"Why do you oppose us?" he asked hoarsely through parched, thirsty lips.

She laughed at him. "You want us to be hospitable to you— when you come to destroy us?"

"Come, Georgalakis, let's kill him and hang his body out the window for the other devils to see," interrupted one of the taller women.

"Let *me* kill him," added a huge, heavyset woman, brandishing a curved Syrian knife in her huge hand. "Why waste a bullet?"

Mrs. Georgalakis, whose husband was a member of the Greek Parliament and was at this time a prisoner somewhere in Athens, put an end to the debate. "No, we're going to send him back, without his rifle or his pistol—and *no water!* Let him tell his leader that unless they surrender to us—the women of Khaniá—we are going to kill all of them!"[6]

Corporal Hans Kreindler joined the two paratroopers who had set up a machine gun behind the protection of a garden wall. When he reached them, he flung himself down to catch his breath. The mad dash over open ground with the enemy shooting at him had been exhausting. The heat had become unbearable, sapping the very core of his strength. He drew his sleeve across his forehead, wiping the perspiration before it dropped into his eyes, and sat still for a few minutes, taking deep breaths.

Suddenly there was a red flash followed instantly by a thunderous, earsplitting explosion. Kreindler felt himself lifted off the ground and slammed down again. He lay there half-dazed, the wind knocked out of him, his ears ringing.

Gradually he raised his head and looked about him. The two machine gunners lay sprawled over their guns—dead. There was a big hole where the wall had been. Carefully Kreindler ran his good hand over his body; he seemed to be unhurt except for the shock. It must have been a shell burst or a hand grenade, he thought. The fact that he was at the other end of the wall had saved his life. He noted that the force of the blast even had twisted the barrel of his tommy gun.

With a painful effort, he raised himself and took his bearings. Some 100 feet to his left was a narrow trail that ran through some trees and seemed to dip toward the valley. In that valley he would find Von der Heydte's paratroopers and the rest of the men from his unit.

Slowly he rose to his feet, only to hear a voice behind him shout, "There's another blighter—still alive!" It was followed by a scattered burst of rifle fire. Kreindler dashed down the trail hoping to lose himself among the trees. At a clearing he ran into three New Zealanders sitting around a fire brewing tea. Before they had a chance to recover from their surprise, Kreindler retraced his steps back up the trail. When he reached the crest of the hill, he followed the trail to the left, past a small chapel and into what appeared to be the village cemetery. He stopped momentarily behind a tombstone to catch his breath. His weary body ached, his heavy paratrooper's combat uniform weighing heavily on him.

From his position Kreindler spotted soldiers at the far wall of the cemetery, firing down the hill, from which came a noisy clamor of rifle and machine-gun fire. It did not take Kreindler long to realize that he was trapped between the Greeks at the cemetery wall and the New Zealanders coming up the trail. Quickly he glanced about him and decided to seek refuge in the small chapel he had just passed at the cemetery entrance.

The iron door opened with a grating squeal, admitting Kreindler into a small, dark chamber, in which he could barely discern a small altar with a cross on it. It was quiet, and the sudden coolness was a relief from the outside heat. He closed the door, shutting out the sounds of battle, and curled up in a corner to rest. He would wait until darkness to make his escape to his own lines. It was a comforting thought, and in a few minutes he was sound asleep.

A sharp pain in the ribs awakened him abruptly. Kreindler rubbed his side and through half-closed eyes distinguished two figures standing before him in the dark. He reached for his pistol, but it was gone.

The two men before him spoke a strange language. It was not English—which he would have recognized—so he assumed them to be Greek. One of them pushed the muzzle of a rifle against Kreindler's chest and motioned him to rise. The second grabbed Kreindler by the collar and pulled him to his feet, half-dragging him out the door. It was still bright daylight outside, and the sudden light hurt Kreindler's eyes. The taller of the two men pushed the German against the chapel wall, and the other closed the bolt and raised his rifle. Kreindler realized that he was going to be executed. He scowled at them, fearful, weary, yet defiant.

As the Greek soldier took aim, a deep, commanding voice stopped him. Both men snapped to respectful attention as a third appeared out of nowhere, tall, pistol in hand, and with the bearing and authority of an officer. Kreindler could not understand what was said, but it was obvious that the officer was reprimanding the two soldiers. Then he turned to Kreindler and said in fair English: "You are a prisoner of war and shall be treated as such."[7]

Manoli Paterakis succeeded in shooting five paratroopers from the "stick" that fell in front of him after the episode with the elderly couple. The rest he lost in the heavy underbrush.

Later that morning he met a group of ten Cretans who had obviously been busy all morning fighting the invader, for they all carried German weapons.

Word reached the Cretans that a column of paratroopers was advancing up the road. After a brief discussion, Paterakis and the rest of the men scattered amidst the high ground that paralleled the road. When the Germans came into view, the Cretans opened fire. It was this sound of battle that attracted Oberleutnant Werner Schiller.[8]

Painfully pushing himself through a thick glade of bamboo, Schiller came to a little rise, beyond which he heard the loud sound of rifle and machine-gun fire. Carefully he crawled to the crest of the knoll and looked down the other side. What he saw frustrated him. There in a shallow hollow was a squad of paratroopers completely surrounded by a group of men without uniforms, looking much like the Cretan he had encountered earlier that morning.

He lay there helpless for about an hour. Gradually the firing from the hollow ceased. When he looked again, Cretans were swarming all over the dead Germans. His comrades had been beaten by civilians. In the brief moment that he was exposed, one of the Cretans spotted him. Schiller rolled down the hill and raced for cover with the Cretans following close behind.

Exhausted, thirsty, out of breath, and weakened by his wound, he pushed himself through the thick underbrush. In a little clearing, he came across a dry irrigation ditch. He crawled in and, with his good arm, dragged some dried bamboo stalks over himself for cover. He lay there for what seemed an eternity, hiding from the approaching Cretan guerrillas.

The Cretans passed without noticing Schiller, the sound of their footsteps diminishing gradually over the uneven, rocky trail. Schiller stayed there, hardly breathing and too weak to stir. Eventually he felt that someone was staring at him. Slowly he opened his eyes, only to peer into the tough, weatherbeaten face of a Cretan standing beside the ditch with a rifle in the crook of his arm. Schiller would never forget that face or the fear that coursed through his body. He closed his eyes again and held his breath, waiting for the bullet that would end his life. It never came, for the Cretan turned and walked away.

The events of the morning were too much for the weakened Schiller, and he lapsed into unconsciousness. When he awakened hours later, he found himself in a German first-aid station.[9]

16

"HENCE, THEY HAVE TO PRESERVE MY HEAD"

MAY 20, 1941

Throughout western Crete on the morning of May 20, the Germans were running into trouble in their struggle with the New Zealand and Greek defenders.

General Eugen Meindl, the commanding officer of the assault regiment fighting in the Maleme area, waited anxiously at his command post for word from his various units. The initial news was not good—in fact, it was demoralizing, even to an officer of his experience. Meindl realized that the situation was going against him. Almost in a daze, he followed the battle developments from scattered reports, watching helplessly as his units were systematically decimated. To this veteran officer it seemed the beginning of a nightmare. He had never conceived the possibility of German troops being so quickly destroyed in the face of enemy resistance. It had never happened before on the continent, and they had not expected it to happen here in Crete.

One of the major problems facing Meindl was the lack of communication with his unit commanders. The wireless sets, shattered during the landings, had not yet been repaired by the communications officer, Oberleutnant Gottsche, leaving Meindl temporarily incapacitated. However, he was not deaf to the sound of battle resonating from the perimeter of the airfield and from Hill 107.

He heard nothing from Major Scherber's ill-fated Third Assault Battalion on the eastern perimeter of the airfield. After the initial storm of battle, the firing from that direction had slackened, yet not a single German paratrooper appeared on the airfield from the east. Meindl had to assume that Scherber was in trouble. He had no way of knowing that Major Scherber had been killed and his whole battalion wiped out.

Of course, the CO of the assault regiment had no inkling that the commanding general of the Seventh Airborne Division, General Suessmann, had also been killed during the flight to Crete. Nor was Meindl able to discern whether Colonel Heidrich's Third Parachute Regiment had been successful in its drop into Prison Valley. Worse yet, he could not communicate with General Student at Luftwaffe headquarters in Athens. It was indeed a hardship to fight a battle without any modern means of communication. Meindl's meager information was derived only from slow, vulnerable runners and from stragglers.

A small reconnaissance patrol sent westward toward Kastelli returned with the news that they had run into stiff opposition from Greek troops outside the town. They added that the fields and valleys east of Kastelli were dotted with empty parachutes and dead bodies. From this fragmentary report, General Meindl assumed that Muerbe and his detachment had failed in their purpose at Kastelli.[1]

Meindl searched frantically for a way to stop what looked like the beginning of a military disaster. In a little less than three hours, he had lost more than half his regiment. It was obvious that the solution lay in the capture of Maleme airfield and its crowning height, Hill 107. Only if the airfield were taken could reinforcements be ferried to Crete. The forces that might be able to turn this pending disaster into victory were the paratroopers of his Second and Fourth Assault Battalions, which had landed successfully west of the Tavronites River.

After a cursory meeting with his two remaining battalion

commanders, Meindl ordered them to attack the airfield and Hill 107. He planned to send the Fourth Battalion, under the command of Hauptmann Walter Gericke—the energetic, intelligent officer who had assumed command after Major von Braun was killed—across the captured Tavronites bridge and attack Hill 107 from the north. Captain Gericke's battalion was composed mostly of heavy machine guns and mortar squads, with few infantrymen. To fill that gap, Meindl assigned one company of paratroopers from the Second Battalion and the survivors of the glider force to join the other three companies of the Fourth Battalion.

The two remaining companies—the Fifth and Sixth Companies of the Second Battalion, led by Major Stentzler—were to cross the Tavronites, circle counterclockwise in an enveloping maneuver, and attack Hill 107 from the south. Meindl's strategy would bring this vital ground under fire from two directions.

As the battalion commanders assembled their troops in their respective staging areas, General Meindl arrived at the line of departure from which his men would begin the attack. Earlier that same morning, he had left for Crete with approximately 2,500 men in his assault regiment. Now he had fewer than 900 troopers.

Lieutenant Colonel L. W. Andrew, commanding officer of the Twenty-second New Zealand Battalion defending Hill 107, had witnessed the parachute and glider landings. At 7:30 A.M. he dispatched a message to brigade headquarters informing General Hargest of the attack. Then, from the command post dug into the side of Hill 107, he tried to maintain contact with his five companies spread out on the crest of the hill and around the slopes leading up to the airfield.

Within the opening minutes of the bombing, the telephone lines to two of the New Zealand companies and to Andrew's Headquarters Company were ruptured. The battalion telephone connection to brigade headquarters in Platanias was next to go. The wireless was Andrew's only communication with Hargest, and from 9:30 A.M. until 10:00 A.M., even that failed.[2]

Meanwhile, the men of Andrew's battalion became engaged in fierce combat. Paratroopers of the Von Plessen detachment were attacking one of the slopes of Hill 107 and, led by Ober-arzt Dr. Weizel, these young soldiers fought with such ferocity that they quickly overran the New Zealanders' platoon positions, killing many and taking few prisoners. Although Von Plessen had been killed earlier, his men pressed their attack from the north and south, exposing the New Zealand troops of the perimeter companies to heavy crossfire.

The major problem now facing the New Zealanders was their dwindling ammunition. When they ran low in hand grenades, they manufactured their own by filling ration cans with concrete and nails and exploding them with gelignite.

Headquarters Company, protecting the area between the villages of Maleme and Pirgos northeast of Hill 107, had a field day shooting Germans. Not a single paratrooper landing in Maleme and Pirgos survived once his feet touched the ground. But many of them did land safely in the fields, and once they concentrated themselves into a striking force, they attacked the clerks and supply men of Headquarters Company. The German assault overran the defenses of one of the company's isolated platoons, but the rest of the New Zealanders rallied behind Lieutenant G. Beaven and held their ground. The hard-pressed Beaven dispatched a runner to battalion headquarters with a note he had received from one of his section leaders, citing his dilemma:

NO MACHINE GUNS, NO HAND GRENADES, EIGHT RIFLES, AND TWO BAYONETS . . .[3]

But the runner never got through.

On Hill 107 itself, the men of A and B Companies were faced by the attack from the scattered troops of Major Koch's glider force. The withering fire set up by the New Zealand defenders extinguished that major threat to their position.

But the Luftwaffe was still present overhead, and periodic attacks by Stuka dive-bombers and strafing ME-109s kept the men of Colonel Andrew's battalion on their toes. As the dust cloud cleared slowly and the increasing heat of day burned off the morning mist, through his field glasses Andrew could see troop movements across the west bank of the Tavronites River. He knew the danger this posed to his own defense position, yet he had no way of knowing how many men had landed in that area.

Before the attack began, Andrew had dispatched several men with a wireless set down to the village of Roponiana across the Tavronites, to act as an outpost. They were based exactly where the Second and Fourth Battalions of the assault regiment had landed. Without a word forthcoming throughout the morning hours, Andrew assumed their outpost had been wiped out, as indeed it had.

Even as he watched the paratroopers moving into position across the Tavronites, sporadic mortar bursts and a few shells from light mountain cannon were hitting the slopes of Hill 107.

At 10:00 A.M. communications with brigade headquarters were restored. Andrew immediately summarized a report of the enemy landings. At 10:55 A.M. he reported to Hargest, without the slightest hint of alarm, that:

> 400 PARATROOPERS . . . LANDED IN THE AREA, 100 NEAR THE
> AIRFIELD, 150 TO THE EAST OF THE AIRFIELD BETWEEN MA-
> LEME AND PIRGOS AND 150 WEST OF THE RIVER.[4]

General Meindl signaled his battalion commanders to begin the first major coordinated attack of the day against a specific defense position in the Maleme area.

At first there was the usual snap of sporadically fired bullets from scattered points on the hill and airfield perimeter. When the platoons were completely exposed, the firing increased to a roar of thunder, with bursts of rifle and machine-gun fire arching down on the paratroopers. Caught in the open, the front ranks were shot dead. Others fell wounded and, lying where they had fallen, they were hit again and again by the spray of bullets. The rest could not proceed; some paratroopers attempting to dash back to the safety of the olive trees were quickly cut down.

Ignoring the initial plight of the attacking platoons, Meindl ordered the assault to continue. But then something caught his eye halfway up Hill 107.

It was a flag signal, and it was German. A group of twenty-four surviving paratroopers from Koch's glider force were holed up in a New Zealand trench they had captured after a brief hand-to-hand skirmish. Once these glider troops had taken the position, they were unable to advance any further; sniper and machine-gun fire cut down anyone who ventured to raise his head above the parapet of the trench. New Zealand fire from farther up the hill was accurate and treacherous.

Looking down toward the airfield, these surrounded paratroopers decided to announce their presence at all costs, hoping that their attacking comrades would relieve them of their plight. When he saw their flag, General Meindl pointed to the spot and enthusiastically shouted over the din: "It must be Koch's men signaling to us!"

Grabbing a green signal flag lying on the ground and starting to wave a reply, he took his staff by surprise. This was the duty of the communications officer, not of the commanding general.

In his enthusiasm to signal Koch, Meindl partly raised himself above the edge of the stone wall behind which he had sought shelter. His aide turned to warn him of the danger, but it was too late. A sharp crack sounded, followed by the singing whistle of a bullet cutting through the air. With hardly a sound the bullet struck the general's hand; the signal flag fell to the ground, covered with blood.

It took a few seconds for the general to realize he had been hit, after which he grabbed his wrist to quell the first stab of pain. In doing so, he rose up again, completely exposing himself a second time. There was a renewed burst of rifle fire with bullets ricocheting off rocks and trees. A few of them ripped into Meindl's body. He slumped forward to the ground, severely wounded in the chest.

His alarmed staff hurriedly gathered around their fallen leader.

Now there was a continuous concentration of fire raking the entire area, making any movement difficult. They dragged his body behind a half-fallen stone wall, where the doctor and his medical assistant began to attend the wounded general.

The staff officers frowned with apprehension as they looked down at the pale face of their commander. They were relieved to hear that the wounds, although severe, would not be fatal.

After his wounds were dressed, Meindl was moved to a nearby farmhouse. He grimaced from the sharp pain that racked his body each time he breathed. It was more painful when he spoke, but he made it clear to his staff that he was still in command and that he intended to remain in command until properly relieved.

"Order the men to attack that damn hill—take it at all costs!" he gasped. "Don't come back until it is in your hands!"

He paused to catch a painful breath, and then with perspiration rolling down his face, he added: "Schnell!"[5]

Meindl's men now struck in full force against the positions on Hill 107. Amid the despoiled foliage and bomb-cratered earth, the paratroopers of the Fourth Battalion raced forward in the face of a rising storm of fire.

Their first ranks were shot down, as were the second and third that followed. But the rest leaped over the bodies of their fallen comrades and raced up the western defense perimeter, gaining a foothold at the base of Hill 107. The whole northern slope of the hill was ablaze with the fire of battle.

The hard-pressed men of the Twenty-second Battalion were taking heavy casualties, but their fire continued unabated. These brave soldiers fought magnificently in the face of the German attack. When their rifles were empty, they resorted to the bayonet, as the first line of trenches became the scene of hand-to-hand encounters.

The Germans could not dislodge the New Zealanders, who clung to their positions as shipwrecked sailors cling to their rafts.

Beneath that blazing hot Cretan sun, the struggle for this valuable hill was to continue throughout the day.

When General Meindl was informed that the Fifth and Sixth Companies of Stentzler's Second Assault Battalion had paused in their attack for a brief respite while search parties went out hunting for wells to get water for the thirsty troopers, he was furious. Although blood was seeping into his lungs from his wounds, and although speech was becoming increasingly difficult for him, he nevertheless gasped out orders that the Second Battalion must continue in the attack without delay.

By 11:00 A.M. shelling from light mountain artillery and heavy mortars, firing from beyond the Tavronites, was accelerated, taking an increasing toll of the men on Hill 107. A wounded straggler from D Company arrived at Andrew's headquarters with the disheartening news—completely incorrect—that D Company had been overrun and destroyed. The inroads that the paratroopers of the Fourth Assault Battalion had made in the defense perimeter at the base of Hill 107 might have indicated to Andrew that even C Company had been wiped out. There still was no word from Beaven and his Headquarters Company at Pirgos. Lacking direct communication with his companies at the defense perimeter of the airfield, Colonel Andrew had no way of knowing that Companies C and D were still holding out despite heavy casualties.

He informed his brigade commander that he had lost communication with his forward companies and could not report on their situation. The report should have alarmed the brigade commander, considering the value of Hill 107.

Colonel John Allen, commanding the Twenty-first Battalion, was also having communication problems. His wireless was inoperable and all his messages had to be dispatched by runner to the Twenty-third Battalion; from there all messages were transmitted to brigade headquarters using the Twenty-third Battalion's wireless. Having destroyed the paratroopers of Major

Scherber's ill-fated Third Assault Battalion earlier in the day, the men of the Twenty-third Battalion were now involved in mopping up the surviving stragglers,

In a message forwarded by the Twenty-third Battalion to brigade headquarters, Colonel Leckie informed Brigadier Hargest that the situation in the area was well under control.[6]

Colonel Allen of the Twenty-first Battalion sent a similar message a short while later.

At brigade headquarters, Brigadier Hargest, the politician-turned-soldier, was pleased with this news. He dictated the following message to the commanders of his Twenty-first and Twenty-third Battalions:

> GLAD OF YOUR MESSAGE . . . WILL NOT CALL ON YOU FOR COUNTERATTACK UNLESS POSITION VERY SERIOUS. SO FAR EVERYTHING IS IN HAND AND REPORTS FROM OTHER UNITS SATISFACTORY.[7]

Thus while Colonel Andrew was hard-pressed in his defense of Hill 107 and hoped for some response to his message, Brigadier Hargest sat down to his noon meal, ignorant and unmindful of the danger that prevailed at Maleme.

King George of the Hellenes and his entourage continued, against great hardships, the climb up the rugged crags of the White Mountains to elude the invading Germans.

Their effort was becoming more difficult with each passing hour. Many times when the group had to pause for rest, they looked down on the panoramic landscape of the northern valleys and fields. It was an appalling sight.

In the northeast, toward Khaniá and Suda Bay, the now-familiar black smoke from burning ships hung like a dark smudge against the blue sky. A light-gray cloud was suspended like a canopy over the airfield to the northwest. The green acres below them were strewn with parachutes that looked like miniature flower petals—red, white, yellow, pink, and black wherever the eye could see. Many were on the ground, and others hung from the trees. There were so many of them that it shocked human imagination for any one nation to have put into effect such a feat of arms as this tremendous air invasion.

When they resumed their climb, the king discarded his tunic and cap. His blouse was drenched with perspiration but it retained the semblance of neatness which was so characteristic of him.

By noon the royal party reached a village cradled in a valley between two huge mountains. This was the village of the Virgin Mary of Keramia.

The men of the village appeared with hoes, axes, and ancient rifles to meet the trespassers. They were prepared to defend their homes. But when the men of the advance guard revealed their identities and those they were escorting, the villagers put down their weapons. Their eyes lit up. "The king is coming here?"

"The king *is* here!"

Immediately the mayor of the village, together with the town elders, rushed forward humbly to greet the royal guest and his party. In no time at all the aroma of barbecued lamb filled the mountain air, fresh warm bread was placed on the tables, and cool red wine filled the glasses.[8]

The German timetable dictated that all the major objectives in the Maleme and Prison Valley areas were to be secured by noon on the day of the attack.

In keeping with this timetable, a Junker-52 transport revved up on Elevsis airfield in Greece. This transport was the first of several that were to fly to Crete carrying the Eleventh Air Corps Airfield Service Company. It was the specific duty of this servicing unit to prepare the airfield for the transports that would carry the first elements of the Fifth Mountain Division as reinforcements that afternoon. It was projected that by nightfall, the troop carriers were to have ferried close to 9,000 men to Maleme. The rest of the Mountain Division was to arrive by sea—the follow-through of the invasion, taking over the fighting from the paratroopers. If the paratroopers represented the spearhead, these mountain troops would be its head and shaft.

Once over Maleme, Lieutenant Colonel Snowadzki, the commanding officer of the unit, sitting in the copilot's seat, scanned the airfield with his field glasses. It was difficult to see clearly through the mistlike layer of dust that hung over the landing strip. He spotted the many downed gliders, lying at grotesque angles in the hills and fields around the airstrip.

As the transport circled the field a second time in a wider sweep, Snowadzki was able to distinguish a huge red banner with its centered white circle upon which was emblazoned a black swastika. It had been placed at the base of the northern slope of Hill 107 by the men of Walter Gericke's Fourth Assault Battalion in order not to be bombed or strafed by their own aircraft. The flag represented the farthest advance by the paratroopers in their penetration of the New Zealand defense perimeter. Snowadzki assumed incorrectly that the flag meant that the airfield had also been captured.

He ordered his pilot to land.

The aircraft slowly lumbered over the field, lining up with the landing strip. It dropped lower and lower, its wheels almost touching the ground. Suddenly the sides of the transport were ventilated by countless holes as bullets bit into the fuselage. A spray of bullets shattered the observation glass behind the pilot's seat. The men in the body of the aircraft were showered with slivers of glass as bullet after bullet smashed through the portholes on both sides. In seconds the transport had become the target of every rifle and machine gun in the area. Streams of tracers arched from all directions at the Junker rolling across the runway.

Startled, Colonel Snowadzki shouted: "Take off!"

The pilot gave the transport full throttle and lifted the plane back into the sky with string after string of tracer bullets following in its wake. He veered and banked his aircraft to avoid enemy fire. In a matter of minutes, he was flying again over the green-blue waters of the Gulf of Khaniá, safely out of reach of enemy fire.

Much to Snowadzki's surprise, Maleme airfield was still in the hands of the New Zealanders. For the first time, the Germans realized that their timetable was inaccurate.[9]

In his headquarters office on the second floor of the Grande Bretagne Hotel in Athens, Kurt Student was anxiously waiting for the first reports of the invasion.

It was difficult to sit blindly 168 air miles from the battle zone, waiting for the first information as to how his paratroopers were faring. The only news he had received was the debriefing reports the transport pilots had given upon their return, after releasing the paratroopers over Crete—and that information was not totally accurate.[10]

Many pilots were not truthful. They did not report that heavy enemy antiaircraft fire caused many transports to veer from the drop zone, resulting in a wide dispersion of the parachute units, possibly decreasing their effectiveness. No pilot wished to indict himself for failing to drop his ''stick'' exactly on target. So for the first hours of the invasion, General Student had nothing more to go on than glowing, albeit inaccurate, information.

Student sat at his desk, checking through his papers. One of them was a transcript from General Gerhard, the Air Service Commander, reporting that the returning transports were having difficulty landing at their home bases because of the heavy dust clouds that reduced visibility to zero in broad daylight. The dried, parched soil, agitated by propeller turbulence, suspended its sandy particles in a dust-filled fog over the airports, making landings hazardous. Several transports had crashed on landing because of this lack of visibility. Other Junker-52's had to fly in circles over their respective airfields as long as two hours waiting for the dust to settle. When they finally did come in for a landing, many of them ran off the runway, damaging their landing gear.[11]

Of the 493 Junker-52 transports that had taken part in the

first-wave assault, two had been lost over Crete, while five had crashed on their return to their home field. Countless others had sustained lesser damage from the difficulties created by the dust clouds. It was a problem that further threatened the German timetable. The question that lodged in Student's mind was whether these troop carriers could be refueled in time for the second phase of the attack on the eastern part of Crete, scheduled for that afternoon.

His thoughts were interrupted by the arrival of his communications officer. The time was a little past noon.

The staff officers who watched Student saw his face begin to pale, a frown furrowing his brow. The message was from Admiral Karageorg Shuster, the commander in charge of southeast naval operations. It forwarded a report from a German E-boat (motor-torpedo boat) patrolling off Aegina in the Saronic Gulf that a glider had crashed on the island. Confirmation of the original report added that the ill-fated glider had been carrying the commanding general of the Seventh Airborne Division and his immediate staff.

Student took the news in stride and immediately issued orders that Colonel Richard Heidrich, commanding officer of the Third Parachute Regiment of the Seventh Airborne Division, then landing in Prison Valley, was to assume command of the airborne division. Heidrich was to be informed as soon as contact had been established with him.[12]

More alarming news followed.

At 1:15 P.M., Student's private telephone rang. He immediately recognized the distinctive voice of Lieutenant Colonel Snowadzki on the other end. Student listened, thanked him quietly, and without the slightest show of emotion, put down the receiver. He sat there for a long time, disregarding the anxious stares from his subordinates and deaf to the constant ringing of the field phones.

Then came the third piece of bad news. Hauptmann Mors of the intelligence section reported a signal from the Maleme area.

Meindl's communications officer, Oberleutnant Gottsche, had finally succeeded in repairing a wireless set. He had spent all morning cannibalizing parts from all the broken sets to produce one that would function. At approximately 4:15 in the afternoon, a weak message began to filter into Athens. It told of an impending military disaster:

ALL MAJOR OBJECTIVES, INCLUDING MALEME AIRFIELD AND HILL 107, STILL IN ENEMY HANDS . . . VON BRAUN, KOCH, SCHERBER, VON PLESSEN, MUERBE . . . KILLED IN ACTION . . . MEINDL WOUNDED SEVERELY[13]

Student sat stunned for many minutes as his staff evaluated the import of this alarming message. Finally he came to a decision, and with a rap of his fist on the arm of the chair, he muttered aloud—more to himself than to anyone else—"I must go there!"

In a burst of energy, he walked hurriedly down the corridor to General Löhr's office. Without waiting for a response to his knock, he entered and briefed his commanding officer. Löhr received the news calmly.

"I must leave for Crete immediately," Student added forcefully, declaring his intent rather than asking permission.

"That is out of the question," snapped Löhr, annoyed at the proposal. "If you go to Maleme, you would be out of touch for the second phase of the attack against Rethimnon and Iráklion. No, your place is here, in case the pattern of fighting should suddenly change."

Crestfallen, Student returned to the map room, informing his chief of staff, General Schlemm, that his request had been denied.

Then, turning toward the tall French windows, Student added, "You see, Schlemm, if this attack fails, they want to be sure I will be around for they will need a scapegoat. If we fail to take Crete, someone has to be held accountable. That is my responsibility. Hence, they have to preserve my head in case it should be wanted at an inquiry."[14]

17

"BE BACK BY 4:30 PM"

MAY 20, 1941

The German timetable for the invasion had indeed gone awry. The 1:00 P.M. deadline for the second part of the assault against the eastern portion of the island was rapidly approaching. In light of the paratroopers' apparent difficulties in the Maleme area, the question of postponing the afternoon attack was raised, along with that of withholding the other two regiments or sending them instead to aid the forces at Maleme.

Student needed time to think this out. Further reports from the Maleme area were scarce, and those from Prison Valley were insufficient for him to order such a dramatic alteration in the detailed plans of the overall assault. He had to wait until his information was more conclusive. One item of bad news followed another: first the item of Suessmann's death on Aegina, followed by Snowadzki's report of the situation at Maleme. At 4:15 that afternoon, Meindl's weak radio transmission put the question to him again.

Now Student recalled the Air Service commander's earlier report about the difficulties the returning transports were experiencing in landing on their home airfields amid the confusion created by the tremendous dust clouds. General Gerhard had expressed concern that this difficulty might delay the refueling of the transports in time to begin the second phase, scheduled for 1:00 P.M. Student hoped that this delay might be a blessing in disguise.[1]

He picked up the phone to call Gerhard's command post, but the line had been cut by the Greek underground. Like Snowadzki, Student had to resort to the use of the civilian exchange, with all its inept difficulties. When he finally got through to the airfield, it was too late. Some transports had already left, while others were on the departure line. Student shrugged his shoulders, somewhat pleased by the news, for now he would not have to change his original plan. Perhaps, he thought, the second phase of the invasion would achieve the immediate success he expected, thus tipping the scales in his favor.[2]

The objectives of the second part of the day's airborne assault were the cities of Rethimnon and Iráklion together with their respective airfields. The seizure of Rethimnon had been assigned to the Second Parachute Regiment under the command of Colonel Sturm. The First Regiment, commanded by Colonel Bruno Brauer, was to capture Iráklion. Their sister regiment of the Seventh Airborne Division had been fighting for its very existence since early morning in Prison Valley.

Colonel Sturm had chosen to divide the attack force of his regiment into three groups. It was an attack pattern similar to the one taken by the assault regiment at Maleme. The western, or right, prong of the attack was assigned to Captain Wiedemann with a force of some 800 men comprised of the Third Battalion of Sturm's regiment, two sections of airborne artillery, and a company of heavy machine guns. His objective was twofold: the seizure of the village of Perivolia and the city of Rethimnon. The capture of Perivolia, some three miles west of the airfield, would cut the northern road and secure the western approach to the field, after which Wiedemann was to wheel westward and take Rethimnon.

The left flank, or eastern prong, of the assault was to be led by Major Hans Kroh, whose force of 550 men consisted of two companies of the regiment's First Battalion, the regiment's heavy weapon detachment of mortars and mountain artillery, in addition to a heavy machine-gun company.

Sturm assumed personal command of the central prong of the attack. He planned to land on the airfield with his headquarters staff and one-and-a-half companies of some 200 paratroopers. From this central command position he planned to coordinate the attack. All three groups were to seize their objectives, and while Wiedemann held Rethimnon, Kroh was to head toward the center and help secure the airfield. With the airfield in their hands, the whole force would then swing to the west and approach Suda Bay from the east.[3]

The whole operation appeared logistically sound, for Sturm's attack group represented a powerful and well-balanced force of some 1,550 men. Flushed with European victories the Germans still considered themselves invincible. What happened in the Maleme sector was still unknown to them, and so Sturm's plan gave little consideration to the possibility that a resolute and determined defense might make the difference between success and failure.

The defending force of Australians and Greeks that was to oppose the landing was outnumbered in men and equipment. But to a scrappy Australian like Lieutenant Colonel Ian Campbell, such a weakness was meaningless. Campbell realized that the most strategic objective in his sector was the airfield located five miles east of the city of Rethimnon. He was determined to deny the Germans that goal.

All Campbell had with which to stop the German attack were two understrength Australian battalions of 600 men each and two poorly trained and equipped Greek regiments of some 2,000 men. He had no antiaircraft guns, only four captured Italian 100-mm cannon and four 75-mm French fieldpieces. The artillery pieces had no sights, in addition to which he possessed only 80 shells for his four three-inch mortars. His men lacked a sufficient amount of grenades and they were even short of rifle ammunition. Of the men in the Greek regiments, many had no rifles and those who did had only ten bullets per weapon. Yet despite all these shortcomings, Campbell was determined to repel the invader.

Campbell surveyed the lay of the land personally during the days before the attack and disposed his units in well-camouflaged positions. So well were they hidden that German photographic reconnaissance aircraft failed to uncover them. In his determination to deny the Germans the airfield, Campbell strung out his units over the uneven terrain surrounding the airstrip. To the east of the landing field there was a steep plateau of broken rock formations that Campbell had penciled on his map as Hill A. A narrow ridge running perpendicular to Hill A and extending approximately three miles westward as far as the village of Platanes was divided by two dried riverbeds; the easternmost, just west of Hill A, the Australians had happily named Wadi Bardia to honor their victory in North Africa. The second riverbed, Wadi Pigi, lay one mile farther west. Between the two riverbeds there rose a small rocky prominence designated as Hill D. The ridge from Hill A continued for two miles in its westerly direction until it terminated in another hilly prominence just south of Platanes. Campbell called this high ground Hill B. Farther west, a mile south of the village of Perivolia, there was yet another rise of ground, standing alone between the village and the city of Rethimnon. This was Hill C.

Along this terrain, well suited for defense, Campbell strung out the companies of his battalions. On Hill A he positioned a company from the First Australian Battalion, which was under his direct command. The rest of the companies were dug in on the ground between Hill A and Hill D. To support the companies of his First Battalion, he had emplaced six of his fieldpieces together with a machine-gun platoon. Dug in on the forward slopes of both hills, they had an excellent range of fire over the airfield.

Campbell's Second Battalion, the Eleventh Australian under

Major R. L. Sandover, was positioned two miles farther west on Hill B, with the remaining two artillery pieces and a machine-gun platoon in support.

Between the two Australian battalions, Campbell put the Fourth and Fifth Greek Regiments. Like the Greek regiments at Kastelli, Alikianou, and Galatas, they were only in battalion strength. The Fourth Greek Regiment, under the command of Lieutenant Colonel John Tryfon, was in the area between Hills A and B, near the coast road just west of Wadi Pigi. The other Greek unit, the Fifth Regiment, commanded by Lieutenant Colonel Serbos, was positioned in the foothills beyond the ridge near the village of Adhele. Campbell hid his two infantry tanks near them on the southern slope of the ridge.

Inasmuch as Campbell had concentrated his men to protect the airfield, he allocated the defense of the city of Rethimnon and its surrounding area to a well-armed, aggressive force of Greek gendarmerie under the command of Major Jacob Chaniotis. These men were to give a good account of themselves in the days ahead.[4]

The communications setup between all these units was intolerably inadequate and incomplete. Campbell established his command post on Hill D in the center of the defense line, from which he had telephone communication with his companies on both Hills A and B. All other areas in the defense perimeter had to depend on runners, who could always fall prey to marauding Messerschmitts overhead. Campbell's single cable line to Creforce Headquarters must have been cut much earlier in the day, for—strange as it may seem—as of four o'clock in the afternoon of May 20, he had not received a single word of the intensive battle in progress in the western part of Crete, a battle then in its tenth hour!

With his battalions well entrenched in their defensive positions, Campbell sat back and waited for the German onslaught.

Zero hour for the attack on Rethimnon and its airfield had come and gone. Unlike the punctuality that marked the morning bombings in the Maleme and Khaniá areas, the afternoon attack rapidly deteriorated into a haphazard affair.

At 4:00 P.M. the fighters and bombers finally made their appearance over the Rethimnon area. The bombing had been assigned, of necessity, to Messerschmitt 109s and the ME-110 light fighter-bombers.

The strafing and light bombing continued for only a fifteen-minute period, after which the aircraft departed. The fuel wasted waiting for the delayed and scattered squadrons to rendezvous over their respective airfields had abbreviated the time allowed over the target. Their departure was followed by an extended lull, the first indication to the defenders that the attack lacked synchronization.

Then a dull drone was heard from the east. At that point, the first of twenty-four JU-52 transports crossed the coastline and turned westward. No sooner had they made their appearance than the Greeks and Australians opened fire. Tracers reached out at the slow, low-flying Junkers like little red fingers, searching for them and digging into their midst. Bren and Lewis guns, firing from high angle tripods, released a hot lead screen that began to take its toll.

One transport, still carrying its human cargo, suddenly banked sharply to avoid ground fire and sliced into another that was just releasing its "stick" of paratroopers. Amidst screams of horror, both men and pieces of aircraft plummeted into the waters beyond the shore. Other transports caught fire and turned back out to sea, trailing smoke. Some had already released their paratroopers, while others continued to release them over the water.[5]

In the center of the attack, Colonel Sturm and the men of his headquarters staff descended with the attached paratroopers in support. They immediately came under fire from Campbell's Australians positioned between Hills A and D on the right and the men of the Fourth Greek Regiment on the left. Lieutenant Colonel Tryfon's Greeks had only ten rounds for each rifle, which they soon used up; thereafter, they did not hesitate in attacking the descending Germans with their bayonets.

Most of the paratroopers who fell in this sector were picked off in that fifteen-second descent that left them so vulnerable. Those who survived the drop were quickly chased off the airstrip, across the road that bounded it on the north, and into the dunes of the sandy beach beyond.

Here Sturm was pinned down and cut off with the other survivors of his force. No man was able to raise his head without being picked off. No runner dared rise to carry out his errand to the scattered men of Sturm's central force. The middle prong of the attack had failed.

For the rest of the day and well into the night, the beleaguered Sturm was to remain with the rest of his survivors, hiding behind dunes and tufts of tall grass in complete isolation from the other two prongs of the attacking force.

On the left, Captain Wiedemann's group did not fare any better. The transport pilots' prolonged delay in dropping Wiedemann's men had strung them out, scattering the paratroopers over a wide area and wiping out their attack-effectiveness. They became easy targets for the intensive fire from the rifles and machine guns of Major Sandover's eager Australians of the Eleventh Battalion, positioned in this area. One "stick" of fifteen men fell in a perfect line, each paratrooper dead before he touched the ground, his body riddled with bullets.

Even the Greeks took part against Wiedemann's men. The company on the left flank of the Fourth Greek Regiment charged the paratroopers as they landed. They captured twenty Germans while they were still shedding their harnesses.

The paratroopers who did succeed in landing safely quickly gathered for protection among the trees and tall grass. Many of the canisters carrying their weapons were too scattered to be reached. Nevertheless, Wiedemann collected his men amidst the protective foliage and returned the fire with what little he had on hand.

As evening approached, Major Sandover decided to end this threat in front of his defenses and ordered an attack. With an excited determination, the Australians left their protected positions and charged the Germans, pushing them back toward the village of Perivolia and beyond, taking some eighty-four prisoners in the rush of the attack.

During the advance, Sandover came across the body of a German officer. A search revealed a list of signal codes. The battalion commander translated the list himself and decided to make use of it. Such resourcefulness was to help Sandover replenish his dwindling ammunition. The next day, German supply aircraft replied well to his coded signal requests for hand grenades, mortar and rifle ammunition—invaluable supplies to be used against Wiedemann's men.[6]

Sandover's knowledge of German was put to good use a second time. From a captured German officer he learned there would be no enemy reinforcements that day. Relieved, he pressed his attack against the paratroopers at Perivolia village.[7]

The second flight of transports released their "sticks" of paratroopers over the same positions. In that fifteen-second interval, it was terrifying for these men to look down at the fields below littered with the dead bodies of their comrades. As they descended, they could see the flaming trajectories of bullets arching up to follow them down.

Major Kroh, however, landed safely with a good portion of his men, despite the heavy concentration of fire from the defense positions of the First Australian Battalion around the slopes of Hill A. Four Australian machine guns, entrenched on the forward slopes of the hill, laid down a devastating fire that pinned the Germans down. For two hours they kept it up, taking a severe toll of the enemy. But then, one by one, the machine guns either ran out of ammunition or jammed from overheating.

Slowly Kroh mustered his men, and as each gun fell silent, the paratroopers advanced toward Hill A. The two companies from Wiedemann's force that had been wrongly dropped in these positions now served to assist Kroh in attacking Hill A. Using the mortars from his heavy weapons detachment, Kroh unleashed a withering barrage against the Australian company that held the hill. In addition to mortar fire, the Germans brought an antitank gun and a howitzer to bear on the Australians. In the face of such heavy fire, the surviving defenders of the hill position had to withdraw from the crest to the reverse lower slope.

At 5:15 Campbell decided to strengthen the counterattack by releasing his only two infantry tanks in support. He ordered them to clear the airfield and strike the Germans on the forward slopes of Hill A from the north. Both failed in their mission: The first crossed the perimeter of the airfield, where its treads got stuck in a gully—without firing a shot; the second succeeded in reaching the eastern slope of Hill A and fired a few rounds at the Germans. Kroh's men were not in the least frightened by the tank's appearance, for they had an antitank gun to counter it. As they wheeled the gun into position, however, the tank backed off and slipped into a deep ravine where it lay useless.[8]

With that threat overcome, the Germans strengthened their hold on Hill A. It was to prove their only success that day in the Rethimnon sector.

By early evening Campbell realized that his position on the hill was in jeopardy; the outnumbered men of his First Battalion were being hard pressed by the better-equipped Germans. If the Germans continued to hold this strategic piece of terrain, they would, in effect, control the airfield. He was determined to dislodge them before any German reinforcements arrived to make the task impossible. Campbell did not know what Sandover had already learned from his prisoners—that there would be no reinforcements.

As it had been since early morning, communication with Creforce Headquarters was still out. At 6:00 P.M., Campbell got his radio working and was able to send a message to Freyberg for help:

> I AM HEAVILY ENGAGED ON BOTH FLANKS AND WOULD APPRE-
> CIATE HELP.[9]

In Athens, Kurt Student faced a dilemma. All day the news from Maleme had been bad, and by 7:00 P.M., he had not had a sin-

gle report from Sturm at Rethimnon. There was not a single response to the regimental call letters sent out repeatedly over the
wireless. In final desperation, Student decided to send a reconnaissance plane to contact Sturm.

Within the hour, a Feiseler Storch monoplane took off from
Athens for Rethimnon. The pilot's orders were simple and direct:
Find out what you can and report back to Student in person. The
plane never returned.

At midnight Ian Campbell finally received Freyberg's reply to
his earlier request for help. It was terse:

REGRET UNABLE TO SEND HELP. GOOD LUCK![10]

Undaunted, Campbell set out to push the Germans off Hill A.
He planned to collect all his men and attack the Germans by
dawn.

Colonel Bruno Brauer decided to land with the men of the First
Battalion three miles east of the Iráklion airfield, where his men
would secure the approaches from the east and from where he
could maintain overall command of the regiment.

A little after 1:00 P.M., Brauer ordered the men of the First
Battalion to board their assigned transports, joining his headquarters staff in the lead plane. He sat down near the open hatch
and waited for the signal to depart.

Brauer seemed calm and undisturbed, yet he wondered what
had caused the delay in the departure for Iráklion. The old war-
horse wanted to get under way. As yet he had no inkling that
the morning attack at Maleme still hung in the balance, dangling
between success or failure. Nor did he know that at this very
moment Kurt Student was desperately trying to contact Elevsis
airfield in an attempt to alter the plan of the operation. Unaware
of all these problems, Brauer sat quietly in his seat, perspiring
profusely in the stuffy confines of the Junker transport, smoking
and waiting.

The signal finally came at 3:00 P.M.

One by one, the huge black trimotor JU-52s lumbered slowly down to the end of the runway, where they rose unmajestically into the air. Once assembled, they pointed their noses to the southeast and headed for Iráklion.

In the early afternoon of May 20, Major A. W. Nicholls, a company commander in the Leicester Battalion, requested permission from his commanding officer to take three of his platoon lieutenants on a reconnaissance of the defense perimeter.

"Get off by two o'clock," the colonel suggested, "but be back by 4:30 P.M.—no later!" It was odd, Nicholls thought, that the colonel should specify a time limit.[11]

Nicholls planned to visit the Greek defense positions in the city, check the Royal Marine gunners at the Bofors batteries, then drive east to the airfield and visit a friend in the Black Watch. It would be a casual trip. No one had mentioned to him—*since no one knew*—that the Germans were landing in force in the western part of Crete. When the colonel set a time limit for Nicholls's reconnaissance, he did not know how prophetic his stipulation would be.

Major Nicholls spent the greater portion of the afternoon completing his rounds. A little after 3:30 P.M., he and his three platoon leaders left their vehicle for the short stroll back to their company positions. A familiar roar was soon audible from the north; within minutes, fighters and bombers crossed the coast signaling the approach of an air attack.

Nicholls's lieutenants raced across Buttercup Field—as the Iráklion airstrip was called—to seek shelter among the rocks and crevices of one of the two heights known as Charlie. Winded, they hid and watched as the bombers began their devastating work.

For less than an hour, ME-109s, ME-110s, JU-87s, and a few JU-88s circled, bombed, and strafed the Iráklion defense positions. Bombs fell on the airfield, the antiaircraft emplacements, and the city with unerring accuracy. When the bombers finished their work, the fighters came down to strafe anything that moved.

From his perch among the rocks, Nicholls watched the bombing spectacle in fascination. The bombers and fighters had a free run, for—following strict orders—not a single shot was fired in opposition. The young pilots smiled with satisfaction, assuming that their bombing runs had silenced the defenders' batteries.

As soon as the bombers turned north over the water, Major Nicholls and his three junior officers made a dash for their company's position within the Leicester Battalion perimeter. At 4:30 P.M. JU-52 transports were sighted flying low over the water. The general alarm was sounded in the Black Watch positions; elsewhere, in the distance, church bells echoed the warning of the enemy's approach.

Slowly the Junkers came in over the coastline and headed for their respective drop zones. The whole sky filled with the slow-moving transports, now settling to their familiar 400-foot height before releasing the paratroopers.

The defenders remained in their entrenchments, watching the tableau before them. It was the first time in their lives that they had witnessed such a colorful aerial spectacle. The air vibrated with the roar of triple-motored aircraft, while the sky filled with thousands of colorful parachutes slowly descending to earth.[12]

It did not take long for the British, Australians, and Greeks to awaken from this spell.

The silent antiaircraft batteries were the first to fire; their gunners at last had the gleeful satisfaction of telling the Germans that they were alive and well. Their announcements had a telling effect on the low-flying transports.

One aircraft took a direct hit, bursting into flames and leaving a black, smoky wake as it plummeted to earth with all its human cargo. Another Junker was hit as it released its paratroopers. The flames scorched some of them before they jumped, while those who were able to get out found their parachutes aflame.

The sky soon filled with the black puffs of shell bursts and the red glows of burning transports. Many Junkers crashed, and others headed out to sea followed by a long smoke trail. From one such blazing aircraft dangled a single paratrooper, his parachute caught in the tail.

Many parachutists, jumping from stricken transports, dropped to earth like rocks, their chutes unopened. Others left their planes, slowly descending to earth below billowing, swaying parachutes, only to meet the ire of the Australian, British, and Greek soldiers.

The defenders now emerged from their hiding places, the crack of their rifles echoing over the fields. Their rattling machine guns struck down the descending paratroopers, rapidly carpeting the fields with German dead and wounded. Most of the paratroopers died before they completed their descent; others hung limply from trees and telegraph wires. Those who were not shot in the air were soon killed on the ground, as the defending patrols sought them out in the fields.

One group of paratroopers hid in a barley field.

"Let's set the bloody barley on fire," yelled one of the Australians.[13]

Several matches were thrown into the dry barley, turning it into a blazing inferno. Hiding among the tall barley stalks, the paratroopers were now caught between two enemies—the Australians at their rear and the raging fire before them. The flames raced through the field, forcing the Germans to flee. One by one or in groups they rose from their positions, only to be picked off by Australian riflemen or to be cut down by machine-gun fire. Not a single German survived.

For three hours the parachute drop continued. As at Rethimnon, where the attack was already in progress, the JU-52 transports arrived over the drop zone in scattered instead of concentrated formations. This staggered drop gave the defenders ample time to seek out and destroy the enemy.

The delays caused by the dust clouds at the airfields on the mainland now took a heavy toll of the battalions of paratroopers at Iráklion, as it had further west at Rethimnon. It proved to be a slaughter.

At 6:15 P.M. General B. H. Chappel ordered his reserve battalion—the Leicesters—to flush out any stragglers hiding in Buttercup Field. The Leicesters pushed the surviving Germans back toward the beaches, where, their backs to the water, they were forced to surrender.

However, five men were determined not to give up. Three survivors from the Sixth Company and two from an attached machine-gun platoon discarded their heavy uniforms and waded out into the surf. They struggled for several hours in deep water, swimming along the perimeter of the airfield until they reached safety well east of the drop zone.[14]

By 8:00 P.M. the Second Battalion was no more. It had lost twelve officers and three hundred men killed, while eight officers and one hundred men lay wounded as prisoners of war.

The Third Parachute Battalion, commanded by Major Karl Lothar Schulz, landed scattered and piecemeal in the hills beyond Iráklion. They were immediately engaged on the outskirts of the city by the Greek battalions. The paratroopers suffered heavily in that first hour, as the Greeks chased them through the fields and orchards with their bayonets.

Major Schulz, a tall paratrooper, quickly collected the survivors and led them in a concentrated attack toward the city gates, against strong Greek resistance. By dusk he had driven his men along Martyron Road toward the northwestern gate, and along Kondilaky toward the western entrance to the city. Once through the gate, several groups of paratroopers succeeded in reaching the harbor docks. With nightfall, however, resistance stiffened as the civilian population picked up arms in a determined effort to throw the Germans out of the city. It quickly became a cat-

and-mouse affair as Cretans stalked Germans through the dark city streets. Every flash from a rifle meant that another sniper had added a victim to the toll. Major Schulz found himself trying to hold his meager gains for the night. He hoped that daylight would turn the battle to his advantage.

Colonel Bruno Brauer landed in Crete with his regiment's First Parachute Battalion, three miles east of the airfield near the village of Gurnes. The battalion's scattered and delayed descent was only lightly opposed, for it had dropped well beyond the eastern extent of Chappel's defense perimeter.

Once on Crete, Brauer was determined to fight in proper dress uniform. From a separate satchel he removed a blue Luftwaffe service tunic, which he immediately put on, making certain that his Ritterkreuz was properly displayed around his neck. In place of the steel helmet he wore the Luftwaffe officer's service cap—the Schirmmütze—and around his waist he strapped his pistol belt, from which hung a holstered Luger. His appearance now assumed that of a field-grade officer on review rather than one who had just landed in a combat zone. With a lit cigarette held smugly in a holder, the dapper, if not eccentric, commander was finally ready to direct the battle fortunes of his regiment.[15]

Turning his attention to the other battalions, Brauer contacted Major Schulz by wireless, only to learn through a feeble signal that the Third Battalion had encountered very stiff resistance in its landing zone. Schulz's casualties were heavy and his progress was slow. The battalion's objective was still in enemy hands.

From the Second Battalion on the airfield, there was no response to Brauer's signals.

Cretan irregulars had arrived on Brauer's eastern and southern flanks. These mountaineers, well accustomed to the field tactics that characterized the basic elements of guerrilla warfare, positioned themselves among the rocks and picked off any paratrooper who showed himself. The accuracy of their fire took a heavy toll of the men in the First Battalion. It was to last into the night and for the many days that were to follow.

By nightfall Schulz signaled that his men had entered Iráklion at two points, but the outcome was still in question. He hoped that his advance unit could hold its position in the city until daylight.

As of nightfall on May 20, at least 1,000 of the 2,000 men of the First Parachute Regiment that had been dropped over the Iráklion sector lay dead.[16]

18

"IF YOU MUST, THEN YOU MUST"

MAY 20, 1941

At 1700 hours—five o'clock in the afternoon—Colonel Andrew lost his patience waiting for Brigadier Hargest's reply to his request for reinforcements. He turned to his executive officer and, in a voice tinged with anger, ordered that another message be forwarded to brigade headquarters.

"Ask Brigade if I can expect reinforcements for a counter-attack—correct that! *Tell* Brigade that I need—repeat, *I need*—reinforcements for a counterattack!"

The executive officer jotted the message on his pad, stopped, and stared at the colonel in mid-sentence. The vehemence of the note was not characteristic of the otherwise subdued battalion commander.

"Dress it up and send it!" was Andrew's only response to his executive officer.[1]

While the battalion commander waited, he evaluated his headquarters staff. The first signs of weariness from the long day's events were beginning to show on their faces. Andrew thought to himself that if his headquarters personnel were tired, what about the lads out there in the trenches under constant fire? At that moment, Colonel Andrew made up his mind: He would counterattack to take the strain off those men, whether he got reinforcements or not.

At 5:20 P.M., twenty minutes later, he received his reply from Hargest:

> THE 23RD BATTALION CANNOT ASSIST YOU BECAUSE IT IS ITSELF ENGAGED AGAINST PARATROOPERS IN ITS OWN AREA.[2]

Turning to his second in command, Major John Leggatt, Andrew ordered, "See what men are available as infantry support for a counterattack. And send a runner to the two 'I' tanks in the field. Tell them that their time has come. I need them!"[3]

In the Prison Valley area, Colonel Kippenberger, the commanding officer of the Tenth Brigade, had taken a brief respite to evaluate the situation.

It was clearly apparent to him that the objective of the German paratroop regiment was the village of Galatas, nestled atop the high ground behind its protective walls. Kippenberger's undermanned brigade had taken a severe lashing during the morning phase of the attack. Yet, despite this, the Germans had been prevented from capturing their objective. As long as Galatas and the surrounding hills were in New Zealand hands, the rear door to Khaniá remained closed.

The Petrol Company of the brigade's Composite Battalion withstood several sharp attacks by the Germans, and their defense of Pink Hill took a heavy toll of the attacking parachute company. But the Germans rallied, and although they lost their company commander, they resumed their attack against the Pink Hill defenders. The Petrol Company commander, Captain McDonagh, kept his men under control until he himself fell dead from a sniper's bullet. Lacking his leadership, the men of Petrol Company withdrew, giving the Germans of Major Derpa's parachute battalion a foothold on Pink Hill.

Kippenberger had not received any word from the Eighth Greek Regiment fighting at Alikianou. From the heavy firing in that direction, he realized they were under attack. A false rumor, carried by a New Zealand runner, informed him that the Eighth Greek Regiment had broken before the German attack and fled from the battlefield. The brigade commander was not to learn until much later of the stout defense mounted by Lieutenant Colonel Peter Karkoulas' men against Major Liebach's Paratroop Engineer Battalion—a defense that caused Liebach to withdraw his force in order to regroup and lick his wounds.

Closer at hand, Kippenberger did not need a runner to tell him that the other Greek regiment attached to his brigade—the Sixth Regiment—was in trouble. In fact, the Sixth faced near annihilation. From the first moment of the paratroop attack in the Galatas area, these green, ill-equipped men had borne the full fury of the assault. They were no match for the disciplined, well-armed Fallschirmjägers.

The regiment's First Company, commanded by First Lieutenant Stavroulakis, had been deployed in a gully west of Cemetery Hill—due south of Galatas village. Within the first hour of battle, this company was surrounded by paratroopers, and when a German flanking thrust captured their commander, the company surrendered.

The same fate befell the Fifth Company, led by First Lieutenant Constantinidis. The men of this unit were surrounded without firing a shot because ammunition had not been distributed to them in time. The prisoners were quickly rounded up and marched off toward Prison Valley.

The regiment's Machine Gun Company, under First Lieutenant Ksirgianakis, put up a stiff wall of fire until their ammunition ran out. When their company commander was killed, the survivors fled toward Galatas village. The Second Company fought stubbornly among the graves and tombstones of Cemetery Hill, but when their company commander, Lieutenant Gianoulakis, fell wounded, the rest of the raw recruits also broke and fled toward Galatas.

Captain Silamianakis' Third Company held its ground east of Cemetery Hill against repeated German attacks. The Third Company's men met each German thrust with a fierce counterthrust. It was the only company of the regiment to hold its ground all day.[4]

When the Fifth Company surrendered, it exposed the Sixth Company's right flank. Captain Emorfopoulos—Captain E—and his executive officer, Lieutenant Kritakis, became aware of this new danger from the right. Having taken severe casualties and running low on ammunition, Captain E ordered his men to fall back behind the cemetery wall. Gathering the survivors of the Second Company who fought in the cemetery, he linked up with a third company and set up a stable defense line. On his right he had contact with the Petrol Company, which had withdrawn from Pink Hill, and on the left he had the New Zealand Nineteenth Battalion. In the hours ahead, Captain E and the survivors of his company were to give a good account of themselves in the face of repeated German attacks up Cemetery Hill.[5]

In order to bolster this defense line, Colonel Kippenberger ordered that the 190 men of the New Zealand Divisional Cavalry Detachment take their place in line along Cemetery Ridge.

Typical of the aloofness exhibited by the British Commonwealth commanders regarding their Greek allies, Kippenberger seemed nonchalant when advised of the troubles faced by the Sixth and Eighth Greek Regiments. Yet he had said nothing when the Petrol Company withdrew from Pink Hill, nor did he admonish the Divisional Cavalry Detachment for having retreated from the foothills above Alikianou village.

As early as 10:40 A.M., he realized that the German attacks toward Galatas were fragmented and that the attackers were off balance. Kippenberger's aggressiveness spurred him to conclude that a sharp counterattack in force against the whole Prison Valley area would throw the Germans back.

Not too far away from Kippenberger's brigade was the Fourth New Zealand Brigade commanded by Brigadier L. M. Inglis.

Inglis was of the same opinion as Kippenberger—an immediate counterattack in force would succeed in clearing Prison Valley of Germans.

Inglis proposed that the Eighteenth and Twentieth Battalions of his brigade mount an attack against the Germans in Prison Valley. The force of the attack should push the enemy out of the valley in confusion and help relieve the beleaguered force at Alikianou village. Once Prison Valley had been cleared, his brigade would wheel northward in a clockwise sweep and attack the Germans at Maleme from the south. The whole advance would follow a course that had been reconnoitered before the battle. Inglis's proposal was a clever, aggressive plan of attack, typical of his nature. It bore that distinct flavor of success, and Colonel Stewart at Freyberg's headquarters liked it. "The plan seems sound, old chap," commented Feyberg's chief of staff, "but you have to put the proposal up to Puttick—after all, you are now under his direct command."[6]

General Edward Puttick, the New Zealand divisional commander, who believed that World War I tactics were equally sound in World War II, did not like Inglis's proposal when he heard it. He considered it too bold a plan, for it depended on many contingencies—such as proper coordination in the face of communications difficulties, movement across open fields while in danger of Luftwaffe attack and, last but not least, the problem of supply. In any case, Puttick took the responsibility off his own shoulders when he remarked to Inglis that he would put the plan before Freyberg.

No sooner had Brigadier Inglis returned to his own headquarters than he received the answer to his proposal:

GENERAL FREYBERG DOES NOT APPROVE THE COUNTER-
ATTACK.[7]

Thus passed General Puttick's first and only opportunity to salvage the day's battle. General Freyberg's failure to approve the proposal and order the counterattack—he did not wish to countermand Puttick's wishes since Puttick was senior in rank—proved to be a costly lost opportunity for early victory.

After repeated messages by Kippenberger requesting a

counterattack, Puttick was finally moved to action only when he was erroneously told that the Germans might clear Galatas valley for a landing field. At 8:00 P.M. Puttick ordered Inglis to attack, yet he failed to tell Kippenberger—the man who would lead the attack!

Kippenberger first learned of the counterattack when he heard the roar of motors as three Vickers light tanks entered Galatas village from the north. In command of these tanks was Lieutenant Roy Farran of the Third Hussars, who brought them hastily over the twisting dirt road into Galatas. He reported to Kippenberger that he was ordered to attack by 8:30 P.M. "but it was not clear what their objective was!"[8]

When the attack finally began, it was almost dark. The three tanks immediately ran into a roadblock just beyond Cemetery Hill. Farran's machines were vulnerable to mortar and machine-gun fire, and he had to exercise great care. By the time the infantry of the Nineteenth Battalion cleared the roadblock, darkness had blanketed the battlefield. Farran pushed his tanks forward hoping to reach Prison Valley and cover the potential landing field with fire, even in darkness. They succeeded in doing so, until a mortar shell blew a track off his tank. Unscathed, Farran left his demolished machine, just missing capture.

Now, in the night hours of pitch blackness, Kippenberger and C. A. Blackburn, the CO of the Nineteenth Battalion, concurred that the attack had begun too late, and was too weak to achieve success. The two remaining tanks and supporting infantry were recalled and the attack cancelled.

Sergeant Dick Fahey was in his foxhole when the runner from Colonel Andrew arrived with the order to move the tanks out.

The crews of the two infantry tanks had dug a series of entrenchments in front of their hidden vehicles. All about these entrenchments lay the lifeless bodies of German paratroopers. Although the tank squad had taken a few casualties, they were still operational, and when Fahey got the message, he and his tankers sprang into action. At last he and his men would see the kind of action for which they had trained, instead of sitting in their foxholes fighting as infantrymen.

Off came the broken olive branches, uprooted cacti, and hunks of sod covering a huge camouflage net. The forward end of the tank pit had been graded like a ramp to facilitate exit. Fahey revved up the motors of the first tank and slowly crawled up the incline into the open, the second tank following right behind. Like two huge metallic turtles, they trundled over the rocky terrain of the eastern slope of Hill 107, heading for the main northern highway. The first element of the counterattack had moved into position.

The second element would be the infantry support. Colonel Andrew's battalion had taken a severe pounding all day, not only from the German ground attacks but also from the ubiquitous Luftwaffe. Although the air attacks had tapered off during the afternoon, pressure on the ground increased. As each paratroop assault was repulsed, the casualties among the defenders increased. By late afternoon, things had reached a point where no men were available to fill the gaps opened in the battalion defense line. And now, amid the fury of battle, these fatigued men would be asked to leave the somewhat supportive shelter of their entrenchments and expose themselves in a counterattack.

It is militarily axiomatic that such a maneuver is most likely to succeed when it is launched with fresh troops. Colonel Andrew had no such reserves available. In view of the increasing pressure exerted from two directions by the Germans, Companies A and B could not be spared from their positions on Hill 107. Company D and Headquarters Company were considered lost by Andrew. Only Company C presented a possible solution to the problem.

Captain S. H. Johnson of Company C had kept two sections of his unit in a secondary defense line along the coast road. These two sections were still intact, and their proximity to the road made them an obvious choice as the source of the men required for the counterattack. Thus, the nineteen battle-weary men of these two sections of C Company were ordered to do the work originally assigned to a whole battalion of 600 men. They were ordered to attack the Germans, rout them, and recapture the bridge over the Tavronites River.

Seeking some possible sign that would confirm the stupidity of the order, the sergeant in command of these seemingly expendable men stared at Captain Johnson while the company commander slowly repeated the orders given to him by the battalion commander. Captain Johnson completed his instructions and looked away; he could not endure the sergeant's penetrating stare, for he acknowledged to himself that it was a suicide mission.

Just then a young officer entered Andrew's headquarters. With a sharp, snappy salute, punctuated by a click of his heels, he presented himself to Major J. Leggatt, the second in command. The enlisted men, noncoms, and officers in the headquarters looked up in surprise at the sound of clicking heels. The sound also drew Colonel Andrew's attention.

"This lieutenant has a detachment of six men who were formerly the crew of a Bofors gun," remarked Major Leggatt, introducing the young officer. "The Bofors is out of action, sir, and he volunteers himself and his six men for the counterattack."[9]

Colonel Andrew nodded assent. "Have him and his men bring up the rear of Johnson's two sections. So now we have twenty-six men for our great attack. Things are looking up, Leggatt!"[10]

South of the main highway just east of the Tavronites River was Captain Campbell's D Company, which Colonel Andrew thought was wiped out. Only forty-seven men remained of this gallant New Zealand company. They were well situated in their defense positions, but their other problems were becoming vastly acute.

At about 5:30 P.M., the roar of motors from the direction of the coast road lightened the spirits of each of the forty-seven men. The sound was the familiar one of tanks; the long-awaited counterattack was finally coming.

The New Zealanders stirred in their trenches, and they noted that German harassing fire was no longer directed at them but toward the coast road. There was much movement and shouting by the Germans as they left their positions in order to repel the approaching counterattack, and the pent-up New Zealanders let loose a deadly fire on them.

One group of paratroopers was pulling a 20-mm mountain gun over the rocky terrain in order to site it on the coast road. A concentration of rifle fire from the flank of the D Company positions dropped each of the Germans around the cannon. Now it was the New Zealanders' turn to pick them off.

The first infantry tank moved slowly along the highway. Rifle fire coming from all directions struck its sides with little or no effect. The sound of ricocheting bullets bouncing off the superstructure made Sergeant Fahey's ears ring.

Through the narrow aperture, he spotted a group of Germans in an irrigation ditch to his right. He ordered that one round be fired at them and rotated the turret in order to sight his gun on the target.

There was no response.

"What the hell you waiting for? Load it!" yelled Fahey over the roar of the tank's motor.

"The shell won't fit—it's too big!" came the reply from the gunner. Hardly believing what he heard, Fahey stepped down from the observer's position, grabbed another shell from the rack, and placed it into the gun's breech. It would not go in. He tried another, with the same result, then another. They had been supplied with ammunition suited for a larger-caliber cannon! Fahey was livid.

"What the bloody hell! Here we are leading an attack and we can't even spit at them!"[11]

The second tank followed the first by an interval of thirty yards. Strung out between them were the twenty-six men serving as infantry support. They were using the tanks for protective cover.

The commander of the second tank had also spotted a good target and ordered his gunner to load the two-pounder cannon. But when he tried to rotate the turret in the direction of the target, he found that it was jammed. Unable to fire his cannon at will, the leader of the second tank ordered it to withdraw from the attack.

Without wireless equipment, when the second tank in the column decided to withdraw, it could not inform the advance tank. Thus Fahey assumed that the rest of the column was following him, and continued onward.

Fahey's Matilda (the affectionate name the Australians called their tanks) churned up the road until it approached the Tavronites River bridge. The Germans felt helpless before the advance of this interloping monster, for their light-caliber weapons could not penetrate its steel skin. One hundred yards from the bridge, Fahey left the road and headed for the river's edge, hoping to strike the Germans from the rear. The tank skidded down the steep embankment and passed under the concrete pylons of the bridge, Germans everywhere running from its path. Although its cannon was mysteriously silent, its machine gun cut a swathe in the fleeing ranks of the enemy.

Fahey continued along the dried-up river bed at the base of the embankment. Directly in his path were three members of a mortar section. Before they could climb out of their shallow entrenchment and run for safety, the tank ran over their position, crushing the men beneath its treads.

Advancing toward the far side of the river, Fahey found the going more difficult when his vehicle entered a muddy patch. The tank struggled forward and then slid into a shallow gully, its spinning treads chewing deeper and deeper into the mud. After exhausting attempts to disengage the tank, Fahey finally realized that it had become hopelessly mired in the muddy soil of the river bottom.

"Bail out!" he yelled, and through the turret and lower escape hatch, the crew wriggled out and raced for the protective cover of the embankment. The Matilda tank was left an abandoned derelict, as it had been once before in the sand dunes of North Africa.

The column of supporting infantry could not keep up with the lead tank, and when the follow-up tank withdrew, they were left in the open, unprotected.

Now a concentration of rifle and machine-gun fire fell upon these hapless men. Those caught in the middle of the road had no chance for survival, and dropped in all the grotesque positions of instantaneous death. Some of the others who were advancing along the side of the road hit the ground at the first volley of enemy fire, rolling into the protective hollow of an irrigation ditch that paralleled the road.

Gone was the lead section from C Company, with its gallant sergeant. Dead were the six volunteers from the Bofors gun crew. Their officer, that young, earnest lieutenant, screamed and shook his fist at the retreating tank, until bullets ripped into his body and he too fell dead.

Of the twenty-six men who constituted the infantry support of the counterattack, only eight demoralized survivors returned from this fruitless and tragic sortie.[12]

Colonel Andrew watched dispiritedly the eight men file past his command post. Suddenly he lost faith in his ability to hold Hill 107.

At 6:00 P.M., he signaled brigade headquarters that his counterattack had failed. Over a wireless set whose weakened batteries were transmitting a fading signal, he repeated his appeal for reinforcements. He added emphatically that in view of the counterattack's failure, if he did not receive reinforcements soon, he would have to withdraw from Hill 107.

To Andrew's surprise, Brigadier Hargest replied, "If you must, then you must."[13]

A curtain of darkness heralded the approach of night. The German commander who opposed Kippenberger also took time to consider his situation. Colonel Richard Heidrich, the newly appointed commander of the Seventh Airborne Division, still commanded the paratroopers of the Third Parachute Regiment in the Prison Valley area.

When Heidrich finished reviewing his position, it left him in a state of "extreme nervous tension."

He issued orders to his Engineer Battalion, recalling them from Alikianou in order to protect his rear in Prison Valley. Derpa's Second Battalion was to remain in place and regroup its men into a cohesive force after the day's bitter losses. To Captain von der Heydte, he issued orders to collect any stragglers from Heilmann's destroyed Third Battalion and together with his own men return and guard Prison Valley on the east, holding the Alikianou-Khaniá road.

Captain von der Heydte was with the battalion field hospital when he received the message to withdraw to Prison Valley. The aristocratic battalion commander, who bore a slight resemblance to the actor Leslie Howard, had spent some time in the hospital assuring himself that his wounded were being as well treated as circumstances allowed. He walked past the litter cases lying in the open under the cooling shade of olive trees and paused before a youthful, badly wounded paratrooper who lay unconscious. Von der Heydte lightly stroked the hair from the young man's eyes and remained kneeling beside him, gazing absentmindedly at his face. The dying soldier reminded the battalion commander of a familiar face from the past. Then he remembered. The youth had once been his aide.

In a hollow, the surgical team had rigged up a canvas top suspended from tree branches, below which stood an old kitchen table stained crimson with blood. This was their operating room.[14]

All night the messages received from Puttick's headquarters overflowed with confidence. Not a single reference had been made to Colonel Andrew's almost monotonously repetitious appeals for assistance. On the basis of the messages, Freyberg assumed that the airfield at Maleme was in no immediate danger.

At 2200 hours—10:00 P.M. that night—Freyberg decided to

inform General Wavell in Cairo of the prevailing situation in Crete at that hour. It was a message tinged with an undercurrent of anxiety:

TODAY HAS BEEN A HARD ONE. WE HAVE BEEN HARD PRESSED. SO FAR I BELIEVE WE HOLD THE AERODROMES AT MALEME, HERAKLION, RETIMO, [RETHIMNON] AND THE HARBORS. MARGIN BY WHICH WE HOLD THEM IS BARE ONE AND IT WOULD BE WRONG OF ME TO PAINT OPTIMISTIC PICTURE.[15]

Shortly after Freyberg dispatched his message to Wavell, a young man appeared at his headquarters. He was Geoffrey Cox, a junior officer attached to Freyberg's improvised intelligence section.

In the first hours of the German assault, Lieutenant Cox had joined a platoon of the Twentieth New Zealand Battalion, which, together with the men of the First Welsh Battalion, were out rounding up the paratroopers of Captain Gustav Altmann's glider force. Later that afternoon, Cox returned to Creforce Headquarters. He sat at the makeshift packing case that served as Colonel Blount's desk. On the desk was a pile of reports scheduled for shipment to Cairo by the first available means. Next to this pile was a captured German officer's briefcase; it did not appear to have been opened. Attached to its handle was a brief notation reporting how the item had come into British possession.

Cox was a journalist by profession, and in the days before the German invasion of Crete, he had edited two issues of a garrison newspaper, the *Cretan News*. Now, as he sat quietly at the desk, his reporter's curiosity got the better of him. He wondered about the contents of the briefcase and decided to glance through it.

It contained maps and an assortment of papers. One document in particular caught his attention. The words TOP SECRET were stamped across the top—with the additional precautionary admonition that it be burned and not carried into battle. Using a pocket-size English-German dictionary, which he had carried since his prewar days as a reporter in Vienna, Cox began to translate the document. It was a tediously slow task that took many hours. As the meaning of each translated word fell into place, he realized the significance of this piece of paper. What he had before him was a carbon copy of a German operational order for the invasion of Crete!

Cox scribbled the last words of his translation hastily, then rushed to Freyberg.

General Freyberg listened attentively to the translation. The words—the phraseology—stirred his memory: A western group would attack Maleme. . . . Group Central was to capture Khaniá. . . . Third Parachute Regiment . . . to seize Prison Valley. . . . Rethimnon and Iráklion to be attacked in the second wave.

The words were all too familiar. Freyberg had heard them before—no, he had read them! But where?

"What is the date of the order?" queried the Creforce commander.

"The eighteenth, sir," answered Cox.[16]

Freyberg remembered. It seemed so long ago, but just yesterday a Greek liaison officer—Major Hector Pavlides—had appeared at Creforce Headquarters, sent from the Greek Army Command in Khaniá, with a captured copy of an order describing the plan for the German attack on Crete.

That was the document taken by a fisherman from two downed German pilots outside Suda Bay. After the Greek commanding general read the captured document, he sent it to Freyberg's headquarters. But Freyberg did not believe that a classified document of such importance would have been carried in a pilot's map case on a flight that ran the risk of being shot down, as indeed had happened. Although the Greek command believed in the authenticity of the captured document, Freyberg had regarded it as a German ploy.

Cox's translation proved that the original document had been authentic. From this translation, Freyberg perceived that the Germans had failed to achieve their major objectives and that they were just holding on. Now was the appropriate time for action—to strike them while they were still weak and off-balance. Yet he issued not a single order to prepare for attack.

For the second and final time in a twenty-four hour period, Creforce Headquarters was informed of the German plans for their military operations in Crete, and for the second time, this valuable information was ignored. It would prove to be a fatal error.

General Student was seated at the broad table that stood in the center of the war room in the Grande Bretagne Hotel. Under a brilliant light, the table's surface was covered with maps, reconnaissance photographs, and official reports. A wisp of smoke rose from an ashtray filled to overflowing with butts and half-smoked cigarettes. Major Reinhardt, Student's staff intelligence officer, stood next to him going over the latest reports. Nearby stood Student's immediate superior, the Fourth Air Fleet commander, General Löhr, together with General Julius Ringel, the commanding general of the Fifth Mountain Division.

The news from Crete continued its disturbing trend; no one felt this tension more than General Student. The success or failure of this operation rested entirely upon his shoulders.

Certainly Adolf Hitler, who regarded the Fallschirmjägers as the ultrasecret weapon of his arsenal, would not look kindly upon the casualty lists incurred in Crete. Hitler must have had little confidence in the success of this operation, even though he approved it, for he had instructed his propaganda minister, Joseph Goebbels, to withhold all press releases of the invasion. Not a word of it had been printed in the German newspapers or reported over the German radio. Had Student realized this on the night of May 20, he would have been frantic. A telephone call from Berlin warned him that detractors in Hitler's capital were even now turning wheels to persuade the OKW to suspend operations in Crete. A brief message mentioned that if an airfield had *not* been secured by the next day:

WE MAY CONSIDER SUSPENDING THE OPERATION . . . AND
WITHDRAW ALL AVAILABLE UNITS.[17]

This struck Student hard. Were he to accede to this "suggestion" his career would be ruined and with it all the work that
had gone into developing the theory that an airborne division could
be effective in an independent military operation. Still, the news
from Crete was not good.

There were no reports from Colonel Sturm and the Second
Parachute Regiment at Rethimnon. This worried Student even
more. Reevaluation of the earlier reports, which described the
problems encountered by the assault regiment at Maleme and by
the Third Parachute Regiment in Prison Valley, revealed that a
great number of senior officers had been killed or wounded.
Student concluded from this that losses in the lower ranks must
have been equally heavy. His depression might have reached its
nadir had he known that in Crete he was destined to lose more
men than had been lost by the whole Wehrmacht since the beginning of the war.

At 2345 hours—fifteen minutes before midnight—Student
received the latest casualty totals for Maleme and Prison Valley.
Major Reinhardt turned to him and softly inquired, "Should I
make any preliminary plan for the possibility of breaking off the
engagement . . . if it seems advisable?"[18]

There it was! His own staff was now asking the same question: Should the attack be suspended? Upon Student's answer
rested the success or failure of Operation Mercury—and of his
career. But Student was an able, conscientious officer who would
not—could not—give up so readily.

He responded with a firm no. The attack would continue;
he would concentrate all his remaining forces upon the Maleme
area.

"Maleme will become the [focus] of the follow-up attack!"
he asserted.[19]

A question still rankled in his mind: Could transports be

landed at Maleme? Colonel Snowadzki's earlier attempt had shown it was impossible; but he had to try again—to be certain. He sent for Hauptmann Kleye, a staff officer with a reputation for dash and cool nerves.

"Fly to Maleme tonight," he ordered Kleye, "and see if you could land on the airfield!"[20]

Within the hour Captain Kleye was in a JU-52 racing for Crete. He reached Maleme and, in complete darkness, put his aircraft down successfully on the western edge of the airfield. Kleye did not encounter the fiery reception that the defenders had given Colonel Snowadzki earlier. He taxied his transport and, with throttles revving the three BMW motors to their full thrust of 830 horsepower, he took off for the return trip to Athens. An hour later he reported to Student that the airfield was usable. That was all Student needed to know. Rapidly he issued a series of orders—the forceful tactician at his best.

He ordered that six JU-52 transports prepare to fly to Maleme immediately carrying medical supplies and ammunition to the beleaguered paratroopers. He also ordered that the Fifth Mountain Division prepare elements of its One Hundredth Regiment to fly to Crete at dawn.

Then, turning to General Ringel, he added, "General, you will be flown to Crete tomorrow to take over the field command!"[21]

With nightfall the sound of battle diminished around Hill 107.

The Germans around the hill were scattered, alone or in small groups. They made no movement, glued to the ground under the olive trees and vines, waiting for whatever the night might bring. They were hungry, thirsty, and tired, but not a single one dared close his eyes. The atmosphere was tense and uneasy.

Like Colonel Heidrich in Prison Valley, the wounded General Meindl at Maleme was equally apprehensive about the expected New Zealand counterattack that could come at any moment during the night.

"What are the [English] waiting for?" he asked of his aide over and over again in a voice so racked with pain that it was difficult for him to speak. Meindl had less than fifty paratroopers holding the lower portion of the western slope of Hill 107.[22]

At brigade headquarters in the village of Platanias, Brigadier Hargest had had second thoughts about Andrew's latest appeal for aid. At last he decided to send reinforcements.

He instructed Colonel Leckie of the Twenty-third Battalion to dispatch one company of infantry to assist Andrew on Hill 107. He was sending a single company on a maneuver originally scheduled for a whole battalion. To bolster the force from the Twenty-third Battalion, Hargest ordered a company from the Twenty-eighth Maori Battalion to proceed to Maleme. These famous New Zealand fighters had been retained at Platanias as brigade reserve.

When Colonel Andrew was informed of Hargest's belated decision, he could not understand the logic of dispatching the Maori all the way from Platanias—a twelve-mile hike in total darkness—while other companies were available from the nearby Twenty-first and Twenty-third Battalions. Nevertheless he was pleased that his daylong appeals for assistance had finally received a positive response although he now feared that it was too late.

By 9:00 P.M. the promised reinforcements had not arrived at Maleme. Andrew ordered A Company to withdraw from its entrenchments on the highest point of Hill 107 and to descend to the lower ridge positions held by Company B. Finally, a half-hour later, the reinforcing company from the Twenty-third Battalion arrived. Colonel Andrew sent Captain C. N. Watson and the new arrivals up to man the positions at the crest of the hill formerly held by A Company.

Hargest never bothered to inform General Puttick, his division commander, that he was sending reinforcements to help Andrew. All day he reported confidently that his brigade was doing well at Maleme. Suddenly, at 11:15 P.M., he requested Puttick's permission to send the Twenty-eighth Battalion together with another battalion to assist the defenders of Hill 107. For the first time, Puttick realized that all was not going well at the airfield.

A little after midnight, the Twenty-second Battalion commander ordered both A and B Companies to leave their positions on the lower slopes of Hill 107. Captain Watson's relief company was to act as rear guard during the withdrawal.

At 0130 hours—an hour-and-a-half past midnight—the Maori company from the Twenty-eighth Battalion finally arrived at Maleme. They had been on the road for six hectic and eventful hours, having left Platanias at 7:00 P.M.

Their twelve-mile march included a brief but hotly contested skirmish with a group of paratroopers. Resolved only by a bayonet charge in the dark, the encounter cost the Maori two of their men. When Hill 107 loomed out of the darkness, Captain Rangi Royal, the company commander of the Maori, sent a scouting party to contact B Company of Andrew's battalion. The scouts found only empty entrenchments, for B Company had already withdrawn.

Captain Royal then took his company south along Xamoudokori Road, where he accidentally encountered Colonel Andrew and his two retreating companies heading eastward toward the defense positions of the Twenty-first and Twenty-third Battalions.

"You are too late, Captain," Andrew remarked dejectedly. "The situation has deteriorated to the point that I have to pull out." [23]

Colonel Andrew never asked Royal if he had encountered the isolated survivors of his headquarters company during the passage through Pirgos. To Royal's report of the bayonet charge, his only comment was, "You are damned lucky to be alive." [24]

At this moment in the battle, Andrew had the opportunity of saving the day at Maleme. He still had 300 unwounded men from his original battalion available for the defense of Hill 107.

Captain Watson's company from the Twenty-third Battalion augmented this to approximately 450 men. Captain Royal and the Maori started out with 114 men, but in picking up many stragglers during the march westward, their strength increased to 180 troopers. With their arrival, the Twenty-second Battalion had a total of 630 men available to defend Hill 107—almost as many as had been available at the onset of battle. But instead of leading the Maori Company, together with his own two companies, back up to the entrenchments on the hill to join Watson's men, Colonel Andrew followed the opposite course.

"It is no use, Captain Royal," he said adamantly. "It's too late. I suggest you take all your men back to Platanias." [25]

The decision to withdraw from Hill 107 was final.

At 2:00 A.M. Captain Watson and his relief company also left Hill 107 and followed Andrew's men back to the defense positions of the Twenty-third Battalion. At this time two runners from Captain Beaven's isolated headquarters company at Pirgos finally broke through to the Command Post of the Twenty-second Battalion, only to find it empty. Surprised, they retraced their steps to Pirgos. Captain Beavan had, however, gone on a personal reconnaissance and, approaching the defense positions of Company B, also found them empty. When he returned to his own command post at Pirgos at about 3:00 A.M., he thought it wise to follow in Andrew's footsteps and withdraw. Taking all the survivors of his company, including the stretcher cases, he withdrew eastward.

Captain Johnson had watched as one section of his C Company was wiped out in the fruitless counterattack late that afternoon. He had also lost the Fifteenth Platoon under Lieutenant R. B. Sinclair earlier in the day's battle on the airfield's perimeter. Yet, in spite of these heavy losses, Johnson was proud of the fifty surviving members of his company. He felt that they "were in excellent heart, in spite of our losses . . . they had not had enough . . . they were first rate . . . and were as aggressive" as when the battle first began. [26]

At 0420 hours, he too ordered withdrawal, sending a runner to inform the Thirteenth Platoon at the northeast perimeter of the airfield of his decision. Ten minutes later, his men moved out in single file. They had been ordered to take off their boots and hang them around their necks—the success of their withdrawal depended on complete silence. The wounded went with them, each man taking his turn carrying the litters in the line of march. As they struggled quietly over the rocky, cratered ground, they could hear the snores of the sleeping Germans on their right flank. They met no opposition and were subsequently allowed to put their boots back on. Along the route of their withdrawal, they came across three men from the Twenty-second Battalion still asleep in their foxholes, unaware that their units had pulled out.

Slowly, quietly, the New Zealand defenders of Hill 107 withdrew. Although ordered off the hill, they were reluctant to leave. These gallant men absorbed severe punishment all day against great odds and proved themselves equal to the task. They felt they had been successful in their defense, and they resented the ill-conceived orders to withdraw. They wanted to stay and fight it out. Most of all, they resented the idea of leaving many of their comrades behind.

By 0500 hours on the morning of May 21, the withdrawal was complete.

As Captain Campbell and his sergeant major stopped momentarily crossing the summit of Hill 107, they, too, heard the grating sounds of Germans snoring—the deep sleep of exhausted men.

"Sleep, would you, you bloody bastards?" muttered Campbell's sergeant major. In one final heave of frustration, he threw a hand grenade into the darkness. The subsequent explosion brought screams of pain from the German positions followed by bursts of machine-gun fire. Campbell and his sergeant major beat a hasty retreat down the opposite slope of the hill.[27]

The Germans were surprised that there was no response to their machine-gun fire; they looked at each other questioningly.

A small patrol went out to infiltrate the New Zealand positions. They returned in a short while with the surprising news that the New Zealand trenches appeared empty.

Oberstabsartzt Dr. Heinrich Neumann, the Assault Regiment's physician and the senior officer of the paratroopers at the base of the hill, quickly appreciated the possible meaning of the silence. The New Zealanders had withdrawn. Exhilarated at this possibility, he led a small group of men up the western slope of Hill 107 to its summit. There he was met by First Lieutenant Horst Trebes, who led a platoon from Stentzler's Second Assault Battalion, approaching the crest from the southern slopes. At the crest of the hill, the two parties quickly consolidated their unexpected windfall.

As the first light of dawn heralded the approach of the second day of the invasion, the strategic Hill 107 had fallen to the Germans. With its capture, the control of the airfield also passed into German hands. What they were unable to capture in daylight through feats of arms, was given to them as a gift during the hours of darkness.

THE
AFTER-
MATH

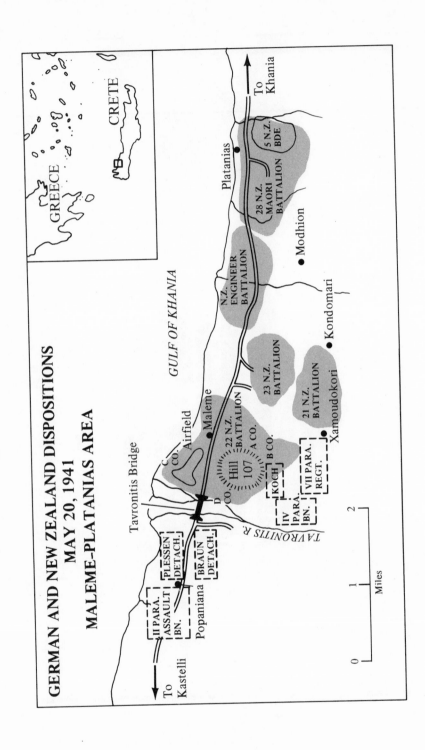

GERMAN AND NEW ZEALAND DISPOSITIONS
MAY 20, 1941
MALEME–PLATANIAS AREA

19

"PRESS ON REGARDLESS"

MAY 21, 1941

In the first twenty-four hours of this historic and dramatic battle, Crete had been won and lost. It had been won by the heroic and determined resistance of the British, New Zealand, and Australian battalions; by the ill-armed and badly trained Greek regiments; and by the proud and hardy Cretan civilians. It had been lost by the vacillating hesitation of the senior commanders in the Khaniá-Maleme area.

It was a day on which no senior officer in those sectors seemed to take the initiative expected of a military commander—to order a counterthrust against the embattled invaders. It was a day on which the commanders followed the safest path—to avoid the onus of responsibility. They passed the buck to the next-higher echelon.

The buck finally reached General Freyberg. Twice in a two-day period, he had been presented with a captured outline of the German plan of attack—and twice he ignored it. The first time he believed it to be a fabrication, a plant, and in light of the influential thinking emanating from the Cairo headquarters of General Wavell, the supreme commander in the Mediterranean, his reaction was acceptable. However, the second rebuff was inexcusable. A closer appreciation of the German operational plan indicated that the invader had failed to achieve his immediate objectives. Furthermore, it showed that the Germans were militarily off balance and outnumbered. A swift, well-supported counterthrust that first night would have overcome the Germans.

That is how close the defenders of Crete came to inflicting upon the German military juggernaut its first land defeat in World War II!

Although the exhausted, outnumbered paratroopers waited anxiously for the anticipated counterattack, it never came. Freyberg hesitated, as did his junior commanders. Instead of issuing immediate orders, Freyberg *invited* his sector commanders to meet him the next afternoon in order to *discuss* plans for a belated counterattack.

On that crucial first night of the invasion, the decision to delay any attack irretrievably lost the immediate opportunity for victory in Crete. After the abandonment of the prized Hill 107 and Maleme airfield, the Germans consolidated their windfall. Using Maleme as a base for men and matériel, they would eventually sweep eastward to inundate the rest of Crete.

Yet the Battle of Crete would last another nine hard-fought days, staining each square yard of Cretan soil with the blood of the attackers and defenders alike. There, under the twisted olive trees, amid the fruit orchards and the verdant fields, and on the rocky, sloping foothills of the White Mountains, a life-and-death drama was to take place that would remain a monument to all men who had ever fought to remain free.

The silence of the night was broken by a challenge: "Halt!" There was a mumbled sound as passwords were exchanged and acknowledged. Then in twos, threes, in fives, followed by larger groups, Andrew's retreating men from Hill 107 passed through the defense perimeter of the Twenty-third Battalion.

The men of the Twenty-third were taken totally by surprise. They were thunderstruck to see their friendly rivals from the Twenty-second struggle through their lines. Even in the darkness of night, they could feel the ordeal that the men of Andrew's battalion had sustained during the previous day's battle. Once the surprise had passed, they greeted them cordially and offered them whatever menial hospitality they could afford.

However, somewhere in the background, a raised voice was heard to ask: "What the bloody hell you doing here—who's guarding Hill 107?"[1]

Colonel Leckie of the Twenty-third Battalion suggested convening a battalion commanders' meeting, and he sent a runner to the headquarters of the Twenty-first to summon Colonel John Allen.

An hour later the meeting began, with Colonel Leckie presiding. Throughout the short conference, Andrew sat slumped dejectedly in a chair. With half-closed eyes he listened to the discussion, nodding his concurrence that the battalions "should hold their positions next day."[2]

Strangely enough, Colonel Leckie made no proposal that he take his Twenty-third Battalion forward, with the Twenty-first in support, to reoccupy Hill 107 and the airfield. Captain Watson's relief company had returned to the Twenty-third's area a few hours after the men of the Twenty-second entered Leckie's defense perimeter. Yet Leckie did not entertain the slightest thought of returning in force and reoccupying the vital hill, nor did he suggest this to General Hargest. Did Leckie derive an inner joy from Andrew's dilemma because of their own personal rivalry? In any event, nothing substantial came out of the meeting except the decision to hold their present positions—a decision that left the airfield open to the Germans.

And Colonel Andrew was too tired to care.

At the airfields in Greece, two companies of paratroopers, approximately 400 men representing Student's reserve, emplaned for the flight to Crete. Colonel Bernhard Ramcke was assigned the overall command of these reinforcements.

A second group of 350 men was also ordered to fly to Crete. These were the "leftovers" who had been stranded by lack of transport to carry them to the attack on Iráklion the previous afternoon.

Kurt Student had decided to drop Ramcke's 400 men in the area west of the Tavronitis River. Once landed, they would reinforce the men of the Stentzler and Gericke assault battalions and attack eastward. Student assumed that the New Zealanders' failure to counterattack the first night, and their subsequent withdrawal from Hill 107, meant they had no reserves available. To capitalize on that weakness, he ordered that the 350 leftover paratroopers be dropped in the Maleme-Pirgos area, where they would secure their positions and wait until the attacking assault troops reached them from the west.

Simultaneously, six JU-52 transports loaded to capacity with ammunition, rations, and medical supplies were to land at Maleme airfield. Right behind them, a task force comprising forty additional transports would ferry about 800 men of the Fifth Mountain Division to Crete. They would represent the first reinforcements that were not part of the original parachute assault force.

This phase of the invasion of Crete began with the floodgate—the abandoned airfield at Maleme—wide open for the Germans to enter.

While the 400 paratroopers under Colonel Bernard Ramcke's command were dropping safely west of the Tavronites River, the second, leftover group of 350 paratroopers was bailing out over the village of Pirgos. Unfortunately for them, they did not have the same peaceful descent as their comrades. What followed was a reenactment of the previous day's slaughter. It was to become the death knell for the Fallschirmjäger in Crete.

This wave of paratroopers was released along the northern coast road, strung out from Pirgos all the way to Platanias. They fell amid the men of the New Zealand Engineer Battalion attached to General Hargest's Fifth Brigade, and among the tough Twenty-eighth Maori Battalion.[3]

No sooner had the "sticks" of paratroopers left their transports than a cascade of rifle and machine-gun fire greeted them. The sporadic firing that had marked the earlier hours of this second day of the invasion now rose to a crescendo.

Captain J. N. Anderson of the Engineer Battalion scanned the sky, watching the paratroopers during their descent. Seemingly out of nowhere, one landed not more than ten feet in front of him. Anderson fired at him point-blank, while the trooper still lay beneath the canopy of his chute. Satisfied that he had disposed of the German, he looked up just in time to duck the feet of another paratrooper dropping right on top of him. At close quarters, Anderson fired the remaining bullets in his pistol into the paratrooper's body.

The New Zealander shook his head in distaste; he had killed the German without giving him a chance to defend himself. "Not cricket," he thought to himself, "but there it is!" With that, he ducked behind an olive tree to reload his pistol.[4]

All along the northern road, parachutes could be seen draped from the branches of olive trees or dangling from the telegraph wires that paralleled the road. From each parachute hung a dead body.

One paratrooper descended slowly, almost majestically, to earth, the path below him seemingly clear and quiet. Suddenly, out of their entrenchments, seven New Zealanders rose with fixed bayonets. When the paratrooper looked down again, what he saw struck terror in his heart. It was the first time that Captain Anderson ever heard a man scream with fear.[5]

Major H. G. Dyer, an officer in the Twenty-eighth New Zealand Battalion, led a group of Maori against the paratroopers.

Racing through a field, Dyer spotted a paratrooper firing at them from a partially filled-in well. He ordered Private Jim Tuwahi to pin the German down with his rifle while Dyer and another soldier approached him from the flank. When the German noted the flanking movement, he feigned death. Taking no chances, Dyer signaled the soldier to bayonet him. The young Maori rushed the well and, as his blade dug into the German's body, he turned his head the other way.

With that obstacle removed, Dyer led the rest of the Maori across the field. Germans were everywhere, clustered at fifteen-to-twenty-yard intervals. One German watched Dyer running toward him and lay down in order to take better aim with his tommy gun. The New Zealander fired a shot at him from the hip, the bullet grazing the paratrooper's buttocks and passing through his open legs. The German took careful aim at Dyer, who now appeared as a perfect target. But before he could squeeze the trigger of his machine pistol, another Maori speared the German with a bayonet. Such hand-to-hand encounters were common during the morning. Dyer continued his sortie against the Germans, many of the scattered paratroopers withdrawing in the face of the fierce Maori bayonet charge. Those Germans who remained behind were either dead or severely wounded.[6]

On the banks of the Platanias River, west of Platanias village, Manoli Paterakis and five other guerrillas had spent all morning hunting Germans. When additional paratroopers fell in their area, Paterakis and his men had a field day shooting them down.

Now a momentary silence fell over this section of the battlefield. Paterakis and the other Cretans stood ankle deep in the shallow waters of the river catching their breath and refreshing themselves from the heat of the day. The braying of a nearby frightened donkey echoed across the fields. For the moment, the area was empty of Germans.

Suddenly Gianni, one of the Cretans, acting as a lookout, gestured toward the road. Paterakis and the others crept carefully to the riverbank, following the lookout's motion. There, coming down the road, was a German officer with a squad of paratroopers behind him.

Major Franz Braun had collected the survivors of a company and was leading them down the road toward the village of Pirgos. When they reached the narrow, stone-arched Platanias

Bridge, Braun spotted the braying donkey and decided to take it with him.

He left the road and crossed the small field to where the donkey stood, passing right in front of Paterakis and Gianni. Unaware of their presence, Braun nonchalantly leaned over and loosened the rope that kept the animal tethered to a stake. At that moment, Gianni pulled the trigger of his rifle.

Nothing happened except for a loud click.

Braun heard the sound, turned, and unholstered his Luger. Before he had a chance to shoot, Manoli Paterakis fired two bullets into his chest, killing him instantly. The shots alerted the squad of paratroopers, who stood idly in the middle of the road waiting for the major. Before they could scatter for cover, the other three guerrillas opened fire with their captured German tommy guns. In a matter of minutes, the paratroop squad was wiped out. No mercy was asked and none was given. The Cretans were not going to allow a single paratrooper to survive to fight them another day.[7]

Of the two companies that had been dropped between the village of Pirgos and Platanias, all the officers and noncoms, together with most of the lower ranks, of one had been killed; from the other, only one officer and eighty men survived the assault. These survivors retreated westward to Pirgos, holing up in stone houses until relief or darkness reached them, whichever came first.

At 1500 hours—3:00 P.M.—Captain Gericke's request for an air strike against the villages of Maleme and Pirgos was finally fulfilled.

For almost an hour, the demonic Stukas subjected the two villages to a blistering bombing. Throughout those endless moments, the air was rent by the shriek of diving Stukas and by the shattering blast of their bombs. When the last plane left, a huge dust cloud hung low over the whole area.

Out of the dust, Gericke's men emerged. They advanced slowly on each side of the main road, moving from the southern edge of the airfield under the shadow of Hill 107, eastward toward Pirgos.

The men felt the rising excitement of victory. However, it was a short-lived exultation. Despite the ferocity of the bombing, there were still pockets of resistance by stubborn Cretans and isolated stragglers from the Twenty-second Battalion. From behind tombstones in Pirgos cemetery, from within the blasted piles of bombed stone houses, from behind walls and trees, armed Cretan civilians, using captured German machine guns and rifles, together with isolated New Zealanders, kept up continuous fire. This harassment slowed the German advance and gradually diminished their thoughts of an easy victory.

The paratroopers continued slowly across the open fields, waded the shallow Sfakoriako River, crossed a narrow valley, and started up the opposite slope—right into the defense positions of the Twenty-third New Zealand Battalion. The New Zealanders spotted them across the fields, their open formation making them perfect targets. They let them advance slowly, silently, into the trap.

At 150 yards, the New Zealanders opened fire.

It did not last long. The crack of rifles and the chatter of Bren machine guns echoed across the fields and valleys as the bullets tore into the ranks of the paratroopers. Occasionally the harsh crump of a mortar shell punctuated the din of battle. What was even more demoralizing for the Germans was the familiar sound of the more rapid-firing Schmeiser machine pistol being used against them.

When the firing finally stopped and the smoke cleared, the slope of the hill was covered with the bodies of German paratroopers. The survivors withdrew to the village of Pirgos, leaving behind them approximately 200 casualties. The advance had been stopped.

While the Germans were licking their wounds in the village of Pirgos, General Freyberg was convening a conference with his brigade commanders in Creforce Headquarters on Akrotiri

Peninsula. This was the conference that was to crystallize a plan to recapture Maleme airfield.

In the dimly lit cavernous dugout that served as Freyberg's war room, the officers assembled around a table, some standing, and others sitting on crates.

At the outset of the conference, Freyberg suggested to his subordinates that the Eighteenth, Twentieth, and Twenty-eighth Maori and the Welsh Battalions be used as the major strike force in the counterattack, and that they in turn be supported by follow-up units. His brigadiers strongly objected to this plan; to accept it at face value meant that each area commander would have to transfer units to Puttick's command. Their personal military pride did not allow them to relinquish control of any unit to another commander. They found innumerable lame excuses with which to circumvent Freyberg's suggestion.

"We must guard against a sea invasion," argued General Weston.[8]

"Let us not dismiss the necessity of guarding our communications from the many isolated enemy in the rear," added General G. A. Vasey of the Australian Brigade.[9] Finally, Freyberg acceded to the suggestions by his subordinates and a compromise plan for a counterattack was formulated.

Receiving no further dictates from his subordinates, Freyberg was pleased to adjourn the conference. He optimistically added that the counterattack would begin sometime between 10:00 and 11:00 P.M. that night.

Kurt Meyer was a German war correspondent who had been assigned to cover the landings of the mountain division in Crete.

As the transport in which he was a passenger approached the coast of Crete, both side hatches were opened and the crew members stood trying to locate a clearing in which to land. The blast of cold air hit Meyer fully, nearly throwing him out of his seat. Through the open hatches, he could see the rooftops of villages and the surrounding green fields. He also observed apprehensively the arcs of tracer bullets coming up at them. The pilot zigzagged the aircraft to avoid enemy fire, all of which made Meyer hold on for dear life.

The transport flew low over the airfield, and the pilot circled and made a second pass. Not a single clear lane was visible; the airfield looked as if a hurricane had struck it. With Junker transports all over the field, settled at various angles and facing in all directions, it resembled a huge parking lot. Some transports were smashed. Many had collided with other transports during the landings. Interspersed between them were a few smoldering hulks of aircraft that had caught fire.

The pilot of the transport carrying Kurt Meyer finally gave up the idea of landing on the airfield itself and swung wide over the water again. He circled and decided to bring the aircraft down along a strip of land near the shore. Slowly the Junker dropped lower to the ground. As it lumbered to touch down, the pilot noticed that the appearance of the strip had deceived him—it was not smooth at all, but interspersed with little rivulets, hollows, and rocks. It was too late to turn back; he had to land.

Just then a blast of machine-gun fire ripped into the right wing. With a last exasperated yell, the pilot warned everyone to hold on. The transport bounced heavily over the uneven ground. Its right wheel struck a rock, and the huge aircraft tilted off-balance to the left. The left wingtip clipped a low cactus and then dug itself into the sandy soil, spinning the aircraft into a half-circle, flinging men and cargo forward into a heap. The huge aircraft came to a sudden stop with one wing dug into the ground and the fuselage half-raised in the air.

Slowly the crew and the troopers separated themselves from the mixed pile of bodies and cargo. Though badly shaken and with some bad bruises, no one was seriously injured. Kurt Meyer's arrival in Crete had a brusque beginning.[10]

George Psychoundakis, the young, dark-eyed Cretan from the village of Asi Gonia, was stationed with ten other Cretans on the sandy shores near the village of Platanias. They had positioned themselves behind a half-fallen stone wall, from where they had a clear view of the shore and the narrow channel that separated the small isle of St. Theodore from the main island. Their assignment had been to protect this sector from a possible German sea invasion.

During the earlier hours of the twenty-first, Psychoundakis and his fellow Cretans had taken a good toll of paratroopers who had dropped nearby. The later hours of the afternoon had been quiet except for the sounds of battle from the west. Now, as late afternoon passed into early evening, six Junker transports began circling overhead. Some disappeared low over the hills, while one of them seemed to land by the shore further west, just out of sight.

Another transport came in low over the water and settled on the sandy strip near the pounding waves. No sooner had it rolled to a stop than the Cretans left the protection of the wall and dashed out to its landing site. Approaching the aircraft from all directions, they fired their machine guns until the barrels turned red. No one emerged from the transport. Finally the aircraft burst into flames.

Psychoundakis looked at the fiery pyre and shook his head, while his comrades danced a jig over their latest success.[11]

Of the six transports from this flight that had decided to land by the shore near Platanias village, not a single one survived the landing. Not a single trooper left his aircraft alive.[12]

All in all, the Germans had lost twelve Junker transports during this operation, but they did safely land 650 mountain troops out of a total of 800 men flown to Crete.

Within an hour after the first group of transports landed on Maleme airfield, Oberstleutnant Snowadzki and his Airfield Service Company were at work clearing the airstrip of wrecked aircraft. Using a captured Bren carrier and one of the abandoned Matilda infantry tanks, Snowadzki and his men pulled and pushed the derelicts to the side of the airfield, thus clearing the path for the arrival of additional reinforcements.

By 7:00 P.M., May 21, Colonel Ramcke arrived in Crete to assume command of all the paratroopers in the Maleme sector.

He succeeded the wounded General Meindl, who had been flown out on a transport earlier in the day.

The hard-driving, aggressive Ramcke was not impressed with the difficulties the paratroopers had encountered earlier and that had halted their advance. As nightfall ended the second day of the battle, he issued sharp and succinct orders to Gericke and to the other commanders in his sector:

PRESS ON REGARDLESS . . . KEEP GOING INTO THE DARKNESS . . . ENSURE THAT THE ENEMY CAN NO LONGER REACH THE AIRFIELD.[13]

By nightfall on the second day of battle, the scales of battle were still evenly balanced.

20

"IT HAS BEEN A GREAT RESPONSIBILITY"

MAY 21, 1941

The news of the German invasion of Crete reached Prime Minister Winston Churchill before noon on May 20. During the early session of the House of Commons, Churchill rose to interrupt a heated debate. The members were somewhat crowded in their temporary meeting hall, having been dispossessed from the Commons chamber by the night bombings of May 10, which had wrecked the Parliament building and Westminster Abbey. In the slow, halting speech so typical of Churchill, particularly when the news bore the urgency of alarm, he addressed the hushed M.P.s.

"I hold in my hand an urgent signal from General Wavell . . . a serious battle has begun in Crete." A murmur ran through the chamber, and when it diminished, Churchill gave a brief resumé based on dispatches. Finally he concluded, "I am confident that the most stern and resolute resistance would be offered to the enemy." [1]

Toward late afternoon he read another report: "After a good deal of intense bombing, enemy troops have landed by gliders, parachutes, and troop-carriers in the Khania-Maleme area . . .

there is a continuous enemy reconnaissance, accompanied by sporadic bombing and machine gunning, chiefly against antiaircraft defenses. . . . It is thought that the enemy were attempting to capture the aerodrome at Maleme . . . so far this has failed . . . the military hospital between Khania and Maleme, captured by the enemy, has now been recaptured.

"It appears," concluded Churchill, "that for the present the military situation is in hand."[2]

The late editions of the *Daily Telegraph* and the London *Times* carried banner headlines of the German attack on Crete. All over Britain people listened to the BBC for news of the invasion. They listened intently, hoping for any word that might forecast a defeat for the Germans.

What surprised Major Karl Lothar Schulz, the commander of the Third Paratroop Battalion at Iráklion, was that the resistance he encountered came not only from British and Greek troops, but also from armed Cretan civilians. Old men, young boys, women, and girls vented their hate on the intruders. The girls threw stones at the paratroopers, while the women collected weapons and ammunition from German dead. The old men fought like youths and the young boys fought like men. From every vantage point, they fired captured German weapons. "They have no right to fight us," protested Major Schulz, "they are not soldiers—they are civilians!"

Oberleutnant von der Schulenberg, an officer in Schulz's battalion, captured one such youthful Cretan and brought him before Major Schulz. Schulenberg remarked that the captive had held one of the platoons pinned down for almost an hour until he had at last run out of ammunition.

The tall battalion commander could not help but admire the youth's courage.

"Why are you fighting us?" he asked him.

The young Cretan did not understand the question, but he must have sensed its meaning. He glared at the German major with hate; in a final display of contempt, he threw his head back, pursed his lips, and spit at Schulz.

Shocked at this disrespect to his rank, Schulz wiped the spittle from his face and walked away—half-angry, half-embarrassed. A short burst from a machine gun denoted the brave young Cretan's fate.[3]

For the remainder of this second day of battle, Schulz's advance had been checked; the resistance had become so stubborn that those little gains were measured in yards. The heat of the day was exhausting, but what was even more alarming was that his paratroopers were running low on ammunition.

Major Schulz had not slept since the night before the invasion. From the moment he landed in Crete, he was constantly in motion—running, shooting, barking orders. Suddenly he felt his strength ebb and decided to rest a few minutes in the cool shade of a stone wall. One of his company commanders, Oberleutnant Kerfin, approached him for orders: "Herr Major?" Schulz shook his head dejectedly.

"If something doesn't happen soon," the battalion commander remarked in a tired voice, "we'll have to evacuate the town."[4]

Kerfin looked at him in disbelief, surprised at his commander's remark. But Kerfin realized what he meant; he knew only too well that if the battalion did not receive a supply of ammunition soon, they might be forced to surrender.

The two men sat in tired silence.

At that moment, a perspiration-soaked Feldwebel snapped to attention in front of the two officers.

"What's up, sergeant?" Kerfin growled, still annoyed at the very suggestion of surrender.

Behind the sergeant were three civilians—a portly elderly man wearing a straw hat, a dark-haired girl, and behind these two a short, dark man dressed in the uniform of a Greek army officer with the rank of major.

"These people want to surrender Iráklion to us," replied the paratroop noncom.[5]

Major Schulz jumped excitedly to his feet; the statement brought a surge of energy to his fatigued body.

The dark-haired girl was the first of the group to speak. In German, she said, "Major Bock!"

Schulz immediately recognized the code word that introduced a German sympathizer.

"Are these gentlemen empowered to make this offer?" he asked the girl directly. She nodded affirmatively.

"The civilian is the mayor of the city and the officer is the Greek commandant of Iráklion. They have come to offer you its surrender."[6]

Satisfied that the two emissaries were officially authorized to act, Schulz immediately dictated the terms of the surrender. Kerfin scribbled hastily on a page taken from a field notebook. With the girl acting as an interpreter, the major and the commandant accepted the terms and signed the paper. Major Schulz then added his signature to the surrender document, making it official.

A new strength raced through Schulz—a strength derived from the knowledge that he had achieved the regimental objective— the capture of Iráklion.

He barked orders to his company commanders. Von der Schulenberg and Kerfin ran to lead their respective companies into the city. Lieutenant Becker was assigned the takeover of the Citadel—a fortresslike, elevated structure in the center of town.

Suddenly the momentary silence was broken by the characteristically slow-firing rattle of a British machine gun. It was followed by a rising crackle of small-arms fire, all coming from the direction of the Citadel. Schulz hastened after Becker.

"What's up?" he asked, angered by this breach of the surrender agreement.

"The British have fired on us," complained Becker, pointing at the bastionlike walls of the Citadel. "They don't accept the surrender agreement!"[7]

Schulz muttered a curse. Just beyond, in the open, he could see the bodies of dead paratroopers from Kerfin's company. The British did not plan to surrender. In fact, the Australians and the British infantry unit defending the town pursued the Germans in a spirited counterattack. Infantrymen from a platoon of the Leicesters Regiment, aided by a platoon from the Yorks and Lancs, drove the Germans back foot by foot.

Taking heavy casualties and running dangerously low in ammunition, Major Schulz had no recourse but to withdraw his men. Leaving a few paratroopers as a rear guard, he took the remnants of his battalion back to the wall at the western gate of the city. All the hard-fought gains of the previous night and early morning had been for naught.

Schulz's retreat left the city of Iráklion firmly in the hands of the Greek and British defenders.

East of Iráklion, Major Schulz's regimental commander was not faring any better. Oberst Bruno Brauer, still in his resplendent dress uniform, ordered several desperate attacks to capture the Iráklion airfield—all of which proved fruitless. During the predawn hours of May 21, Colonel Brauer sent a platoon of paratroopers, led by Oberleutnant Wolfgang von Blücher, to occupy a hillock on the eastern fringe of the airfield. He planned to use that high ground as a base for an all-out attempt to seize the landing strip.

No sooner had this platoon of paratroopers dug themselves into the side of the hill than they were surrounded and isolated by British infantry. Brauer was alert to the platoon's predicament and ordered whatever units were available to break through to the beleaguered paratroopers on the hill. But the German thrusts were piecemeal and easily repulsed by the gallant men of the famous Black Watch Battalion.

Later in the day, the infantrymen of the Black Watch launched a vicious counterattack against the hill. They raced up the slopes with the steel of their bayonets glittering in the afternoon sun.

Not even the wall of fire that greeted them could stem their charge. One German position after another fell in rapid succession until the hill was completely overrun. There were few German survivors and even fewer prisoners.

The reverses suffered by the Germans at Iráklion were similarly dealt to their countrymen at Rethimnon.

Lieutenant Colonel Ian Campbell, whose task it was to defend the airstrip east of Rethimnon, was being hard pressed by the Germans. By nightfall of May 20, the troopers of the Second Parachute Regiment had seized control of a strategic piece of high ground designated as Hill A. This hill was to Rethimnon what Hill 107 was to the airfield at Maleme; whoever possessed it controlled the airfield—the little clearing that served as Rethimnon's airport.

Campbell knew very well that if he were to hold the airfield, he had to regain possession of Hill A. What bothered him was that he had to do it with only the few men available, for there was no possibility of assistance from any quarter. But Campbell was an experienced officer who was not fettered by the stagnant military dogmas of World War I as were Generals Hargest and Puttick. Campbell believed in the military philosophy of maneuver and attack, shortly to be exemplified by General Rommel in North Africa. It was this belief that drove him to do what had to be done: attack with his few men and take the hill.

At dawn of May 21, Campbell sent one company of Australians, commanded by Captain D. R. Channell, against the Germans on Hill A. In the face of heavy small-arms and machine gun fire supported by a deluge of mortar fire, the Australians had to break off the attack. There were many casualties, which included the company commander among the wounded.

Campbell was not disheartened by this failure. His determination and fighting spirit drove him to a second attack. He ordered Captain O. Moriarty and the reserve company to take the hill.

The Australians charged up Hill A with Captain Moriarty in the lead, firing from the hip and yelling wildly over the din of small-arms fire. These sons of soldiers who had fought at Gallipoli showed the same spirit and determination as their commander in the sweep to seize the hill. When the Germans saw the naked steel of the Australian bayonets, they broke and fled— with the attackers in hot pursuit. The charge carried Moriarty's men to the crest and down the other side. The hill was taken and the airfield returned to Colonel Campbell's control.

The eastern half of the isolated paratroopers were soon joined by the German survivors retreating from Hill A. Together they were led by Major Kroh in a withdrawal further east to the village of Stavromenos, where they took shelter within the thick walls of an olive oil factory. Captain Moriarty's men of the First Australian Battalion were close on their heels.

Perhaps the greatest victory of the day for Colonel Campbell's brave Australians was the capture of the commanding officer of the Second Parachute Regiment.

Colonel Sturm had never achieved full command of his paratroopers in Crete. From the first hour of the landing in the Rethimnon area, the command remained separated into two sectors with Wiedemann commanding in the west while Kroh led in the east. Communications failure kept the two regimental forces isolated. It was a situation that did not sit well with the arrogant and aloof Colonel Sturm.

Colonel Campbell's determined series of attacks and tactical maneuvers succeeded in keeping the Germans apart. Unaware of Campbell's rapid advance northward, Sturm found himself suddenly surrounded in his headquarters by the attacking Australians, and was subsequently captured together with his whole regimental staff.

By late afternoon on the twenty-first, Colonel Heidrich in Prison Valley ordered Major Derpa's Second Parachute Battalion to attack Galatas heights again. Derpa grimaced at the order; it seemed to him that his battalion was doing all the attacking. His command was down to a strength of a little less than two companies, and his men were fatigued, thirsty, and hungry. Yet, disciplined as he was to follow orders, he gathered his surviving company commanders for yet another attack.

Major Derpa ordered two platoons from the paratroop company on his right flank to assault Cemetery Hill once again. He reasoned that if he succeeded in seizing Cemetery Hill, he could enfilade the adjacent Pink Hill—held by the New Zealand Petrol Company—neutralize it, and then coordinate an advance on Galatas village.

Captain Emorfopoulos and his executive officer, Lieutenant Kritakis, watched the paratroopers gathering in the protective shadows of a line of olive trees across the meadow that separated the Germans from Cemetery Hill. The veteran commander of the Sixth Greek Company correctly assumed that his men would soon bear the brunt of an assault. Runners bellied out to Lieutenants Piperis and Koulakis, the platoon commanders on the flanks of the company's defense position, with the captain's orders: "Tell them to hold their fire until the Germans get close— and make each shot count."[8]

The Greeks watched anxiously as the paratroopers left the line of trees and crossed the open meadow. They were approaching in almost parade-ground precision, their officers in the lead, noncoms shouting orders. Captain E noted admiringly the coolness of the attackers.

"Those men are real professionals," he commented to Kritakis.[9]

Halfway across the meadow, the paratroopers broke into a trot that quickly brought them up the slopes of Cemetery Hill. The Greeks opened fire.

One squad of Germans led by a big, heavyset sergeant charged toward Captain E and his headquarters staff. Lieutenant Kritakis, positioned behind a tree, aimed and fired his pistol— but not a single one of his targets fell. Captain E was in a prone position, taking unhurried aim with a rifle. He had earlier discarded his pistol as ineffective and had borrowed the rifle from a wounded soldier. He sighted carefully and fired; he ejected the shell, slammed the bolt forward, and fired again. With each shot, a German fell in his tracks.

Kritakis gleefully shouted congratulations to him. The company commander cast him an annoyed glance. The rest of his men followed their commander's example and set up a strong and effective field of fire that finally stopped the German squad. The big paratroop sergeant was the last to fall.

But the German assault on the flanks of the Sixth Company was more successful, forcing Lieutenants Piperis and Koulakos to withdraw their platoons behind the stone wall that separated the cemetery from the road to Galatas. This withdrawal left Captain E and his men exposed. The brave Greek company commander realized his predicament but held stubbornly to his position. He was virtually surrounded, and the German fire was cutting his men down all around him.

"We shall fight to the last man!" he shouted stubbornly to Lieutenant Kritakis, loudly enough for all his men to hear. Private George Katosis, the company runner, dug his hand deep into the side pocket of his tunic. When he opened it, he found that he had only five bullets left. The other men fared no better.[10]

For minutes that seemed like hours, the struggle continued amid the tombstones of the village cemetery.

Suddenly there rose a thunderous shout from beyond the cemetery wall. Everyone heard it over the din of battle; even the paratroopers were momentarily distracted.

In one lusty yell came the cry of "Aera!"

Captain E smiled with relief as did the survivors of his surrounded company. All Greeks knew what that shout meant—the battle cry of the kilted Greek evzones, those specially selected warriors known for their great valor and heroism in Greece's fight for independence. The Greeks were counterattacking.

Like water that bursts from a ruptured dam, so did 200 Greeks of the Sixth Greek Regiment burst over the wall with bayonets held high, shouting over and over again the bloodcurdling battle cry of "Aera!"[11]

In their lead was a tall, fair-complexioned British officer!

Captain Michael Forrester from the Queen's Regiment had reported to Colonel Kippenberger on official business on May 20. The German invasion delayed his return to Creforce Headquarters. All that day he remained at Galatas, finally attaching himself to the Sixth Greek Regiment as its advisor. When the green troops from some of its companies fled in the face of the German assault earlier on the first day of the invasion, Captain Forrester rallied them, scrounged ammunition for them, and planned to use them as a mobile reserve force.

As it become apparent on this hot afternoon of May 21 that the Germans might succeed in capturing Cemetery Hill, he led his 200 Greeks in a stirring bayonet charge that surprised even Forrester by its spirited success.

The charging Greeks raced over the crest of the hill and down its slopes with a passionate determination to avenge themselves for the previous day's retreat. In one continuous rush, like a wind blowing across a field, the Greeks swept from tombstone to tombstone, slashing and killing Germans, and dying in turn while avenging their honor. Not one single German survived the Greek counterattack; not one was taken prisoner.

The German assault against Cemetery Hill failed—as had all the previous attacks against the Galatas heights.[12]

By sunset on May 21, the situation in Crete still remained critical for the Germans. Everywhere throughout the island, the German troopers settled their fatigued, thirsty bodies uncomfortably for the night amid their hundreds of wounded and thousands of dead comrades.

Back in Berlin, Adolf Hitler kept a close watch on the events in Crete. He still had not permitted a single item about the assault to appear in the newspapers or to be broadcast over Radio Berlin. This continued restriction somehow gave the impression that Hitler felt the Cretan operation to be a lost cause, and that he wanted to hide the disastrous facts of this side venture from the German people. Hitler's thoughts were centered on *the* major military operation in the east—Operation Barbarossa—the invasion of Russia. Hundreds of thousands of troops were already positioned on the Russian border, waiting for the word to attack. But this assault on Crete caused a delay in his scheduled invasion of Russia. Spring had come and gone and summer was approaching.

General Kurt Student was very much aware of this increasing anxiety, and of the diminishing faith in his operation. But he still clung to the desperate last hope that the arrival of the Mountain Division in Crete would tip the scales in favor of a German victory.

Toward evening Brigadier Hargest summoned the battalion commanders who would be directly involved in the counterattack to meet with him at brigade headquarters in Platanias. When Colonel George Dittmer, the commanding officer of the Twenty-eighth Maori Battalion, entered the main room of the farmhouse that served as Hargest's headquarters, he was surprised to find one other battalion commander present—Major John Burrows of the Twentieth New Zealand Battalion.

Dittmer frowned, for he knew that the attachment of the Twentieth Battalion brought the Fifth Brigade's strength up to five battalions—a formidable force with which to counterattack. Yet the only other officer present at the conference was General Puttick's staff representative, Lieutenant Colonel W. G. Gentry. Why had Hargest not invited Colonels Andrew, Allen, or Leckie? As the brigade commander reviewed the tactical details of the operation, Dittmer realized why the three other battalion commanders were not present. Hargest had not included their battalions in his plans. The whole burden of the counterattack would rest solely upon the arms of his Maori and upon Burrows's men. Dittmer did not like the plan.

Hargest continued. The operation dictated that the two attacking battalions be at their starting line—a point just west of the Platanias River—by 1:00 A.M. Under the protective cover of darkness, the Twentieth Battalion would advance north of the road, while the Twenty-eighth would cross the territory south of the main highway. Three tanks would advance simultaneously along the highway and give support to the two battalions as required.

Starting time for the advance would be 1:00 A.M. The attack on the first major objective—the village of Pirgos—would begin at 4:00 A.M. Once that village had fallen to the New Zealanders, they would rest for thirty minutes and then advance to clear the airfield and capture Hill 107. Burrows's men would take the airfield while Dittmer's Maori seized Hill 107.

"There it is, gentlemen," Hargest concluded in an optimistic tone of voice.[13]

Dittmer was not as optimistic as Hargest. This operation *might* succeed in peacetime night maneuvers, he thought to himself, but an advance requiring speed and the cover of darkness for success—with one of the battalions waiting to be relieved before it can be brought up to the starting line—all against a determined enemy . . . ! He raised the obvious question: "What if enemy pockets in the territory between the starting line of the advance and Pirgos delay our timetable?"

Before Hargest could reply, Dittmer added: "May I suggest that the detachment of engineers from the Twenty-third Battalion be sent down to clear the path in advance of the main body . . . ?"

Hargest brushed off Dittmer's suggestion with a curt, "It is too late for any clearing up activity!"

It was Burrows's turn to clarify an obvious omission: "Can we expect assistance from the Twenty-third, Twenty-first, or Twenty-second Battalions once we have reached our objectives or if we run into difficulty?"

Hargest looked at Burrows for a few moments before answering. "Oh, I suppose I could send Allen around the left flank

. . . and I might send the Twenty-Third in for a 'mopping-up' role."[14]

Dittmer wanted a more definitive answer: "Could we depend on their assistance . . . ?" But a frown from Hargest cut his question short.

"By the way, Dittmer," added Hargest as an afterthought, "as soon as the operation has been completed, you are to withdraw your Maoris and bring them back here to Platanias . . . you will entrust the defense of Hill 107 . . . to the Twentieth Battalion alone!"[15]

Burrows and Dittmer looked at each other incredulously. Instead of sending the three other battalions forward to consolidate the gains, Hargest was weakening the attack by *withdrawing* one of the attacking battalions! How could a strategy that had failed on the first day with a single battalion on line be expected to succeed two days later with another lone battalion composed of men tired from an all-night attack against a stronger enemy?

Dittmer closed his note pad angrily at the idiocy of the order.

Colonel P. G. Walker, the commanding officer of the Seventh Australian Battalion, had no trucks available to transport his men to Khaniá in order to relieve Burrows's Twentieth New Zealanders. His trucks were to arrive from the motor pool at Suda. Walker, still smarting from Brigadier Inglis's sarcasm that "a well-trained battalion could carry out such a relief in an hour,"[16] wondered if his commander appreciated how many factors could affect the successful completion of such a maneuver. Walker felt that the order was ill conceived and open to many obstacles that might disrupt the whole operation. Disregarding, for the moment, a sky filled with Stukas and Messerschmitts searching for targets, his trucks had to travel some five miles east to his headquarters at Georgeopolis, pick up the troops, then backtrack over the same road (now going westward) to Khaniá in time to relieve the Twentieth Battalion—all this to be accomplished before nightfall.

Walker looked anxiously at his watch as the first trucks arrived in dribs and drabs. He left his executive officer, Major H. C. D. Marshall, to see that the companies got started properly, and he departed for the advance position at Khaniá.

It was well after 5:00 P.M. before the first contingent of Australians was ready for the truck ride to Khaniá. Leaving Lieutenant Halliday to look after D Company, which was still waiting for trucks, Major Marshall led the truck convoy on its eighteen-mile trip eastward.

The sky above was filled with marauding Messerschmitts; once the trucks began to move along the narrow, curving tarmac, the game of tag began.

Aware of the danger, Marshall remembered a trick he had learned during the Battle of Greece. Aircraft require a straight stretch of ground in order to strafe troops. A long, straight road or an open field gave the pilots a perfect run to shoot up their targets. If a target kept zigzagging, however, it often proved difficult to hit. That knowledge could help his convoy get through.

Marshall ordered the drivers to race the trucks at maximum speed along the straight stretches of road, maintaining a safe distance between. He instructed them to keep close to the shoulder of the road and against the walls of the overhanging cliffs wherever possible. At curves in the road, Marshall would stop the convoy and wait for the other trucks to catch up. Above them the aircraft circled, unwilling to chance a run on a curve, with those perilous cliffs rising on one side like a gray wall. Once the convoy started again, the pilots would be waiting patiently for them over the straight sections of the road ahead. Thus the game of tag would resume.

It was an unnerving trip for the drivers, but Marshall—proud of bringing the convoy through without losing a single man or truck to a strafing Messerschmitt—found it an exhilarating experience.[17]

Darkness had fallen by the time the convoy reached the eastern outskirts of Khaniá. Fires were still burning fiercely from daytime air raids, and the debris from the blasted buildings made passage through the streets impossible. To cross to the western gate of the city, the convoy had to make detours that caused additional delays. It was midnight before Major Marshall brought the trucks carrying Companies A and B to the positions of the waiting Twentieth Battalion. Company C was further delayed, for it had lost its way in the darkness of the blackout. No one knew when D Company would arrive.

Night settled over the battlefields of Crete, bringing with it the darkness of a moonless sky. Even the stars seemed dimmer than usual. At 23:30 hours—half an hour before the end of the second day of battle—the black northern sky was ruptured by intermittent waves of light followed by the distant rumble of thunder. The sound grew louder; the light grew brighter. Searchlights stretched white fingers into the darkness, and bright flares turned night into day. Rockets arched into the sky trailing a fuzzy light in their wake. The roll of thunder now became the more distinct sound of shells detonating on target, over and over again. At the center of this spectacular display was a constant glow of flame.

Everyone everywhere in the Khaniá-Maleme area stopped to watch; they all knew what it meant—a sea battle was in progress. For thirty minutes it continued. Then, with one last flicker of light and one last roar of thunder, it ended. The lights disappeared and darkness prevailed once again.

High up on the heights of Akrotiri Peninsula, General Freyberg and his staff members watched the events taking place in the waters north of Crete. Smiles of elation were shared by Freyberg, his chief of staff, Colonel Stewart, and Lieutenant Geoffrey Cox. The fear that had gnawed at Freyberg from the first day he assumed command of the Cretan garrison was finally dispelled. The Royal Navy had saved Crete this night from a seaborne invasion, and at that same hour the New Zealand counterattack should be in progress. By morning, Maleme airfield would be recaptured and the Germans pushed back beyond the Tavronites River. Satisfied with this thought, and breathing a sigh of relief, he turned to his chief of staff: "Well, Jock, it has been a great responsibility." [18]

Captain von der Heydte, commanding officer of the First Parachute Battalion, had watched the same fiery display from a hill south of Galatas.

Although von der Heydte's parachutists had incurred many casualties during the first two days of battle, he was still able to field a battleworthy battalion. He knew that the Third Parachute Battalion had ceased to exist as a fighting force and that Major Derpa's Second Battalion had suffered such heavy losses from its repeated and fruitless attacks on Galatas heights that it was down to less than two companies.

Colonel Heidrich, the commanding officer of the parachute regiment in the Prison Valley area, had ordered Von der Heydte to turn over all his available ammunition to Derpa's battalion. Heidrich wanted Derpa to renew his attack on Galatas heights the next day. If Derpa were to fail again, the whole regiment would have to withdraw into a tight defensive position: There would be no ammunition with which to attack.

The successful arrival of the naval convoy in the Maleme area would offer a solution to the supply problem.

When the bright lights and deep roars of battle diminished in the waters north of Crete, von der Heydte shook his head dejectedly, descending the hill to return to his headquarters. The German hopes for reinforcement and resupply by sea had been unsuccessful. The convoy had been obviously intercepted by the Royal Navy. Tomorrow would be a difficult day for his paratroopers. [19]

21

"THE WHOLE WORLD IS WATCHING YOUR SPLENDID BATTLE"

MAY 22–23, 1941

The major counterattack that was to wrest Maleme airfield and Hill 107 back from the Germans had not yet begun. General Freyberg had envisaged it as starting sometime between 10:00 and 11:00 P.M. on the night of May 21. Now it was approaching 1:00 A.M.—with the third day of battle soon to dawn—and the order to begin the attack had not been given.

Colonel Dittmer, commanding officer of the Twenty-eighth Maori Battalion, moved his men to the starting line as early as 11:30 P.M. on the night of the twenty-first. There they sat for three frustrating hours awaiting the arrival of the Twentieth New Zealand Battalion.

A little before midnight, Colonel Dittmer asked Brigadier Hargest to allow Major Burrow's Twentieth Battalion to move up to the attack line without waiting for the arrival of the tardy Australians. Dittmer realized that each moment's delay during the hours of darkness lessened the counterattack's chances of success. The commander of the Maori Battalion believed the attack should begin as soon as possible, but Hargest could not decide for himself and referred Dittmer's request to the divisional commander, General Puttick. Puttick refused, replying that the

Twentieth Battalion must hold its defense position until the arrival of the *full* Australian battalion to complete the relief. He explained that the Twentieth's position protected that sector from sea invasion, despite the fact that he—like everyone else in the Maleme-Khaniá area—had just witnessed the interception of the German convoy at sea.

Major Burrows, commanding officer of the Twentieth Battalion, shared Dittmer's opinion regarding the need for haste. He decided to skip the chain of command and make the same request—directly to General Puttick. Puttick's refusal was equally direct. To avoid further delay, Burrows decided to sidestep divisional orders. On his own initiative, he ordered the companies of his battalion to move forward to the line of attack as they were relieved, instead of waiting for Walker's entire battalion to arrive.

At 2:00 A.M. Burrows arrived at Platanias with the first two of his relieved companies. He went immediately to see Hargest at brigade headquarters.

He found the old farmhouse that served as Hargest's headquarters on the road ascending toward the church of St. Demetrios. In the main room, he met Lieutenant Colonel W. Gentry, the staff officer from Puttick's headquarters who had been present all evening, and Lieutenant Roy Farran, who was to command the three tanks that would participate in the planned counterattack.

To Burrows, studying the portly, red-faced brigadier who looked more like a country farmer than a brigade commander, it was apparent that Hargest was very tired. His words were uttered slowly and he hardly completed a sentence; the strain of the attack must have weighed heavily on him. Burrows thought it best not to mention the fact that he had arrived in Platanias with only two of his companies.

In the middle of the conference, Hargest abruptly stopped, looked at the three men, and asked, "Must the attack go on?" [1]

Burrows, Gentry, and Farran looked at each other in complete surprise. It seemed that the brigade commander had lost his zeal for the attack. Hargest mechanically picked up the telephone to call Puttick.

Puttick's reply was brief and to the point: "The attack must go on!"[2]

Hargest put down the phone and stared at it for a few minutes, while the three men watched him in silence. Then he turned to them and asked them to wait for half an hour while he had some sleep.[3]

At 3:30 A.M., some three hours delayed, the counterattack finally began.

Through the waning darkness the New Zealanders picked their way across ditches, into ravines, through bushes, past olive trees, and over walls, moving slowly but surely forward.

A stone house near the beach had been converted by the paratroopers into a strong point. When D Company, on the right flank of the Twentieth Battalion, approached the house, the Germans loosed a withering fire that pinned the New Zealanders down and brought the whole company to a halt. Lieutenant P. Maxwell ordered the platoon to work themselves around the house. Dashing in short spurts toward the flanks, many of the men fell victim to the persistent German fire. With great effort, the New Zealanders finally maneuvered themselves into positions from which they set up a heavy concentration of rifle fire on the house from all directions. It was only a skirmish, but the continuous din of rifle and machine-gun fire gave it the sound of a major battle.

With the first crack of dawn streaking the eastern sky, a handful of paratroopers emerged to give themselves up. As a squad of Maxwell's men went forward to accept the surrender, a few diehard Germans opened fire on them from behind a wall. Angered by this breach of military etiquette, the New Zealanders charged the house. The surviving paratroopers threw down their weapons to spare themselves the fury of the New Zealand bayonets.

This lone stronghold was taken at great expense in time and

men. This was one obstacle of many in the path of the major objective ahead, and each would prove to be as strongly fortified. Even worse, the necessary cover of darkness was rapidly disappearing as May 22 dawned.

The din of battle rudely awakened the tired, sleeping Germans. Caught unprepared by the attack, in the confusion some of them rushed out of the houses without their pants while others forgot to put on their boots. But not a single one of them forgot his weapon.[4]

While D Company was clearing its first major objective, its sister company on the left flank was running into even heavier resistance.

From every ditch and from behind every obstacle, rifle and machine-gun fire increased into a heavy concentration against the New Zealanders of C Company. Tracers rained down on them from all directions.

South of the main road, Colonel Dittmer's Maoris advanced steadily against light resistance. Dittmer was surprised to encounter only scattered opposition. The heavy and continuous firing that echoed from the direction of Burrows's two companies, across the road to the north, told him that the advance was not unopposed. Dittmer did not know that in order to avoid the annoying fire from the entrenchments of the Twenty-third Battalion, many paratroopers had shifted their positions to the north of the main road the previous day. Now these paratroopers found themselves deployed in depth before the advancing companies of the Twentieth Battalion. Burrows's earlier suggestion that a reconnaissance patrol precede the counterattack might have pinpointed these emplacements.

Nevertheless, the Maoris did find scattered pockets of resistance in their path, which they quickly eliminated with grenades and handy use of the bayonet.

When the men of Dittmer's battalion crossed the Sfakoriano River, they were joined by Manoli Paterakis and his fellow Cretans—now fighting their own war against the German invaders. They were not the only Cretans to join the attack. As the New

Zealanders advanced, other Cretans slipped like ephemeral shadows from their hiding places and, with captured German weapons, took their own toll of the paratroopers.[5]

Paterakis and his men preferred to follow in the wake of the advancing troops, applying their natural skills in stalking the isolated groups of paratroopers who now found themselves behind the New Zealand lines. These fearless Cretans, who had come from all over Crete to help fight the Germans, were proficient at this game of hide-and-seek. They had spent all their lives in the fields hunting game for sustenance. Now they were ferreting out a new species for their survival, and they were taking no prisoners.

The Maoris continued their advance. A platoon from the company on the right flank entered the southern outskirts of Pirgos against heavy opposition. The fighting had become so fierce that even these brave New Zealanders were brought to a standstill.

On the opposite end of the Maoris advance, the company carrying the left flank crossed the Xamoudokori road and captured that village. This brought them to the base of their major objective—Hill 107.

By now it was broad daylight. The paratroopers on Hill 107 could observe the movements of the Maoris and, from their defense positions, could rain mortar and machine-gun fire on them. With daylight came the Messerschmitt 109s, bombing and strafing anything that moved in the fields. The Maoris had no choice but to dig in and hold.

All along the line, the advance had been stopped.

Lieutenant Roy Farran halted his three Vickers light tanks outside Pirgos and deployed them under some trees for protection from air attack. There he awaited further orders. He dared not advance alone into the village, for he heard that the Germans were using captured Bofors guns as effective field artillery. One shot from a depressed Bofors gun at his thin-skinned vehicles and he would be a tank commander without tanks.[6]

Farran was resting momentarily under the shade of a tree when an angry voice aroused him. It was Captain R. Dawson, Hargest's brigade major. Hargest never left headquarters to visit his forward units, but he relied heavily on his field representatives. Unlike Hargest, Captain Dawson was spirited, vigorous, and aggressive in battle. When the attack faltered, he rushed forward to get it moving again. The first targets of his ire were Farran and his tanks.

Dawson stopped in front of the lead tank and urged the sergeant to move on into the village.

"Get moving . . . there is nothing to worry about except perhaps small-arms fire!" [7]

The sergeant looked back at his troop commander, just then climbing into the second tank. Farran waved him forward. The lieutenant shook his head disapprovingly, knowing that it would be suicide for any tank to venture into that hornet's nest without infantry support.

"I know," he muttered to his driver, "that the first tank will get it!" [8]

The sergeant rode the lead tank down the highway into the village of Pirgos. As he approached an intersection, a Borfors gun roared from behind the cemetery wall. The shell struck the tank just below the turret, wounding the gunner. The driver spun the tank around, and the wounded gunner sprayed the German gun crew with its machine guns. Then a second Bofors barked, hitting the tank broadside, killing the crew and setting it afire.

The tank column was observed by a passing flight of ME-109s. No sooner had the first tank burst into flames than the Messerschmitts dived to strafe them. Their bullets hit the light-armored tanks like molten rivets. The crew members covered their faces to protect themselves from the hot flakes of burning metal flying off inside.

Farran halted his vehicle beneath a tall tree for protection, but to no avail. The bullets ripped through the branches, striking the metallic hull in a persistent patter. Like a huge animal trying to avoid repeated bee stings, Farran spun, turned, and backed his tank, finally crashing into a field bamboo.[9]

One of the tank's bogey wheels was broken, and the frustrated lieutenant inspected the damage that, for the moment, had put him out of action. He ordered the third tank not to proceed, for he feared that it would meet the same fate that had greeted the luckless lead tank.

Long before Burrows's messenger contacted D Company of his battalion with orders to resume the attack, Lieutenant Maxwell and his men had reached the eastern perimeter of the airfield. They had suffered many casualties during their advance along the coastal strip; most of the officers had been killed or wounded. Maxwell considered himself lucky, for he was the only officer to remain unhurt.

When he and the remainder of the company reached the edge of the airfield, they were amazed at what they saw. From their hiding places in bushes and behind trees, they watched in awe as transport after transport circled and landed on the congested airstrip. Disabled Junkers were pushed aside by what looked like a tank. It was in fact an abandoned Matilda—one of the ill-fated infantry tanks from Colonel Andrew's unsuccessful attack on the twentieth—used as a bulldozer to make landing space available for the arriving transports.

No sooner did a transport come to a halt than the hatches on either side opened, twenty-five to forty troopers jumping out. Officers and noncoms in the field guided the new arrivals directly into the battle line. Junker 52s landed, unloaded, and departed, making room for others. The roar of motors was a continuous din that easily drowned out the sounds of battle.

Private Amos knelt next to Lieutenant Maxwell and looked on in frustration. "Sir," he said, "I've carried this antitank rifle all this way and I now am going to have a shot!"[10] With that he loaded the rifle and fired two shots at a transport just as it rolled to a stop. Both shots hit the aircraft: The first one caused it to smoke and the second blew it up. Private Amos smiled proudly.

Now fully aware of their presence so dangerously close to the airfield, the Germans on Hill 107 showered D Company with heavy mortar and machine-gun fire. The concentration was so intense that D Company had to withdraw to less exposed positions away from the airfield perimeter. Lieutenant Maxwell realized that if crossing the airfield in the daylight would be difficult, capturing it would be impossible.[11]

Coming up south of Pirgos, the Maoris Company nearest the highway pressed forward in its own attack on the village. The men from Burrows's C Company had been brought to a standstill in the center, and the Maoris were having an equally difficult time on the outskirts.

Not only were they receiving frontal fire from the houses south of the village, but mortar and machine-gun fire rained down onto their flank from the lower slopes of Hill 107. Nevertheless the hardy Maoris pressed on, disregarding the storm of bullets. It was an indescribable feat of heroism and perseverance in the face of such deadly opposition.

Major H. G. Dyer, the executive officer of the Twenty-eighth Battalion, marveled at the Maoris' drive. He kept repeating to the battalion sergeant major, "We must get forward and get above and around the Germans." Sergeant A. C. Wood nodded his head in agreement as he took aim and fired at a German running between the trees.[12]

Germans were firing their tommy guns from behind every tree, dodging from tree to tree as the Maoris approached. Dyer led his men in small groups against each position, wiping out one only to have two others open fire from another position farther ahead.

Wood, the redoubtable sergeant major, led a shouting group of Maoris in a bayonet charge against a platoon of paratroopers who had set up a strong point in a stone house. It was a wild melee, and when the yells and screams subsided, the Maoris held the stone house. All the paratroopers had been shot or speared by bayonets.

The energetic commander of the Maoris hustled through the field to his battalion's left flank. Colonel Dittmer wanted to know why his advance company—which had already captured Xamoudokori village and reached the southern base of Hill 107—had not seized the hill. Its capture would eliminate the harassing fire that was tearing into the company on the right flank and hindering its advance on Pirgos.

When he reached the company's forward positions, he found the men dug in or under cover. Standing before them with his hands on his hips, in full view of the watchful Germans on the hill, he shouted angrily at his men: "Call yourselves bloody soldiers?" His face got red as he pointed up the hill with his swagger stick. "Let's move!"[13]

With that command, he plunged forward into a storm of bullets and mortar shells, his men following close at his heels.

It did not take long for Dittmer to realize why his brave Maoris had sought cover. The fiery wall of machine-gun and mortar fire was an obstacle too formidable even for them to overcome.[14]

By midday Major Burrows had finally been reinforced by the arrival of his other company, but it was too late. His two attacking companies had taken heavy casualties during the day, and the survivors were dropping from sheer exhaustion. Added to this was the sad fact that the day's battle had depleted the battalion's supply of ammunition, hand grenades, and mortar shells. What might have succeeded earlier with a force of four fresh attacking companies could fail now in the face of increasing German resistance.

Burrows decided to alter his phase of the attack plan. He would bring all his companies south of the road and help Dittmer in an assault that would capture Hill 107. With this idea in mind, he dispatched Lieutenant C. H. Upham to carry the withdrawal order to D Company.

Upham took his batman, Sergeant Kirk, with him. When he reached the D Company positions, he saw the same spectacle on the airfield that had awed Maxwell and his men. When Upham finally returned with D Company behind him, he commented to Burrows, "The mortar and machine-gun fire on the open ground was very heavy, and we were lucky to get back alive." Adding, "With another hour of darkness, we could have reached the far side of the 'drome.' "[15] Now, in broad daylight, it was too late.

Burrows conferred with Dittmer again in the shade of a grape arbor. He was dismayed to learn that the Maoris' advance had been stalled by superior German fire power and by those accursed Messerschmitts. With the Maoris at a standstill, Burrows's revised plan of attack had no purpose. The counterattack was failing, but the diehard Dittmer would not accept defeat.

"No!" he said with determination. "There is a way . . . we need help, and I'm going to get it!"[16]

General Hargest had finally awakened from his severe case of nerves which, the night before, had caused him to request cancellation of the counterattack. Now, with the dawn of a new day, he took a different view of the attack and of its result. He wired his division commander:

STEADY FLOW OF ENEMY PLANES LANDING AND TAKING OFF. MAY BE TRYING TO TAKE TROOPS OFF.[17]

When Lieutenant Farran returned to get the fitters to repair his tank, he reported what happened to his lead tank and the stiff resistance encountered by the attacking battalions.

Other reports indicated that the Germans were landing men in droves and were being supplied artillery and motorcycles from the arriving transports. In spite of these frontline reports, Hargest sent another wire still filled with misguided optimism:

BECAUSE ELEVEN FIRES HAVE BEEN LIT ON 'DROME, IT APPEARS AS THOUGH ENEMY MIGHT BE PREPARING EVACUATION.[18]

Colonel Dittmer quickly covered the three-quarter mile back to the headquarters of the Twenty-third Battalion. If he was going to get help to resume the attack, it would have to come from Leckie's battalion. After all, he thought to himself as he wiped the dust and perspiration from his face, the Twenty-third has not seen action since the first day of the invasion. Leckie's men are rested and fit for combat. He felt certain that their assistance would turn the tide.

He found Colonel Leckie in his headquarters having lunch with Colonel Andrew of the Twenty-second Battalion. Good! he muttered to himself at the sight of Andrew. He knew that Andrew had three companies intact, and they could hold down the fort while the Twenty-third Battalion followed him back to Hill 107.

Colonel Leckie did not share the enthusiasm or aggressive leadership that inspired Dittmer. He was surprised by the request, because he was under the impression—based on incorrect information received from stragglers—that the Twentieth Battalion had withdrawn from the attack.

"My dear Dittmer," he replied, sipping a cup of tea, "I really feel that you chaps cannot make any more progress without more infantry and artillery."

Colonel Andrew muttered concurrence. Dittmer looked at them, incredulous at their lack of enthusiasm. "That's why I am here—for more infantry!"

Leckie turned a deaf ear: "I think the best course would be to hold what ground you have and stop the enemy infiltration that is constantly going on."[19]

Dittmer left Leckie's headquarters angered by this short-sighted refusal. Without the assistance he sought, the counter-attack was doomed to failure.

By early afternoon Hargest's optimism began to wane. All reports indicated that Maleme airfield was the door through which the Germans gained strength in arms and men. At 1325 hours he wired Puttick and admitted that the "situation was confused." He added:

TROOPS *NOT* AS FORWARD ON LEFT AS BELIEVED. OFFICERS ON
GROUND BELIEVE ENEMY PREPARING FOR ATTACK AND TAKING
SERIOUS VIEW.

Yet in spite of all the on-the-spot information reaching him from
the men in the front lines of battle, he went on:

I DISAGREE, OF COURSE.

And instead of hurrying to get a clearer view of the battle situation, he went in the opposite direction, informing Puttick:

[I] WILL VISIT YOUR H.Q. WHEN BRIGADE MAJOR RETURNS.[20]

Colonel Dittmer returned to his battalion still seething over
Leckie's refusal. He informed Burrows of the situation and then
gave orders that his battalion withdraw to the safety of a valley
southeast of Pirgos. The counterattack was over.

As dusk began to fall over the hills and valleys, Colonel Bernhard Ramcke, the new German field commander who had relieved the wounded General Meindl, mustered the newly arrived
mountain troops for an attack.

Three companies from the Second Battalion of the Eighty-fifth Mountain Regiment were ordered to counterattack the New
Zealanders and smash their forward line. Ramcke felt that the
time was ripe and that the exhausted, depleted ranks of the Maoris
would scatter before these newly arrived mountain troops.

The Maoris watched the German preparations from behind the
twisted olive trees of an orchard on the reverse slope of a hill.
Slowly the Germans advanced through the fields. Major Dyer
watched them as they crossed the valley carrying a huge flag
with a black swastika in its center, suspended from two poles.
Dyer reflected that it looked more like a military procession than
men preparing for an attack.[21]

Through the fields, the valley, and up the hill the excited
Germans advanced, some singing, some shouting, some firing.

At the crest of the hill, they threw hand grenades and then charged over the top.

The Maoris were waiting for them. Slowly the gallant New Zealanders, who had already suffered so much that day, opened fire on the Germans. Then, singly or in groups, with knees bent and firing from the hip, they moved forward to meet the charging enemy. Major Dyer watched as force met force on the reverse slope of the hill.

When the Maoris had spent their ammunition, they broke into a run with bayonets held level. From their throats came the Maoris' battle cry, "Ah! Ah! Ah!"

The advance rank of Germans went down to Maori fire, the second and third ranks watching stupefied as the short, shouting men came at them with bayonets held high. Bullets whined into the Maoris' ranks and many fell dead or wounded, but they kept on coming. The Germans could take no more: They turned and fled down the hill and through the valley back to their starting point, with the pursuing Maoris hot on their heels. Dyer, laughing at what he described as the "Huns with their fat behinds to us running for their lives," raced after the Maoris to keep them from going too far.[22]

It had also been a weary, daylong ordeal for the men and ships of the Mediterranean Fleet. The score indicated that the Germans, after an all-out effort, lost only two planes as definites, with six probably lost and five damaged—a mere pittance compared with the Royal Navy's loss of two cruisers and one destroyer, with severe damage to two mighty battleships and swift cruisers. It was *not* an even exchange! When Admiral Sir Andrew Cunningham heard the tragic news of the day's losses, he ordered the whole squadron back to Alexandria. The time had come to take stock, and to review the disastrous results of this day.[23]

Captain Lord Louis Mountbatten, cousin to King George VI of England, left the beleaguered island of Malta on Wednesday

night, May 21, planning to join Admiral Rawlings's force by
10:00 A.M. the next day. However, though they had an uneventful trip, Mountbatten's flotilla of five destroyers—comprising the
flagship *Kelly*, and the *Kashmir*, the *Kelvin*, the *Kipling*, and
the *Jackal*—did not join Rawlings's squadron until 4:00 P.M. on
May 22. They were just in time to take defensive positions against
the German air attacks that had been in progress all day.

Later that night, Rawlings ordered Mountbatten to take the
Kelly, Kashmir, and *Kipling* north in search of survivors from
the *Fiji* sinking. The destroyers *Kelvin* and *Jackal* were dispatched on a similar mission, to seek out survivors of the cruiser
Gloucester. (The British did not know that a German air-sea
rescue operation had picked up as many as 500 of the *Gloucester* survivors.)

After the rescue mission was recalled, Mountbatten regrouped his ships—with the exception of the destroyers *Kelvin*
and *Jackal,* which had left earlier on their own to rejoin Rawlings's group—and pursued an active evening against the Germans.

As May 23 dawned, the *Kelly* became the next target, as 24
dive-bombers now concentrated on the two destroyers. Speeding
and maneuvering at thirty knots, Mountbatten's flagship was
struck by a huge bomb on the rear turret. She stopped dead in
the water, listing heavily to port. Mountbatten watched the
launching of all available rafts and boats before giving the order
to abandon ship. The *Kelly* slowly turned turtle and floated in
that position a half-hour before sinking, giving her survivors ample
time to get clear of the ship.[24]

Now the only remaining destroyer came to the rescue. Commander A. St. Clare-Ford of the *Kipling* lowered all her lifeboats and rafts, still fighting off the ever-present dive-bombers.
During a lull in the attack, she would sweep in to rescue the
Kelly survivors, including Mountbatten. When the German dive-bombers returned, the *Kipling* maneuvered quickly away, dodging bombs as she sped across the water. At the next lull, the
plucky destroyer returned to pick up the *Kashmir* survivors. Sat-

isfied that she had done all she could, she turned and headed for the safety of Alexandria. From 8:20 A.M., when she stood alone after the *Kelly* and *Kashmir* had been sunk, until she departed those perilous waters at 1:00 P.M., the *Kipling* had warded off at least forty individual attacks and avoided some eighty-three bombs. It was a miracle that she survived unscathed.[25]

Back in Athens, in the second floor war room of General Student's headquarters in the Grande Bretagne Hotel, details of the New Zealand counterattack were coming in hourly.

Student followed the reports closely. By late evening on May 22, the commander of the Eleventh Air Corps received the satisfying news that a total of three battalions from the Fifth Mountain Division, together with artillery and a field hospital, had landed safely in the course of the day. Student smiled with relief. To all appearances, the airfield at Maleme was securely controlled by the Germans. Always confident that his plan would work against any adversity if given the chance, he now felt that the danger was over.

Since the evening of May 19, when the invasion of Crete began, Student had taken his meals at his desk in the war room. Now he left to go to dinner.

Seated at his private table in the headquarters dining room with his chief of staff, Student remarked that the scale of battle seemed to be swinging in their favor.

"If the enemy," he added in retrospect, "had made a united all-out effort in counterattacking during the night from the 20th to the 21st, or in the morning of the 21st, then the very tired remnants of the Sturm Regiment . . . could have been wiped out."[26]

In London, Churchill followed the battle closely through dispatches. He was aware that this had been a hard day both for the New Zealanders in Crete and for Admiral Cunningham's Mediterranean Fleet.

At first, he was elated to hear that the German convoy had

been intercepted and destroyed. But his elation was shortlived, for in the course of the day, he was informed of the loss of the destroyer *Greyhound* and of the two heavy cruisers *Gloucester* and *Fiji*. He realized that without an airfield in effective range, he could not order the Royal Air Force into action either to help the New Zealand defense or to fly protective cover for the Mediterranean Fleet.

Deeply concerned that Crete's strategic position be maintained at all costs, his words were emphatic when he wired General Wavell in North Africa:

CRETE BATTLE MUST BE WON.[27]

Anticipating Churchill's concern, Wavell had already ordered that 900 men from the Queen's Royal Regiment, together with the headquarters staff of the Sixteenth Infantry Brigade and some eighteen vehicles, set sail for Crete. In the late afternoon of this third day of battle, the special service ship *Glenroy* left Alexandria for Tymbaki, a fishing village on the southern coast of the island.

While Wavell was at last awakening to the fact that Crete needed reinforcements, Churchill sent off another message to his dear friend General Freyberg:

THE WHOLE WORLD IS WATCHING YOUR SPLENDID BATTLE, ON WHICH GREAT EVENTS TURN.[28]

22

"MALTA WOULD CONTROL THE MEDITERRANEAN"

MAY 23–24, 1941

General Freyberg was disheartened when he heard the counterattack had failed.

Later in the afternoon on May 22, Freyberg summoned Puttick to his headquarters for a conference. The New Zealand divisional commander arrived at 5:00 P.M., at which time Freyberg expressed his wishes for a new counterattack. "I want the Fifth Brigade to attack en bloc!"[1]

The lean-faced Puttick seemed skeptical. Freyberg noticed the hesitation and, to make the idea more acceptable, added: "I shall release to you the Eighth Australians and the Eighteenth New Zealanders from the Fourth Brigade."

Puttick's expression did not change, nor did he appear enthusiastic about the whole idea. The Creforce commander stared at him and, in a firm if not stern voice, intoned: "By my order!"[2]

For the first time since the battle for the island had begun, Freyberg was not diffident in interfering with his subordinate commanders. For the first time, he *ordered* an attack.

Brigadier Hargest listened quietly, but with increasing irritation, as his division commander forwarded Freyberg's order.

Puttick's unenthusiastic mood must have been contagious. After a few minutes of silence, Hargest reacted with a flurry of pessimistic protests.

"My men are not fit for further attack," his tired voice rasped over the phone. It was a remark that would have angered the gallant Dittmer and his brave Maori or the intrepid Burrows and the determined men of the Twentieth Battalion. "Besides," he added, "they are exhausted!"[3]

When Puttick catalogued this report with Hargest's glum picture of the situation, he decided to contact Freyberg and request a reversal of the earlier order to counterattack.

"I do not like the suggestion of a withdrawal, Puttick,"[4] replied the Creforce commander, annoyed at Puttick's suggestion that the Fifth Brigade be withdrawn from its present position. "Why not relieve Hargest's men with the two battalions I released to you and let Hargest pull his men back to reorganize?"

Once again the Creforce commander reverted to his earlier habit of suggesting rather than ordering.

"How could we expect two battalions to hold what five could not?" was Puttick's response. Puttick did not know that Hargest had never utilized the full strength of all his battalions in a concerted effort.[5]

"Very well," Freyberg acceded, dismay evident in the tone of his voice. "I'll send Stewart down to your headquarters, and you can draw up the details for the withdrawal."[6]

Freyberg replaced the phone and slowly resigned himself to the idea that his original order to counterattack had somehow been converted to an order for withdrawal. He realized that with this decision, all hope of recapturing Maleme airfield had to be abandoned.

On the same night that Puttick, Hargest, and Stewart were planning the withdrawal of their forces, Major General Julius Ringel, the commanding general of the Fifth Mountain Division, landed at Maleme airfield. He immediately assumed the command of all German troops in western Crete.

The goateed, nattily dressed former head of the Austrian army's Nazi party, carried with him revised orders from the Fourth Air Fleet. He was instructed to secure Maleme airfield, advance and clear Suda Bay, relieve the surrounded paratroopers at Rethimnon, make contact with Iráklion, and last but not least, occupy the whole island. Ringel planned to fulfill each part of the order exactly as prescribed in his written orders.

Ringel's arrival marked a change in the field command of the whole operation—it was no longer an all-Luftwaffe affair. Ringel was a Wehrmacht officer who carried with him into Crete the support and professionalism of the militarists of the German army. "Now we will see results!" opined the Wehrmacht staff officers of the German Army High Command.[7]

The new commanding general let it be understood that he was in complete control. He sent a radio message to Colonel Heidrich in Prison Valley informing him that effective immediately Group Center and Group West were to be combined into a single force referred to as Ringel Group. All paratroop survivors in the Maleme area were placed into a single group under the command of Colonel Ramcke. Once Ringle's command had been asserted, he sat down to plan the operation that would end the battle of Crete in a decisive German victory.

Ringel explained to his staff that by next morning, he wanted Maleme airfield to be fully operational. That same afternoon ME-109s would use the airfield as a forward base, thus offering continuous air support to the attacking German columns. During the course of day, he expected the arrival of two batteries of the Ninety-fifth Mountain Artillery Regiment, the Ninety-fifth Antitank Battalion with 50-mm antitank guns, the Fifty-fifth Motorcycle Battalion, and the first battalions of the One Hundred Forty-first Mountain Regiment. Within twenty-four hours, he stated that the full strength of the mountain division would be in the battle.[8]

All this would be happening at Maleme airfield, a door that Hargest had left open to the Germans.

It was 10:00 P.M. before General Puttick and Freyberg's chief of staff, Colonel Stewart, completed the details of the withdrawal.

In a series of continuous movements, the whole of the Fifth Brigade would be pulled back to a point east of Platanias, where its left flank would link up with the Tenth Brigade in the Prison Valley—Galatas area. The disorganized Twenty-second Battalion would go in reserve within the ranks of Brigadier Inglis's Fourth Brigade. The Seventh Australian Battalion, which relieved Major Burrows's Twentieth New Zealanders east of Khaniá the night before, would join its sister unit—the Eighth Australians—and protect the New Zealand left flank at the village of Perivolia. Colonel Dittmer's Twenty-eighth Maori Battalion, deployed in the hard-fought positions east of Pirgos and situated closest to the Germans, would be the last to depart. They would fight as the rear guard, protecting the brigade's retreat.

Puttick called the commander of the Fifth Brigade with the news, and related the withdrawal plan to him. Hargest received the new orders with a sigh of relief, and immediately dispatched his brigade major to relay the order to the line battalions.

The first men to hear the news were the medics of the brigade's field ambulance, located on a low hill near Modhion village. Captain Palmer and most of the other off-duty medics awakened to the disappointing orders to pull out. What surprised the sleepy men most was that they thought everything was going well.[9]

Quickly the men transferred the movable wounded to stretchers and then carefully and silently began the long trip. They moved down the hilly slope until they reached the main road and then, turning eastward, headed for Platanias. The wounded who could not be moved were left behind with medical personnel who volunteered to stay and care for them.

When Colonel Dittmer was told that his Maoris had to forsake all the ground they gained through such bitter fighting, his face turned crimson with anger. And when Dawson informed him that his battalion had been delegated to act as the rear guard, the brave colonel became furious.

"My men have fought hard for this ground, and to have to leave it—" Dittmer protested, pointing out the many casualties his unit had suffered. "Now you tell me that I am to be the rear guard!" He continued in a rude vein, expressing himself in well-chosen words that made his sergeant major smile with pride. Dittmer knew that once the Germans discovered the retreat, the full fury of their fire would fall on the rear-guard unit—his Maoris.[10]

The movement began after midnight. The units withdrew slowly, climbing down the steep sides of cliffs, marching through ravines and over hills, past glades of bamboo, through wheat-fields, arbors, and olive groves. The men trekked through terrain that had been painfully won in battle.

They were resentful, but sworn to follow orders, not a single man disobeyed. They trudged eastward mile after mile with a discipline that made their officers proud. The wounded were carried on makeshift stretchers, while the stronger carried the weapons of the fatigued.

The last to receive the order were the men of the artillery units, who were not contacted until 4:00 A.M. It was too late for them to hitch up their guns and move within the protective line of the rear guard, so gun after gun was destroyed before being abandoned. Two 3.7-inch howitzers and three 75-mm field-pieces were included—guns that might have been useful later. A truck with its cannon in tow slipped off the edge of the road and spilled down a ravine. Left without their cannon, the crews joined the Twenty-eighth Maori as infantrymen to help in the rear-guard action.

It was daylight before Captain Dawson, the brigade major, reached the headquarters of the Twenty-third Battalion. The battalion commander took one look at him and saw fatigue written all over his face. Dawson slumped heavily into a field chair, and in a slow, tired voice said, "I have some very surprising news for you."

"What, have they tossed it in?" asked Colonel Leckie, who, seeing the new day dawn peacefully, assumed the Germans had departed during the night.

"You are to return to the Platanias River line," was Dawson's answer. Then he added, with half-closed eyes, "The withdrawal of your battalion was supposed to have started half an hour ago."

Leckie masked his surprise, but before issuing orders for the movement, he gave the sleepy Dawson a blanket, comforting him with, "Here, have a sleep . . . I will awaken you in good time." [11]

By first light the aggressive Colonel Ramcke found the morning stillness unusual, and sensed something afoot. A reconnaissance patrol reported that they had not encountered any opposition—not a shot fired at them and not a New Zealander in sight.

Ramcke slapped his fist down triumphantly. "They have retreated," he declared with finality. [12]

The word that the New Zealanders were retreating raced through the German lines. Kurt Meyer, the war correspondent, had now attached himself to a battalion of mountain troops. He could not believe that the New Zealanders were retreating; he felt that they must have misunderstood the situation.

"Either they overestimated our forces," he noted, "or they supposed that we could go into an attack with only a handful of mountain troops." [13]

"Nonsense," replied Colonel August Wittmann, the commanding officer of the One Hundred Eleventh Mountain Artillery Regiment, newly arrived and unscarred by battle. "They have lost their nerve!" [14]

With the sun rising higher each passing hour, the paratroopers moved slowly and carefully forward through the grim landscape of the battlefield. Wherever they looked, trees were bullet-torn or splintered, fields were scarred by discolored earth churned up by exploding shells, shattered vehicles and dead mules lay all around, the blackened walls of some cottages still smoldered, and worst of all were the hundreds of dead paratroopers.

Captain Gericke, the battalion commander of the Fourth Parachute Assault Battalion, led his paratroopers into an area east of Pirgos and into the fields and groves beyond, and there he solved the mystery of what had happened to Major Scherber and the Third Assault Battalion of the Storm Regiment. The scene was frightful to behold; it was a field of carnage.

It was painful even for an experienced soldier like Gericke to accept the nightmarish vista before him. The green fields had turned blue-gray, carpeted with the uniforms of dead paratroopers. The olive trees were covered with the silk of parachutes from which hung paratroopers suspended from their harnesses, swinging in the breeze. Others lay in the fields where they had fallen, their parachutes half covering them like shrouds. There were still other paratroopers, dead in the grass, singly or in groups, amidst the debris of helmets, ammunition boxes, weapons, grenades, and bandages. All over the corpses, big, fat, blue flies clustered like vultures.

Hardened as they were, many of Gericke's men vomited at the sight.[15]

Ringel's mountain troops in the center were held back by brief and bitter skirmishes with the stubborn Maoris of the Twenty-eighth Battalion. But the Germans were persistent, following close behind the retreating rear guard. Messerschmitts were out in full force, flying overhead in support of their comrades on the ground, but the fluid battle lines made it difficult for them to pick out targets. The Maoris were aided by this close-quarter fighting.

Three times the Maoris had to stop and fight off their pursuers. The Germans towed several captured Bofors guns and manhandled them into line, firing at the Maoris from a range of 300 yards.

Major Dyer, the battalion's executive officer, led his men up to a wooded creek just west of Platanias village, reaching it by midday. Safety was just a few hundred yards away—a dash through a field and up the face of a ridge. Dyer turned to his men: "We must get up that hill—let's move!"

They dashed for the ridge, every man for himself.

The Germans kept up a steady fire, and the captured Bofors barked repeatedly, slamming shell after shell at the Maoris. A shell exploded on Dyers's left, and when he looked, he saw that his sergeant had been decapitated.

In one last rush, the men of the rear guard reached the safety of the new defense perimeter, leaving many of their friends lying in the fields behind them. It was now 2:00 P.M. on the fourth day of battle.[16]

By the side of the road beyond Platanias, where it curves toward Galatas, Colonel Kippenberger, the commanding officer of the Tenth Brigade, stood watching a group of men marching past. When Major Burrows walked by, Kippenberger realized that these men represented the depleted ranks of the Twentieth Battalion—the unit Kippenberger had commanded in Greece.

He saw their torn and dirty uniforms, observed the tired, listless way they marched, and, *for the first time in Crete, recognized the painful signs of defeat.*[17]

If Captain Walter Gericke's advance through the fields east of Pirgos solved the mystery of what happened to Major Sherber's Third Assault Battalion during the first day of the invasion, there now remained a second mystery: Where was Oberleutnant Peter Muerbe and his detachment of seventy-two paratroopers?

When General Ringel completed the deployment of the troops under his new command, he ordered that one Kampfgruppe advance westward toward the village of Kastelli at the base of Kisamos Bay. He ordered Major Schaette and his Ninety-fifth Engineer Battalion to secure those positions.

Schaette's men advanced robustly at first until they came within a few miles of the eastern approach to Kastelli. At that point, their attitude changed, as they crossed the fields where Lieutenant Muerbe and his paratroopers had met the men of the First Greek Regiment.

The grim scene that greeted Captain Gericke east of Pirgos now reappeared in all its horror before Major Schaette and his soldiers. The fields were strewn with the blackened, bloated corpses of Muerbe's men. What shocked the Germans most of all was that many of them had apparently met their deaths not by bullets but by the distinct slashes and punctures of knives and swords—or by having their skulls bashed in. To an impeccable officer like Schaette, this was not warfare but an act of atrocity.

"Obviously," he surmised incorrectly, "these men had been executed after their surrender." [18]

The thought never occurred to him that the defenders had no bullets with which to repel the invaders and had resorted to the age-old weaponry of knife and club.

As the Germans advanced toward Kastelli, they were exposed to sporadic fire from the outlying positions of Battalion A of the First Greek Regiment. It was getting dark, and Schaette did not relish the thought of continuing with his troops into unreconnoitered territory where hidden Cretan snipers could ambush them. He decided to halt his advance for the night. When he reported his position to General Ringel, he made certain to mention the "atrocities."

For three days after Muerbe's attack, the men of the First Greek Regiment rested in the peaceful countryside. They could hear the roar of battle far to the east at Maleme, but there was not a single German near them to disturb the uneasy tranquility; the only Germans around were the seventeen parachutists still detained in the town's jailhouse.

When the outposts reported on May 23 that the Germans were approaching in force, the men of the First Greek Regiment realized their temporary respite had ended.

The next morning the terrors of the sky—the dreaded Stukas and the feared Messerschmitts—appeared over Kastelli. They represented the first blow that General Ringel would use to destroy "those bestial hordes" at Kastelli.

For more than an hour, the Stuka dive-bombers ranged over the town, diving from heights of 4,000 feet to almost treetop level before releasing their bombs,. At such low altitudes, they could not miss. Some squadrons carried 110-pound bombs, which they dropped in clusters of four. Other Stukas came down with 1,100-pound high-explosive bombs, aimed at the buildings in the town.

The men in Battalion A on the eastern perimeter of the town listened to the heavy bombardment and feared for the lives of their wives and children. Some of these men, still considering themselves civilians rather than soldiers, left their positions to seek out their families.

The ferocity of the Stuka attack suggested to Major Thomas Bedding, the New Zealand military advisor to the Greek Regiment, that it was a softening-up process before the renewal of the German ground attack. Just as he turned to give Lieutenant Baigent new orders for the Greek regimental staff, a 1,000-pound bomb exploded outside the coffeehouse, showering the occupants with pieces of masonry and wood and choking them with dust.

At the same time, another bomb hit the jailhouse, knocking out its front wall. The prisoners rushed through the opening, attacking and taking weapons from the surprised guards. Picking up additional rifles along the way, they headed for Bedding's headquarters.

No sooner had Lieutenant Baigent dusted himself off than he left to carry out Bedding's orders. He did not get far beyond the front door when heavy rifle fire forced him to return. Bedding grasped the situation in a moment and led the young lieutenant out the rear door into a narrow alley. One end of the alley was blocked with debris; when they turned in the other direction, they ran into Germans coming at them through the heavy clouds of dust that still filled the air. They ran back into the *kafeníon,* or coffeehouse, only to come face to face with the muzzles of rifles held by paratroopers who had entered through the front door. They were prisoners; the captors had become the captives.

Lieutenants Campbell and York from Bedding's staff learned of their commanding officer's capture and planned to rescue him. They rounded up some Greeks led by a Sergeant Argyropoulos, and together with a few others, rushed the coffeehouse. The Germans, who were enjoying their newly found freedom, had armed themselves with a Bren gun, in addition to Enfields and grenades, and had taken good defense positions amidst the broken walls of the *kafeníon*. The Greek sergeant led his men in a wild charge against heavy fire. His men were easily cut down, but Sergeant Argyropoulos managed to get into the house before the Germans killed him. Lieutenant Campbell was also killed in the skirmish, leaving Lieutenant York no alternative but to withdraw with the survivors. Major Bedding remained a prisoner of the Germans.

Major Schaette's advance from the east resumed as soon as the Stukas completed their devastating work. The men from Battalion A resisted as long as their ammunition held out, resorting to the use of the bayonet once it was spent. Major Nicholas Skordilis, the commanding officer of the battalion, led his men in countless bayonet charges against the well-armed engineers of the mountain division, but they always fell short of the German line. It was a heroic but fruitless effort that left over 200 Greeks, together with their battalion commander, dead in front of the German guns.

By noon, Schaette and his engineers had reached the center of Kastelli.

Major Emmanuel Kourkoutis, who had deployed his men from Battalion B on the western side of the town and around the harbor, continued the resistance for another three days. Making good use of the weapons captured from the ill-fated Muerbe detachment, they made Schaette's men pay in blood for each yard of their advance. But the captured rifles and machine guns used by the Greeks were no match for the artillery brought up by the engineers. What subsequently developed into a house-by-house resistance was methodically crushed by Schaette's men. Shells from antitank guns blasted the houses, which the gallant Greeks had turned into strong points. It was a bitter resistance to the death; the Germans took no prisoners. Those few Greeks who did survive the onslaught slipped off into the southern hills under the cover of darkness.

By May 27 all of Kastelli, including the harbor, had been secured by the engineers of the Ninety-fifth Pioneer Battalion.

In that final attack, which had begun on May 23, Schaette utilized the power of the Stukas and Messerschmitts from above and the massive firepower of machine guns and artillery on the ground against the rifles and bayonets of the outnumbered men from the First Greek Regiment. Yet it still took the Germans four days to secure their objective.

Now that Major Schaette had completed the capture of Kastelli, he turned his attention to the unfinished business of finding a scapegoat upon whom to vent his wrath for the "execution" of the paratroopers from the Muerbe detachment.

The circumstances of their death suggested to him an "atrocity" committed by the local inhabitants. "They must be punished!" he repeated in his report to the commanding general of the mountain division.

From the first hour that Julius Ringel assumed command in Crete, he was informed about the surprising opposition of the civilian population. (Admiral Canaris's Bureau of Military Intelligence—the Abwehr—had reported that the Cretans were Germanophiles who would greet them with open arms.)

The Abwehr's intelligence staff had failed to evaluate the history of Crete in their bitter struggle against another oppressor—the Turk. All that an Abwehr agent had to do was step into a Cretan home—simple and austere as it was—and observe the family photographs that adorned the walls. Portraits of grandfathers, fathers, husbands, and sons—the Kapetans of Cretan tradition—dressed in their native costume, rifle in hand, pistol and knife at the belt, and bandoleers across the chest, would have given him an indication of what to expect.

Though there were international regulations governing the treatment of enemy soldiers in uniform, not a single word referred to civilians—whether men, women, or children—fighting as soldiers without uniforms. When Major Schaette's report about Muerbe at Kastelli arrived, Ringel decided that he had heard enough.

With the finality of a judge rendering a verdict, he concurred that "they must be punished!" [19]

On May 23 a memorandum was issued at the headquarters of the Fifth Mountain Division:

> THE GREEK POPULATION, IN CIVILIAN OR GERMAN UNIFORMS,
> IS TAKING PART IN THE FIGHTING. THEY ARE . . . MUTILATING
> AND ROBBING CORPSES . . . ANY GREEK CIVILIAN TAKEN WITH
> A FIREARM IN HIS HANDS IS TO BE SHOT IMMEDIATELY.

And, finally, the words that would begin a pogrom of senseless executions, first in Crete and later in other occupied countries:

> HOSTAGES (MEN BETWEEN 18 AND 55) ARE TO BE TAKEN FROM
> THE VILLAGES . . . AND IF ACTS OF HOSTILITY AGAINST THE
> GERMAN ARMY TAKE PLACE . . . WILL BE SHOT IMMEDIATELY
> . . . 10 GREEKS WILL DIE FOR EVERY GERMAN! [20]

On the airfield at Maleme, a group of fifteen Cretan civilians had been ordered to help unload the Junker transports that were bringing supplies for the mountain troops. The captives refused the order, and a delegation of three approached an officer at the end of the runway contending that they could not in good conscience obey an order that would aid the Germans against their own people. The German lieutenant turned his back on them and walked away, openly ignoring their persistent protests. The Cretans followed him.

Suddenly the German spun around angrily, pistol in hand.

His Luger coughed three times in rapid succession. Although the sound was smothered by the roar of transport motors, the horror of the scene would be long remembered by the other prisoners. Stepping over the three sprawled bodies, the German motioned the other Cretans back to work.[21]

At Kastelli, Ringel's memorandum was all Major Schaette required to enable him to satisfy his lust for revenge. He was still fuming at the bitter resistance that delayed his capture of Kastelli, an anger compounded by his false impression that atrocities had been perpetrated on the paratroopers of the Muerbe detachment.

Squads of soldiers from his Ninety-fifth Engineer Battalion were ordered to round up all Cretan males in the surrounding countryside and to bring them to his command post in the center of town. Within a few hours, 200 villagers were herded in front of Schaette's headquarters and made to stand in ranks in the dusty, debris-filled town square. Many of them bore the wounds of the recent battle, yet they stood proud and disdainful in the hot sun. They did not know that Schaette had given orders for their execution.

When Major Bedding heard of the order, he protested vehemently. "There is no justifiable reason for these people to be executed," he argued. "Your soldiers were killed in the course of the battle!" The seventeen paratroopers who had been held prisoners in the jailhouse added assurances that they had been properly treated by their captors. Nevertheless, in spite of these protests and assurances, Schaette wanted his revenge. He ordered the executions to begin.[22]

Stavros Beroukakis, a villager who looked older than his years, approached Major Bedding, imploring him to intercede in his behalf. His fourteen-year-old son, John, was among the 200 condemned hostages. Beroukakis was offering himself as hostage in place of John. Would the Germans accept him and reprieve his son?

The German captain to whom Major Schaette delegated the duty of carrying out the executions studied the pleading father who stood before him, hat in hand, tears in his eyes.

"So the Cretans can cry after all," he sneered contemptuously. Then, turning to his sergeant, he snapped, "Shoot them both!"[23]

In groups of ten, the boys and men were marched out into a field, and with short bursts of machine-gun fire, all 201 were slaughtered in order "to teach the rest a lesson."

Word of the New Zealand withdrawal spread rapidly among the Cretan civilian population.

From the villages of Spilia, Voukoules, Gerani, Modhion, Vryses, Fournes, Vatolakos, and Platanias, the message raced through the grapevine faster than any radio: "The New Zealanders are retreating to Galatas."

In Fournes, a village located south of the battlefield, thirteen-year-old Tasso Minarakis heard his father advising the men of the village that the fighting was centering around Galatas, and that all Cretans should go there to fight the enemy.[24]

From the nearby village of Vatolakos, Nicholas Daskalakis took his teenage son, Theodore, with him to help fight the Germans. In his left hand he held an old vintage rifle for which he had only three bullets, while in his right, he carried a heavy bag filled with stones. His son carried two such burlap bags, also filled with stones. These stones were the weapons with which these two Cretans were going to fight the enemy. With knives in their belts, father and son set off for Galatas.[25]

George Christoudakis was a combat veteran of the Albanian front against Italy; his wounds had caused the loss of his left arm. Officially discharged from the Greek army and living in his native village of Vryses, south of Modhion, the embers of a Cretan warrior still glowed in his heart. When word reached him that all men were needed at Galatas, those embers rekindled into a flame.

Christoudakis did not consider the loss of his left arm a handicap, for he still had his right arm. Taping a long knife to the end of a broomstick, he improvised a spear. Holding this primitive weapon under the stump of his left arm and with a revolver in his belt, he departed for Galatas. The crippled Cretan warrior was off to war again.[26]

Manoli Paterakis had spent the last two days ambushing Germans. Following the New Zealand counterattack, Paterakis and the fellow Cretans who made up the band accounted for some two-score Germans in their personal war against the invaders.

Many of these ambushes became hotly fought skirmishes. On one occasion, Paterakis and his group were almost surrounded in a wheat-field. By setting fire to the wheat, they were able to escape under cover of the dense smoke.

Much later, while crossing a field, a passing Messerschmitt spotted them and came down to strafe. The men lay flat in the field. Paterakis dared not move from his place behind a stone wall, changing his position only to avoid the strafer's line of fire.

The day before, Paterakis had taken a pistol from a dead German. What caught his eye was the pistol's unfamiliar shape: It had a short, stubby nose with a wide-cylindered barrel in which was a missile that looked like a shell. Paterakis assumed that it was a specialized antiaircraft pistol; he had never seen or heard of a flare gun.

When the ME-109 came down for another pass, Paterakis fired at it with his new acquisition. His eyes opened in surprise when he saw a green flare shoot up into the air.

"Now you've done it," admonished his friend Gianni. "You've given away our position. He has spotted us!"

The Messerschmitt made a wide circle and came down again, but this time, instead of firing, he dipped his wings. The pilot assumed that the signal had come from a German whom he had mistaken for Cretan. To make amends for the error, he dropped a package of caramels.

As soon as the aircraft disappeared beyond the trees, Paterakis retrieved the package and shared the contents with his friends, after which they resumed their trek toward Galatas.[27]

As the battle progressed into the third day, Freyberg still had no inkling of King George's whereabouts. Considering Freyberg's tactless comment that he would rather the king were wounded or killed fighting for Greece than be taken prisoner, he now faced a frantic period of concerned waiting that added to his considerable troubles.

The members of the royal party continued their flight from the Germans. Struggling upward in the continuous climb toward the near-alpine heights of the White Mountains, the king, Prime Minister Tsouderos, and the whole entourage, buttoned their collars to keep warm as they crossed those peaks on mules.

Once they left the village of Therison, the royal escort of gendarmes was ordered to return north to the battle area. They were replaced by villagers from the mountains who volunteered to become the king's bodyguard.

At one point, villagers brought the king some boiled lamb to eat. There, upon the cold rocks amid the snow, the king and his party sat down and ate the lamb together with freshly baked bread and feta cheese dripping with brine. There was no water available to drink, but that problem was easily solved by melting snow.

From the hour that they had left Therison, the royal party encountered innumerable villagers—old men, old women, and boys and girls—all heading north to fight the invader. The patriotic spirit that compelled them to defend the soil of Crete, instead of staying in the safety of their mountain homes, touched the king and the prime minister to the point of tears.

The trail continued in a southwesterly direction, and as the lower altitudes were reached, the snow gradually disappeared. They had finally crossed the spine of the White Mountain range.

Then began the slow descent over narrow, almost impassable goat trails, until they reached the canyon of Samaria. During the passage through the high-walled, narrow gorge, the king stopped many times to admire the unsurpassed beauty of the flowers amidst the ruggedness of this natural wilderness.

It took several hours before they reached the village of Samaria, located deep in the shadows of the canyon. After a short stay, during which King George and the prime minister prepared a final proclamation for the people of Greece and Crete, they resumed the trip south until the narrow walls of the canyon opened like a huge door on the vast expanse of the Mediterranean beyond.

At 6:00 P.M. on the evening of Thursday, May 22, the king and his party reached the end of their long trip—the village of Aghia Roumeli on the southern coast. There, waiting for the king to arrive, was an advance party that included a British admiral and his staff. Ahead lay the crossing of the Mediterranean and the safety of Egypt.[28]

Late the same day, Admiral Cunningham, in Alexandria, forwarded a message to the commanding officer of Task Force A1, ordering him to send two destroyers to pick up King George and his party. Admiral H. G. Rawlings immediately dispatched the destroyers *Decoy* and *Hero* to Aghia Roumeli.

It was not until 1:00 A.M. on Friday, May 23, that the king set foot on the deck of the British destroyer. Once the whole royal party had embarked, the two warships sped off to rejoin Rawlings's naval squadron.[29]

General Freyberg, back in Crete, knew nothing of this. It was not until May 26 that General Wavell thought of informing him that the king of Greece had finally completed his flight from the Germans.[30]

Four hundred miles to the south, across the Mediterranean and the scorching sands of North Africa, a German general followed the battle of Crete with utmost concern.

Bardia, situated high on the precipitous cliffs overlooking the sea, was a hot and weatherbeaten array of stone houses. Too small to be considered a town and too large to be a village, Bardia first emerged from obscurity as the site of an early British victory against Mussolini's African army. Now it housed the advance headquarters of the German Afrika Korps.

The general who took such intense interest in the events in Crete was in Bardia as the commanding officer of the Afrika Korps, and he knew that whoever controlled the Mediterranean would ultimately win North Africa; his mission in that northern desert was to conquer Egypt and seize the Suez Canal. From the day he assumed command, he wasted no time in exhibiting the military talent that would make his name a household word that would strike fear into the hearts of his enemy.

Through a series of rapid and daring maneuvers, his panzer army won several outstanding victories in North Africa. These feats rapidly transformed him into a hero and earned him the sobriquet of Desert Fox. This corps commander was none other than General Erwin Rommel.

On the evening of May 23, General Rommel joined his staff for the evening meal in the main room of the huge stone house that served as his headquarters in Bardia. His staff felt honored to be eating with their general, whom they respected not only for his military skill and leadership, but also for his spartan traits. Rommel was modest in his taste for food, usually eating the same rations as the men in the ranks. Once in a while, but only on special occasions, he took wine. Tonight he requested some and toasted the ultimate success of his plan to seize the Suez Canal. After meals it was Rommel's habit to retire to the privacy of his quarters and attend to his mail. This night was no exception, and as he left the table, he beckoned his aide to accompany him.

As Rommel's aide, it was Leutnant Heinz Werner Schmidt's duty to make all the necessary preparations for the next day's tour of the front lines, and to make certain that the appropriate memoranda and orders had been issued to the various field commanders. In the evenings, Schmidt had the additional assignment of acting as the general's private secretary.

Schmidt noticed Rommel looking at a recently received communication. Its content must have been of a serious nature, for the general's strong chin was set in apparent disgust as he dropped the paper in the out box. The young aide stood silently in the shadows, watching him.

"Well," said Rommel, acknowledging Schmidt's presence for the first time. "It looks like the Reichsmarshall's paratroopers have attacked Crete."

"Yes, Herr General, I have heard reports about the landings from intelligence."

The general nodded, adding in an almost inaudible mutter, "I suppose that the seizure of Crete could provide a favorable base for operations against the enemy in the desert and in the Middle East . . ."

As his voice trailed off, he rose from his desk and slowly walked over to a huge map of the Mediterranean area hanging on the wall, Schmidt's eyes following him. After a few minutes of silent study, Rommel placed a finger on a speck south of Sicily.

"I tell you, Schmidt, that the occupation of *this* island would be of greater value to us than Crete!"

Schmidt looked hard, trying to determine to what island he was referring.

"This island," continued Rommel, now speaking in a loud, emphatic voice, "lies there like a thorn in our side . . . a constant menace to our lifeline of supply here in North Africa!"

Then, repeatedly tapping the little speck with his forefinger, he concluded: "It is *Malta* and *not* Crete that would control the Mediterranean. That's where Goering should have sent his Fallschirmjägers!"[31]

23

"STAND FOR
NEW ZEALAND!"

MAY 24–25, 1941

With his headquarters less than a mile from the newly formed defense line, General Hargest was able for the first time to see the rising smoke of gunfire. Paradoxically enough, not since the beginning of the invasion had Hargest ventured from his headquarters to visit his forward positions. Now his forward positions had retreated to within a stone's throw of his headquarters. For Hargest, this was too close for comfort.

His most recent apprehensions centered upon the strain under which his men had been fighting since the first day of battle and upon the severity of their estimated losses. In a report he dispatched to the New Zealand Division Headquarters on the night of the withdrawal, Hargest had estimated that the Twenty-second had been depleted to 110 men, while the Twenty-third was only able to muster 250. *In each case he overestimated his losses.*[1]

These erroneous figures were the basis for Hargest's contention that he did not have the capacity to hold the new defense line. By 2:50 P.M. the next afternoon, May 25, he was quite emphatic in his doubts, and the question was raised as to whether he should abandon the Platanias River line. Puttick, his division commanding general, listened to Hargest's argument, but had no fear about his New Zealanders' ability to hold the line against a German frontal assault. His only fear was for the defense line's left flank, which ended in midair, unsupported and indefensible. It was that factor alone that forced Puttick to agree with Hargest that the Fifth Brigade should abandon its new position and move farther east.[2] So it was that when darkness arrived, the plucky but disgruntled New Zealanders of the Fifth Brigade once again began a withdrawal.

This new withdrawal eastward toward Galatas left a void quickly entered by the newly arrived German troopers of the Fifth Mountain Division. In a matter of hours, the larger villages of Fournes, Gerani, Modhion, Vatolakos, Vryses, and Platanias fell to the Germans. With the exception of innumerable New Zealand stragglers and Cretan marksmen—who still harassed the Germans with sniper fire—organized resistance west of Galatas had been virtually eliminated.

As May 24, the fifth day of battle, dawned, the opposing forces faced each other like two gladiators ready for a life-or-death struggle among the hills that ringed the walled village of Galatas.

If Maleme, with its airfield, was the door through which the Germans entered Crete, Galatas would be the gateway for the seizure of the Cretan capital of Khaniá, and thence the remainder of the island.

Galatas was a small village of some twelve whitewashed stone buildings—that had lain in peace for decades amidst its hilltop splendor. Its white houses reflected the sun's rays with the sparkle of jewels, sharply contrasted against the surrounding backdrop of green hills. A natural string of shallow eminences that offered the defenders a favorable position from which to protect Galatas and the roads beyond leading to the capital of Crete, these hills were destined to play a major role in the forthcoming battle.

There were five prominent hills west of Galatas, none of them exceeding a height of 400 feet. They lay in a semicircle whose arc bellied westward. The northern point of the arc began less than a mile south of the main coast road, where the ground rose abruptly to the summit of the first hill—Red Hill—so named for the preponderance of bougainvillea that gave the terrain its color. From Red Hill the arc curved south and east to include Wheat Hill, named for its waist-high crop of wheat, and Pink Hill, with its varicolored flora, finally terminating at its southern tip in the village's Cemetery Hill. Bisecting this arc of hills at its center was a long, low ridge called Ruin Ridge. It extended westward for a quarter of a mile and ended in an abrupt peak—the highest hill of the five. Nestled within the open end of this arc of hills lay the village of Galatas; the surrounding eminences were known as Galatas heights.

The Third Parachute Regiment in Prison Valley was already familiar with these heights and with the men defending them. Now the men of Julius Ringel's Mountain Division were to taste the same bitter fruit.

With his first objective—Maleme airfield—taken, the time had arrived for Ringel to begin the second phase of his operation.

The northern sector of the German attack force would be led by Colonel Ramcke, commanding the remnants of parachutists. From the area immediately above the main northern coast road to a point south of Red Hill, the survivors of Captain Gericke's and Major Stentzler's paratroop battalions took up their positions for the attack.

Exhausted after a continuous five-day battle against a stubborn army under a searing hot sun, these survivors of the original assault regiment now hoped for victory.

In the center of the line, General Julius Ringel placed the fresh troops of Colonel Utz's One-hundredth Mountain Regiment. The regiment's Second Battalion, commanded by Major Schury, took up a position opposite Ruin Hill, while on its right flank, the First Battalion, under Major Schrank, posed itself before Pink Hill in the center and Cemetery Hill on the right.

Far to the south, an enveloping column, using the First and

Third Battalions of the Eighty-fifth Mountain Regiment under Colonel Krakau, was to swing wide, capture Alikianou village, join forces with the Third Parachute Regiment in Prison Valley, and break into the rear of the New Zealand defense line.[3]

As ambitious as the attack plan looked on paper, it had one drawback: The attack was to be a series of separate assaults, starting in the northern sector and continuing down the line, instead of a simultaneous all-out mass attack. It would start with Ramcke's force in the north, be continued by Utz's regiment in the center, and be followed up by Heidrich's parachute regiment in the south later in the day. The main stroke would be borne by Colonel Utz and his battalions in the center of the line. With Krakau's men of the Eighty-fifth Regiment coming up on the Zealanders' rear, it was felt that the defense line would crumble between the jaws of these two factors.[4]

From the Galatas heights, the New Zealand defenders watched these fresh German troops move into position. Wherever they looked, groups of men were digging entrenchments for mortars and machine guns. The Germans were only two miles away, but the New Zealanders were so low on mortar and machine-gun ammunition that they held their fire for the moment when the mountain troops would begin the attack.

When the sun rose on May 24, the Eighteenth Battalion held the high ground from Red Hill south to Wheat Hill. The withdrawn Composite Battalion occupied positions in the rear of the Eighteenth Battalion on Ruin Ridge. The Divisional Petrol Company and the Divisional Cavalry Detachment were all that remained of Kippenberger's original Tenth Brigade on the firing line; both units were combined under the command of Major John Russell and were subsequently referred to as Task Force Russell.

The Petrol Company was dug in on the right of Pink Hill, linking with the Eighteenth Battalion's left flank at Wheat Hill. The Cavalry Detachment held the left forward slope of Pink Hill, where its left flank joined the Fourth Brigade's Nineteenth New Zealand Battalion.

General Hargest's Fifth Brigade was withdrawn far to the rear of the Galatas defense line. The brigade's Twentieth, Twenty-third, and Twenty-eighth Battalions were repositioned near the Galatas turn, just south of the promontory housing the Seventh General Hospital. The Twenty-second and Twenty-first Battalions were held farther east, straddling the coast road and well out of the immediate battle zone.

To protect the extreme left flank, well east of Cemetery Hill where the survivors of the Sixth Greek Regiment had dug in, Puttick placed the Seventh and Eighth Australian Battalions in line on the left flank of the New Zealand Nineteenth Battalion.[5]

On May 23 Colonel Heidrich summoned Von der Heydte and Major Wulf Derpa, the CO of the Second Parachute Battalion, to his headquarters tent. The previous day, the regimental commander had ordered Von der Heydte to give all his ammunition to the Second Battalion and told Derpa to resume his attacks against both Pink and Cemetery Hills. Derpa's battalion subsequently made several spirited assaults on both hills, which ended in failure with heavy losses. As a result, the Second Battalion had been reduced to a strength of only two companies.

On this morning of the twenty-third, Heidrich ordered Derpa to continue his attack on Cemetery Hill, and Major Derpa finally protested.

"Herr Oberst, I question the practicability of these incessant frontal attacks."

Colonel Heidrich glared at the battalion commander, a surge of fury rising within him. The regimental commander's nerves strained to breaking point by the repeated defeats suffered at the hands of the Greeks and New Zealanders, he was in no mood to have his orders questioned.

"You will do as I say, Major," he shouted at Derpa. "Have you no more stomach for fighting—are you afraid to die?"

There was silence in the tent, everyone stiffening at this harsh accusation.

The sensitive, courageous battalion commander paled at the unwarranted insult to his courage. He clicked his heels and through tightly compressed lips, he replied, "It is not a question of my own life, sir; I am considering the lives of the soldiers for whom I am responsible." After a pause Derpa added, "My own life, I would gladly give!"

Colonel Heidrich ordered Derpa to resume the attack.[6]

From the far side of Prison Valley, Captain Von der Heydte sadly watched his colleague and friend leading the remnants of the Second Battalion in a renewed attack against the right slope of Cemetery Hill.

Smoke covered the crest of the hill as the Germans approached the positions held by the right flank of the Nineteenth New Zealand Battalion. The crack of rifles and the deadly rattle of machine guns echoed across the valley. Von der Heydte could see the paratroopers of the Second Battalion charging up the steep hill, where the smoke of gunfire enveloped them. Soon the roar of firing diminished and finally stopped. When the smoke lifted, the hillside was covered by the blue-gray uniforms of dead and wounded paratroopers. The survivors trickled back down the hill; once again the attack had been repulsed.

Still smarting from Colonel Heidrich's insult—which reflected on his men—Major Derpa ordered the survivors to join the remnants of his battalion for a renewed attack. Derpa was very proud of his paratroopers, but they were tired, hungry, and thirsty. The heat of the Cretan sun had taken a heavy toll; most of them had no water left in their canteens and they were still wearing the heavy woolen paratroop uniform. Many of his men had discarded their outer smocks, opened their tunics, and rolled up their sleeves for relief. Others had even cut the legs from their trousers, hoping for some cooling comfort. Their uniforms saturated with perspiration, many of his men had fallen victim to heat prostration.

Derpa requested a few hours of rest for his men, but Heidrich insisted that the attacks continue.[7]

Captain H. M. Smith, whose men had just repulsed the first assault, warned his men to remain on the alert, his intuition telling him that the Germans would attack again. If they attacked on his front, he held no fears: The earlier attack had cost him only a few casualties, and the rest were in good spirits. But Smith did have one concern—his right flank.

That section of the hill defense was protected by the remnants of the Sixth Greek Regiment. Many of the Greeks had been scattered by the earlier German attacks, but the Sixth Greek Company was still holding its own on the rise of ground to the right of Smith's Nineteenth Battalion. If the Germans pressed their attack on the Greek position and succeeded in penetrating their defenses, the New Zealand flank would be turned and the whole hill defense could be lost.

When Derpa's men aimed the thrust of their second attack at the Greek positions, Smith's worst fears were realized. He had no men to spare, and the New Zealand ammunition did not fit the Greeks' prewar Styr guns. But he did send an officer to the commander of the Sixth Greek Company beseeching him to "hold the line at all costs."

"We shall!" replied Captain E.[8]

From behind the olive trees, the Germans emerged at a trot, charging directly up the slope toward the positions of the Sixth Greek Company. Captain Smith ordered his men to commence firing into the attackers' flank, but—realizing that the undulating terrain sent the New Zealand fire well over the heads of the charging paratroopers—he had to rescind the order.

The Germans gathered momentum as they charged up and over the crest of Cemetery Hill, pressing the attack as they approached the village cemetery wall at the top of the rise.

Above the crack of rifles and the rattle of machine guns, there now rose a new sound from the Greek positions—a heart-stopping human cry echoing over the defense positions as it passed from man to man, each Greek in turn repeating it louder and louder until it crescendoed over the hillside, smothering the roar of the German attack. The New Zealanders had heard that call before. It was "Aera!"—the rallying battle cry of the immortal Evzones—and to the Greeks, it had one meaning: "Attack!"

The New Zealanders watched in awe, and Captain Smith uttered to no one in particular, "Why, those bloody crazy Greeks!"[9]

Over the top of the cemetery wall came the madmen. They had no more bullets, but they still had their bayonets, and down the hill they charged, screaming "Aera!" at the top of their lungs, the gleam of their bayonets reflecting the midday sun.

For a moment, the Germans stood in disbelief.

With snarling fury, the Greeks met the Germans head-on, halfway down the rise. They slashed, they butted, and they bayonetted, German after German falling to their piercing stabs. In the lead was Captain E, with Lieutenant Kritakis at his side.[10]

There was a brief moment when the two forces swayed in furious hand-to-hand combat. Then the Germans broke, turned, and ran down the hill, the Greeks in close pursuit.

Captain Smith shook his head, admiring the heroism with which these gallant Greek soldiers had shattered the German attack.[11] The Second Paratroop Battalion had ceased to exist as a fighting force. Severely wounded by a bayonet thrust in the stomach, its commanding officer, Major Derpa, was later to die in the Regimental Field Hospital. He had proved his courage with his life.

But by midday on May 24, the German advance was succeeding. The radio broadcast from Berlin, which finally told the German people that Crete had been invaded, was a good sign. The Fuehrer's public acknowledgement of the battle for Crete meant that victory was at hand. To the embattled, exhausted paratroopers in Prison Valley, this announcement was a shot in the arm.

When Lieutenant Colonel J. R. Gray and his Eighteenth Battalion took over the defense perimeter previously held by the Composite Battalion, they found that this newly assigned position covered a much greater area than a half-strength battalion could properly defend. Gray positioned his men carefully over the mile-and-a-half stretch of hilly terrain that extended from Wheat Hill north to Red Hill, finding the defense line so overextended that he did not have sufficient men to hold its highest point. He decided not to defend Ruin Hill, even though its capture by the Germans would have them breathing down his neck. It was a tactical error, for the hill was to become the weakest link in a relatively weak defense line.

On the morning of May 24, Colonel Utz sent a patrol on a reconnaissance of the New Zealand positions. They found Ruin Hill undefended and immediately brought up mortars. With these entrenched on the reverse side of the hill, the Germans could bring flanking fire to bear on Red Hill to their left front and Wheat Hill to their right. This firing position could make those hilly bastions in the New Zealand defense line almost untenable.

When Utz was informed that Ruin Hill had been seized, he ordered Major Schury of the Second Mountain Battalion to send out a company-strength combat patrol to pierce the line. Advancing slowly and unopposed until it reached the far edge of an olive grove leading into the valley between Red and Wheat Hills. Once it left the protection of the trees, the patrol was caught in a crossfire from the New Zealand defense positions. Pinned down for hours, they finally withdrew, leaving more than half of their number behind. The episode was evidence enough for Colonel Utz to postpone any further attacks until he received proper air support.[12]

That support was already evident in the clear blue skies farther east. However, the Luftwaffe's targets were not the New Zealand hill positions before Galatas, but Khaniá.

From a little past noon until 8:00 P.M., Stukas, Dorniers, and Heinkels, interspersed by marauding ME-109's, kept up a constant bombing of that hapless city. By dusk, flames rose hundreds of feet into the sky, turning the advent of darkness into daylight, and outlining the devastation wrought on that once-beautiful capital of Crete.

In the wake of the torrential rain of death that had drenched the city for an eight-hour period, there remained the scars of uprooted trees, shattered buildings, torn walls, and debris-filled streets, fogged by clouds of pulverized stone eerily reflecting leaping tongues of flame. Amid the rubble lay hundreds of dead civilians, innocent victims of man's ability to wield death from the sky.[13]

On the next day, May 25, General Kurt Student, the overall commander, finally set foot upon Crete. No longer tethered to the stake, he was "off the hook."

Student was greeted at Maleme airfield by General Ringel. The goateed, immaculately dressed commander of the mountain division personally conducted him on a tour of the battlefield. The whole day was spent visiting the regimental headquarters at the forward positions. Student talked and ate with the troops. He listened and observed, finally satisfied that the operation was progressing well, albeit delayed.

There was, however, one aspect of the tour that bothered him. The sight of thousands of corpses of his beloved paratroopers scattered over the fields of Crete shocked him. He had always considered his elite Falschirmjägers to be invincible. Their stinking, bloated corpses lying on soil reddened with their blood would stay with Kurt Student for the rest of his days.[14]

When Captain E, CO of the Sixth Greek Company of the Sixth Greek Regiment, returned to his original position after the counterattack that shattered the German assault of the Second Battalion in which Derpa was killed, he gathered the survivors of his company and reestablished a more concentrated defense line behind the stone wall atop Cemetery Hill. There were not that many of his men left, and that worried him, for if the Germans were to attack again, it would be almost impossible to hold the line.

Nearby, a wounded German paratrooper lay beside a shattered tombstone, feigning death. As Captain E stood in the open, positioning his men, the German slowly and deliberately raised his Luger, carefully aiming at the Greek captain. Kritakis spotted the movement and shouted, pushing the captain out of the line of fire just as the Luger barked. The bullet missed the captain but nicked Kritakis in the arm; at the same instant, Captain E's aide dispatched the German with a quick thrust of his bayonet.

There was no time to thank Kritakis for his alertness, for before any appreciation could be expressed, a flight of Messerschmitts raced past, sprewing bullets all over Cemetery Hill, scattering the men to cover. When the strafing attack passed, Captain E noticed blood on Kritakis' sleeve. He examined the wound, grateful that his life had been saved, and suggested that Kritakis go to the dressing station in Galatas, Kritakis refused. "My place is here with you," he replied.

"My friend, must I *order* you to the dressing station? Go, get away from this hell!" Kritakis reluctantly left the hill position.[15]

A squad of German machine gunners had been ordered out of Schrank's battalion to set up a machine-gun position on a small hillock between Wheat and Pink Hills. The Germans worked their way along the protective edge of an olive grove, crossed a small depression, and reached their objective unobserved by the New Zealanders. But a Cretan civilian noticed them and raced off to report their position.

When the German squad reached the hillock, they immediately went to work digging entrenchments, the squad's two heavy machine guns lying nearby. The guns were to be placed so as to face the flank of Wheat Hill, thus giving protective cover to any German advance in the valley between Wheat and Pink Hills. The olive grove, through which they passed, protected their rear. As they dug their positions, the Germans became aware of a clamoring noise arising from the edge of the olive grove through which they just hiked. The babble of voices was loud enough to distract them and, pausing in their digging, they watched with interest and bewilderment as a motley collection of old men, old women, children, and a few dogs came into view. Some of the men carried what appeared to be long-barreled, muzzle-loading muskets; others carried swords and hoes, while the women bore sickles and sticks. Not to be outdone, the children carried bags of stones and the dogs raced about yipping and sniffing.

The Germans looked at each other, amused; until they saw the leader of this ragged group. His appearance gave them cause for alarm.

He was tall and thin-faced—from his bearing obviously a British officer—dressed as strangely as the people he led. Clad in shorts and wearing a long buff-colored army jacket that reached almost to his knees, he had a yellow bandanna around his forehead. With a service revolver in each hand, he formed the Cretans into a single rank.

He was Captain Michael Forrester, the same officer from Freyberg's headquarters who had attached himself to the Sixth Greek Regiment after the first day of the invasion and two days later led 200 shouting Greeks in a charge that broke up a German attack. Now he was back with this odd collection of civilians.

Here was George Christoudakis, the one-armed veteran of the Albanian War, his spearlike weapon under the stump of his left arm, while his right held the shaft. Here also was the octogenarian from the village of Daratsos, Spiro Gregorakis, bearing an ancient, rusty rifle from the Turkish campaigns.

Forrester turned to the Cretans and, pointing up the hill, waved his arm forward. Before the Germans realized what was happening, these bedraggled civilians charged with the screams of warriors going into battle.

The German machine guns were now in position, but facing the wrong direction, and the ammunition belts had not been passed through the breach. Before the Germans could raise their pistols or rifles, the Cretans were on top of them. It was a costly hesitation based on the belief that such civilians would never dare attack a trained, armed German squad.

Forrester leaped over the trench firing his pistols at the Germans. Christoudakis felt the blade of his spear snap as he drove it into the body of a startled German. Gregorakis came face to face with another German, raised his ancient rifle, and pulled the trigger. The gun's blast tore the German apart, but its kick was enough to topple the eighty-year-old Cretan over the parapet and down the hill.

The women pounded the Germans with their sickles and sticks, while Forrester shouted encouragement. When the bewildered German survivors broke and ran, the children followed them down the hillock, throwing stones in their wake. Even the dogs chased at the Germans, nipping at their heels.

Later that day, eighty-year-old Spiro Gregorakis returned to his village of Daratsos. As he walked up the path to his house, he shouted to his wife Maria and daughter Eleni. When they greeted him, he raised his right arm high, holding before them a captured German tommy gun. He smiled proudly at them with a twinkle in his eye as he stated: "I blew his head off!" [16]

Throughout the night of the twenty-fourth, sporadic firing continued along the whole defense perimeter before Galatas, enough to keep everyone alert and on edge.

Bright and early the morning of May 25, Ramcke formed his paratroopers for the attack. Their movements were readily observed from Red Hill, and word was passed back to Colonel Gray, who ordered an immediate mortar attack on Ramcke's positions. The sudden mortar deluge scattered the paratroopers, causing them many casualties. But this liberal use of mortar shells created a new problem for the men of the Eighteenth Battalion, for it depleted their supply to ten shells. Colonel Gray's request for replenishment was answered with thirty more and a note stating that these were the last shells available in the whole brigade.

The men of the Eighteenth Battalion knew they were sitting on a powder keg. Mortar shells were in short supply; so was their rifle and machine-gun ammunition. A reconnaissance patrol during the previous night had found as many as seventeen German machine guns in one sector alone—more machine guns than the entire Eighteenth Battalion had in the whole one-and-a-half-mile stretch of their defense line.

Colonel Utz had been persistently inquiring about air cover. "When do we get Stuka support?" was the question that he repeatedly asked of General Ringel. He was finally told to expect an air strike by 4:30 that afternoon.

Following Colonel Utz's earlier instructions, Major Schury ordered his Second Mountain Battalion forward without air cover. But a continuous wall of fire from the New Zealanders made an advance almost impossible, and the German need for air support became even more apparent. Thus, for the major part of this day —like the day before—the New Zealand line held the Germans at bay, but they knew the fuse to the powder keg had been lit.

At 4:30 in the afternoon, it exploded.

The sky above the New Zealand forward positions filled with Messerschmitts and Stukas. Even Dorniers joined in the attack, and for half an hour the rain of death continued. In the north, Colonel Ramcke's paratroopers attacked first, driving south between the coast road and Red Hill. To support them Ramcke unleashed a heavy concentration of high explosives from 55-mm antitank guns and some captured Bofors, all firing over open sights. The New Zealanders were taking heavy losses from this direct fire, with no chance for retaliation. The commanding officer of the New Zealand unit on the right flank had been severely wounded and his successor killed, leaving the leadership of the company in the hands of sergeants and corporals. The persistence of the paratroop attack was such that it succeeded in surrounding and cutting off Red Hill, causing a breach in the northern end of the New Zealand defense line. The road to Khaniá lay momentarily open.[17]

Colonel Gray, with rifle in hand, rushed forward with a small collection of cooks and clerks from the Composite Battalion, including the battalion chaplain. He ran into the midst of the fight, yelling, "No surrender! No surrender!"[18] But the paratroop attack, with its devastating mortar and antitank fire, was so intense that Gray had to withdraw the twelve survivors of the forward company, leaving Red Hill securely in German hands.

Now, the second phase of Colonel Utz's tactical plan went into effect. Major Schury, who had been repulsed earlier in the day, sent his men back against Wheat Hill in the center. For the New Zealanders, defending the slopes of the hill, it became a hell on earth. Heavy mortar and artillery shells fell on them in a crossfire from the abandoned Ruin Hill position before them and from the newly captured Red Hill on their right. The whole of Wheat Hill was hidden in a cloud of smoke, as shell after shell burst upon it. Kippenberger watched the devastating fire through his field glasses, yet twice refused requests for withdrawal.[19]

At the end of this fiery two-hour pounding, the men of C Company could take no more. The few survivors pulled out, led by Major R. J. Lynch. Wheat Hill—the third bastion in the New Zealand defense line—had fallen to the Germans.

Further down the line, the third phase of the plan—the attack on the southern part of the position—began.

Even though it was now early evening, Utz felt that to call a halt to the attack because of pending darkness might give the New Zealanders an opportunity to regain their balance and bring in men to reinforce the line. To prevent this, he ordered Major Schrank's First Mountain Battalion to attack and seize Pink and Cemetery Hills, while Schury's Second Battalion would continue the advance in order to capture the village of Galatas.

Major Schrank's men rushed forward to attack the two hills, carrying with them the additional strength of the Engineer Detachment from the Third Mountain Battalion, which had been held in reserve by Utz. The firepower from this reinforced battalion was too much for the depleted and exhausted ranks of the Cavalry Detachment and for the survivors of the decimated Sixth Greek Regiment. As the sun dipped behind the Rodopos Peninsula in the western part of Crete, the mountain troops of Schrank's First Battalion finally captured Cemetery Hill.

But Pink Hill still held.

The gallant Petrol Company struggled desperately to hold this last hill in the New Zealand defense perimeter. This heroic assortment of truckers and supply men had fought for days as bravely as any first-class infantry unit. Now, with Cemetery Hill captured, the mountain troops turned their efforts toward Pink Hill.

Captain H. A. Rowe, the brigade supply officer commanding this gallant company, received some reinforcements to bolster his dwindling ranks. Two platoons arrived from the Nineteenth Battalion, located far on the left flank beyond Cemetery Hill. Lieutenant W. N. Carson joined him with several drivers, and Lieutenant J. P. Dill brought a platoon of gunners.[20]

The deadly deluge of bombs continued to pound them. From the sky ME-109s and Stukas strafed and bombed the hill continuously; from the ground German rifle and machine-gun fire arched into the New Zealand emplacements together with the murderous crash of mortar shells. Their position soon became untenable. When machine-gun fire from Wheat Hill struck them in the rear, Captain Rowe ordered the survivors of the Petrol Company to withdraw to the safety of buildings in Galatas. The men of the Petrol Company fought as they went, even in retreat.

While Lieutenant Kritakis, the executive officer of the Sixth Greek Company, was having his wound treated, two disheveled Greek soldiers brought in a wounded man. Kritakis recognized one of the litter bearers as a man from his own company. When he walked over to see the wounded man, he was shocked to discover that lying on a makeshift stretcher was his commanding officer. Captain E was semiconscious, with a wound in his chest.

One of the Greeks carrying Captain E turned to Kritakis with tears in his eyes, repeating over and over again, "The Germans have overrun our positions!"[21]

The heavy German bombardment of the New Zealand line in the Wheat Hill area had killed more than 100 of Colonel Gray's men, almost decimating the Eighteenth Battalion. The whole western part of the defense line had lost all semblance of cohesion. It had been pierced at many points, and most of the New Zealanders lay in their trenches, completely surrounded, fighting to the death.

But the fiery onslaught was too much for many of them, and they finally broke.

Colonel Kippenberger watched with increasing alarm as the men of his brigade stumbled back. They were wild-eyed, some without helmets and others without weapons. When Colonel Gray emerged from the cloud of smoke looking "twenty years older than three hours before,"[22] Kippenberger recognized the symptoms.

As more of his men came over the hill, he rushed into their midst, waving his arms and shouting over and over again: "Stand for New Zealand!"[23]

Electrified, the men awakened from their momentary lapse. The retreat was stopped before it became a rout.

The Germans continued their advance into Galatas. Maddened with the fury of battle and enraged by the stout resistance of the defenders, the mountain troops fought mercilessly. In the ensuing struggle, furious charge and counter-charge left New Zealand, Greek, and German bodies piled up in the streets of the village. The attackers gave no quarter and none was given in return; captured soldiers were slain on the spot. A group of surrounded New Zealanders raised their hands to surrender, but the Germans burned them alive with flamethrowers. One survivor tried to escape, only to be caught and thrown back into the flames. The street-by-street battle developed into a carnage.

Galatas finally fell to the Germans.

The loss of the village of Galatas was a terrible blow for the New Zealanders. However, the diminutive but aggressive commander of the Tenth Brigade, Colonel Kippenberger, was determined to take Galatas back from the Germans.[24]

Just before dusk Lieutenant Roy Farran appeared out of nowhere with his two light tanks. Kippenberger looked upon them as a gift from heaven. These were the same tanks that had survived the fruitless counterattack on May 22 at Pirgos. When Brigadier Inglis of the Fourth Brigade heard that Wheat Hill had fallen and that the New Zealand line had been breached, he sent Farran forward to see if he could help.

Kippenberger lost no time in putting the tanks to good use. He immediately ordered Farran to take them into the village on a reconnaissance patrol. The two tanks clattered down the dusty road and soon disappeared into the smoke that hung low over the village.[25]

While Kippenberger waited for Farran's return, the remaining two companies of the Twenty-third Battalion appeared over the crest. They also had been sent forward by Inglis to reinforce the New Zealand line.

About 100 yards from the edge of the village, they came upon Colonel Kippenberger, standing in the middle of the road, a pipe in his mouth, waiting for Farran's tanks to return. He lost no time telling them what he had planned for them: "You have to take Galatas with the help of the two tanks. There is no time for reconnaissance," he continued. "You must move straight in up the road and . . . and take everything with you!"[26] Farran's two tanks reappeared.

Farran lifted the lid of his turret and reported to Kippenberger, "The place is stiff with Jerries!" He added, as he hauled himself out of the tank, "They are everywhere in the village!"[27]

"I have two companies of infantry," interrupted Kippenberger. "Would you go in again with them?"[28]

Farran nodded. The infantrymen of the Twenty-third Battalion waited nervously.

Major Thomason of the Twenty-third replacing the wounded Leckie now took his turn to pass instructions to the men of his two companies: "D Company will be attacking on the left side of the road. We have two tanks for support," he added, but cautioned that "the whole show is stiff with Huns . . . it is going to be a bloody affair, but we have just got to succeed.'' Then he added with a wave of his hand, ''Now, for Christ's sake—get cracking!''[29]

There it was—the order to attack!

No sooner had the advance begun than stragglers from other units joined them. Men separated from the remnants of the Petrol and Cavalry Detachments, together with the survivors from the Composite, the Twentieth, and the Eighteenth Battalions, fell in at the rear of the column. More than 250 men had been collected for this do-or-die effort to dislodge the Germans from Galatas.

At first, the infantrymen moved forward at a normal walking pace, but as the tanks increased their speed, the New Zealanders broke into a trot. At that precise moment, a spontaneous shout rose from their ranks. It echoed across the hills and fields like the bloodcurdling scream of a banshee.

Lieutenant Colonel Gray, standing on the eastern outskirts of the village with some survivors from his battalion, heard the shout and thought it was the cry of a wild beast. Lieutenant Farran heard it above the noise of the tank's motors. It even reached Von der Heydte's ears in Prison Valley, and it made his flesh crawl.

It was the shout of New Zealanders on the attack. It was the battle cry of men who were returning with a vengeful wrath.[30]

The Germans were caught off guard by this new attack at twilight. When Farran retreated with his two tanks earlier, the Germans assumed that the battle was over for the night. No sooner did they hear the chorus of shouts than the two tanks were back, this time supported by a flood of wildly charging men.

The slaughter began all over again as the New Zealanders tore into the Germans.

Firing came from all directions—from windows, from rooftops, and from behind trees, chimneys, and walls. Those Germans caught in houses were quickly killed with grenades thrown through windows. Others raced into the streets only to be cut down by New Zealand bullets. Soon the streets were filled with struggling men fighting savagely with bayonets, pistols, rifle butts, and even with bare hands.[31]

A mortar blast crippled Lieutenant Farran's tank, wounding him and killing his driver. As Farran emerged from his tank, he was hit a second time, and now he lay in the gutter next to his disabled vehicle, on the village's main street just off the town square.

A squad of New Zealanders trotted past Farran with Lieutenant Thomas of the Twenty-third in the lead. When they reached the main square, they ran into a group of Germans less than fifty yards away. The New Zealanders opened fire on them, cutting some of them down, but the rest turned and charged.

Lieutenant W. B. Thomas aimed his pistol at a German less than three yards away, whose youthful face had been contorted into a snarl. Thomas fired point-blank at him and, through the flash, saw the youth shudder with surprise as he lunged forward. The German fell dead at Thomas's feet, but not before his bayonet had pierced Thomas's thigh. Thomas now lay wounded, bleeding badly, amid other bodies of Germans and New Zealanders—some groaning in pain, others silent in death.[32]

Through the wild melee and the shouts, he heard a distinct English voice from across the square shouting to the New Zealanders, "Good show, New Zealand—jolly good show—come on, New Zealand!"[33]

The vicious battle continued. It was a bitter struggle that was fought street by street, house by house, room by room, until, in time, the whole village was littered with the bodies of the dead, the dying, and the wounded. Little by little, the Germans were pushed out of Galatas. As twilight lapsed into darkness, Galatas was once more in the hands of the New Zealanders.

24

"WHY IS CRETE STILL RESISTING?"

MAY 26–28, 1941

Stillness finally reigned over the battlefield of Galatas. The streets of the village presented a grim crimson tableau. The dead—the New Zealanders, the Greeks, the Cretan irregulars, and the Germans—were lying one on top of the other. New Zealand medics tended to the fallen, treating friend and foe alike. Volunteering assistance were a handful of Cretan women who offered water and bread to the wounded.

A little after 10:00 P.M., a messenger brought Kippenberger a dispatch from the area brigade commander, General Inglis, summoning him and the brigade's battalion commanders to meet. Ignoring his fatigue, he departed for Inglis's headquarters.[1]

Kippenberger groped through the darkness, stumbling over the rocky terrain past vineyards and ravines, looking for Inglis's command post. He finally found it in a deep hollow, covered by a huge tarpaulin. Inside, Inglis was sitting at a small table, straining his eyes to read a map by the flickering glow of a single candle. In the shadows cast by the dim light, Kippenberger was able to distinguish Burrows of the Twentieth, Blackburn of the Nineteenth, and Major Sanders. Colonel Dittmer of the

Twenty-eighth Maori Battalion was the last to arrive, entering on Kippenberger's heels.

General Inglis glanced at his watch. He had also invited his division commander, General Puttick, to be present. Annoyance appeared on his face, for time was of the utmost importance, and the hours of night would wait for no man.

"Gentlemen," he began, "you realize that if a counterattack is to have any chance of restoring the position, it must be delivered tonight and in as great strength as possible."[2]

The officers wearily nodded their agreement.

"The attack must be carried forth by a fresh force," he continued. "When General Puttick arrives, he could well decide what units to put in to restore the situation."[3]

Kippenberger and the battalion officers knew very well that by a "fresh force," Inglis referred to the use of units from the reserve force located at Suda Bay. To have those units released to Inglis's command, General Puttick would have to ask Freyberg. That would take time, and daylight was only six hours off. Yet Puttick, the only man who could properly make this request of Freyberg, had not arrived, and the hours slipped silently away.

While the men waited for Puttick, the fate of the battle for Galatas hung by a thin thread, and on that flimsy link depended the outcome of the battle for Crete.

Inglis was growing apprehensive about Puttick's absence. Could it mean that there was no possibility of help? If that was the case, then he would have to use any available force at his command. His attention turned to the Twenty-eighth Maori Battalion.

The Maoris had been in reserve during the battle of Galatas. Their ranks had been reduced to 477 men by their unsuccessful counterattack two days earlier at Pirgos, but their morale remained high. Inglis felt that if any unit could attack and restore the situation, it would be the brave Maori, even in their depleted state.

"What do you think?" Inglis inquired, turning to Colonel Dittmer, the Maori battalion commander.[4]

Kippenberger interrupted: "It cannot be done. The terrain is crisscrossed by vineyards and ravines cut at angles to the line of advance. They don't know the ground," he continued, speaking from experience, having just groped his way over the same terrain, "and in the darkness, they will get lost and cut off."[5]

"What choice do I have, Howard?" Inglis replied to Kippenberger's objection. "We are done if it does not come off!"[6]

Then Inglis once again turned to Dittmer. "Can you do it, George?"

"I'll give it a go," replied the plucky Maori commander.[7]

At that moment there was a movement at the entrance to the headquarters tent. The tarpaulin parted and an officer entered. Kippenberger and the others peered through the dim light, hoping to see Puttick. Instead, they recognized Colonel W. G. Gentry, Puttick's staff officer.[8]

When Gentry heard of the plan to use the Maori battalion in a counterattack, he replied with a very emphatic no.[9]

"That is it, then, gentlemen," Inglis remarked, relieved that the weight of responsibility had been taken from his shoulders, yet irked that Gentry's decision meant no counterattack. "Galatas will have to be abandoned!"[10]

Kippenberger stalked out of the meeting, his fatigue forgotten in the heat of his anger. The aggressive young colonel was furious at the thought that no effort would be made to restore the line at Galatas. "After all that fighting—after all that bloodshed!" he murmured to himself. With that thought, he set out to order his men to withdraw to a line east of the village of Daratsos.

From the day that preceded the battle of Galatas, Freyberg had come to the conclusion that Crete could no longer be held. He felt that it was just a matter of time, that no matter how bravely and stubbornly his men fought, it was of no avail against the increasing strength of the mountain troops arriving hourly at Maleme airfield. Nor could they sustain a proper ground defense while the Luftwaffe terrorized them from the sky. Freyberg felt that "at this stage, [it] was quite clear . . . that the troops would not be able to last much longer against a continuation of the air attacks." [11] All reports received from the forward battalions at Galatas forced Freyberg to conclude that the end was rapidly approaching. It was gradually becoming a situation that offered only "two alternatives, defeat in the field and capture, or withdrawal."

He sat down to write these thoughts to his commander-in-chief in Cairo, yet he hesitated to mention the dreaded word "evacuation."

> TODAY HAS BEEN ONE OF GREAT ANXIETY TO ME HERE . . . THIS EVENING AT 1700 HOURS, BOMBERS, DIVE BOMBERS AND GROUND STRAFERS CAME OVER AND BOMBED OUR FORWARD TROOPS AND THEN HIS GROUND TROOPS LAUNCHED AN ATTACK. IT IS STILL IN PROGRESS AND I AM AWAITING NEWS. [12]

Freyberg ended his message with the hopeful words:

> IF WE CAN GIVE HIM A REALLY GOOD KNOCK, IT WILL HAVE A VERY FAR-REACHING EFFECT. [13]

No sooner had he completed this message to Wavell than Freyberg received news from Puttick:

> THE ENEMY IS THROUGH AT GALATAS AND MOVING TOWARD KARATSOS! [14]*

Puttick's report alarmed Freyberg, forcing him to erase the last sentence from his message. In its place, he penciled:

> I HAVE HEARD FROM PUTTICK THAT THE LINE HAS GONE AND WE ARE TRYING TO STABILIZE. I DON'T KNOW IF THEY WILL BE ABLE TO. I AM APPREHENSIVE. [15]

Once again the men of the New Zealand division were ordered to withdraw. Kippenberger glared icily at a junior officer who,

---

*The British referred to Daratsos as Karatsos.

when given the order, replied flippantly, "This is becoming a bloody habit!" [16]

General Freyberg had by now interceded personally in the plan for the withdrawal from Galatas. The Creforce commander ordered that a new defense line be established at the Kladiso River, which ran a few miles west of the Cretan capital. He was determined to hold a line west of Khaniá and Suda until such time as enough food supplies had been received at Suda to enable the quartermaster to set up a series of supply dumps on the road south to Sfakia. This would be the first preparatory step in the withdrawal to the southern beaches for evacuation.

The New Zealander order of battle facing the Germans on the morning of May 26 found half the Fifth Brigade back in the line in the northern sector, with the Twenty-first Battalion holding the right flank, the Nineteenth Battalion in the center, and the Twenty-eighth Maori on the left. Farther south of the Fifth Brigade, Brigadier Vasey's Seventh and Eighth Battalions of his Australian brigade were holding the extreme left of the line.

Far to the rear, the survivors of the Eighteenth and the Composite Battalions, who had fought so desperately the previous day at Galatas, were scattered in isolated groups, unfit to fight as a cohesive force. Most of their comrades had been left behind in the narrow dirt streets of Galatas, either wounded or dead.

Puttick was told by Freyberg that General Weston, the Suda base commander, was to assume command of the whole western defense perimeter. In so doing, Freyberg placed under Weston's control his own detachment of Royal Marines, the Australian brigade, and the Force Reserve. Weston's orders included putting Force Reserve in relief of the New Zealand division that same night. But Freyberg did not clarify what Puttick's status would be with regard to Weston's frontline command.

At 5:45 P.M. that afternoon of the twenty-sixth, General Weston arrived at the New Zealand Divisional Headquarters with his chief of staff, Lieutenant Colonel J. Wills.

In view of the events that were taking place in the front lines, Puttick felt it imperative that his men be withdrawn. When Weston appeared, Puttick greeted him with the news that his flanks were under great pressure and that his forward units would be totally unable "to hold their front after dark."

Weston disregarded Puttick's appraisal, replying only that *the line was to hold* and that Force Reserve would relieve the New Zealand division that night as planned. Lieutenant Colonel A. Duncan, the CO of the First Welsh Battalion, was present at the conference but remained silent during the heated debate that ensued.[17]

Brigadier Inglis, whom Freyberg earlier appointed as CO of Force Reserve, pressed for a withdrawal to a rear position that he had personally reconnoitered. Weston remained adamant that the forward line was to be held as instructed. In a rush of angry language, Weston was prophetically warned that "if he sent Force Reserve forward, he would never see them again."[18] Colonel Duncan did not appreciate the warning for his unit was part of Force Reserve.

When tempers returned to a calmer level and a momentary embarrassed silence prevailed, Weston picked up the phone and called Vasey to hear for himself how the Australians were faring on the left flank. The Australian brigade commander reported that it would not be possible for him to hold his present position for an additional day and that he "considered it necessary . . . in conjunction with the New Zealand division to withdraw to a shorter line east of Suda Bay."[19]

Weston replied that he could not make such a decision but that he would consult Freyberg. Weston departed in search of Freyberg, leaving behind him a command structure that was complex if not totally muddled.

Inglis was in command of Force Reserve, but Weston also controlled Force Reserve. Puttick was in command of the defense perimeter and so was Weston. Weston had been given control of Vasey's Australian brigade, but no one mentioned that to Puttick, who assumed that the Australians were still under his area command. And in a final stroke that was to add more confusion to an already unsettled situation, Weston informed Duncan, the CO of the First Welsh Battalion, that the Ranger and Northumberland Battalions were to come under Duncan's personal command during the relief operation—which brought everything back full circle to Brigadier Inglis's command of Force Reserve.

Weston finally found Freyberg at Suda sometime after 9:00 P.M.—more than two hours after leaving the New Zealand divisional headquarters. Puttick's requests for withdrawal made no impression upon the Creforce commander. He insisted that the line should be held *at all costs* in order to keep the Germans away from the Suda dock area.

Weston remembered to report Vasey's remarks about the Australian brigade's inability to hold for another day. On the basis of Weston's report, Freyberg hastened to issue a strongly worded message to Vasey that concluded with the order that "the Australians were to continue to hold their line at all costs."[20]

As the evening wore on, General Puttick waited at his divisional headquarters for orders from Weston. Each passing hour brought with it new levels of alarm as the roar of battle remained undiminished. If anything, the ferocity of the fighting seemed to increase, which conjured in Puttick's mind the nightmare of a German breakthrough with subsequent encirclement and destruction of his force.

From a little past 6:00 P.M., when Weston had left, until ten o'clock that night, there was no message from Weston. Those hours dragged slowly for Puttick. At 10:00 P.M. he was finally able to reach Creforce headquarters by radio, but still had made no contact with Weston's command post. To his request for orders, Puttick was reminded by the crackling radio voice from Creforce that he was under Weston's command and that General Weston would "issue orders."[21] But Weston was nowhere to be found. At last Puttick could wait no longer and decided to take matters into his own hands. At 10:30 P.M. he issued orders to his forward units to begin a withdrawal at 11:30 P.M. To cover his action, he dispatched Captain R. M. Bell of his staff with a handwritten message for Weston:

> NEW ZEALAND DIVISION URGENTLY AWAITS YOUR ORDERS. CANNOT WAIT ANY LONGER AS BRIGADE COMMANDERS REPRESENT SITUATION ON THEIR FRONTS AS MOST URGENT. PROPOSE RETIRING WITH OR WITHOUT ORDERS BY 11:30 HOURS 26 MAY.[22]

No sooner had Bell left than Vasey called to inform Puttick of Freyberg's stern order that the Australians were to hold "at all costs." Vasey then asked Puttick for an explanation. "In view of Freyberg's order, how is it that you authorize us to withdraw?" Puttick hesitated, momentarily disconcerted by Vasey's question, then retorted gruffly, "I will take full responsibility for countermanding General Freyberg's orders!"[23]

Captain Bell finally found General Weston's headquarters, located in a hollow not far from the Suda docks, an area referred to as Forty-second Street. It bore no relationship to New York City's famous or infamous thoroughfare, but was named after the 42nd Field Company, which had been stationed there before the invasion.

Much to Captain Bell's surprise, he found that General Weston was asleep and no one wished to disturb him. It was not until 1:00 A.M. that the duty officer, at Bell's insistent urgings, decided to disturb the general. Once awakened, Weston read the message, realized that the withdrawal—already in progress—left Force Reserve in "a difficult position," and ordered that they be called back. With that matter taken care of, the seemingly unperturbed Weston went back to sleep![24]

The staff had difficulty finding dispatch riders to carry this all-important message to Force Reserve. Finally three couriers were located, and they raced off with the order. Sometime after 3:00 A.M. they returned, reporting that the message had been handed to officers of Force Reserve. *But Colonel Duncan, the acting CO of Force Reserve, never got the message.*

Weston's sleep was destined for further interruption. General Puttick arrived shortly thereafter with Colonel A. F. Hely of the Suda brigade and angrily inquired why no orders had been sent to him.

"No use sending orders," replied the irritated Weston, who seemed more annoyed by the interruption to his sleep than by the question. Then he sarcastically added, "Your division command had made it very clear that the New Zealand division was retiring, whatever happened."[25]

Puttick and Hely exchanged glances. If Weston accepted the fact of the withdrawal come what may, *why had he waited until 1:00 A.M. to recall Force Reserve?*

By dawn of the twenty-seventh, Force Reserve moved into positions beyond the Kladiso River, with the Rangers and Northumberland Hussars taking up unprepared positions near the river, while the Welsh occupied the same trenches they had dug weeks before. When they were all in position, the battalions formed an arc facing westward, with one end resting on the sea and the other, a-mile-and-a-half south, across the Alikianou road.

At the crack of first light, Force Reserve was in position— all alone. During the night, the withdrawal of the New Zealand division had been completed, and with the New Zealanders went Vasey's Australians and Hely's Suda brigade. However, the men of Force Reserve did not know this and believed that their left flank was well protected. Worse yet, Brigadier Inglis, the *official* CO of Force Reserve, had retired with the New Zealand division, assuming that Force Reserve would also be withdrawn. After all, the command of Force Reserve was in Duncan's hands during the relief, thus his presence would not be required in the withdrawal. Such were the effects of a muddled command system. The end result was that Force Reserve not only stood isolated and alone, but it stood without its commanding officer.

By the time the early morning mist evaporated, 4,500 German troops were ready to launch an assault against the 1,000-odd men of Force Reserve.

General Ringel issued final orders to his unit commanders that they use mortars and machine guns and a maximum effort to break through the enemy's defense positions. He was not yet aware that the New Zealanders and Australians had withdrawn during the night and that the only force before him was an outnumbered combination of three depleted battalions with open flanks.

Once the German attack began, it took little time before Colonel Duncan of the Welsh battalion heard the sound of Spandau machine guns and Schmeisser tommy guns firing at him from his flanks. He was bewildered, for he still was under the impression that the Suda brigade was on his left. Patrols sent to contact the Suda brigade returned reporting no contact—only the presence of Germans. When firing of German tommy guns was heard to his rear, Duncan became alarmed and felt that General Weston should be told of the situation. He sent an officer with a brief but frantic note to Weston, but the messenger never got through the German lines.

The message would have made little difference, even if it had succeeded in reaching Weston's headquarters. At that very hour, General Weston and his staff were well on the road south to Sfakia, having left Force Reserve to fend for itself.

The German fire on Duncan and his men was becoming incessant, as the mountain troops began to close the ring on Force Reserve. Duncan realized that his battalions were completely surrounded and that his companies were being cut to pieces. He ordered that they break out and flee for the rear. Over the echoing roar from the heavy sound of battle, Duncan yelled to his executive officer, Major J. T. Gibson, to muster as many survivors as he could find from the three battalions and lead them back to Khaniá.

In small groups, the tired men of Force Reserve dragged themselves through the olive groves, splashed through the shallow waters of the Kladiso River, and headed through the outskirts of the debris-filled streets of Khaniá. Gibson hoped to reorganize them somewhere on the Suda road, but the Germans gave them little respite, following close behind. Colonel Duncan remained behind with about 200 men of his Welsh Battalion to prevent the withdrawal from becoming a debacle.

By midday the First Battalion of Colonel Jais's One Hundred Forty-first Mountain Regiment had advanced toward Suda, where they ran into the Australians of the Nineteenth Brigade and the New Zealanders of the Fifth Brigade, defending Forty-second Street. As the German column turned north toward the head of the bay, Australians from the Seventh Battalion and Maoris from the New Zealand Twenty-eighth Battalion attacked them on the right flank. There followed a savage and bitter encounter where once again the Maori and Australian bayonets did their deadly work. The Germans broke and fled to the west with the Maoris in close pursuit, bayoneting any German in their path.

In the half-mile retreat that followed, the Germans lost more than 300 men to the Maori and Australian counterattack. The First Battalion ceased to exist.[26]

The counterattack came as a shock to the Germans, but it allowed Duncan and his men to slip past the enemy and reach the Kladiso River bridge. The Germans followed them through the main streets of Khaniá and onto the rocky terrain of Akrotiri Peninsula beyond.

General Hargest of the Fifth Brigade followed the retreat with his field glasses from his position at Forty-second Street. He watched in dismay as Duncan and his Welsh survivors were annihilated in this, their final defense position. Hargest shook his head dejectedly, muttering caustically to his aide, "Whoever sent them forward should be shot!"[27]

Force Reserve had been totally destroyed.

By 3:00 P.M. Colonel Jais and the other battalions of his One Hundred Forty-first Regiment succeeded in reaching the western fringe of Suda Bay. About the same time, Captain von der Heydte led the paratroopers of his First Battalion into the burned-out outskirts of Khaniá from the south. It had taken him eight days to capture his first day's objective.

The capital of Crete had finally fallen to the Germans.

At his headquarters at the Grande Bretagne Hotel in Athens, General Kurt Student stared thoughtfully out the tall windows of his office overlooking Constitution Square. He was concerned. He had just returned from a personal inspection of the battle situation in Crete. It seemed that his field commander, Ringel, had things well under control. His forces were advancing steadily, but their progress was painstakingly slow. And that slowness concerned Student.

Again the paratroop commander pondered the same question that had tortured him during those dreadful first hours of the Cretan invasion, when events were going so badly. "How could our intelligence have been so faulty?" he muttered, reviewing the prebattle predictions made by the Abwehr. Admiral Canaris, the intelligence chief, had reported that the British garrison was ill prepared and too outnumbered, after the Greek fiasco, to offer any extended resistance to the airborne assault.

Student swept his eyes across Constitution Square to the Parliament building beyond and then back to the Tomb of the Unknown Soldier. He steadied his gaze upon the crowds of Athenians crossing Amalia Avenue with utter disdain for the presence of the German troops.

He could not erase from his mind the grim scene of thousands of dead paratroopers littering the island, and he paced nervously from the windows to his desk and back again, hands clasped behind him, his head bowed in deep reflection.

All this misinformation, this faulty intelligence, was the cause of delay in seizing Crete. It was a delay that ultimately reflected upon himself and embarrassed him before his Fuehrer.

Kurt Student had promised Adolf Hitler that he would capture Crete in five days. The attack had been postponed from the original date of May 15 to the seventeenth, and finally to the twentieth. Now, one week later, May 26, Crete was still in the hands of the British. Student was aware that time was most important in Hitler's plan for the scheduled attack on Russia. Even General Franz Halder, chief of staff of the German army, had written a memorandum that the delay in Crete might cause a postponement of Operation Barbarossa.[28] The very thought that all these circumstances prevented him from keeping his word to Hitler rankled.

Finally a voice interrupted Student's solitude. "Herr General!" It was his chief of staff, who handed the general a telegram. Student read it and paled:

FRANCE FELL IN EIGHT DAYS, WHY IS CRETE STILL RESISTING?[29]

It was signed by Adolf Hitler.

About the same time that Kurt Student was reading Hitler's telegram, General Freyberg sat down to write another message to his commander in chief in Cairo:

I REGRET TO HAVE TO REPORT THAT IN MY OPINION THE LIMIT OF ENDURANCE HAS BEEN REACHED BY THE TROOPS UNDER MY COMMAND HERE IN SUDA BAY . . . OUR POSITION IS HOPELESS. PROVIDED A DECISION IS REACHED AT ONCE, A CERTAIN PROPORTION OF THE FORCE MIGHT BE EMBARKED.[30]

But Wavell was not convinced by Freyberg's appeals; evacuation meant defeat, and that was out of the question. Instead he instructed Freyberg to reorganize his force, withdraw eastward toward Rethimnon, and set up a defense at that point. Freyberg was to make every effort to hold the eastern half of the island. Wavell remembered Churchill's earlier message that "Crete must be held."

While the battle in the western part of the island swept to its critical stage, the defenders at Rethimnon maintained a constant pressure on the Germans of the Second Parachute Regiment, caught in a continuous and isolated struggle.

Lieutenant Colonel Ian Campbell, the Rethimnon area commander, made every effort to ensure that the initiative remained with the Australian and Greek units at all times. The
Rethimnon defense garrison now assumed the role of the at-
tacker, while the Germans became the defenders. Campbell meant
to keep it that way.

Unlike General Hargest of the Fifth Brigade, Campbell trav-
elled from unit to unit, always appearing in the front line of battle to make certain there would be no letup against the Germans.
His mode of transportation was a motorcycle, for he had early
discovered that German aircraft ignored solitary cyclists traveling on the dusty roads below. This was a blessing for Campbell,
and the intrepid, aggressive commander appeared wherever the
action was.

By the fourth day of the battle, Campbell's leadership had
succeeded in keeping the enemy force split into two separate
elements, fighting for survival and unable to offer aid to each
other. With the Germans kept apart, the airfield that was their
major objective remained under Australian control. The other
German objective—the city of Rethimnon—was well under the
control of the Greek gendarmerie unit garrisoning the town.

On the western sector of the Rethimnon battle zone, some
four miles west of the airfield and two miles east of the town
itself, the Eleventh Australian Battalion was slowly forcing
Captain Wiedemann's men back toward the eastern fringes of
the village of Perivolia.

On the afternoon of May 21, Australian signalers had laid
out some captured German markers that conveyed a request to
the Luftwaffe to bomb the village.[31] At 5:00 P.M. Stuka dive-
bombers fell for this ploy and bombed the village, raining their
missiles on their own men and forcing them to withdraw further. The Australians pursued the Germans into the village, but
the paratroopers strengthened their position amid the rubble of
the houses and subsequently held the attacking Australians at bay.

With each passing hour, the Germans strengthened their entrenchments, one flank resting in the village houses and the other around the solid granite, walled-in church of St. George, on a prominent rise beyond. From the church's bell tower, the Germans were able to observe the slightest movement by the Australians, making an advance almost impossible.

Lacking artillery, the Australians had no hope of dislodging the Germans. All they could do was to contain them in that line. Even a company of Rangers dispatched by Freyberg from Suda could not force the rear of the German defense line without artillery; the German roadblock set up between Rethimnon and Perivolia was too strong.

In the late afternoon of May 23, German Stukas returned to bomb the Australians for a five-hour session, causing many casualties among the men of the Eleventh Battalion. Then, with the sun to their backs, the German paratroopers left their defense line and rushed forward in a surprise attack. The Australians stood fast, meeting the assault with a stubborn wall of fire. Many of them climbed out of their trenches and, standing in the open, fired from the hip at the charging Germans.

The Germans were repulsed, with so many casualties that they requested a truce to bury their dead and tend their wounded. Campbell granted the truce, and it was strictly enforced, a chivalrous note in a battle that was characterized by so much brutality. Even Campbell's German prisoners were granted permission to collect the German dead, after which they returned to the Australian prisoner-of-war stockade. They were true to their word and their word was their honor.[32]

On the eastern sector of the Rethimnon battle zone approximately one-and-a-half miles east of the airfield, Major Kroh's paratroopers had withdrawn to an olive oil factory in the village of Stavromenos. Inside its thick walls, the Germans established a well-fortified bastion. All efforts by the Australians of the First Battalion to dislodge them had been futile.

On May 22 the aggressive and persistent Colonel Campbell had ordered another attack against the factory by a group of forty

Australians led by Captain G. W. Mann. They were to be supported by a detachment of 200 Greeks from the Fifth Greek Regiment. However, a communications failure kept the Greeks back; when the Australians attacked alone and unsupported, they were quickly repulsed.

Colonel Campbell left the 200 Greeks to keep the factory under fire while he departed for the western sector of the battle zone to help his Australians of the Eleventh Battalion beat off the German attack of May 23.

Two days later Campbell returned to Stavromenos, this time *determined* to capture the olive oil factory. He brought with him a repaired infantry tank and three 75-mm guns. After a short period of point-blank shelling, the Germans indicated that they had had enough. As Captain F. J. Embrey and his men stormed the factory buildings, the Germans surrendered—eighty-two of them walking out with their arms raised. The position had finally been taken, and the eastern sector of the Rethimnon battle zone had been secured.

On the day that General Freyberg was wiring Wavell that the "limit of endurance has been reached by the troops under my command" the Australians of the Eleventh Battalion had broken into the German defense line on the *western* sector of the Rethimnon battle zone and finally captured the redoubts around the Church of St. George.

Colonel Campbell had mustered his men and all available 75-mm guns in order to capture the village of Perivolia and thus break through the German roadblock to the west.

While Freyberg appealed for an evacuation, Campbell was ordering the new attack! It was typical of the Rethimnon area commander. Besides his ground successes, Campbell could also boast of holding 500 German prisoners, including the commander of the Parachute Regiment, Colonel Sturm.

Even though General Freyberg had said before the invasion that he was unimpressed with Campbell, Campbell's fighting leadership caused Freyberg to reconsider his earlier evaluation.

Campbell's successes impressed Freyberg enough for him to wire Campbell:

YOU HAVE BEEN MAGNIFICENT![33]

The Germans at Iráklion did not fare any better than their comrades at Rethimnon.

By the fifth day of the battle, the survivors of the First Parachute Regiment found themselves isolated in two groups, six miles apart, and suffering a humiliating existence. Having arrived as conquerors, they now cowered on the brink of defeat.

Colonel Brauer and his eighty survivors had to hide among the rocks and seek the soothing shade of caves while hoping for some miracle that might save them from this dire predicament.

In the western sector of Iráklion, the second isolated group of German paratroopers fared little better than Brauer's men.

The two major German objectives—the city of Iráklion and its airfield—remained in the hands of British and Greek units. Nor was there any possibility for the Germans to gain their objectives; the German attack on Iráklion had been a failure.

Unfortunately for the defending forces, the commander of the Iráklion garrison, Brigadier Chappel, was too indifferent to appreciate that he had the Germans reeling in defeat.

On May 24 Student sent the last of his "leftover" paratroopers to Crete. Four hundred men who had not made the initial drop on the twentieth because transport was lacking now descended in an area south of the Iráklion defense perimeter. They were quickly surrounded by units of the Argyll and Sutherland Highlanders and either killed or captured. Some survivors fled to join Major Schulz's battalion.

This was the last of any available reinforcements for the attackers at Iráklion. A few subsequent supply airdrops followed but they fell into the welcoming arms of British troops and Cretan irregulars, who thus replenished their own supplies. For the Germans—low on ammunition, food, and water—there would be no more airdrops, for the Luftwaffe aircraft were now needed to fight the Royal Navy at sea.

Unable from their precarious position to mount an attack against the British with any possibility of success, the frustrated Germans of Major Schulz's battalion vented their fury on the civilian population.

On May 22 the paratroopers of the Third Battalion had been forced to withdraw form Iráklion under pressure from the attacking British and the harassing Cretan irregulars. Even the monks from the monasteries took part, carrying water and food to the British. During the withdrawal, Schulz ordered the seizure of forty-two civilians as hostages. He planned to punish the Cretans for their folly of resisting the German conqueror.

He ordered that all forty-two hostages be shot.

On May 24, the hapless Cretans were lined up in ranks of ten for the execution, with little regard for age or sex. Among the hostages were an old man of ninety and a girl of fourteen; there was also a priest, who spent the last moments of his life praying; there were the Katsanevakis brothers and their friend Manoli Gavdiotis, who stood bravely against the wall, glaring unflinchingly at their executioners. And there was one man whose execution gave the Germans a particular delight. He was Rabbi Ben-Israel Sholub.

Raised in Germany, the middle-aged rabbi and his wife fled that country during the early days of the Nazi pogroms. He traveled to Greece to join his relatives in Salonika. When the Germans invaded Greece, he fled once again, boarding a refugee-filled boat for Egypt, but was transported instead to Iráklion. He thought for a while that he had found safety in Crete, but the Nazis followed in his wake. On May 24 his flight finally ended at the execution wall, at the hands of those he had tried so hard to escape.[34]

On May 25 the Luftwaffe returned to reduce the city of Iráklion to dust and rubble, leaving it a stark shambles of shattered buildings, debris-filled streets, and crushed bodies—like its sister city of Khaniá to the west.

At 11:00 A.M. on May 27, Winston Churchill gave a progress report to the House of Commons about the situation in Crete and about the search for the *Bismarck*. (The Commons had been meeting in the Church House ever since the Parliament building had been destroyed on May 10 during a severe German air raid.) No sooner had Churchill finished and taken his seat than he was handed a message. He rose once again and with a touch of dramatic finality in his voice, reported: "I have just received news that the *Bismarck* is sunk." Like their predecessors after the announcement that bore the news of Nelson's victory at Trafalgar, the members stood and cheered.

With the problem in the North Atlantic resolved, the prime minister now turned his undivided attention to Crete. If only the events there would come to an equally successful conclusion. Wasting no time, Churchill telegraphed General Freyberg on May 27, hoping that his words could inspire a victory in Crete:

YOUR GLORIOUS DEFENSE COMMANDS ADMIRATION IN EVERY
LAND . . . ALL AID IN OUR POWER IS BEING SENT[35]

and General Wavell in Cairo:

VICTORY IN CRETE IS ESSENTIAL AT THIS TURNING POINT IN THE
WAR. KEEP HURLING IN ALL AID YOU CAN.[36]

Wavell had made one last effort to reinforce Crete. On May 26, the day before he received Churchill's order to "keep hurling in all aid," Wavell ordered the Second Battalion of the Queen's Regiment to be ferried to Tymbaki aboard the transport *Glenroy*, with the destroyers *Jaguar, Stuart,* and *Coventry* as escorts. Colonel Laycock's commandos were already on their way, but a different fate awaited this convoy. Halfway to Crete the ships were attacked by a heavy concentration of torpedo- and dive-bombers, setting the *Glenroy* afire and forcing the convoy to return to Alexandria. There would be no more reinforcements for the defenders of Crete.

Fighter Command in Egypt dispatched ten Hurricanes to the airfield at Iráklion. Unfortunately, six of the ten were shot down by the trigger-happy defenders. When two other fighters observed their first six comrades shot down because of mistaken identity, they turned back over the sea. Too short of fuel to return to their home base in Egypt, they were never seen or heard of again. The remaining two Hurricanes, which succeeded in landing safely, were destroyed by German strafers the next day.

When the commander in chief returned to his desk, he found a personal message from Freyberg waiting for him. It was another despairing plea for the evacuation of the troops from Crete, couched in terms of hopelessness. To Wavell, these words were an indication of Freyberg's determined state of mind. He realized that he could not force a commander fighting an isolated battle 400 miles away and without hope of receiving reinforcements to continue a struggle he had already deemed lost.

Wavell therefore had no alternative but to accept Freyberg's view of the true state of affairs prevailing on Crete. Reluctantly, he dictated a four-point message to Winston Churchill:

1. FEAR THAT SITUATION IN CRETE MOST SERIOUS . . . THERE IS NO POSSIBILITY OF HURLING IN REINFORCEMENTS.

2. . . . CONTINUOUS AND UNOPPOSED AIR ATTACK MUST DRIVE STOUTEST TROOPS FROM POSITIONS . . . AND MAKES ADMINISTRATION PRACTICALLY IMPOSSIBLE.

3. TELEGRAM JUST RECEIVED FROM FREYBERG STATES ONLY CHANCE OF SURVIVAL OF FORCE IN SUDA AREA IS TO WITHDRAW TO BEACHES IN SOUTH OF ISLAND. . . .

4. FEAR WE MUST RECOGNIZE THAT CRETE IS NO LONGER TENABLE AND THAT TROOPS MUST BE WITHDRAWN AS FAR AS POSSIBLE. . . .[37]

Thus the heroic battle for the island of Crete reached its final stage. Wavell's message to Churchill was a request for permission to evacuate the island. With a heavy heart, Churchill, recognizing that all hope for victory in Crete was gone, authorized the evacuation.

With that authorization began another epic of heroism—by the men of the withdrawing force, by the officers and men of the Royal Navy who rushed to their rescue, and by the Cretans and Greeks who remained behind to continue the fight.

25

"300 YEARS TO BUILD
A NEW TRADITION"

MAY 26–30, 1941

General Wavell did not wait for Churchill's acknowledgment that Crete must be abandoned. While the prime minister and his cabinet mulled over the hard-to-accept situation, Wavell authorized Freyberg to begin the evacuation as soon as possible, assuring him that the Royal Navy would be waiting to embark the troops.

The day before—May 26—General Wavell had met in Alexandria with the other two chiefs of services. Admiral Sir Andrew Cunningham and Air Marshal A. W. Tedder were joined by General Sir Thomas Blamey, the commanding general of the Australian forces in the Middle East, and Peter Fraser, the prime minister of New Zealand. Both Blamey and Fraser voiced deep concern for the Anzac troops that represented their two nations. The sole subject on the meeting's agenda was "the consideration for a possible evacuation from Crete."

A solemn mood filled the air of the conference room. Each man bore a heavy burden of responsibility in his representative position, but the heaviest lay painfully upon the shoulders of the Middle East commander, General Wavell.

Once the decision had been reached to abandon Crete, the question arose if the troops could be evacuated safely or would losses make surrender inevitable? Admiral Cunningham warned that incessant German air attacks could inflict terrible losses upon the men, "and to save lives, surrender might be more humane."[1] At these words Blamey and Fraser looked at each other and then at Wavell as if to remind him that the bulk of the troops on Crete were New Zealand and Australian. Wavell avoided their glance.

Cunningham then added somewhat proudly, "After all, gentlemen, the navy's duty was achieved and no enemy ship, whether warship or transport, succeeded in reaching Crete."[2]

"Does that mean," he was asked, "that the Royal Navy deems it impossible to evacuate the troops in the face of the German air onslaught?"[3]

The Mediterranean Fleet commander hesitated thoughtfully for a moment before replying. On May 21 the destroyer *Juno* had been sunk; the next day the destroyer *Greyhound* and the cruisers *Gloucester* and *Fiji* went down, while the cruisers *Naiad* and *Carlisle* and the battleships *Warspite* and *Valiant* were heavily damaged by bombs. On the twenty-third the destroyers *Kashmir* and *Kelly* together with five motor-torpedo boats had been sunk by German aircraft, and on May 26 itself, the aircraft carrier *Formidable* was severely damaged while the destroyer *Nubian* had her stern blown off. Eleven ships had already been sunk as of May 26, with six of Cunningham's first-line men-of-war badly damaged. *Never before had the Royal Navy suffered such losses in any one single battle.* How many more ships would be lost during an evacuation?

He finally broke the silence: "Whatever the risks, whatever our losses, the remaining ships of the fleet will make an all-out effort to bring away the army."[4]

There was a sigh of relief from Blamey and Fraser, while Wavell forced a pained smile. The Royal Navy would be there once again to rescue the army as it had earlier at Dunkirk and later in Greece.

Cunningham shook his head sadly at the thought of what lay in store for his men and ships. In grave tones he reminded the conferees of the heavy losses suffered by his fleet in the waters around Crete. "This time we evacuate with fewer ships, far less resources, and with our men and ships worn to the point of exhaustion."

"But let us remember, gentlemen," Cunningham continued in a voice infused with the spirit of Nelson, "it takes the navy three years to build a new ship. It will take 300 years to build a new tradition."[5]

Once Freyberg received the authorization to abandon the island, he centered his attention on the business of disengaging the troops and sending them on an organized retreat to the southern beaches of Sfakia for evacuation. The release had not come any too soon, for even the island's Greek commander had seen the handwriting on the wall.

The order to withdraw to the south was quickly passed to the troops. Suddenly everyone—British, Australians, and New Zealanders—felt the urgent desire to leave this once beautiful and peaceful island that the flames of war had converted into a place of death and desolation. The dusty, dirty route south to Sfakia was soon choked with columns of ragged, tired soldiers.

The men moved forward in overheated exhaustion, stumbling over each other in their haste. Many of them discarded their helmets, their weapons, and their ammunition; others removed their tunics and cast them aside. The whole trail was soon littered with the accoutrements of an army in disorderly retreat. Blankets, gas masks, field packs, helmets, and ammo boxes were scattered with related castoffs along the side of the trail.[6]

During the day, trucks passed through the retreating column, bumping from side to side on the hard, rocky, rutted road, spewing dirt and dust on the perspiring, weary marchers. The men cursed the trucks for thus adding to their discomfort.

As the men struggled through the heat and dust, their attention was forever riveted to the sky. Fear of the marauding Luftwaffe was always uppermost in each man's mind. The slightest sound of an approaching aircraft was enough to raise the alarm of "Take cover, take cover," whereupon the men would scatter onto the rocky slopes on either side of the trail.

Today, however, the Luftwaffe was surprisingly absent. It was concentrating its efforts on the ships of the Royal Navy in the waters all around Crete. There were, however, a few strafings by Messerschmitts—enough to keep the retreating troops on the alert.

At night, even the flicker of a match was enough to raise angry shouts. So great was their fear of an air attack that some of the men even fired at the light, with complete disregard for order and discipline.

At dusk on the first night of the retreat, Colonel Kippenberger, at the head of his column of men from the Tenth Brigade, reached a fork in the road. Uncertain which of the two paths led south to Sfakia, he laid his map on the ground and shone his flashlight on it. Careful as he was to cover it, a slight glimmer of light was evident. Instantly there followed a series of curses and shouts from above the trail to "put out that bloody light!"

One outraged soldier rushed up and kicked the flashlight from Kippenberger's hand. Incensed at this gross breach of military discipline, Kippenberger grabbed the trooper and threw him to the ground. The furious brigade commander threatened that if there was any repetition of such discourtesy to an officer, he would shoot the offender.[7]

Throughout the night of May 27 and into the twenty-eighth, a continuous stream of men trudged down the long, rugged mountain trail that led to the southern coast. For most of the tired men, the retreat had become a test of endurance. There was little food left to relieve their hunger; their parched throats demanded water, but water was in even shorter supply than food. Nevertheless the men staggered silently onward, often weaving and ready to drop with fatigue. Their clothes were dusty, dirty, and torn; their boots had been slashed by sharp rocks; their feet were blistered and bleeding, but onward they marched. They had no choice.

Throughout the whole night of the withdrawal from Suda,

Hargest and Vasey felt the dread of an ambush or a flanking German attack on the exhausted column. They could not know that it was a groundless fear, for the Germans were as yet unaware that the defenders were fleeing to the southern beaches.

General Ringel was still following the original order of priorities given him by General Alexander Löhr, the Fourth Air Fleet commander, when Ringel took over field command of the invading forces in Crete. He was to secure Maleme airfield, seize Khaniá and Suda Bay, and capture Rethimnon and Iráklion—in that sequence. In his anxiety to succor his beloved paratroopers at Rethimnon and Iráklion, General Student had never altered this order of priorities. Thus, while the defenders were withdrawing toward the south, Ringel reminded the Eighty-fifth Mountain Regiment of his Fifth Mountain Division that they were not to be "drawn away southward," and that they were still to take Rethimnon.[8]

The orders issued from Ringel's headquarters on May 28 emphasized that "the enemy was to be pursued eastward through Rethimnon to Iraklion without a pause." The first objective would be Rethimnon, followed by the relief of the paratroopers at Iráklion. He ordered Colonel August Wittmann, the former commanding officer of the One-hundred-eleventh Artillery Regiment and now commanding the Ninety-fifth Artillery Regiment, to lead a task force comprised of ancillary artillery units, engineers, and antitank gunners attached to the Ninety-fifth Motorcycle Battalion in the drive eastward.

Ringel's right-hand punch, led by Colonel Krakau's Eighty-fifth Mountain Regiment, was still stalemated by the Eighth Regiment in the shrubs and broken hills around Alikianou village. Krakau was following Ringel's edict not to be drawn to the south, but his battalions could not move eastward either. The Greeks of the Eighth Regiment, joined by the Cretans, continued their fierce resistance, keeping the Germans at bay. First it was the Engineer Battalion of Heidrich's Third Parachute Regiment that was kept in check; five days later, it was Krakau's battalions of the Eighty-fifth Mountain Regiment.

The Greeks and the Cretan irregulars repulsed the Germans over and over again, day in and day out. These were the men to whom Kippenberger had referred as "malaria-ridden little chaps." This was the unit that had been reported destroyed in the first day of battle, yet seven days later, it was still holding the Germans in the hills around Alikianou.

The British command was not to realize until much later that the courage of the Eighth Greek Regiment was another factor enabling the Commonwealth troops to withdraw to the south. If the Greeks and Cretans had fled on the first day of battle as incorrectly reported, there would have been no chance of a withdrawal—instead, the whole New Zealand command would have been surrounded and wiped out. For these two reasons—Ringel's adherence to his priority of orders and the resolute resistance of the Eighth Greek Regiment at Alikianou—the Commonwealth defenders were now able to move south for evacuation.[9]

Finally, on May 27, the depleted ranks of the Eighth Greek Regiment dispersed and fled to the hills to continue the fight as guerrillas in the resistance movement that was to follow during the German occupation. At last the three reinforced battalions of Krakau's regiment were able to advance eastward, breaking through to Stilos only to find Hargest's men already there. As a detachment of the Second Battalion climbed the slope of a hill west of Stilos, they were met by withering fire from the New Zealanders, who had arrived some hours earlier. Thanks to the gallant defense of the Eighth Greek Regiment, The Germans arrived at Stilos twenty-four hours too late. *That delay made the evacuation possible.*

At 10:00 P.M. that Tuesday, May 27, the Creforce skeleton staff abandoned their headquarters compound. The wireless station had been destroyed and the codes burned; the men wearily mounted the trucks and headed south.

When Freyberg finally arrived in Sfakia, he established his headquarters in a cave high in the cliffs above the village. He immediately forwarded an urgent message to Alexandria for the evacuation to begin. At his first opportunity, he sat down and penned an assessment of his situation. He planned to have the message carried to Alexandria by his personal aide, Lieutenant John White:

> WE HAVE HAD A PRETTY ROUGH TIME. THE TROOPS WERE NOT BEATEN BY ORDINARY CONDITIONS, BUT BY THE GREAT AERIAL CONCENTRATION AGAINST US . . . WE WERE HANDICAPPED BY LACK OF TRANSPORT, COMMUNICATIONS, AND LACK OF STAFF. EVERYBODY TRIED HARD IN MOST DIFFICULT CIRCUMSTANCES. I AM SORRY CRETE COULD NOT BE HELD.[10]

Then, in a final sentence, he assumed complete responsibility for the debacle:

> IT WAS CERTAINLY NOT THE FAULT OF THE TROOPS.[11]

Everywhere the men of the retreating column saw the destruction wrought by the Luftwaffe. Fields were pitted with bomb craters, stone cottages lay shattered, and roads were littered with burned-out, strafed vehicles—many still filled with the corpses of fighting men. Corpses lay everywhere, at roadsides and in the fields; with them lay the badly wounded and those too exhausted to continue. The retreating men looked straight ahead, as if these horrible sights of defeat were invisible.

Strangely, this movement in broad daylight was unimpeded by a single German aircraft. Most of the Stukas and Messerschmitts were involved in attacks on the ships of the Royal Navy. Other Luftwaffe squadrons had already been withdrawn to the eastern front, for Hitler had at last decided that the invasion of Russia would begin on June 21, now that the campaign in Crete was nearing a successful conclusion.

Under a clear sky, Hargest rode up and down the column in his Bren carrier giving his men encouragement and admiring their unfailing spirit. The men hiked through the village of Babali Hani, six miles beyond Stilos, and then another six miles to Vrises. There they paused to rest in the cool shade of olive, oak, and plane trees and to quench their thirst with the cool waters that gave the village its name.[12]

From prisoners taken when isolated pockets of resistance were overrun, German intelligence finally learned that there was a mass movement of troops toward the southern coast of Crete. Still following Ringel's orders to advance eastward toward Rethimnon, Colonel Wittmann dispatched only the Third Battalion from his Eighty-fifth Mountain Regiment in pursuit.

Their heated, day-long skirmish with Commonwealth rearguard troops attracted German reinforcements. By nightfall, the whole of Wittmann's Kampfgruppe turned south to give battle.

It was time for the commandos to withdraw.

By 10:00 P.M. that night, Colonel Young of the commando battalion successfully disengaged his men from battle and turned to follow the retreating New Zealanders.

The advance group of the retreating mass of exhausted men burst through the massive barrier of the White Mountains and reached the southern coast. The rock-strewn mountain path terminated on an escarpment 500 feet above shore; from there a faint goat trail meandered down the steep side of the rugged cliff to the white stone houses that lay in its shadow.

This was the fishing village of Sfakia.

Off the narrow strip of sandy beach that touched the sparkling cool water of the inlet, the ships of the Royal Navy were soon to drop anchor and begin the evacuation. They would be a welcome sight to the men who had suffered the ordeal of battle this past week.

From his headquarters atop the cliffs, approximately a mile above the beach at Sfakia, General Freyberg made systematic plans for the evacuation. He decided that the troops should embark during the three hours after midnight. This would allow the ships a safety margin of darkness—four hours to reach Sfakia, three to embark the troops, and another four to steam beyond the reach of enemy aircraft—before dawn.

Freyberg ordered that all Creforce personnel from the Suda Bay area be evacuated from the beach at Sfakia, while Chappel's troops at Iráklion would be embarked from the city's harbor. Lieutenant Colonel Campbell's Australians at Rethimnon were to retire to the south and be evacuated from the tiny village of Plaka.[13] With typical indifference, there was no concern for the evacuation of the Greek regiments.

In the early predawn hours of Saturday, May 31, General Freyberg, following Wavell's orders, left Crete with the naval liaison officer, Captain J. A. V. Morse, in a Sunderland flying boat. As the huge craft lifted off the waters off Sfakia, Freyberg looked back in dismay. His first and only senior command had ended in defeat. It was a bitter pill for this fine soldier who held so many honors; moreover he felt great concern for the men he was leaving behind.

That same day, having arrived safely in Alexandria, Freyberg with New Zealand Prime Minister Fraser went to plead that an additional effort be made to evacuate the rest of the men on Crete. He begged that the ships "take aboard at Sfakia every man [they] could pack."[14]

After consulting with his officers, Admiral Cunningham decided to send additional ships back to Crete in what was destined to be the last rescue mission.

With food and medical supplies transferred from the ships to the beaches of Sfakia, the embarkation began. In a matter of a few hours, as many as 3,710 men had been ferried out to the waiting ships. Well before dawn on Sunday, June 1, the last ship of the force left Sfakia for the final journey to Alexandria.[15]

When Prime Minister Churchill learned late on the thirty-first that the rescue operation was to be terminated while British troops still remained on Crete, he protested to the Navy vice-chief of staff. In turn, the Admiralty urged Cunningham to continue the evacuation, but the Mediterranean Fleet commander was adamant in his decision. His fear of what Luftwaffe air superiority could do to his ships made his decision final.

Cunningham was to describe the whole evacuation operation as one of "great tension and anxiety such as I have never experienced before or since."[16]

His decision to end the evacuation sealed the fate of more than 11,000 men still on the southern beaches of Crete. For them, the fighting was over.

26

"CRETE HAS BECOME THE GRAVEYARD OF THE GERMAN PARATROOPER"

MAY 30–31, 1941

The ships of Admiral Cunningham's Mediterranean Fleet succeeded in evacuating approximately 16,511 men from the beaches
of southern Crete during those last days in May.[1] However, that
those fortunate men were available for embarkation was due in
large part to the resolute resistance of the rear guard in the ravines and rocky passes of the southern mountains above Sfakia.

As more troops were evacuated each night, the defense perimeter was gradually contracting. Despite the German flanking
maneuvers, the stubborn rear-guard defense brought the German
mountain troops to a standstill. Each day the crack of rifle and
machine-gun fire echoed through the mountains as skirmishes
turned into bitter battles. The Germans were unable to breach
the defense line. Colonel Utz of the One hundredth Mountain
Regiment concluded that he could not successfully press the attack without proper air cover and artillery support. While he
waited for this help, he decided to postpone any renewed attacks
for at least two more days. By June 2, he felt, his reinforcements would have arrived, and his flanking companies would
reach the coast. All would be in readiness for the final assault

to break the rear-guard defense and cast the defenders into the sea.

When General Freyberg was ordered to leave Crete on Saturday, May 31, he turned over the command of Crete's defense to General Weston. Weston's first act as commander was to wire Wavell that some 9,000 men remained on the island ready for evacuation. He optimistically added that he felt he would be able to hold Sfakia for at least two more days, enough time to get these men off the island. It was not until later that afternoon that Weston received word of Cunningham's decision to terminate the evacuation with the departure of Admiral King's ships later that night. The message included orders for Weston to leave Crete aboard a Sunderland flying boat that would arrive the same night. The final sentence in the message advised Weston to "authorize the capitulation of any troops who had to be left behind."[2] The end was near.

Weston summoned Colonel Laycock to his headquarters and informed the commando leader of the decision to end the evacuation. "I am ordered out tonight," he told Laycock, "and I have been instructed to pass the command to the next senior officer."

Laycock shifted his stance nervously and clasped his hands behind him. He had a premonition of what was to follow. "I am *offering* you the command of the remaining troops," continued Weston, "and am authorizing you to negotiate their surrender at your convenience anytime after tomorrow."

Colonel Laycock bowed his head momentarily in thought. After a silence that seemed eternal, he snapped to attention and looked into the general's eyes. "I respectfully decline the offer, sir!"

Weston understood. He had not *ordered* Laycock to take command, he had *offered* him the command.

"I did not come to Crete," explained Laycock, "to surrender to the Hun. I believe I can be of greater service with my Commando Brigade than as a prisoner of war."

"Very well, then, Laycock, *you* pick the officer who is to negotiate with the Germans."

This time, Weston's words were a command.[3]

Colonel Laycock passed the responsibility to an officer in his command. He ordered Lieutenant colonel G. A. D. Young, whose brave leadership of D Battalion had kept the Germans at bay during the rear-guard action, to take command of the remaining troops when he and Weston departed. Unlike Laycock Young was not *offered* the command; he was *ordered* to assume it. Thus it was to fall to this unfortunate officer to surrender the island to the Germans.[4]

The hours passed quickly that last afternoon, and the ships of Admiral King's task force would soon arrive. General Weston made one last decision before turning the command over to Young. He ordered that the men who had been engaged in the fighting since the first day of the invasion should be given first evacuation priority.

He ordered Brigadier Hargest's Fifth Brigade of New Zealanders and Vasey's Australian brigade to prepare for departure.

As the sun began to dip in the western sky, Hargest made his preparations. He gathered the 1,100 survivors of his brigade and gave specific orders to the officers. The only New Zealanders who were to be evacuated were those wearing helmets and carrying rifles; all others were to be considered stragglers. It was a painful but necessary decision.

Hargest sent Colonel Andrew and the Twenty-second Battalion—the defenders of Hill 107—down to the beach to clear a path for the rest of the brigade. "Have your men fix their bayonets if you have to," he instructed Andrew, "but keep the path to the beaches clear."[5]

The men were ordered to shave, bear rifles, and carry haversacks on their backs as if on parade. When darkness finally blanketed the island, the New Zealanders of the Fifth Brigade began the long descent down the trail to the beach and ultimate rescue by the ships that were already dropping their anchors in the waters beyond.

When Colonel Walker and his Seventh Australian Battalion reached the trail to the beach, he found confusion all around him, with large groups of noncombat soldiers sitting down on the trail, effectively blocking it. A self-appointed movement-control officer informed Walker that only a single file could pass at this point and that the Australians would have to wait in line.

Walker was furious and was almost tempted to order his men to draw their bayonets and force a passage to the beach. Instead he decided to take a detour.

For the next five hours, the men of his battalion, led by the second in command, Major H. C. D. Marshall, struggled in the darkness over the broken ravines and rugged mountain terrain seeking an alternative path to the beach.

The men staggered onward spent with fatigue; they had fought so many days, and now when rescue was within their grasp, they had to undergo this additional ordeal. They had to fight not only darkness and the mountains but, more important, they had to struggle against time.

One Australian fell, too exhausted to move, and pleaded to be left where he had fallen. Major Marshall picked him up and supported him for miles until they reached the beach. Throughout the arduous trek, Marshall also pushed and even threatened his men to keep up a "fast and proper pace."

When the battalion finally reached the beach, they lined up quietly in orderly ranks waiting to be evacuated, but it was too late. From the last departing barge, the officer aboard could see the Australians waiting on the beach for his return.[6]

Major Marshall found his CO, Colonel Walker, sitting dejectedly on the stone sea wall as the last ships in the bay weighed anchor for departure.

Realizing that it was all over for them, some of the noncombatant stragglers raised white flags. At the sight of this surrender signal, two of Walker's NCO's rushed over to him and angrily asked, "Shall we shoot the bastards?"

"No," he replied slowly, "we may not like it, but we might as well pack it in!"[7]

By 3:00 A.M. the last of Cunningham's ships had sailed for Egypt.

Lieutenant Colonel Young, designated by Laycock to assume command of the remaining troops, opened the sealed envelop that represented General Weston's final order before departure. It was addressed, "Senior Officer left on the Island." [8]

Young ran his eyes down the six paragraphs of the order. The fourth was brief and to the point: "No more evacuation is possible," [9] and the sixth and final paragraph clearly indicated what he was expected to do: "You are ordered to make contact with the enemy and arrange capitulation." [10]

The colonel folded the order and put it in his breast pocket. With a heavy sigh at the distasteful task before him, he picked up a white flag and went out to meet a German officer.

The battle for Crete was finally over.

Although most senior officers reluctantly obeyed the order to capitulate to the Germans, there were many New Zealanders, Australians, and British troopers of all ranks whose fighting spirit would not allow them to surrender, to spend the rest of the war in a German prison camp. When it became evident that no more rescue ships would arrive, many men decided to seek their own means of escape.

In the early morning hours of the first day of the surrender, a group of stranded soldiers found an abandoned landing barge. The men knew little or nothing about handling the boat until Private Harry Richards, an Australian, offered to act as boat commander. A New Zealander, Private A. Taylor, volunteered to be the navigator. The rest of the group, made up of Australians, New Zealanders, and British, helped maneuver the barge into a huge cavern to keep it out of sight until nightfall. That night they set sail on what they hoped would be an easy and rapid trip to Egypt. It was destined to be neither.

The next morning the barge ran aground on Gavdos, an island south of Crete. Although repairs were made quickly, Private Richards, acting as skipper, realized that the boat was over-loaded and asked for volunteers to remain behind.

The journey resumed early that evening, lighter by ten men. A day's journey later, the barge ran out of fuel. In desperation, an oar was rigged up as a mast, and a worn blanket as a sail. The trip became intolerably slow, with the danger of attack from the air ever present. What little rations and water they had were soon gone, leaving the men under the hot sun, hoping for the slightest breeze to billow the sail. They weakened, and often tempers flared in their misery. Finally, on June 8—one week later—with hope almost gone, they reached the rocky beach of Sidi Barrani in North Africa. The landing site proved to be near a British camp, from which the troopers rushed out to welcome them.[11]

While Richards's group of escapees struggled to cross the waters to North Africa, another group of 137 Royal Marines under Marine Major R. Garrett set forth on a similar journey. Garrett and his men had also found an abandoned barge and launched it for their escape. Paralleling Richards's saga, Garrett's barge also ran out of fuel one-third across, and his group, too, resorted to makeshift mast and sails. Their rations dwindled to a half tin of water and one teaspoonful of bully beef daily. When the wind died down, the men would jump into the water to push the barge forward. They endured an excruciating nine-day trip before they reached Sidi Barrani—a trip during which one soldier died from exhaustion and another committed suicide.[12]

The flight to avoid capture was not confined to large groups of men. Many others made the attempt, singly or in pairs; some met with success but most failed.

Major Sandover, the Australian who led his Eleventh Battalion so gallantly at Rethimnon, meant it when he told his commanding officer, Brigadier Campbell, that he would not surrender. He led a group of Australians from his unit across the mountains to a point east of Sfakia from whence he made his escape to North Africa.[13]

Private D. McQuarrie of the Eighteenth New Zealand Battalion had lain wounded in a hospital encampment in Suda. Cretan civilians kept him alive for two weeks by tending to his wounds and by feeding him and the other patients in the encampment. Deprivation and hardship followed soon after the Germans took over the area. McQuarrie was transferred to a hospital in Khaniá where he personally witnessed the wounded die from hunger and lack of care. He decided to escape on June 18. Trekking south to the village of Meskla, high in the White Mountains, he stayed with a Cretan family for two weeks; he ate well and his wounds had an opportunity to heal.

However, the Germans were closing in and threatening death to any Cretan who offered shelter or assistance to a British soldier. Fearing for the safety of his hosts, McQuarrie left for the surrounding hills. There he met another New Zealander, Private B. Carter, who had escaped from the prison camp at Galatas on July 1.

The two wandered about the mountains for a week and then headed north, back to Suda. They were joined by two Australians and finally reached the coast, where they found an abandoned dinghy. On July 16 they began their long trip across the waters to North Africa.

As soon as they set sail, they realized why the dinghy had been abandoned. They used their socks and shirts to plug the many holes, and each man took a turn sitting on a larger hole in the stern while the rest bailed water. Locomotion was provided by a makeshift setup of lashed oars for a mast and tied blankets for a sail. Luckily for them, a strong gale prevailed throughout the trip, blowing them the 400 miles to Sidi Barrani within four days. When the British soldiers at Sidi Barrani waded out to help them, the dinghy fell apart. It was a miracle, they thought, that this delapidated craft had remained seaworthy long enough to complete such a tempestuous sea voyage.[14]

Lieutenant R. Sinclair of the Twenty-second New Zealand Battalion and Lieutenant Roy Farran of the Third Hussars Tank Regiment had fought hard in the eleven-day battle in Crete. Sinclair had been involved in combat around Hill 107 from the first day of the invasion, and Farran had led the unsuccessful New Zealand counterattack against Pirgos with his three light tanks on May 22. With his tank, Farran also led the counterattack to recapture Galatas. Now Sinclair and Farran were prisoners of the Germans.

Both men had been shipped from the prison compound in Prison Valley to Kokkinias Prison, on the mainland near Athens. It was from Kokkinias Prison that they made their escape. The Greek underground got them onto a thirty-foot caïque bound for Alexandria, together with ten other Greeks and three soldiers. As the caïque entered the straits between Kaso island and Crete, a heavy storm struck them with high winds and mountainous waves. Only the captain's skill kept the caïque from being swamped, but the effort soon exhausted their fuel. The same dilemma that confronted Richards's and Garrett's groups now presented itself to Sinclair, Farran, and the rest. Makeshift sails were used to catch what little wind prevailed. Rations diminished daily. By the ninth day, the men lay in utter exhaustion—thirsty, hungry, too weak even to speak. That night they were picked up by a passing British destroyer. Sinclair and Farran finally reached the safety of Alexandria.[15]

As the months passed, the Germans tightened the cordon and increased their search for these stragglers, whom they called "deserters." The Germans did not hesitate to shoot any civilian aiding an escapee, nor did they hesitate to burn whole villages in retribution. Yet despite these brutal measures, the Cretan population continued giving guidance and sustenance to the New Zealand, Australian, and British stragglers and escapees who roamed the hills and mountains of Crete.

Some 1,000 Commonwealth soldiers were eventually able to escape from the stricken island. Those soldiers who made no such effort or were unsuccessful remained as prisoners of war. These numbered approximately 11,835 men, many of whom were first confined in makeshift compounds at Aghia and Prison Valley and later transferred to the mainland. However, by the end of the year, there were still about 500 escapees at large and roaming the hills, having filtered into the safety of the mountains, seeking and receiving shelter from the Cretans.

During the four long, dreary years of the German occupation that followed, the people of Crete were to suffer heavily under the tyrannical rule of the Nazi oppressor. From the first day of the occupation, which began on June 1, 1941, the Cretan population faced a terrible trial of terror for their resistance. Countless thousands of Cretans were gathered for execution upon the slightest pretext. A constant sense of fear pervaded the island as squads of Germans marched from village to village collecting hostages at random. The more fortunate villagers were mustered into labor gangs; the less fortunate were sent to the execution wall. Over 2,000 Cretans were executed in the first month of the occupation. During the next four years, more than 25,000 islanders were marched before German execution squads. Considering the island's census of 400,000 residents, this was a decimating toll. It was also a hell of which the outside world knew nothing.

Men like Nicholas Manolakakis from Spilia village, who had seen his wife and son slain by the Germans on the first day of the invasion, waged a one-man campaign against the destroyers of his quiet family life. In the ten days that followed, he personally killed some forty German paratroopers. Now the SS were looking for him. They announced that if Manolakakis did not surrender himself immediately, they would execute at random ten hostages from his village for each day's delay. When Manolakakis heard of this proclamation, he left the safety of the White Mountains and, returning to his village, surrendered himself to the Germans. The SS had Manolakakis dig his own grave, and when he finished, they executed him. The same fate befell Kostas Manousos, the six-foot six-inch Cretan from Sfakia, who had seen his father slain on the first day of the attack. When he learned that a similar bounty had been placed upon his head, he made the same decision as Manolakakis. His surrender would prevent a wholesale slaughter of villagers from Platanias. His personal revenge accounted for forty-three Germans, and now he had to pay the price. He kissed his wife and son tenderly before making the long trek north to Platanias.

Not a single village, not a single home, not a single family remained unscarred by this wanton execution of relatives and friends. In time, the whole of Crete was draped in black, and a floodtide of mournful tears fell from the eyes of the bereaved.

High in the mountains of southern Crete, ranging from the White Mountains in the west to the Lasithi Mountains in the east, bands of men and women, old and young, roamed the slate-gray escarpments of those rugged heights fleeing the yoke of German oppression. They banded together into an army of patriots who fought a continuous battle against their enemy. In the four years of occupation that followed the invasion, these Cretans were the nucleus of the Cretan resistance movement against the German occupiers.

Crete was the last place in Europe to be freed from the German swastika. When the Germans finally departed on May 15, 1945—one week *after* hostilities had ceased on the European continent—they left thousands of dead soldiers behind.

In London the population heard the final reports of the tragic events that turned an opportunity for victory in Crete into another defeat for British arms. Churchill announced to the House that the evacuation had been terminated and that the only cause for satisfaction was the heroic effort of the Royal Navy. He did not detail, however, the cost in personnel and in ships.

In the United States, a small article in the *New York Times* mentioned that Crete had finally succumbed to the German airborne onslaught. Little reference was made to the gallantry of the Commonwealth soldiers, to their plight in the withdrawal, or to the heroic exploits of the Cretans in fighting side by side with the New Zealanders and Australians. Certainly no reference was made to the Cretan hostages being executed daily for their resistance to the invader.

Across the Aegean Sea in Athens, the Greeks listened attentively to reports of the battle taking place. Some of their information came from American Embassy personnel, while most of it was heard over BBC news reports received on clandestine radios. By the end of May, the tone of the reports forecast defeat in Crete for the Allies. The Greeks believed the Germans had received a rude and costly shock.

In July 1941 General Kurt Student was summoned from Athens to appear before Hitler at the Fuehrer's new underground headquarters near Rastenberg, in the dark gloomy forest of East Prussia. It was from there at the Wolfsschanze—the Wolf's Lair—that Hitler now directed the campaign against Russia which had begun at 3:30 A.M. on June 22.

Student was instructed to bring several of his senior commanders with him so they might be decorated. Hitler greeted them warmly in the conference room of his headquarters. Following a simple ceremony in which he awarded the Knight's Cross to some of the paratroop officers, he congratulated them on their success.

"You have accomplished an essential task," Hitler informed them, "which could only have been undertaken by an airborne assault." [16]

Student was proud of his men; all those early hours of pending defeat were now forgotten. He did not wish to review the heavy losses incurred in the battle. The paratroop commander did not wish to be reminded that he no longer had a combat-worthy parachute division. Given time, the division would be reinforced, reequipped, and revitalized. It would be given greater strength for greater military deeds in the days ahead. At Corinth and certainly in Crete, the parachutists had proven their mettle. If Keitel, Jodl, and Halder agreed with Hitler, then Student's paratroop corps would be given the support it so richly deserved. As coffee was being served, Hitler turned to Student, but his remarks were to shatter the paratroop commander's hopes.

"Of course, you know, Student, that we shall never order another airborne operation. Crete has proved," Hitler continued without a pause, "that the days of the parachute troops are over." [17]

Student was thunderstruck by the remark. "But why, mein Fuehrer?" he stammered in his typical, slow drawl.

Hitler ignored Student's obvious dismay, giving the reason for his decision: "The parachute force as a weapon is one that relies entirely on surprise. The element of surprise has exhausted itself."

Hitler rose and gave the general his hand in dismissal. "It is unfortunate, Student," Hitler concluded, "but Crete has become the graveyard of the German paratrooper." [18]

Lieutenant General Kurt Student, the first and last commander of the German Parachute Corps, was taken prisoner in 1945 by the Allied Forces. The man who had planned and commanded the Cretan invasion had been promoted to Oberstgeneral after Crete, and subsequently commanded various army groups on the eastern and western fronts during the rest of the war.

The high point of Student's military career was the airborne invasion of Crete, which resulted in a Pyrrhic victory for the Germans. Hitler never forgot the heavy toll of casualties—one in every four perished, totaling some 6,116, of which 1,990 were officially listed as killed.

After Crete, Student proposed a plan to launch an airborne invasion of Cyprus as a stepping-stone for an attack on the Suez Canal from the east. Hitler rejected the proposal, citing the heavy casualties in Crete.[19]

Student remained undaunted by this rejection and in April 1942 proposed an air invasion of Malta. The ultimate plan called for a combined air and seaborne assault, with a tentative date set for June 10. This plan was favorably received by the German General Staff, and the program moved into full operation. Student was to command the combined German-Italian airborne forces that were to be used in the attack. He would command his original Fliegerkorps XI, which would be comprised of the reconstituted Seventh Air Division, the Italian Folgore Parachute Division, and a light air-landing support division, all to be ferried to Malta in 300 JU-52s and HE-111s, together with 155 Savoia-82s of the Italian Regia Aeronautica. In addition, ninety gliders were to be used as an advance attack force.

As June 10 approached, Hitler had misgivings that led to a delay. Student flew to Hitler's headquarters for a personal conference, hoping to obtain final approval for Operation Herkules, as it had been designated. Once again Hitler rejected the proposal. The reminder of the casualties suffered on Crete rose again like a nightmare. "The affair will go wrong," he declared to Student, and in a tone that meant that his decision was final, he added: "It would cost too many lives!" Crete had left a deep scar on Hitler.[20]

It must have been a bitter pill for Student to swallow when he personally witnessed the massive Allied airborne assault on Holland in September 1944. The very thought that the Allies had copied his creation and were using it against him must have made him envious on the one hand and angry at Hitler's shortsightedness on the other.

Student's anguish over the fate of his beloved paratroopers was deepened when in 1944 he lost his only son, also serving in the Luftwaffe. With the war's end came the end of Kurt Student's military career. A military tribunal cleared him of any complicity in war crimes, releasing him in 1948, whereupon he returned to his home to live out his days in postwar Germany. Student died in 1978 at the age of eighty-eight.

For the remainder of the war, the German parachute units fought with distinction *as infantry* on all the major fronts. And they were well respected by all Allied units that opposed them. The survivors of the battle of Crete were regarded as an elite group. They were given permission to wear a special patch bearing the word *Kreta* on their sleeve-cuffs.

General Freyberg returned to battle in North Africa, where he was wounded again during the British withdrawal to El Alamein. His failure in Crete was to deprive him of any future independent command for the rest of the war. He subsequently served as a senior staff officer in North Africa and later in Italy.

Wherever he went, Freyberg's fame as Great Britain's most decorated soldier preceded his shadow by a mile. Yet the outcome on Crete seemed to bother him. Throughout the war he continued to give reasons—not always the same—why Crete should never have been defended.

Freyberg must have asked himself repeatedly why he had not ordered a counterattack on the night of the first day of the German invasion; or why he yielded to the wishes of his individual senior sector commanders instead of ordering them to attack; or why he had not armed the civilian population with the weapons stored in the warehouses in Khaniá. What a formidable civilian army they would have made!

After the war Freyberg continued to serve his sovereign. In 1946 King George appointed him to be governor-general of New Zealand. At the end of this tenure, he returned to England to become lieutenant governor of Windsor Castle and to serve in the House of Lords. His service to his country continued until his death in 1963.

The greatest tribute that could be given to the Australians and New Zealanders—both officers and enlisted men—who fought so bravely on Crete was accorded by the Cretan people. When asked what they thought of these men who came from so far away below the Southern Cross to defend their island, the Cretans smiled admiringly and replied: *"They were fighters!"*

The passage of time has obliterated many of the deep scars that war brings to the land, but the wounds of the heart endure. Those wounds forge the creation of monuments that decades later stand as an epitaph to the deeds of both invaders and defenders. Today the whole island of Crete remains a memorial to the battle that was fought there.

The English memorial to their fallen heroes is located not far from the Suda docks where they first set foot on Cretan soil.

In a sprawling green meadow, the symmetrical lines of tombstones radiate from a central granite cross. The cool breezes wafting in from the water carry the fragrance of the flowers that surround the Suda Bay War Cemetery, the final resting place for Freyberg's men. Here lie the New Zealanders, the Australians, and the British of the Commonwealth. Perhaps most poignant of all is the inscription at the cemetery gate reminding the visitor that "As the sun sets low over Suda Bay, we shall remember them."

The German dead are buried at the new military cemetery— the Deutscher Soldatenfriedhof—which was opened in 1974 atop Hill 107, overlooking Maleme airfield. Beneath a 25-foot wooden cross are buried, under flat tombstones in tidy lanes amidst blossoming red flowers, those who came to Crete to stay.

The Cretans gathered their dead and buried them in the cemeteries of the villages in which they had lived.

Of all these grim reminders of battle, of all the monuments that have been erected as memorials to the dead, one, perhaps, stands out because of its simplicity.

On a high hill not far from Khaniá, there is a huge black wooden cross that marks the gravesite of a fallen soldier. No one knows whether that slain warrior was a Greek, a New Zealander, an Australian, or an Englishman, for time and the elements have expunged his name from the marker on the cross. His identity is known only to God. Daily several Cretan women dutifully ascend the hill and place a bouquet of flowers at the base of that cross, to honor the memory of this unknown soldier.

Somewhere in Hades, where the fallen of Greek mythology go when they depart this earth, Leonidas and his 300 Spartans— renowned heroes of the ancient battle of Thermopylae—must have been proud to accept into their ranks this gallant warrior who fought a modern Thermopylae in May 1941. Like Leonidas and his Spartans, he fought fiercely; and like them he died bravely for liberty.

EPILOGUE

Fortune touched each person involved in this battle differently.

Kurt Student's immediate superior, General Alexander Löhr, was not so fortunate as Student. The commanding general of the German Fourth Air Fleet, whose air force command was involved in the Balkan operations against Yugoslavia, Greece, and Crete, was held for trial as a war criminal in Belgrade after the war. Accused of complicity in the opening-day bombardment of the Yugoslavian capital, in which 17,000 civilians were killed, he was executed on December 27, 1947.

Another officer who served in Crete and who met the same fate as Löhr was Colonel Bruno Brauer, commanding officer of the First Parachute Regiment, which landed in Iráklion on May 20. After the battle Brauer remained as commander of the occupation force, with headquarters at Khaniá. He bore the onus of responsibility for the brutal mass executions undertaken by the SS against the Cretan civilians during the four-year occupation. Tried in Athens as a war criminal, he was executed on the anniversary of the invasion of Crete—May 20, 1947. Buried in Kokkinias Prison cemetery near Athens until 1974, his remains were reinterred in a grave at the new German military cemetery at Maleme in Crete.

General Wolfram von Richthofen, who commanded the aircraft that rained continuous death upon Crete, survived the war only to die of natural causes in an Allied prisoner-of-war camp.

Major General Eugen Meindl, commanding officer of the assault regiment, who had been severely wounded in Crete, recovered in Germany and returned to command a battle group on the western front during the Allied invasion of Normandy in June 1944.

Another officer in the assault regiment who survived wounds received on Crete was Major Walter Koch. It was Koch who commanded the glider companies that landed on Hill 107 on May 20. After Crete, Koch rose to command the elite Fifth Parachute Regiment serving in North Africa, which was built around the surviving officers and NCOs of General Meindl's assault regiment. Koch was killed in an automobile accident in Germany in October 1943.

Most of the German officers who survived the battle in Crete achieved advancement in rank. Colonel Richard Heidrich, who commanded the Third Parachute Regiment in Prison Valley, rose to become a general in command of the reconstituted Seventh Airborne Division. In a major reorganization of the airborne units, the veteran Seventh Airborne was renamed the First Airborne Division and, with Heidrich commanding, fought the Allies brilliantly and stubbornly at the epic Battle of Cassino in Italy.

Commanding his old regiment was one of Heidrich's former battalion commanders, Colonel Ludwig Heilmann. Heilmann's former Third Parachute Battalion had been wiped out on the first day of battle in Crete.

Another of Heidrich's battalion commanders in Crete was Baron von der Heydte. A captain in Crete, Friedrich August Freiherr von der Heydte rose to a colonelcy and served on the eastern and western fronts. He commanded a special task force in the Battle of the Ardennes in 1944, and he was captured by

American troops. After the war, he returned to Würzburg where he taught international law.

Colonel Bernhard Ramcke, the aggressive parachute officer who succeeded the wounded General Eugen Meindl in field command of the paratroopers in the Maleme area, led a brigade in the battle at El Alamein. As a major general he commanded the newly formed crack Second Parachute Division and moved into Brittany in June 1944. His defense of the encircled city of Brest held many American divisions at bay during that long siege, until he was forced to surrender in mid-September.

Captain Walter Gericke, who commanded the Fourth Assault Battalion in the Maleme area, subsequently rose in rank and saw combat service in North Africa, Sicily, and Italy. After the war Gericke became commanding general of the first West German airborne division in 1962.

Many of the soldiers of lower ranks also survived the war. Werner Schiller recovered from the wound he received in Crete and returned to combat duty in North Africa and later in Italy and France. He survived the war to become an engineer.

Corporal Hans Kreindler was released from captivity when the Germans took Galatas. Returned to combat duty, he fought in North Africa and Italy and was wounded at Cassino. He survived the war and emigrated to South America and thence to the United States.

Perhaps the greatest disappointment among the paratroopers who fought in Crete was Max Schmeling, the former world heavyweight boxing champion. He saw little or no action in Crete because of a stomach disorder. Nevertheless he became a central figure of Joseph Goebbels's propaganda machine, depicted in photographs and posters as a hero-Fallschirmjäger. Veterans of the Cretan campaign scoffed at this image. Schmeling survived the war and became a businessman in West Germany.

In Crete the officers and men of the Australian, New Zealand, and British units wrote the finest pages in their war history.

However, in some cases the battle records men established on Crete tended to affect their destiny for the remainder of the war, and for some senior commanders, Crete had a telling effect on the rest of their military careers.

General Edward Puttick, who headed the New Zealand division in Crete, found that his actions there left a shadow on his ability as a leader in battle. He continued to command the division for a brief period after Crete, but when the division was transferred to Italy, Brigadier Howard Kippenberger took over.

Brigadier James Hargest of the Fifth New Zealand Brigade, the farmer-turned-politician-turned-soldier, could not overcome the lethargy he had shown during the first night of the invasion, when he allowed Hill 107 to be abandoned. Even his fine leadership during the withdrawal to Sfakia did little to erase his earlier conduct.

Colonel Howard Kippenberger, the feisty commander of the Tenth New Zealand Brigade in Prison Valley and at Galatas, proved that he had a penchant for fighting the enemy. In North Africa, Kippenberger was given command of a brigade, and in Italy he rose to command the New Zealand division. Wounded at Cassino, he survived the war with the rank of major general and was later knighted for his exemplary service.

The man who succeeded Kippenberger as commander of the Twentieth New Zealanders—Major John Burrows—eventually commanded a brigade. Major Sandover, the Australian from the Eleventh Australian Battalion who escaped from Crete, also rose to command a brigade by the end of the war. However, his immediate superior, Brigadier Ian Campbell, remained to surrender at Rethimnon and had to spend the next four years in a German prison camp. Lieutenant Thomas, who led a platoon from the Twenty-third New Zealand Battalion at Galatas, was captured by the Germans as he lay wounded. Like Lieutenants Sinclair and Farran, he was transferred to the Greek mainland and later escaped to North Africa.

Another officer who rejoined his regiment and saw additional service in the campaigns in Europe was Captain Michael Forrester, whose exploits on Crete became legendary.

Some officers who escaped from Crete met sad ends on other battlefields. Colonel John Allen of the Twenty-first New Zealand Battalion fought and died in North Africa. Lieutenant Colonel John Gray, who aged perceptibly during the hot battle at Galatas, was also killed in action in Europe. Many others also escaped from Crete only to die in other theaters of war.

Of the Greek soldiers who fought with the New Zealanders and Australians at Galatas, Alikianou, Rethimnon, and Iráklion, most remained to become prisoners of the Germans. Very few Greeks were evacuated from Crete with the British forces, for no provision had been made. Some did escape to join the Cretans in the mountains and to fight in the resistance.

Captain Emorfopoulos—Captain E—survived the wounds he received defending Cemetery Hill before Galatas. For the rest of the war, he was a German prisoner. His adjutant, Lieutenant Aristides Kritakis, was also captured and spent four years in a prison camp in Germany. After the war he returned to Greece and resumed his profession as a correspondent.

The civilians in the story fared better.

Major John Drakopoulos, the "maintenance engineer" in the Grande Bretagne Hotel whose covert activities discovered the German intent for Crete, continued his work for the British until 1943. When the Gestapo uncovered his status as a double agent, he was forced to flee. He returned to Athens after the war where he lived until he died in 1977.

It is worth mentioning that the British had been aware of the pending operation against Crete from another source. An apparatus known as Ultra had enabled them to intercept and decode German messages originating in the highest German command echelons. As early as April 28, Churchill had informed General Wavell that an airborne invasion of Crete was to be anticipated. Nevertheless, General Wavell's replies to the prime minister indicated that he did not believe these reports. He felt strongly, as did the Imperial General Staff, that the impending attack on Crete was a ruse, and that the major assault would be directed elsewhere. By the time Wavell accepted the fact that the Germans did intend to invade Crete, it was too late to take stronger measures to defend of the island.

The man who hired Drakopoulos as the maintenance engineer for the Grande Bretagne, George Canellos, survived the war and became director of the hotel.

As an afterthought, SS Colonel Heinz Gellermann, the Gestapo officer who interviewed Drakopoulos and approved his employment in German headquarters, remained in Athens until 1943. He was later transferred to the Russian front, and there is no evidence that he survived the war.

Athanasios Tziotis, the teenager who carried messages to the British secret wireless transmitter at 5 Canaris Street, also survived the war. In later years he married a coworker at the Grande Bretagne.

Most of the Cretans who fought the Germans and survived took to the mountains during the occupation. From there they continued the fight as members of the resistance. George Psychoundakis and Manoli Paterakis were no exception.

Psychoundakis, the lithe, olive-eyed shepherd from the village of Asi Gonia, became a runner for the British secret agents who were sent into Crete to work with the Cretan resistance. Paterakis became a legend. After fighting the Germans during the invasion, he continued the fight as a guerrilla during the occupation. He was awarded the Military Medal of the British Empire, and the walls of his home are adorned with letters of commendation from such famous people as Field Marshal Sir Harold Alexander, among others.

The West German National Federation of War Memorial Associations—Volksbund Deutsche Kriegsgräberfürsorge—purchased the ground of Kavsakia Hill at Maleme, better known as Hill 107, and in 1974 opened a military cemetery there. They reburied the 4,465 paratroopers who were killed during the Battle of Crete and those who died during the occupation. As caretakers for this new cemetery the Germans chose Manoli Paterakis and George Psychoundakis!

When Psychoundakis left his home village of Asi Gonia in 1941 to fight the Germans, he swore that he was "going to bury a German officer." He never had the opportunity to fulfill that vow during the battle or later during the occupation. But by an ironic quirk of fate and time, Psychoundakis was the caretaker when the Germans transferred the remains of General Bruno Brauer from the Kokkinias Prison cemetery in Athens, where he had been buried after his execution in 1947, to the military cemetery at Maleme. It was Psychoundakis who actually reinterred Brauer's remains into the new gravesite. After thirty-three years, George Psychoundakis had finally fulfilled his vow—he had buried a German officer.

NOTES

CHAPTER 1
NO, IT IS WAR!

1. Archer, *The Balkan Journal*, 117–120.
2. Liddell Hart, ed. *History of Second World War*, Vol. 1, 272.
3. *Ibid.*, 272.
4. *Ibid.*, 263.
5. Wason, *Miracle in Hellas*, 13.
6. *Ibid.*, 14.
7. Papagos, *The Battle of Greece*, 275.
8. Liddell Hart, ed., 1:264.
9. Stewart, *The Struggle for Crete*, 31.
10. Papagos, 414.
11. Trevor-Roper, *Hitler's War Directives 1939–1945*, 90.
12. Smith, *The Great Island: A Study of Crete*, 1–89.

CHAPTER 2
WAR COMES TO THE LAND OF MINOS

1. Thomas, *Nazi Victory, Crete 1941*, 53.
2. *Ibid.*, 54.
3. Ritchie, *East of Malta, West of Suez: The Official Admiralty Account of the Mediterranean Fleet 1939–1943*, 101.
4. *Ibid.*, 102.
5. Liddell Hart, ed., 3:1327.
6. Lenton, *Navies of Second World War: British Cruisers*, 72, 73.

CHAPTER 3
MERCURY IS BORN

1. Farrar-Hockley, *Student*, 88.
2. Manvell, *Goering*, 127.
3. Townsend, *Duel of Eagles*, 173, 238.
4. Frischauer, *Rise and Fall of Hermann Goering*, 187.
5. *Ibid.*, 188.
6. Whiting, *Hunters From the Sky*, 48.
7. Frischauer, 189. Frischauer is quoting the diary of General Karl Bodenschatz, Goering's military aide.
8. Clark, *The Fall of Crete*, 48.
9. Frischauer, 190. Quoting Bodenschatz.
10. Bekker, *The Luftwaffe War Diaries*, 261.
11. Halder, *Kriegstagebuch*, entry April 24, 1941.
12. Frischauer, 191.
13. Manvell, 66
14. Windrow, *Luftwaffe Airborne and Field Units*, 28.
15. Farrar-Hockley, 6–80.
16. *Ibid.*, 81.
17. Student, *Crete*, 55.
18. *Ibid.*, 55.
19. Bekker, 261.
20. *Ibid.*, 261.
21. Student, 55.
22. Clark, 51.
23. Student, 55.
24. *Ibid.*, 60.
25. *Ibid.*, 60.
26. Clark, 51.
27. Farrar-Hockley, 81.
28. Frischauer, 195.
29. *Ibid.*, 195.
30. Trevor-Roper, 117.

CHAPTER 4
DETERMINE THE NEXT GERMAN OBJECTIVE

1. Churchill, *The Second World War*, Vol. 3, 246.
2. *Ibid.*, 244.
3. *Ibid.*, 246.
4. *Ibid.*, 247.
5. *Ibid.*, 246.
6. *Ibid.*, 251.
7. *Ibid.*, 261.
8. *Ibid.*, 272.

9. Cameron, *The Valorous Island: Malta*, 23.
10. *Ibid.*, 31.
11. Whiting, *The War in the Shadows*, 40.
12. *Ibid.*, 40.

CHAPTER 5
ANY DAY AFTER THE SEVENTEENTH

1. Waller, *With the 1st Armored Brigade In Greece*, 19.
2. Canellos, George. Interview with author. Athens, July 10, 1976.
3. Whiting, *The War in the Shadows*, 28.
4. Drakopoulos, John. Interview with author. Athens, July 14, 1976.
5. Tziotis, Athanasios. Interview with author. Athens, July 8, 1976.
6. Thompson, *Assignment: Churchill*, 218.
7. Churchill, 3:280.

CHAPTER 6
SCORCHER ON COLORADO

1. Churchill, 3:227.
2. Winterbotham, *The Ultra Secret*, 104.
3. Churchill, 3:271.
4. *Ibid.*, 272.
5. Churchill, 2:548.
6. Churchill, 3:273.
7. Clark, 30.
8. *Ibid.*, 31.
9. *Ibid.*, 31.
10. *Ibid.*, 31.
11. *Ibid.*, 32.
12. *Ibid.*, 33.
13. Churchill, 3:274.
14. *Ibid.*, 273.
15. *Ibid.*, 273.
16. Stewart, 73.
17. Churchill, 3:277.
18. *Ibid.*, 281.
19. *Ibid.*, 280.
20. Clark, 33.

CHAPTER 7
JUST A CIRCLE ON THE MAP

1. Lazerakis, Peter. Interview with author. Khania, June 30, 1977.
2. Stewart, 93.
3. Manolikakis, *The Golgotha of Crete*, 55.

4. Davin, *Crete*, 469.
5. Manolikakis, 57.
6. Stewart, 93.
7. *Ibid.*, 121.
8. Clark, 84.
9. Gyparis, *Heroes and Heroism in the Battle of Crete*, 99.
10. Kippenberger, *Infantry Brigadier*, 50.
11. Kritakis, Aristides. Interview with author. July 10, 1978.
12. Kazantsakis, Vasili. Interview with author. July 16, 1978.

CHAPTER 8
THE HUNTERS FROM THE SKY

1. Clark, 57.
2. Kurowski, *Der Kampf Um Kreta*, 18.
3. *Ibid.*, 20.
4. Windrow, 3.
5. *Ibid.*, 4.
6. Liddell Hart, ed., 2:504.
7. Farrar-Hockley, 47.
8. *Ibid.*, 52.
9. Kurowski, 19.
10. Bekker, 123.
11. U.S. Department of the Army. *Airborn Operations—A German Appraisal*, MS P-051, 88, 89.
12. Bekker, 120.
13. *Ibid.*, 264.
14. *Ibid.*, 264.
15. Von der Heydte, *Daedalus Returned*, 40.
16. *Ibid.*, 43.

CHAPTER 9
IT IS ONLY A RUMOR

1. Manolikakis, 12.
2. Rose, Thomas. Interview with author. London, August 12, 1974.
3. Michas, George. Interview with author. Khania, July 13, 1977.
4. Pavlides, Hector. Interview with author. Athens, July 20, 1976.
5. Gyparis, 110.
6. Pavlides, Hector. Interview. Athens, July 20, 1976.
7. Churchill, 3:272.
8. Kritakis, Aristides. Interview. Athens, July 10, 1978.
9. Kreindler, Hans. Interview with author. Vienna, August 20, 1974.
10. Schoerner, Karl. All information on Schoerner was furnished by Kreindler. Vienna, August 20, 1974.
11. Clark, 44.

12. Ryder, John. Interview with author. London, August 13, 1974.
13. Stewart, 130.
14. *Ibid.*, 131.
15. Ryder. Interview. London, August 13, 1974.
16. Stewart, 132.
17. Farrar-Hockley, 91.

CHAPTER 10
MERCURY IS AIRBORNE

1. Von der Heydte, 14.
2. Thomas, *Nazi Victory,* 143.
3. *Ibid.*, 143.
4. Bekker, 263.
5. U.S. Department of the Army. Ms. B-639, 184.
6. Kreindler. Interview. Vienna, August 20, 1974.
7. Clark, 59.
8. Von der Heydte, 14.
9. Hausser, Franz. Interview. Vienna, August 21, 1974.
10. Bekker, 271.

CHAPTER 11
THEY ARE COMING!

1. Stephanides, *Climax in Crete,* 95.
2. Kritakis. Interview. Athens, July 15, 1978.
3. Stewart, 148.
4. Stephanides, 144.
5. *Ibid.*, 149.
6. Clark, 61.

CHAPTER 12
IT WAS LIKE A TERRIBLE DREAM

1. Kurowski, 32.
2. Bekker, 267.
3. Clark, 64.
4. *Ibid.*, 63.
5. *Ibid.*, 64.
6. Schiller, Werner. Interview with author. Zurich, August 22, 1974.
7. Davin, 130.
8. *Ibid.*, 129.
9. Clark, 65.
10. Striker, Ray. Interview with author. London, August 13, 1974.
11. Clark, 65.
12. Bekker, 270.

CHAPTER 13
IT WAS MAGNIFICENT, BUT IT IS NOT WAR

1. Stewart, 182.
2. Clark, 66.
3. Stewart, 182.
4. Kurowski, 24.
5. Bekker, 271.
6. Von der Heydte, 59.
7. *Ibid.*, 62.
8. Kreindler. Interview. Vienna, August 20, 1974.
9. Von der Heydte, 69.
10. Clark, 62.
11. Bekker, 273.
12. Clark, 85.
13. *Ibid.*, 84.
14. Vlahakis, Mixali. Interview with author. Khania, July 19, 1978.
15. Manolikakis, 39.
16. *Ibid.*, 42.
17. Bedding report quoted in Clark, 86.

CHAPTER 14
THAT THE GERMAN SHALL NOT PASS!

1. Kippenberger, 52.
2. *Ibid.*, 53.
3. *Ibid.*, 52.
4. Davin, 147.
5. Schiller, Werner. Interview. Zurich, August 22, 1974.
6. Clark, 69.
7. Davin, 148.
8. Stewart, 157.
9. Davin, 142.
10. Kreindler. Interview. Vienna, August 20, 1974.
11. Clark, 71.
12. Davin, 143.
13. Gyparis, 99.
14. Stewart, 185, 186.
15. Manolikakis, 39.
16. Wie Wir Kampfen, *Parachute Engineers in the Battle of Crete,* 13.

CHAPTER 15
WITH AXES, WITH SHOVELS,
AND WITH THEIR BARE HANDS

1. Manolakakis, Manolis. Interview of brother with author. Khania, July 10, 1978.
2. Paterakis, Manolis. Interview with author. Khania, July 11, 1978.

3. Manolikakis, 54.
4. Davin, 468.
5. Bekker, 271.
6. Georgalakis, Maria. Interview with author. Athens, July 5, 1978.
7. Kreindler. Interview. Vienna, August 20, 1974.
8. Paterakis. Interview. Platania, July 12, 1978.
9. Schiller. Interview. Zurich, August 22, 1974. Schiller again met Paterakis in 1975 while visiting the German cemetery at Maleme. He recognized Paterakis as the Cretan who had stopped to stare at him in this episode. Paterakis denies seeing Schiller, but he claims that he paused to urinate. He adds that had he seen Schiller hiding in the bamboo glade, he would have shot him.

CHAPTER 16
HENCE THEY HAVE TO PRESERVE MY HEAD

1. Stewart, 166.
2. *Ibid.*, 171.
3. Henderson, J. *22nd Battalion, Official History of New Zealand in World War II, 21.*
4. Stewart, 167.
5. Bekker, 270.
6. Clark, 68.
7. Ross, *23rd Battalion, Official History of New Zealand in World War II,* 67.
8. Manolikakis, 54.
9. Bekker, 272.
10. Fredericks, Franz. Interview with Author. Fort Lee, N.J., June 6, 1979.
11. Bekker, 273.
12. Stewart, 193.
13. Bekker, 273.
14. Clark, 107.

CHAPTER 17
BE BACK BY 4:30 P.M.

1. Bekker, 273.
2. Student, 92.
3. Clark, 83.
4. Gyparis, 100.
5. Clark, 91.
6. *Ibid.*, 86.
7. *Ibid.*, 86.
8. Stewart, 216.
9. *Ibid.*, 217.
10. *Ibid.*, 217.
11. Underhill, *The Royal Leicester Regiment,* 55.
12. *Ibid.*, 55.
13. Buckley, *Greece and Crete 1941,* 205.

14. Stewart, 206.
15. Feist, *Fallschirmjäger in Action*, 16.
16. Stewart, 209.

CHAPTER 18
IF YOU MUST, THEN YOU MUST

1. Henderson, 52.
2. Clark, 69.
3. Henderson, 53.
4. Gyparis, 182.
5. Kritakis. Interview. Athens, July 15, 1978.
6. Clark, 75.
7. *Ibid.*, 76.
8. Kippenberger, 57.
9. Clark, 70.
10. *Ibid.*, 70.
11. Davin, 110.
12. *Ibid.*, 110.
13. Clark, 71.
14. Von der Heydte, 87.
15. Churchill, 3:286.
16. Davin, 180.
17. Clark, 99.
18. *Ibid.*, 99.
19. *Ibid.*, 100.
20. Bekker, 275.
21. Clark, 100.
22. Stewart, 238.
23. *Ibid.*, 224.
24. Cody, *28th (Maori) Battalion: Official History of New Zealand in World War II*, 95.
25. Henderson, 54.
26. Davin, 118.
27. *Ibid.*, 118.

CHAPTER 19
PRESS ON REGARDLESS

1. Stewart, 247.
2. Clark, 101.
3. *Ibid.*, 105.
4. Davin, 188.
5. *Ibid.*, 188.
6. *Ibid.*, 190.
7. Paterakis. Interview. Platania, July 11, 1978.
8. Clark, 104.

9. *Ibid.*, 104.
10. Meyer, *Battle for the Stronghold of Crete*, 90.
11. Psychoundakis, George. Interview. Tavronites, Crete, July 15, 1978.
12. Davin, 189.
13. Kurowski, 95.

CHAPTER 20
IT HAS BEEN A GREAT RESPONSIBILITY

1. Stewart, 229.
2. *Ibid.*, 229.
3. Prüller, *Diary of a German Soldier*, 32.
4. Kurowski, 90.
5. *Ibid.*, 91.
6. Manolikakis, 71.
7. Kurowski, 91.
8. Kritakis. Interview. Athens, July 15, 1978.
9. Kritakis. Interview. Athens, July 15, 1978.
10. Kritakis. Interview. Athens, July 15, 1978.
11. Kritakis. Interview. Athens, July 15, 1978.
12. Kippenberger, 57.
13. Clark, 121.
14. Cody, 104.
15. *Ibid.*, 105.
16. Clark, 105.
17. Long, *Australia in the War 1939–1945*, Vol. 2, 235.
18. Clark, 120.
19. *Ibid.*, 119.

CHAPTER 21
THE WHOLE WORLD IS WATCHING
YOUR SPLENDID BATTLE

1. Davin, 215.
2. *Ibid.*, 215.
3. Farran, *Winged Dagger*, 95.
4. Davin, 216.
5. Paterakis. Interview. Khania, July 11, 1978.
6. Farran, 95.
7. Stewart, 297.
8. Farran, 97.
9. *Ibid.*, 97.
10. Clark, 126.
11. *Ibid.*, 126.
12. *Ibid.*, 127.
13. *Ibid.*, 127.
14. Ross, 72.

15. Davin, 216.
16. Clark, 129.
17. *Ibid.*, 127.
18. *Ibid.*, 127.
19. *Ibid.*, 129.
20. *Ibid.*, 128.
21. Cody, 105.
22. Dyer, *The Way of the Maori Soldier*, 73.
23. Pack, *The Battle for Crete*, 117.
24. Thomas, D., 168.
25. *Ibid.*, 169.
26. Stewart, 309.
27. Churchill, 3:293.
28. *Ibid.*, 293.

CHAPTER 22
MALTA WOULD CONTROL THE MEDITERRANEAN

1. Davin, 238.
2. Clark, 130.
3. *Ibid.*, 130.
4. *Ibid.*, 131.
5. *Ibid.*, 131.
6. *Ibid.*, 131.
7. Wittmann, *Von Kreta, der Insel der Rätsel*, 6.
8. Clark, 137.
9. Stewart, 351.
10. Clark, 134.
11. *Ibid.*, 134.
12. Stewart, 353.
13. Meyer, K., 110.
14. Wittmann, 6.
15. Gericke, *Da Gibt Es Kein Zurück*, 85.
16. Dyer, 60.
17. Kippenberger, 61.
18. Long, 240.
19. *Ibid.*, 241.
20. Stewart, 316.
21. Filipakis, Tasso. Interview with author. Khania, July 17, 1978.
22. Long, 241.
23. Beroukakis, George. Interview with author. Khania, July 25, 1978.
24. Minarakis, Tasso. Interview with author. Khania, July 18, 1978.
25. Mourellos, *Battle of Crete*, Vol. 1, 412.
26. *Ibid.*, 412.
27. Paterakis. Interview. Khania, July 11, 1978.
28. Manolikakis, 54.
29. Thomas, D., 161.

30. Davin, 328.
31. Schmidt, *With Rommel in the Desert,* 76, 77.

CHAPTER 23
STAND FOR NEW ZEALAND!

1. Clark, 130.
2. *Ibid.,* 131.
3. *Ibid.,* 138.
4. *Ibid.,* 139.
5. Kippenberger, 63.
6. Von der Heydte, 120.
7. *Ibid.,* 120.
8. Kritakis. Interview. Athens, July 15, 1978.
9. Davin, 235.
10. Kritakis. Interview. Athens, July 15, 1978.
11. Davin, 235.
12. Clark, 141.
13. Stephanides, 100.
14. Von der Heydte, 123.
15. Kritakis. Interview. Athens, July 15, 1978.
16. Kippenberger, 59. Also reported by Clark, 132, 133 quoting A.Q. Pope of the 4th RTM Company; commented on by Kritakis in interview with author; commented on by Mrs. Eleni Beroukakis (nee Gregorakis).
17. Kippenberger, 63, 64.
18. Davin, 301.
19. *Ibid.,* 303.
20. *Ibid.,* 306.
21. Kritakis. Interview. Athens, July 15, 1978.
22. Kippenberger, 65.
23. *Ibid.,* 65.
24. *Ibid.,* 66.
25. *Ibid.,* 67.
26. *Ibid.,* 66.
27. Farran, 101.
28. Kippenberger, 67.
29. Clark, 147.
30. Thomas, W. B., *Dare To Be Free,* 24.
31. Stewart, 390.
32. Thomas, W. B., 26.
33. *Ibid.,* 28.

CHAPTER 24
WHY IS CRETE STILL RESISTING?

1. Clark, 152.
2. Kippenberger, 68.

3. *Ibid.*, 68.
4. *Ibid.*, 68.
5. *Ibid.*, 68.
6. *Ibid.*, 68.
7. Clark, 153.
8. Kippenberger, 69.
9. Clark, 153.
10. *Ibid.*, 153.
11. Davin, 294.
12. *Ibid.*, 325.
13. *Ibid.*, 325.
14. *Ibid.*, 326.
15. *Ibid.*, 326.
16. Kippenberger, 73.
17. Clark, 153.
18. *Ibid.*, 153.
19. Davin, 344.
20. *Ibid.*, 346.
21. Stewart, 411.
22. Davin, 348.
23. *Ibid.*, 349.
24. *Ibid.*, 361.
25. Clark, 154.
26. Davin, 378.
27. Stewart, 421.
28. Halder, entry dated May 27, 1941.
29. Manolikakis, 72.
30. Churchill, 3:295.
31. Stewart, 362.
32. *Ibid.*, 363.
33. Long, 265.
34. Manolikakis, 79.
35. Churchill, 3:295.
36. *Ibid.*, 295.
37. *Ibid.*, 295, 296.

CHAPTER 25
300 YEARS TO BUILD A NEW TRADITION

1. Cunningham, *A Sailor's Odyssey*, 385.
2. *Ibid.*, 385.
3. *Ibid.*, 386.
4. *Ibid.*, 387.
5. Churchill, 3:299.
6. Stephanides, 213.
7. Kippenberger, 76.
8. Stewart, 436.

9. *Ibid.*, 159.
10. *Ibid.*, 453.
11. *Ibid.*, 453.
12. Davin, 399.
13. Stewart, 432.
14. *Ibid.*, 463.
15. Cunningham, 387.
16. *Ibid.*, 390.

CHAPTER 26
CRETE HAS BECOME THE GRAVEYARD
OF THE GERMAN PARATROOPER

1. Pack, 124.
2. Davin, 446.
3. *Ibid.*, 446.
4. *Ibid.*, 447.
5. Stewart, 467.
6. Clark, 161.
7. *Ibid.*, 162.
8. Davin, 447.
9. *Ibid.*, 447.
10. *Ibid.*, 447.
11. Clark, 178.
12. *Ibid.*, 178.
13. *Ibid.*, 166.
14. *Ibid.*, 169.
15. *Ibid.*, 181.
16. Farrar-Hockley, 101.
17. *Ibid.*, 101.
18. *Ibid.*, 101.
19. Stewart, 477.
20. *Ibid.*, 477.

BIBLIOG-
RAPHY

Abshagen, K. H. *Canaris*. London: Hutchinson, 1956.

Addington, Larry H. *The Blitzkrieg Era and the German General Staff, 1865–1941*. New Brunswick, N.J.: Rutgers University Press, 1971.

Ansel, Walter. *Hitler and the Middle Sea*. Durham, North Carolina: Duke University Press, 1972.

Archer, Laird. *The Balkan Journal*. New York: W. W. Norton and Co., 1944.

Argyropoulos, Kaity. *From Peace to Chaos*. New York: Vantage Press, 1975.

Bailey, George. *Germans*. New York: Avon, 1972.

Bailey, Ronald, Ed. *World War II: Partisans and Guerrillas*. Alexandria, Virginia: Time-Life Books, 1978.

Baldwin, Hanson. *Battles Lost and Won: Crete—The Winged Invasion*. New York: Avon, 1968.

Barry, Gerald. *The Parachute Invasion*. London: Blackwoods, 1944.

Baumbach, Werner. *The Life and Death of the Luftwaffe*. New York: Ballantine Books, 1967.

Bekker, Cajus. *The Luftwaffe War Diaries*. New York: Doubleday & Co., 1969.

Bohmler, Rudolf. *Fallschirmjäger*. Munich: Verlag Hans-Henning Podzun, 1961.

Bragadin, Commander Antonio. *The Italian Navy in World War II*. Annapolis: U.S. Naval Institute, 1957.

Buckley, Christopher. *Greece and Crete 1941*. London: Her Majesty's Stationery Office, 1977.

Caidin, Martin. *ME 109. New York: Ballantine Books, 1968.*

Cameron, Ian. The Valorous Island: Malta. New York: Arbor House, 1963.

Carell, Paul. *Hitler Moves East 1941–1943*. London: G. Harrop & Co., 1964.

Cecil, Robert, et al. *Hitler's War Machine*. Secaucus, New Jersey: Chartwell Books, Inc., 1975.

Churchill, Winston S. *The Second World War, Vol. 2: Their Finest Hour*. Boston: Houghton Mifflin, 1950.

――――. *The Second World War, Vol. 3: The Grand Alliance*. Boston: Houghton Mifflin, 1950.

Ciano, Count Galeazzo. *Ciano's Diary 1939–1943*. Garden City, New York: Doubleday & Co., Inc., 1946.

Clark, Alan. *The Fall of Crete*. London: Anthony Blond Ltd., 1962.

Cody, J. F. *28 (Maori) Battalion: Official History of New Zealand in the Second World War 1939–1945*. Wellington: Department of Internal Affairs, War History Branch, 1956.

Collier, Basil. *The Battle of Britain*. New York: Berkley Medallion Books, 1969.

Collier, Richard. *Duce!* New York: Popular Library, 1971.

Comeau, M. G. *Operation Mercury*. London: Kimber, 1961.

Congdon, Don, Ed. *Combat, World War II*. New York: Arbor House, 1963.

Cooper, Matthew. *Uniforms of the Luftwaffe 1939–1945*. London: Almark Publishing Co., Ltd., 1974.

Cunningham, Admiral of the Fleet Viscount of Hyndhope. *A Sailor's Odyssey*. New York: Dutton, 1951.

Davin, Daniel M. *Crete (Official History of New Zealand in the Second World War, 1939–1945)*. Wellington, New Zealand: Department of Internal Affairs, War History Branch, 1953.

Davis, Brian L. *Luftwaffe Air Crews 1940*. New York: Arco Publishing Co., Inc., 1974.

――――. *German Parachute Forces 1935–1945*. New York: Arco Publishing Co., Inc., 1974.

De Courcy, Captain J. *The History of the Welch Regiment 1919–1951*. Cardiff: the Western Mail, 1952.

Delarue, Jacque. *The Gestapo*. New York: William Morrow, 1964.

Dobiasch, Sepp. *Gebirgsjäger Auf Kreta*. Berlin: Stocker, 1942.

Dyer, Major H. G. *The Way of the Maori Soldier*. London: Stockwell, 1957.

Edwards, Roger. *German Airborne Troops 1936–1945*. New York: Doubleday and Co., Inc., 1974.

Farran, Roy. *Winged Dagger*. London: Collins, 1948.

Farrar-Hockley, Anthony. *Student*. New York: Ballantine Books, Inc., 1973.

Feist, Uwe, et al. *Fallschirmjäger in Action*. Michigan: Squadron/Signal Publications, Inc., 1973.

Fergusson, Bernard. *Wavel: Portrait of a Soldier*. London: Collins, 1961.

――――. *The Black Watch and the King's Enemies*. London: Collins, 1950.

Fielding, Xan. *The Stronghold*. London: Secker and Warburg, 1963.

Fisher, Graham, and McNair-Wilson, Michael. *Black Shirt*. New York: Belmont Books, 1961.

Fitzgibbon, Constantine. *Secret Intelligence in the Twentieth Century*. New York: Stein and Day, 1977.

Frischauer, Willi. *The Rise and Fall of Herman Goering*. New York: Ballantine Books, 1951.

Galland, Adolf. *The First and The Last*. New York: Ballantine Books, 1973.

Galland, Ries and Ahnert. *The Luftwaffe at War*. Chicago: Henry Regnery Company, 1973.

Gardner, Hugh H. *The German Campaigns in the Balkans (Spring 1940)*. Washington: Office of Chief of Military History, Department of the Army, 1954.

Gericke, Walter. *Da Gibt Es Kein Zurück*. Munster: Fallschirmjäger-Verlag, 1955.

German Air Force Handbook 1944. *Wie Wir Kampfen*. (Parachute Engineers in Battle of Crete) Berlin: 1944.

German Intelligence Digest, World War II. Stamford, Connecticut: Blacksmith Corporation, 1943.

German Mountain Troops Corps H-Q., *Gebirgsjäger in Griechenland und auf Kreta*. Berlin: 1941.

Gibson, Major T. A. *Assault from the Sky, Crete 1941*. London: Journal of Royal United Services Institute, 1961.

Gill, Hermon. *Royal Australian Navy 1939-1942, Vol. 1*. Canberra: Australian War Memorial Press, 1957.

Gyparis, Paul. *Heroes and Heroism in the Battle of Crete*. (in Greek) Athens: 1954.

Halder, Col. Gen. Franz. *Halder: Kriegstagebuch*. Stuttgart: Kohlhammer, 1963.

Heckstall-Smith, Anthony and Vice-Admiral H. T. Baillie-Grohman. *Greek Tragedy, 1941*. New York: W. W. Norton and Co., Inc., 1961.

Heiden, Konrad. *Der Fuehrer*. Boston: Houghton Mifflin Co., 1944.

Henderson, J. *22 Battalion, Official History of New Zealand in the Second World War 1939-1945*. Wellington, New Zealand: War History Branch, Department of Internal Affairs, 1958.

Herzstein, Robert Edwin, Ed. *World War II: The Nazis*. Alexandria, Virginia: Time-Life Books, 1978.

Hetherington, John. *Airborn Invasion: The Story of the Battle of Crete*. New York: Duell, Sloan and Pierce, 1943.

Hibbert, Christopher. *Mussolini*. New York: Ballatine Books, 1972.

Howell, Wing Commander Edward. *Escape to Live*. London: Longmans, 1947.

Irving, David. *The Memoirs of Field Marshal Keitel, Chief of the German High Command, 1938-1945*. New York: Stein and Day, 1966.

———. *Hitler's War*. New York: Viking Press, 1977.

Ismay, General Lord. *The Memoirs of Lord Ismay*. London: Heinemann, 1960.

Keitel, Wilhelm. *Memoirs*. London: Kimber, 1965.

Kippenberger, Major General Sir Howard. *Infantry Brigadier*. London: Oxford University Press, 1949.

Koutsoulas, Dimitrios. *The Price of Freedom*. Syracuse, New York: Syracuse University, 1953.

Kurowski, Franz. *Der Kampf Um Kreta*. Herford und Bonn: Maximilian-Verlag, 1965.

Lavra, Stephen. *The Greek Miracle*. London: Hastings House, 1943.

Leach, Barry. *The German General Staff*. New York: Ballantine Books, 1973.

Lenton, H. T. *Navies of the Second World War: British Cruisers*. New York: Doubleday and Co., Inc., 1973.

Lewin, Ronald. *The Chief: Field Marshal Lord Wavell 1939-1947*. New York: Farrar, Straus and Giroux, 1980.

———. *Rommel as Military Commander*. New York: Ballantine Books, 1970.

———. *The War On Land: The British Army in World War II*. New York: William Morrow and Co., Inc., 1970.

Liddell Hart, B. H. *History of the Second World War.* New York: G. P. Putnam Sons, 1971.

———, Ed. *History of the Second World War, Vol. 1.* London: Marshall Cavendish Ltd., 1973.

———, Ed. *History of the Second World War, Vol. 2.* London: Marshall Cavendish Ltd., 1973.

Lochner, Louis, Ed. *The Goebbels Diaries.* New York: Doubleday and Co., Inc., 1948.

Long, Gavin. *Australia in the War 1939–1945, Vol. 2., Greece, Crete, and Syria.* Canberra: Australian War Memorial Press, 1953.

Macksey, Kenneth. *Panzer Division: The Mailed Fist.* New York: Ballantine Books, Inc., 1972.

———. *The Partisans of Europe in Second World War.* New York: Stein and Day, 1975.

Manolikakis, I. G. *The Golgotha of Crete.* (in Greek) Athens: Efstathiadis, 1951.

Manvell, Roger. *Goering.* New York: Ballantine Books, Inc., 1972.

Mathioulakis, C. Z. *Crete: Mythology and History.* Athens: Mathioulakis, 1974.

Mayer, S. L., Ed. *Signal: Years of Triumph 1940–1942.* Englewood Cliffs, New Jersey: Prentice-Hall, Inc., 1978.

Meyer, Kurt. *Battle for the Stronghold of Crete.* (War Correspondent with 100 Mountain Regiment) Berlin: 1941.

Mosley, Leonard. *The Reich Marshal: A Biography of Herman Goering.* New York: Dell, 1975.

Mourellos, J. D. *Battle of Crete.* Iraklion: Erotocritos, 1950 (in Greek)

Muller, Gunther. *Sprung Über Kreta.* Oldenberg: Stalling, 1944.

Neumann, Robert. *The Pictorial History of the Third Reich.* New York: Bantam Books, 1962.

Newton, Don, and Hampshire, Cecil. London: William Kimber and Co., Ltd., 1959.

Pack, S. W. C. *The Battle of Crete.* Annapolis: Naval Institute Press, 1973.

Papagos, General Alexander. *The Battle of Greece, 1940–1941.* New York: New World Publishers, 1946. (in Greek)

Payne, Donald. *Malta: Red Duster, White Ensign.* New York: Doubleday & Co., Inc., 1960.

Pia, Jack. *Nazi Regalia.* New York: Ballantine Books, Inc., 1971.

Playfair, Major General I. S. O. *The Mediterranean and Middle East: Vol. 2: The Germans Come to the Help of Their Ally (1941).* London: Her Majesty's Stationery Office, 1956.

Poolman, Kenneth. *The Kelly.* London: William Kimber and Co., Ltd., 1954.

Price, Alfred. *Luftwaffe: Birth, Life and Death of an Air Force.* New York: Ballantine Books, 1969.

Pruller, Wilhelm. *Diary of a German Soldier.* New York: Coward-McCann, Inc., 1963.

Psychoundakis, George. *The Cretan Runner.* London: John Murray, 1955.

Ringel, Gen. Julius. *Hurra Die Gams.* Berlin: Leopold Stocker Verlag, 1965.

Ritchie, L. A. *East of Malta, West of Suez: The Official Admiralty Account of the Mediterranean Fleet 1939–1943.* Boston: Little Brown, 1944.

Rokakis, Manousos. *The Story of Crete, 1941–1945.* Khania, Crete, 1953.

Ross, Angus. *23 Battalion, Official History of New Zealand in Second World War 1939–1945.* New Zealand: War History Branch, 1959.

Rothberg, Abraham. *Eyewitness History of World War II.* New York: Bantam Books, Inc., 1962.

Rudel, Hans Ulrich. *Stuka Pilot.* New York: Ballantine Books, 1973.

Russell, Francis, Ed. *World War II: The Secret War.* Alexandria, Virginia: Time-Life Books, 1978.

Schmidt, H. W. *With Rommel in the Desert.* New York: Ballantine Books, 1967.

Sheffield, Major O. F. *The York and Lancaster Regiment 1919–1953.* Aldershot: Gale and Polden, Ltd., 1956.

Shirer, William L. *The Rise and Fall of the Third Reich.* New York: Simon and Schuster, 1960.

————. *Berlin Diary.* New York: Popular Library, 1941.

Singleton-Gates, Peter. *General Lord Freyberg, V.C.* London: Joseph, 1963.

Smith, Michael Llewellyn. *The Great Island: A Study of Crete.* London: Longman, Green and Co., Ltd., 1965.

Speer, Albert. *Inside the Third Reich.* New York: Avon Books, 1971.

Stephanids, Theodore. *Climax in Crete.* London: Faber and Faber, Ltd., 1946.

Stevenson, William. *A Man Called Intrepid.* New York: Harcourt, Brace, Jovanovich, 1976.

Stewart, I. McD. G. *The Struggle for Crete: 20 May–1 June, 1941.* London: Oxford University Press, 1966.

Student, General Kurt. *Crete (Kommando).* South Africa: Ministry of Defence, 1952.

Sulzberger, C. L., Ed. *The American Heritage Picture History of World War II, Vol. 1.* New York: Simon and Schuster, Inc., 1966.

Thomas, David A. *Crete 1941: The Battle at Sea.* London: New English Library, 1976.

————. *Nazi Victory: Crete 1941.* New York: Stein and Day, 1972.

Thomas, W. B. *Dare to Be Free.* London: Wingate, 1957.

Thompson, Walter H. *Assignment: Churchill.* New York: Farrar, Straus and Young, 1955.

Toland, John. *Adolf Hitler.* New York: Doubleday and Co., Inc., 1976.

Townsend, Peter. *Duel of Eagles.* New York: Simon and Schuster, 1971.

Trevor-Roper, H. R., Ed. *Blitzkrieg to Defeat: Hitler's War Directives, 1939–1945.* New York: Holt, Rinehart and Winston, 1965.

Underhill, Brigadier E. W. *The Royal Leicestershire Regiment 17th Foot: A History of the Years 1928–1956.* South Wigston, Leics., Regimental Printing Office, 1958.

U. S. Department of the Army. Office of the Chief of Military History. *The German Campaigns in the Balkans-Spring 1941.* Washington: 1953. Ms 20-260.

U. S. Department of the Army. Office of the Chief of Military History. *General Hans-Joachim Rath, 1st Stuka Wing (February–May 1941). Washington: 1953. Ms No.* D-064.

U. S. Department of the Army. Office of the Chief of Military History. *Airborne Operations—A German Appraisal.* Washington: 1952. Ms No. P-051.

U. S. Department of the Army. Office of the Chief of Military History. Major General Rudiger Von Heyking, *Commitment of Parachute Troops by the Second Air Transport Wing (Special Purpose): Crete, 21 May 1941.* Washington: 1953. Ms No. B-639.

U. S. Department of the Army. Office of the Chief of Military History. *Warlimont, General of Artillery: Answers to Questions Concerning Greece, Crete, and Russia.* Washington: 1953. Ms No. B-250.

Von der Heydte, Baron F. *Daedalus Returned, Crete 1941.* London: Hutchinson and Co., 1958.

Von Mellenthin, Major General F. W. *Panzer Battles: The Balkan Campaign.* New York: Ballantine Books, Inc., 1973.

Von der Porten, Edward P. *The German Navy in World War II.* New York: Apollo Edition, 1972.

Von Wittmann, A. *Von Kreta, Der Insel Der Rätsel.* Munich: Die Gebirgstruppe, 1954.

Waller, Lt. Col. R. P. *With the 1st Armored Brigade in Greece.* London: Journal of Royal Artillery, 1945.

Warlimont, Gen. Walter. *Inside Hitler's Headquarters 1939–1945.* New York: Praeger, 1964.

Wason, Betty. *Miracle in Hellas.* New York: The Macmillan Company, 1943.

Waugh, Evelyn. *Officers and Gentlemen.* London: Chapman and Hall, 1955.

Weeks, John. *Assault from the Sky.* New York: G. P. Putnam's Sons, 1978.

Whipple, A. B. C., Ed. *World War II: The Mediterranean.* Alexandria, Virginia: Time-Life Books, 1978.

Whiting, Charles. *Canaris.* New York: Ballantine Books, 1973.

———. *The War in the Shadows.* New York: Ballantine Books, 1973.

———. *Hunters from the Sky.* New York: Ballantine Books, 1974.

White, Leigh. *The Long Balkan Night.* New York: Charles Scribner's Sons, 1944.

Wilmot, Chester. *The Struggle for Europe.* New York: Harper, 1953.

Windrow, Martin. *Luftwaffe Airborne and Field Units.* London: Osprey Publishing Ltd., 1972.

Winterbotham, F. W. *The Ultra Secret.* New York: Dell, 1976.

Winterstein, Ernst Martin, and Jacobs, Hans. *General Meindl und Seine Fallschirmjäger.* Munich: Gesammelt und Neidergeschrieben, 1949.

Woodhouse, C. M. *The Struggle for Greece: 1941–1949.* London: Hart-Davis, Mac-Gibbon, 1976.

Wunderlich, Hans Georg. *The Secret of Crete.* New York: MacMillan Co., Inc., 1974.

Wykes, Alan. *SS Leibstandarte.* New York: Ballantine Books, 1974.

———. *Hitler.* New York: Ballantine Books, 1970.

Young, Brigadier Peter. *Atlas of the Second World War.* New York: Berkley Publishing Corp., 1977.

Zotos, Stephanos. *Greece: The Struggle for Freedom.* New York: Thomas Y. Crowell Co., 1967.

INDEX